THE OXFORD HANDBOOK OF

# DANCE AND
# REENACTMENT

# THE OXFORD HANDBOOK OF

# DANCE AND REENACTMENT

*Edited by*

MARK FRANKO

OXFORD

UNIVERSITY PRESS

# OXFORD
UNIVERSITY PRESS

Oxford University Press is a department of the University of Oxford. It furthers
the University's objective of excellence in research, scholarship, and education
by publishing worldwide. Oxford is a registered trade mark of Oxford University
Press in the UK and certain other countries.

Published in the United States of America by Oxford University Press
198 Madison Avenue, New York, NY 10016, United States of America.

Library of Congress Cataloging-in-Publication Data
Names: Franko, Mark, editor.
Title: The Oxford handbook of dance and reenactment / edited by Mark Franko.
Description: New York, NY : Oxford University Press, 2017. |
Includes bibliographical references.
Identifiers: LCCN 2016050922 | ISBN 9780199314201 (hardcover : alk. paper) |
ISBN 9780197533895 (paperback : alk. paper)
Subjects: LCSH: Choreography. | Dance—History. | Dance—Study and teaching.
Classification: LCC GV1782.5 .O84 2017 | DDC 792.809—dc23
LC record available at https://lccn.loc.gov/2016050922

# Contents

# PART III. PROLEPTIC ITERATION

# PART IV. INVESTIGATIVE REENACTMENT: TRANSMISSION AS HEURISTIC DEVICE

# PART V. ENACTING TESTIMONY/PERFORMING CULTURAL MEMORY/SPECTATORSHIP AS PRACTICE

# Acknowledgments

I wish to express my gratitude to all the contributors to this volume, who responded so generously to my initial proposal and accompanied me on this long and fascinating journey. Very helpful in the development of this project was the two-year speaker series on Reenactment (2010–2012) that I curated as Director of the Center for Visual and Performance Studies during my tenure at the University of California, Santa Cruz. The Reenactment Workshop held at the University of California, Santa Cruz, in January 2013 was another event at which research was shared and the volume began to take on shape. I wish also to thank those who were present but who did not in the end contribute to this volume: Hayden White, Rebecca Schneider, Margaret Brose, Janice Ross, Deana Shemek, Ted Warburton, and Shannon Jackson. Special thanks are extended to the Arts Research Institute of UCSC and Oxford University Press for providing funding that made the workshop possible. I wish to thank my graduate assistant at UCSC, Jenna Purcell, for assisting me with the speaker series and the workshop. I could not have managed the logistics of this volume without the supportive editorial assistance of my graduate students in the Dance Department of Boyer College of Music and Dance, Temple University, Colleen Hooper, Charmian Wells, Macklin Kowal, and Carolyn Pautz. I want to offer special thanks to Alessio Franko for his translations of many of these chapters. Last but not least, I am thankful to my editor at Oxford University Press, Norman Hirschy, for his support and his encouragement of this project from the very start.

# CONTRIBUTORS

**Anurima Banerji** is an Associate Professor in the Department of World Arts and Cultures/Dance at University of California, Los Angeles. She holds a PhD in Performance Studies from New York University. Her articles and book chapters have been published in *About Performance, EPW, e-misferica, Women and Performance*, and *Planes of Composition: Dance, Theory, and the Global*, edited by André Lepecki and Jenn Joy (Seagull, 2009).With Violaine Roussel, she served as co-editor of *How to Do Politics with Art* (Routledge, 2016). She has trained in Odissi, a South Asian classical dance; her monograph on the form is forthcoming from Seagull Books.

**Fabián Barba** was born in Quito in 1982, where he studied dance and theater and worked as a professional performer. Parallel to his artistic formation, Fabián took classes in communications and literature. In 2004 he went to Brussels to join PARTS, after which he became a founding member of Busy Rocks. He has created two solo performances: *A Mary Wigman Dance Evening* and *a personal yet collective history*. In collaboration with Mark Franko, he worked on *Le marbre tremble* (2014) and with Esteban Donoso on *slugs' garden*. He also works as a dancer for Zoo/Thomas Hauert. Due to his ongoing research on the legacy of colonialism and dance history, he has been invited to give seminars and workshops in several European countries, the United States, Brazil, and Chile. His articles have been published in *Dance Research Journal* and *NDD l'actualité en danse*.

**Maaike Bleeker** is a Professor of Theatre Studies in the Department of Media and Culture Studies at Utrecht University. She graduated in Art History, Theater Studies, and Philosophy at the University of Amsterdam and obtained her PhD from the Amsterdam School for Cultural Analysis (ASCA). She taught at the School for New Dance development (SNDO) in Amsterdam and worked as dramaturge with various theater directors, choreographers, and visual artists. She was the organizer of the 2011 PSi world conference titled *Camillo 2.0: Technology, Memory, Experience* (Utrecht, May 25–29, 2011) and President of Psi (2011–2016). She has published extensively in international journals and edited volumes and has edited several books, including *Anatomy Live: Performance and the Operating Theatre* (AUP, 2008), *Performance and Phenomenology: Traditions and Transformations* (Routledge, 2015) and *Transmission in Motion: The Technologizing of Dance* (Routledge, 2016). Her monograph *Visuality in the Theatre: The Locus of Looking* was published by Palgrave in 2008.

**Ramsay Burt** is Professor of Dance History at De Montfort University, United Kingdom. His publications include *The Male Dancer* (1995, revised 2007), *Alien Bodies* (1997), *Judson Dance Theater* (2006), with Valerie Briginshaw, *Writing Dancing Together* (2009), *Ungoverning Dance* (2016) and *British dance: Black routes* (2016) with Christy Adair. With Susan Foster, he was founder editor of Discourses in Dance. In 1999 he was Visiting Professor at the Department of Performance Studies, New York University. In 2010 he was Professeur Invité at l'Université de Nice Sophia-Antipolis, and he is a visiting teacher at PARTS in Brussels.

**Seeta Chaganti** is an Associate Professor of English at the University of California, Davis, who specializes in late medieval literature and culture. She published her first book, *The Medieval Poetics of the Reliquary: Enshrinement, Inscription, Performance*, in 2008. She also edited the essay collection *Medieval Poetics and Social Practice*, which was published in 2012. Her articles have appeared in *PMLA, Dance Research Journal, New Medieval Literatures, Romance Studies, postmedieval, Exemplaria, Australian Literary Studies*, and other journals and collections. Her second monograph, *Strange Footing: Poetic Form and Dance in the Late Middle Ages*, will be published by the University of Chicago Press in 2018.

**Timmy De Laet** is a postdoctoral researcher at the University of Antwerp and the Research Centre for Visual Poetics. He had an actor's training at the Royal Conservatoire of Antwerp, graduated in theater studies at the University of Antwerp, and studied dance theory at the Freie Universität Berlin. He obtained his PhD in 2016, for his dissertation on reenactment in European contemporary dance. Timmy has been a Fellow of the Research Foundation Flanders (FWO) and winner of the Routledge Prize. He worked as a Visiting Professor at Ghent University (S:PAM—Studies in Performing Arts & Media) and as a lecturer at the Royal Conservatoire Antwerp. Supported by a Fulbright Postdoctoral Award and a Fellowship of the Belgian American Educational Foundation (B.A.E.F.), Timmy is joining the Institute of Dance Scholarship at Temple University (Philadelphia) as a Visiting Scholar (2017–2018). His research interests are the reiterative nature of live performance in relation to archivization, documentation, and artistic reenactment. He has published on these topics in journals such as *Performance Research, Tanz*, and *Muséologies*, as well as in the edited collections *Bewegung Lesen/Bewegung Schreiben* (2012), *Performing Memory in Art and Popular Culture* (2013), *Moments: A History of Performance in 10 Acts* (2013), *Performing Memory in Art and Popular Culture* (2013), and *Moments: A History of Performance in 10 Acts* (2013).

**Kate Elswit** is Reader in Theatre and Performance at the Royal Central School of Speech and Drama and author of *Watching Weimar Dance* (Oxford University Press, 2014) and *Theatre & Dance* (Palgrave Macmillan, 2017). She is winner of the Gertrude Lippincott Award from the Society of Dance History Scholars, the Biennial Sally Banes Publication Prize from the American Society for Theatre Research, and honorable mention for the Joe A. Callaway Prize, and her research has been supported by many sources, including a Marshall Scholarship, a postdoctoral fellowship in the Andrew W. Mellon Fellowship of Scholars in the Humanities at Stanford University, and the 2013 Lilian Karina Research

Grant in Dance and Politics. Her essays appear in *TDR: The Drama Review, Theatre Journal, Modern Drama, Art Journal, Performance Research, Dance Research Journal,* and *New German Dance Studies,* and *The Oxford Handbook of Dance and Politics.* Recent performance collaborations include *Future Memory* and *Breath Catalogue.*

**Susanne Foellmer** is Reader in Dance at Coventry University, Centre for Dance Research (C-DaRE). Her research focuses on contemporary dance and performance, as well as the Weimar era with respect to theories of aesthetics and corporeality. Further research fields are dance in connection to media and visual arts, and historicity of performance. Since 2014 she has been directing the research project "On Remnants and Vestiges: Strategies of Remaining in the Performing Arts" (DFG/German Research Association). Publications include *Valeska Gert: Fragmente einer Avantgardistin in Tanz und Schauspiel der 1920er Jahre* (Transcript, 2006), *Am Rand der Körper. Inventuren des Unabgeschlossenen im zeitgenössischen Tanz (On the Bodies' Edge. Inventories of the Unfinished in Contemporary Dance;* Transcript, 2009), and "Re-Cyclings: Shifting Time, Changing Genre in the Moving Museum," in *Dance Research Journal, Special Issue Dance and the Museum* 46(3), December 2014.

**Susanne Franco** is an Assistant Professor at Ca' Foscari University of Venice. Her publications include *Martha Graham* (Palermo: L'Epos, 2003), and several essays on modern and contemporary dance. She edited *Audruckstanz: il corpo, la danza e la critica,* a special issue of the Italian journal *Biblioteca Teatrale* (Bulzoni, 2006); and, with Marina Nordera, she co-edited *Dance Discourses. Keywords in Dance Research* (Routledge, 2007) and *Ricordanze. Memoria in movimento e coreografie della storia* (Utet Università, 2010). She is the editor of the book series "Dance for Word/Dance Forward. Interviste sulla coreografia contemporanea" in which her volume *Frédéric Flamand* (L'Epos, 2004) appeared. She is a member of the editorial board of the Italian journal *Danza e ricerca* (University of Bologna), of *Recherches en danse* (the journal of the French association of dance scholars, aCD), and of the Centre Transdisciplinaire d'Epistémologie de la Littérature et des Arts vivants: Littérature, Musique, Théâtre, Danse (CTEL) at the University of the Côte d'Azur (Nice). As a dance curator she has worked for the Fondazione Querini Stampalia (Venice), the François Pinault Foundation—Palazzo Grassi (Venice), and with Roberto Casarotto for the Hangar Bicocca (Milan).

**Mark Franko** is Laura H. Carnell Professor of Dance and Chair of Dance, Boyer College of Music and Dance, Temple University. He is founding editor of the Oxford Studies in Dance Theory book series and was the editor of *Dance Research Journal* (Cambridge University Press) from 2008 to 2017. In 2011 Franko received the Congress on Research in Dance award for Outstanding Scholarly Research in Dance. His monograph *Martha Graham in Love and War: The Life in the Work* (Oxford University Press) is now in paperback. His other books include *Dance as Text: Ideologies of the Baroque Body; Dancing Modernism/Performing Politics;* and *The Work of Dance: Labor, Movement, and Identity in the 1930s.* He edited *Ritual and Event: Interdisciplinary Perspectives,* and co-edited *Acting on the Past: Historical Performance across the Disciplines.* His choreography has been produced at Lincoln Center Out-of-Doors Festival, Berlin Werkstatt Festival, Getty Center, Montpellier Opera, Toulon Art Museum, Haggerty Art Museum (Milwaukee), Akademie der Künste (Berlin), Mozarteum (Salzburg), STUK festival (Leuven), and in New York City and San Francisco dance venues. He is currently working with Alessandra Nicifero on *Choreographing Discourses: a Mark Franko Reader* (forthcoming at Routledge) and *Serge Lifar, Politics, and Neoclassicism in French Dance* at Oxford University Press.

**Jens Richard Giersdorf** is Professor of Dance Studies at Marymount Manhattan College. Giersdorf's research focuses on choreographies of nationhood and locality in a global context, as well as epistemological investigations in dance studies. He has published in a number of journals, including *Dance Research Journal, Theatre Journal, GLQ—Gay & Lesbian Quarterly, Forum Modernes Theater, Jahrbuch für Tanzforschung,* and *Maska.* His work has been translated and anthologized in the United Kingdom, Switzerland, Italy, Serbia, and Germany. His monograph *The Body of the People* (University of Wisconsin Press) is the first study of dance in East Germany. The German translation is published by Transcript Verlag as *Volkseigene Körper.* In co-authorship with Gay Morris, Giersdorf edited *Choreographies of Twenty-first Century Wars.* Giersdorf is a member of the editorial boards of the Society of Dance History Scholars and *Dance Research Journal.*

**Yvonne Hardt** is a Professor of Dance Studies and Choreography at the University of Music and Dance Cologne, Germany. She was also Assistant Professor at the Department of Theater, Dance and Performance Studies at the University of California, Berkeley. Her main research areas are dance history and the critical investigation of its methodology and use in performative practices, gender and media in dance, and more recently, the praxeological investigations of dance training and educational systems. She also works as a choreographer investigating the possibilities of linking her scholarly research with her choreographic endeavors. Selected book publications: *Choreographie-Medien-Gender* (2013, ed. with M. Angerer/A. Weber); *Choreographie und Institution: Zeitgenössischer Tanz zwischen Ästhetik, Produktion und Vermittlung* (2011, ed. with M. Stern); *Tanz— Metropole—Provinz. Jahrbuch der Gesellschaft für Tanzforschung,* Bd. 17, (2007, ed. with K. Maar); *Politische Körper. Ausdruckstanz, Choreographien des Protests und die Arbeiterkulturbewegung in der Weimarer Republik* (2004).

**Sabine Huschka,** a dance and theater scholar, has served as head of the DFG research project "Transgressionen. Energetisierung von Körper und Szene" (Transgressions. Energizing Body/Scenery) at the Inter-University Centre for Dance/University of the Arts, Berlin, since 2015. She was recently a visiting professor at the Institute for Movement-Science/Performance Studies of the University of Hamburg (2016–2017). In 1998, she attained her doctorate in the field of cultural sciences at the Humboldt Universität at Berlin and did her Habilitation Treatise at the University of Leipzig in 2011 with a study on "Wissenskultur Tanz: Der choreografierte Körper im Theater" (Knowledge Culture Dance: The Choreographed Body in Theatre), accompanied by studies on reconstruction and reenactment in dance and theater. She has held diverse national and international visiting professorships for theater and dance studies (University of Hamburg, Free University of Berlin, University of Bern), also at the UdK (University of the Arts) in Berlin, where she is now an Associate Researcher of the postgraduate program "Das Wissen der Künste" (Knowledge of the Arts). Recent book publications include *Wissenskultur Tanz. Historische und zeitgenössische Vermittlungsakte zwischen Praktiken und Diskursen* (2009) and *Moderner Tanz. Konzepte—Stile— Utopien* (2002/2012).

**Branislav Jakovljević** is an Associate Professor and Chair of the Department of Theater and Performance Studies at Stanford University. He specializes in avant-garde and experimental theater, performance theory, theater history, and performance and politics. His articles have been published widely in the United States and Europe. He was the recipient of Association for Theatre in Higher Education (ATHE) 2009 Outstanding Article Award for the essay "From Mastermind to Body Artist: Political Performances of Slobodan Milosevic" (published in *TDR* 52:1, 2008). His first book *Daniil Kharms: Writing and the Event* was published by Northwestern University Press in 2009, and his second book *Alienation Effects: Performance and Self-Management in Yugoslavia, 1945–1991* was published in 2016 by University of Michigan Press.

**Susan Jones** is Professor of English Literature at the University of Oxford and Fellow of St. Hilda's College. She has published widely on Joseph Conrad, nineteenth- and twentieth-century women's writing, the periodical press, and modernism. Formerly a soloist with the Scottish Ballet, Glasgow, she also writes on the history and aesthetics of dance. She is the founder and director of Dance Scholarship Oxford and author of *Literature, Modernism, and Dance* (Oxford University Press, 2013).

**Ketu H. Katrak** born in Bombay, India, is a Professor in the Department of Drama at the University of California, Irvine (UCI) and affiliated with the Departments of English and Comparative Literature. Katrak is the author of *Contemporary Indian Dance: New Creative Choreography in India and the Diaspora* (Palgrave Macmillan, 2011, paperback, 2014), *Politics of the Female Body: Postcolonial Women Writers* (Rutgers University Press, 2006), and *Wole Soyinka and Modern Tragedy: A Study of Dramatic Theory and Practice* (Greenwood Press, 1986). Katrak has a forthcoming book (in progress) entitled *Jay Pather: Performance and Spatial Politics in South Africa*. Katrak's published essays in drama, dance, and performance, postcolonial theory, and African and postcolonial women writers appear in journals such as *Amerasia, Modern Fiction Studies*, and *South Asian Popular Culture*, among others. Katrak is the recipient of a Fulbright Research Award to India (2005–2006), University of California, Humanities Research Institute's Fellowship (2002), The Bunting Institute Fellowship (1988–1989; Harvard University, Radcliffe College), and the University of Massachusetts Chancellor's Award for Multiculturalism (1993). Katrak was on the Fulbright Senior Specialist roster (2010–2015).

**Anthea Kraut** is Professor in the Department of Dance at the University of California, Riverside, where she teaches courses in critical dance studies. Her first book, *Choreographing the Folk: The Dance Stagings of Zora Neale Hurston*, was published by the University of Minnesota Press in 2008, and she received a Special Citation from the Society of Dance History Scholars' de la Torre Bueno Prize® for distinguished book of dance scholarship. Her second book, *Choreographing Copyright: Race, Gender, and Intellectual Property Rights in American Dance*, was published by Oxford University Press in 2015 and won the Congress on Research in Dance's Oskar B. Brockette Book Prize for Dance Research, The Association for Theatre in Higher Educations's Outstanding Book Award, and the Biennial Sally Banes Publication Award from the American Society for Theatre Research. Her articles have been published in the edited volumes *The Routledge Dance Studies Reader* and *Worlding Dance* and in *Theatre Journal, Dance Research Journal, Women & Performance: a journal of feminist theory, The Scholar & Feminist Online*, and *Theatre Studies*.

**Randy Martin** was Professor of Art and Public Policy and founder of the graduate program in Arts Politics at New York University. He is the author of *Performance as Political Act: The Embodied Self; Socialist Ensembles: Theater and State in Cuba and Nicaragua; Critical Moves: Dance Studies in Theory and Politics; On Your Marx: Relinking Socialism and the Left; Financialization of Daily Life*; and *Empire of Indifference: American War and the Financial Logic of Risk Management*. He has edited collections on US communism, sport and academic labor, and, most recently, *Artistic Citizenship: A Public Voice for the Arts* (with Mary Schmidt Campbell) and *The Returns of Alwin Nikolais: Bodies, Boundaries, and the Dance Canon* (with Claudia Gitelman). Dr. Martin holds degrees in sociology from the University of California, Berkeley, the University of Wisconsin, Madison, and the City University of New York. He has studied, taught, and performed in dance, theater, and clowning in the United States and abroad. Previously, he served as Professor and Chair of Social Science at Pratt Institute, Associate Dean of Faculty at Tisch School of the Arts, Chair of the Department of Art and Public Policy, and as an editor of the journal *Social Text*.

**Richard Move** is Artistic Director of the performance collective *MoveOpolis!* He is an Assistant Professor of Dance at Queens College, City University of New York, and a TED Global Oxford Fellow. Move's commissions include works for Mikhail Baryshnikov's White Oak Dance Project, Martha Graham Dance Company, PARADIGM, Opera Ballet of Florence, New York City Ballet's Helene Alexopoulos, Guggenheim Museum, Parrish Art Museum, European Cultural Capitol, Deborah Harry, Dame Shirley Bassey and Isaac Mizrahi. Move's award winning films include *Bardo, BloodWork—The Ana Mendieta Story, GhostLight* and *GIMP. Martha @ . . .* , Move's performances as Martha Graham, received two New York Dance and Performance Awards, tours globally, and was named "Best of 2011" by *ARTFORUM International, Time Out*, and other publications. Recent performances include the Museum of Modern Art in New York, Singapore's Asian Civilizations Museum, and Italy's Ravello Festival. Move received his

MFA from the City College of New York and is a PhD Candidate (ABD) in Performance Studies at New York University.

**Martin Nachbar** is a choreographer, dancer, researcher, and teacher in Berlin. Among his pieces are *Urheben Aufheben*, which includes a reconstruction of Dore Hoyer's *Affectos Humanos; Repeater*, in which Nachbar invited his non-dancer father to dance with him; "The Walk," which takes the audience for a performative walk around the block; and "Animal Dances," which explores human-animal relations through movement. Martin tours internationally with his works, and he teaches regularly at places such as SNDO, HZT Berlin, TRINITY LABAN, FU Berlin, University Hamburg, SEAD, and PARTS Martin has published essays and reports on his research in numerous magazines and publications in Germany, Belgium, the United Kingdom, and the United States.

**Rani Nair** works as a choreographer and dancer with a special interest in postcolonial ideas and the body in social contexts. She has developed her own work in Morocco, Mexico, Vietnam, Iceland, and South Africa, among other places, many of them as part of the artistic trio WE Insist. She has performed at festivals including Spielart in Munich, ImPulsTanz in Vienna, the Ignite! Festival of Contemporary Dance in Delhi, Singapore International Festival of Arts, Avignon Festival, and the Gothenburg Dance and Theatre Festival. As a dancer she toured with Shobana Jeyasingh, Jayachandran Palazhy, Roger Sinha, and Julie Nioche. Nair is a dance advisor at Riksteatern, a national touring network in Sweden. She has been a collaborator with the network Sweet and Tender Collaborations, and on the editorial team of *Ful*, a queer feminist art collective that produces art magazines. The collective made the anti-nationalistic cabaret *Europa Europa* about the inhuman migration politics of Europa in collaboration with the electronic duo The Knife.

**Carrie Noland** is Professor of French and Comparative Literature at the University of California, Irvine. She has published three monographs: *Poetry at Stake: Lyric Aesthetics and the Challenge of Technology* (Princeton University Press, 1999); *Agency and Embodiment* (Harvard University Press, 2009); and *Voices of Negritude in Modernist Print* (Columbia University Press, 2015). Her work focuses on gestural and inscriptive artworks that integrate media technologies. Supported by fellowships from the Guggenheim Foundation and the Clark Art Institute, she is currently completing a book on Merce Cunningham.

**Anna Pakes** is Reader in Dance Studies at the University of Roehampton, London. Her research is focused on the philosophy of dance, with a particular interest in analytic aesthetics. She has published on a range of philosophical themes as they relate to dance, including the mind-body problem, Husserlian phenomenology, and the epistemology of practice as research. Her monograph on the ontology of dance works is forthcoming from Oxford University Press.

**Frédéric Pouillaude**, after training in ballet and contemporary dance, studied philosophy at the École normale supérieure de Paris. He has been an associate professor in the philosophy of art at Paris-Sorbonne University since 2007. He has published *Unworking Choreography: The Notion of the Work in Dance* [2009] (Oxford University Press, 2017, translated by Anna Pakes). He has been a junior *membre* of the Institut Universitaire de France since 2013.

**VK Preston** is an Assistant Professor at the University of Toronto's Centre for Drama, Theatre and Performance Studies. Her work engages dance, gender, economic, ecological and performance histories of colonization in the Americas, focusing on movement as a site of political and historiographical labor. She completed the research for her contribution to this volume during an arts residency at *La Cité internationale des arts*. She thanks the curators and directors of the *Département des Arts graphiques* at the Louvre Museum for their expertise and support, as well as the Early Modern Conversions Project, the Institute for the Public Life of Arts and Ideas, and the Social Sciences and Humanities Research Council (SSHRC). A version of this essay, workshopped at Interdisicplinary Performance Studies at Yale, appears in her current book project. VK earned her PhD at Stanford University's Theatre and Performance Studies program and holds a PhD minor in History.

**Anita Ratnam**, based in Chennai, India, is highly respected as a performer, writer, speaker, and arts entrepreneur and culture mentor. Her four-decade career, with over a thousand performances in twenty-seven countries, intersects the varied disciplines of dance, theater, storytelling, feminist themes, arts production, music, and costume design. Dr. Ratnam's Neo Bharatam repertoire distills the classical dance traditions of her Bharatanatyam training, with a focus on ritual traditions reinterpreted for the modern concert stage. Using voice, singing, Vedic hymns, drumming, contemporary mythology, and devised movements, her various choreographies include *Seven Graces, Ma3ka, A Million Sitas,* and *Neelam.* In 2000, Ratnam created narthaki.com, the largest web portal on Indian dance featuring articles, reviews, directories of events and information on Indian dancers in India and beyond. In January 2017, Dr. Ratnam was awarded the International Arts Award by UK-based Milapfest for her role in initiating and nurturing this significant dance portal over the past seventeen years. As a respected dance advocate interested in cultural policy, Ratnam served on the executive board of several Indian national arts organizations such as the Ministry of Culture (Grants Committee), ICCR (Indian Council for Cultural Relations), and Sangeet Natak Akademi. Anita Ratnam is a voting member of the Dance Critics Association, United States, and a Fellow of the World Academy of Arts and Sciences, United Kingdom.

**Lucia Ruprecht** is a Fellow of Emmanuel College and an affiliated Lecturer in the Department of German and Dutch, University of Cambridge, United Kingdom. She is researching and teaching across literature, dance, and film studies. Her *Dances of the Self in Heinrich von Kleist, E.T.A. Hoffmann and Heinrich Heine* (2006) was awarded Special Citation of the de la Torre Bueno Prize. She is editor of a Special Issue of *Performance*

*Philosophy*, entitled *Towards an Ethics of Gesture* (2017), and co-editor of *Performance and Performativity in German Cultural Studies* (with Carolin Duttlinger and Andrew Webber, 2003), *Cultural Pleasure* (with Michael Minden, 2009) and *New German Dance Studies* (with Susan Manning, 2012). From 2013 to 2015, she was an Alexander von Humboldt Fellow at the Institute of Theater Studies, Free University Berlin. In 2016, she was the inaugural Visiting Research Scholar at Boyer College of Music and Dance, Temple University, Philadelphia. She is currently completing the manuscript of a book entitled *Gestural Imaginaries: Dance and the Culture of Gestures at the Beginning of the Twentieth Century*, under contract with Oxford University Press. Together with Bettina Brandl-Risi, she is co-editing the *Handbuch Literatur & Performance*.

**Gerald Siegmund** is Professor of Applied Theater Studies at the Justus-Liebig University in Giessen, Germany. He studied theater, English, and French literature at the Goethe University in Frankfurt/Main, where he also received his PhD with a thesis on *Theatre as Memory*. Between 2005 and 2008 he was Professor of Contemporary Theatre at the University of Berne, Switzerland. Gerald Siegmund is the author of numerous articles on contemporary dance and theater performance, as well as editor of the book *William Forsythe—Denken in Bewegung*, published in 2004 at Henschel Verlag, Berlin. His most recent monograph is *Abwesenheit. Eine performative Ästhetik des Tanzes* (Transcript, 2006). It includes in-depth studies of the work of Jérôme Bel, Xavier Le Roy, Meg Stuart, and William Forsythe. Among his most recent publications are *Dance, Politics, and Co-Immunity* edited with Stefan Hölscher (2013) and *The Oxford Handbook of Dance and Politics* edited together with Rebekah Kowal and Randy Martin (Oxford University Press, 2017). His monograph *Jérôme Bel: Dance, Theatre, and the Subject* will be published by Palgrave Macmillan in 2017.

**P. A. Skantze** writes, directs, and teaches theater in London and in Italy. She is a founding member of the performance group Four Second Decay, whose work seeks to create "an aesthetic of taking one's time, attempting by so doing to instigate a relationship between artists and audience based on an ethics of attention." Four Second Decay has performed internationally, most recently in New York with a production of *afterKleist*. Currently a Reader in Performance Practices in Drama, Theatre, and Performance Studies at Roehampton University, she is the author of *Stillness in Motion in the Seventeenth-Century Theatre* (Routledge, 2003), as well as many articles on race, gender, sound, and theater. Her most recent book, *Itinerant Spectator/Itinerant Spectacle*, was published in December 2013 by Punctum Books. The book forms a part of her current explorations in the epistemology of practice as research.

**Catherine M. Soussloff** has written books, articles, and essays in art history and the related fields of performance studies, Jewish studies, the history of photography, and contemporary visual studies. Known for her comparative and historiographical approaches to the central theoretical concerns of art history and aesthetics, Soussloff's most recent publications have focused on the aesthetic theories of the French philosopher Michel Foucault. Her edited volume *Foucault on the Arts and Letters: Perspectives* *for the 21st Century* appeared in 2016. Her book on Michel Foucault and painting theory in the twentieth century will be published by University of Minnesota Press in 2017. Lectures on Foucault given at the Collège de France in Paris (2015) may be accessed at www.college-de-france.fr. Soussloff teaches at the University of British Columbia, where she is also an Associate of the Peter Wall Institute for Advanced Studies. She taught for twenty-four years at the University of California, Santa Cruz, where she held a University of California Presidential Chair in Visual and Performance Studies and the first Patricia and Rowland Rebele Chair in the History of Art. She has been awarded fellowships from The National Endowment for the Humanities, The Getty Research Institute, The Sterling and Francine Clark Art Institute, the University of California Humanities Research Institute, the Herbert D. Katz Center for Advanced Judaic Studies, University of Pennsylvania, the Institute for the Humanities at New York University, and the Institut National d'Histoire de l'Art in Paris.

**Christel Stalpaert** is a Professor at Ghent University (Belgium), where she is Director of the research centers S:PAM (Studies in Performing Arts and Media) and PEPPER (Philosophy, Ethology, Politics and Performance). Her research interests are corporeality and intermediality in performance, dance, and new media arts (from the historical avant-garde to the present day) at the meeting point between philosophy and ethics. She has published on these topics in *Performance Research, Text & Performance Quarterly, Contemporary Theatre Review*, and *Dance Research Journal*. She has edited *No Beauty for Me There Where Human Life Is Rare: On Jan Lauwers' Theatre Work with Needcompany* (Academia Press, 2007); *Bastard or Playmate? Adapting Theatre, Mutating Media and the Contemporary Performing Arts* (Springer, 2012); and *Unfolding Spectatorship: Shifting Political, Ethical and Intermedial Positions* (Academia Press, 2016).

**Christina Thurner** is Professor of Dance Studies at the Institute for Theater Studies at the University of Bern. Main areas of research include the history and aesthetics of dance from the eighteenth century to the present, contemporary dance and performance, historiography, gender, and theories of physicality and temporality. Recent book publications include *Beredte Körper—bewegte Seelen. Zum Diskurs der doppelten Bewegung in Tanztexten (Speaking Bodies—Moving Souls. On the Discourse of the Double Movement in Texts on Dance)* (2009), *Original und Revival. Geschichts-Schreibung im Tanz (Original and Revival. Historiography in Dance)* (2010, edited with Julia Wehren), *Tanzkritik. Materialien (1997–2014) (Dance Criticism. Material (1997-2014)* (2015), *Rhythmen in Bewegung. Äußere, eigene und verkörperte Zeitlichkeit im künstlerischen Tanz (Rhythm in motion. Outer, inner and embodied temporality in performance dance)* (2017).

THE OXFORD HANDBOOK OF

# DANCE AND REENACTMENT

CHAPTER 1

····································································

# INTRODUCTION

*The Power of Recall in a Post-Ephemeral Era*

····································································

MARK FRANKO

IT is not easy to say with certainty when and where reenactment as a distinctly new choreographic strategy and dramaturgical modality first made its appearance on the dance concert stage.[1] It may have been Susanne Linke's reconstruction of Dore Hoyer's *Affectos Humanos*, which drew my attention in 1988 for containing a new self-critical attitude toward reconstruction.[2] Although Linke was performing the solo cycle *Affectos Humanos* (1962) of her predecessor Dore Hoyer (1911–1967), Linke's performance stood apart from conventional reconstructions of earlier work through its unusual framing device, which forecast a fundamental shift in the way the dancer positioned herself with respect to the historical material she had reconstructed. The concern was no longer to demonstrate how the dance could be redone by simulating the original dance and the dancer's appearance; the emphasis was rather on what it was like to *do* it again. Linke dramatized this experience on stage by distancing herself from the illusion of the past dance in between its sections, as she changed in full view of the audience before a costume rack at the back of the stage. This seemingly simple but, in 1988, unprecedented gesture signaled a dynamic shift by virtue of the acknowledgment of distance over the desire for and pretension toward proximity that can mark impersonation and/or failed identification.[3]

---

[1] The term *reenactment* itself was first used by R. G. Collingwood in 1928. See Dray 1995. See Chapter 10 by Maaike Bleeker in this volume for a discussion of Collingwood in relation to danced reenactment.

[2] I first wrote about Linke's performance, which premiered on June 15, 1988, at Forum Niederberg in Velbert (then West Germany), in Franko (1989).

[3] Although the theme of this *Handbook* is not the evolution of reenactment since the 1980s, I wish to accent this fact here, and I return to it in Chapter 24. It is nothing short of ironic that Susanne Linke's own choreography *Wandlung* was taken up for reenactment by Jérôme Bel in *Le dernier spectacle* (*The Last Performance*) to explore what had to be reenacted in 1999 because it could no longer be performed. Linke herself was, like Hoyer, a student of Wigman. See Chapter 23 by Gerald Siegmund in this volume.

Hoyer herself was formed as a dancer by the teaching of Mary Wigman (1886–1973) in Germany, but in the postwar and postmodern era Hoyer herself cut an anachronistic figure. As a belated exponent of German *Ausdruckstanz* (German expressionist dance), Hoyer's work did not meet with cultural acceptance in postwar Germany given the sympathies between Nazism and *Ausdruckstanz* during the Hitler era and the subsequent upsurge of ballet in postwar Germany.[4] As Jens Richard Giersdorf has described, Arila Siegert also reconstructed *Affectos Humanos* in East Germany in 1988, and there too, albeit for different reasons, a return to dance modernism had not previously been well received (Giersdorf 2013, 85–87). Hence, the return to Hoyer's work in the 1980s raised complex political issues around German dance that, as Giersdorf has remarked, were not always being addressed. More recently, Martin Nachbar has also taken up Hoyer's *Affectos Humanos* in his *Urheben/Aufheben*,[5] which is discussed at length in this volume by a number of contributors, Nachbar and myself included.[6] The point is not necessarily to locate the origin of danced reenactment in historical time, but to ask whether the choice of Hoyer—an artist performing in the aftermath of modernism and hence one whose very presence was already displaced in historical time during the end of her own lifetime in the late twentieth century—might not inform the entire tendency of reenactment in dance today.

This is because the case of Hoyer, in my view, reveals a double displacement, or a double quality of being out of place: first, her work was out of place in the moment of the late 1980s when it was reenacted in both East and West Germany; second, it was always already out of place at the time of its premiere in 1962.[7] In other words, to grasp Hoyer's historical out-of-placement, one has to grasp her historical displacement, and it is the general significance of this very fact that could be said to characterize the reenactment effect that reverberates in the present moment. The reenactment of dance is always already enmeshed in overlapping temporalities, thanks to which the notion of historical time as chronicle time becomes destabilized by an uncertain historicity hinging on gesture. One of the hallmarks of danced reenactment is that historicity is always invested in complex temporalities whose modalities are those of spatiality rather than narrative.[8]

One commonality of all the Hoyer reenactments is that all drew on a film of the dance. The importance of media to the accessibility of earlier work, as well as media's role in the felt necessity to return to the past, is also undeniable in reenactment (see, in this

---

[4] Hoyer did find a warm welcome in South America (Müller, Peter, and Schuldt 1992, 46–50).

[5] It premiered in May 2008 at Kampnagel Theater in Hamburg. See Nachbar (2012) and Chapter 2 in this volume.

[6] On Nachbar's work on Hoyer, see also, in this volume, Maaike Bleeker, Chapter 10; Susanne Foellmer, Chapter 13; Gerald Siegmund, Chapter 23; and Sabine Huschka, Chapter 30.

[7] And, as Chapter 23 by Gerald Siegmund points out, Nachbar in dancing Hoyer is displaced from his own bodily form and identity as well. The transition from one being into another is also discussed in Chapter 4 by Richard Move.

[8] Certain features of narrativity in literature help us to understand the complex concept of historicity as explored by the *Handbook*'s various notions of reenactment. See, in particular, Chapter 22 by Susan Jones in this volume.

volume, Bleeker, Chapter 10; Siegmund, Chapter 23), yet it should be added that the temporal phenomena of reenactment in dance can themselves be uncovered in early modern choreographic poetics (Changanti, Chapter 25). That dance plays with our perception of time in a variety of contexts, thanks to its unique investments in corporeality and space, may be a structural possibility always susceptible to be mined, but it is one that reenactment highlights and brings urgently to our attention in the present moment. The ontology of historical displacement is at the core of a contemporary dance that is no longer mesmerized by presence. In fact, the present itself can be decentralized as a warrant of contemporaneity.[9] Hence, the whole subject of dance and reenactment is taken up in this handbook largely from the perspectives of historicities, temporalities, and spatialities.[10]

The point is frequently made that reenactment is an act in the present, and this point is meant to show that the present, from the perspective of the historian, is historically defective. When it comes to dance, let us emphasize that it is also an act that reclaims *space* for movement. Because of the prominence of gesture in dance, space also has certain claims on historicity. The carving of space in particular choreographic actions cannot be identified uniquely with the present, no matter when the actions are performed, because formally defined uses of space do not evoke a temporal so much as a rhythmically shaped dimension. Further, the idea of remains or the remainder is based on materiality, and hence cannot do without space and spatiality. Any remainder is a proposition for space and, if it is a performative remainder, for spatial practice. The reader should be attentive throughout the following chapters to the relative weight given to space and time by the contributors in their specific analyses. Temporal displacement of choreographic thought may work with, but also against, the spatial *mise en scène* of the choreographic act. Reenactment uses space and time in intentional counterpoint. The subject of reenactment is an occasion to elaborate and nuance dance theory with respect to the tried and true—but until now somewhat overly abstract—categories of time and space. It is the potential of this new field of study not only for dance practice as such, but also for critical dance theory, that has been the principal impetus for bringing this volume into existence.[11]

Examples of dance reenactments explored in the chapters to follow are Fabian Barba's *A Mary Wigman Dance Evening*; Olga de Soto's *Débords: Reflections on The Green Table*; Philippe Decouflé's *Panorama*; Christina Ciupke and Anna Till's *undo, redo and repeat*, the reconstruction of Merce Cunningham's *Crises*; Richard Move's *Martha@*; recreations of the dances of Rudolf Laban; Olivia Grandville's *Le Cabaret Discrépant*; the Kirov Ballet's 1999 reconstruction of *The Sleeping Beauty*; Trajal Harrell's *Antigone Sr./Twenty Looks or Paris Is Burning at The Judson Church (L)*; Wim Vandekeybus's *Booty Looting*;

[9]  In this sense, reenactment in dance resembles Rosalind E. Krauss's analysis of the grid in modernist art. See "Grids" (Kraus 1985, 9–22).

[10]  See the last section of this Introduction.

[11]  In addition, several chapters focus on the early modern, thus raising the question of whether thinking through reenactment does not affect how we theorize dance prior to contemporary production. See Chapter 14 by VK Preston and Chapter 25 by Seeta Chaganti.

Beyoncé's *Countdown*; Janez Jansa's reconstructions; *Of a Faun (fragments)* by the Knust Quartet; Rani Nair's *Future Memory*; and the reconstruction of Yvonne Rainer's *Continuous Project/Altered Daily*. The general traits that emerge from the iconic example of Hoyer, however, can be outlined as follows: (a) the sense of a primary displacement in the non-contemporaneity of the past with itself; (b) the evocation of complex historical temporalities and the choreographic situation whereby these temporalities enter into the present of performance (the historicity of performative temporalities), creating a complex sense of historicity interacting with the present; (c) dissatisfaction and/or call for reinterpretation and reconceptualization of past art in light of the present creative agenda, which gives the emergence of these temporalities and historicities the aspect of a contemporary intervention.

In sum, danced reenactment places the dance work in a configuration of asymmetrical historical temporalities; it is hence likely to unsettle our assumed grounding in a linearly progressive past, or to unsettle the notion of modernity and/or contemporaneity as something achieved by virtue of the overcoming of a past in a geographical location understood as occupying the global center.[12] These are all signs that reenactment as a general phenomenon has seriously compromised the notion of periodicity, as well as that of the cultural-geographic center and periphery. Need it be stressed that the authors of this volume do not envisage preservation per se as the ultimate goal of reenactment? The fact that reenactment transcends issues of preservation alone is indicated by the evident extensions of the problematic beyond concert dance into areas such as plagiarism (see Kraut, Chapter 18), the inherent contradiction in attempts to preserve the avantgarde (see Noland 2013), the heuristic and pedagogic value of reenactment (Jakovljević, Chapter 11; Hardt, Chapter 12), choreographic interventions in literary texts that raise questions and ideas about the historicity of danced reenactments and the nature of the production of the narrative voice in literary modernism (Jones, Chapter 22), the problem of reproducing a distributed body in an altered physical environment (Banerji, Chapter 21), the entwinement of reenactment with religious belief (Banerji, Chapter 21; Katrak and Ratnam, Chapter 15), the relation of the canon to cultural geography (Barba, Chapter 20), the dialectic between reenactment and the image (Soussloff, Chapter 29; Staelpart 2011), the role of reenactment in spectatorship and research (Skantze, Chapter 16; Preston, Chapter 14), and, ultimately, the question of the relationship of reenactment to historiography itself (Pakes, Chapter 5; Siegmund, Chapter 23; Franko, Chapter 24; Thurner, Chapter 26) as well as to the politics of dance's circulation in a globalized world (Burt, Chapter 17; Kraut, Chapter 18; Staelpart, Chapter 19; Barba, Chapter 20; Giersdorf, Chapter 27; Martin, Chapter 28). Rather, it seems to us that beyond the effects of preservation and/or reinterpretation of dances past, reenactment engages more fundamentally with a critical, polemical, and philosophical reflection on temporality and spatiality in relation to dance's pasts.

---

[12]  Reinhart Kosseleck has identified temporality as the specificity of historical epistemology. Time, for Kosseleck, "leads to the disclosure of history as an epistemological object" (1985, 94).

Danced reenactment leads us into the historical investigation of the relation of dance to pastness at many different levels.[13] The year 1980 was named Heritage Year (*L'Année du Patrimoine*) in France, which brought about significant funding for an important historical dance company, *Ris et danseries*. The work of the Albrecht Knust Quartet in France experimented with danced reenactment in the early 1990s (see Launay 2012). There has since been significant financial support in Western Europe (particularly in Germany) for creative work on the dance heritage of the twentieth century, particularly through the *Tanzfonds Erbe* (Dance Heritage Fund) established by the *Kulturstiftung des Bundes* (The German Federal Cultural Foundation) after the *Tanzplan* ended in 2011 (Siegmund, Hushka). Chapter 23 in this volume, by Gerald Siegmund, contains a good deal of information on work and initiatives in Germany during the decade of the 1990s. A significant number of artists discussed in these pages are for this reason either German or have worked in Germany. But danced reenactment is not presented here exclusively as a response to state funding or as an exclusively European phenomenon. The UNESCO initiatives of the 1990s, which included dance as immaterial culture, identified movement and gesture as valued and endangered aspects of world heritage: dance was central to this initiative globally. The *Handbook* includes chapters on East and South India and South America.

*The Handbook of Dance and Reenactment* explores how the preoccupation of contemporary choreographers with the dances of predecessors has emerged in the new millennium at the vanguard of contemporary dance. Although this phenomenon has wide-ranging implications for dance in relation to concepts of the past, historicity, and memory, the handbook is not intended to convey a definitive viewpoint on the subject, which at the time of this writing proves to be as diverse as the protagonists—dancers, choreographers, and scholars—individually and collectively engaged with it. The term *reenactment* is one of many other terms used in the chapters that follow: *re-performance, remake, citation, the distributed body, alternative histories, acheiropoietics, restructuring touch, re-actualization, the derivative, cover*, and so on.[14] The category of reenactment itself, while it has been explored in performance art,[15] film,[16] and photography (Soussloff, Chapter 29), extends in the case of dance beyond dance history per se to questions of practice as research, archival phenomenology, spectatorship, legacy,

---

[13] On the relevance of pastness to the notion of historical performance, see Franko and Richards (2000).

[14] This last term is adopted from music and is analogous to versioning.

[15] The retrospective of the performance art of Marina Abramovic at the Museum of Modern Art in New York several years ago brought to wide public attention the phenomenon of reenactment in the world of contemporary art. Abramovic's performance works of the 1970s were returned to the museum space as living artifacts, as if they now existed outside of historical time, as objects to be displayed. Her show "The Artist Is Present" raised public consciousness of a broader trend currently taking place in contemporary dance and performance; it also reopened debates about the return of past work (Jones 2011).

[16] An early example of filmed reenactment is Doug Hall, Chip Lord, Doug Michels, Jody Procter, *The Eternal Frame* (1975) produced by T. R. Uthco and Ant Farm. See also Mellencamp (1999).

heritage, plagiarism, singularity, and political action, as well as to historiography, pedagogy, witness-hood, transmission, cultural geography, and the experience of inter- and
hetero-temporalities. Each part of this *Handbook* attempts to define the major concerns
that relate chapters to one another under a given rubric. Yet, despite these rubrics, which
impose thematic categories on the wealth of material reflected upon in these chapters,
all of the authors represented here engage in a vigorous theorization of the significance
of danced reenactment for contemporary culture, a theorization that militates against
self-enclosed categories. It is this theorization of a new field of contemporary creative
activity and its relationship to scholarship—an unprecedented relationship bringing
performance and research together—that is analyzed here.

Scholars of performance art have underlined the relation to reenactment of the
document—most particularly of the photographic document—as a major axis of
inquiry and theorization. As Boris Groys has noted, "Increasingly, in art space today
we are confronted not just with artworks but with art documentation" (Groys 2012,
209). Groys goes on to explain that it is actually the document that is the living art or
"life form," whereas the work of art itself is a documentation of the image.[17] That dance
and dance studies have not accorded comparable attention to the photographic document is due to the particularity of dance practice or, one might say, its medium specificity, wherein (unlike performance art) research into corporeality plays a crucial role
for which the still image is inadequate, and where before the question of the work can
arise, the question of a technique of repetition must be examined. So, for example,
Fabián Barba's reenactment of Mary Wigman's dance evening for her 1929–1930 tour of
the United States took research into corporeality as "a crucial addition to archival and
textual sources" (Barba 2011, 84). In addition, a set of modalities already exists in the
dance field with a preexisting relationship to reenactment. Here, I refer to activities such
as revival, reconstruction and/or reinvention, and adaptation or reworking.[18] For example, a revival implies the return to a work that has ceased being performed but within
an institutional context, such as a ballet company, that is able to provide institutional
and personal memory; reconstruction implies, to the contrary, a return to work whose
performative traditions have been essentially lost; whereas reinvention, reworking, and/
or adaptation imply other sorts of strategies for and theories of historical evocation.
Because of this already fairly complex layering of possibilities for historical reflection in
danced performance, crucial issues of the artist's identity, the work's identity, and historical consciousness tend to take precedence over the instrumentality of the visual document per se in dance.[19]

---

[17] "Art documentation . . . marks the attempt to use artistic media within art spaces to refer to life
itself, that is, to a pure activity, to pure practice, to an artistic life . . ." (Groys 2012, 210).

[18] For further discussion of these categories, see Midgelow (2007).

[19] This fact has much to do with the specificity of dance's histories and ideologies in relation to the
field of reenactment. The fact that dance in the Western canon has long been associated with a belief
in the uniqueness of the present moment—the now—is what reenactment as contemporary creativity
challenges. In a preface to her seminal essay on minimalist dance, Yvonne Rainer wrote: " . . . [I]t is
unclear to me whether the present generation is knocking its head against the walls of their predecessors,

# After Ephemerality

In many ways, reenactments tell us the past is not over: the past is unfinished business.[20] By insisting upon the return to actions following precise aesthetic procedures, reenactment troubles our sense of what is past in the past. By bringing back movements that were thought to have expired with their inaugural contexts—movements that are both strange and familiar, forgotten and recalled—danced reenactment unsettles the closure of history, the conviction that new movements do effectively supersede earlier ones. The notion of the work is not only recalled but also destabilized; the belief in authenticity is both confirmed and turned on its head; the return to the past becomes an avant-garde gesture; the notion of tradition is invoked, but also criticized; references to time past are multiplied and only understood as a constellation (Christina Thurner, Chapter 26 in this volume, also calls it a *network*); the tools of time and space essential to dance composition are intellectually retooled.

Nothing militates more against the claim of dance over its own history than the notion that dance is fundamentally ephemeral. Were we to accept the ephemerality of dance, then the history of dance itself becomes unnamable. Reenactment in dance testifies to the overturning of a long-standing trope of dance history and theory: dance has been much vaunted, but also subtlety maligned, as the quintessential art form of the immediate, transient, and vanishing present. Movement and vanishing are both contained in the phrase "the moment." But many dancers are now actively engaged with reclaiming their past rather than flying from it, and in this process they challenge the irremediable nature of dance's storied transience. What has reenactment done to ephemerality? The aura that ephemerality has cast on the dance work in modernity is perhaps finally succumbing to its own intellectual and artistic mortality because of reenactment. This death of ephemerality opens a space for recalling—in the sense both of remembering (or wishing to remember) and summoning back. For these reasons, reenactment should be understood as post-ephemeral: it may emphasize the presence of the dancing subject in dialogue with history, but the dancing subject herself is not presented in a "before"; the status of the lost past and that of the vanishing present are equally under erasure: a double disappearance is revoked (Schneider 2011). In their place, the stage is filled with inter-temporal gestures wherein the spatial positions necessary to this operation can be

---

or just writing on them" (Rainer 1999, 28). At this remove we can affirm that they are not just writing about predecessors: they are also reenacting them. But does such reenactment constitute writing? As Susan Foster noted in 1993 of the brawl between Clio and Terpsichore: "*Clio and Terpsichore . . . roll up their sleeves and begin to write (or is it dance?)*" (Foster 1995, 19). Whatever the case may be, the supersession of the predecessor in the teleology of modernism has been jettisoned. If George Balanchine reputedly stated, "There is nothing but now," as proclaimed on the banner hanging on the wall of the State Theater announcing the current 2016 New York City Ballet season in New York, it seems that the now is being crowded out by a series of other theres or other wheres.

[20] I am grateful to Charmian Wells for this formulation.

dramatized and hence rendered visible and understandable. This is the imaginary cho-reographic template that many reenactments engage us with. Intertemporal relational-ity of gesture is the spatial grid (Kraus 1985) that militates against progressive change, characterized by modernism; it is thus not by chance that modernists themselves are frequently the subjects of reenactment. This is why danced reenactment is not strictly a heritage activity, even if it has been funded under these auspices. And this is also why our subject does not fit neatly into François Hartog's framework of presentism.[21]

## RECONSTRUCTION/REENACTMENT

Reenactment and cognate activities referred to and conceptualized in these pages con-stitute a challenge to the mode of presentation of dance as traditionally reconstructed in the twentieth century. This refers not to the method of reconstruction per se, but to the mode of theatrical presentation that the reconstructive method lends itself to.[22] The dis-tinction and overlap between reconstruction and reenactment reside in the difference between reconstruction as methodology of recovery and reenactment as dramaturgy of presentation. Reconstruction is the activity necessary to restore the movements of a dance in their completeness through the strict decoding of notation (if there is any) and the requisite filling in of knowledge gaps where they occur (reconstruction as method-ology); reenactment encompasses the theatrical and dramaturgical devices with which the effect of the dance as a representation of itself in the past is shaped and manifested in performance. Reconstruction, despite its uncertainties of interpretation, remains a core discipline unless it is not entirely rejected as irrelevant (Siegmund, Chapter 23); reenact-ment has fundamentally reformulated how to stage reconstructive results.[23]

The goal of reconstruction was to create a "dance museum," a way to view the past accomplishments of dance as if preserved within the medium of live performance. But the notion of movement preservation was in conflict with the phenomenology of dance that affirmed dance's immediate appearance in the present—its phenomenality—as an unavoidable requirement of its power. Indeed, one could go so far as to say that the very medium of dance was thought of as the present body, also called the lived body.

Reconstructions were always afflicted by a double vision: they were live performances reproducing a transpired past in the present. Perceived in this way, they were unable to fully realize the immediacy of dance in its phenomenal presence. Consequently, they engendered a gap between themselves and the very terms in which the original

---

[21] See the discussion of Hartog in what follows.
[22] See Chapter 20 by Fabián Barba on the structural balance between reconstruction and reenactment; see Chapter 6 by Carrie Noland in this volume for an argument in favor of reconstruction and against reenactment.
[23] For a more pointed critique of reconstruction in the case of Renaissance dance, see Franko (1986, 6–7).

had embodied its originality. Reconstruction, in other words, unwittingly presented dance as always already historical. Although it developed a methodology for the historical reconstitution of choreography, it faced by that very fact a contradiction inherent in its theatrical mode of reproduction, a contradiction whose focal point was the dancer's body. In its valiant attempt to save dance from oblivion, reconstruction struck at the very corporeal heart of dance itself. The main critique was that, despite the rigor of the research undergirding it, reconstruction came across as a simulacrum rather than as a historical experience. This may be due to what Simone Willeit has called "the historical positivism" implied in reconstruction considered as a "historiography of practice" (Willeit 2010, 47; my translation).[24] This positivism consists in the assumption that only textual evidence can suffice to fill the gaps in knowledge and that no other form of reflection might be useful. What is rarely taken into consideration is that the passage of time, in itself, has wrought changes in the dancer's bodily morphology, technique, and aesthetics, as well as in the spectator's expectations.[25] Unable to account for these, the reconstructed work appeared to exist outside of time—time here understood as the medium within which dance transpires—despite claims for the value of the reconstructed work as timeless, eternal, and hence highly valuable: worthy of being remembered. Reconstructions lacked persuasive presence in the visceral terms of dance itself.

Reenactment represents a significant corrective to reconstruction's undertheorized theatricality that was also beset with assumptions about authenticity. It is worth recalling to mind here the critique of immediacy in modern art by Georg Lukács, who wrote of the modern literary schools: "[T]hey all remain frozen in their own immediacy; they fail to pierce the surface and to discover the underlying essence, i.e. the real factors that relate their experience to the hidden social forces that produce them" (Lukács 1980, 36–37). While it is not evident that reenactment is a new form of realism enabling us to free ourselves of modernism's frozen immediacy, it is clear that reenactment actually replaces the frozenness of reconstruction with the immediacy of the present in such a way that a critical dimension is able to arise from the ruins of impersonation and under-theorized reproduction.

Reenactments generally manage to uphold the claims to historicity that cannot be reasonably abandoned in the dance field, while at the same time relinquishing the pretense to the reproduction of the past as a copy. Reenactments do this by treating the past dance as something that exists in the present. Although not entirely divorced from reconstruction as a methodology, the current phenomenon of reenactment in the dance field intrepidly alters what we dare call the ideology of reconstruction as the possibility of witnessing the past again as past. The conceit of the museum has disappeared, inasmuch as a contemporary dancer now reconstructs earlier work as part of his or her contemporary creative activity, rather than as removed from it by historical

---

[24] " . . . [I]dentifiziert sich doch eine Historiographie der Praxis—im landläufigen Sinn als Tanz-Rekonstruktion gefasst—über eine 'bodily investigation.' "
[25] As Gerald Siegmund remarks in Chapter 23, these differences reveal the very conditions of the possibility of reconstruction itself.

reflection.[26] Furthermore, the distinctions between history and memory bifurcating the reconstructive field have splintered. The re-enactor of a past dance is no longer necessarily a dance scholar, first of all, and the relation of the re-enactor to personal memory is no longer that of the eyewitness/participant, as the dancer frequently works through the memory of a custodian of the work or through other types of training. Where the reconstructor assumed distance from the past through recourse to documents, the re-enactor assumes closeness to the past through the body itself as archive; where the reconstructor assumed closeness to the past through witness-hood, the re-enactor assumes distance from the past through temporal estrangement. This would particularly be the case with Martin Nachbar's reenactment of Dore Hoyer. Yet, in Fabián Barba's relation to Mary Wigman through his expressionist dance training in Ecuador and in Richard Move's relation to Martha Graham by virtue of a very personal sense of channeling, there are varying scenarios of affinity and kinship also at work.[27]

Perhaps this explains how and why the issues broached here under the aegis of reenactment extend well beyond those normally associated with reconstruction and preservation. Throughout the chapters to follow, connections are made between what is happening on the concert stage and elsewhere in the global "performative" environment: commercial performance, ritual performance, pedagogy, the financial and art markets, spectatorial reception, visual art, the phenomenology of archival research, and the field of history as an academic discipline. Despite this, some very familiar issues are still apparent: What counts as a document? What is an archive with respect to embodied memory? How do memory and memory transference operate in the absence of first-person experience? What is a score? What are the limits of interpretation, and why? What is the relationship of past dance to futurity? Just as reenactment overhauls the reconstructive project by way of asking new questions and devising new responses, so the breadth and depth of questions surrounding reconstruction and authenticity are opened up to wider inquiry regarding repeatability and reproduction.

Dance, as a time-based art, exists within a historical temporality that comprises historically determined conditions of reception, styles and modes of gesturality, tastes with their concomitant cultural contexts, and technologies of display, all of which are productive of uniquely defined aesthetic experiences. With its emphasis on the recovery of movement vocabulary, sequence, and music of the original work, reconstruction could not incorporate the conditions of production and reception within which the work made its claim to time as historically present.[28] Yet, what reconstruction can accomplish is irreplaceable. Many reenactments subsume reconstruction within a

---

[26]  It is perhaps ironic that one of the sites in which this has become possible is precisely the art museum, which continues to play a role in the production of dance reenactments, introducing a new twist into the museal aspect of reconstructions generally. See Franko and Lepecki (2014); Franko (2016).

[27]  See Chapters 4 and 20, by these two artists, in this volume.

[28]  "Traditional studies of past dance practices typically ask questions about movement vocabulary, dance's relationship with music, coordination with scenic/visual elements, and dancers' training and careers" (Tomko 2004, 328).

dramaturgical and conceptual frame that removes the implicit claim to authenticity from the reconstructed dance.

In reversing the ideological premises of reconstruction while conserving its methodology, re-enactive dancers have taken the representation of the past into their own hands, and accordingly have transformed it. This appropriation of the historical function can be interpreted in a number of ways: (1) as the "right of return" to earlier work; (2) the use of performance as a historiographical medium with a discursive dimension; and (3) self-staging as a contemporary agent in confrontation with this project, hence a willful theatricalization of the entire situation.[29]

# HISTORICITY, TEMPORALITY, AND WORK WITHIN WORK

The questions of time and space, long the staple terms with which dance has been discussed in formal terms, are now the very terms engaging actively with what François Hartog has called "regimes of historicity." For Hartog, a regime of historicity or temporality is "ultimately a way of expressing and organizing—that is, ways of articulating the past, the present, and the future—and investing them with sense." (Hartog 2015, 106). The displacement of reconstruction by reenactment in dance history signals a change in regimes of historicity at the level of how the past of dance can be understood to occur as dance again. Reenactments are related not only to the rediscovery and restaging of particular past works, but also to the relationship of those works to the present in which they are reproduced. What is (re)produced by many reenactments is not only a work per se, but also the knowledge of history necessary to the work's very reappearance. The presence of knowledge production in performance can be related to the lecture-performance format prevalent in many reenactments. As Maaike Bleeker has remarked,

> [L]ecture performances emerge as a genre that gives expression to an understanding of dance as a form of knowledge production—knowledge not (or not only) about dance but also dance as a specific form of knowledge that raises questions about the nature of knowledge and about practices of doing research. (Bleeker 2012, 233)

The problematic of dance as historical research into dance, of dance production as the performance of a research product, and of the set of relationships that ensue between present and past that can also be said to constitute knowledge or conscious reflection—all this differentiates reenactment in dance from reenactment in other media.

[29] André Lepecki's insistence on the "will to reenact" in the title of his article that introduced the notion of the body-archive is important in this respect. Lepecki (2010) also argues against the idea that reenactment has anything to do with a nostalgia for the past. He also discusses this very nostalgia with respect to the phenomenon of choreography in Lepecki (2004).

One of the particular qualities of a reenactment is that the past of dance is no longer apprehended as irrevocably past, and the present no longer apprehended as uniquely phenomenal. When Hartog speaks of the presentism of our regime of historicity since the 1980s, he defines presentism as "the present's immediate self-historicization" (2015, 193). A close analysis of reenactment in dance nevertheless reveals spatiotemporal processes at work in dance that are more complex than self-historicization. In reenactment, dance historical material is being treated as the object of knowledge, rather than as a mechanism of self-historicization. Therefore, it is not the present that historicizes itself in danced reenactments, but the past that "presentifies" itself through particular protocols of research and the theatrical manipulation of time and space in that dramaturgical process. Indeed, reenactments engender an awareness that dance occupies a unique time and space between past and present. Just as there is variability within historical time, as Reinhart Koselleck has shown, so there is variability in the experience of historical time or the experience of time within performance as historical. To experience time as historical in performance is not equivalent to reading historical narrative: It is to be engaged with an experience in/of the present, which contains pastness *in actu* (Kosseleck 2002, 127). Areas of inter-temporality are germane to our subject when it comes to dance. On behalf of the authors of this *Handbook*, I am gesturing here toward their intervention into the theory of history from the perspective of dance theory.[30] This is, first of all, because the notion of history as it is performed in danced reenactment is not founded on the necessity for narrative or for a visual artifact because such dance knowledge makes the claim to embodiment. In this sense, the use of the document by dancers is closer to what Paul Ricoeur referred to with the document as trace. "[T]he notion of documentary proof, placed at the forefront of the investigation refers directly to the problem that concerns us, that of knowledge through traces" (Ricoeur 1984, 6). Ricoeur goes on to explain that documents are the trace of the "inside" of events, which when correlated to the "outside" of events leads to *action*:

> The twofold delimitation of the concept of "historical evidence" by means of the notion of the "inside" of the event and that of the "thought" of the historical agent leads directly to that of re-enactment. (1984, 7)

Reenacted dance presents us with a history of dance in its own terms—a dimension of self-reflexivity, rather than the pretense toward reproduction of the "outside" alone, and existing in the mode of present performance as an action with this twofold dimension. With no textual or material artifact upon which to ground its relationship to history, dance requires the body itself as a mediator of knowledge: it is both historical agent and bearer of historical action. Reenactments shift the history of dance into the present as performances that appropriate the project of historiography by *acting on* that which seemed heretofore to belong only to the register of language (the *writing* of history).

---

[30] Dialogue with the theory of history is rarely recognized as a characteristic of dance theory.

Reenactments reintroduce lived experience of the event into what would otherwise be a historical representation—a representation of the past as "history," resulting in the status of representation as history.

This understanding of reenactment in relation to history has been, of course, controversial. When historian Vanessa Agnew makes the distinction between historical reenactment and history proper, she challenges us to understand how this distinction operates in relation to choreography. In her article "What Is Reenactment?" Agnew states, "Reenactment's central epistemological claim that experience furthers historical understanding is clearly problematic: body-based testimony tells us more about the present than the collective past" (Agnew 2004, 335). It should be considered, however, that when dance itself is the historical "object," body-based testimony at the level of *savoir faire*, to use Barba's term, is crucial to research and complementary to textual and visual sources. Moreover, research into corporeality cannot be dismissed so easily as "body-based testimony" precisely because it is research. In dance, the presence of scores and/or documents that constitute traces, in Ricoeur's sense, can be reanimated by "techniques of repetition," one of Derrida's requirements for the very existence of the archive.[31] In this sense, the position of the re-enactor, like that of the historian, is in the present. As Michel Foucault has noted, "Historians take unusual pains to erase the elements in their work which reveal their grounding in a particular time and place . . . . " (1977, 156).[32] But what is significant about this present, as Ricoeur points out with respect to Collingwood, is that reenactment abolishes "the temporal distance between the past and the present by the very act of rethinking what was once thought" (Ricoeur 1984, 10). And, one could add, by the very act of re-dancing what was once danced, with the proviso that the choreographic and performative logic of a particular dance (in Chapter 10, Maaike Bleeker, following Collingwood, speaks of "the logic of thought embodied in the dance") has been retrieved in following the trace of documentary evidence and by further understanding that trace in the context of the corporeal logic that makes it re-doable. This is precisely where the importance of dance's medium specificity as practice becomes salient. A dance is itself a specific kind of event. Reenactment, unlike bodily testimony, is the recalling (in the active sense of summoning) of a past action as a particular event in the present. In this sense, one can say that memory remains not in the body, but in the event as it becomes accessible by doing. In dance, to reenact is to relive eventfulness in/as the work. But, by "work" is meant here two things: the work of dance itself, understood as the labor that makes up the dance; and the dance itself as a work of art, the product of that labor. In other words, danced reenactment is the reestablishment of

---

[31] "No archive . . . without techniques of repetition" (Derrida 1995, 11).

[32] Susan Leigh Foster explored the relation of the historian to the past of dance as a desire on the historian's part to "consort with dead bodies" (Foster 1995, 6). "This affiliation, based on a kind of kinesthetic empathy between living and dead, but imagined bodies, enjoys no primal status outside the world of writing" (7). Following this logic, it would seem that reenactment brings dance closer to writing. Foster's concern in this piece was the historian's body, but the gap between the historian's body and the dancer's body has since narrowed.

the live artwork as the work within the work. As work remains visible within the work, the work of reenactment produces dance as self-reflexively performative knowledge of itself for an audience, and hence, as historically in the present moment, rather than as a reproduction of ephemerality outside of time. The way in which this conceit is conveyed to an audience as "historically in the present moment" (which I consider to be significantly different from in the present moment *tout court*) constitutes danced reenactment as both theatrical modality and political strategy.

## Works Cited

Agnew, Vanessa. 2004. "What Is Reenactment?" *Criticism* 46(3) (Summer): 327–339.

Barba, Fabián. 2011. "Research into Corporeality." *Dance Research Journal* 43(1) (Summer): 83–89.

Bleeker, Maaike. 2012. "Lecture Performance as Contemporary Dance." In *New German Dance Studies*, edited by Susan Manning and Lucia Ruprecht, 232–246. Urbana, Chicago, and Springfield: University of Illinois Press, 2012.

Derrida, Jacques. 1986. *Archive Fever: A Freudian Impression*. Translated by Eric Prenowitz. Chicago and London: University of Chicago Press.

Dray, William H. 1995. *History as Re-enactment: R. G. Collingwood's Idea of History*. Oxford: Oxford University Press.

Foster, Susan Leigh. 1995. "Choreographing History: Manifesto for Dead and Moving Bodies." In *Choreographing History*, 3–21. Bloomington: Indiana University Press.

Foucault, Michel. 1977. "Nietzsche, Genealogy, History." In *Language, Counter-Memory, Practice: Selected Essays and Interviews*, edited by Donald F. Bouchard, 139–164. Ithaca, NY: Cornell University Press.

Franko, Mark. 1986. *The Dancing Body in Renaissance Choreography (c. 1416–1589)*. Birmingham, AL: Summa Publications.

Franko, Mark. 1989. "Repeatability, Reconstruction and Beyond." *Theatre Journal* 41(1) (March): 56–74.

Franko, Mark. 2016. "Anti-Museum, Super-Museum, and Heterotopia in Boris Chamatz's *20 Dancers for the XX Century*." In *Corpus* (Spring 2017): http://www.corpusweb.net/der-tanz-von-museum-und-performance.html.

Franko, Mark, and André Lepecki. 2014. "Dance in the Museum." *Dance Research Journal* 46(3) (December): 1–4.

Franko, Mark, and Annette Richards, Editors. 2000. *Acting on the Past: Historical Performance across the Disciplines*. Middletown, CT: Wesleyan University Press.

Giersdorf, Jens Richard. 2013. *The Body of the People: East German Dance since 1945*. Madison: University of Wisconsin Press.

Groys, Boris. 2012. "Art in the Age of Biopolitics: From Artwork to Art Documentation." In *Perform, Repeat, Record: Live Art in History*, edited by Amelia Jones and Adrian Heathfield, 209–219. Chicago: University of Chicago Press.

Hartog, François. 2015. *Regimes of Historicity: Presentism and Experiences of Time*. First published in French in 2003. Translated by Saskia Brown. New York: Columbia University Press.

Jones, Amelia. 2011. "'The Artist Is Present': Artistic Re-enactments and the Impossibility of Presence." *The Drama Review* 55(1): 16–45.

Kosseleck, Reinhart. *1985. Futures Past: On the Semantics of Historical Time.* Translated by Keith Tribe. Cambridge, MA: MIT Press.

Koselleck, Reinhart. 2002. *The Practice of Conceptual History, Timing History, Spacing Concepts.* Translated by Todd Samuel Presner et al. Stanford, CA: Stanford University Press.

Kraus, Rosalyn. 1985. *The Originality of the Avant-Garde and Other Modernist Myths.* Cambridge, MA: MIT Press.

Launay, Isabelle. 2012. "Citational Poetics in Dance: . . . *of a Faun (Fragments)* by the Albrecht Knust Quartet, before-after 2000." *Dance Research Journal* 44(2) (Winter): 173–194.

Lepecki, André. 2004. "Inscribing Dance." In *Of the Presence of the* Body, edited by André Lepecki, 124–139. Middletown, CT: Wesleyan University Press.

Lepecki, André. 2010. "The Body as Archive: Will to Re-enact and the Afterlives of Dances." *Dance Research Journal* 42(2) (Winter): 28–48.

Lukács, Georg. 1980. "Realism in the Balance." In *Aesthetics and Politics,* edited by Ronald Taylor, 28–59. London: Verso.

Mellencamp, Patricia. 1999. "Death, Shock, Art: Kennedy, Walter Benjamin, and *Eternal Frame.*" In *High Anxiety. Catastrophe, Scandal, Age and Comedy,* 99–103. Bloomington: Indiana University Press.

Midgelow, Vida L. 2007. *Reworking the Ballet: Counternarratives and Alternative Bodies.* London and New York: Routledge.

Müller, Hedwig, Frank-Manuel Peter, and Garnet Schuldt. 1992. *Dore Hoyer Tänzerin.* Köln: Deutsches Tanzarchiv/Edition Hentrich.

Nachbar, Martin. 2012. "Training/Remembering." *Dance Research Journal* 44(2) (Winter): 5–12.

Noland, Carrie. 2013. "Inheriting the Avant-Garde: Marcel Duchamp, Merce Cunningham, and the 'Legacy Plan.'" *Dance Research Journal* 45(2) (August): 85–123.

Rainer, Yvonne. 1999. "The Mind Is a Muscle." In *A Woman Who . . . Essays, Interviews, Scripts,* 27–46. Baltimore, MD, and London: Johns Hopkins University Press.

Ricoeur, Paul. 1984. *The Reality of the Historical Past.* Milwaukee: Marquette University Press, 1984.

Schneider, Rebecca. 2011. *Performing Remains: Art and War in Times of Theatrical Reenactment.* London: Routledge.

Staelpart, Christel. 2011. "Reenacting Modernity: Fabián Barba's *A Mary Wigman Dance Evening* (2000)." *Dance Research Journal* 43(1) (Summer): 90–98.

Tomko, Linda J. 2004. "Reconstruction." In *The International Encyclopedia of Dance,* edited by Selma-Jeanne Cohen, vol. 5, 328. New York and Oxford: Oxford University Press.

Willeit, Simone. 2010. "Stolpern und Unzulänglichkeiten. Interferenzen in Tanz-Rekonstruction." In *Original und Revival. Geschicts-Schreibung im Tanz,* edited by Christina Thruner and Julia Wehren, 47–58. Zürich: Chronos.

# PART I

# PHENOMENOLOGY OF THE ARCHIVE

CHAPTER 2

........................................................................................................................

# TRACING SENSE/READING SENSATION

## *An Essay on Imprints and Other Matters*

........................................................................................................................

MARTIN NACHBAR

## A DOUBLE BEGINNING

........................................................................................................................

WHEN I found the VHS videotape of *Dore Hoyer tanzt—eine Gedenksendung* (*Dore Hoyer Dances—A Broadcast in Commemoration*) in the library of PARTS (Performing Arts Research & Training Studios) in Brussels in 1999, I didn't know I would be working with it and thinking about it for some time, as I do in this chapter.[1] But when I started writing this chapter, focusing on questions around the archive in general and the dance archive in particular, I realized that I had to include experiences and insights from a more recent work of mine: *Repeater—Dance Piece with Father* (2007). Though working on Hoyer's dances made me aware of how history can be in dialogue with contemporary bodies, it was the process of research toward *Repeater* that made the imprint of experience on the body actually palpable to me (*spürbar*). This is not merely an idle phrase, since the word for trace (*spur*) also includes in its meaning the fact of sensation. In this sense, the trace is an actual fact that we live with long before we become aware of it. In this chapter I want to look at and better understand the interactions between these bodily imprints and the documents in dance archives, as I have experienced them during my reconstruction of Dore Hoyer's *Affectos Humanos*, which I undertook from 1999 to 2008.[2]

........................................................................................................................

[1]  Hoyer premiered *Affectos Humanos* in Berlin in 1962.
[2]  This is the revised version of a text first written in German on invitation of Janine Schulze, then director of the German Dance Archive, Leipzig. The earlier version was published in *Are 100 Objects Enough to Represent the Dance. Zur Archivierbarkeit von Tanz* (München: epodium 2010).

It is common knowledge that our bodies store consciously learned movement sequences. As children, we learn postural, behavioral, and movement patterns from our adult models: we incorporate strata of experiences and movement knowledge in our bodies, which we can then excavate layer by layer, as would an archaeologist who searches for what occurred in earlier times; traces of events that we can uncover by chance or through research and reading, much like a forensic criminologist in search of evidence of guilt or innocence; or patterns that can be talked about and interpreted during a psychotherapeutic session.

In the context of this chapter, archaeology, forensic work, and psychotherapy share four relevant features. Each of them deals with a place, where something has been put and has been stored. Then the stored things—historical objects, traces, behavioral patterns—surface, either coincidentally or through a careful search. After this, the things found are examined and interpreted. And eventually, the findings are related to the present—in order to understand history and culture better, as in archaeology; to convict the guilty party, as in forensic work; or to come to an understanding of oneself, as in psychotherapy. These similarities may seem obvious and unimportant at first. But they are what give us the clues with which to examine the dance archive as a place where documents of past dances are stored, from the particular point of view of a dance artist, whose intention is to bring the study of documents into movement.

The archive as a place is derived from the Greek *acheîon*: a house, the villa of an *árchont*, a high-ranking civil servant of the city-state, custodian of the official documents of the state, and the one authorized to interpret these documents (Derrida 1995, 2). But to consider the archive not only as a place, where documents are stored systematically and researched and interpreted intentionally, but also as a site, where things emerge accidentally, might shed new light on what differentiates the dance archive from other archives. As I understand it, the problem of the dance archive is at the same time its scope: The documents that are collected in it always contain references to events that took place in the form of dances, performances, or workshops, or other events in the life of a choreographer. Thus, before a dance scholar studies and interprets these documents, there has already been a transfer from the medium of dance to a medium that can be archived in the usual sense. And this transfer is not only a technical, but also a conceptual one, which takes something away from the dance to be archived or adds something to it, depending on the tastes and interests of those involved.

At the same time, the dance archive competes with exactly those bodies that have experienced specific dance forms and choreographies and that have, most importantly, stored them as so-called tacit knowledge, almost as securely as an archive stores its documents. I am speaking of dancers, dance teachers, choreographers, and spectators, whose experiences themselves constitute a dance archive in which they are stored. This ambiguity makes the dance archive a "place" where no ultimate interpretation can be achieved. Instead, it asks for a continuous doubling of the approach to the dance archive: The body that enters the archive in order to find documents of dance is itself already a carrier of movement knowledge. The knowledge stored in dance archives has to be constantly aligned and realigned with this bodily knowledge. In this sense, the dance archive that I am at pains to describe is not "placed" in space as a conventional archive would be: it is multi-sited.

And I am not speaking of documenting so-called oral history or filming moving bodies because I mean more specifically the interactions between archived and remembered movement knowledge. These interactions necessitate a constant and conscious dealing with the ambiguity of the researcher's body entering, finding, studying, reimagining, and interpreting the documents that speak of past bodies creating, studying, imagining, and interpreting dances. And in doing so, we might be hovering over a double bottom without noticing it, until suddenly a yet unseen document or unfelt sensation flies up like a magician's dove from a seemingly empty box.

## The Dance Archive as Work/Space

My reconstruction of Dore Hoyer's *Affectos Humanos* first consisted of the reconstruction of three dances, *Desire, Hate,* and *Anxiety*, for a piece called *affects* (see note 5). Shortly after the staging of *affects*, I did a lecture-performance entitled *ReConstruct*, in which I talk about the meaning of reconstruction in contemporary dance and then show the three dances. Both works toured extensively throughout Europe and South America. In 2007, I began the work on the remaining two dances, *Vanity* and *Love*, in order to stage them together with the other three dances in a piece entitled *Urheben Aufheben*, which premiered in May 2008 at Kampnagel Theater in Hamburg. At this time, I taught one of the dances for the first time to a dance student in Cologne.

After touring *Urheben Aufheben* throughout Europe, Japan, and Australia, I started working with French-Brazilian choreographer Paula Pi on her reconstruction of all five dances. Paula Pi began working with Hoyer's dances during her master's studies at EXERCE (Master's degree choreographic studies "research and performance") in Montpellier in France. At first, she asked me to be her mentor for her research project, in which she experimented with repetitions and loops of the original material and with crossdressing as a man (which I found particularly interesting, as Hoyer herself looks androgynous in the costumes she wears in the film). Now Paula Pi is producing her reconstruction in France and Germany, and we still work regularly on her reconstruction,

I am no longer performing the reconstruction, but I am still teaching workshops on reconstruction. In these, I regularly use the film I used for my reconstruction, inviting students to study a few seconds or minutes in depth, rather than teaching them the dances. Filmed in black and white in 1967 by the German broadcasting station Hessischer Rundfunk, the film of Hoyer dancing the solo cycle was first shown in 1968 after Dore Hoyer had committed suicide. First we see dance critic Klaus Geitel, reading an obituary. He is sitting in a chair, reading from a manuscript on his lap. He speaks about the earnestness and sobriety of Hoyer's art and relates it to her tragic end. As he speaks, Geitel's image is overlain with photographs of Dore Hoyer, a thoughtful woman, whose gaze persistently looks beyond the camera's lens into the distance, while she shows great energy and concentration in her dancing poses. The result is the image of an underestimated, poor, almost tragic artist, whom we can observe dancing once again in the wake of her obituary.

Then we see her dancing the five short solos, each dealing with one human affect or emotion: *Vanity, Desire, Hate, Anxiety*, and *Love*.[3] She is accompanied by percussion and piano by Dimitry Wiatowitsch, but she seems to be all alone in space, as he remains outside the picture frame. Dressed in wide costumes that flow around her thin body, with white makeup on her face and wearing a black skullcap, Dore Hoyer looks androgynous, a black-gray-white figure that unfolds her choreographies in a gray-white space, which is lit in such a way that no edges, corners, or walls are visible. A human lost in an endless space, following the traces of her affects and emotions all alone, drawing and redrawing themes and variations, she is so deeply absorbed in her task that she no longer hears Klaus Geitel's obituary. It is as if she withdraws from the world, a feeling for which we find visual evidence in shots of the last two dances: A camera tilt upward and away from the shivering figure, who lifts her arms in despair at the end of *Anxiety*, as Dore Hoyer disappears downward, as if sinking into the ground. And in the last sequence of *Love*, the light fades out slowly until the kneeling dancer with folded hands is swallowed in darkness. At the end we read the credits, white cursive script on black ground: "Dore Hoyer danced a cycle."

This solemn cinematic portrait, which seeks to create a direct link between dance and death, together with Dore Hoyer's meticulous movement research that surfaces in the film and has helped her dances to survive, forms the document that has made the choreography of the five dances of the *Affectos humanos* archivable. But the film is not only a document of the choreography and its interpretation by the dancer. It is also a document that shows how Klaus Geitel and the film director Rudolf Küfner saw Dore Hoyer and her work at the time of making the film. There are, for example, the choice of words in the obituary, the camera work, the space design, and the lighting. Surely, these are not considered news for the science of the archive. But considering the ambiguity of the dance archive, we have to point out that it is exactly these processes of translation that can make dealing with archived material productive. But I am getting ahead of myself.

Let us go back to finding the VHS tape in 1999 in Brussels. Present were Thomas Plischke, Alice Chauchat, Hendrik Laevens, Erna Omarsdóttir, and I. The title on the back of the VHS cassette caught my attention because a colleague at the SNDO[4] in Amsterdam had given a talk about Dore Hoyer in 1992. As I had only seen photos of Hoyer, I was curious about what her work would look like in motion. So I suggested to the group that we watch the recording. I remember that it was Thomas Plischke and myself—the two Germans of the group—who were particularly fascinated by the

---

[3]  Dore Hoyer made the *Affectos humanos* after reading Baruch de Spinoza's *Ethics* in 1962.

[4]  *School voor Nieuwe Dans Ontewikkeling*, Dutch for School for New Dance Development. Founded in 1975, the school has an international reputation. Well-known graduates include, among others, Sasha Waltz, Thomas Lehmen, Nicole Beutler, and Ivana Müller.

dances. We were about to move back to Germany after several years of living abroad, and I believe we were looking for reference points that would help us not just to go back geographically but also to understand the artistic implications of our return. What was our cultural heritage beyond the training and formation we had received outside of Germany? We decided, together with dramaturge Joachim Gerstmeier, to work with Dore Hoyer's material, and there were two reasons for this decision: the documented meticulousness of Dore Hoyer's movement research and the pathos with which the film-makers had endowed it.

Without being able to explain in detail how our roles evolved, Joachim Gerstmeier ended up as the dramaturge, Thomas Plischke as artistic director, and Alice Chauchat as assistant, while I took on reconstructing and dancing Hoyer's dances.[5] For me, this meant the significant step into the dance archive. As far as I remember, it was dance scholar and dramaturge Susanne Traub who knew that the copyright of *Affectos Humanos* was with the German Dance Archive in Cologne. Thus, the first thing to do was to call them. Frank-Manuel Peter, the archive's director, explained to me that the archive held the copyright. But the decision about who may work with the dances had been transferred to an old friend of Dore Hoyer's, the then eighty-four-year-old dance pedagogue Waltraud Luley, living in Frankfurt am Main. This meant that the second step was to call this woman, a total stranger, who wanted to know right away why I wanted to work with Hoyer's dances and where I had gotten my professional training. She liked the fact that a twenty-eight-year-old man wanted to reconstruct the dances of a woman, who had made them at fifty-one years of age. The phone call ended with her giving me the task to reconstruct two or three dances by myself and then call her again.

No sooner said than done. Four weeks later, Thomas Plischke and I met with Waltraud Luley in her dance studio in Frankfurt am Main. In the office, she served us coffee and coconut macaroons while talking to us about dance history in general and our staging ideas in particular. Then we went into the dance studio and I showed the dances *Desire* and *Hate*. Afterward, Luley commented on what she had seen: "Well, Mr. Nachbar, concerning the gestures and steps, you have worked well. But concerning the intensity needed for these dances, you have achieved no more than twenty percent." I swallowed hard. Thomas Plischke was asked to leave the studio. And Waltraud Luley began to work with me on the first movements of the dance *Hate*.

I am standing in front of her, my with legs slightly turned out, my gaze directed downward, looking at clawed hands hanging from arms stretched long in front of my body. Then I very quickly lift my long right arm until I hold it like an exclamation mark above my right shoulder. Then I tear it straight down into its beginning position. At the

---

[5] This collaboration ended up in the piece *affects*. It was a kind of experimentation setup, in which we juxtaposed historical and contemporary dance materials in order to explore how perception and dance aesthetics might be connected and might have changed over time. Interestingly, we changed the staging of *affects* many times, from a multimedia setup in three spaces, each containing intensively affective material, to a minimalist stage piece for three performers. We needed several tries to finally get to a meaningful version. The result was consequently called *affects/rework*.

same time, I lift my left lower arm with the clawed hand in front of my chest. After that, I slowly bring the left lower arm back to its beginning position. Once it has arrived, my legs suddenly implode into a demi-plié, both lower arms and clawed hands fly up in front of my chest, and my head violently pulls backward as I looked upward in exasperation. I feel strange in Dore Hoyer's movements, not just because of Luley's comment. Trained in postmodern release techniques that favor an economic use of the body, I feel that my dancing of Dore Hoyer's dances has very little in common with her aesthetics. Something feels wrong—too sloppy maybe, or not well placed.[6] The intensity and modulation of bodily tension applied by Hoyer are completely foreign to me. Luley sees this, and jumps out of her chair and yells, "Mr. Nachbar! This is hate! The whole body is in a cramp!" Thomas Plischke sits outside of the studio and fears that Luley is one of these expressionist dance dragons who draw self-esteem from humiliating their students— according to our prejudiced view of that generation. But during the direct exchange with her in the studio, I notice immediately that she wants to clarify a vital aspect of the dance. And for this, she needs to jump up and yell at me. So, I put myself once again into the beginning position and try to tense my whole body, so that it is a cramp. But I forget to claw the little fingers, which instead stick out straight in front of me. She immediately comments, "The little fingers, Mr. Nachbar, the little fingers!"

In the further course of the rehearsals until the premier of *affects* in February 2000, I do consult other sources as well, but I concentrate on the film document and on Luley's memories and body knowledge. She was trained in similar dance practices and techniques as Hoyer, which allows me to learn these practices, and begin to see how I can use mine in order to get into hers. This makes three main sources: the film, Waltraud Luley, and the dance knowledge stored in my body. I let them meet, push into, and mix with each other. Eventually, this results in the reconstruction of three of the five dances: *Desire, Hate*, and *Anxiety*. Doing so, I rewind the VHS tape many times; I replay scenes in slow motion; I let Waltraud Luley correct me time and again and get her to tell me stories about Dore Hoyer; I look for numerous ways to sneak my contemporary body into the dances of 1962, while letting the dances smuggle their implicit training and other habits into my own body, full of patterns and imprints. I make a conscious effort to understand and learn Dore Hoyer's dance technique and choreographic knacks and to bring them in contact and friction with my techniques and knacks.

The dance archive proves itself here to be a workspace or workshop where bodies are constructed, taken apart, and put together anew. This always also comes with ideas about bodies, how they should move, and what they should look like. Past dances get

---

[6] I always find it difficult to explain the differences between Dore Hoyer's practices and resulting aesthetics and mine without showing them with my body. A short way of describing might be that Dore Hoyer comes from and develops practices that seek to explore feelings and emotions and their physical expression, while I have studied practices that focus on the creative potential of exploring the human anatomy and motor system. My practice from the time of the reconstruction until today is based on these studies, and mixes them with specific dramaturgical practices that I do not discuss in this chapter for lack of space.

compared and calibrated with contemporary bodies. In this process of continuous construction, deconstruction, and repair, the strange aspects of the past keep pushing into the picture: Why, for example, does Dore Hoyer shape her hands like claws in *Hate*? Why doesn't she focus on the hip swings in *Love*, using swan-shaped hands at the beginning and at the end? This can be understood intellectually. Documents from the archive shed light on the decision-making criteria at the base of the dances. But when I dance them, I feel as if something is wrong. Something feels strange and stays foreign to me— not only in the dances' shapes, but also in how the dances feel to my body. Paradoxically, it is in this feeling of estrangement that the past is able to come closest to the present. By accepting the kinesthetic differences and by putting the temporal and aesthetic distance on display, the space between then and now appears, revealing the points of contact between the two. To show this, we deliberately refrained from the original music and from reconstructing the costumes when staging *affects* in 2000. At the same time, and at first unconsciously, we traced the black-and-white film by putting on dark costumes and dancing on a white and brightly lit stage.

And this kind of tracing, which is a kind of translation process, allows for exactly the kinds of vagueness that are productive for the dance archive. Of course, meticulous study of source material is necessary, especially in dance. In my reconstruction of Dore Hoyer's dances, I tried to physically understand her movement principles as precisely as possible. But if the dance archive is supposed to exceed the bounds of stored documents, it depends on a direct exchange with embodied movement knowledge. And this is also exactly the opportunity the dance archive presents, as opposed to other kinds of archives: documented and stored movement knowledge meets embodied movement knowledge. This is how the dance archive begins to dance itself and thus takes place beyond its bounds. It places itself in movement. However, the problem of corporeal movement knowledge is that it is not tattooed or printed on the body's skin as the letters of this text are printed on a white sheet of paper. It is not even a bruise. Movement knowledge is rather an imprint. It is based on the conscious and unconscious imprint of postural patterns and movement sequences. The imprint, which is the (neuronal) network of singular cells to whole sequences, remains invisible and only surfaces in movement and behavior. For much of the time, it stays somewhere deep inside the body, under the skin, waiting in the dark for activation—not easy to detect, but often palpable, and in movement sometimes also visible and even legible.

## THE BODY AS DANCE/ARCHIVE

But what does legibility mean in dance, as a definite interpretation often can be missed? How can we imagine that the impressions a spectator has when watching a dance piece become legible? Can we speak of legibility when dealing with these impressions? In short, does dance form and leave signs?

In November 2006, I started working with my father. The piece premiered on November 8, 2007, at the Sophiensale in Berlin.[7] In the beginning, my motivation was of a more pragmatic nature: After my father had invited me several times in vain to visit him in his birth- and now weekend-house in the countryside, I felt like spending more time with him, but without having the feeling of wasting potential freelance working time. The simplest solution seemed to be to make a piece with my father. This also had the advantage of my being able to show him what he had been trying to understand without ever really grasping: dancing. I am still astonished by how easily my father agreed to join in. Similar to the reconstruction of the *Affectos humanos*, the first active step was a phone call. My father at the other end of the line responded immediately: "Well, yes, sure, if you know what I have to do, I will join in." His only constraint was that as a sixty-nine-year-old pensioner, he could no longer do all the things that a dancer might have to do. That this phone call was also a big step into the dance archive was not yet clear to me. But, again, I am getting ahead of myself.

First we got together in a dance studio to see what could be possible together. From mid-September to mid-October 2006, I worked during a four-week residency at PACT Zollverein in Essen. It was a good opportunity to try out a few things with my father, who lives not far from Essen, in Cologne. He came and stayed for three days. We worked each of these days in the studio. It felt strange to me to touch him again after an interim of twenty-five years. And it was odd to tell my father what he had to do. We did simple contact improvisation exercises, pulled faces at each other, introduced ourselves to each other by explaining each item in our wallets, improvised with each other along abstract scores, and we danced in front of each other using concrete themes such as the blossoming and withering of a flower. It was moving to see how and with what curiosity my father became involved in the tasks, and how eager he was to do them well. But, as the retired wholesaler that he was, he could not avoid asking for each exercise's use to the piece. He wound up complaining each time I dropped choreography from the day before. One year before the planned premiere, however, I had no answers to such questions and comments. So I thought about what to do to get us into the same boat in a spirit of shared research.

The solution came in form of a dance book: *Der moderne Ausdruckstanz in der Erziehung: Eine Einführung in die kreative tänzerische Bewegung als Mittel zur Entfaltung der Persönlichkeit*, in which one of the godfathers of modern and contemporary dance in Europe, Rudolf von Laban, made accessible in print on paper the movement knowledge imprinted in his body and his experience as dance pedagogue, which knowledge could then enter the (dance) archive. Among other things, he describes eight efforts in the book: pressing, flicking, punching, floating, wringing, dabbing, slashing, and gliding.

---

[7] In *Repeater—Dance Piece with Father*, my father, who has never danced on stage before, and I, the professional choreographer and son, perform on stage together. Inspired by the collaborating dramaturge Jeroen Peeters, we were concerned with physically exploring the father-son relationship in a sort of laconic dialogue without words. The piece has toured internationally, as well as to the village my father comes from.

My dance studies and work had also been involved with movement qualities, but not with these particular ones. I actually knew them as little as my father did. Therefore, they seemed to be a good base from which to fathom the "wiggle room" of our shared work and research.

I brought the book to the rehearsals of our second meeting, which took place in February 2007 in Berlin. We read the description of each movement quality and tried them out in solo and duet improvisations. Afterward, we would discuss the experiences and the outcomes. In the rehearsal phase, the crossings-over contained in the project clearly came to light. First my father agreed to reverse the usual teaching and learning process between father and son, becoming my student in the world of dance. Then I put myself in the lineage of Rudolf von Laban, not presumptuously, but rather as if compensating for the father that was now missing once he had become my student. And finally, there was a moment on the second day of this second meeting, which imprinted itself on my memory—an image or a wink that German film director Oskar Roehler describes as follows:

> The great thing about images that move us is that we feel in an instant that everything is in us. They are able to activate our memory that normally moves in narrow trails. [ . . . ] Triggered by the image, they [the memories] vaguely reemerge and light an afterglow that is filled with a moment from our life. "Wink"—the ambiguity of the word is the nature of the image. (Roehler 2002; my translation)

As we were improvising together on "pressing," my father ran out of ideas and started to imitate me. I noticed this out of the corner of my eye, and I was briefly irritated by the situation. I interpreted it as my father being unimaginative. But then I recognized within my father's imitation of me a similarity that is much older than the one in our improvisation. I saw that a problem throughout my dance career, which I have always thought to be my individual one, is actually a shared one. Both my father and I have a line of muscular tension that runs from the thumbs along the upper side of the arms and the top of the shoulders to the throat. For years, I have tried to release this line of tension to gain more space for the movement of my arms and head. Now I see that I learned this pattern a long time ago from my father. Despite all my dance and body knowledge, I am surprised and moved by how corporeal the crossovers are when father and son learn from one another. It is a wink that literally imprints itself on my memory, and one and a half years later, when I am thinking about the text you are reading, I realize that I opened the door to another kind of archive back in February 2007. It is different from the dance archive. And at the same time, it is closely connected to it. It is an archive of imprints, of imprinted and engraved surfaces beneath the surface of the skin.[8] This is somewhat

---

[8] To understand this thought better, it might be helpful to consult an image that I adopt from Steve Paxton, who said during a workshop I took with him in winter 1998 at PARTS in Brussels: "If I start to draw a line on the skin of one of my thumbs, I can continue along my hand, arm, shoulder, throat, and chin all the way to my mouth, where I can go on along the mucous membranes and down the esophagus until the stomach and through the whole digestive track to its end, where the pen exits from the anus and

similar to André Lepecki's notion of the "body as archive" (Lepecki 2010, 34), especially in "its precariousness" and in how it "replaces and diverts notions of archive away from a documental deposit" (34). But while Lepecki stresses its "muscular tremors, [ ... ] [and] bleedings" (2010, 34), I would like to suggest a body system other than muscles and blood circulation, one that is not to be controlled in the first place, like muscles can be, and that does not ooze out of the body once it is cut. I am speaking of fascia tissue, which runs under the skin as well as around the organs, muscles, and muscle fibers. Most of the body's proprioceptors are situated here. Long neglected by Western medicine, fascia tissue is now found to be holding many of the tensions that cause back pain and other aches, almost like a storage of movement or traumatic memories, running through the whole body and connecting its different parts (Luczak 2015). The advantage of such a physical archive is that it is linked to sensation as much as to movement, and we do not need to cut the body open in order to access it.

At the time of rehearsing *Repeater—Dance Piece with Father* I was thirty-five years old. My father gave me not only his participation in this project, but also insight into an old habit that he had given me thirty to thirty-five years earlier. The gift of my father's presence carried an imprint that came to light in a wink while improvising together. The imprint became legible to me. Maybe the therapeutic aspect that so many spectators had been assuming in many of the talk-backs on tour was to be found there: not in any change in the relationship, but in the recognition of long lost ways of passing an imprint that consisted of no more than a line of tension in the body, which now became the sign of a bond: "You descend from me, and this is what you have learned from me," the father tells the son by dancing with him.

In *Archive Fever* Jacques Derrida talks about a similar present, made by Jakob Freud to his son Sigmund:

> It is an inscription in the form of a dedication. It was written by the hand of Jakob, son of R. Shelomoh Freud, the arch-patriarch, the grandfather of psychoanalysis, and addressed to his son, Shelomoh Freud, on the day of his thirty-fifth birthday, in Vienna, the sixth of May, 1891. (29 Nisan 5651). A gift *carried* this inscription. What the father gives to the son is at once a writing and its substrate. The substrate, in a sense, was the Bible itself, the Book of books, a Philoppsohn Bible Sigmund had studied in his youth. His father restores it to him, after having made a present of it to him; he restitutes it as a gift, with a new leather binding. To bind anew: this is an act of love. Of paternal love. (Derrida 1995, 21)

Although the incident described here by Derrida carries other implications and bears different consequences than my improvising with my father, I perceive a strange kinship: In a certain way my father also gave me an old habit studied in my body at a young

---

can go via buttocks, back, shoulders, arm, and hand all the way back to the thumb, where I have started the line. I have drawn on the same surface throughout the journey, even if I went from outside to inside and back out again." But I don't just mean the surfaces of the digestive track, but the surfaces of all the tissues inside the body.

age, in a new binding, a new skin—namely, the one of improvising with me. In a certain way, he gave me a present by dancing with me except that it was not an inscription in a book, but an imprint in a body.

The parallel drawn here is admittedly associative rather than scholarly. But at this point, it allows me to think through a connection between the dance archive and the dancing body. It was Sigmund Freud who developed an early attempt to describe the complexity of human memory with the Mystic Writing-Pad model. With it, Freud describes how memories become inscribed into a piece of wax, one layer on top of the next, overlaying, superimposing, and erasing each other, not unlike palimpsests, which are among the first paper or papyrus documents we know of (Freud 1961 [1925], 229–232). This connection between a person's intimate imprints in her body, on the one hand, and, let us say, her archived memories written down or printed on paper, on the other, is important for the dance archive, precisely because the dance archive must grapple continuously with the paradox of archivable documents and non-archivable but repeatable body knowledge. "But where does the outside commence? This question is the question of the archive. There are undoubtably no others" (Derrida 1995, 8).

In order to answer this question from a choreographer's perspective, I would like to return to the house of the *árchont*, which was not only the place where official documents were kept, but also the residence of a civil servant's family. Habits got passed along here, imprints were made and respectively suffered, and Mystic Pads were inscribed upon. Similarly, albeit with less emotional intensity, kinship gets produced during dance studies: through constant observation, emulation, and repetition of movement ideas and sequences, specific habits, skills, and biases are constructed in the body. The fact that these processes are not documented or archived doesn't mean that they don't take place. They literally do, outside the body, in a dance studio, on stage, and elsewhere.

The chiasmus from the rehearsal process of *Repeater—Dance Piece with Father* makes this clear. "The archive takes place at the place of originary and structural breakdown of the said memory." (Derrida 1995, 11) But no archive takes place if it isn't put to work by a memory with all its structural weakness, that is, through producing, reading, and interpreting the very documents of the archive. Derrida is right when he says, "*There is no archive without a place of assignation, without a technique of repetition, and without a certain exteriority. No archive without outside*" (Derrida 1995, 11; italics in original). But dance opens up a perspective from which we can understand the line of tension in my father's body and my body as consigned and repeatable through specific techniques of observation. Movement qualities and techniques are somewhat external to bodies, different from yet similar to written or printed texts, films engraved in external hard drives or DVDs, or photographs printed on paper. At this point, legibility becomes a question of the reading or perception techniques at hand, as well as of the definition of what writing might be.

After all, the dance archive collects documents of an art form that writes body knowledge into space: choreography, the repeatable inscription of or in space by a knowledgeable moving body. Choreography is not only the object to be saved from forgetting by the dance archive (as an external place of an internal memory), but it is also the dance archive's counterpart written into space. And one might think that choreography as an externalized writing of imprints under the skin doesn't need the documents of its having-taken-place stored in the archive.

# BACK TO THE DANCE ARCHIVE'S
# DOUBLE BOTTOM

But forgetting in this way would mean to exclude the memory data carriers specific to the dance archive, with their ability to bridge distances in time and to help develop a critical distance from dance as a research object, from the practice of contemporary choreography. The latter would lose an opportunity for self-reflection. Conversely, banning choreography and dance strictly from the spaces of the dance archive (imagined, thought, or actual) would mean reducing the documents stored in the dance archive to mere objects of scientific knowledge.

Because the dance archive is a collection of documents of bodily knowledge, that is, difficult to fathom yet repeatable, the dance archive should seek the exchange between (printed) documents and (imprinted) bodies. In the end, all the forms of writing, printing, engraving, or imprinting that are involved are mutually dependent: The imprint of the body depends on choreography, because the latter makes the first visible; choreography depends on its documentation outside of bodies, because some evidence of dances becomes more readable in their documentations; and the documentation of the dances depends on its translation back into impressions and bodily imprints, because they might otherwise congeal into mere signs within the dance archive.

The dance archive is therefore perhaps more than just double: it actually has many spaces folded between the surfaces, carrying much information, and many documents to be discovered between dance knowledge that is immediately transferred across the generations, and dance knowledge that is bridged over many years through documents stored in the dance archive. In thinking this way, it is not a matter of looking at every form of knowledge and experience in the same way. On the contrary, I am interested in differentiating between the different forms of knowledge in order to make their exchange possible and productive. And I have experienced the dance archive as precisely the place where such a differentiation and exchange between print and imprint, between sensing and reading, and between choreographing and writing can take place as an example from which other archives can, in fact, learn.

## WORKS CITED

### Books

Derrida, Jacques. 1995. *Archive Fever: A Freudian Impression*. Translated by Eric Prenowitz. Chicago and London: University of Chicago Press.

Freud, Sigmund. 1961 [1925]. "A Note Upon the 'Mystic Writing-Pad.'" *In the Standard Edition of the Complete Psychological Works of Sigmund*, translated by Freud and edited by James Strachey (London: the Hogarth Press, 1961), vol. XIX, 225–232.

Laban, Rudolf von. 1981. *Der moderne Ausdruckstanz in der Erziehung: eine Einführung in die creative tänzerische Bewegung als Mittel zur Entfaltung der Persönlichkeit.* Wilhelmshaven: Heinrichshofen's Verlag.

Lepecki, André. 2010. "The Body as Archive: Will to Re-Enact and the Afterlives of Dances." *Dance Research Journal* 42(2) (Winter): 28–48.

Luczak, Hania. 2015. "Der innere Halt." *Geo* 2 (February): 96–119.

Roehler, Oskar. 2002. *Die Unberührbare: das Original-Drehbuch; sowie Rezensionen und Materialien.* Cologne: Kiepenheuer und Witsch.

## Film

Geitel, Klaus, and Rudolf Küfner. 1968. *Dore Hoyer tanzt—eine Gedenksendung.* Frankfurt am Main.

## Performances

Chauchat, Alice, Joachim Gerstmeier, Waltraud Luley, Martin Nachbar, and Thomas Plischke. 2000. *affects.* Frankfurt am Main.

Chauchat, Alice, Joachim Gerstmeier, Waltraud Luley, Martin Nachbar, and Thomas Plischke. 2000. *affects/rework.* Paris.

Hoyer, Dore, and Dimitri Wiatowitsch. 1962. *Affectos humanos.* Berlin

Nachbar, Klaus, and Martin Nachbar. 2007. *Repeater—Dance Piece with Father.* Berlin.

## Workshops

Paxton, Steve. 1999. *Material for the Spine.* Brussels.

....................................................................................

# CHAPTER 3

# GIVING SENSE TO THE PAST

*Historical D(ist)ance and the Chiasmatic Interlacing of Affect and Knowledge*

....................................................................................

TIMMY DE LAET

IT is often assumed that reenactment is more concerned with feeling the past than with understanding history. "Reenactment," as historian Jerome de Groot puts it, "offers a range of *experience* within history" (2009, 107). Whether historical events are replayed on the battlefield, on television shows, in video games, or on a theater stage, reenactment is both hailed and scorned for the corporeal, sensorial, emotional, and psychological engagement with the past it is claimed to offer as an alternative to the allegedly more distant and primarily discursive access provided by history books or archival documents. Cultural historian Vanessa Agnew voices this dual stance in a widely cited article that has set the tone for much of the current discourse on reenactment. While appreciative of the more general "affective turn in history," of which the growing popularity of reenactment from the 1980s onward is but one important symptom, Agnew ultimately doubts whether reenactment has the "capacity to further historical understanding" (2007, 301), precisely because of its "emphasis on affect" (299) as well as its "tendency to collapse temporalities" (309).

Agnew's critical stance toward the epistemological potential of reenactment is hardly surprising when one takes into account the manner in which affect is generally defined in so-called affect theory, which began to emerge across several branches of the humanities shortly after the turn of the millennium.[1] Lisa Blackman, who in *Immaterial Bodies* (2012) examines the relationship between affect and subjectivity, explains that the increasing interest in affect is principally geared toward the "making explicit of those

---

[1] Patricia T. Clough and Jean Halley's edited volume *The Affective Turn* (2007) is usually cited as the first to identify the intensified interest in affect across the humanities. Mitigating the novelty sometimes ascribed to this kind of turn, Anu Koivunen convincingly shows that the roots of the attention to affect reach further back, going so far as to claim, provocatively, that "an affective turn never happened" (2010, 23).

registers of experience that are at work in objects, artefacts and practices" and "which might variously be described as non-cognitive, trans-subjective, non-conscious, non-representational, incorporeal and immaterial" (4). Blackman's description highlights the way in which affect is commonly conceptualized as a category that stands outside, if not in opposition to, discursive understanding and consciously registered experience or emotions. This distinction between affect and emotion is key to Brian Massumi's influential theorization of affect in *Parables for the Virtual* (2002). In his view, "an emotion is a subjective content, the sociolinguistic fixing of the quality of an experience" and, as such, it should be distinguished from "the irreducibly bodily and autonomic nature of affect" (28). In their editorial introduction to *The Affect Theory Reader* (2010), Melissa Gregg and Gregory J. Seigworth similarly maintain that affect designates "visceral forces beneath, alongside, or generally *other than* conscious knowing, vital forces insisting beyond emotion" (2010, 1). Even though they acknowledge that "affect and cognition are never fully separable—if for no other reason than that thought is itself a body, embodied" (2–3), the primary appeal of affect does seem to be that it provides a name for those supposedly unmediated sensations that elude conscious registering.

In a sweeping critique of the affective turn, Ruth Leys contends that most affect theorists—despite their claims to the contrary—adhere to a Cartesian dualism between body and mind. She argues that "shift[ing] attention away from considerations of meaning or 'ideology' or indeed representation" in order to refocus on "the subject's subpersonal material-affective responses" installs an antagonistic relationship between meaning and affect (2011, 450). Leys considers this a fundamental flaw that weakens affect theory in general, even if different intellectual traditions have led to distinct approaches among scholars dealing with affect. Leys more specifically distinguishes between the neuroscientific "Basic Emotions Paradigm" vis-à-vis others who rather align themselves with the philosophies of Baruch Spinoza, Henri Bergson, William James, or Gilles Deleuze and Félix Guattari (439–442).[2] According to Leys, what binds these two main strands of affect theory together is "their shared anti-intentionalism" or the "single belief . . . that affect is independent of signification and meaning" (443). Expounding on Leys's critical standpoint, social scholar Margaret Wetherell asserts that "complex acts of *meaning-making* and *representation* are involved in the spreading of affect, no matter how random and viral it appears" (2015, 154). In her account of the role of affect in the formation of cultural memory, Sharon Macdonald also maintains that "dismissing discourse can only mean that we ignore much that matters" (2013, 81). In her

---

[2] In their introduction to *The Affect Theory Reader*, Gregg and Seigworth count no less than eight different perspectives from which theorists are currently exploring the notion of affect (2010, 6–8). These include, next to the Tomkins-Ekman paradigm and the philosophically inflected branch mentioned by Leys, (post-)phenomenology; cybernetics and neuroscience; political theory; cultural, social, and performance studies; critical research on emotions, also from a postcolonial perspective; science studies and new materialism. For a similar outline of different directions in affect theory—in the case amounting to twelve perspectives—see Elkins (2013, 10–13).

view, naming what one feels is equally important—*and* affective—as feeling what allegedly cannot be named.

In light of these critical interventions in the prevalent definitions of affect, Agnew's characterization of reenactment as a form of affective history is at once more significant and more troubling than she herself admits. Rather than merely wanting to sense the past, reenactment can also aim to make sense out of it. As such, reenactment exposes a deeper conflict between knowing and feeling, a tension that has been haunting philosophy, historiography, and critical theory, as well as dance studies. Especially in the wake of poststructuralism and deconstruction the predominance of discourse and representationalist points of view have threatened to eclipse the role of embodiment, both in being and in thinking.[3] With regard to reenactment, then, the main problem seems to be, as historian Mark Salber Phillips points out, that "reenactment has generally been characterized as an experiential approach to history, with little concern for the conceptual issues characteristic of more traditional historiographies" (2013a, 12). In other words, as long as reenactment is figured as a popular and bottom-up immersion in the past, it continues to stand in opposition to academic historiography as an intellectual and top-down process that keeps a reflective distance and finds its expression primarily in print.

Could it be that the common equation of reenactment with a search for affect has fostered a rather one-sided perspective that disregards how reenactments can stimulate epistemic faculties and provoke critical reflection on how it is we come to know the past? While it is certainly true that some popular forms of living history are less concerned with raising historical consciousness about how the past is continuously *re*construed every time it is brought back into the present, the ways in which contemporary choreographers have been appropriating the format go in a markedly different direction. In the hands of certain dancers, reenactment exceeds the status of a mere pastime, insofar as their work acknowledges the passing of time and yet still tries to pass on what risks getting lost as time passes. Affect, or the getting in touch with history, obviously plays an important part in this endeavor, but—as I will argue in this chapter—the affective engagements that propel choreographic reenactment are as much about feeling the past as about understanding mechanisms of historicization. Crucial in this regard is the idea of historical distance, which is generally understood as the temporal difference between the past and the present, but which, in dance reenactment, grows into something broader and more flexible than merely an indicator of time's transience.[4] The

---

[3] As Patricia T. Clough explains, "the turn to affect . . . returned critical theory and cultural criticism to bodily matter, which had been treated in terms of various constructionisms under the influence of poststructuralism and deconstruction" (2010, 206). According to feminist scholar Clare Hemmings, however, the constructionist attitude so heavily denounced by affect theorists actually also applies to their own position. She claims that scholars such as Eve Kosofsky Sedgwick and Brian Massumi create their own enemy, since they need to uphold that "poststructuralist epistemology [has] ignored embodiment, investment and emotion" in order to assert that affect offers a "way out" of the theoretical dismissal of pre-discursive life (2005, 556–557).

[4] In taking the idea of historical distance as a central hinge of my discussion, I am in fact pursuing a cross-disciplinary dialogue between dance studies and the theory of history. While the practice of

mobilization of distance, whether by amplifying or compressing it in terms of formal aesthetics and affective response, is what the two dance reenactments that I discuss in the following put at stake.

Exploring the correlations between affect, form, and distance in dance reenactment, I will draw on Hans Ulrich Gumbrecht's distinction between "presence" and "meaning," as introduced in his 2004 book *The Production of Presence*. Ultimately, current debates on affect do seem to serve the same need as the recent revaluation of the notion of "presence" in the humanities. "Any accounting of affect theory," James Elkins writes, "would have to include the [recent] history of the rediscovery of presence" and the fact that "after the poststructural critiques of unmediated presence, there has been an accelerating awareness of the necessity of rethinking presence" (2013, 13). Combining Gumbrecht's conceptual pair with the function of historical distance in dance reenactment allows me to ask to what extent the concept of affect can help to make the workings of dance reenactment insightful and, vice versa, how the practice of reenactment necessitates redirecting some of the predominant aspirations of affect theory.

# Hyperbolic Imitation

In *A Mary Wigman Dance Evening* (2009), the Ecuadorian dancer and choreographer Fabián Barba reconstructed a dance recital as the German expressionist dancer or *Ausdruckstänzerin* Mary Wigman would have performed it in the early 1930s. Adopting Wigman's format of a dance program featuring several solos, Barba compiled what he described as "a dance evening as it *could have taken* place in the first half of the 20th century" (2011, 84; my emphasis). While the subjunctive mode of Barba's statement indicates that he was well aware of the impossibility of recreating the past as it *actually* happened, he nevertheless went to great lengths to re-embody the choreographic movements, while also reproducing the original costumes, music, and even *mise en scène*. When the audience enters the auditorium, they see a red curtain closing off the stage, as well as two chandeliers hanging above their heads. As if to complete the illusion, spectators find on their seats a program leaflet with the titles of the successive solos in an archaic typography, similar to the one used in Wigman's time.[5] When the curtain opens, a young male dancer appears who, during the piece, performs a series of six- to

---

reenactment seems to invite this quite naturally, it is surprising how both domains have been operating rather isolatedly from each other in coming to terms with the rise of reenactment, both in the arts and beyond, even though this connection might be beneficial. I therefore draw on the renewed attention historical distance has received in the theory of history. See, for instance, den Hollander et al. (2011); Lorenz and Bevernage (2013).

    [5] According to the program leaflet, Fabián Barba performs the following solos: *Anruf, Seraphisches Lied, Gesicht der Nacht, Pastorale, Sturmlied* and *Sommerlicher Tanz* (from the cycle *Schwingende Landschaft*); *Raumgestalt* and *Feierliche Gestalt* (from the cycle *Visionen*); and *Drehmonotonie* (from the cycle *Feier*).

FIGURE 3.1. Fabián Barba in Mary Wigman's *Drehmonotonie.*

Photo: Dieter Hartwig.

seven-minute solos, each followed by a bow and a short pause, after which he returns wearing a different costume, ranging from distinctly female dresses to more theatrically abstract layers of fabric (Figures 3.1 and 3.2).[6] The dances in themselves strike contemporary audiences as quaintly anomalous, due to the dramatic, even histrionic, movements that spring from a remarkable bodily tension, sometimes combined with sudden outbursts of energy, at other times suffused with a refined grace.

The overt evocation of Wigman's aesthetic universe, by means of both *mise en scène* and dancing, made some spectators wonder why a young dancer would devote his time and energy to re-embodying a dance style that is historically outmoded. This sort of reaction, however, fails to recognize the suggestive but significant cracks that puncture Barba's mimetic approach and which undercut the supposedly complete identification with Wigman. At those moments when Barba appears dressed in a strapless evening gown—modeled after Wigman's later costumes—his hairy male legs and his slightly too muscled arms are tellingly visible. Also, the music that accompanies the piece—some of which Barba adapted from archival videos of Wigman's dances—sounds distant, as

---

[6] In a 2010 essay on *A Mary Wigman Dance Evening*, Barba explains that the different types of costumes he wears during the piece are reminiscent of a remarkable change in the aesthetics of Wigman's solos. Whereas, in her early career, she was dressed in costumes that masked her female body, from 1929 onward (the year in which the dance cycle *Schwingende Landschaft* was created), Wigman started to appear in distinctly female dresses (see Barba 2010, 102, 104; see also Manning 2006, 41–43, 140–146).

**FIGURE 3.2.** Fabián Barba in Mary Wigman's *Gesicht der Nacht.*

Photo: Dieter Hartwig.

if it were played on an old gramophone, covered by the dust of history. Barba's skill-ful manipulation of these theatrical elements—and the reactions they evoke in the spectator—interfere with the enticing time machine that he also creates and signal how his aim reaches further than that of merely producing a blunt copy of Wigman's dances and aesthetics, or what we might consider a reconstruction.

Rather than attempt a straightforward mimesis, Barba's performance turns reenact-ment into what I propose to call a strategy of "hyperbolic imitation," not unlike Judith Butler's suggestion that "a repetition of the law into hyperbole" might be a way of sub-verting tacit conventions (1993, 122). Barba's strategic use of reenactment stems most obviously from his refusal to impersonate Wigman fully: his incorporation of the dances does not intend to be seamless and instead dissociates her dances from any harsh alignment with her female persona, exposing ways of moving that we habitually regard as a feminine style of dancing. Yet the perhaps most astute effect of Barba's approach is that, by replicating the generic conventions of traditional dance reconstructions as such, he eventually overturns them—even if this is a thin line to walk. Barba's endeavor to achieve a formal resemblance with Wigman's work can be easily misinterpreted as a reinforcement of what Mark Franko, already in 1989, denounced as the main flaw of dance reconstructions, the kind that delivers "staid and antiquated presentations" by "merely animating an historical artifact" (57). To find a way out of the apparent stasis of reconstruction, Franko used the term "reinvention," which in his view "sacrifices the reproduction of a work to the replication of its most powerful intended effects" and thus may involve a noticeably more liberated and critical attitude toward historical sources (58).

Franko's distinction between reconstruction and reinvention anticipated the direction of dance reenactment as it has been emerging since the 1990s, insofar as most of these works that return to the past take a reinterpretive stance toward the sources they aspire to resuscitate. In this context—and nearly twenty-five years after Franko's intervention—Fabián Barba's *A Mary Wigman Dance Evening* takes up a more than remarkable place, as the piece demonstrates how a reflective reinvention of historical dance works can also be achieved by means of a strategic reproduction of their formal features. But precisely because Barba's decided choice for the road of resemblance goes against the dominant current of reinterpretation, his *Dance Evening* might trouble contemporary spectators who more likely expect to see a clear signature of the artist-as-author that guides their reading of the reenactment. In Barba's case, the clues are more difficult to discern, which explains why the piece, even though it was hugely successful and has toured worldwide, provoked mixed receptions, as for some spectators his strategy was clear, while for others it was a mere exercise in epigonic and presumably faithful imitation.[7] Recognizing the strategic intentions behind Barba's reenactment, however, does not attenuate affective involvement in the piece. To the contrary, it adds to the manner in which Barba attempts to give sense to the past, in the double meaning of attributing meaning to, as well as of adding sensoriality to, history in its traditional forms. It is by disentangling this mixture of discursive interpretation and emotive response that we might get a clearer idea of the role affect has to play in dance reenactment.

For those spectators who did not dismiss Barba's *Dance Evening* as a mere reproduction of Wigman's work, his reenactment produced shifting figures in which his contemporary body confusingly blends with the historical image of Mary Wigman. This dynamic becomes perhaps most clearly visible in the solo *Pastorale*, which involves a subtle, arguably feminine elegance as the choreography consists mainly of detailed movements of hands and arms while the body remains lying, sitting, or turning on the ground. Especially at the moment when Barba sits straight up, showing his back to the audience, with his long, brown, voluminous hair reaching his shoulders, he seems to conjure up the spectral presence of Mary Wigman. For a second, spectators might be puzzled by the hybrid persona they are looking at, speculating whether it is Wigman they see, or Barba, or both at once. But as soon as Barba turns around, the doubt is likely to dissipate, since the sight of his masculine face and physical constitution makes the body image shift again into the young, contemporary dancer incorporating and externalizing Wigman's expressionist dancing style. Various reviews suggest indeed how

---

[7] A telling example of the mixed reception to Fabián Barba's *A Mary Wigman Dance Evening* can be found on a blog on the website of the Turkish iDans festival, which documents various responses to the piece after it was shown in Istanbul in 2010 (see https://idansblog.org/tag/a-mary-wigman-dance-evening/ [last accessed July 29, 2016]). Also Susanne Foellmer refers to both positive and negative reviews in her discussion of the work (see Foellmer 2014, 87–88 n. 29).

Wigman's spectral presence shimmered through Barba's physical appearance, praising him for how he "didn't just re-enact Wigman, but was Wigman" (Miller 2009, para. 8), or for the fact that it is "Mary Wigman in person [who] performs" (Witzeling 2009, para. 1; my translation). While such admittedly exalted accounts lose sight of the manner in which it is not only Wigman who reappears through Barba, but also the other way around, this dialectical back-and-forth movement is more aptly invoked by theater scholar Christel Stalpaert. Describing her viewing experience, Stalpaert recounts how several likenesses—such as "the poses, the muscular qualities of *Ausdruckstanz*, the similar haircut, the costumes"—make it seem "as if the icon Mary Wigman has returned to life," but this conjuring up of her specter is ruptured by small details that come with Barba's individual bodily constitution—including "the large feet . . . , the empty bosom, the broad-shouldered torso"—with the result that you find yourself "catapulted away from your own mental image or cliché of the way you remember Mary Wigman" (2011, 91).

Whether or not one is able to remember Wigman and to discern her spectral presence through Barba's body depends, of course, to a large degree on the knowledge or memories one has of her work or even of her persona in general. But even without any previous awareness of who Wigman was or what she or her oeuvre looked like, one is able to grasp what Barba's *Dance Evening* aims to achieve. In an essay on the early reenactments of the French collective the Albrecht Knust Quartet, dance scholar Isabelle Launay suggests how the intentionality behind dance reenactment also permeates the staging of the work and how this, by consequence, might also affect the perception of the audience:

> What appears onstage is as much the history and the memory of the work, with its many masks, as it is the history of the dancers dancing. The performers are staging, as much as dancing, the difficulties of grappling with movement that predates their own: the places and moments of confrontation, revelation and pleasure, impossibilities and resistances, even dissociations from the self. (Launay 2012, 65)

Fabián Barba's *Dance Evening* similarly plays upon the frictions between different histories and memories, which are not limited to Mary Wigman's historical legacy or to his own personal background as a dancer, but also include the memory work the audience performs during the piece.[8] Essential in this respect are the short breaks that follow after

---

[8] With regard to the idea that dance reenactment brings different histories into dialogue, it is interesting to note that Fabián Barba and Mark Franko collaborated on a piece, first shown in 2014, in which they both revive *Le marbre tremble* (*Marble Trembles*), a solo that Franko created in 1988 and which he, more than 25 years later, transmitted to Barba. Their joint dancing of fragments from the solo is framed by monologues in which Barba and Franko unfold some of their personal histories as dancers and how their mutual interest in the persistence as well as the possible "reinvention" of dance history led to their encounter and the decision to collaborate on this work. As such, *Le marbre tremble* poignantly demonstrates how dance reenactment creates new genealogical lineages while revisiting older ones. For spectators, this might even trigger different links across several works. For instance, it is meaningful that Fabián Barba, after having danced as Mary Wigman and before working with Mark Franko, also appears as one of the performers in Olga de Soto's *Débords*. What starts to emerge here is a genealogical network

each solo (with a longer one in the middle of the performance) and which insert caesuras into the flow of the work, spurring spectators to reflect on the sequence they have just seen, as well as on Barba's intention in general. "These constitutive gaps," as Franz Anton Cramer writes, "may simply follow from the desire for a precise and detailed reconstruction" of how Mary Wigman would structure a dance evening, but "they nonetheless demonstrate that even the highest level of empathic understanding of the historical work ultimately only conceals the gaps in knowledge" that haunt any attempt to revive the past, whether in reenactment or reconstruction (2010, para. 11; my translation). While the so-called gaps are thus a structural principle of Barba's *Dance Evening*, they also install a certain distance between his attempt at reincorporating Wigman's technique and aesthetics vis-à-vis the possibility that spectators might want to feel totally immersed in the illusionary world that is created on stage. From this perspective, Barba's reenactment, despite its formal reproduction of Wigman's work and the physical resemblances between Wigman and Barba, does not bridge but instead emphasizes the historical distance between expressionist *Ausdruckstanz* and contemporary dance. Herein resides the true dialectical nature of Barba's *Dance Evening*: while approximating Wigman, it also distances us from the tradition she represents, as well as from the contemporaneity that Barba, by default, is supposed to embody by virtue of being alive.

Somewhat counterintuitively, then, "distance" emerges here as the key term to understand the affectivity at play in Barba's reenactment. This linkage, however, becomes more plausible against the background of what Mark Salber Phillips calls "the plasticity of historical distance" (2013b, 9). According to Phillips, historical distance ought to be reconceived as a versatile concept that exceeds the function it has long fulfilled in traditional historiography. In the wake of nineteenth-century historicism, he explains, distance was narrowly defined as the temporal gap that separates the past from the present and which was consequently privileged as the indispensable condition that makes presumably objective knowledge possible. Only with the passage of time, so it was assumed, can one take a detached and affectively neutral stance toward the past. As an alternative to this influential view that, apart from being limited, also "carries a heavy weight of prescription" (2013b, 5), Phillips proposes to transform historical distance from a restrictive doctrine into what he terms a "liberal heuristic" (6). Instead of a normative prerequisite for historiography, historical distance should be used as a flexible interpretive instrument to analyze how "every representation of history, whatever its genre, incorporates elements of *making, feeling, acting*, and *understanding*" (6).

These four parameters—which Phillips also describes as the "formal, affective, summoning, and conceptual" modes of distance (2013b, 14)—invite us to consider in what manner dance reenactment deals with historical distance as a concept that is not only about differences in time, but also about construing, feeling, *and* understanding the past. Barba's strenuous endeavor to mimic Wigman's dances and aesthetics as faithfully

---

of danced reenactments in which cross-connections can be drawn between choreographic practices that may seem to be remote in time but which become closely affiliated in the concern to work with existing dance traditions.

as possible suggests that, at least on the level of form, his performance is aimed at reducing the historical distance between himself and his precursor. But the same effect does not necessarily apply to the perception of the audience. Whenever one believes that one sees, however momentarily, the spectral presence of Mary Wigman on stage, the formal reduction of historical distance finds its correlate in the spectator's affective response. Yet from the moment one focuses on the minor details that bespeak Barba's male body or on his skillful manipulation of the theatrical machinery (including light, sound, costume, and dance), his literal imitation is likely to be perceived as historically distant, which diminishes the initial identification of Barba with Wigman. At some points, then, the past of Wigman may seem truly remote, whereas at others, we gladly familiarize ourselves with it and appropriate its characteristic codes. These shifting viewpoints ensue from Barba's play with historical distance, which—following Phillips—not only is a matter of time, but also manifests itself both in form and affect, leading spectators to believe and disbelieve that Wigman's presence might flash forth through Barba's body. This demonstrates that Bertolt Brecht's classical *Verfremdungseffekt* is not necessarily about establishing formal distance, but can also be achieved through strategic proximity.

To the extent that Barba's *Dance Evening* is a balancing act between belief and disbelief, combining what art critic Michael Fried described as "absorption" and "theatricality" (1980), how do both dimensions amplify, rather than mitigate, one another? In *Production of Presence* (2004), Hans Ulrich Gumbrecht opens up the possibility of what he calls a "presentification of the past," which can be obtained through "techniques that produce the impression (or, rather, the illusion) that worlds of the past can become tangible again" (94). While Gumbrecht does not specify what these "techniques" might entail, he does provide an important clue when stating that, in our current rationalized cultural climate, presence may only occur by virtue of an "oscillation between meaning effects and presence effects" (49). As Western cultures have never been able to shed the Cartesian privileging of mind over body, "presence could never become perfect if meaning was excluded," even while meaning seems to be incompatible with presence, insofar as "meaning perhaps never does emerge without producing effects of distance" (137). What Gumbrecht distinctly calls "'*effects of* presence'" (106; my emphasis) can therefore only occur when they are in "oscillation" or a "productive tension" with effects of meaning, which requires "a specific framework" (107), most likely to be found in aesthetics and history, insofar as each of these domains implies "a marked distance from our everyday worlds" (125).

Once again, distance emerges as a prerequisite not only for the attribution of meaning, but also for the occurrence of presence effects, which suggests how both registers are always already, if not necessarily, imbricated within one another. Perhaps the distinctive feature of contemporary dance reenactment is that it acknowledges the role of meaning in producing effects of presence, whereas traditional dance reconstruction is solely concerned with reproducing presence without regard to the representational mechanisms that undergird this endeavor. The complexity of Fabián Barba's *Dance Evening* derives from its confrontation of presence with meaning, with the result that both dimensions begin to oscillate with one another. This helps explain the mixed perceptions provoked by Fabián Barba's *Dance Evening*. Resolutely focusing on the outward look and choreographic techniques of the historical dances, Barba does not set out to extract a given meaning from the work or to impose a certain interpretation upon it. Instead, laboring to create a literal re-embodiment, he infuses the solos with his corporeal presence. But the resultant hyperbolic imitation also gives meaning to this apparent attempt to achieve a "presence effect," since recognizing the strategic impetus behind the reconstruction induces an acute awareness of the time-bound character of expressionist dance and the ways this legacy is largely absent from contemporary stages in both Europe and the United States. As Barba turns reenactment into an artistic strategy by hyperbolically imitating both Wigman's aesthetics and the conventions of reconstruction, his *Dance Evening* thus acquires a meta-historical dimension, revealing its own procedures to awaken and appropriate a specific part of the history of dance. This suggests how reenactment takes Hayden White's famous *Metahistory* (1973), in which he excavates the underlying patterns of historiography, beyond a primarily linguistic understanding of history, to include performative and embodied practices, such as dance reenactment.[9]

Echoing Vanessa Agnew's concerns about reenactment's "tendency to collapse temporalities" (2007, 309), dance scholar Kate Elswit worries that "projects that draw upon twentieth-century German dance"—and Barba's *Dance Evening* is one of the examples she mentions—"may ultimately take an ahistorical turn, flattening certain temporal economies that should remain destabilized, even as it disrupts others" (2014a, 12). To the extent that Barba's re-embodiment of Mary Wigman's dances does not directly challenge, for example, the general label of *Ausdruckstanz*—which, as Susanne Franco (2007) has argued, has been rather monolithically and retroactively applied to a variety of practices—he can indeed be suspected of subscribing to a flattened history of dance. There are, however, other temporalities at play beneath the work's perceptible surface and which follow from the manner in which Barba confronts his own personal history as a dancer with the canonized history of dance. One of the arguably most significant "meanings" Barba came across in his allegedly "presence"-oriented engagement with Mary Wigman's solos is the insight that the tradition of expressionist dance expanded and developed at different rhythms in other parts of the world. When Barba first saw Wigman dancing on video, he claimed to have "experienced a vague, ambivalent feeling of recognition," which prompted him to think that the past of European dance might be the present of Ecuadorian dance (2011, 83). As he explains in Chapter 20 of this volume, however, this initial scheme of thought actually endorsed the linear narrative of dance's canonized history, whereas, in reality, some dance traditions do continue to coexist in different places, as evidenced by the enduring influence of modernist dance on the

---

[9] In *Metahistory* (1973), Hayden White writes that "the style of a given historiographer can be characterized in terms of the linguistic protocol he used to prefigure the historical field prior to bringing to bear upon it the various 'explanatory' strategies he used to fashion a 'story' out of the 'chronicle' of events contained in the historical record" (426). Approaching reenactment as an artistic strategy—as I have been proposing—leads to a similar kind of reading of these works, which articulates how the past is intentionally and often self-reflectively re-plotted on the stage.

contemporary dance scene in Ecuador. Ultimately, then, Barba's *Dance Evening* uncovers a cartography of dance that troubles the chronological distinction between past and present as a means to historicize dance and as the foundation of historical distance.

# Unorthodox Faithfulness

Identifying how historical distance is at work in Barba's *Dance Evening* gives some idea of the interactions between presence and meaning, as well as the fluctuating temporalities that arguably undergird dance reenactment in general. In order to refine our understanding of this shifting dynamic, which Barba's performance brings to the fore, I would like to juxtapose his work with another dance reenactment, one that enters this field from an entirely different angle.

As opposed to Barba's formal imitation in *A Mary Wigman Dance Evening*, the Brussels-based Spanish choreographer Olga de Soto opts for the deviant route of reinterpretation in *Débords: Reflections on The Green Table* (2012). As she said in an interview, "I am not interested in producing an identical reconstruction" (Imbault 2012, 28; my translation). While de Soto was drawn to revisiting Kurt Jooss's canonical dance work *The Green Table* (1932) because of the lasting impression it made on her, she considered it superfluous to create yet another facsimile, knowing that already "more than fifty companies have realized more than eighty different productions" of the piece (de Soto 2015, 25; my translation). Instead, de Soto's approach focused on the reception, rather than the actual staging, of the original work. In *Débords*, the stage is populated by various projection screens that turn out to be the main protagonists, despite the physical presence of six dancers who, all dressed in black, seem to merge with the conspicuously dark scene, primarily serving as facilitators of the testimonies we see on the projected videos. The people that appear on the screens were interviewed by de Soto and recount their memories of *The Green Table*, a piece they either attended as a spectator or in which they performed as a dancer.[10] As we hear them talking in German, English, French, or Spanish, the variety of languages evokes how Jooss's work—after its successful 1932 premiere at an international dance competition in Paris—started to travel across

---

[10] For *Débords*, de Soto expands on the documentary method she already employed for her 2004 performance *histoire(s)*, in which she revisited Roland Petit's ballet *Le jeune homme et la mort* (1946). As with the work of Kurt Jooss, she was not interested in restaging Petit's piece in its original form, but rather in tracing its impact by interviewing people who had attended its premiere in Paris. For an explanation of the rationale behind *histoire(s)*, see de Soto (2011). Enlarging her scope for *Débords*, de Soto focused not only on the moment of the premiere of *The Green Table*, but also on the period before and after in order to find out how the piece affected people from different generations, also outside of Europe (see de Soto 2015). Interviewees featured in *Débords* are Juan Allende-Blin, Jeanne Brabants, Jacqueline Challet-Haas, Edith del Campo, Françoise Dupuy, Fernando García, Christian Holder, Ann Hutchinson Guest, Bruno Jacquin, Philip Lansdale, Michèle Nadal, Marina Grut, Toer van Schayk, Nora Salvo, Hanns Stein, Joan Turner Jara, Andras Uthoff, Jeanette Vondersaar, and Gerd Zacher.

various countries, leaving its traces in several minds and bodies at different points in time. Watching these fragments, it soon becomes clear that, as the interviewees are attempting to recollect the content of specific scenes, their memories unwittingly slip into the larger impact that Jooss's work had on their individual lives and how *The Green Table* was able to measure the tensions of the inter-war period, as well as the anxiety that followed the end of World War II.[11]

Kurt Jooss's piece indeed became renowned as a fierce anti-war ballet that used choreography to evoke and denounce the grim reality of war. The thirty-five-minute performance consists of eight tableaux in which various figures—such as diplomats, partisans, or the profiteer—run through the course of warfare, including its emergence, effects, and aftermath. The famous opening scene shows a group of politicians gathered around a diplomatic table, gesticulating frantically but not able to arrive at a consensus. The sequences that follow are the unfolding consequences of the political inability to ward off war. In a chronological succession, the scenes depict moments such as "The Farewell," "The Battle," and "The Refugees," while the next two sequences zoom in on the resistance of a partisan woman and the oppression of women in a brothel. The seventh tableau, "The Aftermath," enacts a *Totentanz* (a dance of death) that demonstrates the fate to which the people are condemned. The last scene brings us back to the beginning, as the exact same situation of diplomats negotiating around a table is reprised. Because Jooss did not stage a specific war situation but rather a generalized and deliberately cyclical depiction of the common features of warfare, some even saw in *The Green Table* a universal condition of humankind. For Marcia B. Siegel, for example, the piece evoked "a sort of generic war, a set of circumstances that produce the same result no matter where or when they are played out" (1989, 17).

As de Soto's *Débords* stubbornly refrains from showing a single step of Kurt Jooss's choreography, her performance instantiates what can be called an "imaginative" type of reenactment, which brings it close to the function R. G. Collingwood foresaw for reenactment in historiography. In his posthumously published *The Idea of History* ([1946] 2005), Collingwood famously proposed that genuine historical understanding is only acquired when "the historian re-enacts in his own mind the thoughts and motives of the agents whose actions he is narrating" (115).[12] Due to the underlying premise that

---

[11]  In *Watching Weimar Dance*, Kate Elswit points out that the common linkage of *The Green Table* with the specific sociopolitical context in Germany during the interwar period could not be overestimated, since it was only after World War II that the piece was performed regularly in Germany (Elswit 2014b, 128). An interesting difference between de Soto's performance and Elswit's study—even though they both take the reception of Kurt Jooss's *The Green Table* as their primary focus—is that, according to Elswit, Jooss's work came to be inscribed into "a narrative of cultural recovery" (137) that aimed to restore a linkage with the past. Contrastingly, the testimonies we hear in de Soto's *Débords* emphasize how *The Green Table* was inexorably connected to the traumatic experience of war, provoking instead the impression that history is destined to repeat itself.

[12]  The fact that Olga de Soto's *Débords* seems to put Collingwood's early definition of reenactment into practice could raise the question of whether Collingwood is describing memory, rather than history. As the tension between history and memory has been a recurrent topic of debate in historical theory (see, for instance, Cubitt 2007), it would be interesting to explore how dance reenactment confronts both dimensions.

historians are, at least on a rational level, able to close the gap between the past and the present through mental and reasoned reconstructions, Collingwood's reenactment theory has been criticized for adhering to a naïve belief in the possibility of returning to the past as it actually was.[13] A more careful reading of *The Idea of History*, however, shows that Collingwood is not discarding historical distance, but rather is foregrounding what Mark Salber Phillips calls its "plasticity." "Any imaginative reconstruction of the past," Collingwood explains, "aims at reconstructing the past of this present, the present in which the act of imagination is going on, as here and now perceived" ([1946] 2005, 247). Collingwood's understanding of reenactment as an "act of imagination" that revisits the past from the viewpoint of the present could be used to describe the process that unfolds in de Soto's *Débords*. Emphasizing the mnemonic dimension of reenactment, the piece reimagines Jooss's work in order to trace its significance for those who were in contact with it when the memory of war was still vividly alive.

Since Olga de Soto turns reenactment into a reimagination of the work, rather than a re-embodiment as did Fabián Barba, her piece provides another angle from which to observe the interaction between presence and meaning that, following Gumbrecht, underlies any attempt at "presentifying" the past. Instead of focusing on the layers of presence, or the outward appearance of *The Green Table*, de Soto's reenactment concentrates on the meaning of the work, quite literally, as the only way by which the audience comes to know Jooss's piece is by the interpretive memories that are recounted in the interviews. Crucially, however, even this indirect approximation of *The Green Table* via the route of meaning does not hamper the effects of presence from coming into play. Perhaps the greatest surprise of de Soto's *Débords* is that the piece does succeed in conveying some of the experiential impact Jooss's work had on its audiences. When *The Green Table* was first performed in the interwar period, its outward evocation of warfare made a strong appeal to spectators who, after having lived through the atrocities of World War I, were in a state of devastation and uncertainty about what the future might bring. Moreover, in retrospect, Jooss's piece proved to be an uncanny anticipation of World War II, which would follow after Adolf Hitler's accession to power in 1933. With *The Green Table*, Jooss gave expression to a *Zeitgeist*, in a manner that was both specific and general enough to make this work into a long-standing exemplum of political art.[14]

[13] Recent scholarship on Collingwood has tried to absolve him from this accusation. Guiseppina D'Oro, for example, argues that Collingwood "uses terms such as 'reenactment,' 'inside/outside' in a highly metaphorical way to explain the nature of historical explanation" (2002, 110). See also Browning (2004, 14, 75). The most extensive study on the role of reenactment in Collingwood's thought is William Dray's *History as Reenactment* (1995). Not surprisingly, the rise of reenactment in the arts has prompted performance and theater scholars to revisit Collingwood's ideas on the function of reenactment for history. Maaike Bleeker, for instance, turns to Collingwood to argue that artistic reenactment is about reviving the *logic* of a work of art, more than about copying its outer appearance (see Bleeker 2012). Also theater historian Bruce McConachie attempts to restore the validity of Collingwood's thinking by showing how recent findings in cognitive science corroborate many of his insights (see McConachie 2010). See Maaike Bleeker, Chapter 10 in this volume.

[14] In contrast to the fairly explicit political content of *The Green Table*, Kurt Jooss seemed to be quite resistant to this kind of interpretation. As he stated in a 1982 interview, "I am firmly convinced that art

This history lives on, not so much in the extensive descriptions and notations of *The Green Table*, but rather in the memory of those who, from the early 1930s onward, had seen the piece, or had performed in it.[15] As de Soto tellingly states, "there is a lot of affect in these interviews" and "what impressed me is the manner in which the message has traveled through time" (2014, para. 3; my translation). This living legacy, which can hardly be accounted for in traditional historiography—although it is by contrast the domain of oral history and performative ethnography—takes center stage in *Débords*, making both the work and the disastrous consequences of war arrestingly present, again. These effects of presence become most tangible when the interviewees resort to gestures and singing when describing particular scenes. Especially the memories about the seventh tableau—the "Aftermath," which shows how Death rips away the lives of people not responsible for the outbreak of war—seem to prompt means of expression other than words in order to make palpable the import of this devastating sequel. De Soto astutely marks this impact by swiftly crosscutting between video fragments that demonstrate how several of the interviewees are at a loss for words in talking about this scene, and begin to gesticulate and to hum the music. This brief accumulation of non-verbal expressions offers yet another angle to the memories that are recounted during the interviews.

De Soto's strategic use of reenactment as a mode of remembrance creates what Ramsay Burt calls a "virtual dance piece," a performance that restages choreography by relying on imaginative memories, rather than reconstituting the work step by step (2009, 443). Significantly, Burt describes the effect of such pieces in terms of affect and reflection. "The virtual power of memory," he asserts, allows choreographers "to create a virtual community" of audience members who might find themselves "sensitive" to the manner in which a given work provokes "affective sensations" (457). These affects may also "engender reflection," since they not only "intensify beholders' experience," but also "encourage them to reflect on who they are and how they relate to others" (457–458). From this perspective, de Soto's *Débords* infuses history with affect by means of memories, clearly not to entice the public, but to confront them with a particular historical reality, which in this case includes the work being mentally reenacted, as much as the interwar context that impregnates it.

It must be acknowledged that even though de Soto's *Débords* invites spectators to reimagine *The Green Table*, not every audience member is able or willing to do this. For some, and especially those who have never seen the piece or even heard about it,

---

should never be political . . . I don't think any war will be shorter or avoided by sending audiences into *The Green Table*" (Jooss quoted in Walther 1993, 60).

[15] Kurt Jooss's *The Green Table* has been fully documented in Labanotation by Ann Hutchinson Guest and was made publicly available in a book she developed in collaboration with Jooss's daughter Anna Markard (2003). For another detailed description, see Walther (1993). For a personal reflection on how the legacy of Jooss has been passed on between practitioners, see Lidbury (2004).

**FIGURE 3.3.** Dancer Mauro Paccagnella handling a screen that shows the interview with Joan Turner Jara in Olga de Soto's *Débords*.

Photo: Gautier Deblonde.

the actual absence of the dance might be an insuperable hindrance that only high-lights how far Jooss's work is removed from us in time. Yet, even when spectators are not drawn into the stories told in *Débords*, this is not so much a failure of the work as it is another instance of the "plasticity of historical distance" (Phillips 2013b, 9). It seems obvious that distance is built into the formal aesthetics of de Soto's *Débords*, not the least because the physical presence of the dancers is ostentatiously subju-gated to the mediated screenings of the conversations. During the piece, the per-formers hold the screens as if to give support to the testimonies, while also moving them around or slightly manipulating them (Figure 3.3). The continuous replacing and handling of the screens by the dancers highlights how *Débords* does not want to retell a pregiven, stabilized narrative, suggesting instead how the story is construed right before the audience's eyes. But even though de Soto exposes the framework of the stage, amplifying its representational and performative nature, the formal dis-tance thus established between the memories we hear and the way in which we see them staged does not vitiate the affective engagement on the part of spectators, but rather demonstrates how affect can be deepened by illuminating the mechanisms that bring it about. In much the same manner that Fabián Barba's *Dance Evening* hov-ers between identification and defamiliarization, Olga de Soto's *Débords* is about the effort to reach out to a past that, despite the affective force of memory, seems to be out of reach. The difficulties that some of the interviewees experience in recalling certain parts of *The Green Table* reflect the way in which history tends to recede from sight, or becomes blurry once recalled.[16]

# AFFECTIVE CHIASMS

Taken together, the works of Fabián Barba and Olga de Soto reveal how the relationship between aesthetic strategies and affective responses seems to follow the structure of a chiasm: while formal immediacy generates affects of distance (Barba), the emphasis on mediation gives way to affective proximity (de Soto).[17] What complicates this general scheme is that the same chiasmatic dynamic between proximity and distance is at work within each of the performances. Both pieces are able to produce the seemingly contrasting affects of identification and defamiliarization, insofar as the experience of spectators is likely to shift between recognizing the past and feeling distanced from it. This internal shifting primarily highlights that audience members are not entirely absorbed in believing that the past *is* made present again in the exact same manner as it supposedly once was.

It is telling that Rebecca Schneider, in *Performing Remains* (2011), also resorts to the figure of the chiasm in elaborating her view on the temporality of reenactment, both in the arts and popular culture. Reenactment brings to light, she argues, how "any approach to history . . . engages temporality at (and as) *a chiasm*, where times cross and, in crossing, in some way touch" (37; my emphasis). The notion of affect plays a pivotal role in Schneider's attempt to rethink the passing of time. In her opinion too, however, there is no salvation in regarding affect as a predominantly non-rational, self-governing intensity, which convinces her to "do away with arguments, such as Brian Massumi's, about affect's autonomy" (34).[18] Instead, she explicitly positions both her book and reenactment as "an exploration of affect *as* inquiry" (2011, 2), which implies that the experiential

---

[16] See Chapter 13 by Susanne Foellmer in this volume.

[17] This general scheme, which I will also complicate, is buttressed by Gumbrecht's argument that in a "meaning" culture, any outward appeal to presence is suspicious because it plays too easily into emotional involvement. It should be noted that "meaning," in this sense, corresponds not only to theory as such, but also to taking a formal distance. Even in entertainment culture, which often strongly appeals to a direct immersion of viewers, there is a certain tendency toward a (sometimes ironizing) self-awareness, as evident, for example, in the play with conventions in genres such as horror or science fiction. This indicates how contemporary audiences are sensitive to the manner in which genres from the past are not merely replicated, but are also conscious of their own codes and conventions.

[18] Instead of endorsing Brian Massumi's influential theorization of affect as an autonomous force, Schneider relies on feminist and queer theory, where affect is defined in emphatically relational terms. In these domains, affect is granted the ability to "jump" between and across different bodies, times, and spaces (Stewart 2007) and thus figuring as an object of "transmission" (Brennan 2004). These approaches, which pull affect out of the enclosed sphere of the subconscious, inspire Schneider to envision a nonlinear temporality that is affective precisely because it is "not to be autonomous, but to be engaged in a freighted, cross-temporal mobility" (2011, 36–37).

side of reenactment must have a distinct discursive impact that also *affects* historical understanding.

While Schneider's account of the chiasmatic and affective nature of reenactment is suggestive, I would like to take the chiasm beyond the mainly rhetorical function it fulfills in her reconsideration of time and affect. By pushing the chiasm to its full analytical potential, we might arrive at a better understanding of how dance reenactment refuses to commit what Vanessa Agnew denounces as "a collapsing of temporalities," prompting instead an array of interactions between the past and the present, thinking and feeling, form and response, presence and meaning. In this respect, it is important to bear in mind that, literally speaking, the chiasm not only consists of the point where two crossing lines meet, but also where they are most remote. The formal structure of the chiasm thus carves out a middle zone that conjoins opposites without collapsing them.

The ability of the chiasm to evoke a dual—but not dualistic—dynamic is also why phenomenologist Maurice Merleau-Ponty, in his unfinished and posthumously published *The Visible and the Invisible* ([1964] 1968), grasped upon this figure in envisioning a new model of being, which he designated as *la chair*, or "the flesh." For Merleau-Ponty, the chiasm provides a figure of thought that goes beyond the traditional dichotomies between body and world, mind and matter, or subject and object, since it embodies a mode of reasoning that acknowledges the deep encroachment and mutual impact of these seemingly opposite poles, while also maintaining a certain distance between them. Merleau-Ponty elucidates the imbricating dynamics of the chiasm through the by now classical example of one hand touching the other:

> If my left hand is touching my right hand, and if I should suddenly wish to apprehend with my right hand the work of my left hand as it touches, this reflection of the body upon itself always miscarries at the last moment: the moment I feel my left hand with my right hand, I correspondingly cease touching my right hand with my left hand. But this last-minute failure does not drain all truth from that presentiment I had of being able to touch myself touching: my body does not perceive, but . . . it is, as it were, prepared for a self-perception, even though it is never itself that is perceived nor itself that perceives. (Merleau-Ponty [1964] 1968, 9)[19]

Depending on where we focus our attention, the feeling of our left hand touching and our right hand being touched easily slips into the reverse sensation. Despite this apparent reversibility, however, neither of these perceptions can ever occur at exactly the same time, which suggests that there is an overlapping but irreducible relationship between

---

[19] The example of one hand touching the other already appears in Merleau-Ponty's earlier *Phenomenology of Perception* ([1945] 2012), but it is only in *The Visible and the Invisible* ([1964] 1968) that it acquires an ontological dimension and becomes a model for being as such. It should also be mentioned that Merleau-Ponty actually takes this example from Husserl, who refers to it in his *Ideas II*, §36 ([1952] 1989, 152–154). Juho Hotanen points out that an even earlier description of "the double sensation of the touching hands" can already be found in Maine de Biran's 1859 *Essai sur les fondements de la psychologie* (2014, 97 n. 33).

both. This double interaction constitutes what Merleau-Ponty calls *écart* (distance), which names a kind of difference that holds the middle ground between convergence and divergence. "I never reach coincidence," Merleau-Ponty writes, "the coincidence eclipses at the moment of realization" ([1964] 1968, 147).[20]

With Merleau-Ponty's theorization of the chiasm in mind, the idea that times may cross—as Schneider suggests—can be taken quite literally, in the sense that different temporalities might not only converge, but also diverge, as in the structure of a chiasm. Most important, Merleau-Ponty helps us to understand how a genuinely chiasmatic time should not be confused with a mere collapsing of temporalities, since it is both about the potential proximity *and* the irrevocable distance between the past and the present. Taking this further, dance reenactment not only induces a chiasmatic imbrication of different times, but it also engages with affect as a non-coinciding intertwining of feeling and knowledge.

## KNOWING AFFECT

Dance reenactment mobilizes both form and affect to generate a certain consciousness about the operations by which choreography is—or can be—historicized. In *Engaging the Past* (2015), historical scholar Alison Landsberg similarly points to this reflective potential in an attempt to counter Vanessa Agnew's skepticism about reenactment's exclusive focus on affect. According to Landsberg, "the experiential or affective mode, in conjunction with more explicitly cognitive modes, can play a role in the acquisition of historical knowledge" (2015, 10).[21] Opposing the idea that affect only comprises a sense of sheer immediacy (whether in terms of presence, intensity, or autonomy), Landsberg asserts that the impact of affective history becomes truly effective only when its underlying mediating operations are made explicit:

> The real potential for the production of knowledge about the past in these nontraditional formats occurs in those instances when a delicate balance is maintained between

[20] The term *écart* is difficult to translate without losing the resonance it has in French. While Alphonso Lingis, the English translator of *The Visible and the Invisible*, felt that this recurrent notion "has to be rendered variously by 'divergence,' 'spread,' 'deviation,' 'separation'" (Merleau-Ponty [1964] 1968, 7 n. 4), there is much to say for Lawrence Hass's opinion that "the word *écart* defies felicitous substitution and should probably remain untranslated," just as, in his view, Derrida's *différance* ought to be adopted without modification (2008, 129).

[21] Aiming to show how the appeal to affect in popular forms of history can foster reflection on how we come to know the past, Landsberg too draws on R. G. Collingwood and his favoring of reenactment as a methodological tool for practicing historians. Opposing the critique that Collingwood was a naïve historical thinker, Landsberg emphasizes how, in his view, "there is a strong *experiential* component," as well as "a meta- or self-reflexive component to the production of historical knowledge" (2015, 5). After all, Collingwood clearly stated that history is "a form of thought possible only to a mind which knows itself to be thinking that way" (quoted in Landsberg 2015, 10). See Maaike Bleeker, Chapter 10 in this volume.

drawing individuals into specific scenarios/crises/issues of the past in an affective, pal-pable way and yet also relentlessly reminding them of their distance and difference from the past—which is also often achieved affectively. (Landsberg 2015, 118)

Alternative forms of historiography are, in this sense, able to combine thinking and feel-ing, producing what Landsberg calls an "affective engagement," which she emphatically differentiates from mere "identification" (2015, 20). In terms similar to Gumbrecht's understanding of presence, she describes affect as "the oscillation between proximity and distance, alienation and intimacy," which, in turn, "provoke[s] analytical or cogni-tive processing and meaning making" (29).

But what exactly does it mean to describe these interactions in terms of an "oscilla-tion," as both Gumbrecht and Landsberg propose, beyond the mere fact that feeling and knowing are always already in some way connected? I suggest that reenactment triggers meaning and experience chiasmatically, exposing a vital epistemological side to affect that, in its current theorization, is often downplayed, if not directly devalued. If, as I have shown, the cross-temporality evoked by the reenactments of Barba and de Soto includes affects of proximity *and* distance—albeit in varying degrees—they can only achieve this by engaging—simultaneously—with the faculties of feeling and knowing, as well as by shifting the spectator's reception—continuously—between *having* a sensorial experi-ence of this cross-temporal dynamic, on the one hand, and *making* sense out of this sen-sation, on the other hand.[22] These performances can therefore make the past effectively felt as present, while beholders remain aware of the representational setting in which it is conjured up. This consciousness is amplified by the fact that choreographers such as Fabián Barba and Olga de Soto frame their reenactments *as* reenactments. In the case of Barba's *Dance Evening*, this is primarily achieved by means of what I have termed the "hyperbolic imitation," which is punctured with minor details that betray Barba's mas-culine physicality. In de Soto's *Débords*, it is rather the salient act of remembering, or the *Erinnerungsarbeit*, that emphasizes the status of this piece as reenactment. Neither of these works makes an ontological claim to bring back the past as it presumably once was, building in a reflective distance that nuances the mere sensorial immersion often associated with reenactment as a practice of living history.

# A DOUBLE SENSE

While affect is rightly valued for its unruly nature, we can only gauge its impact by trac-ing the steps, trajectories, or interactions through which affect moves and by which

---

[22] In distinguishing between *having* a sensation of and *making* sense out of dance reenactment, I am inspired by film scholar Vivian Sobchack who, in her book *Carnal Thoughts* (2004), traces a similar type of dual consciousness with regard to the watching of movies. She too draws on Merleau-Ponty to argue that we are "embodied and conscious subjects who both 'have' and 'make' sense *simultaneously*" (2004, 75).

it moves us. When it comes to danced reenactment, the figure of the chiasm offers a particularly illuminating way to rethink not only the cross-temporality, but also the function of affect in these practices. As the performances of Fabián Barba and Olga de Soto exemplify, artists turn to reenactment because it allows, indeed, for a mediation of the past that is arguably more immediate and affective than history in its tradition-ally written forms. However, in its artistic adaptation, reenactment often discloses the mechanisms and strategies by which it re-presents the past, acquiring a self-reflective dimension that constitutes—as I have called it elsewhere—"metamemories" (De Laet 2012). Making explicit the unavoidably representational nature of reenactment means that its historical evocations will always remain "as if" the past were rendered by turns either present or distant. But even if contemporary dance metamorphoses reenactment into a self-reflective practice, this does not undercut the actual realness of the cross-temporal affects it may engender. On the contrary, the attribution of meaning and the awareness of interpretive frameworks are rather chiasmatically intertwined with sen-suous experience and emotional involvement. Affect and understanding thus stand in a relationship of reversibility, whereby each dimension not only induces or amplifies, but also requires the other. Therefore, if reenactment epitomizes a form of affective his-tory, it must be acknowledged that, when used strategically, reenactment is all about the endeavor to make sense out of sensing the past.

## WORKS CITED

Agnew, Vanessa. 2007. "History's Affective Turn: Historical Reenactment and Its Work in the Present." *Rethinking History: The Journal of Theory and Practice* 11(3): 299–312.

Barba, Fabián. 2010. "Reconstructing a Mary Wigman Dance Evening." In *Are 100 Objects Enough to Represent the Dance? Zur Archivierbarkeit von Tanz*, edited by Janine Schulze, 100–115. Munich: Epodium Verlag.

Barba, Fabián. 2011. "Research into Corporeality." *Dance Research Journal* 43(1): 83–89.

Blackman, Lisa. 2012. *Immaterial Bodies: Affect, Embodiment, Mediation*. London: Sage.

Bleeker, Maaike. 2012. "(Un)Covering Artistic Thought Unfolding." *Dance Research Journal* 44(2): 13–25.

Brennan, Teresa. 2004. *The Transmission of Affect*. Ithaca, NY: Cornell University Press.

Browning, Gart K. 2004. *Rethinking R. G. Collingwood: Philosophy, Politics and the Unity of Theory and Practice*. Houndmills, UK: Palgrave Macmillan.

Burt, Ramsay. 2009. "History, Memory, and The Virtual in Current European Dance Practice." *Dance Chronicle* 32(3): 442–467.

Butler, Judith. 1993. *Bodies That Matter: On the Discursive Limits of "Sex."* New York and London: Routledge.

Clough, Patricia Ticineto. 2010. "The Affective Turn: Political Economy, Biomedia, and Bodies." In *The Affect Theory Reader*, edited by Melissa Gregg and Gregory J. Seigworth, 206–225. Durham, NC, and London: Duke University Press.

Clough, Patricia Ticineto, and Jean Halley, eds. 2007. *The Affective Turn: Theorizing the Social*. Durham, NC, and London: Duke University Press.

Collingwood, Robin George. [1946] 2005. *The Idea of History*. London: Oxford University Press.

Cramer, Franz Anton. 2010. "Hilflose Rekonstruktion." http://www.corpusweb.net/hilflose-rekonstruktion.html (accessed July 30, 2016)

Cubitt, Geoffrey. 2007. *History and Memory*. Manchester and New York: Manchester University Press.

De Groot, Jerome. 2009. *Consuming History: Historians and Heritage in Contemporary Popular Culture*. London and New York: Routledge.

De Laet, Timmy. 2012. "Dancing Metamemories." *Performance Research: A Journal of the Performing Arts* 17(3): 102–108.

de Soto, Olga. 2014. "D Festival: Olga de Soto remonte le fil." Interview by Gilles Bechet. http://www.agendamagazine.be/en/blog/d-festival-olga-de-soto-remonte-le-fil (accessed August 22, 2015).

de Soto, Olga. 2015. "Danses de mots, Danses fantômes." *NDD: L'actualité de la danse* 62: 24–25.

den Hollander, Jaap, Herman Paul, and Rik Peters, eds. 2011. "Historical Distance: Reflections on a Metaphor." *History and Theory* 50(4): 1–149.

D'Oro, Guiseppina. 2002. *Collingwood and the Metaphysics of Experience*. London and New York: Routledge.

Dray, William. 1995. *History as Reenactment*. Oxford: Clarendon Press.

Elkins, James. 2013. "Introduction." In *Beyond the Aesthetic and the Anti-Aesthetic*, edited by James Elkins and Montgomery Harper, 1–16. University Park: Pennsylvania State University Press.

Elswit, Kate. 2014a. "Inheriting Dance's Alternative Histories." *Dance Research Journal* 46(1): 5–22.

Elswit, Kate. 2014b. *Watching Weimar Dance*. Oxford and New York: Oxford University Press.

Foellmer, Susanne. 2014. "Re-enactment und andere Wieder-Holungen in Tanz und Performance." In *Zitieren, Appropriieren, Sampeln: Referenzielle Verfahren in den Gegenwartskünsten*, edited by Frédéric Döhl and Renate Wöhrer, 69–92. Bielefeld: Transcript Verlag.

Franco, Susanne. 2007. "Ausdruckstanz: Traditions, Translations, Transmissions." In *Dance Discourses: Keywords in Dance Research*, edited by Susanne Franco and Marina Nordera, 80–90. London and New York: Routledge.

Franko, Mark. 1989. "Repeatability, Reconstruction, and Beyond." *Theatre Journal* 41(1): 46–74.

Fried, Michael. 1980. *Absorption and Theatricality: Painting and Beholder in the Age of Diderot*. Berkeley: University of California Press.

Gregg, Melissa, and Gregory J. Seigworth, eds. 2010. *The Affect Theory Reader*. Durham, NC, and London: Duke University Press.

Gumbrecht, Hans Ulrich. 2004. *Production of Presence: What Meaning Cannot Convey*. Stanford, CA: Stanford University Press.

Hass, Lawrence. 2008. *Merleau-Ponty's Philosophy*. Bloomington and Indianapolis: Indiana University Press.

Hemmings, Clare. 2005. "Invoking Affect: Cultural Theory and the Ontological Turn." *Cultural Studies* 19(5): 548–567.

Hotanen, Juho. 2014. "From the Embodied Cogito to the Flesh of the Cogito." In *Corporeity and Affectivity*, edited by Karel Novotný, Pierre Rodrigo, Jenny Slatman, and Silvia Stoller, 91–101. Leiden: Brill.

Husserl, Edmund. [1952] 1989. *Ideas Pertaining to a Pure Phenomenology and to a Phenomenological Philosophy. Second Book: Studies in the Phenomenology of Constitution.*

Translated by Richard Rojcewicz and André Schuwer. Vol. III, Edmund Husserl, *Collected Works*. Dordrecht: Kluwer Academic Publishers.

Imbault, Charlotte. 2012. "Fouiller la Mémoire." *Mouvement* 66: 24–30.

Koivunen, Anu. 2010. "An Affective Turn? Reimagining the Subject of Feminist Theory." In *Working with Affect in Feminist Readings: Disturbing Differences*, edited by Marianne Liljeström and Susanna Paasonen, 8–27. London and New York: Routledge.

Landsberg, Alison. 2015. *Engaging the Past: Mass Culture and the Production of Historical Knowledge*. New York: Columbia University Press.

Launay, Isabelle. 2012. "Citational Poetics in Dance: . . . of a Faun (Fragments) by the Albrecht Knust Quartet, before and after 2000." *Dance Research Journal* 44(2): 49–69.

Leys, Ruth. 2011. "The Turn to Affect: A Critique." *Critical Inquiry* 37(3): 434–472.

Lidbury, Clare. 2004. "The Jooss Legacy: One Perspective." *Dance Research Journal* 36(1): 224–230.

Lorenz, Chris, and Berber Bevernage, eds. 2013. *Breaking up Time: Negotiating the Borders between Present, Past and Future*. Göttingen: Vandenhoeck & Ruprecht.

Macdonald, Sharon. 2013. *Memorylands: Heritage and Identity in Europe Today*. London and New York: Routledge.

Manning, Susan. [1993] 2006. *Ecstasy and the Demon: The Dances of Mary Wigman*. Minneapolis: University of Minnesota Press.

Markard, Anna. 2003. *Kurt Jooss, The Green Table: The Labanotation Score, Text, Photographs, and Music*, edited by Ann Hutchinson Guest. London and New York: Routledge.

Massumi, Brian. 2002. *Parables for the Virtual: Movement, Affect, Sensation*. Post-Contemporary Interventions. Durham, NC, and London: Duke University Press.

McConachie, Bruce. 2010. "Reenacting Events to Narrate Theatre History." In *Representing the Past: Essays in Performance Historiography*, edited by Charlotte M. Canning and Thomas Postlewait, 378–403. Iowa City: University of Iowa Press.

Merleau-Ponty, Maurice. [1945] 2012. *Phenomenology of Perception*. Translated by Donald A. Landes. London and New York: Routledge.

Merleau-Ponty, Maurice. [1964] 1968. *The Visible and the Invisible*. Edited by Claude Lefort. Translated by Alphonso Lingis. Evanston, IL: Northwestern University Press.

Miller, Daniel. "Tanzkongress 2009: The Second Edition of the German Dance Congress." https://frieze.com/article/tanzkongress-2009?language=de (accessed July 30, 2016).

Phillips, Mark Salber. 2013a. "Introduction." In *Rethinking Historical Distance*, edited by Mark Salber Phillips, Barbara Caine, and Julia Adeney Thomas, 1–18. Houndmills: Palgrave Macmillan.

Phillips, Mark Salber. 2013b. *On Historical Distance*. New Haven, CT: Yale University Press.

Schneider, Rebecca. 2011. *Performing Remains: Art and War in Times of Theatrical Reenactment*. London and New York: Routledge.

Siegel, Marcia B. 1989. "The Green Table: Sources of a Classic." *Dance Research Journal* 21(1): 15–21.

Sobchack, Vivian. 2004. *Carnal Thoughts: Embodiment and Moving Image Culture*. Berkeley and Los Angeles: University of California Press.

Stalpaert, Christel. 2011. "Reenacting Modernity: Fabián Barba's *A Mary Wigman Dance Evening* (2009)." *Dance Research Journal* 43(1): 90–95.

Stewart, Kathleen. 2007. *Ordinary Affects*. Durham, NC: Duke University Press.

Walther, Suzanne K. 1993. "The Dance of Death: Description and Analysis of The Green Table." Edited by Suzanne K. Walther. *Choreograpy and Dance (Special Issue: The Dance Theatre of Kurt Jooss)* 3(2): 56–81.

Wetherell, Margaret. 2015. "Trends in the Turn to Affect: A Social Psychological Critique." *Body & Society* 21(2): 139–166.

White, Hayden. 1973. *Metahistory: The Historical Imagination in Nineteenth-Century Europe.* Baltimore, MD, and London: Johns Hopkins University Press.

Witzeling, Klaus. 2009. "Hommage für Tanzlegende Mary Wigman." *Hamburger Abendblatt,* November 6. http://www.abendblatt.de/kultur-live/article107585022/Hommage-fuer-Tanzlegende-Mary-Wigman.html (accessed July 30, 2016).

# CHAPTER 4

# MARTHA@ . . . THE 1963 INTERVIEW

## Sonic Bodies, Seizures, and Spells

### RICHARD MOVE

We drink sound through our throats; our throats are activated, brought to
life, by what we hear. Listening is a reciprocation; grateful for what the ear
receives, the throat responds by opening.

—Wayne Koestenbaum, *The Queen's Throat* (2001, 14)

THIRSTILY, like Wayne Koestenbaum's experience of the operatic diva, I have gratefully
listened to the late Martha Graham and have responded with my reproduction of her
voice since 1996—an overwhelmingly alluring and charismatic voice that is, for me,
more powerful than any other and fills me with the compulsive agency to replicate it.
Beginning with the first of my *Martha@ . . .* performances, it has been said by critics,
scholars, and audience members alike that I incarnate Martha Graham. I attribute this
sensation of incarnation to the linguistic dance and sonic embodiment of my vocal performance that facilitates the emergence of Graham's personae—a paralinguistic vocal
emergence at times so powerful that its affective transmission has, at least momentarily, cast a spell and convinced even those who knew Graham intimately that they were
hearing and experiencing Graham herself. This medium-like transference of her voice
speaking through my body is the privileged point of entrance into my reenactments.
This is especially true of the 2011 iteration of my odyssey with Graham, *Martha@ . . . The
1963 Interview*, a production based upon an audio recording of Graham's 1963 onstage
interview with dance critic and historian Walter Terry at the 92nd Street Y in New York.
With this chapter, I trace the process of capturing Graham's voice with a study of her own
language at the age of sixty-nine and the methods used to reproduce it at this particular

moment in her career. It is the voice of Graham at the decline of her dancing power, near retirement from the stage, and approaching what she called her "first death."[1]

As the author, I am keenly aware the reader will notice what may surely be a glaring omission to some; I do not address expressions of gender. Nor do I situate expressions of gender within the realm of queer theory. Gender, as has been proven, is unstable, fluid, and subtly nuanced. The stubborn trope of the male/female binary is steadily becoming undone. The complex spectrum of gender and gender identification, now part of the popular culture's conversation, is an understanding I have long had, lived with, lived beside, lived inside, and lived outside. There is, of course, great attention paid to each detail of costuming and maquillage that help facilitate my physical transformation. It is, indeed, an important component of my enaction. Nonetheless, it is a singular component. As I hope will become clear, more central to this transformation, and the focus of my analysis, is the bodily absorption of mediated archival matter and its transmission. This focus is especially critical to my examination of the media at the heart of *Martha@ . . . The 1963 Interview*. The corporeal absorption, secretion, and its circulating affect, as I set out to establish, transcend the limitations imposed by the male/female binary.

The material that comprises my performances as/of Graham, in text and dance, is derived and developed from my admittedly obsessive relationship to the mediated archival matter that I have collected and that has been gifted to me. This archival matter includes Graham's images, texts, photographs, recorded films, video and audio, as well as the aural history generously shared with me by many older company members and other persons in Graham's Olympus-like inner orbit. My body has become, as André Lepecki asserts, ". . . an attractor of Graham's most intimate collaborators, friends, and former dancers. And, as an attractor, that is a critical point—he started to be treated by them as an archive" (Lepecki 2010, 43).

# THE GIFT

As an attractor, I received another extraordinary gift and call to enact—a vital gift and an addition to my archive that had enough of the force, enough of the event of Graham, that it became part of ". . . an archive that could unleash Martha's voice, as well as her body, presence, dance, eroticism, creativity, and works" (Lepecki 2010, 42). This time it arrived in the form of an audio recording of Graham's 1963 onstage interview with

---

[1] In *Blood Memory*, Graham wrote, "A dancer more than any other human being, dies two deaths: the first, the physical when the powerfully trained body will no longer respond as you wish" (1991, 238). I utilize this "first" death to underscore Graham's belief that the inability to dance is equated to death, that she considered herself a dancer first and choreographer second; thus I name her passing on April 1, 1991, her "second" death. I use the "second" death throughout the chapter to convey the afterlife that, I contend, follows both Graham's "first" and "second" deaths to advance my analysis.

Walter Terry at the 92nd Street Y. The interview with Martha Graham was presented by the 92nd Street Y at the Kaufmann Concert Hall on March 31, 1963, and was the last of Terry's sixty-six "Dance Laboratory" programs. In 2010, I was contacted by John-Mario Sevilla, of the 92nd Street Y Harkness Dance Center's DEL (Dance Education Laboratory), about the discovery of the audio recording, which would soon give life to a fully realized production, *Martha@ . . . The 1963 Interview*. Sevilla had the audio recording transcribed. With the audio and its transcription in my possession, the inescapably alluring animism of Graham's voice, prompted by Terry's over the course of approximately seventy minutes, immediately demanded from me an aesthetic and corporeal rebirth.

Surprisingly, according to the 92nd Street Y, there is not a single photograph, let alone a filmic document, of this event—an absolute anomaly considering how Graham had been so consistently, widely photographed and was a celebrated public figure at the time of the interview. However, as I will describe in detail, nothing of the archival felt missing. I longed for no other media.

For a clear understanding of the mechanism and enaction of this transmission from recorded object to archival body and to the stage, I turn to the study of sound anthropology, specifically, research of the soundscape and voicescape. I draw upon this scholarship as a resource in my investigation of the archival audio recording, its embodiment, and its circulating afterlives. I also employ the poetic prose of Roland Barthes's and Wayne Koestenbaum's explorations of the voice to advance my efforts to demonstrate that the archival recording lives on within me and my collaborators, and extends beyond our bodies to the performance event's spectators. Additionally, the central tenets of Erin Manning's trans-disciplinary research on thoughts in motion and movement's connectivity to language assist in the clarification of my exploration that the affective force of language is inextricably linked to the gesture of dance. Manning's work, in part, extends the philosophies of Gilles Deleuze and Felix Guattari, and I call upon Deleuze in support of my investigation of the eternal returns of the distinct force that is Graham, made evident with *Martha@ . . . The 1963 Interview*.

## BECOMING SOUND BODIES

This archival recording, buried, forgotten, then discovered and animated nearly fifty years later, demonstrates that the sonic archive may live not only as a technology of memory, but may be trans-temporally activated. As a performance anthropologist, I fully engaged in the "search for traces of the aural and practices of listening in literatures of [a] different historical period" (Samuels et al. 2010, 333).

I sought to create a sensorial soundscape experience, at once a present-day pursuit and a theatrical rendering based upon the recording. In this manner, I ". . . sought to abstract sound from its immediate surroundings while noting its connectivity to place" (Samuels et al. 2010, 330). Although the work was presented at the Dance Theater Workshop and

New York Live Arts in 2011 and at the Singapore International Festival of the Arts in 2014, actor and playwright Lisa Kron, as Terry, welcomed the viewer to another place, the 92nd Street Y, while speaking into a replica of an early 1960s microphone. Terry also invited the audience to another time with the mention of the date of the interview, March 31, 1963. Composer Pierre Schafer's "schizophonia" (Samuels et al. 2010, 331) is achieved as the recorded source from the past was transposed to present time, through the dialogue of Terry and Graham, the sounds produced by the dancers, and the ambient sounds of the audience, evoking Schafer's "time and place-shift" (Samuels et al. 2010, 331). The performance elicits both a specificity of "here" and "now" and a multiplicity of "heres" and "nows" through mediatization, creating newness of time and place, rather than a mere reproduction. We treated the sound on tape as a "sound object" (Samuels et al. 2010, 331) and lived its originary source through enactment. With the development and presentation based upon on the study of their recorded voices, we entered into an "acoustic construction of knowledge" (Samuels et al. 2010, 331).

Embodiment with theatrical gesture connected to language was combined with the nonverbal, highly rigorous choreography of Graham's vocabulary, performed by Katherine Crockett, then a senior principal with the Martha Graham Dance Company, along with Catherine Cabeen, a former Graham Company member. Further animating the interdisciplinary work is the digital media scenic design of Gabriel Barcia-Colombo. These elements combined to create a multisensorial event, with the sonic in the form of the dialogic as the production's genesis and center.

## LISTENING TO GRAHAM AND TERRY

The first and foremost method in our process of actualization is a most attentive and refined practice of listening, which was used throughout the entirety of the rehearsal process and in preparation for each performance. This practice, in accordance with Roland Barthes, is "[b]ased on hearing, listening (from an anthropological viewpoint) is the very sense of space and time, by the perception of degrees of remoteness and of regular returns of phonic stimulus" (1995, 246). The listening is stimulated by and through temporalities and spaces of the once analog, reel-to-reel recording, now digitized. Yet, some fifty years later, even new software cannot erase the Victrola-esque quality of the recorded voices, at least not without partially erasing the orators as well. Our listening to and through the audio objects' pops, hisses, crackling, and disturbances, toward achieving aural intimacy, ". . . is a physiological phenomenon; listening is a psychological act" (Barthes 1995, 245). Our hungry, hyper-alert, diligent ears, are perfectly poised and perfectly constructed, anatomically, to listen. Auricles miraculously ". . . made for this capture of the fleeting index . . . the folds and detours of its shell seem eager to multiply the individual's contact with the world . . ." (Barthes 1995, 248). Enrapt, we listen to receive the voices, and by this reception, the intimate interiority of the very beings of those speaking. Once they were disembodied voices lying in rest at the 92nd Street Y. The voices of Graham and Terry are no longer dormant in recorded stasis. Their voices find in our willing corporeal vessels the opportunity for prosopopeia and a home of unique agency—a newness of dwelling that will soon fully transform our bodies and will be listened to by audiences in New York and Singapore, resembling the statement of Deleuze, "That is why it is properly called a belief in the future. Eternal return affects only the new, what is produced under the condition of default and by the intermediary of metamorphosis" (1995, 90).

Kron and I listen as medium-like intermediaries, with silent, yet soon to be animate bodies as ". . . listening is the very operation of metamorphosis" (Barthes 1995, 248). Transmission and transformation via the sonic commence. This transmission may, at first, seem phenomenological. However, our method toward this metamorphosis more closely follows Erin Manning's position: "Yet there is no question that articulation through language is capable of conveying a certain complexity, bridging the worlds of sensory eventness with the affective tonality of language in the making such that a dialogue between these co-arising worlds can begin" (2009, 214).

We began by listening to a sentence, or what we deem a complete thought, as this interview, like most conversation, does not follow conventional syntax. I named these sentences "choreo-thoughts" as a means to assist and inform our decisions of analyzing and working with the audio and its accompanying written transcript. These "choreo-thoughts" are complete with stutters, pauses, breaths, and silences, expressing much more than what appears on the page. The written transcript offers substantially less detail when compared to this close listening. It becomes evident the most direct point of entry into Graham and Terry, and them into us, is the extra-vocal. "The injunction to listen is the total interpellation of one subject by another: it places above everything else the quasi-physical contact of these subjects (by voice and ear): it creates transference: "*listen to me*" means *touch me, know that I exist . . .*" (Barthes 1995, 251).

Gradually, the hearing and the listening take hold of our bodies. We then repeat aloud each of the "choreo-thoughts" as closely as possible. The interiority and intimacy of first listening alone with earbuds to their voices, then repetitively speaking as precisely as possible what we've just heard out loud to each other, serves several purposes of utmost value to staging this document. First and foremost, "[l]istening to the voice inaugurates the relation to the Other: the voice by which we recognize others . . . indicates to us their way of being, their joy, or their pain, their condition; it bears an image of their body and, beyond, a whole psychology . . ." (Barthes 1995, 254).

This repetition of transmission also serves as means of memorization. But, most important, it allows us to uncover and physically meet the Other through the study of the Other's own language. It is important to reiterate that there is no filmic record of the event, not even a single still photograph, only the audio recording. It is the disembodied voice of the dead (at first), and this alone, that is our source material, revealing that "[r]ecords are tokens of disappearances and comeback: they are also portraits" (Koestenbaum 2001, 50).

We internalize aurality: "To hear is metaphorically to be impregnated—with thought, tone and sensation" (Koestenbaum 2001, 16). This process of silent hearing, listening, then repeatedly reciting aloud each and every "choreo-thought" provides the bridge toward our ultimate inhabitation of them, by us and each other; demonstrating the "[c]orporality of speech, the voice is located as the articulation of body and discourse, and it is in this interspace that listening's back-and-forth movement might be made" (Barthes 1995, 255).

As Terry/Kron and Graham/I deliver their parts, we pay keen attention to the audio and written transcript, correcting the other when the language has not been produced with the utmost precision. Every "uh," "um," or stutter, every breath, every slip of the tongue, every word, audible and inaudible, as well as the perceptible thoughts that are found in their sighs, silences, and reflexive pauses, are repeatedly rehearsed and ultimately presented in this meticulous manner. We have begun to ". . . feel sound rhythmically. We find ourselves thinking sound. Sound becomes a concept for language in the making" (Manning 2009, 224).

As human discourse is unpredictable, the live interview finds the interlocutors at moments caught off guard, mid-thought, sometimes adrift, changing the subject, striving for the right words and always in the present moment. This technique allows us to *truly* hear and produce the interview as a living, organic discussion, even though it took place over fifty years ago.

Through their speech patterns becoming our own, patterns of being begin to emerge through rhythmic repetitions of their voices. We are ensconced in a visceral, linguistic dance of sonic embodiment. Our process connects us to the reflection of Deleuze that "[r]epetition is the power of language, and far from being explicable, it implies an always excessive Idea of poetry" (1995, 291). The excess of Graham and Terry's poetic language accompanies us to a heightened place of transduction.

Graham herself practiced the most attentive listening. We learn this over the captivatingly rhythmic course of the interview. It is hearing and listening to voices and sounds that provide the catalyst for some of Graham's greatest dance-plays' most decisive and dramatic moments. In the interview she recounts, or rather lives, such a moment with Jocasta in her 1947 *Night Journey*: "And then, there's a moment when she hears something, and this is very definite, very concrete to me. She hears a child cry, although she's in the arms of her lover . . . and, she is constantly torn between—she's not torn, no, but she's bewildered."[2]

Another example of Graham's listening to visual stimuli is when she tells of visiting a church in France, where she simultaneously finds the inspirational voice to create her Joan of Arc and becomes Joan of Arc:

The sunlight came in and the church was very dim. And I thought perhaps she stood there, perhaps she, she stood there because she was in this place, she walked through

---

[2] The audio recording and its transcription are from my archive. The transcription by Elizabeth Jean Marie Foster was completed May 17, 2009, and was given to me with the audio recording, courtesy of the 92nd Street Y Harkness Dance Center. The excerpts from the transcript appear in this chapter exactly as they appear on the pages of the transcription.

these doors. And perhaps the sunlight hit her and at that moment she felt that it was St. Catherine or St. Michael or St. Margret or the voice of God. (Graham 1963, 21)

Graham makes no differential between visiting the church to study Joan in preparation to create the ballet, and, via a beam of the sunlight's voice, becoming Joan, just as Graham believes Joan could have become Joan. For Graham, sights as sounds synthesize with choreographic action.

When in discussion of her technique, Graham refers to another sort of listening, again just as concrete:

> WT:    But I—I was wondering if inherent in your technique, uh is the uh—are the tools for characterization?
> MG:    I like to think they are but what you have to do then is you listen to your own pulse after you have learned the exercises enough. (8)

For Graham, the organ of repetition is the heart. As a dancer, one is only privileged enough to "listen to your own pulse" after an arduous period of rigorous training and repetition. With close listening, Graham's pulse is actualized with the pulsating beats of her speaking and dancing heart.

## GRAHAM'S GRAIN

What is it about Graham's voice that speaks so clearly, so directly, as if to be calling to me to speak for her, to make her voice heard once again and time and time again? What makes it the only voice with enough resonant power to distinguish itself from all the other voices I've ever heard? What pulls me into the force that is Martha Graham and inspires me, along with her singular body and body of work, to become her? I listen, like Koestenbaum to the opera singer, with a ". . . listener's inner body [that] is illuminated, opened up . . . she exposes the listener's interior. Her voice enters me, makes me a 'me,' an interior, by virtue of the fact that I have been entered" (Koestenbaum 2001, 43).

Like Barthes, I must ask, ". . . am I alone in perceiving this? Am I hearing voices within the voice? But is it not in the truth of the voice to be hallucinated? Is not the entire space of the voice an infinite space?" (Barthes 1995, 272). Perhaps somewhere in the recesses of immeasurable memory is another voice I once heard, which could have resembled Graham's own valence and have been of great enough significance to continually embark on this phantastical journey, full of glorious "[m]oments of being pierced, of being surrounded by sound, being called . . ." (Koestenbaum 2001, 16). It has emerged as a solitary voice from the choir of the mnemonic to the extent that it decidedly takes root. Graham's truthful voice arises from the cacophony of others that I must act upon, transformatively bringing it into the present-future to share publicly. Her voice and personal narrative have become inscribed onto my own body.

Perhaps this inescapable attraction may best be described with Barthes's use of "... the grain of the voice, when the voice is in a double posture, a double production: of language and of music" (Barthes 1995, 269). I listen to Graham's language musically, and it is Graham's "grain" that accounts for the excitement that I continuously experience listening to it. Her voice and its grain, the formerly ineffable thing, now made material, overwhelmingly lures me in from the moment of its grand entrance—an entrance, it seems, without exit.

Graham's grain may be especially more pronounced, as it is a dancer's vocal utterance. It emerges as more pertinent, poignant, and more hyper-embodied, as the utterance is viscerally felt, especially as Graham recounts her virtuosic, wordless, and dramatically communicative roles. In this manner, like Barthes's description of a Russian cantor, Graham's corporeal voice for me is "... brought by one and the same movement to your ear from the depths of the body's cavities, the muscles, the membranes, the cartilages ... as if a single skin lined the performer's inner flesh ..." (Barthes 1995, 270).

Throughout the interview, I am in tune with Graham and the "... materiality of the body speaking its mother tongue" (Barthes 1995, 270) and, in turn, the zone of my body. It is "[t]he *geno-song* ... the space in which the significations" germinate "from within the language and in its very materiality ..." (Barthes 1995, 270). The diction of her language is choreographic speech, as she is communicating what is articulated through the gesture of dance. Graham's speech, like her art, is exceedingly, excessively expressive. Each utterance of her philosophies, theories, and thoughts are expressed with grain; in cadences and rhythms rife with theatrically calculated pauses and carefully selected words, she constructs phrases for the greatest erudite delivery and impact. Her diction is vividly bountiful with the resonance of her breath. "By her noises, Nature shudders with meaning passion" (Barthes 1995, 250). In fact, Graham states in the interview that the creative impulse for certain roles begins with shudders that she refers to as "seizures" (1963, 4) that she can sense come "at her out of the atmosphere" (1963, 4). This is the truth of her language—a truth that allows me, through her impassioned vocal shudders and seizures, to escape my own voice and transcend physical and psychic boundaries.

# VOICESCAPE AND LINGUISTIC
# CHOREOGRAPHY

The entrancing, melodious, and activating embodiment of voices, I came to understand, is its own musicality. Sound ecologist Henry Johnson opposes the traditional binary separating speech and music "... based on the two extremes where speech is seen to be at one end of a continuum and song at the other. However, there is no mention of the performed intricacies of, for example, breathing, vibrato, register, and pitch, in many everyday utterances that bridge the continuum between speech and song" (2004, 26). The text had exposed itself as so musical that I, along with dramaturge Joshua Lubin-Levy and our collaborators, came to realize that a decision must be made whether or not to employ traditionally defined music anywhere in the production.

I experimented with incorporating extracts of Graham's own musical scores within several of the dances staged for the project with the two dancers for three purposes: first, to present to the audience the essence of the ballets' distinctive soundtracks; second, to underline and support the dances in a manner to approximate Graham's use of these musical compositions; and third, to dramatize my belief that while Graham verbally recounts, in detail, the performance of her roles, she is *listening* to fragments of the accompanying music she danced with.

Remarkably, throughout the entirety of the interview, neither Graham nor Terry ever mentions her exceptional use of music. At first, this may seem like a glaring omission, considering her renowned commissions from some of the twentieth century's greatest composers. Graham's particular use of music is certainly essential to the study of her vast oeuvre, but the focus of this interview remains on her philosophical intent, the development of her technique, and the employment of that technique to actualize the interdependent, personal, and dramatic narratives fundamental to the creation of the roles. For these reasons, the soundscape remains devoid of music in the usual sense, in keeping with the form and content of the interview, and instead we utilize our "voicescape" (Johnson 2004, 26) as the project's soundscape.

The voices are musical. The language is musical. There is nothing of the quotidian about their vocalizations. They are idiosyncratic in word choice, intonation, inflection, and expression, especially in the intensified context of a public interview that Johnson lucidly defines:

> That is, it is the social interaction of humans in meaningful situations that provides the conceptual framework for the voice to be performed in musical ways. It is through social performance that the voice is used as a musical instrument, which expresses literal and symbolic meaning through every style of voice production. (Johnson 2004, 26–27).

The focus on the voicescape and music of the text would also allow the unveiling of another of the layers of the interview's dramatization that is normally hidden, the sound of the dancers physicality. These dances are usually presented with fully orchestrated scores that almost hermetically seal the sounds emitted by the dancers. Sounds such as the barefoot turning, jumping, landing, or sliding on the stage floor, along with Graham's signature floor work—including the seated turns, skittering *pirouettes*, spins and crawls on the knees, standing falls backward, foreword, and sideward to the floor, and other body parts that make contact with the stage in her complex vocabulary—all create a rich variety of diegetic sound with a musicality of its own.

There is also the dancer's breath. For Graham, breath, again linked to the pulsating beat of the heart, is an essential principle. The vocabulary cannot be accomplished without an understanding of the specifics of movement's connection to breath. The basis and fundamental core of her technique—the contraction, followed by the release—are premised upon the intently focused exhalation and inhalation of breath to initiate, complete, and transition from one movement to the next. This breath rhythm contributes yet another musical layer to the soundscape.

The voicescape of Terry and Graham, with the soundscape of the two dancers, allows the viewer to more viscerally experience the dances while maintaining the emphasis on the dialogic. These sounds, along with the musical speech, accentuate that Graham, at sixty-nine, can no longer perform these works and that "[l]anguage must be called forth as a layering with of the affective tonality of expression" (Manning 2009, 215). She made these same sounds, and her bodily archive relives the physical sensation that accompanied them, while being transduced verbally.

For Graham, language is choreographic and resides in the voice as much as in the mute gesture: "Bridging a vocabulary of movement with one of language requires concepts for thinking affective resonance within linguistic enunciation" (Manning 2009, 216). Dance and spoken word are inextricable, performative texts of equivalent significance. The choreographic is preceded by thought and speech. This principle of Graham's process is evident in Terry's very first question and her answer:

> WT:    Um, when you steep yourself in <AUDIO DISTURBANCE> and you almost need to know what they had for breakfast. Uh, let's say in the case of, uh, Medea, uh, I assume you read all the versions of the Medea story, how—how, far does the steeping actually go? Uh—I mean does that go beyond Medea and go into a period of—of history oh—uh that she lived in and the circumstances and so on?
> MG:    Uh yes, of course you read as much as you can about the existing woman— the plays. But also the country that she lived in, the countryside that she lived in. (Graham 1963, 1)

There is simultaneity to the intertextual. The process of creating a dance begins with all manner of scholarship and copious reading and writing on a character. Before making a gesture, Graham immerses herself in the Classic literature, historical epoch, and geographic texture of her soon-to-be-realized work. It is a literary and verbal approach to physicality. For Graham, "[l]anguage does not replace the sensual exploration of the relational environment: it moves with it, becoming one more technique for composition. Words are an extra component of the experience of articulation, not its final form" (Manning 2009, 215).

## LINDA HODES AND GESTURAL VOICES

The union of voicescape with truthful, moving gesture discloses itself throughout the discourse encompassing Graham's "choreo-thoughts," her body, and her body of work, and "[t]his dance of movement sound prepares the way for the creation of a complex emergent environment that comes to life through the conjunction of objects, sound, and gesture" (Manning 2009, 213). This dancing union of voice and bodily gesture is observed, discovered, rehearsed, and refined with the collaborative, ongoing super-vision of one whom I attracted and who treats me as a sort of archive, Linda Hodes, who first worked with me as my rehearsal director in 2001 on my staging of *Phaedra* for *Martha@Town Hall.*

Hodes, now eighty-three, began as a student in the children's program at the Martha Graham Center for Contemporary Dance. By her teen years, she advanced through the technique classes to the advanced level. Graham took notice of the young dancer and invited her to join the company. Hodes began performing as a part of the chorus in such masterpieces as *Night Journey* and as one the quartet of women "Followers" in her *Appalachian Spring.* After only a few years, Hodes was promoted to soloist and then principal dancer, performing leading roles internationally.

She danced in nearly each of the works that Terry and Graham discuss, including Graham's own roles and originating others. "In Phaedra, of course, I had my great role as "Pasiphae" (Tracy 1996, 177), as Hodes recounts, "I can distinctly remember Martha choreographing *Phaedra*" (Tracy 1996, 177). *Phaedra,* which premiered in 1962, was the most recent work Graham had made at the time of the interview, and she discusses it with Terry.

Hodes remained in Graham's orbit and eventually became director of the Graham school. By the early 1970s, Hodes became artistic co-director of the company. She then remained by Graham's side in this capacity for more than two decades and maintained her position as artistic director for several years after Graham's "second" death in 1991. The philosophy, technique, vocabulary, repertory, and person of Graham live within Hodes. In another temporal synchronicity, several weeks into rehearsal, Hodes realized that her first performance with Graham had taken place sixty years earlier, in 1951, at the 92nd Street Y, in Terry's interview with Graham for an earlier installment of his Dance Laboratory series.

Hodes became an extension of Graham herself, who was unable to demonstrate and often could not verbally articulate the choreography for the last ballets she is credited with having made for the company. In this way, she imbued within Hodes the ability and responsibility to complete her "choreo-thoughts" and to embody the choreogra-phy that Graham valiantly attempted to communicate in those years. Hodes, entirely steeped in the work from a young age, became an appendage-like extension of the frail, aging legend, whose body was riddled with painful rheumatoid arthritis that had begun, by the mid-1960s, to disfigure her once unimaginably strong, articulate hands and feet. Although many dancers dedicated years or even decades to Graham, her vision, and the company, Hodes is the sole figure that grew up in the Graham studios, rose through the ranks of the company, directed the school, and then ultimately became Graham's voice and body as artistic co-director. Hodes eloquently told *The New York Times:*

> "I was always so amazed when we did press conferences on tour at how articulate she was about what she was doing," said Ms. Hodes, who is helping Mr. Move refine his gestures in the piece. "She could charm everybody and relate everything to these

great issues in life: love and jealousy and desire. She could make everybody feel like they were taking part in a poem." (Kourlas 2011)

Our work together began by first listening to particular moments of the recording where Graham is gesturing while speaking. We paid foremost attention to the moments when Graham demonstrates, either from her seat, or when she gets out of her chair. I reiterate here that Graham thought of herself as a dancer first and choreographer second, even at sixty-nine. We worked as Hodes had always worked with Graham: "In Martha's case, the dancers were choreographing within a certain prescribed scenario and syllabus that Martha herself had created" (Tracy 1996, 177). Our intertextual syllabus takes shape with Hodes present to guide me through the gestures of the dancing voice, from a subtlety in the placement of my hand upon the chair to choreographing Graham's speech while demonstrating.

Speaking while dancing is not unique to the interview. It is a training methodology used in the classroom where a first exercise Graham taught to students unites the voice with a *port de bras* of the arms. As she lecture-demonstrates in the interview:

> Now when we start the first exercises with the arms, uh, I think you have to start with yourself first. When you do something <MG WALKS AWAY FROM THE MICROPHONE> which is just uh, lifting the arms and opening them. And we've done this and we do it <from there we say how>. My name is Martha, simply. And you start from that—then what you do on top of that is another matter. (Graham 1963, 1)

She is illustrating how either in a standing position or while walking across the floor, the start of class begins with the arms down near the pelvis as the word "My" is stated. As the arms travel up to the chest area and the heart, the word "name" is spoken. The arms then continue to the head, where the word "is" is said. Finally, the dancers simultaneously opens their arms above the head, lift the chest, focus their gaze upward on a high diagonal, and proclaim their own name. That Graham started technique classes in this manner, from the children's beginning classes to those taken by the professionals in her company, provides an understanding that in order for dance to communicate, it is imbued with language.

Later in the interview, Graham describes the contraction, which is the very essence of her vocabulary and elemental to her technique and choreography. And she clarifies that this contraction must communicate something to the audience:

> WT:   Mhm, could—would—would it be possible to, for instance, you—you uh said the principle contraction is used for laughter or fear or love or hate. Uh, could you give an example of it or would you rather do it within the frame work of your . . . [characters]?
>
> MG:   Well I feel that in—in uh. A contraction is essentially, drawing something back into yourself, taking a hold of it, and then giving it out. Now that can be a delight, something that has delighted you or you s-say I—I adore you, ya know. You don't

say I adore you <WT AND AUDIENCE LAUGH>. It can't get out that way. There is no place for you [to] take the adorable into your arms, you gotta find a little place in here <WT AND AUDIENCE LAUGH>. And uh it can mean any of those things, but what it must do is to be not just be used as a contraction. (Graham 1963, 10)

For this passage, Hodes recalled that Graham used this narration in the classroom and taught me the accompanying gesture that Graham exhibited while speaking these words, with the arms connected to the back while contracting, creating a lush, circular, and all-encompassing embrace of the space. Hodes, also a longtime friend of Terry, provided invaluable insight for Kron's actualization of him.

# WALTER TERRY IS LISA KRON

As Kron and I first encounter Terry, we are struck by the (seemingly, at first) dearth of existing archival material of Walter Terry, the person. We know he was a well-known dance historian and dance critic for *The New York Herald Tribune* and *Saturday Review* and that his nearly fifty-year career was pivotal not only to the development of dance criticism, but also, from the 1930s onward, to the development of modern dance itself. Anna Kisselgoff wrote of Terry's crucial contributions in his obituary in *The New York Times*, published on October 6, 1982:

> Mr. Terry's newspaper reviews, especially in *The Herald Tribune*, served an equally important function in the United States itself. His initial career as a critic coincided with the development of a native American dance tradition and Mr. Terry spent a great deal of his time explaining modern dance and ballet to people in the 1930s and 40s.... (Kisselgoff 1982)

Terry was also instrumental in educating international audiences on his State Department tours with lectures on American modern dance that provided an introduction to "... puzzled ballet-oriented audiences" (Kisselgoff 1982).

It was Graham, at the forefront of the burgeoning art form, that Terry most regularly conversed with, as we learn throughout the interview's references to their previous discussions having taken place over the course of much of their careers. About halfway into their dialogue, there is a playful exchange between them when Terry asks of Graham:

WT:  Yes. Um, on the uh, coming now on the basis of what you were saying about, <sigh> opening yourself, meeting face on with the characters that uh are to become a part of your theater. Uh we had called this—at your suggestion—certain dark ladies portrayed in dance. Now I think we'd all like to know uh where the phrase, "dark ladies," came from.

MG:  It was stolen <WT: clears throat>. Uh, see that—

WT:    By you?

MG:    By me.

WT:    Yeah.

MG:    It—uh, well it was borrowed, let's put it that way. There's a book called *Dark Ladies* written by Ivar Brown . . . . And these—I had thought of doing um I must say you stole it from me too, cause I let you in on this and [of] course, Walter Terry just leapt on it like that and I know then—

WT:    You gave me clearance as I recall.

MG:    Yes I did, <OVERLAP> but I wanted to </OVERLAP> do a group of the— of characters, now I'll never do it because I've spoken of it and I never speak of anything that I'm going to do. (Graham 1963, 8)

This passage discloses a detail of their ongoing discourse on Graham's work and, with Terry's admission, that he published writings incorporating Graham's own theories. Their conversant, longtime friendship both influenced Terry's writing and informed Graham's linguistic expression of her choreographic ruminations.

Graham, a prominent public figure at the time of the interview, had been photographed extensively. To the contrary, aside from the rather unremarkable publicity photos accompanying the jackets of his book covers, there are few enlightening visuals of Terry, with the exception of a 1952 ink on manila sketch by Andy Warhol that eloquently discloses his particular manner of dress; a prominent, modish watch, large ring, and cigarette with a flowing plume of smoke held in Terry's delicate hand, set in a long, stylish, cigarette holder of the period. In strikingly few strokes, Warhol captures the silhouette of an elegant, sophisticated, and fashionable man. Unlike the publicity photos, where Terry is seen in a somewhat nondescript suit jacket, tie, and nearly expressionless face, Warhol's spare rendering provides distinct insight. Our discovery of this drawing led us to integrate these telling accoutrements into Terry/Kron's costume design and provided an awareness of the expressiveness of his hands through Warhol's rendering of a single gestural utterance.

However, it is the captured and animated voice of Terry that provides all the detail required to find new life in Kron's body:

> There's a fantastic Andy Warhol drawing of him, which is the thing that really makes him look like a dandy, Ms. Kron said. But the real way you feel him is through his voice. He has a fantastically melodious effete, Southern gay way of talking, and I'm not an incredible mimic, but I'm really interested in the musicality of the way that he talks. (Kourlas 2011)

We discover once again that the voice is portraiture. There is, for us, no sense of lack in the absence of more visuals. Through our creative process, Terry, like Graham, is met anew via transduction.

For Kron and I, our experiential, aural intimacy is as simpatico as the relationship of Terry to Graham. A rapport of mutual trust, respect, and great warmth was evident throughout this, their last public conversation. "Recreating timing and cadence from the recording, she lets Terry's slightly camp persona emerge through the words. His admiration, even veneration, for Graham, his anxiety about asking the right questions and desire for the audience to like her are transparent" (Sulcas 2011).

## GRAHAM CASTS HER VIBRATING SPELLS

As outlined, the production's sound and voicescape are diegetic. However, I made one significant exception. Nearly an hour into the approximately seventy-minute work, a recording of myself and Kron, duplicating the dialogue of Graham and Terry, suddenly enters the soundscape for an important dramaturgical purpose: to allow Graham to dance again, momentarily free of the constraints of the interview setting and her declining body. As her body had begun failing her in the years leading up to the time of this interview, she persisted in performing. In the interview, both in the original recording in which you hear her leave the microphone's range to leave her seat and dance, and in our staging, Graham, the impassioned, oracular, and poetic speaker, is dancing the text. It is Graham the dancer that defines her. Thus, we chose to record a section of the interview where she speaks of one of her favorite roles, the Bride in *Appalachian Spring*. This both enhanced the meta-theatrical staging and provided a sort of cathartic climax for the production, as Graham is granted, by the production and through me, her desire to fully relive the role and dance, unencumbered, as the Bride. Although it is a three-and-a-half-minute segment, this proved to be an exceptionally resonant moment, with our voices engineered to qualitatively sound as if an excerpt is being played from the original recording. The affect was tremendous. Despite the fact that Kron's voice is heard during this section, along with mine as Graham, many audience members thought it was the original recording, including individuals who personally had known Graham and her voice for decades, such as Stuart Hodes, ex-husband of Linda Hodes, who danced with Graham from 1947 to 1958. His principal roles included the Husbandman, partnering Graham herself as the Bride in *Appalachian Spring*. Like Linda, Stuart's relationship with Graham continued well beyond his tenure as company member and up until and beyond her second death, as friend, sometime rehearsal director, and, for a short while, as director of the school. Stuart, in our post-performance conversation, commended me for including an excerpt of the "original" recording in the performance. Stuart had (like us), been trans-temporally transported, and, until I informed him otherwise, had been under the illusion of having been presently in the past. So entranced with this dialogue, Stuart listened and believed this recorded passage was Graham herself and Terry himself. The original is momentarily displaced: "This is the point at which the ultimate origin is overturned into an absence of origin in the always displaced circle of the eternal return" (Deleuze 1995, 282).

Hodes was not the only one to think the three-and-a-half-minute recording was the archival original. So did critic Quinn Batson, who wrote in *OFFoffoff* that "[i]n mid-midstage interview, a portion of the original interview is played as the action freezes, a clever touch that both confirms the accuracy of the Martha-ness onstage and breaks up the evening artfully" (Batson 2011). The affect of the engineered effects—the white noise, the static, and audio engineering by sound designer Chris Tabron replicating the recording as it sounded then—convinced many contemporary ears accustomed to high-quality sound, devoid of such defects, that they were hearing the original.

I attribute this largely to the affect of sound as dance and dance as the vibrating matter of sound. Graham herself perceives the "movement thought" of dance as a vibration and equates the dancer's body to a stringed instrument: "But in any event what you—you are like—like a string vibrating on a certain note and that—the vibration at that point is something in the nerves of the body" (Graham 1963, 9). The vibration of sound—our listening, the audience's listening, and the very anatomy of the ear interpreting sound by means of the vibratory—travels in a circulatory fashion among the audience.

Sound is sensation made material with the dancer's body. Transmission of vibration through aurality becomes concretized. I experience it throughout the rehearsal process, but most especially onstage, where the voice and its bodily vibratory transmission between myself, my colleagues, and the audience are heightened, entirely palpable, and very real. The dialogic script, combined with the sounds emitted by the two dancers, resonated for the entirety of the production. The embodiment of the sonic and its projection of language united to gesture create a sensorial, medium-like transference and exchange with the spectator.

Our critical, dramaturgical choices and detailed connections of gestures during the performance to appropriate sections of language also contribute to a shared sonic space with the audience—a place in the present, while conjuring a historical moment. Our voices at once memorialize these persons and the occasion of their interview, while generating a circular trans-temporal play with time and place. The work's paralinguistic dances, gestures, posture, breath, and other indicators of body language while listening, and while silent, further create and transmit meaning around, between, and through the voice.

The key to the transmission of Graham's voice specifically has a spell-like affect. Graham herself is under the spell of the heroines of whom she speaks and dances. Graham makes this abundantly clear at the very beginning of the interview, when carefully dissecting her process of becoming the Greek sorceress Medea in *Cave of the Heart* (1946):

> Everyone in life has tragic happenings; everyone has been a Medea at sometime. That doesn't mean that you've killed your husband or that you've killed your children. But in some deep way uh the impulse has been there to cast a spell—to use every ounce of your power, and that's true of a man as well as a woman, for what one wants. (Graham 1963, 13–14)

For Graham, (seemingly) unthinkable acts of violence, such as Medea's murder of her children, can be universalized with her understanding and explanation of jealousy—a jealousy that, to varying degrees, is inherently basic to the human condition, transcending gender. The archetypal commonality resides in a desire for power induced by jealousy "to cast a spell."

Terry and the Y audience are under her spell. Her voice has the creative team, and myself, spellbound. The affect of the production's voice extends to the audience. Although other theatrical elements are employed in the performance, it was, to quote Roslyn Sulcas's review in *The New York Times*, our performances, which centered on sonic incarnation, that evoked the affect: ". . . the straightforward conviction with which Mr. Move and Lisa Kron (as Walter Terry, in another sex reversal) played their parts slowly exerted its spell" (Sulcas 2011).

Not surprisingly, "spell" appeared in other critiques and again points to the affect of our voices—from the recording, through our bodies, and to the spectators' bodies. Leigh Witchel also describes this in *The New York Post*, ". . . her tales here—more incantations than answers to her interviewer's questions—weave a spell all their own" (Witchel 2011). I posit that Graham's own use of the "spell" early in the dialogue, along with the production's aural intimacy, creates the conditions that enable the once dormant audio objects' activation to cast these spells and to facilitate such potent transmission.

## THE AFTERLIFE OF AFTERLIVES

The force that is Graham, the life and afterlife of her archive, *Martha@ . . .* , and *Martha@ . . . The 1963 Interview*, cast continually reverberating spells. Several weeks after the premiere, I received, again as an attractor, yet another call to action. This time it materialized in the form of an email from Stuart Hodes, asking me to write the introduction for his autobiography, *Part Real Part Dream—Dancing with Martha Graham*:

> Dear Richard,
>
> For years I had Francis Mason, a longtime supporter of Martha and publisher of *Ballet Review,* in mind as the one to write this Intro. He had read an early version and was strongly encouraging. After his loss, I made a list, but as soon as your name was added, all other choices faded. You and I share one overwhelming essence—we are both still under Martha's spell.
>
> I make a strong distinction between those who loved and served her like Bertram Ross, Francis Mason, Robin Howard, Halston, myself, and you, and those I consider commandeered personalities—Erick Hawkins, other dancers, Leroy Leatherman, Craig Barton, Ron Protas.
>
> You, like me, still under Martha's spell happily and gratefully, are thus are the only one I can turn to who will understand from within, that is, "where I'm coming from," as it is said.
>
> Below is the Foreword written by Paul Taylor for my earlier book, *A Map of Making Dances*. I'll have a copy of the book in the mail to you by tomorrow, but here is Paul's

Foreword, which, I note, may be a better word, since it is casual, pleasantly offhand, and short. If this is impossible, I'll cry, but will understand.

Love, Stuart[3]

Again, the spell, and its "overwhelming essence," situated within my body, had left its affective impression. For Stuart, there was no one else he could "turn to" and I obligingly composed the book's foreword. I happily deemed it my duty to him, to Graham, and to my project.

That Stuart counts me among the likes of Bertram Ross, Graham's longtime company member and partner onstage, speaks with its own powerful voice to the event and force that is *Martha@* . . .—a voice of transmission, a voice Stuart names "love." As do I. It is a symphonic repetition of the transmission of voices: Graham's, mine, *ours*.

I hope that I have been successful in convincing the reader that originals do transform through our embodiment of the archival, recorded audio, and its processual metamorphosis into a vibrant and living work. And that the actual, virtual exchanges of our bodies with the bodies of our subjects were granted full voice in the temporal zones of the afterlives of afterlives, revealing new possibilities and meanings of the original through our discovery, allowing, in the words of Deleuze, "the present that it was, but also the present present which it could be" (1995, 85).

Although my goal has been to concretize this method of corporeal capture and transmission, I choose to close by acknowledging that there remains something mysterious and magical of the aura of aurality that resides in the (perhaps) less concrete realms of my fidelity, faithfulness, and commitment to Graham, pulsating with the proposition that "[t]he domain of laws must be understood, but always on the basis of a nature and a spirit superior to their own laws, which weave their repetitions in the depths of the earth and of the heart, where laws do not yet exist" (Deleuze 1995, 250).

## Works Cited

Barthes, Roland. [1977] 1995. *The Responsibility of Forms: Critical Essays on Music, Art, and Representation*. Translated by Richard Howard. Berkeley: University of California Press.

Batson, Quinn. 2011. "Making Martha Matter." *OFFOFFOFF.com*. (April 14). http://www.offoffoff.com/dance/2011/richardmovemartha1963.php (accessed August 15, 2015).

Deleuze, Gilles. [1968] 1995. *Difference and Repetition*. Translated by Paul Patton. New York: Columbia University Press.

Graham, Martha. 1991. *Blood Memory: An Autobiography*. New York: Washington Square Press.

Graham, Martha, and Walter Terry. 1963. Interview. Transcribed by Elizabeth Jean Marie Foster.

Hodes, Stuart. 2011. Email to author (April 26).

[3] Stuart Hodes, email message to Richard Move, April 26, 2011.

Johnson, Henry. 2004. "Voicescapes: The Enchanting Voice and Its Performance Soundscapes." *The Journal of Acoustic Ecology: Soundscape: The Experience of Music in Daily Life* 5(11): 26–28. http://wfae.proscenia.net/journal/scape_9.pdf (accessed August 15, 2015).

Kisselgoff, Anna. 1982. "Walter Terry, A Dance Critic, Author and Lecturer, Is Dead." *New York Times* (October 6). http://www.nytimes.com/1982/10/06/obituaries/walter-terry-a-dance-critic-author-and-lecturer-is-dead.html (accessed August 15, 2015).

Koestenbaum, Wayne. 2001. *The Queen's Throat.* Cambridge, MA: DeCapo.

Kourlas, Gia. 2011. "He's the Shade of Martha Graham." *New York Times* (March 27). http://www.nytimes.com/2011/03/27/arts/dance/richard-move-still-portrays-martha-graham.html (accessed August 15, 2015).

Lepecki, André. 2010. "The Body as Archive: Will to Re-Enact and the Afterlives of Dances." *Dance Research Journal* 42(1): 28–48.

Manning, Erin. 2009. *Relationscapes: Movement, Art, Philosophy.* Cambridge, MA: MIT Press.

Samuels, David W., Louise Meintjes, Ana M. Ochoa, and Thomas Porcello. 2010. "Soundscapes: Toward a Sounded Anthropology." *Annual Review of Anthropology* 39: 329–345.

Sulcas, Roslyn. 2011. "Martha Graham Lives, and Is Interviewed." *New York Times* (April 1). http://www.nytimes.com/2011/04/01/arts/dance/richard-moves-martha-graham-at-dance-theater-workshop-review.html (accessed August 15, 2015).

Tracy, Robert. 1996. *Goddess: Martha Graham's Dancers Remember.* New York: Limelight.

Witchel, Leigh. 2011. "Move to Keep Icon Alive." *New York Post* (April 1). http://nypost.com/2011/04/01/move-to-keep-icon-alive/ (accessed August 15, 2015).

# PART II

## HISTORICAL FICTION AND HISTORICAL FACT

# CHAPTER 5

# REENACTMENT, DANCE IDENTITY, AND HISTORICAL FICTIONS

ANNA PAKES

## THREE REENACTMENTS AND AN INTRODUCTION

FABIÁN BARBA's *A Mary Wigman Dance Evening* (2009) consists of nine short solo works, separated by brief musical interludes to enable the performer, Barba, to change costume (offstage). Barba describes having learned three of the solos from extant films of Wigman dancing, then deepening his understanding of the corporeal textures of Wigman's work through studies with her former students, Susanne Linke, Irene Siebern, and Katherine Sehnert (Barba 2011, 83–84). The embodied understanding he developed, he claims, enabled him to reimagine other solos from the same dance cycles of which no film records apparently survive. Within the *Dance Evening*, the Wigman solos and Barba's Wigmanesque choreographies sit alongside one another without signaling their different origins. All are performed with sincerity and a careful attention to detail, and there are only faint traces of the irony that pervades some other kinds of cross-gender performance (the work of the Ballets Trockadero de Monte Carlo, for example, or some of Richard Move's impersonations of Graham). But Barba's gender does create a distancing effect that heightens audience consciousness of the theatrical illusion, especially given that these solos "belong" to an iconic female performer. This heightened consciousness spurs reflection on the retrievability—or perhaps irretrievability—of lost dance. Is performance repeatable, and to what extent can dances persist through time?

In Philippe Decouflé's *Panorama* (2012), fragments of past works by Decouflé, dating back to 1983, are woven together into a new evening-length show that presents a "creative retrospective" of the history of his company, DCA. Young dancers re-embody the actions of their sometimes iconic predecessors (Muriel Corbel, Christophe Salengro, Michele Prélonge, and others), and the distinctive style of the earlier work is transmuted through these new performers' very different bodily habitus. Earnest and full-bodied, virtuosic commitment to the material displaces the ironic performance mode of the original dancers' movement. This, along with changes in the number of performers for particular sequences, alters the dynamic energy and effect of the original dances. Gender swapping is evident here too as roles previously performed by men are taken on by women, and vice versa. The publicity and program notes explicitly acknowledge the distance between past and present incarnations: this is "variation plus que reprise" (DCA 2013) and "a live reworking of past creations rather than a backward-looking exhibition of what has passed" (Sadler's Wells 2012). Such descriptions suggest a certain skepticism about the value, if not the possibility, of past dances returning. They also imply acceptance, even celebration, of the transformations wrought by those dances' present re-envisioning. Nostalgia for what was is simultaneously indulged and displaced, at least for viewers who can recall the dances' first performances. Though the originals are still visible in the different guise they assume in this current excursion, the past fragments also appear "other" in their contemporary modulation.

In the Kirov Ballet's 1999 production of *The Sleeping Beauty*, Petipa's choreography was restaged by Sergei Vikharev from early twentieth-century notations of the 1890 work. The Maryinsky's acquisition of these scores, compiled by Nicholai Sergeyev using the Stepanov system, made it possible to create a version of this ballet "as close as possible to the Petipa original" (Vaziev and Vikharev 1999, 18). The new production proved controversial, not least because of its claims to authenticity, and the challenge it posed to the Kirov's "traditional" *Sleeping Beauty*, as re-choreographed by Konstantin Sergeyev in 1952. In Tim Scholl's view, the 1999 production was politically and artistically charged in that it questioned "the Soviet ballet's faithfulness to the classical inheritance [ ... ] and the company's diligent efforts, over decades and under a variety of conditions to preserve that legacy authentically" (2004, 132). In the process of developing the new-old version, Sergeyev's notations were analyzed in detail and cross-referenced, in quasi-philological manner, with five different twentieth-century productions, all in the effort to produce an authoritative movement "text" (Vaziev and Vikharev 1999, 19). Meanwhile, archival documentation of the original's costumes and set (designs and contemporary photographs, as well as verbal descriptions and actual costumes) enabled the visual detail of Petipa's work to be rediscovered (Owen 2000; Vaziev and Vikharev 1999, 21). The production promised a reincarnation of a landmark moment in dance history, but also pointed up the temporal and aesthetic distance (not to say gulf) between that moment and the present. As Scholl (2004) attests, there was a significant tension between the training and expectations of late twentieth-century Kirov dancers and audiences, and what the new-old Petipa ballet demanded of them—so much so, in fact, that the life of the production appears to have been short. The Kirov-Maryinsky retains Konstantin Sergeyev's "traditional" *Sleeping Beauty* in its repertoire, rather than the Vikharev production, and to date has not produced a commercial DVD of the 1999 staging. As in the previous two examples—the works by Barba and Decouflé—the production reveals significant *discontinuity* between past dance and its current return, even as the restaging seems in some sense to make that dance present again.

The three cases just described pose questions about the nature of the dance past, and about its accessibility through both the archive and the mechanism of reperformance. In so doing, the dances participate, in various ways, in a recent trend toward performance "reenactment." The past two decades have witnessed numerous artists returning to historical materials in order to reinvent and reimagine those dances within the contemporary moment (Burt 2003; Lepecki 2010). And this trend in the context of theater performance parallels developments in popular (general) history, where increasing interest in and prevalence of historical reenactments (of jousting tournaments, life in Viking settlements, American Civil War battles, and so on) represent a concerted attempt to bring history to life for participants and tourists (see Schneider 2011, 2).[1] Such practice in the context of theater dance is arguably not new: the reconstruction and re-envisioning of works from the past have been important elements of dance performance and scholarship throughout the twentieth century, and are evident in various forms in previous centuries as well.[2] Yet several theorists offering commentary on contemporary reenactments identify the current trend as distinctive in the manner and mode of its return, sometimes casting reenactment in opposition to older models, like reconstruction (Burt 2003; Franko 1993; Lepecki 2010; Schneider 2001, 2011; Stalpaert 2011).

In this chapter, I am interested in ontological and identity issues raised by recent practices of reenactment in dance, and in probing the ontological implications of the scholarly commentary on the phenomenon. My particular focus is on whether it is possible to be more precise about *what* recurs and *how* in recent dance reenactments. The theoretical literature on performance reenactment highlights diverse examples of the practice, as does this volume. Indeed, my own sample cases, described at the beginning of this chapter, represent different kinds of endeavor. Thus, Barba's *A Mary Wigman Dance Evening*, focused on recreating a concert of shorter solo works of the kind Wigman toured in the United States in 1930–1931, seems a different order of thing to Decouflé's *Panorama*, in which older choreography is reused, recycled, and repackaged in a new frame, and supplemented with new materials by the original choreographer. Meanwhile, the Kirov Ballet's 1999 *Sleeping Beauty*, though it raises similar philosophical issues, places significant emphasis on authenticity and visual similarity to an original. As such, it perhaps appears to be an instance of more traditionally conceived "authentic" reconstruction than of reenactment as it is characterized in recent performance theory (what

[1] On the relationship of living history and reenactment practice to academic history, see Agnew (2004, 2007), as well as Cook (2004).

[2] For example, one aim of those developing the *ballet d'action* in the eighteenth century was to restore the art of ancient pantomime. Marius Petipa reworked, adapted, and restaged nineteenth-century ballets such as Coralli and Perrot's (1841) *Giselle* and Saint-Léon's (1870) *Coppélia* (Scholl 1994, 5–7; Collins 2009). In late nineteenth-century England, a revivalist movement emerged that sought to reenact and reinstate social dances of the seventeenth and eighteenth centuries, as well as folk dance traditions (Buckland 2011). On reconstruction in twentieth-century Western theater dance, see Palfy, ed. (1993) and Jordan, ed. (2000).

this production is and the plausibility of the reconstruction/reenactment distinction are discussed further in what follows). But while it may be problematic to generalize across this variety of practices, the recent prominence of the term "reenactment" and claims for what it achieves do suggest an emerging conception of a new kind of redoing. Here, I attempt to offer a critical analysis of what might be going on, and of the way this is discussed in the literature. The chapter by no means seeks to define "reenactment" (in terms of necessary and sufficient conditions, for example). Rather, I want to reflect on what the term implies, ontologically speaking, especially as regards the relationship between contemporary performances and the dances they claim to reiterate.[3]

## DANCE TYPES AND TOKENS

According to one standard dance ontological picture, dance works are *types* of which there can be many possible performance *tokens* (Davies 2011, 29–32; McFee 1992, 88–111, and 2011; Sparshott 1995, 399–404). Thus Decouflé's *Triton* (1990) is a type of which the performances in Avignon (in June 1990) and the performances in Angers (in December of the same year) are all tokens. The type-token view maintains that performances must obey certain minimal constraints, or adequately meet the identity conditions pertaining to that work, if they are to count as being *of* that dance. For example, the identity conditions for Wigman's *Seraphisches Lied* (from the 1929 *Schwingende Landschaft* cycle) might include the movement material, or at least elements of it, such as its spatial organization and distinctive motifs (the reverence with hands joined in the opening minute, for example); the piano score by Hans Hastings; and probably the long dress and shawl-like drapery, which emphasizes the angularity of the movement and the spiritual theme. Without these elements being present in performance, I would question whether I were watching *Seraphisches Lied*. That I do not do so when watching Fabián Barba dancing this work suggests that his performance meets its identity conditions: it is a token of the *Seraphisches Lied* type.

On first glance, this type-token model may appear inappropriate to the phenomenon of reenactment, as least as it is theorized in the recent literature. There, considerable emphasis is placed on how reenactment moves beyond or bypasses mimetic reproduction of an original dance. For example, Stalpaert values Barba's work because it avoids "the magic and static circle of clichéd reproduction" (2011, 94). Franko argues that, whereas (some) reconstruction offers " 'still life' reproduction [which] generates performance museums," *construction* (the prototype for reenactment[4]) "*sacrifices the reproduction of a work* to the replication of its most powerful intended effects" (1993, 135; my

---

[3] The chapter also thereby offers a coda to the longer-form reflection on the nature of dance works in my monograph (Pakes forthcoming in 2018), where issues of identity and reperformance are discussed in more detail, though the specific phenomenon of reenactment is not analyzed in depth.

[4] See Franko, Chapter 24 in this volume.

emphasis). Schneider argues more generally of performance reenactment that it is a form of oral history, a practice that evidences "an approach to saving that is not invested in identicality" and that thereby avoids "the habit of approaching performative remains as a metaphysic of presence that privileges an original or singular authenticity" (2001, 103–104). Such commentary, then, rejects the conception of reenactment as a process of imitative reproduction of an original work.

In fact, the type-token view similarly rejects this conception. Its emphasis is on tokens meeting the conditions for numerical identity (for whether it is *that* dance, e.g., *Seraphisches Lied*, or not), and not on *qualitative* identity between the new token and a previous performance (say, Wigman's performance captured on film).[5] It is accepted— indeed considered a crucial and valuable feature of performing art—that tokens differ from one another in important respects. "[W]ork identity cannot require indistinguishability," claims Graham McFee, which is "neither possible nor fully intelligible" as a way of characterizing reperformance, partly because the empirical differences between performers inevitably manifest in the way they dance a work (1992, 92). Thus, Barba's gender is a significant difference between his performances of *Seraphisches Lied* and those of Wigman. But unless there is evidence to suggest that the dancer being female is one of the identity conditions of this dance, that difference does not discount the reenactment as a token of the type. The nature of a dance work's identity conditions will vary depending on the genre and on what is choreographically salient about that particular piece. So the gender of the performers might be essential to reperformance of a dance in some cases, but not in others. Likewise, the movement shape, structure, dynamics, and sequence might be very precisely defined for some dances, but variable in others: perhaps a work involves structured improvisation, so the movement varies each time it is performed, though the principles governing the generation of that movement are (expected to be) respected. In such cases, the principles—not the movement as such— furnish the identity conditions for the dance.

This raises the question of how and by whom identity conditions are determined. If only some properties of a dance are work-identifying, who selects which, and by what process? On McFee's view, the choreographer sets the type-constraints (1992, 94–99; see also 2013). But problems arise because it is not always clear what those type-constraints are—in other words, whether such features as soundscore, stylistic qualities, or the particular sequence of the movement material are essential to the reperformance of a given dance.[6] Often, such uncertainty stems from a choreographic decision not to articulate them independently of their embodiment in performance. Hence, for McFee,

---

[5] McFee (1992) comments: "identity questions are characteristically questions across time: questions relating what we see now to what we saw then. Second, they are not questions about similarity [ ... ] the man is short, bald, old; and the boy was tall (for his age), hairy, young and so on. We know the boy did not look as the man does, but, still, are they the same person? This is an identity question: A *numerical* identity question" (90). On the issue of numerical versus qualitative identity, see also McFee (2011, 36–42).

[6] On this issue, see Armelagos and Sirridge (1978).

notation—and, derived from it, the idea of "notationality"—plays a key role (1992, 97–99; 2011, 70–95). Type constraints are clear where an adequate score exists—at least when that score is intended as a mechanism to enable reperformance.[7] The variety of scoring practices in dance is extensive and growing, and possible modes of description are widely divergent. The Labanotation scores held by the Dance Notation Bureau, for example, contrast markedly in mode and degree of analytic detail with verbal schemas like that for Steve Paxton's *Satisfyin' Lover* (Banes 1987, 71–74). Both can qualify as adequate scores, however, if they effectively articulate type constraints. As such, they do not capture all features of a dance, but do (if they are adequate) articulate what is important to its reperformance. In practice, they may not articulate everything that is work-identifying, but that does not necessarily render reperformance impossible. There might be some implicit choreographic prescriptions, of which those who are knowledgeable about the practice (that way of making dances, that particular dance style, perhaps) are aware.[8] Respecting these implicit prescriptions, as well as what is explicitly stated, is typically necessary to the appropriate interpretation of scores. Hence, foundations such as the Balanchine Foundation employ former dancers to direct or contribute to the process of revival, on the basis of their immersion in and ability to teach the appropriate style, which could not be learned exclusively from the notation (Stoddart 2002; Yeoh 2012).

A similar set of considerations applies to the practice of learning a dance from film. Film is considered by McFee to be a less reliable means of reviving a dance (2011, 76–77). The film shows us one performance of the work, rather than the work as such. Hence, as I teach myself the dance from film, I might embody characteristics of the original performer's interpretation, rather than offering a new interpretation of the same choreographic structure. In other words, I might treat as type-constraints things that were actually variable when the work was set, and miss what is choreographically important because I have been distracted by the earlier dancer's idiosyncrasies. However, this appears less likely when the new dancer is reasonably knowledgeable in relation to the choreographer's style, and/or can cross-reference the film with other recordings or traces of the work. In any case, the same potential for misunderstanding is arguably a feature of score-interpretation in dance too. Scores need knowledgeable interpreters. Moreover, because they are often not written by the choreographer in the manner of a work-prescribing score in music composition, dance scores may not record (just) work-constitutive properties; cross-referencing with other sources of information may be necessary to determine identity constraints. The widespread use of film and video to learn and restage older dances suggests a consensus within the practice that such

[7] On the variety of types of notation, only some of which constitute work-prescribing scores, see Davies (2001, 99–150) and Pakes (forthcoming in 2018). Hutchinson-Guest (1989) and Franko (2011) examine a range of dance notation systems dating back to the fifteenth century. A critical analysis of the role of dance scores is developed in Hecquet and Prokhoris (2007) and Pouillaude (2017, particularly Part 3). There has been considerable interest recently in the practice and functionality of scoring choreography: see, for example, the website of the Motion Bank project (http://motionbank.org) and Cvejić and de Keersmaeker (2012, 2013).

[8] On implicit versus explicit prescriptions for musical performance, see Davies (2001, 103–107).

records can be effectively employed to enable reperformance. But, as in the case of Barba seeking advice from former students of Wigman, the oral and embodied tradition frequently plays a role here, too, in enabling new performers to understand somatically what the film presents visually, two-dimensionally, and from a spectator's perspective. Seeking out the testimony and embodied knowledge of original or earlier dancers is common in restaging and reconstruction projects: these early performers help remember the dance. On the type-token view, they thus contribute to producing new tokens of the dance work type by ensuring that implicit as well as explicit choreographic specifications are fulfilled in performance.

# CHOREOGRAPHER SPECIFICATIONS, INTENTIONS, AND THE ARCHIVE

The very idea of a normative choreographic specification is challenged by the theoretical commentary on performance reenactment, however. Indeed, some argue that reenactment itself, in treating the body as a kind of archive, overturns the constraints imposed by choreographer specifications as to how work should be performed. Ramsay Burt, for example, comments on dancers redoing a solo by Susanne Linke in Jérôme Bel's (2000) *The Last Performance* and also on Martin Nachbar's reenactment of solos by Dore Hoyer in *Affects/Rework* (2000). The dancers performed what "by association, looked the sort of dancing that conventionally suggests emotional expression" but without its intended dynamic or expressive force (Burt 2003, 38). The Linke choreography in *The Last Performance* was learned from a video of poor quality: the performance was "a version of a version of a version" and offered "an open-ended series of displaced differences, rather than being tied in a closed subordinate relationship to a unique transcendental choreographic original" (Burt 2003, 38).

There is a way to describe what is going on here in terms of a type-token view. That the original choreography is still recognizable might indicate that its minimal identity constraints have been respected (since otherwise they would not have been recognizable as *those* dances), although the performance was unlike other, previous tokens of this dance type. The radical element in these reenactments, then, appears to be their capacity to reveal performance possibilities not previously evident, though implicit in the type as abstract object. But Burt's argument goes beyond the claim that this is just one more (albeit an unusual and inventive) performance-token. The dance artists in question re-embodied the material (at some level), but deliberately *flouted* some of what would appear to be the work's identity constraints (particularly as regards style). Indeed, it seems, on Burt's view, rather that these artists *thematized* their refusal or failure to abide by work identity-constraints, while still retaining enough of the form of the work for the choreography to be recognizable (Burt cites Nachbar: "to find out the puzzling difference, you have to be the same"; 2003, 38). The result highlighted the "uniqueness of the live moment of performance," in a process (according to Burt) with much more general political implications: "troubling the author function seems to have contributed towards releasing the performer from the normative meanings inherent in the expressive qualities of the movement performed, and allowed each of them [ . . . ] a freedom from the disciplinary and controlling structures of repressive representational regimes" (Burt 2003, 39).

André Lepecki similarly theorizes choreography as an "apparatus of capture" (2007) and argues that documentary archives collude in the "domiciliation" of the work (2010, 35). He is concerned with liberating the "still non-exhausted creative fields of 'impalpable possibilities,'" within past dances, which he suggests are barred by the archive (2010, 31). Because it treats "the author's intention as commanding authority over a work's afterlives" (2010, 35), the archive limits and controls, on Lepecki's view. Reenactment, meanwhile, "suspends economies of authoritative authors who want to keep their works under house arrest" because it celebrates the transformations and transmutations that works undergo as they pass through the bodies of new performers (Lepecki 2010, 35). As in Burt (2003), the emphasis is on the multiplicity of the work's possible realizations. Although, as explored earlier, variation in performance is perfectly compatible with a type-token model of the work-performance (or work-reenactment) relation, and the rhetoric employed by Burt and Lepecki makes clear their resistance to the idea of normative type-constraints linked to choreographic intention. And they see such resistance as an important element of the practice of reenactment.

Two key issues arise here. One concerns whether dance work type-constraints are indeed connected with choreographic intention in the manner suggested: In other words, is the identity of the work fixed by how the choreographer intended it to be? And second, does the (documentary) archive in fact inscribe and reinforce choreographic intention (and the type-constraints that appear to flow from it), shoring up "economies of authoritative authors who want to keep their works under house arrest" (Lepecki 2010, 35)?

On the first issue, the language of both Burt (2003) and Lepecki (2010) implies a radical anti-intentionlism influenced by Barthes (1977). The latter's target was interpretative intentionalism, that is, the thesis that authorial intention constrains the meaning of a work in some way—a stance that has been extensively challenged by literary and critical theory. Regardless of where one stands on this issue, however, it is not clear that interpretive intentionalism is necessarily implied by what might be termed "ontological" intentionalism, or the view that intention shapes the nature (including the identity conditions) of a work. One might hold the latter view but not the former; in other words, one could argue that choreographic intention constrains what a dance is without limiting what it means. Lepecki, following Silvia Benso, characterizes artworks as "self-sufficient objects" but recognizes that they are "humanly made": their self-sufficiency, once established, "erases the presence of the artist in them" (2010, 44). This appears compatible with ontological intentionalism, in that it recognizes the artist's influence on the object's emergence, though not its meaning or afterlife.

In any case, the connection between type-constraints and authorial intention seems less clear in dance than in some other art forms. Dances are not (typically) made by choreographers writing a specification, which is then handed over to performers to enact. Creative processes in dance often involve experimentation and improvisation around ideas or tasks, with dancers contributing to the generation of movement, to decision-making about what kinds of actions will be performed, and to the way in which these actions are "fleshed out." The choreographer may be a participant in this process or may take more of an observer-, dramaturgical role, editing and shaping the emerging materials.[9] In most creative processes, there comes a point where the material is "set" (and that might mean setting the structure of improvisation, rather than a given sequence of identified movement). When a work is "set" and rehearsed as a defined structure of action, its parameters are somatically internalized by the performers. In some cases, those parameters are also articulated in a score, though there remains a lack of consensus about whether works *should* be notated or otherwise documented, and the extent to which either notation or film effectively captures work identity conditions. Not all dance artists have the means or will to use these methods to preserve their work, and many either accept that their work will not have an afterlife, or rely on the memory of the dancers who have embodied the principles governing the work. Because dancers can teach the material they know to others, new performers can come to internalize the constraints of the dance-type. Thus dances are disseminated and sustained through time in an oral and embodied tradition, rather than (just) through documentary archives (see also Hodes 1993 and Pouillaude 2017, 265–286). Indeed, from the mid-eighteenth century at least until the advent of modern systems of notation, the oral and embodied tradition has been the *principal* means of transmission of Western theater dances across generations.

The "body-as-archive" (Lepecki 2010), then, appears to be a long-standing feature of dance practice, and choreographic specifications are filtered across time through the embodied personalities of the dancers who internalize and transform them. There is ample evidence of choreographers accepting (even celebrating) the transformations wrought by new performers, new bodies, on old works. Indeed, the enduring skepticism in dance about the value of notation, and the failure of any of the many systems devised to widespread use and integration in the practice in the longer term, indicates a kind of broad historical consensus that dances are malleable and always capable of being transformed through their re-embodiment. There is, then, an already fluid relationship between dancer embodiment and choreographic specification, evident before and beyond the particular phenomenon of contemporary reenactment. One of the reasons why the Kirov's 1999 *Sleeping Beauty* proved contentious was that the new-old choreographic "text" challenged an embodied tradition used to a version of the ballet

---

[9]  On the basis of this editing and decision-making role, McFee argues that choreographers are authors of their works, hence dance "artists," where dancers are not; the choreographer is, he argues, responsible for the final form of her dance, that is, for the type or set of constraints by which performers abide in order to embody it (2011, 167–184; 2013).

handed down from dancer to dancer, through the Maryinsky's coaching system (Scholl 2004, 153). On Burt and Lepecki's view, the project might be characterized in reactionary terms as an attempt to reimpose repressive control by reverting to an exhumation of Petipa's choreography, and hence to his intentions as commanding authority over the work. But, in this particular case, the political polarity appears to be reversed: reliance on the archival documentation rather than dancer bodies-as-archives seems the more artistically (and politically?) radical strategy in challenging entrenched hierarchies and the "carefully cultivated public image of the Soviet ballet as the vigilant guardian of tradition" (Scholl 2004, 152).

Lepecki argues that "in its constitutive precariousness, perceptual blind-spots, linguistic indeterminations, muscular tremors, memory lapses, bleedings, rages, and passions, the body as archive re-places and diverts notions of archive away from a documental deposit or a bureaucratic agency" (Lepecki 2010, 34). But it is not obvious—turning now to the second of the two issues identified earlier—that the (documentary) archive in dance inscribes choreographic intention any more clearly than the dancer's body. Dance archives do not just house scores (whether notational or in some other mode). Indeed, in many cases, they do not contain scores at all, or any other clear articulation of the choreographic specification for the dances in question. They may contain film and still photographs (at least in cases post-dating the advent of the relevant technology), drawings, designs, verbal notes (by choreographer and others involved), reviews, or programs; indeed, they are often composed of performance "ephemera," loose collections of fragments, not necessarily in any particular order (certainly, rarely in an order imposed by the choreographer), which happen to have survived. Although such fragments can be used to reconstruct a past work, it seems doubtful they could impose authorial control on its reperformance, given the lack of such control over what makes its way into the archive in the first place.[10] In many cases, invention is part and parcel of reconstruction because the archive is "gappy": the fragmentary nature of the record, as well as the attempt to make an old work "live" in the present, means that the reconstructor has to invent. Invention, then, occurs at two levels: at the level of the performers' modulations of the work each time someone new engages with the material; and at the level of the choreographic, to bridge archival gaps and to rework the piece for the contemporary public.

The degree of invention—particularly choreographic invention—involved in reconstruction and reenactment compromises the plausibility of the type-token view. In some respects, though, it does seem able to adequately account for the *what* and *how* of reenactment. Although the malleability of dance works complicates their characterization as types (in ways I have touched upon but cannot fully explore here). Barba appears

---

[10] Exceptions might be identified here among the legacy programs of prominent modern choreographers, such as Cunningham (Yeoh 2012). Even there, however, for all the archival information that is stored, and whether by choice or oversight, there is not always any clear identification of constitutive, as distinct from contingent, features of the dances preserved. See Chapter 6 by Carrie Noland in this volume.

concerned to "get right" the three Wigman solos he learned from film. Part of that process was to consult former dancers to ensure that corporeal memory and transmission can help reconstitute what the film record omits but is nonetheless essential to re-instancing this choreography. His actions seem focused on offering *genuine* tokens of the types of those three dances, which meet the choreographic prescriptions even while they throw new light on them via his distinctive performance interpretation. Similarly, movement sequences from particular works by Decouflé are recognizable in *Panorama*: They appear differently when embodied by the new dancers, but these variations are arguably within the range of acceptable interpretations that the choreography permits. The same claim might be made about aspects of the Kirov's (1999) *Sleeping Beauty*: The company dancers reinterpret the Petipa "text" that Vikharev has reassembled in a performance style that accords with contemporary ballet training and aesthetic values. As a result, the work is danced differently from the way it would have been danced in 1890, but the new performance might still respect the identity constraints (step sequences, order of dances, narrative structure, musical score) of the Petipa *Sleeping Beauty*. In other words, one might claim that it is still a token of that type, though it provokes audiences to think differently about the dance work because it contrasts markedly with more conventional restagings.

There are limits, however, to the plausibility of this ontological characterization of reenactment. Even leaving aside the issue of whether dances are best conceived as types in the sense of normative choreographic specifications, these limits are evident in significant features of the Barba and Decouflé examples. In the Barba case, the audience is presented not just with the dances learned from film, but with other Wigmanesque choreographies invented on the basis of the fragmentary remaining evidence. These other dances are reimaginings of Wigman's works, rather than tokens. Neither is Decouflé's *Panorama* simply a case of re-instancing, or producing a new token of, a choreographic type, at least at the level of the dance work overall. Here, the audience is presented with *extracts* from earlier dance works, not those dances as such, and a new work is constructed from those fragments. Audiences are (now) watching *Panorama*, not *Triton, Decodex*, or *SHAZAM!* though *Panorama* is an assemblage of elements from those other dances. Thus type-token relations are probably involved at some level—that of the individual "numbers" that are re-instanced in order to make up the new show—but something else is going on at the level of that show, treated as an entity or as an event in its own right.

## Reliving Events

So can reenactment and its relationship to past works be construed in another, more plausible, way than on a type-token view? It might be instructive here to follow the lead of the term "reenactment" itself, as it contrasts with the term and concept of "reconstruction." Whereas "reconstruction" suggests the piecing back together of an *object* (a building, say, or a dance *work*), the term "reenactment" implies the redoing of an *event* of some kind. In English, certainly, the verb "reenact" seems to collocate more naturally with "event" (and perhaps "ritual") than with "object" or "work." Indeed the *Oxford English Dictionary* spells out this collocation in its definition: to "re-enact" is "to act out (a past event)," as in the sample usage *"bombers were gathered together to re-enact the historic first air attack"* (OED, 3rd edition, online). Perhaps, then, rather than conceiving of reenactment as a token of an abstract choreographic specification, it is preferable to think of it as a redoing of a particular performance event. This distinction between redoing an event and remaking an object is borne out in the case of Fabian Barba's Wigman: his primary declared aim is not so much to reassemble Wigman's solo works from their archival fragments as to produce a "reenactment of a dance evening as it could have taken place in the first half of the twentieth century," specifically modeled on programs during Wigman's first tour to the United States in 1930–1931 (Barba 2011, 84). Decouflé's *Panorama*, though constituted largely by preexisting fragments of other dances, selects these because they are significant *events* in the choreographer's career trajectory. Eventfulness is also emphasized by the Kirov's (1999) *Sleeping Beauty*, the length and structure of which seem to have been among the most surprising characteristics, revealing how the ballet might have been experienced durationally and aesthetically as an evening's entertainment (Dorris 1999; Scholl 2004, 162–163; Stupnikov 1999).

Conceiving reperformance as the reiteration of events rather than the retokening of types also makes sense in terms of the way works are typically made in dance: that is, many dances are not created through writing a text or score of some kind, but rather through the creation of token instances—performances that take place in the absence of, or prior to, their documentation via a score or other textual anchor. That dances can be performed and reperformed without being notated lends plausibility to a "canonical performance view" of dance identity (Conroy 2013, 119–123).[11] On this view, earlier or original performances—or perhaps a single one of those performances—serve as models for future reiterations. Instead of an independently articulated choreographic specification determining what counts as a performance of a given work, performances (i.e., the dance events) themselves fix the identity constraints by which other performances should abide. To illustrate: a proponent of the canonical performance view might claim that Wigman's own performance, of *Seraphisches Lied*, captured on film, sets the parameters for subsequent performances, including Barba's reenactment; and that the 1890 première of Petipa's *The Sleeping Beauty* is the model to which new *Sleeping Beauties*— whether the Vic Wells Ballet's 1939 or the Kirov's 1999 production—should conform.

There are numerous practical difficulties with the process of reperformance implied by adopting this view, however. The fragmentary nature of dance archives has already

---

[11] The "canonical performance view" is one of three contrasting positions considered in Renee Conroy's discussion of dance work identity (i.e., of what makes two performances both performances *of the same* work), alongside Graham McFee's notationalism (1992, 2011) and Julie Van Camp's legal model (1981, 2006). Conroy offers a critique of each, endorsing none, but in the process clarifying the issues that a plausible theory must address.

been discussed. How can the reconstructor or re-enactor derive a sufficiently detailed picture of the canonical performance from the scraps of information that are often all that remains (in the body-memories of dancers as well as the documentary archive)? Perhaps in the majority of cases (and certainly those that have not been well filmed) she cannot, rendering reperformance impossible on the canonical performance view. As Conroy points out, there are also conceptual difficulties, arising from the fact of differences between performances that purport to be *of* the same dance. Someone trying to reconstruct or reenact a dance might well be faced with conflicting information from one performance to another, and may be forced to make a choice to follow the model of the first rather than the second (or vice versa). That means treating a *single* performance—the first, say—as fixing the identity constraints for subsequent iterations. But how to explain why *that* single performance is preferable as a model to all others? The academic convention of dating a work from its first performance seems to favor the *first* as the canonical instance, but it is not obvious that or why it should set the conditions for subsequent instances (after all, things can go wrong on a first night, and it may take a performance run or several before the work takes a definitive shape). As Conroy suggests, "[i]f one performance event is metaphysically basic, then no reasons can be given for why *that* performance sets the relevant constraints on the abstract dance art object" (2013, 122); its identification as such appears ad hoc. Conversely, if reasons can be given for preferring one performance over another, then it is those reasons that capture what is metaphysically core to the work, not the event as such.

Even if this issue could be resolved—and sound reasons provided for why a single performance is the canonical performance—there remains a question concerning *which* properties of the performance event constrain subsequent performances. If *all* properties of the event constitute the dance, then it becomes impossible to re-instance: no two events can be strictly qualitatively identical since, at the very least, they are differently located temporally and/or spatially. Perhaps this is the point being made in discussions of reenactment that seek to explode the "old myth of repeatability" (Franko 1993). Certainly, as noted earlier, contemporary practice and theory resists the idea that reenactment is a mimetic reproduction of an earlier dance. As Schneider claims, "[i]n performance *as* memory, the pristine sameness of an 'original' [ . . . ] is rendered impossible" (2001, 102), while Franko contrasts construction and theatrical theory with reactionary reconstruction, which, "seeking the truth in its own 'still life' reproduction [ . . . ] generates performance museums" (1993, 150). Emphasis particularly is on reenactive performance exploding the idea of *visual* similarity with past performance. Schneider considers performance to be "less bound to the ocular" than the archive (2001, 106), while Barba describes his efforts to develop "a working approach based not on an external image but on proprioception of my own body" (2011, 86). Indeed, the directors' attention to reproducing the scenography, costumes, and other visual aspects of the 1890 performances of Petipa's *The Sleeping Beauty* is one reason why it seems problematic to think of the Kirov's 1999 production *Sleeping Beauty* in terms of reenactment. Although it has some of the same effects as the Barba and Decouflé cases, encouraging comparable reflection on the possibility and desirability of retrieving the dance past, it

seems to have been intended "authentically" to reproduce the look of an earlier performance, rather than acknowledging or celebrating the "inevitable failure to be faithful to
an original" (Burt 2003, 38).

Does this imply treating the visual properties of a performance as contingent, where
other features are identity-constitutive? This may be appropriate for some dances, but
not all, given than some works (such as Decouflé's) involve scenography at a deep level.
In other words, the scenography does not just function as "background," but is integral
to the action and its effect. And once again, the claim that some properties are constitutive where others are not requires grounding in reasons if it isn't to appear ad hoc.
Such reasons cannot be provided without relying on some prior conception of what the
work is. This compromises the plausibility of the canonical performance view, because
it indicates that it is not the event *as such* setting the identity constraints, but whatever
motivates the selection of constitutive properties. Reenactment, insofar as it is concerned with reliving the dance as event, is often described as not aiming to reproduce
the latter's surface details, but rather to enable an experiencing of its dynamic contours
or affective charge. Or, like Franko's "construction," it is interested in how the theatrical effects of earlier works might play out affectively in the present. As theorized in
the literature, reenactment offers an eventful reimagining rather than event reiteration,
in the process foregrounding lived experience. It does so both in the sense of trying
to recreate something of the original's *affective* dimension (or, at least, to refer to this
affective dimension in some way) and in the sense of enabling participants and viewers
to have a present experience of live *recurrence*. As Barba comments, "lived experience
is what is at stake during the actual performance: the public and the dancers should
be involved in a mutual, subjective experience mediated by the dance" (2011, 85). The
reenactment restores "the experiential realm of dance [that] appears to get lost once
it is transposed into words" (2011, 86). Reenactment is thus conceived as reanimating
and reasserting the realm of lived experience, as it appears to do also in practices of historical reenactment, "a body-based discourse in which the past is reanimated through
physical and psychological experience" (Agnew 2004, 330). By participating in a jousting tournament, or dressing up as a Civil War soldier and acting out a famous battle,
the past seems to come alive again, and more directly than in the experience of reading
and imagining.

Is there more at stake here than engaging a public who might otherwise tend to think
of dance history as a dry, academic pursuit? Alexander Cook (2004) comments on the
growing predilection for including a reenactive element in general history programs on
TV: "just" historical documentary telling the story of (say) Captain Cook's journey to
Australia and then Hawaii is no longer enough; instead, historians and other volunteer
participants are shown learning to sail an eighteenth-century frigate and undergoing
the hardships of a lengthy sea voyage aboard it. Part of the rationale for including reenactive elements is that they bring history to life for the TV viewer who might otherwise
think it boring. But Cook also discerns a further motivation, based on the notion that
"one can learn something about history from the experience that would be less accessible using conventional methods for studying the past" (2004, 488). In this respect, the

reenactment has an investigative purpose—it is concerned with finding out about the past, not just with making its presentation more entertaining.

# CORPOREAL INVESTIGATIONS

Dance reenactments have a similar investigative dimension—they are not simply bringing past dance to life, but are contributing to our understanding of the works, practice, or historical moment concerned.[12] This is explicit in Fabian Barba's description of his "research on corporeality [ . . . ] as a crucial addition to archival and textual sources" (2011, 84). By learning to embody the particular textures of muscular tone associated with Wigman's practice, Barba claims to understand her idiom in a different way from textual dance scholarship—his corporeal investigation is another kind of work, producing a different order of insight, to that involved in mining the archives of verbal and filmed documentation. Philippe Decouflé, meanwhile, declares his curiosity about how his new choreography-assemblage represents the older works, articulating an investigative purpose: "I [ . . . ] wanted to return to the particular energy of my first works [ . . . ] . The world has changed, so what about all these gestures? How have they come through the passing of time?" (Sadler's Wells 2012). For all its emphasis on authenticity with regard to the *visual* environment, the 1999 *Sleeping Beauty* clearly also had an investigative dimension with regard to kinaesthetic experience: the dancers' struggle with the challenge of the movement as notated revealed the gap between the contemporary Russian-trained ballet habitus and the corporeal norms of the late nineteenth century; while difficult to bridge somatically, this gap is historically significant in disrupting claims about the continuity of the classical tradition. What is more, the visual environment of the work itself must have set material constraints on the movement, constraints that themselves are potentially instructive about the shaping conditions of the period's choreography: the weight, construction, and capacity for movement of the costumes made a difference to how it was possible to dance.

Insofar as dance exploits an embodied medium, re-embodying past dances is important to understanding what they were. It seems clear that the attempt to engage somatically with a dance style or idiom from the past is going to teach the researcher something that cannot be gleaned from more conceptual and abstract attempts to reimagine it. It also appears self-evident that, because dance is an embodied medium, the testimony of others who have somatically inhabited a given choreography will be relevant to grasping its character and scope. The textual record gives only partial, if any, information about the kinaesthetic characteristics of past dances, while film may be difficult to interpret, and may flatten or erase precisely the effects that were most salient in live performance. Long-standing practices of disseminating dances

---

[12] On the heuristic value of reenactments, see Chapter 11 by Branislav Jakovljević in this volume.

from performer to performer, via oral traditions, seem as much concerned with communicating the qualia of movement idioms as with preserving choreographic structures. In seeking the advice of former pupils of Wigman, for example, Barba uses the resource of others' past experience to inform his own corporeal engagement. But this is not a practice specific to contemporary reenactment; it is evident also in more traditionally conceived reconstruction projects, for example, Millicent Hodson's conversations with Marie Rambert about the movement and movement qualities of Nijinsky's *Sacre du Printemps* (Hodson 1996). In some cases, oral testimony of earlier dancers can even be sought out to test received ideas about dances transmitted through oral tradition. An example might be Elsa Marianne von Rosen's discussions with Ellen Price de Plane in the process of restaging Bournonville's *La Sylphide*, first for the Scandinavian Ballet and then for London's Ballet Rambert (Clarke 1962, 208). Consulting a dancer from an earlier generation allowed elements of Bournonville's choreography and style that had been eroded, even erased, over time—within the supposedly continuous Royal Danish Ballet tradition—to resurface and challenge contemporary movement norms.

This suggests an important qualification to claims in the theorization of reenactment about the body-as-archive, and the oral-embodied tradition as counter-memory.[13] Schneider is critical of archivists, claiming "you lose a lot of history" through relying on oral and embodied modes of transmission. "Such statements assume that memory cannot be housed in a body and remain, and thus that oral story-telling, live recitation, repeated gesture, and ritual enactment are not practices of telling or writing history" (2001, 101). Equally, it is important not to assume that oral traditions, qua practices of history, give unproblematic access to an authentic past or a set of historical truths where archives do not. For all the value of corporeal investigation of past dance, the act of embodying an older style is fraught with practical and epistemological difficulties. How can the kinaesthetic characteristics of lost dances be known or retrieved, given the significant changes in bodily habitus across time? In each of my three cases of reenactment, questions arise about stylistic difference and displacement. Christel Stalpaert, for example, claims Barba's mode of dancing Wigman highlights the "corporeal gap with the archival material" (2011, 91). Despite the commonalities between the Wigman idiom and Barba's own training history—in Ecuadorian modern dance and subsequently in Belgium—his habitus does not melt into the Wigman style but remains visible, even as he embodies her choreography. Aside from the (interesting) issue of how it is possible to see two styles juxtaposed in one person's dancing, there is also a question here about how we can know the features of the Wigman idiom in the first place, except through the film records, reenactments, and the embodied heritage of her pupils, all of which are already implicated in Barba's process. Thus reenactment may contribute to sustaining the myth of a style, as well as potentially drawing attention to its disjunction with contemporary ways of moving.

---

[13] On oral transmission, see Chapter 13 by Susanne Foellmer.

So, if corporeal engagement with past dances has an investigative dimension, what it teaches about those dances must be corrigible, as is information gleaned from other modes of inquiry. In the same way that textual archives can create a misleading impression of the dances they represent, re-enactors and their audiences can also be mistaken in what they discover about the past through the processes of redoing and reliving. Perhaps that doesn't matter, if the value of reenactment is its capacity to open up creative possibilities for the future. But it does matter to the extent that reenactment (as the very term suggests) concerns also a return to, and revisiting of, the historical. To emphasize the corrigibility of history is not to assert wholesale skepticism about the very possibility of understanding the past. Such skepticism is sometimes implied in theorizations of reenactment,[14] though it is not always clear whether the underlying claim is metaphysical or epistemological: In other words, is the argument that the past does not exist as an objective fact or set of facts? Or that it does, but remains inaccessible—in other words, that something happened, but one cannot hope to know what? In relation to dance history, the metaphysical position appears difficult to sustain (as it probably is more generally, though there is no space to develop that view here). Even if there is no single way these dances were, there do seem to be ways they were not or cannot have been; hence the past is not wholly indeterminate. Equally, epistemological access to how things *weren't* seems possible, even if knowledge of how they were is more difficult to come by. And good (as well as bad) guesses at how things were are enabled by careful reading of *both* archival traces and what has come down through oral and embodied traditions.

The implication of some theorizations of reenactment is that the latter is more sophisticated than "traditional" reconstruction because it *asserts* skepticism about the existence or possibility of knowledge of the past. But it also seems important not to assume that audiences only appreciate the provisional, partial, and constructed character of history when their attention is explicitly drawn to it. Here the parallel of historical fiction is instructive. When I read a novel like Hilary Mantel's *Wolf Hall* (about the English king Henry VIII and his relationship with his advisor Thomas Cromwell), I don't naïvely think that I am accessing the past thoughts of Cromwell, or reading the words he would have spoken. Like other readers, I am well aware that the dialogue and details of plot and character are largely made up. Despite this, I feel that the novel gives me insight into the historical period, because it tests out the way things might have been, or what the experience of living in these circumstances, among these historical agents, might have been like. The historical accuracy of the detail is important, but only up to a point. Given a certain willing suspension of disbelief, both reenactment and reconstruction can function as a kind of thought experiment that tests our understanding of, and assumptions about, the past. Again, Barba exemplifies the tendency, though I am suggesting that this is a feature of reconstruction as well as reenactment: "though I care about accuracy," he says, "I mainly strive to reproduce a theatrical illusion, with all the fiction that implies,"

---

[14] For example, Stalpaert writes of Barba "not attest[ing] to a clear-cut past, as evidence of 'a' dance movement, 'a' culture or 'a' [*sic*] identity" (2011, 94).

producing "an imaginative proposition that something might have been this way [ . . . ] grounded on [ . . . ] rigorous research" (2011, 84, 86).

There is an interesting parallel here with general historical reenactment. In contrast to the assumption that they naïvely believe they are inhabiting a past, Rebecca Schneider emphasizes the complex attitudes of the American Civil War reenactors she spent time with while researching her book *Performing Remains*: "Problems of ambivalence, simultaneous temporal registers, anachronism, and the *everywhere* of error were not lost on any of the reenactors with whom I spoke, despite their common depiction as, by and large, simple or naïve 'enthusiasts'" (2011, 8). And she comments that "many of them find reenactment to be, if not the thing itself (the past), somehow also *not not* the thing (the past), as it passes across their bodies in again time" (8). This ambivalence seems to be characteristic also of dance reenactors, as well as my own experience as an audience member of their productions. Theorizations of dance reenactment may stress its rejection of imitation, identity, and the "old myth of repeatability" (Franko 1993), but they also recognize that—to be reenactment at all—it must seek to repeat something, at least to some extent. Filtered through the preoccupations of the present though it invariably is, reenactment also hazards and tests historical claims.

# THREE HISTORICAL FICTIONS AND
# A CONCLUSION

In *A Mary Wigman Dance Evening*, Fabián Barba constructs his "theatrical illusion, with all the fiction that implies," by various means. The auditorium is adorned with a golden chandelier hanging from the ceiling and a luscious red velvet curtain, which opens with a swish to reveal the stage. The bare performance space accentuates the presence of the solo figure who dances there. A curious feature of the performance— one that may have been anticipated by those knowledgeable about Wigman's concert practice, but which is striking when relived durationally—is its episodic structure: dances last just a few minutes, their brevity concentrating the potency of their particular statements. The short span of the individual dances also catches the audience off-guard: after the first, they are unsure whether to applaud, or whether that will destroy the developing tone and momentum of the performance. When they acclimatize and start to clap at the end of each solo, the curtain calls are taken with a ritualistic formality on the part of the dancer. His straight-faced demeanor reinforces the serious spiritual purpose of the choreography. The pauses between dances to allow costume changes, meanwhile, become noisier and noisier as the audience members share thoughts about what is happening, giggle, and speculate on what will come next. The event has a distinct patterning as a social, as well as a spiritual, ritual and these two dimensions coexist in an odd sort of tension through the performance as a whole.

Philippe Decouflé's *Panorama* unfolds through a series of familiar and unfamiliar stage pictures and dances, offering (as the title promises it will) a broad vision of a choreographic practice over several decades. The inventiveness and humor characteristic of Decouflé's practice is clearly in evidence. The dancers by turns stride across the stage, backs curved forward in purposeful concentration, their long, floppy arm extensions carving the space in front. Three seated male dancers have a rhythmic play-flight, full of slapstick impacts and exaggerated facial expressions. A couple on bungee ropes engage in a vociferous argument while exploring the movement possibilities that their new relation to gravity opens up, the duet ending with an emotional reconciliation in an spinning embrace. Matthieu Penchinat, wearing giant flipper feet, verbally addresses the audience in an intervention as surreal as his furry dog costume donned at another moment. Some parts of the performance, which reenact dances from early works like *Vague Café* (1983) and *Jump*, vividly recall the period idiom of 1980s visual culture, their "graphic, comic-book style" (Decouflé in Sadler's Wells 2012) and simple unison structure wavering between (faux?) naivety and irony. But the irony is also softened by deliberately poignant moments of human intimacy and by the earnestness of the performers. Whereas I recall the earlier dancers performing as if standing at some internal distance from their actions, the current company invests in and fills the movement. Their full-bodied engagement is touching, and reveals a humanistic element of this work that seemed (to me) less evident in its earlier incarnation.

Many minutes of the Prologue from the Kirov Ballet's 1999 *Sleeping Beauty* are occupied by the slow procession of a series of groups of supernumeraries, who gradually fill up the stage. The characters parade rather than dance, their costumes in a myriad of vibrant colors accentuating the increasingly busy stage picture. Eventually, the King and Queen appear, and the milling of the court resolves into relatively elaborate sequences of mime, interspersed with dances that draw geometrical patterns on the space in their choreography of the dancers' massed ranks. As one Russian commentator notes, compared to the "traditional" *Sleeping Beauty*, this is "not just a different ballet, but a spectacle that relates to a significantly different type of ballet theatre [ . . . ] . It is a *ballet à entrées*. Classical dance arises here out of ceremonial ritual" (Yaroslav Sedov, cited in Scholl 2004, 162–163). Aside from the more extended sequences of pantomime (and even here, the gestures themselves seem relatively familiar), the movement material is not significantly different in appearance or quality from that of the Konstantin Sergeyev *Sleeping Beauty*. This is perhaps because the dancers have retained their contemporary technical approach to the vocabulary, rather than trying to rediscover a late nineteenth-century movement idiom. But the structural organization *is* different, and the spectacle proceeds at another pace: "[in] the aesthetic of Petipa's theater[,] there is time to pose, to mime, and to dance" (Vaziev and Vikharev 1999, 20). The scenography is surprising as well, the garish colors and visual overload rendering a "carnival kitsch" that explodes "the myth of the nineteenth-century ballet's good taste" (Scholl 2004, 163).

These reenactments, then, appear to be neither simple tokens of dance work types, nor simple reiterations of past performance events. They are inventive and in some cases subversive; yet, because they refer explicitly to past dances, they are unlike inventive (and subversive) dance creations, which do not. The referential relationship to other, older dances is key, but apparently not established (merely) through re-instancing or replication, though there might be an element of both these processes in contemporary reenactments. The latter are (also) doing something else, however. In engaging with dance history, each of these performances gives an account of a past dance, an account that aims partly at reflecting its reality and partly at reinventing it for the present moment. These dance reenactments are forms of historical fiction—they tell a story about the dance past, grounded in archival and corporeal research, but inventing and modulating according to contemporary idioms and concerns. In historical terms, the function of such fictions is to test how things might have been without necessarily committing to the claim that this is how they were. In that sense, reenactments present thought experiments about dance history, allowing performers and audiences to envisage possible pasts. Lepecki sees reenactment as evidence of "choreographic will to archive," or "a capacity to identify in a past work still non-exhausted creative fields of 'impalpable possibilities'" (2010, 31). But a focus on the historical- as distinct from the future-orientation of reenactment implies recognition of the multiplicity of ways a dance might have been, not just the variety of contemporary actualizations it makes possible now.

So, the *what* of reenactment might be a work, an event, a style, or a period of dance history. And the relation between that *what* and the present performance is one of representation, rather than re-instancing. The representation characterizes, but also fictionalizes and invents. But the framework provided by relevant archival materials, both documentary and bodily, grounds the fictions so that they remain clearly *of* or *about* the work in question. They shape my understanding of those dances because they test how they might have been, and in that sense function not just as pretexts for contemporary creation, but as history too.

## WORKS CITED

Agnew, Vanessa. 2004. "Introduction: What Is Reenactment?" *Criticism* 46(3): 327–339.

Agnew, Vanessa. 2007. "History's Affective Turn: Historical Reenactment and its Work in the Present." *Rethinking History* 11(3): 299–312.

Armelagos, Adina, and Mary Sirridge. 1978. "The Identity Crisis in Dance." *Journal of Aesthetics and Art Criticism* 37(2): 129–139.

Banes, Sally. 1987. *Terpsichore in Sneakers: Post-modern Dance*. Rev. ed. Hanover, NH: Wesleyan University Press.

Barba, Fabian. 2011. "Research into Corporeality." *Dance Research Journal* 43(1): 82–89.

Barthes, Roland. 1977. "The Death of the Author." In *Image, Music, Text*, 142–148. London: Fontana.

Buckland, Theresa Jill. 2011. *Society Dancing: Fashionable Bodies in England, 1870–1920*. Basingstoke, UK: Palgrave Macmillan.

Burt, Ramsay. 2003. "Memory, Repetition and Critical Intervention: The Politics of Historical Reference in Recent European Dance Performance." *Performance Research* 8(2): 34–41.

Clarke, Mary. 1962. *Dancers of Mercury: The Story of Ballet Rambert*. London: A & C Black.

Collins, Willa. 2009. "The Petipa Problem." In *Proceedings of the Society of Dance History Scholars Annual Conference*, 66–70. Stanford University and ODC Dance Commons, June.

Conroy, Renee. 2013. "The *Beat* Goes On: Reconsidering Dancework Identity." In *Thinking through Dance: The Philosophy of Dance Performance and Practices*, edited by Jenny Bunker, Anna Pakes, and Bonnie Rowell, 102–126. Binsted, UK: Dance Books.

Cook, Alexander. 2004. "The Use and Abuse of Historical Reenactment: Thoughts on Recent Trends in Public History." *Criticism* 46(3): 487–496.

Cvejić, Bojana, and Anne Teresa de Keersmaeker. 2012. *A Choreographer's Score: Fase, Rosas Danst Rosas, Elena's Aria, Bartók*. Brussels: Mercartorfonds.

Cvejić, Bojana, and Anne Teresa de Keersmaeker. 2013. *En Atendant and Casena: A Choreographer's Score*. Brussels: Mercartorfonds.

Davies, David. 2011. *Philosophy of the Performing Arts*. Malden, MA: Wiley-Blackwell.

Davies, Stephen. 2001. *Musical Works and Performances*. Oxford: Clarendon Press.

DCA/Philippe Decouflé. 2013. "Spectacle en tournée: Panorama." http://www.cie-dca.com/fr/spectacles/panorama (accessed June 10, 2014).

Dorris, George. 1999. "The Kirov in New York." *The Dancing Times* (September): 1081–1083.

Franko, Mark. 1993. "Epilogue: Repeatability, Reconstruction, and Beyond." In *Dance as Text: Ideologies of the Baroque Body*, 133–152. Cambridge: Cambridge University Press.

Franko, Mark. 2011. "Writing for the Body: Notation, Reconstruction, and Reinvention." *Common Knowledge* 17(2): 321–334.

Hecquet, Simon, and Sabine Prokhoris. 2007. *Fabriques de la Danse*. Paris: Presses Universitaires de France.

Hodes, Stuart. 1993. "Dance Preservation and the Oral History Paradigm." In *Dance Reconstructed, Conference Proceedings*, edited by Barbara Palfy, 97–108. Rutgers University, October 16–17, 1992.

Hodson, Millicent. 1996. *Nijinsky's Crime against Grace: Reconstruction Score of the Original Choreography for Le sacre du printemps*. Stuyvesant, NY: Pendragon Press.

Hutchinson-Guest, Ann. 1989. *Choreo-graphics: A Comparison of Dance Notation Systems from the Fifteenth Century to the Present*. New York: Gordon and Breach.

Jordan, Stephanie, ed. 2000. *Preservation Politics: Dance Revived, Reconstructed, Remade, Conference Proceedings*. University of Surrey Roehampton, November 8–9, 1997. London: Dance Books.

Lepecki, André. 2007. "Choreography as Apparatus of Capture." *The Drama Review* 51(2): 119–123.

Lepecki, André. 2010. "The Body as Archive: Will to Re-Enact and the Afterlives of Dances." *Dance Research Journal* 42(2): 28–48.

McFee, Graham. 1992. *Understanding Dance*. London: Routledge.

McFee, Graham. 2011. *The Philosophical Aesthetics of Dance*. Alton: Dance Books.

McFee, Graham. 2013. "'Admirable Legs'; or, the Dancer's Importance for the Dance." In *Thinking through Dance: The Philosophy of Dance Performance and Practices*, edited by Jenny Bunker, Anna Pakes, and Bonnie Rowell, 22–45. Binsted, UK: Dance Books.

Mantel, Hilary. 2009. *Wolf Hall*. London: Fourth Estate.

Owen, Michael. 2000. "The Logistics of Bringing the Kirov to London and the Russians' Hopes for the Season." *The Dancing Times* (May): 690–691.

Pakes, Anna. Forthcoming in 2018. *Choreography Invisible: The Disappearing Work of Dance*. Oxford: Oxford University Press.

Palfy, Barbara, ed. 1993. *Dance Reconstructed, Conference Proceedings.* Rutgers University, October 16–17, 1992.

Pouillaude, Frédéric. 2017. *Unworking Choreography: The Notion of the Work in Dance.* Trans. Anna Pakes. New York: Oxford University Press. Originally published in French as *Le Désoeuvrement Chorégraphique*, Paris: Vrin, 2009.

Sadler's Wells. 2012. "Compagnie DCA/Philippe Decouflé's *Panorama*." Program for performances at Sadler's Wells Theatre, London, November 2–4.

Schneider, Rebecca. 2001. "Archives Performance Remains." *Performance Research* 6(2): 100–108.

Schneider, Rebecca. 2011. *Performing Remains: Art and War in Times of Theatrical Reenactment.* London: Routledge.

Scholl, Tim. 1994. *From Petipa to Balanchine: Classical Revival and the Modernization of Ballet.* London: Routledge.

Scholl, Tim. 2004. Sleeping Beauty: *A Legend in Progress.* New Haven, CT: Yale University Press.

Sparshott, Francis. 1995. *A Measured Pace: Towards a Philosophical Understanding of the Arts of Dance.* Toronto: University of Toronto Press.

Stalpaert, Christel. 2011. "Reenacting Modernity: Fabian Barba's *A Mary Wigman Dance Evening* (2009)." *Dance Research Journal* 43(1): 90–95.

Stoddart, Amy Lynn. 2002. "The Balanchine Trust: The Inherent Ironies of Authentic Preservation." *Proceedings of the Society of Dance History Scholars Annual Conference*, Temple University, Philadelphia, June.

Stupnikov, Igor. 1999. "Letter from St Petersburg." *The Dancing Times* (July): 899–901.

Van Camp, Julie. 1981. *Philosophical Problems of Dance Criticism.* PhD dissertation. Philadelphia: Temple University

Van Camp, Julie. 2006. "A Pragmatic Approach to the Identity of Works of Art." *Journal of Speculative Philosophy* 20(1): 42–55.

Vaziev, Makhar, and Sergei Vikharev. 1999. "A Sleeping *Beauty*." *Ballet Review* 27(1): 15–21.

Yeoh, Francis. 2012. "The Choreographic Trust: Preserving Dance Legacies." *Dance Chronicle* 35(2): 224–249.

CHAPTER 6

........................................................

# BOUND AND UNBOUND

## *Reconstructing Merce Cunningham's* Crises

........................................................

CARRIE NOLAND


"WE don't need to be afraid to say that *Crises* is dramatic," Jennifer Goggans begins her short speech delivered during an intermission between two workshop showings of her reconstruction of the dance Cunningham made in 1960. Standing before an audience of Cunningham students and admirers in November 2014, she prepares us for what we will see: "John Cage once said that connection creates drama. You may have noticed something strange about this piece—that the dancers are connected by elastics. Here, they are literally connected, so there is lots of drama!"[1]

Indeed. *Crises* is one of Cunningham's most overtly dramatic works. To engage in its reconstruction requires that one rethink his interest in drama from the considerable distance afforded by the passage of time. The critical literature on Cunningham, which leans heavily on what he himself stated in print, has tended to neglect the dramatic as a mode or area of possible experimentation. During the 1950s and 1960s, Cunningham wanted to turn the focus away from drama for several reasons: so that his work might be seen as a sequence of movements rather than as a narrative (reliant upon literary sources); and so that personal meanings would not be mapped onto the actions produced on stage. But it is important to recall that Cunningham himself had a theatrical

[1] Cunningham also stated that "drama is produced by contrast, something against something else" in Jacqueline Lesschaeve, *The Dancer and the Dance: Merce Cunningham in Conversation with Jacqueline Lesschaeve* (New York: Marion Boyars, 2009, 82). Two Workshop performances on November 7, 2014, were recorded and can be accessed for webstreaming at www.tischdanceandnewmedia.com/MCT/ondemand.html. For information on the workshops supported by contributions to the Merce Cunningham Trust, consult mercecunningham.org. I am greatedly indebted to Jennifer Goggans for allowing me to attend the rehearsals of the *Crises* workshop during October and November of 2014. I would also like to thank the workshop dancers in both casts: Benny Olk, Pareena Lim, Tess Montoya, Jenna Lee Hay, Amy Blumberg; and Ernesto Breton, Erin Dowd, Lindsey Jones, Vanessa Knouse, Rebecca Hadley.

training, wrote plays, was an avid reader of Artaud, and cared more than we might suspect about the dramatic impact of his dances on the spectators viewing them.

Jennifer Goggans may not have been aware of Cunningham's background in theater
when she staged *Crises*, but she was highly aware of his interest in the dramatic tensions
that could be generated between individual dancers on the stage. Having observed the
choreographer over the course of her twelve years in the company, she learned a good
deal about how he would choose and coach the partners of his duets, and that knowledge
was passed on to the dancers who reconstructed *Crises* in 2014. It has frequently been
argued that dance reenactments, because they reinterpret and recast the dance, present
the opportunity to open up a new critical approach to the choreographer, whereas more
traditional projects of reconstruction merely attempt to reproduce the original. But in
the case of the reconstruction of *Crises*, the mere act of bringing the dance back into
the repertory had the result of encouraging a new perspective on Cunningham's work.
Dancers and audiences (and certainly witnesses of the reconstruction, such as myself)
were given the opportunity to discover a new Cunningham, one whose complexities
could be manifested simply by taking up the work again in a context less limited by the
framing discourses Cunningham and Cage had sought so hard to erect. The simple fact
that time has passed, that new audiences are not in the grip of the same *idées reçues*,
means that a dance—even reconstructed in a spirit of fidelity—can divulge something
not seen or registered before. And fidelity itself is complicated; Goggans clearly wished
to remain faithful to the precise movement content of the dance (the actual steps), but
she also hoped to impart some of Cunningham's way of working with his dancers. It
is this subtler knowledge that can be activated when a former company member participates in a reconstruction, especially when the dance being reconstructed has been
passed along from one dancer to the next in a process requiring a variety of interpretive
work rarely associated with Cunningham and his aesthetic.[2] It is even possible that the
decision to reconstruct early dances such as *Crises*—and more recently, the controversial and rarely performed *Winterbranch*—is itself subversive in nature.[3] The most overtly
dramatic works in Cunningham's repertory were often made for specific dancers (whose
idiosyncratic, expressive qualities the choreographer appreciated), and thus they were
retired from the repertory when that dancer left the company. To reprise these works
is tacitly to challenge our understanding of the choreographer and his way of creating
drama—not through plot, but through an exploration of choreography as a practice
charged with the drama of relations between particular human beings. Insofar as any
reconstruction takes place at a later date than the original, it can be said to participate in
the larger project of reenactment. That is, a reconstruction holds the potential to release

[2] I direct readers to Isabelle Launay's marvelous reflections on the oral transmission of dances from
one generation to the next, "Poétiques de la citation en danse, d'un faune (éclats) du Quatuor Albrecht
Knust, avant-après 2000," in *Mémoires et histoire en danse*, ed. Isabelle Launay and Sylviane Pagès (Paris:
Harmatton, 2010).
[3] Jennifer Goggans reconstructed *Winterbranch* (1964) for Benjamin Millepied's L.A. Dance Project
in 2013 and for the Opéra Ballet of Lyon in March–April 2016.

"agencies" formerly latent in the work, whether such a goal is an explicit intention of the reconstructors or not.

Merce Cunningham's death on July 26, 2009, sent tremors throughout the dance world. Artistic communities in general lost an important innovator, a choreographer whose influence had spread well beyond the shores of the United States. Yet at the same time, Cunningham's disappearance also offered multiple opportunities to assess his works anew. Decisions made prior to Cunningham's death—such as the folding of his company—opened up the possibility that his works might enjoy a rich but unpredictable afterlife. A licensing program put together by the Merce Cunningham Trust has encouraged numerous restagings of his works, while dance scholars have found new archives readily accessible online at mercecunningham.org and on Youtube.[4] At least two new generations of choreographers have arrived on the scene since the formation of Cunningham's company in 1953, making it possible—and even reasonable—to place in question the account he himself gave of his own work. Is it really true, one could ask, that Cunningham's dances are about nothing but the movement? Did he short-circuit our access to drama as pugnaciously as, say, Yvonne Rainer did in *Trio A*? Did he develop an aesthetic agenda as radically anti-theatrical as the one she set out in her "No Manifesto" of 1964?[5] Could he have authored Boris Charmatz's "Manifesto for a Dancing Museum" (2009) and placed in question the nature of a dance's temporality (or the dancer-choreographer relation) in the same way?[6]

## CRISES IN THE 1960S

The reconstruction of *Crises* offers an ideal example of the way in which reconstructions—and not just reenactments—may revise our approach to a choreographer's creative process. Not only is *Crises* a dramatic work, but, in addition, it was made to feature Viola Farber, one of Cunningham's most dramatic dancers. Even the costumes designed by Robert Rauschenberg, tonally fiery and intense, highlighted the dramatic nature of the material: four dancers wore leotards and tights dyed different shades of red, while Viola Farber wore golden yellow, "an exaggerated extreme of red,"

---

[4]  On the closure of the Merce Cunningham Dance Company, see my essay, "Inheriting the Avant-Garde: Merce Cunningham, Marcel Duchamp, and the Legacy Plan," *Dance Research Journal* 45(2) (August 2013): 85–122.

[5]  The conceit of *Trio A* (1966) is that each gesture should be executed only once and always in the same monotone way. The "No Manifesto" contained the directives "No to virtuosity," "No to spectacle," and "No to involvement of performer or spectator." See Yvonne Rainer, *Work 1961–1973* (Halifax: Press of the Nova Scotia College of Art, 1974).

[6]  See Boris Charmatz, http://www.borischarmatz.org/en/lire/manifesto-dancing-museum; also republished as "Manifesto: Dancing Museum" in *Danse: An Anthology*, ed. Noémie Solomon (Monts, France: Les Presses du réel, 2014): 233–240.

wrote Cunningham.[7] Uncharacteristically, the choreographer directed the women to wear their hair down—and there is a good deal of hair swinging in the piece. According to his account, he chose the music—*Rhythm Studies* by Conlon Nancarrow (#1, 2, 3, 4, 5, 6, and part of 7)—"after the dance was choreographed," thus ensuring that the movement was at least originally conceived as independent of the score. However, further notes in the "Choreographic Records" at the New York Public Library suggest that at some point he began to cue the transitions in the dance to the transitions in the music.[8] Drawing the movement closer to the score constituted a significant deviation from his stated practice, but it was only the first deviation of many. Intention clearly played a role early on. Far from assigning movements or phrases arbitrarily, Cunningham carefully selected an individuated movement "gamut" for each dancer.[9] Although rarely commented on, this was actually a practice he developed early on, one which he followed throughout his career and which he explicitly linked to *Crises* in his treatise on choreography, *Changes: Notes on Choreography*.[10] Critics have (over-)emphasized his reliance on chance operations, neglecting to note that it was only *after* selecting the gamut of movements with a certain dancer in mind that he would then toss coins to determine the movements' sequence, or "continuity." For *Crises*, a process of "random selection" determined not only the sequence of the movements, but also the timing and the placement of contact between the dancers; coin tosses indicated to the choreographer whether two dancers would be "attached," and "if so, how, by holding each other, or by elastic, [and]

[7] Cunningham quoted in *Merce Cunningham, Fifty Years*, Chronicle and Commentary by David Vaughan, ed. Melissa Harris (New York: Aperture, 1997), 124. Cunningham makes it clear that Rauschenberg matched the costumes to the dance; as in a traditional collaboration, he was "responding" to the "disquieting quality of the dance movement" (124).

[8] According to Carolyn Brown, the dancers didn't hear Nancarrow's score until the first performance. See *Chance and Circumstance: Twenty Years with Cage and Cunningham* (New York: Knopf, 2007), 276.

[9] It is for this reason that I find many of the accounts of Cunningham's practice that rely on Gilles Deleuze's notion of a "Body w/o Organs" to be misleading. See, for instance, Camilla Damkjaer, *The Aesthetics of Movement: Variations on Gilles Deleuze and Merce Cunningham* (PhD dissertation, Department of Musicology and Performance Studies, Stockholm University, 2005, in cotutelle with Université de Paris VIII); José Gil, "The Dancer's Body," in *A Shock to Thought: Expression After Deleuze and Guattari*, ed. Brian Massumi (New York and London: Routledge, 2002); and Sabine Huschka, *Merce Cunningham und der Moderne Tanz. Körperkonzepte, Choreographie und Tanzästhetik* (Würzburg: Königshausen & Neumann, 2000). All of these works are valuable insofar as they place Cunningham in the context of pertinent philosophical ideas, but they tend to generalize what was merely one moment of his practice and therefore distort the record. The terms "gamut" and "continuity" come from John Cage; he developed these terms (and the methods associated with them) throughout the early 1950s; see, in particular, "Experimental Music: Doctrine" and other essays collected in *Silence* (Middletown, CT: Wesleyan University Press, 1973).

[10] Merce Cunningham, *Changes: Notes on Choreography*, ed. Frances Starr (New York: Something Else Press, 1968). To cite Cunningham himself on this issue: "So from the beginning I tried to look at the people I had, and see what they did and could do .... Because it isn't only training, although that has a great deal to do with it. It has to do with temperament and the way they see movement, the way they are as persons and how they act in any situation; all that affects the dancing. It's all part of it" (Lesschaeve, 65). On Cunningham's special way of mobilizing dancers as "persons," see Emily Coates, "Beyond the Visible: The Legacies of Merce Cunningham and Pina Bausch," *PAJ: A Journal of Performance and Art* 32(2) (May 2010): 1–7.

where it might go."[11] Cunningham chose to allow the elastic band to be a choreographic agent: it was involved in crafting the quality of the movement, in initiating the coupling of dancers (and thus creating duets), and it served as a stage prop ripe with symbolic meanings that his choreography could exploit.

The sets of individuated movement gamuts, one for each dancer, reflected Cunningham's intimate knowledge of his dancers, their movement qualities and body types. The conceit of the elastic band ensured that at various points in the dance, two different movement qualities and body types would meet and interact. Encounters between dancers were thus treated as just another spatial variable, governed not by a narrative arc but by an aleatory result: "Where these contacts came in the continuity, or where they were broken," Cunningham explains, "was left to chance in the composition and not to personal psychology or physical pressure."[12] Despite Cunningham's disclaimer, however, the title, *Crises*, evokes directly some type of psychological or physical "pressure"—perhaps the pressure of too much enforced intimacy during those summer months when *Crises* was being made during the Merce Cunningham Dance Company's residency at Connecticut College. The word "crisis" is a Greek noun meaning a crucial turning point in a disease. Originally from the verb *krinein* (to separate, judge, or discriminate), "crisis" refers to a moment of decision. Over time, it took its place in a specifically theatrical lexicon, indicating the turning point in a situation or plot. It is important to note that "crisis" shares several meanings with the related noun, "climax," which also denotes a point of extremity or a critical juncture. Few of Cunningham's titles reference psychological or theatrical states in just this way, a fact that allows us—even encourages us—to seek a dramatic meaning in the proceedings on the stage.[13]

Much about this work might strike us as atypical, a surprising departure from what audiences have been taught about Cunningham's practice. Indeed, Cunningham's explicit rejection of the dramatic arc with its "crisis," "climax," and *dénouement* ("Climax is for those who are swept by New Year's Eve," he quipped[14]) might very well make it difficult for us to consider *Crises* as anything other than an odd exception, perhaps one that confirms the rule. Nevertheless, I believe that *Crisis*, even with its overt sexual pantomime and what one critic called its "sleaziness," is less an exception to, than a revelation of, Cunningham's choreographic style.[15]

---

[11] Notes to *Crises*, Merce Cunningham, "Merce Cunningham Choreographic Records," *MGDMZ 295, Box 3, Folder 8, Jerome Robbins Collection, New York Public Library. All subsequent references will be to this folder.

[12] See Merce Cunningham, *Changes: Notes on Choreography*, ed. Frances Starr (New York: Something Else Press, 1968), n.p.; quoted in Vaughan, *Fifty Years*, 122.

[13] Cunningham may have been referencing the title of one of Martha Graham's early solos, *Moment of Crisis*, from 1944. The critical literature on Graham often describes her dances as centering on a moment of crisis in a woman's life; Cunningham's careful use of the plural ("Crises") can be read as a not so subtle parody—by means of multiplication—of Graham's themes and structuring devices. I thank Mark Franko for this observation.

[14] Merce Cunningham, "Space, Time and Dance," 39.

[15] See Wilfred Mellers, review of *Crises* for *The New Statesman*, July 31, 1964 (160).

There is more eroticism—and more drama—in his work than we have been led to expect.[16]

But how was *Crises* regarded in the 1960s? According to multiple reviewers, audiences in the early 1960s found *Crises* more comical than dramatic.[17] This audience reaction can be explained, at least in part, if we resituate the dance in its performance context. Commissioned by the American Dance Festival, *Crises* was juxtaposed on the Festival's program with Pearl Lang's *Shira*, a Graham-inspired dance with a religious theme. Reviewing the dance, Doris Hering called *Shira* "an ecstatic utterance" accompanied by a "lush score"; it "confronted the theme of mortality" through a series of clearly symbolic gestures.[18] In contrast, Hering found the Nancarrow score for *Crises* "unbearably" jarring, concluding that Cunningham had "turned his back on dramatically motivated dance."[19] No wonder that, in this context, *Crises* struck viewers as incongruous and even slightly slapstick. The jangle of the player piano and the odd movement vocabulary would have evoked nervous titters among viewers primed to appreciate more thematically coherent and musically transparent fare.

Yet, as I have suggested, the dramatic material embedded in *Crises* was not ignored (or misunderstood) by audiences simply because it differed from that which animated the works of Graham, Limón, and their followers. Cunningham's variety of dramatic intensity was less available to contemporary audiences because its presence was obscured by the discursive frame Cunningham himself had wrought, the rhetoric of emotional neutrality he tirelessly circulated from the early 1940s onward. The recent reconstructions of *Crises* remind us once again that a discourse always surrounds and influences the reception of a work, and therefore that movement can never be "just movement," the human body exposed in all its inalienable pre-discursive essence.[20] Ever since Cunningham wrote in 1952 that movement need not have an "actual or symbolic reference to other things,"[21] scholars and reviewers alike have in large part accepted the notion of a

[16] That *Crises* may be an important work in Cunningham's corpus is suggested by the greater attention it has received in recent months; not only was it chosen for reconstruction by Jennifer Goggans but it was also prominently featured by the Whitney Museum in its Conlan Nancarrow Festival of June 2015. The newly relocated Whitney Museum in New York City put on a series of concerts, "Anywhere in Time: A Conlan Nancarrow Festival," June 17–28, which included two performances of *Crises*, reconstructed by Jennifer Goggans and danced by members of the original workshop that I attended.

[17] See Carolyn Brown, *Chance and Circumstance: Twenty Years with Cage and Cunningham* (New York: Knopf, 2007): "The general audience response was outright laughter plus much ill-suppressed giggling" (276).

[18] Doris Hering, "Silences and Sounds: Thirteenth American Dance Festival, August 18–21; Connecticut College, New London" in *Dance Magazine* (October 1960), 22.

[19] Doris Hering, "Silences and Sounds," 24.

[20] See Mark Franko, "The Readymade as Movement: Cunningham, Duchamp, and Nam June Paik's Two Merces," *RES: Anthropology and Aesthetics* 38 (Autumn 2000), 211–219; "There is, I suspect, an institutional investment in keeping North American dance, even in its most 'avant-garde' manifestations, non-discursive" (214).

[21] Merce Cunningham, "An Impermanent Art (1952)," quoted in Vaughan, 86. See also Jacqueline Lesschaeve, *The Dancer and the Dance: Merce Cunningham in Conversation with Jacqueline Lesschaeve* (New York: Marion Boyars, 2009): "movement comes from something, not from something expressive but from some momentum or energy" (68); and "Space, Time and Dance" in *Merce*

non-referential, semantically denuded dance vocabulary. In 1986, for instance, Susan Leigh Foster summarized what had become a critical consensus, explaining that for Cunningham, "the dance could simply be about human bodies moving and nothing more"; he "emphasized the arbitrariness of any correlation between movement and meaning."[22] In short, Cunningham (and to a great extent his critics) both urged us and forbade us to associate any particular movement with any particular symbolic meaning or affective resonance. There are critics to this day who reiterate faithfully Cunningham's semiotics of movement, believing that the choreographer was interested in—and managed to present—movement abstracted from any meaning, reference, or dramatic narrative whatsoever.[23]

Since 2001, however, the mantra "movement means movement" has begun to unravel.[24] Foster herself developed an alternative discourse on Cunningham in "Closets Full of Dances: Modern Dance's Performance of Masculinity and Sexuality." Here, she challenges what she takes to be his implicit contention: that movement can be "unmarked." For Foster, to maintain that male and female bodies—or white and black bodies—are equivalent vehicles is to ignore the social meanings attached to specific moving bodies. But I would argue that Cunningham was never blind to those social meanings and that he was, in fact, interested in just how powerful they could be, even when their traditional supports—narrative context, gestural syntax, and musical accompaniment—had been effaced. Although he overtly discouraged symbolic and autobiographical readings, he also found ways to solicit them, leading us toward the very contexts his statements would appear to exclude. Nowhere is this interest in the limits of his stated aesthetic program of decontextualization more evident than in the duets he choreographed for *Crises*.

We are fortunate to have greater access to these duets than we previously had: a 16-mm film made by Helen Priest Rogers of an August 14, 1961, performance at Connecticut College is now available online through the Merce Cunningham Trust website; in addition, Cunningham's Notes for the dance may be found at the New York Public Library, Jerome Robbins Collection. The first thing one observes when watching the 1961 film

*Cunningham: Dancing in Space and Time*, ed. Richard Kostelanetz (New York: A Cappella Books, 1992): "What is seen, is what it is" (39).

[22] Susan Leigh Foster, *Reading Dancing: Bodies and Subjects in Contemporary American Dance* (Berkeley and Los Angeles: University of California Press, 1986), xiv, 168.

[23] Nancy Dalva, who has been particularly alert to the presence of "passion" in Cunningham's work, nonetheless subscribes to the dictum that, as she puts it, "[h]e made the viewer the *auteur*" (see Nancy Dalva, "The Way of Merce," nancydalva.com/p/way-of-merce_29.html).

[24] See Susan Leigh Foster, "Closets Full of Dances: Modern Dance's Performance of Masculinity and Sexuality," in *Dancing Desires: Choreographing Sexualities on and off the Stage*, ed. Jane C. Desmond (Madison: University of Wisconsin Press, 2001): "His approach presumed an absolute equivalence of male and female bodies, and black and white bodies . . . . Through this determined inquiry into physicality, Cunningham perpetuated the tradition of a nonsexual dancing instigated by the earliest modern choreographers. He also sustained its inherent racism . . . . The very project of locating identity in a physicality that denied racial difference could only be supported by a tradition that presumed its own universality" (174).

is the degree to which the style of the dance draws attention to the idiosyncratic movement qualities of the original company members—especially Viola Farber, Carolyn Brown, and Cunningham himself. The choreographer has underscored the dancers' idiosyncratic ways of moving, not merely by exaggerating them, but also by setting them into close relation during the duets. In performance, the elastic bands that periodically tie two dancers together freight their encounters with an added charge; the bands tend either to accentuate the tension between the two dancers as they move in opposed directions or to exaggerate their intimacy as their bodies are pressed close. Two different (and idiosyncratic) movement styles are thus forcibly joined—not at the hip (although that is suggested at the end of the dance)—but at other joints, such as wrists and ankles. Whereas other dances of the same period—*Summerspace* (1958), *Antic Meet* (1958), *Rune* (1959), and *Aeon* (1961)—all contain quirky or unusual movements and movement patterns, *Crises* is particularly replete with the sinuous extensions and eye-catching curves of Viola Farber for whom, by all accounts, the dance was made. More on this presently. Watching the 1961 video, we become alert to what Cunningham himself referred to in his notes as "quivering gestures," "wiggling," and "shaking,"[25] thereby indicating his desire to capitalize on the dancing body's fleshiness, its presence on stage as a carnal rather than abstract substance.

We have been conditioned as Cunningham viewers to experience the coolness, the clarity, and the cleanliness of a Cunningham dance. Although we might be seated very near the edge of the stage during a theatrical performance, and although we might end up in close proximity to the dancers during a museum event, we rarely remark on the trembling of their sweaty bodies as they struggle to maintain a pose. Nor do we attend consciously (or hermeneutically) to moments when two dancers enter into genital contact in the process of executing a move. *Crises*, however, develops in us different habits of viewing—or at least it could. Instead of distancing us from the intense affect of sensuous gestures—"reobjectifying" them through fragmentation, randomization, decontextualization, and parataxis—*Crises* manages to bring that affect up close, almost rubbing our noses in it.[26] Over the course of the twenty-two minutes of the piece, we are encouraged to read a relationship, an explicitly erotic relationship, into the exchanges between the dancers. In the duets especially, there is what Cunningham called in "Space, Time and Dance" a "surfeit" of climaxes, a surfeit of "crises."[27] Yet this surfeit does not produce a leveling effect; it does not dissipate the erotic tension or the affective intensity of the individual moments of the dance. Instead, that surfeit, the multiplication of "crises," tempts us to find a climactic energy in every contact, every encounter we see. *Crises* encourages

[25]  Notes to *Crises*, "Choreographic Records."

[26]  See Joan Acocella, "Cunningham's Recent Work: Does It Tell a Story?" in *Choreography and Dance*, special issue on Merce Cunningham, ed. David Vaughan, 4(3) (1997): 3–16. Writing about *Trackers*, Acocella notes: "Whatever his grief about the end of his dancing career, in this piece it had been reabsorbed into comedy, reobjectified" (13–14).

[27]  Cunningham, "Space, Time, and Dance" in Kostelanetz, 39: "There is a tendency to imply a crisis to which one goes and then in some way retreats from."

a different kind of spectatorship, a kind of eroticized version of a Buddhist awakening in which each moment of life, or at least of performance, promises an encounter of heightened (carnal) intensity. Cunningham: "Now I can't see that crisis any longer means a climax, unless we are willing to grant that every breath of wind has a climax (which I am)..."[28]

Cunningham is suggesting in the preceding quote that we might find drama even in those encounters that strike us at first as indifferent, unremarkable, neutered of all sexual charge. Just as "every breath of wind has a climax," so too any corporeal contact might set off electric sparks. In short, one need not try to be dramatic; the sheer presence of two bodies on stage is enough. But there is evidence from the staging of *Crises* that points us in a different direction. We know that in *Crises*, the choreographer intentionally increased the volume on all the elements that make a dance dramatic. Cunningham and Rauschenberg dressed the dancers in various shades of red and dictated that the women's hair would be loose and wild. (During the reconstruction, Goggans directed the women to "throw [their] hair around.") Meanwhile, the music, which materializes the clash between at least two (and up to thirteen) independent, rhythmically distinctive piano riffs, forces us to experience dissonance at a more visceral, sonic level. Finally, the prop, the elastic band that literalizes the connection between the dancers, visually draws our eye to exact points of contact between bodies, underscoring both sensuous and conflictual modes of touch.[29] It is as though everything in *Crises*—the movement, the prop, the costumes, and the music—conspires to undermine the objectivist conceit propagated by Cunningham and Cage. Even Cage's comment on *Crises*—that the relationships rendered "explicit" by the elastic band remain "mysterious"—seems slightly off.[30] It is precisely because the relationships showcased in *Crises* are *not* so mysterious that it appears to us exceptional, a departure from the coolness and abstraction that we associate with Cunningham's work.[31]

## RECONSTRUCTING *CRISES* IN 2014

When Goggans taught the dance to the workshop dancers, she was careful to avoid explicit references to Cunningham's personal relationships with his dancers, but she

[28]  Cunningham, "Space, Time, and Dance," in Kostelanetz, 39.
[29]  The idea for the elastic may have come from Maude Barrett, his first dance teacher in Centralia. Apparently, for some performances she would put a big rubber band over her skirt and then walk on her hands.
[30]  John Cage's comments are relayed in Vaughan, *Fifty Years*, 123.
[31]  Mark Franko argues persuasively that the seeming neutrality, coolness, and depersonalization of movement that critics have noted in Cunningham's work is not a necessary aspect of his aesthetic but began to creep into performances during the late 1970s; see "Expressivism and Chance Procedure: The Future of an Emotion" in *RES: Anthropology and Aesthetics* 21 (Spring 1992): 142–160. See also Franko, *Dancing Modernism, Performing Politics* (Bloomington: Indiana University Press, 1995).

did focus a good deal on Viola Farber's movement idiosyncracies, which the student dancers could access through Rogers's film. Goggans had danced Carolyn Brown's role in the first reconstruction of *Crises* undertaken in 2006 under the guidance of Robert Swinston and Carol Teitelbaum (Holley Farmer played Farber's role; Rashaun Mitchell played Cunningham's). The 2014 reconstruction of *Crises* that I observed was thus "three generations away" from the original production, as Carolyn Brown put it when recollecting the sequence of performances and reconstructions in which she had taken part.[32]

Carolyn Brown's memoir of her years with the Merce Cunningham Dance Company, *Chance and Circumstance*, suggests that at least three conflicts were coming to a head during the months preceding the making of *Crises*. First, it appears that Cunningham was secretly planning to exclude Remy Charlip, the only other male dancer in the company, and *Crises* was the first dance in which he did not appear. It is no accident that *Crises* focuses on the rather intense and competitive relationships between the remaining company members. Second, she reports that he was increasingly uneasy while choreographing the commissioned work during a residency at Connecticut College in the summer of 1960. In one of her letters she notes:

> Merce is in decline at last . . . . He seems very, very sad, despondent, lonely . . . . He is so alone—with no one to talk to. Pearl Lang has her husband José his wife. Etc. Merce has no one—no friends and although I try to be helpful, something, someone more is needed.[33]

With Cage absent, Cunningham was left on his own to navigate what was at the time an alienating environment. It is no wonder that he would have fallen back on his relationships with company members—relationships that might have been intensified by their isolation in the countryside. Another of Brown's letters reports:

> Viola and I think he's making a witches' dance. It is all quite sinister, wild and strange. Once Viola said to Merce she'd like to be a witch in a dance. So who knows? Maybe he is granting a wish (witch).[34]

By all accounts, Viola Farber was a moody person, and this may have contributed to Cunningham's decision to make a "witches' dance" for her, one that would explicitly pit her type of energy against Brown's. Although there are no solos in *Crises* (except very brief ones by Cunningham and Judith Dunn), it is by no means an "ensemble piece." The dancers, except when engaging in duets, appear isolated, in their own worlds. The duets, however, are unmistakably instances of partnering, gestural expressions of close

---

[32]  These are Carolyn Brown's words from a telephone interview with the author, November 20, 2014.

[33]  *Chance and Circumstance: Twenty Years with Cage and Cunningham* (New York: Knopf, 2007), 272. The letter is dated August 1, 1960.

[34]  *Chance and Circumstance*, 272. The letter is dated July 27, 1960.

involvement. When partnering Farber, Cunningham is at times responsive and physically intimate, at others, manipulative and bossy. In contrast, when partnering Brown, he takes on the more traditional tasks of the *pas de deux*, such as supporting her *developpés* and *pirouettes*. Finally, when partnering Dunn, he is solicitous, chivalrous, almost a supplicant at her side. It is as though he were choosing not just between different women, but also between different ways to move, different ways to *be*.

In this vein, I would speculate that the third "crisis" to which the title alludes might have had something to do with Cunningham's ambivalence with respect to his sexual preferences, broadly understood. That is, the competing drives Cunningham exposes (or performs) in *Crises*, his sequential interest in the three women he partners, could have been a mask for an erotic ambivalence of a different sort. Just because Cunningham carried on a long-term homosexual relationship with Cage does not mean that he never felt erotic urges toward others—both male and female. Speculation aside, though, what the duets with both female dancers plainly reveal is that Cunningham, as a choreographer, could draw on a variety of relationship types for inspiration. In the *Crises* duets he allowed himself to explore a broad array of movement styles, shifting the way he moved to accommodate his partner to the point where he ended up pushing the envelope of what might be considered appropriate male dancing behavior within the frame of the traditional couple genre. Put differently, by accommodating and imitating his partner, he could trouble the gendering of his movement vocabulary without leaving the duet structure behind. As I have indicated, much has been said about Cunningham's effort to evacuate narrative, and certainly, Cunningham rarely foregrounded a plot per se. But the very nature of the duet as a form is to suggest an intimate relationship, one that almost inevitably bears the seed of a larger drama. Cunningham knew this. Not only did he make the duet one of his lifelong preoccupations—a study of which would require yet another essay—but in *Crises* he focused on the potential for coupling to excite narrative expectations by figuring conflict as kinetic contrast, that is, by exaggerating the different movement qualities of each of his leading ladies and by responding to each one in a different way.

As many have noted, Farber possessed a highly distinctive way of moving that deeply affected the flavor of Cunningham's work during the period she worked with him (from 1953 to 1965). In the choreographer's words:

> One of the special characteristics of this dance [*Crises*] was due to Viola Farber. Her body often had the look of one part being in balance, and the rest extremely off. Now and again it was like two persons, one there, another just ahead or behind the first. This was coupled with an acute rhythmic sense.[35]

Farber was certainly one of the dancers for whom the movement gamut was "individualized to a great degree." The other dancer who was distinguished in a similar fashion

---

[35] Notes to *Crises*, "Choreographic Records."

was Carolyn Brown. In contrast, Marilyn Wood and Judith Dunn perform phrases that seem more generic, perhaps for the simple reason that they are often given basically the same moves to perform. What is odd is that the only male dancer—Cunningham—does not always have a vocabulary (or "gamut") sharply distinguished from that of the women's. During the period leading up to *Crises*, Cunningham almost invariably gave himself more challenging, awkward, and idiosyncratic movement to perform in his solos than he assigned to his female dancers. For *Changeling* (1957), for instance, he invented lots of small hand and head gestures, moving like an otherworldly creature, half-animal, half-man.[36] But in *Crises*, Farber and Brown also perform a wider range of material, much of it uncodified and difficult to describe. That is, some of the material would not fall under the categories we associate with Cunningham: "ballet," "modern," "popular" (e.g., vaudeville), or "folk" (e.g., the jig or the polka). Instead, he choreographed movements for Farber, Brown, and himself that seem to undermine the very notion of technique—although watching the 2014 reconstruction demonstrated the difficulty of the movement, despite the fact that it was not technically codified. What I mean by "uncodified" movement is actions that are not "everyday" or task-oriented. The movement vocabulary of *Crises* includes a range of micro-motions that disturb the pose, whether balletic or modern. When describing what these dancers do, words like "jerk," "wobble," "slither," "undulate," and "punch" come to mind. Cunningham's own notes contain descriptives such as "quiver," "wiggle," and "glide," and the term "Kurati fists" [*sic*] is used to evoke the strange, rhythmic punching moves he makes during two of the duets.[37]

*Crises* opens with a duet that clearly highlights and derives from Farber's signature style. But her "sensuous" contribution to the duet only begins after a lengthy period of suspense.[38] Cunningham specifies in his notes that a tape of the first of Nancarrow's *Rhythm Studies* should start even before members of the audience are settled in their seats. Then the house lights should go down and the curtain rise to reveal Farber standing at down stage right, facing Cunningham, who is located at down stage left, facing the audience. After five seconds, Cunningham abruptly turns to face Farber. As he swivels his hips back and forth, back and forth, hands held rigidly to his brow, she kicks violently toward him from across the stage in a low contraction and then turns to face upstage and begins her next phrase: a slow extension of her leg to the side while undulating her arms, achieving a precarious balance in *relevé*. "Quivering" her torso (Cunningham's word), she repeats the extension from *passé* five times. After the fourth time, Cunningham crosses the stage in *chené* turns and comes to stand behind her, making circles around

---

[36] Audiences will soon be able to view Cunningham's movements in *Changeling*; filmmaker Alla Kovgan recently discovered a 16-mm film, which includes *Changeling* and duets from *Springweather & People* and *Suite for Five*, in an archive of a Hamburg radio station. See, for details, http://www.nytimes.com/2015/06/19/arts/design/long-lost-merce-cunningham-work-is-reconstructed-in-boston.html?_r=0. I am very grateful to Ms. Kovgan for allowing me to view the film.

[37] Notes to *Crises*, "Choreographic Records."

[38] "Sensuous" is the term Jennifer Goggans used to describe Viola's movements when teaching the duet to workshop dancers Lindsey Jones and Tess Montoya.

her head with small "Kurati" punches into the air [*sic*]. After the fifth extension, Farber then lowers herself into a split, her torso "quivering"—again, Cunningham's term— while her hands reach to the back of her head in a position reminiscent of Cunningham's hand position at the beginning. As she completes the split downstage, Cunningham also begins a split behind her, leading with the opposite leg, his hands folded together at the level of his navel. Slinking down, his "head shakes unevenly," Cunningham's notes tell us, "in proportion to Viola's body shaking." This is no small detail: the shaking that takes place in her body is communicated to his. It is as though her crackling energy were able to spring, like an electric spark, across the air into his body, giving the impression that their bodies are connected by an invisible cord.

Indeed, immediately after this sequence, the first elastic band appears, literally material- izing the connection they have already established on kinetic grounds. Cunningham hauls Farber up from her split, sets her straight, and then inserts her right hand through an elastic band that has been placed around his waist. The audience has probably not noticed the elas- tic band until this moment since it is the same color as his costume, a dark red. The gesture by which he inserts her arm into the elastic band appears undancerly; it has the slightly awk- ward but matter-of-fact air of theatrical blocking during a rehearsal. "Now I put your hand here, see?" But although Farber has to pause ever so slightly to allow herself to be manipu- lated, inserted into the prop, the actual connection loses none of its dramatic character since it has been rendered symbolic by the heat generated between them. Cunningham inserts her hand from the top of the elastic downward, thus drawing attention to his lower pelvis region. Facing him squarely now, Farber lifts her left leg and, in a thrusting gesture, wraps it around his torso. She arches dramatically away from him, but he lifts her and swings her around in what has become an iconic moment of the piece (see Figure 6.1).

The photograph of this moment in the duet was most likely taken during a studio session/photo shoot and not during an actual performance. Yet it still manages to convey the conflictual nature of their duet: Farber pulls away from the central axis of Cunningham's body, the point at which she is tied, literally, to his waist. The smiles of the dancers in the photo belie what is the far less sanguine tone of the dance, for a strug- gle is clearly taking place. This is another moment when the power relation between the two dancers appears to switch. At the beginning, Farber calls the shots—Cunningham moves "in proportion" to her movements; his jerkiness is a direct result of her own. Next, he takes control by forcing a more literal connection, tying her to him with the elastic band. But in the next phrase Farber turns the tables. She uses the fact that Cunningham is tied to her by the waist to spin him around in circles. After she makes three kicks in his direction, they try to pull apart. She releases herself from the elastic but remains attached to him, hand in hand. Exerting equal weight and pressure, they both subside to the floor. Once entirely prone, the second elastic comes into play: this time, Cunningham puts his right hand through another elastic that has been placed on Farber's upper arm. In a kind of awkward tug of war "par terre,"[39] they each take turns pulling the other along the floor

---

[39] "Par terre" is Cunningham's term for floor work. When planning out his dances, he often used the variables "en l'air," "en planche," and "par terre" as elements of the chance operation. The results of a coin

**FIGURE 6.1.** Viola Farber and Merce Cunningham, *Crises* (1960).

Photograph by John Wulp.

toward stage left. A photograph of this part of the duet taken by Bill Griffin (Figure 6.2) shows how close the two dancers were; here , Cunningham seems to be burying his face in Farber's hair.

After six of these pulls across the floor—Farber always leading the way on her left side and Cunningham, on his belly, sliding after her—Cunningham flips himself over and Farber climbs onto him. She curls up in a ball, her back stacked up on his torso, and they

toss—say one head and one tail—would produce a specific orientation of the body—say, in this instance, "par terre." Cunningham used these variables in the construction of *Crises*. The vocabulary Cunningham uses in his description/notation of the dance found in the "Choreographic Records" reveals that a chance operation determined that the tug-of-war movements would be performed on the floor.

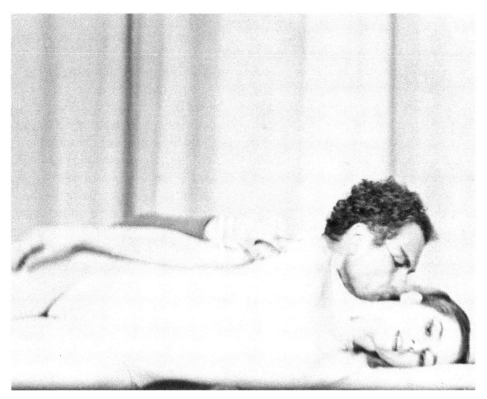

FIGURE 6.2. Merce Cunningham and Viola Farber in *Crises*.

Photograph by Bill Griffin. Reproduction by the New York Public Library; permission granted by the Merce
Cunningham Trust.

rotate in a circle until, simultaneously, they both sit up. She abruptly executes a frontal
split across his thighs, ending up facing the audience. A second later, he concludes the
phrase dramatically by striking a high arch, his hand still gripping hers and his lower
body pinned to the floor by her weight.[40]

The duet between Viola and Merce is arguably one of the most awkward and inventive parodies of the sexual act to be performed on a modern dance stage. Everything
is there except the bump and grind: the bodies side by side, one on top of the other,
pushing and pulling away, with the abrupt release at the end. But who ends up on top?
As Cunningham arches ecstatically, Farber dominates majestically from above. At this
point in the piece, Nancarrow's score is confined to a repeated four-note melodic line,
somewhat like a jagged Joplin rag that adds to the sense of comic slapstick. In contrast to
more traditional ballet choreography that approaches dance as a sublimation of the sexual act, this duet ironically displaces and channels sexual energy *without elevating it to*

---

[40] A photo of Farber and Cunningham in the positions just described can be found in *Changes: Notes
on Choreography*.

*a sublime form.*[41] The yanking and hauling of bodies along the floor suggests none of the grace of a classically sensuous duet. Ultimately, the connection between the two dancers is not exactly erotic, but it is not *not* erotic either.

The end of the duet consists of a sequence of short runs. After all the twisty, jiggly, quivery movement of the previous passage, the running sequence seems clear and crisp. Rhythmically, however, the runs are anything but regular. The sequence bears the distinct signs of having been choreographed by chance means—and in fact, the notes disclose that Cunningham determined by tossing coins in which direction the dancers would run, how many steps they would take in each direction, and whether they would start the run with the right or the left foot. A separate group of pages in the notes titled "Crises Numbers" contains a list composed of three columns: a column listing two numbers, either 3 or 4 (indicating the number of steps); a column listing the initiating foot ("R" or "L"); and a column with arrows pointing up, down, sideways, or diagonally (the direction of the run). The final running pattern—which Cunningham specifies should be executed while Farber's right arm is still connected to Cunningham's right hand by an elastic band—directs the dancers in a complex, metrically uneven pattern: "3, 3, 4 (hold 4 counts); 4, 4, 4, 4, 3 (hold 2 counts)"; and so on.

Although the pattern of the running was arranged by chance, the running itself could not be purged of all affective resonance. Speedy running always suggests a compulsion to escape, to catch, or to lead. It thus remains relatively easy to read into the running sequence a clear meaning. For instance, during the 2014 rehearsals of the reconstruction, Jennifer Goggans told the dancers of the duet: "She's in charge." To the male dancers (there were double casts), Goggans explained, "It has a tugging feeling. She's really pulling *you.*" "Stay close," she insisted, as the woman's pace challenged the man's; "She's changing her directions and you're like whaaaa?!" Goggans entreated the two female dancers to "take bigger steps so that you're really pulling him." When the dancers were learning the complicated sequence, executing it at a slower pace, it appeared mechanical and drill-like. However, when speeded up, the running sequence inevitably caused a relationship to emerge between the two dancers. Goggans was merely asking the dancers to exaggerate what was already present in the placing and pacing of the steps: the initiating action of the woman. Since the woman runs quickly, determining which way they will turn, she causes the man to look as though he were being dragged behind. And a woman dragging a man behind her conveys a drama, what Vaughan would call "a human situation on stage."[42] The very last gesture of the duet compounds the sense a spectator might have of a lover's quarrel, or, more accurately perhaps, an erotic chase. As Farber exits down stage left at a run, Cunningham stands, legs together, with his back to

[41] For a wonderful send-up of this conceit, see Susan Leigh Foster's "The Ballerina's Phallic Point," in *Corporealities, Dancing Knowledge, Culture and Power* (New York and London: Routledge, 1995).

[42] David Vaughan, *Merce Cunningham: Fifty Years*: "Cunningham has not been interested in telling stories or exploring psychological relationships: the subject matter of his dances is the dance itself. This does not mean that drama is absent, but it is not drama in the sense of narrative—rather, it arises from the intensity of the kinetic and theatrical experience, and the human situation on stage" (7).

the audience upstage left. At a fast-action pace, Cunningham raises his arms overhead and opens them wide, bringing his gaze abruptly to the ceiling as if in an exclamation of pain or surprise. In Goggans's words, "Oh no! Viola's escaped." She's gone.

If the slow motion of Cunningham's earlier duets (in *Suite for Five*, for instance) tends to add *gravitas* to the dancers' co-seduction in the duet, the fast pace of this last running sequence shifts the choreography toward a Keystone-cops comic register. The final gesture Cunningham performs, that of a lover abandoned by his beloved, strikes us as both satiric and genuine at once. As is always the case in *Crises*, there are at least two ways to read what is happening. On the one hand, the duet is a lyrical dance, an artistic reworking of the movements typical of a lover's quarrel (of which chance is merely an extreme case). Accordingly, we can experience the gestures as part of a recognizable vocabulary of narrative ballet. On the other hand, the duet is a farce, a reworking of typical movements that distances us from identifying (with) the action. The pace at which the runs are executed, the intentionally quirky, off-balance, hippy motions, and the literalization of human connection by means of the prop are all deeply estranging; they prevent us from taking the "passion" too seriously. And yet, when performed under the right conditions, the heat of passion is still there. *Crises* enables us to experience both at once—the heat of erotic conflict and the comic relief provided by the prop.

# CHOREOGRAPHY AS CONTAGION, NOT CAPTURE

Whenever a choreographer choreographs for a specific dancer—as Martha Graham did for Erick Hawkins, as George Balanchine did for his many "étoiles," as Cunningham did for Farber—one is tempted to read an autobiographical narrative into what happens on stage. *Crises* plays with that temptation on more levels than one. The *pas de deux*, which might be an allegory for a choreographer's relationship with his lead dancer, takes on an even greater charge in *Crises* since, in the original 1960 production, the choreographer actually played the male lead. The precise nature of the physical relationship staged between Farber and Cunningham—she initiates, he chases after her—lends itself easily to an allegorical or biographical interpretation. Could it be that there really was an erotic tension between them? Did he feel like he needed to constrain her? Was he ambivalent about how close he wanted them to be? Did he feel both controlling and controlled?

According to Farber's husband of nine years, Jeff Slayton, Cunningham and Farber carried on a particularly intense relationship, what he called a "love-hate relationship" that continued throughout her life until she died in 1998.[43] At one point, "Merce was

---

[43] This and what follows are quotations from the telephone interview with Jeff Slayton conducted by the author on May 20, 2015. According to Slayton, Merce was angered ("he was jealous") when Viola married him; Merce wouldn't talk to either of them for several years. Finally, they made amends and saw

in love with Viola," Slayton stated in a 2015 interview; and "Viola was madly in love with him, but he couldn't satisfy her in that way. Their dancing on stage was their love affair."[44] Slayton claims that many gay men fell in love with Viola, himself included. This was due to her "extraordinarily feminine and yet masculine" persona. She was simultaneously "intriguing and aloof," evoking in her fellow company members an ambivalent response. If Slayton's assessment is accurate, then the multiplicity of urges Cunningham felt toward her could have produced the "crises" referred to in the title. In general, Cunningham's relationships with both of his (often competitive) lead dancers, even if they were not particularly erotic in nature, could be complex and intense, a possibility that the multi-hued costumes (Farber wore golden; Brown pink; Dunn and Marilyn Wood red; and Cunningham an even darker red) underscore in visual terms.

It is always dangerous to speculate on the autobiographical content of a work of art, and I feel particularly uncomfortable approaching Cunningham's choreographies as acts of self-exposure. The critical literature on Cunningham has been extraordinarily circumspect with regard to his private life; however, it is likely that the tide will soon turn. Excerpts of Cunningham's journals are being edited for publication by Laura Kuhn, and one of his most knowledgeable reviewers, Alastair Macaulay, is preparing a biography. I do not wish to turn audiences and scholars toward a primarily autobiographical approach. What I do wish to do is argue that the autobiographical was always one of the poles that Cunningham was interested in exploring, if only because of the striking contrast it could make with the impersonal nature of his aleatory processes. Was it merely by chance that Viola and Merce ended up prone, side by side, on the floor? Was the prop—an elastic band—chosen randomly, or did it allegorize in performance a relationship that the dancers were struggling with in real life?

We are not likely to find answers to these questions, and, from at least one angle, they are beside the point. For the relationship staged in the duet lends itself to an allegorical reading of an entirely different kind. The connection that Cunningham and Farber establish in the initial duet may indeed serve as an allegory not simply for a choreographer's relationship with another dancer (that is, not simply for a man's relationship with a woman) but for the practice of choreography itself. That is, the control Farber has over Cunningham as she leads him across the stage may indicate her ability to compel him—or, in more positive terms, her ability to inspire him—to forge a dance vocabulary that suits *her* way of moving. More crucially still, the duet may point to her ability to compel (or inspire) him *to imitate her way of moving*, to absorb her unique motricity into his own way of moving as a dancer. It could be said that in *Crises*, we witness a kind of contagion, an absorption of movement qualities associated with a female partner (Farber, for instance) into the very body of the male (Cunningham).

one another socially. When Viola lay dying at age sixty-seven in a Bronxville hospital, Merce came and sat by her bed for an hour, crying. Slayton's memories suggest that the choreographer had very complex feelings about one of the first dancers in his company. I thank Mr. Slayton for his remarkable candor.

[44] Telephone interview with Jeff Slayton conducted by the author on May 20, 2015.

How, precisely, does Farber's way of moving flow into and alter Cunningham's? After the initial duet, what happens to her way of moving in the rest of the piece? A few examples are in order. Following the initial duet, and after a trio sandwiched between two quartets, Cunningham enters into a duet with Judith Dunn. He reprises the punching motions he used at the very beginning of the piece (to create a halo around Farber's head with "Kurati fists"), only this time he is hunkered down in a deep *plié* in first position, from which he pivots to face Dunn. In between the crouching punch sequence (the rhythm of which is also carefully patterned, probably according to a random number sequence), Cunningham rises up on one leg and extends the other into an attitude in second. Just as Farber had (during her opening phrase), Cunningham also quivers and wobbles, thereby imitating the off-balance quality he attributes to her in his notes. It is as though he had caught Farber's body—had caught the *quality* of her body—not just by gripping her wrist but also by a kind of osmosis or contagion. Through his physical intimacy with Viola, he has contracted her way of moving, revealing that the connection between two bodies can produce the intermingling of their qualities.

We might recall an earlier instance of such contagion: the passage in the opening duet, when Cunningham jerks his head "in proportion to" Farber's jerks and wobbles. *Crises* contains many such moments, when Farber's sudden contractions and wobblings are mirrored by Cunningham, causing him to fall. Even though there are passages in the dance when Cunningham clearly assumes the dominating role, Farber's peculiar quality of movement seems to hover over the entire piece, imposing itself on different bodies like an insistent motif. Yet Farber's is not the only body to have an influence on Cunningham's. In his duet with Carolyn Brown, we see once again how partnering can spur a kind of contagion, an intimacy that troubles the barrier between two dancers and their ways of moving. His duet with her occurs midway through the piece, immediately following a brief solo in which he executes a leaping combination typical of the male virtuosic interlude in the *pas de deux* of narrative ballets. Eating up stage space with soaring *sautés* in second position, Cunningham seems to be energetically reasserting his dominance just before Brown steps onto the scene. He joins her as she enters from down stage left and begins a virtuosic phrase of *développés* while leaning back in an extreme arch, all the while walking backward diagonally toward upstage right (see Figure 6.3)

After these repeated arch-walks, he "pick[s] her up by waist and carr[ies] her DSR," Cunningham writes in his notes. The choreographer specifies further that while held by the waist Carolyn, should "mov[e] everything but [her] torso." He captures her and holds her horizontal and thus perpendicular to his upright carriage. To the spectator, it looks as though Brown were dangling like a ganglion, gently waving her arms and legs in all directions. Cunningham firmly sets her down, then holds her left ankle to the floor as she lunges forward and continues wiggling away from his grip. Again, her motions are willowy and sensuous, her arms reaching forward and away. She is clearly trying to escape from the hold of the man who has captured her, but she does so without the aggressiveness of Farber's earlier "quiverings" and kicks. A few moments later in the duet, Cunningham seems to take on the very quality of movement that Brown has just exhibited. Both have ended up stage center: as she reprises a variation on the iconic pose

**FIGURE 6.3.** The arch-walk from *Crises*, Carolyn Brown and Merce Cunningham.

Photograph by John Wulp.

from *Summerspace*, falling onto her knees repeatedly—from the left, from the right—Cunningham executes a series of falls from on high. In his notes, Cunningham writes: "I fall from arabesque position with wiggling (4 x's)." Both, in other words, are falling, she from her knees, he from *relevé*, at syncopated rhythms and both are "wiggling." The gangly movements Brown executed near the beginning of the duet (while Cunningham held her horizontally off the floor) now enter into *his* movement vocabulary. He falls out of the arabesque due to the instability of the balance caused by the variety of wiggles and tremors that his female dancers have introduced. These off-center movements, exaggerations of the kind of involuntary trembles that accompany any dancer's attempt to achieve or hold a pose, and thus accentuations of their carnal being, have become the very theme of their duet. Whereas the off-balance character attributed to Farber's way of dancing might be seen by some as a liability, Cunningham treats it as a force, a possibility to be explored, a color to be added to the mix. Each dancer presents a different hue of that color: Farber is the fortified, aggressive version—a red so hot it has become gold; Brown emphasizes the vulnerability and fluidity of an off-balance stature, producing in her version a kind of aqueous wavering; and Cunningham makes "quivering" and "wiggling" into motions that border on the obscene.

## "Whatever Stirs and Makes Us Stir"

These exchanges between Farber and Cunningham, or Brown and Cunningham, transform movements—first introduced by a woman, we might note—into genderless choreographic units that either of the sexes may perform. Cunningham's adoption of a particular woman's way of moving not only suggests her intermittent dominance but also counteracts the highly gendered nature of the classical *pas de deux*. Although Cunningham has been criticized by some scholars for retaining traditional gender roles, distributing tasks (such as lifting for men, being lifted for women) in a manner consistent with the most traditional ballet choreographers of his day, it is indeed possible to identify many moments when he seeks to escape from such a strict segregation of movement styles.[45] To be sure, dances such as *Suite for Five* (1952–1958) and *Duets* (1980) use partnering to create sharp contrasts between male and female dancers. Yet in *Crises*, Cunningham offers the duet as an exercise in commingling, an exchange in which the movement style of one dancer influences—or contaminates, to prolong our pathological metaphor—that of another. What occurs at times in *Crises* is a loss of gestural differentiation, an elimination of gender marks from specific motions, and a reduction of both dancers to flesh. To say that Cunningham's body is "feminized" when he assimilates some of the movement qualities of his female partner is not quite correct since these qualities are distinctively *hers—that* dancer's—not "feminine" in some general sense. Farber's embodiment can be seen to alter Cunningham's embodiment; her body activates in his a sympathetic (mimetic) response. He is imitating (or absorbing, miming sympathetically) her off-balance stance. The result of the duet's intimacy is to unchain a particular movement or movement quality from a particular body (and from a particular gender), allowing movements and qualities to circulate from one body identified as female to another body identified as male.[46]

---

[45]  See, for instance, Jill Johnston, "Jigs, Japes, and Joyce," in *Art in America* (January 1987): 103–105; and Ramsay Burt's subtle reflections in *The Male Dancer: Bodies, Spectacle, Sexualities* (New York and London: Routledge, 2007).

[46]  At least one critic saw the influence flowing the other way: Clive Barnes wrote after seeing *Crises* that Farber's "body" was like "pliable putty"; "Merce Cunningham's greatness as a dancer is projected with a penetrating intensity particular to himself, although his characteristic quick, intense style has been captured most closely by Viola Farber" (quoted by Jeff Slayton in *The Prickly Rose: A Biography of*

*Crises* could be said, then, to revision choreography as a practice in which the choreographer's body—as a dancer's body—is saturated, overwhelmed, and transformed by movement qualities attributed to someone else. In consequence, *Crises* encourages us to place some pressure on the definition of choreography itself, at least as it has been presented most recently by André Lepecki in *Exhausting Dance: Performance and the Politics of Movement* (2006).[47] In this book, Lepecki is primarily interested in investigating the use of stillness and other forms of arrested motion in contemporary dance. I could take issue with his approach—especially his attribution to contemporary choreographers of what he considers to be the most radical challenges to the traditional definition of dance *as movement*, for it seems clear to me that the very instances of stillness he attributes to postmodern choreographers such as Trisha Brown, Xavier Le Roy, and Jérôme Bel are in fact already explored in works by Cunningham. However, that is not my mission in this chapter. Instead, what concerns me here is Lepecki's bold but also rather unfair comparison of choreography to forms of "tyranny."[48] For Lepecki, there is a "strange power at the core of the choreographic that subjects the dancer to rigorously follow predetermined steps . . . ."[49]

Lepecki's idiom is intentionally polemical and (melo)dramatic, probably because he wants to make a point about what Adorno might have called the "total administration" of daily life under capitalism, or the movement regime of modernity. But his lexical extremism ("tyranny," "tyrannical machine") calls out for some correction, especially in light of what we find in *Crises*.[50] On the face of it, Lepecki's formulations seem like an unnecessarily critical way to describe what a choreographer actually does. After all, dancers are not "subjected" to the choreographer in the same way that children are subjected to physical discipline or punishment. Nor are the dancers in reconstructions "tyrannically" subjected to the past. Dancers choose to be dancers, audition for companies, work for a particular choreographer, participate in reconstructions. They may be "interpellated"—to stretch Althusser's term—insofar as their bodies are shaped by the techniques to which they respond. But as Marcel Mauss taught, the techniques of the

---

*Viola Farber* [Bloomington, IN: AuthorHouse Press, 2006], 50). Brown's "wiggles" can also be seen as movements that lose their gender-specific quality once they are taken up by Merce.

[47] (New York and London: Routledge, 2006).

[48] André Lepecki, "Choreography as Apparatus of Capture" *TDR* 51(2) (2007): (119–123): "Why is it that the habits of tyranny, the identification of a tyrannical machine operating at the core of Western dance, appears in so much writing and in so many dance-related practices derived from the tradition of Western theatrical dance?"

[49] Lepecki, *Exhausting Dance*, 46.

[50] According to Lepecki, the recent anti-movement bias in choreography is driven by a reading of poststructuralist critiques of "modernity" and "capitalism." But to my mind, this bias ends up generating dances that fit all too neatly into the trap of the (capitalist) museum establishment. Places like the MoMA in New York and the Tate Modern in London want to "acquire" dance, but they have neither the infrastructure nor the architecture to accommodate dances that really move. As Claire Bishop notes in "The Perils and Possibilities of Dance in the Museum: Tate, MoMA, and Whitney," "only certain lineages of dance are embraced by museums and the art world in general: a conceptually oriented practice that refuses narrative, character, and expressionism"; *Dance Research Journal* 46(3) (December 2014): 72.

body are not a homogeneous group, all equally unavoidable, oppressive, and limiting. A particular culture may enforce oppressive regimes of gender coding, but few (if any!) demand that a youth learn modern choreography or else suffer exile or death (Mauss [1935] 1992).[51] Techniques acquired at birth are not the same as highly skilled techniques voluntarily sought after and mastered by a privileged few. There is a coercive element to any bodily discipline, but without that element there can be, as Deleuze and Guattari fully acknowledge, no body at all.[52]

There are other objections one could put to Lepecki, but I will confine myself here to one last observation of relevance to the case of Cunningham.[53] If the first model of choreography that Lepecki advances places emphasis on the (tyrannical) power of the choreographer over his dancers, the conclusion of his book offers quite a different model, one that seems far more generative for our purposes. Discussing dance's fragile temporality, Lepecki suggests that choreography, *as* an "apparatus of capture," can be mobilized to preserve dance, and thus combat that fragility. "Choreography," he states, "activates writing in the realm of dancing to guarantee that dance's present is given a past, and therefore, a future."[54] In this revision, the dancer's "subjection" to pre-inscribed steps is the cost to be paid for the preservation of creative modes of moving.[55]

In his more modulated conclusion, then, choreography becomes that which "makes us stir"—and, in doing so, exerts an element of coercion. But in "making us stir," choreography also swells the present with a past and future, and thus opens our being to, as Lepecki puts it, "becoming." In other words, choreography becomes a process of subjection that is in turn subjected to transformation *by the present of its own performance or reconstruction*. This is, I think, what Lepecki means by "becoming." It is as though a work, conceived originally for a different audience, discursively framed in a different way, bore in its very DNA the possibility of evolving along other lines. The aesthetic of the reconstructor, the kinetic particularities of the dancers, and the attitude of the

[51] Marcel Mauss, "Techniques of the Body," in *Incorporations*, ed. Jonathan Crary and Sanford Kwinter (New York: Zone, [1935] 1992): 455–477.

[52] Deleuze and Guattari, *A Thousand Plateaus: Capitalism and Schizophrenia*, trans. and foreword by Brian Massumi (Minneapolis: University of Minnesota Press, 1987), 162: "a body without organs that shatters all the strata, turns immediately into a body of nothingness, pure self-destruction whose only outcome is death . . . . "

[53] For instance, it is all very well and fine for white postmodern choreographers like Jérôme Bel to reject a "compulsion" to move that they associate with powerful institutions of classical and modern dance, but what about black choreographers just coming into their own? Does their adherence to the role of choreographer, the primary inventor and arranger of movement, make them into tyrants? What are the politics of saying that Ronald Brown (or Arthur Mitchell, or Alvin Ailey, or Bill T. Jones, or Ralph Lemon, or Kyle Abraham, or Bebe Miller) "subjects" his/her dancers to choreography?

[54] Lepecki, 125.

[55] At this point in his argument, Lepecki turns to the work of Henri Bergson, allowing, through his influence, for a less negative assessment of what choreography has to offer dance: "If the past's pure passivity is its encounter with ontology, then whatever stirs and makes us stir (a force, an affect, a memory, an image) no matter whether visible or invisible, at hand or at a distance, physical or metaphysical, linguistic or visceral, constitutes a present understood as becoming" (*Exhausting Dance*, 129).

contemporary audience all pull the choreography further in a direction latent in the choreography. *Crises*, then, could be seen as an allegory of this more nuanced understanding of choreography, for the dance suggests that choreography may be a tug of war, a critical struggle, between (at least) two bodies, (at least) two subjectivities, and (at least) two kinesthetics. On the one hand, choreography is a giving-to-dance, as Mark Franko has felicitously put it.[56] In this vein, Brown reports in her autobiography that she experienced learning the steps of a Cunningham dance as a liberation, not a constraint. His choreography offered novel ways to experience the body in movement; it constituted the gift of a new "I can." On the other, choreography is itself informed by the dancers with whom the choreographer works; that is, the gift goes both ways. *Crises* overtly stages this transfer of motile qualities. It is a dance about the process whereby movement is given from one subject to another. The process is indeed fraught with peril—and it is sometimes out of balance—for that giving can turn into manipulation. But the process can also provide both choreographer and dancer with a chance to extend themselves, to become present again in another (each other's) form. A reconstruction follows this path at yet one more remove: The reconstruction submits the dancers to a script, but they in turn inform how it will be realized in the present. As opposed to members of the original company, the dancers of the reconstruction will not necessarily have been trained by the choreographer, nor will they have had the chance to inform how that choreographer moves.

## "WHETHER THEY ARE ATTACHED, IF SO, HOW"

It would be inaccurate, however, to conclude that *Crises* projects an entirely sanguine attitude toward the choreographer-dancer relation. Whereas Cunningham's interest in Farber's way of moving may have played a large role in determining the movement gamut he gave her, she also became an object of choreographic manipulation at various moments in the work. That is, the control she exerts on Cunningham's movement gamut is only part of the story; he, too, exerts control in ways we have yet to examine.

There are in fact two duets in *Crises* in which Cunningham plays the role not of sympathetic emulator, responding kinetically to the qualities of his partner, but rather of dominatrix, a controlling, manipulating force. Near the beginning, he partners with Judith Dunn, strapping her right foot to his left hand. Over the course of the duet, he manipulates her legs into an attitude in *plié*; lifts her leg back up into a forward

---

[56] In "Given Time: Dance and the Event," Mark Franko describes the transmission of dance from choreographer or master practitioner to student as a "gratuitous gift," tenderly bestowed rather than tyrannically imposed (*Of the Presence of the Body: Essays on Dance and Performance Theory* [Middletown, CT: Wesleyan University Press, 2004], 119).

extension; turns her and lowers her to the floor, eventually hinging under her right leg, as if it were a bridge extended above him. Even when he lies down at her feet at the end of the duet, it is up to him to release her foot and allow her to walk away. Similarly, the second *pas de deux* with Farber near the end of the dance transforms the female partner into a kind of toy. Instead of submitting his body to her "quivering," absorbing her quality as if it were a traveling electric spark, Cunningham takes charge in a matter-of-fact and entirely unambiguous manner. First he grabs hold of her left foot with his left hand and clasps her two hands together with his right hand over her head; then he proceeds to flip her back and forth from an attitude front to an attitude back, finally guiding her as she awkwardly hops off the stage. The relation between the two dancers resembles more closely that of a puppeteer to his puppet than that of a cavalier to his ballerina (although the suggestion here is that the latter is simply an exaggerated version of the former). The literalized connection between Farber and Cunningham promptly loses its romance, its intimate, albeit conflictual, quality, generating instead a repeated mechanical phrase.

Cunningham may merely have intended to point out the manipulative aspect of his relation to his dancers, the way choreography does indeed involve, as Lepecki has argued, a degree of tyrannical blocking. But the women in *Crises* are ultimately a cross between puppet and dominatrix. We would be reducing what is a complex depiction of the choreographer's project were we to characterize the contact in *Crises* as uniform, for the choreographic contact as depicted here is both a form of tyranny *and* an example of contagion. Merce—the figure of the choreographer—is by turns a lover subjected to his muse and, alternatively, a puppet master subjecting his puppet to manipulation.[57]

The transfer of movement qualities from one body to another requires a good deal of observation and contact, a togetherness that is portrayed in the dance as both creative

---

[57] Yet another motive might have influenced the choices Cunningham made for this dance: with *Crises*, Cunningham might have been entering into a dialogue with George Ballanchine's *Agon* of 1957. Balanchine began *Agon* in collaboration with Igor Stravinsky in 1953 but didn't complete the dance until four years later. During the interim, his lead dancer and wife, Tanaquil Le Clercq, was striken with polio and lost all use of her legs. During the year following Le Clercq's crises, Balanchine worked closely with the now crippled ballerina, trying to heal her through modified Pilates routines. He invented his own exercises, manipulating her limbs in the mad hope of restoring to her transformed body the use of her muscles. His efforts were not successful, but they did inspire a change in the way he choreographed for women. Jacques D'Amboise, among others, has suggested that the *pas de deux* of *Agon*, the first piece Balanchine completed once he returned to choreography in 1957, transports to the stage the relation between Le Clercq and the choreographer that they had established in the exercises. The gentle manipulation to which Arthur Mitchell subjects Diana Adams in the original version of *Agon* not only evokes the quality of engagement that had occurred between Balanchine and Le Clercq; it also suggests a variety of connection that Cunningham would explore in his duets with Viola and Judy. Cunningham knew Le Clercq and might have followed her slow (and incomplete) recovery, as well as Balanchine's temporary departure from the dance world. The metaphor of choreography as contagion thus takes on a more sinister connotation when we consider the possibility that *Agon* might have influenced the making of *Crises*. There is clearly something pathological in a dancer who has been struck down with a contagious disease and can no longer move her legs; but there is also something pathological about a choreographer who insists that that dancer move, that despite neurological damage, she still submit to being "stirred."

*and* pathological. Commingling may in fact augur a danger for the dancer whose movement quality is being emulated, as well as for the choreographer who emulates that quality. Further, the addition of a prop, an elastic band, that actively informs the morphology and dynamics of the movement raises the question of choreographic agency: Precisely who, or what, is determining the shape and feel of the dance? In the duet between Merce and Viola, who is the choreographer? Merce Cunningham? Viola Farber? The elastic band? Or an assemblage of all three?

"The dance is full of violence," Cunningham observed in reference to *Crises*. "How that came about through the above proceedings I don't remember, except if you have to bend and turn, attached or not to someone, and they are turning differently from you and at a greater or lesser speed, some violence might occur."[58] Cunningham is referring here to the fact that chance "proceedings" (and not plot or psychology) determined if and when two dancers would enter into contact, either attached by an elastic band or not. Initially, Cunningham might have meant for *Crises* to be a dance about "togetherness," but the procedures he applied ended up producing a situation in which "togetherness" looks a lot like collision, an accidental or forced contact between bodies, rather than their motivated and rational (or passional) union. What we can glean from Cunningham's notes is that he used a chance procedure (probably coin tosses) to determine where on the body of each dancer the contact would take place: "Throw to indicate parts of the body *not* to be used/or to be used//," we read on a sheet of graph paper in the file.[59] But the point on the body where the contact would take place might have been the very last element to be determined, even though it would play a large role in the shape of the movement, given that a bend or turn would begin its arc from that spot. On the same page, under the heading "Procedure," Cunningham lists five different elements of the dance to be determined by chance:

1. toss for 1 or more predominant species
2. toss for which one or ones [8 = 4+4 = 2+2 = 1+1]
3. toss for which time length (or fraction of)
   a. toss for possibility of non-use
4. toss for part of body not to be used
5. toss for duet or trio or quartet.

Elsewhere, we find a list of eight movement types that might have constituted the "species" to which Cunningham refers in procedure #1 above: "Bend/ rise/ extend/ turn/ glide/ dart/ jump/ fall." The finished dance does indeed include these eight "species," and one or two seem to "predominate" in certain parts of the dance. If procedure #1 told him how many "predominant" movement "species" there would be in the phrase (the examples he gives always use either one or two), then procedure #2 would identify

---

[58] *Changes*, n.p., and Vaughan, *Fifty Years*, 122.
[59] Notes to *Crises*, "Choreographic Records"; original emphasis.

which "one or ones" would be used (e.g., "bend"; "rise"; "extend"; and so on). Procedure #3 indicated the length of time that would be devoted to that particular phrase (or combination of "species"). Procedure #4 is the procedure that would determine what body part would not be used (or, alternatively, if all could be used). And procedure #5 determined whether the section of the dance would be a duet, trio, or quartet.[60]

Another list in the folder suggests that Cunningham determined in advance a number of ways in which two bodies could be connected: "Body to: hips/waist/chest"; "head to: neck/chin/brow"; "R. arm to: wrist/elbow/shoulder"; "L. arm to: wrist/elbow/shoulder"; "R. leg to: Foot/knee/thigh"; and "L. leg to: Foot/knee/thigh." The finished piece contains a total of seven connections by means of an elastic band; however, body parts of two dancers enter into contact many other times over the course of the dance without being literally tied together. When Cunningham republished his comments on *Crises* he added a sentence in parentheses in order to clarify his procedure. "Made in the summer of 1960 at Connecticut College," he explains,

> I decided to try a dance where, instead of being separate, the dancers could be together, one could hold another, that is, contact one another some way, but further not just by holding, or being held, but through being attached by outside means. I used elastic bands around a wrist, an arm, a waist, and a leg. (These places on the body were found by chance means *as the choreography proceeded*), and by one dancer inserting a hand under the band on another's wrist, they were attached but also, at the same instant, free.[61]

The added sentence suggests that the part of the body that would be strapped was determined after the other features (numbers 1 through 5 listed earlier) had been chosen by random selection. This meant that drama, the conflictual moments, would result as much from the place where the two dancers were connected as from the nature of the movements in which they were involved. The "*outside* means," in other words, created the illusion of an *inner* motivation. "Bending" could become "pulling away"; "running" could become "escaping"; and "turning" could become a tug of war.[62]

As stated, *Crises* includes, in all, seven instances of actual binding by means of an elastic band. The first six bindings involve, in order, (1) Cunningham's waist to Farber's right hand; (2) Cunningham's right hand to Farber's right upper arm (during the slides along the floor and the running sequence); (3) Wood's right ankle to Dunn's left ankle; (4) Cunningham's left hand to Dunn's right foot (during their duet); (5) Cunningham's upper ribs to Brown's hands (during the spins in their duet); and (6) Cunningham's right wrist to Brown's right wrist (in their harmonious *pas de deux*). At times, the two

---

[60] In *Changes: Notes on Choreography*, Cunningham provides some examples of how the collected results of these five chance determinations might be combined to produce the rudiments of a phrase.

[61] This account is found on typewritten sheets in the NYPL folder for *Crises*; added emphasis.

[62] *Crises* is thus a good example of what Mark Franko has presented as Cunningham's revision of the expressionist aesthetic: a physical rather than an emotional "impression" motivates the movement; see Franko, "Expressionism and Chance Procedure," 147–148.

connected dancers seem to be enjoying a bond that facilitates their unison movement, as in the final duet between Cunningham and Brown. At others, the dancers seem to be resisting a bond that hinders their freedom, as in the duet between Dunn and Wood in which they turn clockwise around each other, executing "alternating leg swings," from front to back or back to front, like interdependent parts of a mechanical toy.

The last—and perhaps most important—instance of a binding takes place at the very end. As the dance draws to a close, with all four women on stage, Cunningham enters from stage left and proceeds toward the center stage in a series of *chené* turns; he then descends into a crouch (a hunched over *plié* in fourth) and turns to face first toward Dunn, then toward Brown, then toward Dunn again, then toward Brown again, in what looks like a frenzied effort to interest one of them in his movements. As he speedily switches directions, he also lowers the elastic band from his waist to his knees and extends it with his right hand in the direction of whichever woman he is facing, as if inviting her to come near, to connect, to insert her hand. Suddenly, as he extends the elastic toward Carolyn, the stage lights are extinguished, leaving us to wonder which—if any—woman accepts his offer of connection. This last use of the elastic band is different from all the others, for it seems to signify the refusal of a connection, the rejection of an invitation to closeness. Here, the elastic band becomes a sign of a frustrated and incomplete rather than successful binding.[63]

As I mentioned earlier, however, it is not always the case in *Crises* that connections between bodies are literalized by means of an elastic band. For instance, at one crucial point in the duet between Brown and Cunningham, he grasps her left foot with his right hand, forcing it down to the floor *without* the restraint of an elastic band. Brown struggles to escape, lunging away repeatedly from the point at which he directs her heel toward the floor. In the middle of the duet, he lets go and moves downstage to execute a series of falls on his own. Surprisingly, even though released from his grip, she continues to lunge away from the point where he had held her heel to the floor. That is, she continues to behave as though trapped in the position in which he first placed her until he returns to grab her foot once again. Her inability to escape from him, even when he has let go, suggests that a connection between them remains in her body even when he is not there.[64] It is as though the elastic band signified not only a synchronic "togetherness,"

[63] A note on sexuality might be appropriate here, given the highly suggestive nature of this last binding. Queer theorists such as Eve Kosofsky Sedgwick and Lauren Berlant have freed us from the need to determine Cunningham's preferences in an ironclad way. While this is not the place to do a full reading of Merce's eroticism in *Crises*, I would like to suggest that Vaslav Nijinsky is his model here. Cunningham has often been compared to Nijinsky, and indeed, his initial pose in *Crises* bears a resemblance to the archaic two-dimensionality as well as the faun-like suppleness associated with the earlier dancer/choreographer. The de-sublimated, animal-like pan-eroticism of Nijinsky's Faun is a model for many of the roles Merce danced throughout his career. Merce doesn't exactly masturbate at the end of *Crises* (as Nijinsky was purported to do at the close of *L'Après-midi d'un faune*), but his gesture of extending the elastic from his knees toward anything in a skirt (so to speak) is a not so subtle reminder of Nijinsky's famous feat.

[64] At another point, toward the end of *Crises*, Merce grabs Viola's left upper arm with his right hand while they are seated. What transpires as she ascends into *relevé* on her left leg can only be called a tug of war, even though no elastic band is involved.

two people connected by physical proximity, but also a diachronic "togetherness," two people connected by muscle memory, as are choreographer and dancer across time.

The status of the prop is thus a curious one in *Crises*, for its function seems both practical and allegorical at once. The elastic band literally holds two bodies together, but it also suggests emotional attachments that are conflictual in nature. On a more abstract level, the elastic band could be read as allegorical of the way in which meaning is so often imposed on—or attached to—dance movement. Cunningham tended to depict meaning-making as a kind of "connection" that he wished to break. Commenting on dance of the 1950s, he once stated: "It was almost impossible to see a movement in the modern dance . . . not stiffened by literary or personal *connection*."[65] And in "The Impermanent Art," Cunningham stresses that movement should not be burdened by such connections: "In dance it is the simple fact of a jump being a jump . . . . This attention given the jump . . . helps *to break the chains that too often follow dancers' feet around*."[66] The grip that holds Carolyn's foot to the floor, the elastic band that straps Viola's arm to Merce's hand—these are like the chains of meaning that prevent movements from being just what they are. Inasmuch as they demand interpretation as such, they are allegorical. The elastic band in *Crises* is a literalization of a danger that always threatens—the danger of being entrapped in relations or meanings, the danger of being chained down.

Bondage, however we may interpret it, is a recurrent theme in Cunningham's work, one that is often literalized through a prop that limits or entraps. He toyed with the idea of using a chair as a form of bondage as early as 1951, while making plans for *Sixteen Dances for Soloist and Company of Three*.[67] In *Antic Meet* (1958) he actually did dance with a chair strapped to his back and described the chair in his notes as "a large mosquito that won't go way . . . like a leech . . . ."[68] *Aeon* (1961) also plays with literal bondage; Cunningham employs a rope designed by Robert Rauschenberg, tying Carolyn Brown's feet together at one point, encircling her waist at another.[69] *Winterbranch* (1964) integrated a piece of fabric that was used to drag people off stage. "There is a streak of violence in me," Cunningham stated in relation to his use of the prop in *Winterbranch*.[70]

[65]  Vaughan, *Fifty Years*, 69; added emphasis.

[66]  Vaughan, *Fifty Years*, 86; added emphasis.

[67]  See notes to *Sixteen Dances for Soloist and Company of Three*, "Choreographic Records," Box 13, Folder 1: "adjust in chair . . . collapse in chair . . . get out of chair . . . start to drag it off . . . walk off dragging chair . . . crawl off dragging chair." Photographs of *Nocturnes* (1956) indicate that Viola wore two bands on her right thigh. In *Signals* (1970), Cunningham had the sweatsuits worn by the dancers wrapped around with black tape; Cunningham's idea was "to give the figure more definition," Vaughan explains. Photographs, though, make the dancers look as though they were tightly bound.

[68]  Vaughan, *Fifty Years*,105.

[69]  Vaughan, *Fifty Years*, 126: "Brown also had a belt made of a rope to which various objects—a tin can, a sneaker—were attached." Robert Rauschenberg was responsible for Cunningham's props between 1954 and 1964; he might have been inspired to make *Elgin Tie* (1964) as a result of working with Cunningham. On the rope for *Aeon*, see Abigail Sebaly, "Between Performance and the Present: Robert Rauschenberg's Belt for Merce Cunningham's *Aeon*," at walkerart.org.

[70]  Vaughan, *Fifty Years*, 135.

Although the fabric didn't exactly bind the dancers, it directed their movements, transforming them into a kind of package (or another prop) to be brusquely displaced. The function of the prop as a form of entrapment was literalized to an even greater extent in *Place* (1966); Cunningham ends the piece by struggling to emerge from a large plastic bag.[71] Even the stools used for *Roaratorio* (1983), which dancers transport from one side of the stage to another at various points in the dance, were envisioned as creating limits to movement. Patricia Lent, who reconstructed the 2010 version, calls the stools "baggage," like weights (or "chains") the dancers have to bear.[72]

Cunningham is by no means the first choreographer to use a prop as a trap, a bind, or a prosthesis, one that influences in significant ways the choreographic act. Loie Fuller immediately comes to mind as the foremost manipulator of props that extend and shape the dancer's movement. Ruth St. Denis's dances with veils also belong in this tradition, as do Doris Humphrey's dances of the period 1919–1924, such as *Scarf Dance* (or *Valse Caprice*) and *Soaring*. Humphrey later satirized modern dance's reliance on scarves, binding herself up comically in a long fabric band in *Theater Piece* of 1936. Then, of course, there is Martha Graham's *Lamentation* (1930), described by Graham herself as a work in which a "tube of material" compels the dancer "to stretch within [her] own skin."[73] Dance has always engaged the prop as a kind of prosthetic or binding element that exerts what Alfred Gell would call "secondary agency."[74] Adrian Heathfield has remarked astutely that performance practitioners did not need to wait for theorists of "Thing Theory" or "The New Materialism" to arrive on the scene before attending to the affordances of objects and responding to their interpellations.[75] Choreographers, dancers, theater directors, and actors have always been aware of the ways in which movement and action are conditioned by things. They attend to the agentic properties of objects, exploiting their role as *actants* in the assemblages we call "performance."[76]

[71]  When Rauschenberg returned to design the set and costumes for *Travelogue* in 1977, he again relied on a host of various fabrics and ropes to guide and direct the dancers.

[72]  Author's interview with Patricia Lent, March 10, 2011. The "Choreographic Records" for *Roaratorio* contain a passage that reads as follows: "stools—beasts of burden/ packs on backs/ wagons/ goods + chattels" (Box #10).

[73]  See Martha Graham, *Lamentation*, an interview and performance, at https://youtu.be/ xgf3xgbKYko. We might think also of Cunningham's parody of *Lamentation* in *Antic Meet* (1958), the scene in which he struggles to put on a many-limbed sweater.

[74]  Alfred Gell, *Art and Agency: An Anthropological Theory* (Oxford: Oxford University Press, 1998).

[75]  Adrian Heathfield in conversation with the author, April 26, 2015. On the interpellation by objects, see Robin Bernstein, "Dances with Things: Material Culture and the Performance of Race," *Social Text 101* 27(4) (Winter 2009): 67–94. Bernstein speaks about the way things "hail" us, providing a script which we then act out.

[76]  On human and nonhuman assemblages, see Jane Bennett, "The Agency of Assemblages," in *Vibrant Matter: A Political Ecology of Things* (Durham, NC, and London: Duke University Press, 2010); on the "actant" and the theory of distributed agency, see Bruno Latour, *Reassembling the Social: An Introduction to Actor-Network-Theory* (Oxford: Oxford University Press, 2007): "When we act, who else is acting? How many agents are also present? . . . Why are we all held by forces that are not of our own making?" (43); "This is exactly what the words 'actor' and 'person' mean: no one knows how many people are simultaneously at work in any given individual" (54).

The vital role of the prop in *Crises* was underscored several times during the rehearsals for the 2014 reconstruction. At one point, a young dancer named Ernesto Breton asked Goggans whether, during a particularly difficult set of arches and turns, his partner Erin Dowd (playing Brown) could clasp his hand instead of him clasping hers, which might have changed the placement of the elastic band. Goggans answered with a categorical "No." As she explained, who is clasping whom matters, for the nature of the clasp determines who initiates the turn and thus affects the way the turn looks. Again, in the case of the running sequence, the placement of the elastic band produces a situation in which it looks as though the man were being forcefully dragged by the woman. As Goggans noted, the elastic band assures that a drama will occur; as a form of connection determined by a chance operation, the elastic band scripts the dance.

Since the location and timing of the connection was, according to Cunningham, determined by chance, then chance must ultimately be considered an *actant* in the assemblage as well. In other words, chance should be seen as an active collaborator, although Cunningham does not tend to present it as such. To be precise, however, we are considering two sorts of collaboration here. At one extreme, Cunningham and his artistic collaborators—Cage, Rauschenberg, Tudor, Johns, Feldman, and so on—worked separately and in isolation such that their contributions would inflect one another as little as possible. At the other extreme, Cunningham, the dancers, the chance operations, and the prop all worked together in close proximity and constant exchange. They formed an assemblage in which each agent would necessarily affect all the others. If in rehearsal Cunningham found that a phrase determined by chance could not be executed by a dancer the first time around, he would often alter that phrase to suit the dancer's capacities.[77] If Cunningham observed and partnered a dancer for too long, *his* own movement vocabulary would be altered by *her* form of kinesis. If a prop enforced a particularly dynamic action, then that action—and its dramatic implications—would be preserved in the finished dance.[78] A directive to move could pass from inscription to prop, from prop to body, and from body to body in a chain of intimacies that Cunningham must have at times found unbearable. As opposed to the clean, remote connections established among Cunningham and the various musicians and artists with whom he collaborated, the connections between Cunningham and his materials were often messier, stickier, potentially leading to more "crises," or critical points where decisions had to be made.

---

[77]  See Viola Farber's account in Slayton, *The Prickly Rose*, 30–35.

[78]  The software program *LifeForms*, which Cunningham began using in 1991, is an "actant" or collaborator in the second sense as well. The way that the program broke down the human body into parts exerted a bind on the way Cunningham could articulate movement. But it should be recalled, yet again, that he used *Lifeforms* both to build up phrases, movement by movement, *and* to store in the computer's "memory" entire phrases *not* constructed by means of chance.

# RECONSTRUCTION AS CONTAGION

Ultimately, the unbearable and yet desirable nature of connection is the major structuring principle of *Crises*. It is also what makes the dance a peculiar choice for reconstruction. Any reconstruction implicitly raises questions about its own ability to connect to what that dance originally was, but *Crises* raises even more difficult issues, since its movement gamuts are so intimately bound up with the physical personalities of specific dancers in that original production. We should recall that Cunningham dropped *Crises* from the repertory for many years before he finally brought it back to the stage in 2006. Apparently, Cunningham felt the dance was associated with Viola Farber to such an extent that it shouldn't be danced by anyone else. He retired it from the repertory in 1965, only allowing it to be performed once in 1970 on the occasion of Farber's temporary return.[79]

No dance can remain exactly the same over time; it is re-authored to some extent by every new dancer who revives a role in it. But *Crises* asks us to place even greater pressure on the concept of author by presenting the transfer of movement from one body to another as a kind of contagion. When Merce "catches" Viola's "quivering gestures" in his own, is she then the original author of his movement? The question could be asked even more broadly: Is the style Cunningham developed throughout the 1950s, the one to which he affixed his signature, entirely his? Or did Viola Farber and Carolyn Brown both play crucial roles in its inception? It may be that, in a very real way, the Cunningham technique, now taught throughout the world, owes a good deal to what *their* bodies were able to achieve. Further, although Farber and Brown had quite distinctive movement qualities, the fact is that they both shared a single training, having studied for years with Margaret Craske, the English ballet mistress who offered classes at the Metropolitan Opera School of Ballet from 1950 to 1968. Craske, in turn, had had "a long career as a ballerina with the Ballets Russes during the time of Diaghilev and Cecchetti."[80] The authorship of Cunningham's movements in *Crises* might belong to that balletic lineage as well as the many other lineages—tap, vaudeville, folk, ballroom, Graham—assembled to form his style.

---

[79] For details concerning Viola Farber's departure from the Merce Cunningham Dance Company, see the transcript of her taped interview with Rose Anne Thom, Oral History Project, Dance Collection, New York Public Library, conducted in 1991 (*MGZMT 3-1839). Farber states here that she left the company in 1965 for a variety of reasons: (1) she had sustained several serious injuries during the 1964 tour (38); (2) she was not enjoying being on stage and was unhappy with her performance (38); and (3) she wanted to do other things, such as choreography (39). She intentionally did not leave in 1964, when many others did so, because she wanted to support Cunningham. Another factor in her decision to leave may have had to do with her disappointment concerning a dance Cunningham had made for her. Slayton reports that Viola only agreed to stay longer if Cunningham would choreograph a dance just for the two of them, which turned out to be *Paired*. When Cunningham took *Paired* out of the active repertory after only two performances, "Viola left in a huff" (Slayton).

[80] See Slayton, *The Prickly Rose*, 34.

So what happens when a new group of dancers attempts to bring *Crises* back to life? To whom—or what—can we attribute the dance that emerges from their efforts? When approaching these questions, it is important to remember that not all reconstructions are alike. The reconstruction I observed—and that serves as my sole example—involved young dancers, workshop students at the Cunningham Studio, who were either apprenticing with other companies or just starting their careers. Their professional training and experience were limited (although their dancing was highly skilled) and their time in the studio was curtailed (they had only ten rehearsals). For these reasons, their treatment of Cunningham's movement material should not be considered exemplary of what can happen when professional companies with greater means attempt to reconstruct his works. At the same time, however, I believe that the challenges the student dancers faced in the workshop framework were indicative of the challenges many dancers encounter when removed from the intimate circle of Cunningham's dancing peers. We can still learn something about *Crises* by attending to its reconstruction, especially one directed by a dancer linked to Cunningham for over eleven years.

Jennifer Goggans began the first rehearsals by teaching the steps in blocks that the dancers could absorb. Frequently, she directed the dancers to watch pertinent phrases on the small screen of her laptop or cell phone. Technically or mnemonically more challenging sections were taught at a slower pace, then brought up to speed later. Most dancers caught on to the movement quickly; only the running and punching sequences, which follow no consistent or logical rhythm, were difficult to absorb. Veterans of the Cunningham Trust's Workshops (and thus slightly more experienced with respect to Cunningham's technique), the women especially had little trouble learning their parts. With a little coaching from Goggans, they could approximate the affect and dynamics of movement initially performed by Farber, Brown, Dunn, and Wood. What they had some trouble with, though, was the use of the gaze. Repeatedly, Goggans had to coach them on how to use their eyes to intensify the drama of the passage: "Scan the room as if you were after someone," Goggans told the women playing Dunn's part; "your focus is nasty," she told her Violas. Goggans' coaching confirmed what Mark Franko has observed, namely that "the quality of the dancer's gaze was an important element of [Cunningham's] early style. That gaze was intent, at times smolderingly intense, while avoiding explicit dramatic statement."[81] Here, though, Goggans did not *want* to avoid "explicit dramatic statement"; in fact, at one point when attempting to enliven a performer's glance, she coached, "think evil thoughts!" She was self-conscious, however, about giving the dancers the kind of directions—what to feel, what to think—that Cunningham was known *not* to provide. At one point during Brown's duet with Cunningham, she cautioned the women playing Brown, "I don't want to tell you what to feel, but for *me*, I was thinking 'Oh my god, I want to get away!'"

On the one hand, then, Goggans was adding to the reconstruction something Cunningham would not have provided during the original rehearsals. In other words,

[81] Franko, "Expressivism and Chance Procedure," 150.

she was interpreting the movements in a way that Farber might not have, and thus she was veering closer to the type of dramaturgy that might be called for in a reenactment (a self-conscious distancing of the dancer from the historical circumstances of the original performer). On the other hand, she was trying to be faithful to the piece in a larger sense, working to create human situations that recalled, as much as possible, lived relationships between the original members of the Company, relationships that the workshop students didn't have time to develop among themselves. Interestingly, the dancers of Goggans's generation *did* dance as though they had had the time to develop those relationships. A student of Cunningham's who had just made it into his Repertory Understudy Group (RUGS) the year he died conveyed to me in an interview that he thought the choreographer often paired dancers for a duet based on the electricity he witnessed between them when they were dancing together. "He sought out dramatic pairings," Timothy Ward recalls, suggesting that even in his later years Cunningham relied on the relationships already burgeoning among company members to enliven the movement he gave them to perform.[82]

Many observers have noted that during the 1980s, especially, Cunningham's dancers seemed to have lost some of the qualities that had enlivened the performances during the earlier decades. Some critics believe that those same enlivening qualities returned to the company's performances in the last years of its existence.[83] Perhaps, though, what really changed over time were not the intrinsic qualities of the dancers themselves, but rather the degree of permission they were granted *to relate to one another on stage*.[84] Be that as it may, Goggans, who joined the company in 2000, certainly belongs to a generation of dancers who developed an uncanny ability to channel the energies of Cunningham's earliest dancers, skipping generations to retrieve the qualities of intimate connection that those dancers enjoyed (and suffered) during the first decade of the company's existence. Note that the training in Cunningham technique that the *Crises* reconstruction workshop dancers had received (both at Westbeth and at the new City Center Studio) was not, on its own, enough to give them a visceral understanding of what *Crises* required. As I observed while watching the rehearsals, oral coaching combined with enacted example had to be contributed by dancers who had worked closely with Cunningham and, in Goggans's case, with Carolyn Brown. Reviving *Crises* with relatively inexperienced dancers was indeed a tall order for Goggans to fill. Yet while nuances of tone were sometimes difficult for the Farbers of 2014 to master, the biggest challenge was clearly reserved for the male workshop students who had to play

---

[82]   Timothy Ward, interview with the author, June 14, 2015.

[83]   See, for instance, Mark Franko's reflections on the different decades of the Merce Cunningham Dance Company in *Dancing Modernism/Performing Politics* (Bloomington: Indiana University Press, 1995).

[84]   It is also possible that a social factor intervened: by the dawn of the twenty-first century, emotional neutrality and "indifference" might no longer have been perceived by Cunningham as politically relevant or aesthetically compelling. On Cunningham and Cage's "aesthetics of indifference" as a response to the 1950s, see Moira Roth with Jonathan D. Katz, *Difference/Indifference: Musings on Postmodernism, Marcel Duchamp, and John Cage* (New York and London: Routledge, 1998).

FIGURE 6.4.  Rashaun Mitchell, *Crises* (2006), with Julie Cunningham and Andrea Weber in the background.

Photo by Briana Blasko, 2006.

Cunningham himself. They simply couldn't acquire—either by studying the 1961 film or by dialoguing with Goggans—the reptilian quality of Cunningham's movements, the supple yet seamier aspects of his actions. The problem came to a head while Goggans was attempting to teach Cunningham's last entrance, one that he makes while crawling forward, one leg extended at a time, belly up. Goggans had to call in Rashaun Mitchell, the dancer who had partnered her in the 2006 reconstruction (and who had been with the company since 2004) to show the men how it should be done (see Figure 6.4).

Mitchell's performance of Cunningham's entrance was spellbindingly different from that of the student dancers.[85] Although they, too, had tried to slither (as instructed by Goggans), Mitchell added a syncopated quality to his advance. He intentionally varied the pace of his steps, as if he were imagining a scenario in which he had to take advantage of moments when he was not being watched to cover as much ground as possible. That is, Mitchell managed to evoke the sneaky animality as well as the confidence, speed, fullness, and power of Cunningham's dancing, even as he slightly altered the movement to suit his own frame.

[85]  Deborah Jowitt reviewed the 2006 performance at the Joyce Theater for the *Village Voice*; she writes of Mitchell's last entrance, "crawling on his hands and feet, belly up, imagine a stallion sniffing out a bunch of mares" (*Village Voice*, October 10, 2006).

In fact, what made Mitchell's performance memorable, and thus allowed him to increase our interest in the dance, was not that he copied exactly the movements Merce had made. Rather, he was able to make the movement his own, to be fully present to each situation he was in, while partnering each woman with an absolute, unwavering, and, one wants to say, ravenous attention.[86] In other words, he was willing to be the-atrical. Mitchell's way of supporting the female dancer was at once more efficient and more expressive; he was actually *doing* something, relating to her in a very specific way, while also making each movement a performance, a presentation of virtuosity and speed. It was as though he were sounding the full physical (and thus dramatic) conse-quences of each step, each hold, each clasp or bind. Luckily, one of the male dancers playing Cunningham understood what he was seeing immediately; from then on, his Cunningham was more determined, less hesitant, "more subtle and really creepy," as Goggans had directed him to be. The power of Mitchell's performance, mirrored by the younger dancer, inhered both in the way he asserted his physical relationship to his part-ner, responding to her as if linked by an *affective* as well as material bond, and in the way he created a movement flow, extending a long vein of energy from one position to the next without pause. The latter was simply a byproduct of a more mature technique and a greater familiarity with the movement; the former, the evocation of an affective bond, was due to a grasp of the theatricality required by this particular Cunningham dance.

# CONCLUSION

It is perhaps too vague to say that *Crises* is a dance about creating bonds. Yet that is pre-cisely what Mitchell and Goggans showed it to be. They suggested that Cunningham was interested in bonds of many kinds, in both their negative and positive connotations. In kinetic terms, the bond could encourage flow between bodies, creating intimacy—a contagion of movement—and thus potentially suppressing the boundaries that ensure difference. An affective bond could provide support, but it could also allow one dancer to dominate another, to become entrapped in a snare. On a semantic level, the bond could connect gesture to feeling, thereby allowing expression to occur but also threaten-ing to congeal the meaning of the dance.

Carolyn Brown's remarks on reconstructing *Summerspace* seem pertinent in this regard. She speaks of the "quivering animal alertness" that she sought to impart when working with dancers at the Paris Opera Ballet and of her attempts "to rediscover the initial spirit that informed the dance in the process of its creation."[87] But she rejects the notion that drama or affect were behind this process, or that they informed that "initial

---

[86] Goggans picked up on this attitude, telling one male student: "you must be secure in whatever event you're in."

[87] Carolyn Brown, "*Summerspace*: Three Revivals" in *Dance Research Journal* 34(1) (Summer 2002): 76.

spirit": "Not narrative ideas, not emotional ideas—but movement qualities!" she insists. But I would counter that perhaps drama ("narrative" and "emotional ideas") and "movement qualities" are precisely what *cannot* be unbound. Or rather, if the dance is to be dance, a "human situation on stage," they can only be unbound to be bound again in a new way. And the qualification "new way" is vital. The state of a reconstruction may be similar to the state of the dancers in *Crises*: they are bound to a past version by a prosthesis, by an elastic band that makes them move; but they are also, as Cunningham puts it, "at the same instant, free." That is, a good reconstruction—or let's just say a reenactment—is one that reanimates a past work; it does not rely on exact imitation, on being bound too tightly to an original. In fact, reconstructions that base their casting on the physical attributes of the original dancers or that insist on exactitude in execution are often less successful. Rashaun Mitchell, a young African American, does not resemble Merce Cunningham, nor does he move in the same ways. Yet in *Crises* Mitchell was able to establish relationships, *dramatic* relationships, with his female partners that, even if they were different in nature from those Cunningham maintained with Brown and Farber—even if they were merely fantasized in a theatrical way—nonetheless produced the very image of involvement and drive. Mitchell brought, if not the exact relations, then *relationality* (that is, connection, and thus drama) into the staging of the dance, showing that the past continues into the present as an open-ended rather than foreclosed experiential possibility. In doing so, Mitchell, along with Goggans, produced "a challenge to the positivistic historicism of reconstruction through an acceptance of the fragmentariness of the past work as well as through a questioning of the categories original, work and author," as Franko writes in the "Introduction" to this volume.

*Crises* constitutes a kind of limit case, an extreme version of what is implicit in many of the dances Cunningham made. Like these other dances, *Crises* is essentially about encounters. *Crises* does not deposit these encounters along a plot line, but rather allows them to multiply, to become "crises" in the plural, points in a drama at which decisions must be made. As Douglas Dunn put it, "Merce is dedicated to the image of a decision."[88] Because these critical encounters are not situated in a plot, these decisive, climactic moments remain nothing more than "images"; but they are not, by that fact, drained of their flavor. On the contrary, Cunningham's great accomplishment as a choreographer is to have succeeded in creating "images" of drama without plot through a combination of variables, one of which is the full investment of each dancer in exploring the images of affective relation that the other variables can yield.

In a revealing interview with Jacqueline Lesschaeve, Cunningham discusses how drama comes about in his work. Speaking of *Locale* (1979), he explains:

> You see a man and a woman dancing together, or being together, it doesn't have to be thought of this way [as dancing "together"], but you make a gesture which can suddenly make it intimate, and you don't have to decide that this is an intimate gesture,

[88] Douglas Dunn quoted by Deborah Jowitt in *Time and the Dancing Image* (New York: William Morrow, 1988), 281–282.

but you do something, and it becomes so . . . . Gesture *is* evocative: those moments which are not intended to express something, but are nevertheless expressive.[89]

He goes on to offer a specific example from *Locale* in which he wanted to choreograph a passage where a man "leap[s] toward a girl who's then pulled up by another man so it's a continuous movement."[90] His first interest, he emphasizes, was in choreographing a "continuous movement," that is, in making a visual and kinetic shape. But as he worked on the sequence with Catherine Kerr and Joe Lennon, certain possibilities began to appear:

> I must get her [another dancer] back to him, so I had her come and do the gesture over him, and I thought, what if she is down over him? . . . She went and, bending over him, she turned her head so that the side of her face touched his chest and I thought, that works very well, but it isn't as though I set out to make an intimate connection. It just came out that way.[91]

Cunningham's account of his procedure finds resonance in many other examples; he would start with a movement idea, and then be happily surprised by the kinds of relationships the results would evoke. "Gesture *is* evocative," as he admits. What he doesn't say here is that much more is involved in locating that gesture such that its evocative power might be tapped. That is, where the gesture is placed in the sequence (its "locale") matters. Cunningham saw himself as providing the circumstances in which such intimate moments *could* occur. According to his account here, he did not set out to create those moments of "intimate connection." However, his actions while making *Crises* and many other dancers—*Suite for Five in Time and Space* (1956–1968), *Nocturnes* (1956), *Summerspace* (1958), *Aeon* (1961), *Winterbranch* (1964), *Variations V* (1965),[92] and so many others—indicate otherwise. Granted, he may not have set out to create those *specific* moments of "intimate connection," but he certainly did set out to create situations in which such moments would occur. (How could the question Cunningham

[89] Lesscheave, 106.
[90] Lesschaeve, 107. At this stage of his career (1980), Cunningham still called his female dancers "girls" and his male dancers "men," an artifact of an earlier era that doesn't seem to have been reflected in the level of respect he showed his female dancers, but does betoken a latent conventionality.
[91] Lesschaeve, 107.
[92] The Notes to *Variations V* state that the variables he was working with—"separate + dependent"— contain "seeds of bondage"; see Merce Cunningham, "Choreographic Records," Box 15, Folder 11; Box 16, Folder 1. Later dances also work on a similar principle: for *Trails* (1982), Cunningham choreographed separate phrases for the two dancers in a duet, allowing them to encounter each other as their paths crossed without planning it in advance. *Polarity* (1990) may have been composed according to a similar principle: he lists body parts and movements in a way that suggests contact between dancers was governed by random combinations. See "Choreographic Records," Box 11, Folder 1. *Enter* (1992) also made "together in space" and "'touch' close" variables to be determined by chance. Such examples could be multiplied.

asked himself—"what if she is down over him?"—*not* produce an erotically charged situation?!) Although he states in his interview with Lesschaeve that "you don't have to decide," in fact such situations of chance encounter *do* create crises, moments when the choreographer has to make a decision. "What if she is down over him?" is posed as a question, but if the position and gesture are evocative of intimacy, Cunningham *chooses* to retain that position and that gesture.

Cunningham once said of *Nocturnes* that he intended it to be a "series of rendez-vous." I think this is a telling way for him to describe not only *Nocturnes* but many other works as well. In the case of *Crises*, it was the movement "species" privileged in the phrase ("bend," "turn," and so on) as well as the chance-derived location of a prop or grip that determined to some degree the *tenor* of the "rendez-vous." That is, the basic rudiments of the encounter itself were scripted into the dance; accordingly, the encounter, as a unit of movement, could be *taught*. But what the workshop reconstruction of *Crises* illustrated is that, while encounters are an intrinsic part of the choreography that future dancers inherit, the way they respond to those encounters (as "togetherness," "violence," "rendez-vous," or "bondage") is only partially governed by the choreography and the prop. Not all motivation can be generated and scripted by "outside means."

Admittedly, in *Crises*, Cunningham set out to inscribe motivation into movement more overtly than in the other dances for which he is known, making decisions from the start about the casting, the nature of the movement, and the qualities of the prop that would overdetermine the affective tenor of the dance.[93] As he himself said, it is very hard for two dancers to turn speedily in two different directions while tied by an elastic band to *not* emote tension, to *not* imply conflict, simply because their physical conduct is associated culturally (and perhaps even experienced viscerally) as tense and conflictual.[94] *Crises* comes as close as any Cunningham dance ever could to revealing the "evocative" nature of gesture, the (almost) ineradicable connections we make between movement and meaning, even when that gesture has been generated by "outside means." Still, even the steps of *Crises* could not, on their own, evoke the drama generated by the original dancers, the original relationships. Such drama required something more: it required a dramaturgy, a set of interpretive decisions made by dancers invested as much in a present as in a past. This indicates that a gap always remains between movement and meaning; that no choreography can root a reconstruction in an original; and that no choreographer can entirely control (or "tyrannize") a dancer since that dancer—whether the original dancer or the dancer of the reconstruction—may link movements to meanings in new ways.

[93]  Compare *Crises* to *Summerspace*, for instance: as Deborah Jowitt has pointed out with respect to the encounters in *Summerspace*, "this is no climax of desire; it is a witty converging of two paths" (278).

[94]  Similarly, in the case of *Locale*, Kerr's head turning may have been necessitated by her proximity to Lennon—she may not have wanted to crush her nose on his chest!—but our culture teaches us to interpret the contact of cheek to chest as signifying tenderness and rapport.

# EPILOGUE

It is probably no accident that the only dance company that has shown a serious interest in reconstructing *Crises* is the company once trained by Martha Graham. In 2014, the Martha Graham Dance Company began negotiations to license the dance. Perhaps it is appropriate that a company known for its comfort with drama, for its ability to elicit expression from gesture, should take an interest in *Crises* in particular. Perhaps the Graham Company's version will reveal within Cunningham's choreography the dramas he always resisted but to which—despite and through chance procedures—he remained bound.

## WORKS CITED

Acocella, Joan. 1997. "Cunningham's Recent Work: Does It Tell a Story?" *Choroeography and Dance*, special issue on Merce Cunningham, edited by David Vaughan, 4(3): 3–16.

Bennett, Jane. 2010. *Vibrant Matter: A Political Ecology of Things*. Durham, NC, and London: Duke University Press.

Bernstein, Robin. 2009. "Dances with Things: Material Culture and the Performance of Race." *Social Text 101* 27(4) (Winter): 67–94.

Bishop, Claire. 2014. "The Perils and Possibilities of Dance in the Museum: Tate, MoMA, and Whitney." *Dance Research Journal* 46.3 (December): 63–76.

Brown, Carolyn. 2002. "*Summerspace*: Three Revivals." *Dance Research Journal* 34(1) (Summer): 74–82.

Brown, Carolyn. 2007. *Chance and Circumstance: Twenty Years with Cage and Cunningham*. New York: Knopf.

Burt, Ramsay. 2007. *The Male Dancer: Bodies, Spectacle, Sexualities*. New York and London: Routledge.

Cage, John. 1973. "Experimental Music: Doctrine." In *Silence*, 13–17. Middletown, CT: Wesleyan University Press.

Charmatz, Boris. 2014. "Manifesto: Dancing Museum." In *Danse: An Anthology*, edited by Noémie Solomon, 233–240. Monts, France: Les Presses du réel. http://www.borischarmatz.org/en/lire/manifesto-dancing-museum.

Coates, Emily. 2010. "Beyond the Visible: The Legacies of Merce Cunningham and Pina Bausch." *PAJ: A Journal of Performance and Art* 32(2) (May): 1–7.

Cunningham, Merce. [1952] 1977. "An Impermanent Art." In David Vaugan, *Merce Cunningham, Fifty Years*, edited by Melissa Harris, 86–87. New York: Aperture.

Cunningham, Merce. [1952] 1992. "Space, Time and Dance." In *Merce Cunningham: Dancing in Space and Time*, edited by Richard Kostelanetz, 37–39. New York: A Cappella Books.

Cunningham, Merce. 1968. *Changes: Notes on Choreography*. Edited by Frances Starr. New York: Something Else Press.

Cunningham, Merce. 1944–2009. "Choreographic Records." Jerome Robbins Collection, New York Public Library: *MGDMZ 295, Box 3, Folder 8.

Dalva, Nancy. 2015. "The Way of Merce." nancydalva.com/p/way-of-merce_29.html. (accessed May 2015).

Damkjaer, Camilla. 2005. *The Aesthetics of Movement: Variations on Gilles Deleuze and Merce Cunningham*. PhD dissertation, Department of Musicology and Performance Studies, Stockholm University, in cotutelle with Université de Paris VIII.

Deleuze, Gilles, and Félix Guattari. 1987. *A Thousand Plateaus: Capitalism and Schizophrenia*. Translated and foreword by Brian Massumi. Minneapolis: University of Minnesota Press.

Farber, Viola. 1991. Interview with Rose Anne Thom, Oral History Project, Dance Collection, New York Public Library (*MGZMT 3-1839).

Foster, Susan Leigh. 1986. *Reading Dancing: Bodies and Subjects in Contemporary American Dance*. Berkeley and Los Angeles: University of California Press.

Foster, Susan Leigh. 1995. "The Ballerina's Phallic Point." In *Corporealities, Dancing Knowledge, Culture and Power*, 1–24. New York and London: Routledge.

Foster, Susan Leigh. 2001. "Closets Full of Dances: Modern Dance's Performance of Masculinity and Sexuality." In *Dancing Desires: Choreographing Sexualities on and off the Stage*, edited by Jane C. Desmond, 147–208. Madison: University of Wisconsin Press.

Franko, Mark. 1992. "Expressivism and Chance Procedure: The Future of an Emotion." *RES: Anthropology and Aesthetics* 21 (Spring): 142–160.

Franko, Mark. 1995. *Dancing Modernism/Performing Politics*. Bloomington: Indiana University Press.

Franko, Mark. 2000. "The Readymade as Movement: Cunningham, Duchamp, and Nam June Paik's Two Merces." *RES: Anthropology and Aesthetics* 38 (Autumn): 211–219.

Franko, Mark. 2004. "Given Time: Dance and the Event." In *Of the Presence of the Body: Essays on Dance and Performance Theory*, edited by André Lepecki, 113–123. Middletown, CT: Wesleyan University Press.

Gell, Alfred. 1998. *Art and Agency: An Anthropological Theory*. Oxford: Oxford University Press.

Gil, José. 2002. "The Dancer's Body." In *A Shock to Thought: Expression after Deleuze and Guattari*, edited by Brian Massumi, 117–128. New York and London: Routledge.

Graham, Martha. *Lamentation*, an Interview and Performance. https://youtu.be/xgf3xgbKYko (accessed May 2015). Filmed in 1943 at Bennington College.

Hering, Doris. 1960. "Silences and Sounds: Thirteenth American Dance Festival, August 18–21; Connecticut College, New London." *Dance Magazine* (October): 22.

Huschka, Sabine. 2000. *Merce Cunningham und der Moderne Tanz. Körperkonzepte, Choreographie und Tanzästhetik*. Würzburg: Königshausen & Neumann.

Johnston, Jill. 1987. "Jigs, Japes, and Joyce." *Art in America* (January): 103–105.

Jowitt, Deborah. 1988. *Time and the Dancing Image*. New York: William Morrow.

Jowitt, Deborah. 2006. "*Crises.*" *Village Voice*, October 10: 1–2.

Kostelantz, Richard, ed. 1992. *Merce Cunningham: Dancing in Space and Time*. New York: A Cappella Books.

Launay, Isabelle. 2010. "Poétiques de la citation en danse, d'un faune (éclats) du Quatuor Albrecht Knust, avant-après 2000." In *Mémoires et histoire en danse*, edited by Isabelle Launay and Sylviane Pagès, 23–72. Paris: Harmatton.

Latour, Bruno. 2007. *Reassembling the Social: An Introduction to Actor-Network-Theory*. Oxford: Oxford University Press.

Lent, Patricia. 2011. Interview with author, March 10.

Lepecki, André. 2006. *Exhausting Dance: Performance and the Politics of Movement*, 2nd ed. New York and London: Routledge.

Lepecki, André. 2007. "Choreography as Apparatus of Capture." *TDR* 51(2): 119–123.

Lesschaeve, Jacqueline. 2009. *The Dancer and the Dance: Merce Cunningham in Conversation with Jacqueline Lesschaeve*. New York: Marion Boyars.

Mauss, Marcel. [1935] 1992. "Techniques of the Body." In *Incorporations*, edited by Jonathan Crary and Sanford Kwinter, 455–477. New York: Zone Books.

Mellers, Wilfred. 1964. "Review of *Crises*." *The New Statesman*, July 31: 160.

Noland, Carrie. 2013. "Inheriting the Avant-Garde: Merce Cunningham, Marcel Duchamp, and the Legacy Plan." *Dance Research Journal* 45(2) (August): 85–122.

Rainer, Yvonne. 1974. *Work 1961–1973*. Halifax: Press of the Nova Scotia College of Art.

Roth, Moira, with Jonathan Katz. 1998. *Difference/Indifference: Musings on Postmodernism, Marcel Duchamp, and John Cage*. New York and London: Routledge.

Sebaly, Abigail. "Between Performance and the Present: Robert Rauschenberg's Belt for Merce Cunningham's *Aeon*." walkerart.org (accessed May 2015).

Slayton, Jeff. 2006. *The Prickly Rose: A Biography of Viola Farber*. Bloomington, IN: AuthorHouse Press.

Slayton, Jeff. 2015. Interview with author, May 20.

Vaughan, David. 1997. *Merce Cunningham, Fifty Years*. Edited by Melissa Harris. New York: Aperture.

Ward, Timothy. 2015. Interview with the author, June 14.

# CHAPTER 7

........................................................................................

# THE MOTION OF MEMORY, THE QUESTION OF HISTORY
### Recreating Rudolf Laban's Choreographic Legacy

........................................................................................

SUSANNE FRANCO

THE subject of this chapter is the dance works created by Rudolf Laban (1879–1958) in Germany in the early twentieth century, some of which have recently been recreated by Valerie Preston-Dunlop in the United Kingdom. Laban, one of the leaders of *Ausdruckstanz*, the German dance of expression was a protean figure who worked as a dancer, choreographer, ballet-master, writer, educator, movement analyst, and director of cultural institutions. Preston-Dunlop, one of Laban's best-known pupils, who in the 1950s studied with him in Great Britain, thus becoming a leading figure of the Laban tradition, recreated selected works by Laban in partial collaboration with the choreologists and movement analysts Alison Curtis-Jones and Melanie Clarke, both former students at the Laban Centre (London) and later members of the teaching staff at the Trinity Laban Conservatoire of Music and Dance. This institution is the only one in Europe still carrying Laban's name,[1] and derives from the merger in 2005 of the Laban Centre for Movement and Dance in London with the Trinity Conservatoire of Music.[2] These recreations, all performed by students first of the Laban Centre and later of the Trinity, have been partially recorded on a series of DVDs, each available independently, which include interviews with Preston-Dunlop and her collaborators, reflecting on the need to document and disseminate knowledge about creative processes as opposed to simply recording reconstructed performances.[3]

---

[1] The only other institution is the Laban/Bartenieff Institute of Movement Studies (New York), established in 1978 by Irmgard Bartenieff, a Laban pupil and a senior member of the Dance Notation Bureau (New York).

[2] The Laban Center was founded in 1975 in London and derived from the Art of Movement Studio founded in Manchester in 1946 by Laban and his pupil and partner Lisa Ullmann.

[3] The complete collection of recorded versions of these recreations is held at the Archive of the Trinity Laban, and the commercial DVDs have been published by Dance Books (London). A standard program

Laban worked in Switzerland during the 1910s, and in 1920s and the early 1930s had an intense artistic career in Germany; he moved to Great Britain in 1937, where he spent the rest of his life teaching and researching movement. Preston-Dunlop recreated only his solos and group pieces produced in the 1920s by the two companies Rudolf Laban founded: the *Tanzbühne Laban* (Laban Dance Group), and the related smaller Laban *Kammertanzbühne Laban* (Chamber Dance Group).[4] Until Preston-Dunlop's recreations, Laban's pupils and scholars gave little attention to his choreographic work and the dance repertoire he created between 1912 and 1936, which did not survive as a living repertoire. The emphasis was rather on the master's conceptual thinking on dance and movement as evidenced in his English-language publications,[5] which became the basis for British modern educational dance and which are still a relevant influence on international contemporary dance.[6] Nevertheless, it is striking that Laban's work as a choreographer should have received so little attention as a significant part of his legacy until the late 1980s. But, where can the traces of Laban's choreographic work be?

of the Chamber Dance Group included dances defined as ornamental, eucinetic [cinematic?], ecstatic, ritual, rhythmic, monumental, grotesque, satiric, country, and stylistic, and some longer dance poems. The recreations of Laban's repertoire by Preston-Dunlop include solos such as the ornamental dance *Orchidée* (*The Orchid*, 1922), the grotesque dances *Marotte* (*Obsessed*, 1925) and *Mondäne* (*The Chic Thing*, 1925); and the monumental dance *Rosetten* (*Rosettes*, 1925); duos, such as the ornamental dance *Krystall* (*The Crystal*, 1925), the grotesque dance *Bizarre* (*Bizarrer*, 1923), the ecstatic dance *Ekstatischer Zweimännertanz* (*Ecstatic Male Duos*, 1924); a quartet, such as the rhythmic dance *Marsch* (*March*, 1923); and a group piece such as the tragic-comic pantomime *Oben und Unten* (*Above and Below*, 1922). In 2008, in collaboration with Alison Curtis-Jones, Preston-Dunlap recreated two other pieces, the grotesque pantomime *Die Grünen Clowns* (*The Green Clowns*, 1926) and, in 2009, the dance play *Night* (*Nacht*, 1927).

[4] The first names given to the main dance group were "Ballett Laban" and *Gruppe für neuen Bühnentanz* (Group for New Dance), then "Kammertanzbühne Laban," and finally "Kammertanzbühne Bereska-Laban," co-directed with his partner Dussia Bereska. The name and the concept of the Kammertanzbühne derive from the tradition of chamber music and therefore the emphasis is on a reduced theatrical scale.

[5] Laban's first book in English, *Effort*, was the outcome of his experiment in industrial work together with Frederick C. Lawrence (London, 1947; 4th edition, 1967), but he wrote most of his English books to sustain his teaching, and they were the outcome of his close collaboration with Lisa Ullmann, who also revised some of them after Laban's death: *Modern Educational Dance* (London, 1948; 2nd ed., 1963); *The Mastery of Movement on the Stage* (London, 1950); *The Mastery of Movement* (London, 1950; 2nd ed. of *The Mastery of Movement on the Stage*, revised and enlarged by Lisa Ullmann, 1960; 3rd ed., 1971; 4th ed., 1980; 1st American ed., Boston, 1971); Ulmann also published the posthumous *Choreutics* (London, 1966), later republished as *The Language of Movement: A Guidebook to Choreutics, by Rudolf Laban* (Boston, 1974), and *A Vision of Dynamic Space*, compiled by Lisa Ullmann (London, 1984). She edited as well the translation of Laban's autobiography *A Life For Dance: Reminiscences* (London, 1975), originally published in German in 1935. *Laban's Principles of Dance and Movement Notation* (London, 1956; 2nd ed., 1975) was annotated and edited by Roderyk Lange.

[6] On the website of the Trinity Laban Conservatoire of Music and Dance, Laban's short biographical profile reports that he provided a basis for development in the twenty-first century "in studio practices and theoretical methods driven by movement practice," and a spirit of inquiry "that unites the scattered and diverse body of people who use his work" rather than in outstanding theater works of dance. See http://www.trinitylaban.ac.uk/about-us/our-history/rudolf-laban.

Laban invented a system of movement notation called *Schrifttanz* (dance writing) and later Kinetography or Labanotation, which is still in use. Despite the huge potential of his system, his dance pieces have been notated only sporadically, and fragmented scores were dispersed in several archives with other kinds of documents (notes, reviews, letters, pictures, and drawings). Laban also speaks about his dances in many publications, but only some of these have been translated into English; therefore some of his writing is inaccessible for readers unable to read German. Whereas Preston-Dunlop's personal memories and archival research, as those of other former Laban pupils, have contributed substantially to the rediscovery of his theories and practice between the 1960s and the late 1990s (Maletic 1987; Hodgson and Preston-Dunlop 1990; Preston-Dunlop 1966–1967, 1979, 1983, 1989, 1990, 1993, 1998), her recreations are still the only such experiment. A more recent attempt to collect the rich archival documentation concerning Laban's choreographies, albeit not supported by a clear critical scrutiny, has been carried out by the German scholar Evelyn Dörr (2004, 2008), who also published two biographies of Laban, one in German that included his years in Great Britain but without any scholarly apparatus (2005), and one in English, limited to his German years, but containing detailed references (2007).[7] The absence of footnotes in both Preston-Dunlop's and Dörr's contextualization of Laban's theories and choreographic works makes these volumes appealing for a large readership, though rather problematic for historians. Finally, *Rudolf Laban: Man of Theatre* by Preston-Dunlop has provided a theoretical compendium of her recreations (2013).

In this chapter I argue that Preston-Dunlop made her recreations a central tool in reviving his repertoire, but simultaneously applied a very specific interpretation of the ideological substance of Laban's thought and practice to them. Preston-Dunlop's recreations aim at making some of Laban's dance pieces available to contemporary audiences and new generations of students. However, in so doing she has focused exclusively on dance pieces created by Laban in the 1920s and has highlighted selected aesthetic and ideological features, interpreted as innovative and progressive, while disregarding the most reactionary and controversial aspects of his dances, which have been uncovered by other studies based on archival research and now widely shared methodologies (Guilbert 2000; Karina and Kant [1996] 2003). More specifically, these scholars worked in the archives of the Propaganda Ministry of the Third Reich, bringing to the surface many forgotten aspects of Laban's life and career. These studies foregrounded hitherto unfamiliar aspects of the ideological scope of Laban's dance theories, particularly his political engagement with the Third Reich, and furnished detailed explications for his departure from Germany in 1937. They also agree that Laban's involvement with the regime lasted for a period long enough to allow him to play a crucial role in the transformation of German dance and body culture into a powerful tool for the diffusion of Nazi ideology (Guilbert 2000; Kant 2016; Karina and Kant [1996] 2003).

---

[7] More recently, Evelyn Dörr has also edited a book with a selection of Laban's correspondence. See Dörr (2013).

Preston-Dunlop, like other former pupils and dance scholars, has recognized Rudolf Laban's engagement with the Nazi regime, but interpreted it as a consequence of a difficult political contingency (Preston-Dunlop 1989), rather than as a more complex genealogy of both Laban's theoretical and ideological foundation and of German culture (Baxmann 2000; Guilbert 2000). Her recreations, ultimately, reveal her defensive attitude with respect to her master and to a dance tradition that she herself has contributed to. A clear symptom of the emotional dimension of memory and of the lasting effect of repression is Preston-Dunlop's assertion, made in the documentary on her recreation of *The Swinging Temple* filmed in 2012, that in 1935 Laban, who at that time held an important position inside Nazi cultural institutions, was in danger in Germany (Preston-Dunlop DVD 2012).

Preston-Dunlop's research work and recreations are the outcome of the entanglement of (auto)biographical and historical narratives. It is not inconsequential that all the dance pieces recreated by Preston-Dunlop were chosen by her because of her link with both Laban and her teacher Sylvia Bodmer, who was also a member of the Laban Chamber Dance Group. Preston-Dunlop affirmed that her discovery of Laban's repertoire was based on embodiment, described as "a process which gives tangible form to ideas [ ... ] involves the whole person [ ... ] perceiving oneself [ ... ] with kinaesthetic awareness of creating and controlling the movement [ ... ] requires that the dancer identifies him/herself with the technique's culture" (Preston-Dunlop 2002, 7). She specifies that she was able "to engage with the archival evidence with a muscle memory and perspective informed by four years of close practice with Laban" (Preston-Dunlop and Sayers 2011, 12), but also through what she learned from other teachers and dancers who worked with him (mainly Lisa Ullmann, Sylvia Bodmer, and Albrecht Knust), and from a study of dance pieces of that time, especially by Kurt Jooss (Preston-Dunlop 2013, 31–41). I argue that the tendency to refer only to a genealogical line of direct pupils of Laban, which Laure Guilbert defines as "the magical circle of direct affiliations" (Guilbert 2000, 428; my translation), also reveals the aim of these pupils to redeem a legendary vision of modern dance and of Laban's legacy.

Preston-Dunlop's recreations are the only attempts to breathe new life into Laban's repertoire, and as such they represent a precious occasion to investigate how memorial and historical narratives are at work in the contemporary (and performative) dimension of the repertoire. But can his works be effectively recreated while disregarding their ideological underpinnings? Such disregard is precisely the limitation of Preston-Dunlop's model of recreation, and it is a consequence of her limited vision of dance studies itself since it disregards well-established approaches to Laban's history.

In this chapter I will discuss how a dance legacy can be carried on by both historical research and collective and personal (bodily) memories, two approaches to the past that answer to different needs and that articulate different temporal models. To focus on how Preston-Dunlop's personal embodied memory transmits a limited idea of Laban's legacy, I will follow Aleida Assmann's suggestion that "active cultural memory" is the outcome of what the institutions charged to preserve the "past as present" do perform as relevant, whereas the archive preserves the "past as past" or what has been forgotten, missed and unused (A. Assmann 2008, 100). The transmission of Laban's vision of dance and of his career still suffers from a binary opposing his pupils' personal memories (both bodily and oral) to historical analyses performed by scholars in the archive. Aleida Assmann's model envisions instead an articulation of memory with history, based on their reciprocal recognition and on the idea that historiography and memory should be considered as complementary modes of cultural memory.

I will argue that Preston-Dunlop's recreations confirm the selective nature of her personal memory and the defensive attitude of her engagement with Laban's legacy, one that inevitably produces an anti-historical reconstruction of the past. This chapter investigates as well how to reconsider the articulation of memory and history by taking advantage of the debates conducted in the new field of danced reenactment, considered as a creative and theoretical approach to both the restoration of past dances and the rewriting of history.

## PRODUCTS, PROCESSES, AND THE PERFORMANCE OF THE AUTHENTIC

As opposed to reconstructions, which aim at reproducing a specific dance work in the present as it supposedly was, Preston-Dunlop self-consciously focuses on the relationship between the past work and the present in which they are re-performed. She names her experiments "recreations" precisely to distinguish them from reconstructions:

> If *reconstruction* is defined as seeking to repeat the parameters of an original performance, by *recreation* is meant practices that establish a freer relationship to an original work and an enhanced dialogue with the past. (Preston-Dunlop and Sayers 2011, 30)

On the one hand, Preston-Dunlop aims to return to dance pieces whose performative traditions have vanished: her embodied knowledge of Laban's theories allows her to act in the absence of living traditions. This approach assumes that bodily memory is an archive that allows her to (re)create something out of what no longer exists, and to bring about the possibility of what she describes as the potential for "a freer relationship to an original work." On the other hand, her recourse to other forms of archival documentation and to theories about historical narratives is insufficient to mark a critical distance from the past (what she defines as "to enhance a dialogue with the past"). In other words, her recreations seem more like ahistorical reconstructions of dance pieces of the past than theory-based critical reenactment.

In a recent article, Preston-Dunlop specifies that with her recreations she aimed at bringing into focus "this forgotten heritage" and at providing "a tranche of cultural, aesthetic, and choreographic discourse valuable and challenging to scholars and practitioners" (Preston-Dunlop 2011, 9). Preston-Dunlop's point of departure was her belief that Laban Dance Group's and Chamber Dance Group's repertoire could enrich the contemporary dance scene, the audiences of the twenty-first century, and dance scholarship. From her perspective, recreations are an effective tool to connect generations of students and teachers to the sources of their tradition. She has pointed out that her approach to earlier works is at once in-depth analytical and highly creative. More precisely, she affirms that recreations restore complex and multilayered creative processes to their prominent place by using the same movement and choreographic principles that Laban created for his dance pieces (Preston-Dunlop 2011, 43). She considers these recreations a testament to the endurance of Laban's choreological and choreographic principles, which have survived as embodied practices especially thanks to his pupils. For this reason, Preston-Dunlop is convinced that she could retrace a consistent part of this legacy by interviewing as many former members of Laban's companies as she could, and other pupils to whom he transmitted his theories about movement.[8] Preston-Dunlop adapted some elements of these experiments, such as duration, costumes, and music scores, to stage solutions that she felt more suitable for a contemporary audience.[9] Despite her attention to the creative process vis-à-vis the dance piece itself and the emphasis on the present, Preston-Dunlop does not explore theoretically the ways in which her recreations mediate knowledge by combining corporeal research with archival documentation. More specifically, her recreations set a past work in motion to relive it, but fail to critique it and to problematize the ways in which aesthetics and politics are mutually implicated in this repertoire. Rather, by presenting Laban's dance pieces and thought simply as a clear example of the most powerful period of *Ausdruckstanz* during the Weimar years, she demonstrates the evidence of their implicit political progressive value. Together with her own historical writings and the recording of these recreations, she also expects to enable contemporary readers and spectators to "judge for themselves" the value of Laban's choreographic production (Preston-Dunlop 2013, 4). Preston-Dunlop's attitude toward Laban's work in her recreations is ambiguous because she presents them in an apparently ideologically neutral or simplified way in order to make them understandable to contemporary audiences: this constitutes an erasure of the history of which they were a part and expression and implies that Laban's tradition is closer to a progressive and democratic than to a reactionary and, to some extent, proto-fascist oriented conception of culture (Green 1986). The theoretical frame for these recreations is what Preston-Dunlop defined as "archaeochoreology," a new disciplinary formation based on the archaeological method used to recover lost dances (Preston-Dunlop and Sayers 2011, 5). As an archaeochoreologist, Preston-Dunlop affirms that her

---

[8]  Preston-Dunlop mentions the following names: Fritz Klingenbeck, Kathe Wulff, Gertrud Snell, Ilse Loesh, Aurell Miloss, Beatrice Mazzoni, Sylvia Bodmer, Albrecht Knust, Kurt Jooss, and Lisa Ullmann. She never met personally Laban's two main performing partners: Dussia Bereska and Ruth Loeszer. See Preston-Dunlop (2013, 33–38). See also the interview between Sylvia Bodmer and Valerie Preston Dunlop while watching a performance of Laban Kammertanz (ca. 1986).

[9]  See also the interview by Martin Hargreaves of Valerie Preston-Dunlop in *Recreating Rudolf Laban's "Der Schwingende Tempel 1922"* (2012).

aim was to discover from the sources what kind of reconstruction, representation, or simulation was appropriate for Laban's dance pieces, but her only reference is the concept introduced by Mike Pearson that "[a]rchaeology is not just excavation (analysis). It must in some way synthesize (reconstruct, represent, simulate) the past" (Pearson and Thomas, 1994, 135).

Archaeochoreology is part of what Laban named "choreology," a kind of grammar and syntax of the language of movement dealing not only with its outer form, but also with its mental and emotional content (Laban [1939] 1966). As described by Preston-Dunlop, a choreological perspective

> moves beyond theories of reading dance that place either the creator, the performer or the audience in a privileged position. It proposes a triadic perspective which examines the inter-relationship of these three positions given the distinct fact that dance [ . . . ] is mediated by living, intending, feeling, thinking "bodies." (Preston-Dunlop 2002, 11–12)

In other words, choreological studies are an "intrinsic" theoretical and practical approach to dance form and content, and are considered by Preston-Dunlop as complementary to "extrinsic" studies such as politics, sociology, and aesthetics of dance, "which bring the methodology of their own discipline to bear on dance" (Preston-Dunlop 1979, 20). As Mark Franko has pointed out, an approach that aims at functioning as closely to dance as possible has "a brand of anti-historical impulse" with great debt to the eternal present implied in phenomenology, whereas "the historical conditions of its possibility are displaced in the name of dance's immediacy" (2006, 9–10).

Preston-Dunlop's recreations are the result of multiple shifts from the past to the present, from the product to the process, and from the original work to the "authentic" bodily performance. Moreover, a recreation should contain something that is not necessarily bound to its time in order to facilitate the contemporary viewers in making theatrical sense out of its original context (Preston-Dunlop and Sayers 2011, 6). The shift from the past to the present also prompts awareness of the impossible task of retrieving a lost work in its original form, precisely because the very act of retrieval produces a new work. Therefore these recreations occupy a strange status in which they are supposed to be recognized as a representation of a work of the past while signaling that they are a representation of what is in reality a contemporary work. The presence of several generations of Laban practitioners—Preston-Dunlop, Curtis-Jones, Melanie Clarke, and their students—forms an additional layer in the relationship these works establish with their historical background and the personal memories connected to it.

As Preston-Dunlop has affirmed, in recreating a dance piece from the archival traces, the bodily memory of the dancers considered as a living archive plays a special role in locating the authenticity of the past (original) work. In Laban's repertoire, she sees the authenticity in both the creative process of his choreography and in the experimental nature of his works, and she aims at reliving it performatively in the present (Preston-Dunlop 2013, 33).

# RETRACING LABAN'S CHOREOGRAPHIC
# AND IDEOLOGICAL LEGACY

The body of Laban's choreographic repertoire is large and covers three decades, from the 1910s to the 1930s. In *Rudolf Laban: Man of Theater*, Preston-Dunlop explains why her recreations are limited to Laban's dance pieces of the 1920s by quoting Alfred Schlee, an important German publisher and dance critic at that time, who affirms that this was the most remarkable period of *Ausdruckstanz* (Preston-Dunlop 2013, 2). She does not explain, however, to what extent this chronological limitation involves the possibility of dodging the production of the 1910s and the early 1930s. Before and during World War I, Laban made his first major experiments in Monte Verità, near Ascona, where choreography and dance were considered important tools to forge a new anti-bourgeois "cultural community" that would be able to carry the seeds of a social reawakening (Laban 1920). Here his thought and practice were markedly imbued with occultist and mystical themes and were oriented toward the building of a cultic community, and he shared his experiments with disciples of other trends and cults (among them nudists, theosophists, vegetarians), and joined the *Ordo Templi Orientis*, a version of occult Freemasonry. By adapting its teaching to the art of the body, Laban focused on his ideas of a *Festkultur* (festival culture) and also created new forms of ritual dance such as *chorische Fest* (choral festival) (Kew 1999). In 1930 Laban was appointed director of movement and dance at the State Theaters in Berlin (a role that included the position of ballet-master at the Berlin State Opera); after the National Socialists came to power in 1933, he took a leading role in reorganizing German dance, becoming the head of its most important institutions, including *Deutsche Tanzbühne* (German Dance Theater), the *Deutsche Meister-Stätten für Tanz* (German Master Studio for Dance), and the *Deutsche Tanzfestspiele* (German Dance Festival). Laban's vision of a choral (mass) dance for a cultic community was taking its ultimate form with the commission of *Vom Tauwind und der Neuen Freude* (*Of the Spring Wind and the New Joy*), one of the artistic events planned for the opening of the Berlin Olympic Games in 1936. The movement choir was a new genre Laban created in the 1920s primarily for lay dancers; it embodied his ideal of the communitarian dimension of both dance and society. This movement choir was conceived for more than one thousand participants and was disseminated via notated scores to lay dancers in thirty German cities. *Of the Spring Wind and the New Joy* was cancelled, however, at the last moment by Joseph Goebbels, the Nazi Enlightenment and Propaganda minister, who officially justified the decision by claiming that Laban's approach was overly "intellectual," though the cancellation was more the result of interpersonal conflicts than of ideological differences between Laban and the Nazi bureaucracy (Guilbert 2000, 221–342). Despite this disappointment, Laban aspired to maintain his politically advantageous positions, but newly appointed officials at Goebbels's ministry curtailed his leadership. In 1937, facing political isolation, he decided to leave the country, and the following year he migrated to Great Britain, where he portrayed himself as a victim of the regime and where he spent the rest of his life teaching and developing his theories. His artistic career was over. On her side, Preston-Dunlop, like many other pupils and some scholars, depicts Laban's practice and theory as part and parcel of an aesthetically revolutionary and politically progressive European modern dance and claims that the Nazis misused and exploited the irrational component of Laban's thought for their own ideological purposes (Preston-Dunlop 1988, 1998). Preston-Dunlop's decision to work exclusively on Laban's repertoire of the 1920s indeed functions to reiterate this interpretation of Laban tradition as aesthetically and politically progressive.

In the 1920s, Laban started to collaborate with important theaters in Germany, founded a network of schools called *Labanschulen*, an institute named *Choreographisches Institut* (Choreographic Institute), and his two dance companies. In this context, the participants of his movement choirs became immersed in the flow of movement, taking pleasure in what Laban envisioned as a mystical merging in a cultic celebration. The context of these productions, the years of intense political instability and artistic and cultural efflorescence of the Weimar Republic, is what Preston-Dunlop assumes as the political frame with which to explain the ideological substance of Laban's dance pieces of that time. In doing so, rather than questioning their transformation in the present, her recreations contribute to determining the ways in which figures of thought and regimes of practice are received in the present time and are perceived as dispossessed of the discursive foundations of their historical background. This is even more problematic given the importance Laban accorded choreography as a way of experiencing and knowing the world, and embodying practices as ways of establishing social relations. Preston-Dunlop's recreations do understand dance as a form of knowledge production, but they do not recognize its potential to raise questions about the nature of the very knowledge and practices that are the object of her research.

# RECREATIONS BETWEEN PAST AND PRESENT, AESTHETICS AND POLITICS

An interesting example of how the multiple problems raised by Preston-Dunlop's approach to Laban's dance pieces intertwine is her latest experiments, the recreation of *Der Schwingende Tempel* (*The Swinging Temple*, 1922). Originally created during the Weimar Republic for the Laban Dance Group, and performed in two versions during the 1920s, the piece also represents a unique case in Laban's repertoire because it was partially recreated in 1952 by Lisa Ullmann with Diana Jordan and Sylvia Bodmer using non-professional dancers during a summer school in Great Britain. Probably they were stimulated by the same problem experienced by Preston-Dunlop and Melanie Clarke, who selected it to better understand and explain Laban's controversial spiritual research. Recently, Preston-Dunlop also collaborated on a movement choir dance film event performed at the amphitheatre of the Trinity Laban and featuring musicians and one hundred dancers aged nine to eighty. This choir is based on *The Swinging Temple* and on the *Dying Procession* from the second section of *Die Grünen Clowns* (*The Green Clowns*, 1926) called *War*, both considered by the recreators as examples of Laban's response to war's aftermath, chaos, and suffering.[10] Their simplistic interpretation of the structure and the meaning of the piece and their use of it to commemorate the Great War's centennial are revealing of the a-historical perspective of their own work and of their difficulties in transforming this material into a contemporary performance suitable for spectators who have little knowledge of Laban's theories and his history. The outcome is that the historical complexity of Laban's thought and work does not materialize precisely because Preston-Dunlop's recreations and the audience's lack of context fuel one another, thus expanding a memory gap that becomes increasingly difficult to fill.

In his autobiography *Ein Leben für den Tanz*, published in German in 1935 and translated into English only 40 years later, many chapters of which are named after a particular choreography,[11] Laban writes about *The Swinging Temple* as an image of a community whose goal was to find the perfect harmonic dimension after having experienced individuality and diversity depicted as a negative interlude of human evolution. In this text, Laban affirms as well that this is his vision for the future. Preston-Dunlop and Curtis-Jones refer to this book as one of the major primary written sources for many recreations, and consider the descriptions and critical inputs that Laban gives about some of his choreographies as a starting point to understand their structures and meanings. The genre of this work (an autobiography), the chronological distance between the first productions of these pieces and Laban's descriptions, and the fact that the book appeared in a radically different political context are all unexplored issues in their research work. It would be certainly too easy to claim that Laban only saw in the Third Reich an opportunity to fulfil his artistic vision since it was also a question of his survival. On the other hand, Preston-Dunlop and Curtis-Jones do not properly evaluate the historical context that made his words acceptable for publication.

Laban's goal throughout his life was certainly to compose "works in praise of the community and of dancing together" (Laban 1975, 67) as much as to create communities or school networks where what he addressed as a new harmony could be experienced. Likewise, he decided to invest in dance in a specific historical context, post–World War I, where the search for a new and true spiritual content for all the arts was a major interest, enforced by the need to discover a meaningful alternative to the evils of destruction and a way to deal with modernization. He was persuaded that through the ecstasy of dance, human beings could dwell in the realm of pure spirit. Laban's artistic and spiritual vision of the world rejected rationality and preached the

---

[10] *In Memoriam 2014* (2015, 30). For a description of the project, see http://inmemoriam2014.org.uk/about.html.

[11] The chapters named after a particular choreography are *Nacht* (*Night*, 1927), *Der Schwingende Tempel* (*The Swinging Temple*, 1921), *Gaukelei* (*Illusions*, 1923), *Der Spielmann* (*The Fiddler*, 1916), *Titan* (*The Titan*, 1927), and *Alltag und Fest* (*Everyday and Festival*, 1929), in which he discusses the life experiences that were the impetus for each work.

possibility of transcendence (Laban 1920). His Masonic aspirations are mentioned by his pupils and by scholars, yet the social and political implications of this liaison have not been fully considered by his pupils. Not only did he never depart from the framework he constructed in his youth, but his active affiliation with the Masonic order and his engagement in this philosophy nourished his way of thinking about movement, dance, and choreography. For Laban, the communal body was necessary "to incorporate the crucial knowledge about harmonic relationships into the individual human being's activity," and harmony was a goal to overcome bodily matter and to access a new spiritual dimension (Kant 2002, 46).

*The Swinging Temple* is an example of his commitment to this specific spiritual dimension, dealing with the transformation of a group of people not only from the primordial chaos, as Laban named it, to reality and the celebration of differences, but also from the affirmation of individualism, which led society into tensions and conflicts, toward final transcendence and harmony. An oscillating group of people stands here for a communal moving body, able to create a virtual temple, a sacred space. The piece, like many others performed by the Dance Group, combined abstract forms and organic movements, using principles of contrast and counterpoint, synchrony and asynchrony between individuals and the group, and structured improvisations based on the kinetic intention.

In Preston-Dunlop's recreation, *The Swinging Temple* is presented as a dance piece nourished by Laban's spiritual attitude and profound mystical religious commitment, whose traces she has recovered in the sources of his creative process, such as prayer exercises and gestures, the trance-like revolving of the Dervishes, and his Rosicrucian knowledge. She explains Laban's attraction for this spiritual dimension and his tension toward an ideal and ultimate harmonic status of a human being as a typical expression of the German cultural and social context of the early 1900s, but she never binds them to the racist views that were the expression of the reactionary modernism of that time, and of Laban's (and others) aspirations to build a cultic community (Guilbert 2011, 55; Kant 2002). Neither does she inquire into them for their potential in transmitting Laban's occult practices and knowledge through embodiment and actions, and therefore in providing a formal structure for not only his spiritual vision, but also his social and political vision. It is not surprising that in the documentary on her recreation of *The Swinging Temple*, Preston-Dunlop admits to have introduced "delicately" these issues to the students learning, performing, and experiencing it. She recognizes as well the difficulties she confronted in transforming the sense of Laban's spirituality into inspiring material for them. This approach to the most problematic and lesser known aspects of Laban's practice and theory is not transmitted as part of a complex historical discourse, but rather as a simplified version of her personal critical perspective.

The way in which Preston-Dunlop and Curtis-Jones display Laban's choreographic patterns, making them occupy a cultural and artistic space in our time, renders their recreations even more problematic. Laban's approach to dance was radically new at that time not only because it produced unfinished ongoing fleeting works, but also because it involved the dancers in the creative process. Both companies were resident (in Stuttgart and later in Hamburg), both treated dance as a theatrical art form, and both challenged the audience with choreographic experiments that were often the results of an intense collaboration between Laban and his dancers that also included work on the costumes and the basic stage designs. The Chamber Dance Group, however, was specialized and could be defined as a small-scale repertoire addressed to an audience that followed the entire season and that expected to see a great number of new and varied productions. For this reason, each dance piece could have been repeated on different occasions with totally different costumes, music, and title, performed by a man and then by a woman, and adapted to different spaces and number of dancers. Often, some choreographic sequences and even entire parts of a previous dance piece were adapted to the new one with few changes. Laban did not invent a dance technique, as much as a way of moving the body, a way of looking at it and conceptualizing it through a basic vocabulary of expressive movement and a series of exercises based on correspondences between spatial directions and dynamic qualities and the concepts of weight, time, space, and flow. Improvisation and creativity were considered as crucial as movement theory since Laban's goal was to make dancers aware of internal impulses and their relationship with the possibilities of moving the body.

Since most of the pieces were not created entirely by Laban, who also promoted the dancers' creative autonomy, they made authoriality a fluid issue. Together with the performative quality of both these unstable artifacts and the process of recovery, the collaboration between the dancers and the choreographer is one of the aspects that Preston-Dunlop seems to have appreciated more about Chamber Dance Group's productions and that convinced her to make them the core of her recreation work. What makes her project problematic—in presenting these pieces and their creative process to a contemporary audience—is the way she links them to dance history and to its political dimension. The parallel she suggests between Laban's *Ausdruckstanz* and the postmodern methods of the two twenty-first-century artists is her way of attributing to the dancer-choreographer relationship of the 1920s the democratic political dimension of the 1960s and the 1970s and its "relish for exploring process rather than making a fetish of the product" (Preston-Dunlop and Sayers 2011, 7). Not only did postmodern dancers in the United States avoid framing dance within the institutional and commercial demands of their time, and took part in civil society's movements against government policies, driven by the need for a better model of democracy and a expanded vision of freedom, but with their practices and performances they also radically challenged the hierarchical model that governed most relationships between choreographers (authors) and dancers (performers) from ballet to modern dance, which involved a collective identification with the desires of one person (Banes 1987, 1993; Burt 2006). Laban's communitarian projects were not a model for egalitarian relationships that entailed the challenging of power dynamics, and the delicate balance between the dancers' autonomy and dependency on the master was one of the ambiguous features of the pedagogic model of (German) modern dance (Guilbert 2000, 49).

# CIRCULAR MEMORIES, HISTORICAL NARRATIVES, AND THE REPRESENTATION OF TEMPORALITIES

The relationship between archive and (bodily) memory has been largely debated in recent years, and the notion of dance and performance as anti-archive has become central to maintaining that their most constitutive component is ephemerality (Phelan 1993). Other scholars (Franko 2007; Franco and Nordera 2010; Roach 1996; Schneider 2001, 2011; Taylor 2003) have asked what kinds of political and epistemological opportunities are lost, precisely by considering performance as ontologically ephemeral. Together with a new inquiry into reconstruction and authenticity that starts from a conceptual reconsideration of repeatability and reproduction, the field of danced reenactment offers a new practical-theoretical approach to what an archive is with respect to embodied memory. More specifically, in his Introduction to this volume (Chapter 1), Mark Franko asks how the transference of memory operates in the absence of first-person experience. If, as suggested by Rebecca Schneider, reenactments are a form of "counter-memory" and of "re-documentation" (2001, 106), we are entitled to ask whose memory is at work in Preston-Dunlop's recreations. And what do they document beside her explicit intentions? In other words, to what extent does the affection for her mentor and the psychological implications of being one of the last of Laban's pupils still involved in the transmission of his vision of dance (but who did not dance them originally) enrich and/or limit her critical perspective on the historical dimension of this legacy? And, last but not least, how could such great oblivion of Laban's choreographic body of work—and more generally *Ausdruckstanz*, which is considered by scholars and artists as a central phenomenon for the development of European modern dance—have followed for so long (Vertinsky 2010)?

For a long time the majority of studies concerning Laban's life and career followed an account of the history that resulted from unclear distinctions of roles and professional profiles between artists, critics, and dance scholars. Laban's direct and indirect pupils have transformed their personal experiences and their bodily memories from primary sources into historical narratives, which have been received as authentic by the readership by virtue of the genealogical line of transmission of their knowledge. The mode and timing of Laban's departure from Germany had an important impact in this situation. As he was unable to carry all his personal papers, which were then at the Berlin Opera, they were stored in a private archive until the 1970s and then at the Dance Archive in Leipzig, where they were almost inaccessible for foreign scholars until the fall of the Berlin Wall. Another portion of the documents was held in Great Britain by John Hodgson, a former student of Laban, and became part of his private archive that only in recent years has been made accessible to the public at Leeds University Library. Other documents belonging to Laban and written in several languages were spread in many private archives, whose heirs in recent times donated to public institutions. In Great Britain the documents that Laban brought with him and those he collected until he died were passed on to Ullmann, who donated them to the National Resource Centre for Dance at the University of Surrey, where the Laban Archive was opened in the mid-1980s, and other material has been acquired by the Laban Centre (Franco 2007). Together, these archival situations explain why the oral transmission of Laban's theories and practices became dominant in respect to the historical approach to his thought and career. Moreover, despite the work of historians who have questioned these narratives and structural models by bringing to the surface the constructed and fragmented nature of individual and collective memory, Laban's historiography can still count on studies based on what is considered firsthand knowledge of this dance tradition. The resistance demonstrated by these authors to different versions of what they assume Laban's history to be should be taken as an integral part of his tradition.

Historical research on Laban's choreographic legacy, carried out by Preston-Dunlop, was stimulated by a desire to retrace the historical background of what she knew mainly as a personal (bodily) memory of her education, and by the first extensive archival studies conducted by Vera Maletic, in her book dedicated to the development of Laban's thought and theories (Maletic 1987). A more recent example of this scholarly attitude is the *The Laban Sourcebook* (2011) edited by Dick McCaw,[12] who conceived it as a tool for Laban practitioners and dance scholars. This *Sourcebook*, which presents a series of English translations of texts written by Laban and previously available only as archival documents or published in the original German, was also an important reference for Preston-Dunlop as her last recreations of Laban's repertoire. The editor, who is not a scholar, legitimizes himself in this publication by claiming to have become a bodily archive through his practical learning (McCaw 2013, 407). In his general introduction, the son of Sylvia Bodmer, Walter, affirms that he can authoritatively speak about this tradition precisely because of his direct affiliation with it, and all the authors, with the exception of Dörr and Stefanie Sachsenmaier, who have selected and introduced the texts are defined as "Laban scholars" by virtue of their personal relationship with Laban, as students or dancers (McCaw 2011, 2).[13] For a dance scholar, *The Laban Sourcebook* and *Rudolf Laban: Man of Theatre* represent a dangerous model of the circularity of memory, rather than precious resources. Here cultural memory informs historical writings that then become the reference point for recreations structured mainly around embodied knowledge.

Preston-Dunlop's personal embodied memory is part of a collective memory, which, following Jan Assmann, is the combination of communicative and cultural memory

[12]  McCaw comes from a background as a theater festival organizer, has arranged Geraldine Stephenson's private archive (one of the first students in 1946 at the Art of Movement Studio in Manchester), and took some practical lessons with her, and later worked on the Laban archive in Leeds. He is currently a Lecturer in Drama and Theatre at the Royal Holloway University of London.

[13]  Vera Maletic, Roderyk Lange, Valerie Preston-Dunlop, Warren Lamb, Anna Carlisle, Marion North, Janet Kaylo, and Carol Lynne Moore.

(J. Assmann 2008, 117). Whereas communicative memory lives in everyday interaction and communication, and is not supported by any institutions or cultivated by specialists, cultural memory carries events of the past and can be mediated by specific dances and performances as much as by texts. Cultural memory is passed on by teachers, artists, and scholars, among others, and it reaches back only so far as the past can be reclaimed as "ours" (and not as it is investigated by archaeologists and historians). For these reasons, the participation of a group in communicative memory is diffuse, whereas the participation of a group in cultural memory is always highly differentiated. Moreover, Aleida Assmann calls "active cultural memory" the interplay of religion, art, and history, resulting from processes of selection and collection managed by institutions charged to preserve the "past as present" (A. Assmann 2008, 100). These processes, which we call "canonization," secure for certain artifacts a lasting place in the cultural "working memory of a society" or "functional memory," a form of future-oriented memory (A. Assmann 2012, 127). Conversely, the institutions of "passive cultural memory," such as archives, preserve the "past as past," and therefore can be considered as the "reference memory of a society" or as "storage memory." In other words, the archive preserves what has been neglected and creates a meta-memory, a formally organized repertoire of missed opportunities, alternative options, and unused and unincorporated material. Laban's heritage is a combination of active cultural memory (the "past as present"), still transmitted after his death by different generations of teachers in the institution(s) carrying his name, and of passive cultural memory (the "past as past"), stored in various archives.

By preserving the "past as present," Preston-Dunlop's recreations produce a selection of Laban's choreographies that makes possible their reception as canonical. More specifically, in Preston-Dunlop's recreations an embodied memory, perceived as a-temporal, and a choreological approach driven by an anti-historical impulse generate what Guilbert defines as "a selective memory functioning at the expense of the awareness of the work that history does to the bodies and that produces the oblivion" (2000, 428; my translation). In other words, these recreations certainly work not only as systems of storing knowledge of both the past and the present, but also as forms of an active remembering that produces an active forgetting of many aspects and events of this very past. Jacques Derrida reminds us of the extent to which oblivion leaves traces and recommends that institutions should preserve the memory of what they tend to exclude, to avoid the possibility that they can be marked precisely by what they expel because it has been experienced as a threat (1990, 17). But how would it be possible to imagine a dimension where memory—and the memory of what has been excluded—can interact with history, and embodied knowledge with archival research?

Following the idea that history is a "dynamic continuity rather than a series of completed events," Preston-Dunlop engaged anew in the creation of a series of works, rather than bringing to the stage dance pieces that have been preserved in their original form. She affirms as well that her recreations can "reveal the work's potential for future performances" (Preston-Dunlop 2013, 39–41), precisely by securing a lasting place in a future-oriented memory, the "working memory of a society." This practical and theoretical model is close to what Diana Taylor suggests in her seminal study when she specifies that the range of cultural memory embodied and transmitted through performances and bodily techniques is coextensive with the performed embodied repertoires repeated in a "constant state of againness" (2003, 21). From a different theoretical perspective, to trouble our sense of "what is past in the past," Mark Franko envisions the possibility of reenactments connecting embodied memory and the archive "in and through choreography" (Chapter 1 in this volume). This is precisely the missing point of Preston-Dunlop's recreations.

Distancing herself from a traditional way of conceptualizing the relationship between memory and history as a form of binary opposition or in terms of an equation, Aleida Assmann points out that there is no historiography without some form of memory and that they should rather be seen as two complementary modes of cultural memory (A. Assmann 2012, 123). To link them to each other, she has envisaged a structure made of foreground and background, which should secure a prospective relationship that is able to account for the dynamics of change in personal and cultural memory. This structure allows making the elements of the two memories interchangeable, and their patterns of meaning alterable, by keeping the borders between storage memory and functional memory permeable. It is precisely the border traffic between these different realms of cultural memory that can illuminate and transmit the complexities of history, as much as the traffic between bodies and ideologies acquired through the dancing and the ways it is experienced, conceptualized, and, last but not least, historicized. Preston-Dunlop's recreations cannot ensure for Laban's legacy a shared dimension where those who claim to transmit it as a form of embodied memory and those who approach it as history do not experience conflicts. On the contrary, the spatial model described by Aleida Assmann allows for multiple shifts of different memories, which, in turn, can fuel reenactments that challenge our assumptions about representations of historical temporalities by incorporating a critical dimension to the past of dance pieces that have been forgotten, allowing their conceptual and ideological substance to rise to the surface in performance.

## WORKS CITED

Assmann, Aleida. 2008. "Canon and Archive." In *Cultural Memory Studies: An International and Interdisciplinary Handbook*, edited by Astrid Erll and Nünning Ansgar, 97–107. Berlin: De Gruyer.

Assmann, Aleida. 2012. *Cultural Memory and Western Civilization: Functions, Media, Archives.* Cambridge, UK: Cambridge University Press (1st ed., 1999. *Erinnerungsräume: Formen und Wandlungen des Kulturellen Gedächtnisses.* Munich: C. H. Beck Verlag).

Assmann, Jan. 2008. "Communicative and Cultural Memory." In *Cultural Memory Studies: An International and Interdisciplinary Handbook*, edited by Astrid Erll and Nünning Ansgar, 104–118. Berlin: De Gruyer.

Banes, Sally. 1987. *Terpsichore in Sneakers: Post-Modern Dance.* Middletown, CT: Wesleyan University Press.

Banes, Sally. 1993. *Democracy's Body: Judson Dance Theatre, 1962–1964*. Durham, NC, and London: Duke University Press.

Baxmann, Inge. 2000. *Mythos: Gemeinschaft. Körper- und Tanzkulturen der Moderne*. München: Wilhelm Fink Verlag.

Burt, Ramsay. 2006. *Judson Dance Theater: Performative Traces*. New York: Routledge.

Derrida, Jacques. 1990. *Du droit à la philosophie*. Paris: Galilée.

Dörr, Evelyn. 2004 [2nd expanded version 2008]. *Rudolf Laban: Das choreographische Theater*. Norderstedt b. Hamburg: Books on Demand.

Dörr, Evelyn. 2005. *Rudolf Laban: Die Schrift des Tänzers: Ein Portrait*. Norderstedt b. Hamburg: Books on Demand.

Dörr, Evelyn. 2007. *Rudolf Laban: The Dancer of the Crystal*. Lanham, MD: The Scarecrow Press.

Dörr, Evelyn. 2013. *Also, die Damen voran! Rudolf Laban in Briefen an Tänzers, Choreographen, und Tazpädagogen*. Vol. 1, *1912–1918*. Norderstedt b. Hamburg: Books on Demand.

Franco, Susanne. 2007. "*Ausdruckstanz*: Traditions, Translations, Transmissions." In *Dance Discourses: Keywords in Dance Research*, edited by Susanne Franco and Marina Nordera, 80–98. New York and London: Routledge.

Franco, Susanne, and Marina Nordera. 2010. "Contro l'effimero." In *Ricordanze: Memoria in movimento e coreografie della storia*, edited by Susanne Franco and Marina Nordera, xviii–xxxv. Torino: Utet Università, 2010.

Franko, Mark. 2006. "Dance and the Political: States of Exception." *Dance Research Journal* 38(1–2): 3–18.

Green, Martin. 1986. *Mountain of Truth: The Counterculture Begins, Ascona, 1900–1920*. Hanover, NH: University Press of New England for Tufts University Press.

Guilbert, Laure. 2011 *Danser avec le IIIe Reich Les danseurs modernes et le nazisme*. Paris: André Versailles. (1st ed., Bruxelles: Complexe, 2000).

Hodgson, John, and Valerie Preston-Dunlop. 1990. *Rudolf Laban: An Introduction to His Work and Influence*. Plymouth, MA: Northcote House.

Laban, Rudolf. 1920. *Die Welt des Tänzers*. Stuttgart: Verlag Walter Seyfert.

Laban, Rudolf. [1939] 1966. *Choreutics*. Annotated and edited by Lisa Ullmann. London: MacDonald and Evans (published in US as *The Language of Movement: A Guide Book to Choreutics*. Boston: Plays).

Laban, Rudolf. 1975. *A Life for Dance: Reminiscences*. Translated and annotated by Lisa Ullmann. London: Macdonald and Evans. (1st ed., 1935. *Ein Leben für den Tanz*. Dresden: Carl Reissner Verlag).

Kant, Marion. 2002. "Laban's Secret Religion." *Discourses in Dance* 1(2): 43–62.

Kant, Marion, 2016. "German Gymnastics, Modern German Dance, and Nazi Aesthetics." *Dance Research Journal* 48(2): 4–25.

Kew, Carole. 1999. "From Weimar Movement Choir to Nazi Community Dance: The Rise and Fall of Rudolf Laban's Festkultur." *Dance Research* 17(2): 73–96.

Karina, Lilian, and Marion Kant. 2003. *Hitler's Dancers: German Modern Dance and the Third Reich*. Oxford and New York: Berghan Books (or. ed. *Tanz unterm Hakenkreuz*, Berlin, Henschel, 1996).

Maletic, Vera. 1987. *Body-Space-Experience: The Development of Rudolf Laban's Movement and Dance Concepts*. Berlin, New York, and Amsterdam: Mouton de Gruyter.

McCaw, Dick, ed. 2011. *The Laban Sourcebook*. London: Routledge.

McCaw, Dick. 2013. "Danger UXB, or My Career in Archives." *Contemporary Theatre Review* 23(3): 403–410.

Pearson, Mike, and Julian Thomas. 1994. "Theatre/Archaeology." *The Drama Review* 38(4): 133–161.

Phelan, Peggy. 1993. *Unmarked*. London: Routledge, 1993.

Preston-Dunlop, Valerie. 1966–1967. *Readers in Kinetography Laban*, 3 vols. London: MacDonald & Evans.

Preston-Dunlop, Valerie. 1979. *Dance is a Language, isn't it?*. London: Laban Center.

Preston-Dunlop, Valerie. 1983. "Choreutics Concepts and Practice." *Dance Research* 1: 77–88.

Preston-Dunlop, Valerie. 1988. "Laban and the Nazis: Towards an Understanding of Rudolf Laban and the Third Reich." *Dance Theatre Journal* 6(2): 4–7.

Preston-Dunlop, Valerie. 1989. "The Making of the Modern Dance. Rudolf Laban: The Seminal Years in Munich, 1910–14." *Dance Theatre Journal* 7(3–4): 11–16.

Preston-Dunlop, Valerie. 1990. "The Making of the Modern Dance: Laban's Dance Activities in Munich and Ascona in 1913 and 1914." *Dance Theatre Journal* 10(4): 10–13.

Preston-Dunlop, Valerie. 1993. "The Making of the Modern Dance: The Nightmare Years in Zurich 1914–1919." *Dance Theatre Journal* 10(3): 14–19, 33–35.

Preston-Dunlop, Valerie. 1998. *Rudolf Laban: An Extraordinary Life*. London: Dance Books.

Preston-Dunlop, Valerie. 2002. "Issues in Revivals and Re-Creations: A Choreological Enquiry." In *Dance and the Performative*, edited by Valerie Preston-Dunlop and Ana Sanchez Colberg, 197–217. London: Verve Publishing.

Preston-Dunlop, Valerie. 2013. *Rudolf Laban: Man of Theatre*. London: Dance Books.

Preston-Dunlop, Valerie, ed. 1979. *Dancing and Dance Theory*. London: Laban Centenary Publication.

Preston-Dunlop, Valerie, and Lesley-Anne Sayers. 2011. "Gained in Translation: Recreation as Creative Practice." *Dance Chronicle* 34(1): 5–45.

Roach, Joseph. 1996. *Cities of the Dead: Circum-Atlantic Performance*. New York: Columbia University Press.

Schneider, Rebecca. 2001. "Archives Performance Remains." *Performance Research* 6(2): 100–108.

Schneider, Rebecca. 2011. *Performing Remains: Art and War in Times of Theatrical Reenactment*. London: Routledge.

Taylor, Diana. 2003. *The Archive and the Repertoire: Performing Cultural Memory in the Americas*. Durham, NC: Duke University Press.

Vertinsky, Patricia. 2010. "From Dance under the Swastika to Movement Education: A Study of Embodied Culture." In *Performative Body Spaces: Corporeal Topographies in Literature, Theatre, Dance, and the Visual Arts*, edited by Markus Hallensleben, 43–55. Amsterdam and New York: Editions Rodopi.

## Videos

Bodmer, Sylvia. 1986. "Interview with Valerie Preston-Dunlop Whilst Watching 'Laban Kammertanz 1986.'" https://vimeo.com/79971880 (accessed June 5, 2016).

*In Memoriam 2014*. 2015. Trinity Laban Conservatoire of Music and Dance, DVD, London.

*Laban Dance Works: Recreations from Laban's Chamber Dance Repertoire, 1923–1928: Documentary*. 2002. Valerie Preston-Dunlop, DVD, London, Verve.

*Recreating Rudolf Laban's Die Grünen Clowns, 1928: Performance and Documentary*. 2008. Alison Curtis-Jones and Valerie Preston-Dunlop, directed by Lesley-Anne Sayers, Trinity Laban, DVD, London, Barefoot-Dancer Productions and IDM.

*Recreating Rudolf Laban's "Der Schwingende Tempel" 1922: Performance and Documentary*. 2012. Melanie Clarke, Robert Coleridge, Valerie Preston-Dunlop, Trinity Laban Conservatoire of Music and Dance, DVD, London, IDM.

*Recreating Rudolf Laban's "Nacht" 1927: Performance and Documentary*. 2012. Alison Curtis-Jones and Valerie Preston-Dunlop, Trinity Laban Conservatoire of Music and Dance, DVD, London, IDM.

*Recreating Rudolf Laban's Solos and Duos (Mondäne, Krystall, Marotte, Orchidée, Ekstatische, Rosetten, Bizarre): Performance and Documentary*. 2013. Alison Curtis-Jones and Valerie Preston-Dunlop, Trinity Laban Conservatoire of Music and Dance, DVD, London, Verve.

# PART III

## PROLEPTIC ITERATION

CHAPTER 8

························································································

# TO THE LETTER

*Lettrism, Dance, Reenactment*

························································································

FRÉDÉRIC POUILLAUDE

THE application of Lettrist principles to dance, attempted by Isidore Isou and Maurice Lemaître between 1953 and 1965, is something that neither historians of dance nor experts on the avant-garde know very much about. Indeed, these forays into choreography seem to have been insignificant on two fronts: that of dance (they had scarcely any impact on the history of twentieth-century choreography) and, comparatively speaking, that of Lettrism itself, which was much better known for work in the fields of poetry, art, and cinema, or for its political and philosophical doctrines. A recent piece, however, staged by the choreographer Olivia Grandville, and entitled *Le Cabaret discrépant*,[1] had the great merit of introducing the public to these experiments in Lettrist dance, now wholly forgotten, and to the theoretical and poetic texts that accompanied them. It is this piece that I intend to examine here, following two lines of analysis: on the one hand, the use of quotation that forms the basis of Olivia Grandville's approach, and on the other, the effect of temporal indeterminacy produced by quotation used in this way.

## LETTRIST DANCE?
## WORKS AND TEXTUAL SOURCES

First of all, a brief inventory of "Lettrist choreographic works" is necessary. This inventory will also be an opportunity to detail the various textual sources still available to contemporary artists or theoreticians.

---

[1] *Le Cabaret discrépant*, inspired by Isidore Isou, created by Olivia Grandville, lighting and artistic collaboration by Yves Godin, with Vincent Dupont, Hubertus Biermann, Olivia Grandville, Catherine Legrand, Laurent Pichaud, Sylvain Prunenec, Pascal Quéneau, and Manuel Vallade. Production in July 2011 at the Festival of Avignon.

In 1953, in an issue of the *Revue musicale* devoted to ballet, Isidore Isou published an article entitled "Manifeste de la danse ciselante" (Manifesto of Chiseling Dance), also known as "Manifeste de la danse isouïenne" (Manifesto of Isouan Dance).[2] One year later he applied the principles of this manifesto to a theatrical work entitled *La Marche des jongleurs* (*The Walk of the Jugglers*), and considered this to be his "first gestural accomplishment." For his part, Maurice Lemaître staged two choreographic works in 1959: the *Fugue mimique n°1* (*Mimic Fugue no. 1*) (January 1959, Théâtre du Tertre) and the *Premier sonnet gesticulaire* (*First Gestural Sonnet*) (June 1959, Théâtre Récamier, as part of the Experimental Dance Theater directed by Dinah Maggie, a prominent dance critic of the 1950s). In 1960, he published *La Danse et le mime ciselants, lettristes et hypergraphiques* (*Hypergraphic, Lettrist, and Chiseling Dance and Mime*),[3] in which these first two pieces are taken again and presented in the form of verbal scores. This book is introduced by a long preface, both historical and theoretical, by Isou: "La danse et la pantomime de l'Antiquité aux Lettristes" (Dance and Pantomime from Antiquity to the Lettrists). Finally, in 1965, Isou published his own "choreographic summa," collecting all his ballets under the general title of *Ballets ciselants, polythanasiques, hypergraphiques et infinitésimaux* (*Chiseling, Polythanasic, Hypergraphic, and Infinitesimal Ballets*).[4] This book contains, in the form of theoretical texts and verbal instructions, ten choreographic works, some of which were never publicly performed, at least by the time the work appeared: *14 Petits ballets ou somme chorégraphique; La Danse hermétique des doigts et des jambes; Étude de langue; La Promenade; Essai d'anti-ballet; Déclaration sur la personne humaine* (*Ballet à peine existant*); *Le quasi anti-ballet; Manifeste de la danse a-optique ou de la danse-débat; Recherches pour un ballet infinitésimal;* and *Ballet provocation* (*Simple, Double, Bivalent et Polyvalent*) (*14 Little Ballets or Choreographic Dream; The Hermetic Dance of the Fingers and Legs; Tongue Study; Walk; Anti-Ballet Experiment; Declaration on the Human Person (Ballet hardly existing); The Quasi Anti-Ballet; Manifesto of the A-Optic Ballet or the Debate Dance; Research for an Infinitesimal Ballet; and Provocation Ballet [Single, Double, Bivalent, and Polyvalent]*). Because of a quarrel between Dinah Maggie and Isou, the *14 Petits Ballets*, initially accepted by the Théâtre de l'Essai de la Danse for performance in June 1960, were not in the end put on until December 1960, in the Galerie des quatre saisons, as part of the Festival d'Avant-garde.[5] *La Danse hermétique des doigts et des jambes*, the *Déclaration sur la personne humaine*, and the *Manifeste de la danse a-optique ou de la danse-débat* were performed in May 1961 before the selection committee of the Théâtre d'Essai de la Danse, in the rehearsal room of the Théâtre des Champs-Elysées.[6] The other ballets

---

[2] Isidore Isou, "Manifeste de la danse isouienne, " *Revue musicale*, 219 (1953), Paris.

[3] Maurice Lemaître, *La Danse et le mime ciselants, lettristes et hypergraphiques*, preceded by "La danse et la pantomime de l'Antiquité aux Lettristes" by Isidore Isou (1960).

[4] Isidore Isou, *Ballets ciselants, polythanasiques, hypergraphiques et infinitésimaux (1960–1964)* (1965).

[5] On this point see Isou, *Ballets ciselants, polythanasiques, hypergraphiques et infinitésimaux* (1965, 5); see also, for Maurice Lemaître's point of view on this affair, Lemaître, *La Danse et le mime ciselants, lettristes, hypergraphiques* (1960, 41–42).

[6] Ibid.

were not performed until February 1965, during an event staged at the Maison du spectateur, which brought together all the choreographies of Isou published in the work mentioned earlier.[7]

Such then is the Lettrist corpus, both artistic and theoretical, as regards dance. It is on this corpus that Olivia Grandville's piece draws; in taking up, in particular, the score for the dancer in the *Premier sonnet gesticulaire* by Lemaître (originally performed by Colette Desbrosses), all of Isou's *14 Petits Ballets*, and five of the other pieces collected in the *Ballets ciselants, polythanasiques, hypergraphiques et infinitésimaux* (*La Promenade, Manifeste de la danse a-optique, Ballet provocation, Recherches pour un ballet infinitésimal, Le quasi anti-ballet*, and *Déclaration sur la personne humaine*).

## LETTRIST THEORY AND THE HISTORY OF DANCE

Before describing the structure of the *Cabaret discrépant*, it is necessary to set out the main features of what could be called the Lettrist or Isouian Theory of Dance. To do so, I will make use of the preface to Lemaître's book, written in 1960 ("La danse et la pantomime de l'Antiquité aux Lettristes"[8]), which is didactic and rather dogmatic, rather than the 1953 Manifesto, which is quite abstruse.

In this preface, Isou identifies four great phases or periods in the history of dance, which are marked by a clear and rather violent caesura: the first period includes all dance that preceded Lettrism, from antiquity to the present day, and the three other phases cover dance's future development, once it has become wholly Lettrist, which, according to Isou, is the only way it could escape from the aesthetic dead end it has been in since the beginning of the twentieth century at least.

The first phase, which consists of the entire history of dance before Isou, is called the "amplic phase," which is "composed of external general forms, that are subject to a superior anecdote."[9] Isou had already applied to other arts, particularly poetry and painting, this notion of an "amplic phase," which is characterized by two main features: on the one hand, the presence of elements of vocabulary that are comprehensive forms not broken down to the root (the words of language, the steps of academic dance), and on the other, the use of these comprehensive forms in the service of a general purpose extrinsic to the artistic medium itself (anecdote, story, fable, etc.). Romantic or academic ballet, with its traditional vocabulary and its subjection to the libretto, is the perfect example of such an "amplic phase."

---

[7] Ibid.

[8] Isou, "La danse et la pantomime de l'Antiquité aux Lettristes" in Lemaître, *La Danse et le mime ciselants* (1960, 9–40).

[9] Ibid., 18.

This "amplic phase," characterized by synthetic unity and indifference to the specificity of the medium, must be succeeded by the first truly Lettrist phase, namely the "chiseling phase," whose function is predominantly negative and analytical. On the one hand, this will involve, in a way not unlike the practice of Clement Greenberg or Merce Cunningham, a purification of the medium: the elimination from dance of everything that is not dance (story, music, scenery, etc.). On the other hand, in a manner not unlike the approach of Rudolf Laban, there will be a breaking down to the atomic level of the comprehensive forms passed down by tradition: the attainment of a sort of "alphabet of movement," in this case based on a distinction between the "lifeless parts" (*sections inertes*) and the "mobile parts" (*sections mobiles*) of the human body. This, I would suggest, is the closest Isou comes to analysis and to Laban, even if (of course) this "chiseling phase" does not lead to any concrete system for analyzing movement, or even to any kind of system of written notation. The distinction between "lifeless parts" and "mobile parts" remains deliberately vague, and the "scores" offered by Isou and Lemaître are entirely verbal.

This chiseling phase, which is essentially analytic and negative, and which seeks to isolate—on the model of the phoneme or the letter—the elementary particles of movement, must then be followed by a new "amplic phase," this time a strictly Lettrist one. This is the "hypergraphic phase," "in which each bodily particle represents a sign, and in which ballet becomes a *message in letters*."[10] Or again, as he goes on to say, "the second amplic phase will have to change each gestural particle into a letter, that is to say, into a symbolic hypergraphic sign, with each work constituting a *message in letters*."[11] The idea that the letter or the graphic symbol can in itself be meaningful, before any association with language, or any kind of conventional code, is in some way the basic tenet of all Lettrism. And if one were called upon to suggest off the top of one's head an actual choreographic equivalent of this "hypergraphic phase," one might—to some extent arbitrarily, admittedly, but not without artistic and aesthetic justification—think of Dominique Bagouet, and particularly of the movements in *Déserts d'amour*, which in their time could legitimately be described as "hypergraphic" (not in Isou's sense) or as "chiseled" (not in Isou's sense, but even so, the coincidence begins to seem remarkable) movements, which in Bagouet's work were from the start conceived of as meaningful, before or beyond any expressive intention. The notion that an abstract bodily graph can in itself be meaningful is the very basis of all Bagouet's work as it has developed since *Déserts d'amour*. And it is without doubt no accident that Olivia Grandville, interpreter of Bagouet's work from 1988 to 1993, came to take an interest in the Lettrist choreographic experiments twenty years later. It is therefore not absurd to suggest that Olivia Grandville, being familiar with Bagouet's work, had already had plenty of opportunity to encounter the "hypergraphic phase," and that this happened before she read Isou, and without there being any need to postulate any direct influence from Lettrism on Bagouet.

[10]  Ibid.
[11]  Ibid., 22.

Finally, this "hypergraphic phase" must be followed by the final phase, in which dance accepts its own destruction so that there can be fresh experimentation; this is the "infinitesimal phase":

> Then, foreseeing that physical hypergraphy too would come to an end, Isou[12] came up with a yet newer land that is infinitesimal choreography, in which any expression only exists insofar as it allows another nonexistent particle to be imagined, or opens the way to conceiving of an impossible body part.[13]

If one seeks to continue the parallel with actual choreographic examples, this "infinitesimal period"—in which movement no longer exists except in terms of the non-apparent, the invisible, the imaginary, and what is simply hinted at—inevitably makes one think of the development of European dance, and French dance in particular, during the last fifteen years, and of what has been mistakenly and clumsily called "non-dance." And if one had to give a more precise name to this invisible, impossible, and purely imaginary movement, one could think of Laurent Pichaud's work, of his invisible piece of 2000 (*Echo anticipé*) or of *Feignant* (2002), in which the performers showed only the intention and the initiation of the movement and not the actual movement itself. And, here again, it is no accident that Laurent Pichaud was one of the main performers of Olivia Grandville's piece.

Such is the four-stage scheme of dance, as conceived by Isou: amplic (pre-Isou), then chiseling, hypergraphic, and infinitesimal. This theoretical construct must of course be interpreted in two ways: as a matter of the greatest doctrinal seriousness, with pseudo-scientific value, and at the same time as simply a huge joke, self-destructing in its outrageousness. Isou constantly delights in combining theoretical hysteria with pure and simple practical jokes, with all the undermining and critical effect that immediately arises from humor, irony, and excess. In other words, one needs to be able to take on board two apparently contradictory propositions: this construct is indeed just a joke, and yet it can equally well be looked at with the utmost theoretical seriousness. One of the great strengths of Olivia Grandville's piece is that it succeeds in keeping these two threads constantly together: the jokes and schoolboy humor (which in today's choreographic context is all to the good), and the extreme power and seriousness of Isou's propositions, which interrogate our own choreographic present, and even—it could be said—document it in advance.

## *LE CABARET DISCRÉPANT*: DESCRIPTION AND STRUCTURE

Olivia Grandville's piece is made up of two quite distinct parts. The first part consists of a series of installations/performances at various scattered points in the theater (the

[12] It is Isou who is writing here, speaking of himself in the third person, of course.
[13] Ibid., 18–19.

bar, foyer, staircases, etc.), but always points that are away from the stage; the spectators are invited to wander through them. These installations/performances, coming sometimes one after another, occasionally, simultaneously, expose the audience to various Lettrist-inspired texts of many different kinds: poems (by François Dufrêne in particular), manifestos, theoretical, political and aesthetic proclamations, and so on. This wandering about is thus like a sort of historical and contextual immersion, enabling one to feel, in a way that is inevitably fragmentary and incomplete, the radical potential of the Lettrist propositions in the 1950s and 1960s. This first part, in which there is hardly ever any suggestion of dance, thus constitutes, in the form of a heterogeneous and scattered happening, a sort of historic airlock that provides context, preparing the spectator for the second part.

This second part takes place in the theater, with staging that could not be more classical and frontal. Furthermore, the generic and scenographic conventions adopted tend to decontextualize the set of dances and "ballets" performed, or rather to surreptitiously make them part of our own present: the minimalist lighting, the absence of scenery, and the inevitable white linoleum of "French dance in the 2000s," together with the no less inevitable form of the "dance lecture," immediately make it impossible to understand this second part as being just historical reconstruction, and compel one to think that the choreographic propositions being performed, although deriving from the 1950s and 1960s, are just as much ideas of the early 2010s. The structure of two sharply separated parts thus produces a remarkable effect of dissociation between historical and contextual immersion on the one side, and abstract and decontextualized presentation of choreographic and textual quotations on the other. All the historical markers having been taken care of, or overturned, in part one, the second part can spread itself out in a sort of temporal no man's land in which it becomes very difficult to identify the historical moment to which the artistic and choreographic statement belongs. To be more precise, in part two the spectator constantly oscillates between two interpretive poles, sometimes seeing discourse and dance as mere reenactment of past experiments (with all the distance—at times ironic or dated—which that implies[14]), and sometimes—in quite the opposite way— forgetting the origins of the discourse and the performance, and accepting them as absolutely contemporary statements. This oscillation between past and present is undoubtedly facilitated by the general structure of quotation, which makes it possible to state something without having to explicitly adopt it as a subject for discourse, but it also seems to me to be intensified by a certain number of formal and scenographic choices (the two-part structure, the dance-lecture form, the scenographic conventions, etc.). I will have occasion to return at length to this effect of decontextualization and temporal indeterminacy.

Part two opens with an exercise in collage or simultaneous quotation, which is both discursive and choreographic: on one side there is the preamble Isou wrote to his *14*

---

[14]  Cf. Isou's preamble played on an old cassette recorder at the start of part two.

*Petits Ballets*,[15] pre-recorded by an actress and played on an ancient cassette recorder; on the other, the part of the dancer in Lemaître's *Premier sonnet gesticulaire*,[16] originally danced by Colette Desbrosses, and here performed by Laurent Pichaud.[17] If part two seems like a simple string of quotations, one should notice the extent of the modifications and distortions with which it opens. In the first place, what we have is not a straightforward performance of Lemaître's *Premier sonnet gesticulaire*, since a trio has become a solo, eliminating the two mimes (one male, one female) who originally accompanied the dancer. Second, and this is doubtless the most obvious detail, a female dancer is replaced by a male one, in accordance with work on gender, which has by now become very familiar to us. Finally, by superimposing one on the other—Isou's discourse and Lemaître's dance, which were not in the least made to be seen together—an artifact has been created that, strictly speaking, never existed. This is the case, in the first place, from the point of view of authorship. For this opening is neither by Isou, nor by Lemaître, but it is not by Olivia Grandville either, except for the collage process. Equally, as far as the content itself goes, since the bringing together of these two disparate elements inevitably causes shifts and upheavals in one and all, this chance meeting very often produces unexpected effects in meaning, which are generally comic. What might still have seemed serious in the discourse and the dance, as long as each was taken in isolation, now dissolves into an absurd whole, which is both over- and under-significant, and in which it is difficult for the dancer not to overplay the comedy by highlighting the chance effects in meaning.

Part two, then, opens with a subject that cannot really be placed, historically or in terms of authorship, setting up this temporal no man's land that is its main feature, and which will remain until the end. However, what immediately follows goes back to a distinctly more literal use of quotation.

After the part of the female dancer is repeated in *Premier sonnet gesticulaire*, all the performers, wearing formal clothes (a dress or suit and tie), arrange a table and chairs on the front of the stage and sit down facing the audience, thus suggesting something like a colloquium or a dance-lecture. From that point on, the whole performance more or less faithfully follows Isou's work of 1965. Table 8.1 shows Olivia Grandville's selection and chosen order, in comparison with the source book.

The *14 Petits ballets*, read and performed simultaneously, demonstrate the various Lettrist phases proposed by Isou. The first nine (lip ballet, eye ballet, finger ballet,

---

[15] Isou, *Ballets ciselants, polythanasiques, hypergraphiques et infinitésimaux (1960–1964)* (1965, 7–12). The content of this preamble is very close to the preface written by Isou in 1960 for Lemaître's book *La Danse et le mime ciselants, lettristes et hypergraphiques.*

[16] Lemaître, "Premier sonnet gesticulaire," *La Danse et le mime ciselants, lettristes et hypergraphiques* (1960, 53–59). To give a simple idea of the score and the verbal instructions it offers, I will quote the beginning: "FEMALE DANCER'S part/1 stretch out motionless on the ground, opposite the mimes, head towards the audience/2 ditto/3 ditto/4 ditto/5 ditto/6 ditto/7 the left arm lifts perpendicular to the ground, the hand and fingers stretching out stiffly/8 the forearm lifts at a right angle, the hand remaining stiff, in line with the forearm/[ . . . ] 13 raise the head/14 raise the trunk/[ . . . ] 16 cross the legs [ . . . ]."

[17] Or by Sylvain Prunenec, depending on the tour dates.

Table 8.1 Comparison of the Structures of Isou's *Ballets ciselants* and Olivia
Grandville's *Le Cabaret discrépant*

| Isidore Isou, *Ballets ciselants, polythanasiques, hypergraphiques et infinitésimaux (1960–1964)*, 1965 | Olivia Grandville, *Le Cabaret discrépant*, Part two |
| --- | --- |
| 1. *14 Petits ballets ou somme chorégraphique* | 1. The female dancer's part from *Premier sonnet gesticulaire* by Maurice Lemaître, accompanied by a reading of the preamble to Isou's *14 Petits ballets* played on a cassette recorder |
| 2. ~~La Danse hermétique des doigts et des jambes.~~ | |
| 3. ~~Étude de langue~~ | |
| 4. *La Promenade* | 2. The *14 Petits ballets* read and performed in the form of a dance lecture |
| 5. ~~Essai d'Anti-Ballet~~ | |
| 6. *Déclaration sur la personne humaine (Ballet à peine existant)* | 3. *La Promenade* |
| 7. *Le quasi anti-ballet* | 4. *Manifeste de la danse a-optique ou de la danse-débat* (not read but performed) |
| 8. *Manifeste de la danse a-optique ou de la danse-débat* | 5. *Ballet provocation* |
| 9. *Recherches pour un ballet infinitésimal* | 6. *Recherches pour un ballet infinitésimal* |
| 10. *Ballet provocation (Simple, Double, Bivalent, Polyvalent)* | 7. *Le quasi anti-ballet* |
| | 8. *Déclaration sur la personne humaine (Ballet à peine existant)* (using the lighting from *quasi anti-ballet*) |
| | End. Dark stage. |

hair ballet, toe ballet, ballet of the mucous or liquid elements in our bodies, improvisation ballet, animal ballet, and ballet destruction) quite clearly belong to the chiseling phase, which has to do with the analytic dismantling of the global entities of the amplic phase, and destroying all unexamined choreographic conventions. Ballets 12 and 13 (hypergraphic ballet and a-hypergraphic ballet) belong, as their titles suggest, to the hypergraphic phase, and to its destruction. Finally, ballets 10, 11, and 14 (immobility ballet, nothingness ballet, and infinitesimal ballet) belong, again in an obvious way, to the infinitesimal phase.[18]

I will not describe the later sections in detail, but will instead concentrate on the structure of part two as a whole, and particularly on the management of tone and intensity. Up to and including *Ballet provocation*, which consists of a pitched battle in which performers and spectators hurl artificial flowers and real vegetables at each other, one can speak of a crescendo of comedy, laughter, and more or less puerile transgression.

---

[18] I will here quote almost in full the text of the last ballet, which, besides the fact that it's relatively clear about the infinitesimal phase, gives a remarkably good description, although by anticipation, of one of the protocols set out by Laurent Pichaud in *Feignant* (2002): "So this ballet imagines a third territory that is yet newer, and is defined as that of infinitesimal choreography, in which each move only exists insofar as it makes it possible to imagine a nonexistent gesture or a movement that is impossible for the body as it now exists, and possible at the most for the body of the future. In this choreography the visible must be ignored, for it serves as a springboard for the invisible. One shows movements to convey the fact that the dance is elsewhere[ . . . ]." Isou, *Ballets ciselants* (1965, 23–24).

The *Ballet provocation* therefore constitutes a real climax where the mounting humor comes to a head with a huge burst of laughter and a vast carnival bazaar. After this there is a complete change of tone.

The final quarter of an hour of the show is marked by a steady reduction of perceptible intensity (of sound, light, and choreography), accompanied by a seriousness that is increasingly genuine, and even by a certain lyricism connected with effacement and disappearance. I will just quote the text of the penultimate section, *Le quasi anti-ballet*, read by Manuel Vallade alone on the stage, facing the public:

> A dance made up of a series of very precise details—tightly linked together—will be performed on the stage *plunged in darkness* or behind *a curtain of transparent tulle*, which will prevent complete and perfect visibility of the work, thwarting the spectators' desire to see what is being expressed before them.
>
> From this mass of shadows will rise, every now and then, certain movements or certain figures, like the limbs of a floating corpse, appearing and then immediately taken away again, sucked in and repossessed by the depths of the night.
>
> Perhaps behind the tulle curtain occasional movements will make ripples in the material, making some lines stand out in relief from the annihilating flatness; one might also light a lantern or a torch at regular intervals, or even better, a match, which, moving for a few seconds in the darkness, would show writhing forms, or some wonderfully expressive movement, briefly glimpsed, its disappearance arousing the sense of enchantment and regret one feels at the sight of the pieces of an unfinished sculpture by Rodin or the broken fragments of a wonderful ancient statue.[19]

The poetic and theoretical beauty of this text and the sudden seriousness of the statement lead the spectator to abandon a mode of reacting that hitherto has been geared to comedy and irony, and to consider the possibility of a serious, literal reading. This seriousness further increases in the last section, in which the choreography and lighting of the *Quasi anti-ballet* is directly adopted (again by Manuel Vallade, in the upstage garden), while the text entitled *Déclaration sur la personne humaine* is played from the stage, until all the lights go out. The treatment of the infinitesimal and of the almost imperceptible, together with the extreme beauty, yet again, of the text[20] rules out a

---

[19] Ibid., 45.

[20] I will quote some extracts: "I would like to make a work involving movement which is like a Malevitch picture, composed of a simple white square on a big white canvas, or like these modern panels that are completely blank, with a few scratches or marks in one corner: a kind of Debussy that is even more nonexistent than Debussy, a few notes, or one note, and then nothing more. /The dancer will be already on the stage when the curtain rises, or will come on stage in total darkness so that his appearance does not lead to movement, or produce that movement which is the most dangerous enemy of dance, especially when it is given in massive doses, as it has been in all ballet up to the present day./Meaningless movement, which is what happens in choreography can at a pinch still be used sparingly, like a fine line, or in such a quantity that, by its very concentration, it becomes incomprehensible, a block that is as opaque as immobility or silence. [ ... ]

The feeling that such a ballet should arouse is that of despair at the impossibility of satisfaction from the ordinary beauties of life and from the usual emptiness one must accustom oneself to contemplate,

reading that is solely comic. Admittedly, one still laughs a bit, but more from inertia than anything else, since one knows very well that what is now being performed is extremely serious. Or rather, these odd bursts of laughter, against the background of general seriousness that is wholly voluntary, are perhaps just the reverse echo of a seriousness that was already surfacing amid the carnival uproar. In other words, far from suggesting a binary structure that would make the serious follow the comic, the second part as a whole constantly takes advantage of the ambiguity of the association of the two, by progressively inverting their respective weight: one laughs at the beginning, but one knows it is serious; one is serious at the end, but the fact of the beginning cannot fail to color what one sees and hears.

# Quotation: Discursive Ambiguity and Temporal Indeterminacy

Such ambiguity already permeates the discourse of Isou and is an integral part of his artistic and theoretical approach. But in this case it is diluted by the very structure of the quotation. One does not exactly know what Olivia Grandville is saying in this piece, which is essentially only an enormous verbal and choreographic quotation: it is very difficult to identify anything like an authorial point of view. Olivia Grandville is neither for nor against Lettrism; she is content to bring up to date, out of their original context, a certain number of statements and choreographic scores. Quotation therefore appears at first to be a strategy of self-effacement on the part of the author-subject who, abandoning any clear, unequivocal idea of "meaning," is able to escape the requirement for non-contradiction and non-ambiguity. If in "my" words it is not "me" who is speaking, statements are both reduced to their strictly literal meaning ("this means what this means") and dispersed into the multiplicity of their potentially discordant, or indeed contradictory, meanings ("this can mean A and not-A").

Now this strategy of withdrawal by means of quotation, which makes ambiguity and contradiction possible, becomes key if one thinks of this piece as also being a discourse on European dance of the last fifteen years—what might have been called "new dance," "conceptual dance," or even, very clumsily and unjustly, "non-dance." Olivia Grandville, thought of as a former dancer of the Paris Opéra and former interpreter of Dominique Bagouet, has to an extent remained outside the conceptual movement of the early 2000s—this being the case despite the fact that her own choreographies have always been closely related to the artistic avant-garde, and to Dadaism in particular. Thus it is that the strategy of self-effacement and widespread quotation enables Olivia Grandville

while waiting for the day one might perhaps go further and find other forms." Isou, *Ballets ciselants* (1965, 41–43).

to adopt a certain number of statements and artistic doctrines that, but for the ambiguity of her approach, would be totally irreconcilable and contradictory.

What, ultimately, can this widespread quotation mean, once it is put back into its pragmatic context? I suggest the following interpretation:

1. The innovations of the "conceptual dance" of the early 2000s do not actually date from those years. They had already been put forward by the Lettrists at the end of the 1950s, and dance, as often happens, is in this case forgetful of its own history.
2. These propositions, by their very radicalness, obviously have a comic aspect: Where "conceptual dance" went wrong was to forget this undermining potential of humor, and simply to take itself too seriously, unintentionally becoming ridiculous.
3. However, this conceptual stage of reflection and self-destruction (the "infinitesimal") is indispensable to the development of all art. It is only surprising that, in the case of dance, it came fifty years later.
4. This negative stage is not only historically necessary, but also has its own greatness and inherent beauty and its own power of poetic and aesthetic evocation (as in the last quarter of the show).

These ideas, which are difficult to reconcile, make their presence felt simultaneously throughout the piece, precisely because of the under-determination of meaning that quotation involves. Because quotation does not "mean" anything, because it does not have one clearly identifiable "intention" behind it, it can also "say everything." Olivia Grandville's response to the "conceptual dance" of the early 2000s, the position she takes up, is to be found precisely in this strategy of evasion and retreat into quotation, with ambiguity becoming her assumed artistic posture.

Nevertheless, the approach taken by Olivia Grandville cannot be reduced to a simple position, even if ambiguous, as regards the choreographic present, just as one cannot for a moment consider it as a simple attempt at historical recreation. Discursive ambiguity here also becomes temporal indeterminacy. Neither a present-day entity, nor an archaeological reconstruction, the whole piece holds together this vagueness, which makes it impossible to connect a time to what one sees, thus giving it the powerful attraction of *timelessness*. This feeling of timelessness, which attaches in the first place to the thing itself (the show), in the end seeps into the two terms it relates to, creating for them, as it were, an imaginary past and future, suggesting forebears and descendants that have never existed. The Lettrist enterprise as regards dance is, from a strictly historical point of view, a dead letter, yet our present works on it retroactively, inventing for it an origin that is perfectly unreal and untimely. Conversely the "conceptual dance" of the early 2000s was completely ignorant of Lettrism, and yet Lettrism, in a sort of advance anachronism, ended up becoming its perfect contemporary. The past and the present are never *simple*. Through the crossing and erasing of temporal indications, *Le Cabaret discrépant* invites us to abandon the peremptory reality of the *indicative* mood, in favor of a stranger, rarer tense, *the past unreal*, which offers the "feeling of regret for *what could have been* and that would cease to be if it continued until one tired of it."[21]

## Works Cited

Isou, Isidore. 1953. "Manifeste de la danse isouienne." *Revue musicale* 219.

Isou, Isidore. 1965. *Ballets ciselants, polythanasiques, hypergraphiques et infinitésimaux (1960–1964)*. Paris: Altmann-Isou.

Lemaître, Maurice. 1960. *La Danse et le mime ciselants, lettristes et hypergraphiques*. Paris: Jean Grassin.

[21] Ibid., 43.

# CHAPTER 9

# LETTERS TO LILA AND DRAMATURG'S NOTES ON FUTURE MEMORY

## Inheriting Dance's Alternative Histories

### KATE ELSWIT WITH LETTERS BY RANI NAIR

Stockholm—Munich March 5th 2010

Dear Lilavati!

I am writing this letter on a plane en route to Germany. I would like to ask you if we could write to each other, as a way of communicating, perhaps as the beginning of a collaboration. I have so many questions I want to ask you. And I have a feeling that you like getting letters. I heard that you came to Sweden that way, through the love letters that Bengt wrote to you, Bengt, who you later married. It would be a way for us to grow closer. In my imagination you answer me, though you no longer are in this world.

I am wondering what this means—me on a plane to the country that Kurt Jooss comes from. Does it mean anything at all? Though I like thinking that it does, that there is some significance in me visiting the country where he took his first dancing steps. I am travelling with the Swedish Arts Grants Committee to support a Swedish project for choreographers: "The History of Swedish Dance Redux." Am I meant to perform Dixit Dominus there? Is there a way to introduce it into the program, to make it part of Swedish dance history?

Sometimes I doubt that the piece is exciting at all. That it still has qualities that we, today, would find exciting. Then I feel bad, as if I am behaving badly towards you. Like I am letting you down, betraying your artistic ambition. That I am betraying the dream you had of performing this piece all over the world, dancing it for the United Nations. I cannot accept that I could rightly judge your work as uninteresting. Even though I feel this way about many works from the past, that they feel so old, so full of dust, that it is difficult to find the "urgency" in these works today.

I'm thinking about Akram Khan, the choreographer. In the beginning of the 2000's, when I was living in London, I could see Khan's experiments with Indian dance forms in modern compositions and I thought that his work was so exciting! That's what made it so interesting to discover that you and Jooss, already in Dixit Dominus in the early '70's, were searching for a contemporary expression for Indian dance, a way to break with traditional restraints and let the dance find a new life in a new form. But today I'm not as keen on the choices Khan made, in the direction of his artistic development. As if he wanted to market the multicultural, global dance all over the world, as a politically correct product, without asking critical questions in regard to diversity and exoticism. Making things harder for us "foreigners" by setting us apart.

I no longer wish to be associated with that dance. I see no meaning in the experiments you made either, or rather; I see that this is not the solution—it can't be the right way to go. I am judging these attempts you made in the past and you are not here to defend yourselves. And then I judge myself, and that is what is making it so hard to begin.

I can recognize myself in the descriptions of you from newspaper articles. Your battle between the Indian and the Swedish in you, your experience of wanting, struggling to find yourself in this gap between two cultures, between East and West. It surprises me that we today, haven't come further. That I find myself faced with the same questions you tried to answer many years before. Are we victims of the projections of other people? Are we ourselves playing a part in the creation of the exotic picture? Do the two of us have things in common other than the Swedish and the Indian? We are both dancers. We live in Sweden. We've studied classical Indian dance and trained modern dance. We've danced solo a lot. We both have long hair. And your clothes fit me almost perfectly!

I remember how uncomfortable it was for me the first time I tried on your costumes. It felt like a great responsibility just to take possession of them, even when I carried them in Bengt's leather bag and in those other plastic bags from his favorite shop, Lindgren's Fish and Shellfish at the market hall in Östermalm. But after that, they hung in my closet on hangers, side by side with my normal clothes, my cotton dresses and jeans and silk shirts and pashima shawls.

Bengt said, "When you inherit the piece, you inherit everything belonging to the piece." But they hung there for almost a year before I dared to put them on. And it was extra special that one particular item, the one in pink shirt silk sewn by haute couture tailors, wasn't it designed by someone famous? Was it Bernard Deyder? It was the most exquisite with all those in-sewn pleats and detail work. The one you and Kurt Jooss really didn't like and you never wore it and nobody had ever seen it. Then there is the one that Swedish TV made when they recorded the performance, the one in wool. I never used that one. I thought in the beginning that I would, but nobody that I asked thought that I should. Most of them thought I should use the one that you performed in the most, the red stretchy one, the simplest of them all: a red unitard in lycra with a zipper in the back and sweat cushions under the armpits.

**FIGURE 9.1.** 1975 promotional image of Kurt Jooss and Lilavati Häger rehearsing for *Dixit Dominus.*

Photo by Folke Hellberg for *Dagens Nyheter.* Courtesy Rani Nair.

We're landing soon and the captain says that I have to turn off my computer. I promise to write again soon. I have plenty more questions to discuss with you! I hope you are well, and that wherever you are, you are free from pain. I hope that these letters will bring us closer.

Warmest wishes—Rani

A decade ago, Rani Nair reconstructed *Dixit Dominus*, a 1975 collaboration between German choreographer Kurt Jooss and Swedish-based Indian dancer Lilavati Häger (Figure 9.1).[1] Set to part of Händel's "Dixit Dominus," a filmed version from 1977 shows a piece in which stylistic features of Jooss's modern movement intertwine with Häger's training in multiple classical Indian forms. The choreography was themed around a

[1]  Elswit's essay is part of a larger writing project supported by the Lilian Karina Foundation's 2013 Research Grant in Dance and Politics, and a shorter version appeared as a stand-alone piece in *Dance Research Journal* 46(1) (2014). Some of Nair's letters to Lilavati Häger were initially published in *Ful* as "RANI <3 LILAVATI FRÅN 1975 TILL 2020" (2010). For this revision, parts of Nair's letters were translated from Swedish by Edward Buffalo Bromberg with funding from Konstnärsnämnden.

"message" Jooss found: "What you take for yourself, shall be lost to you—what you give, will remain with you forever" (Jooss/Westerberg 1977).[2] It consisted of two parts: the first aggressive, greedy, and full of "false heroism," in contrast with the second, which was lyrical and based on giving (see Häger's description in Pikula 1981). The movement of the piece from Jooss to Häger to Nair further extends this underlying idea. After Lilavati Häger's death in 2002, her husband, the impresario and dance champion Bengt Häger, passed it on to Nair. Bengt Häger knew that his wife had always wanted to pass on the work and that, after seeing Nair dance for British Asian choreographer Shobana Jeyasingh shortly before her death, Lilavati Häger mentioned having found the dancer for *Dixit Dominus*. Bengt told Nair, as she writes in the letter from March 5, 2010, "when you inherit the piece, you inherit everything that goes with it." Yet, wearing Häger's costumes and hearing stories about her, while attempting to do her movement, made Nair feel farther from, rather than closer to, *Dixit Dominus* and its original creators. This ultimately led to the second phase, *Future Memory* (2012/14), a second-order performance—a performance about a performance—that explores how else she might engage with that inheritance. Jooss's concept returns to structure the grounding question of the *Future Memory* project: How does one accept a gift and care for it by finding new ways to pass it on? To do nothing before giving it away would be to reject the gift, whereas to do too much risks "taking" for oneself.[3]

The last fifteen years have been full of "reenactments," "recreations," and "reinventions," to name a few classifications, all preoccupied with reusing the material of past performances.[4] Describing what he calls the "archival impulse" in contemporary art more generally, Hal Foster suggests that such work fulfills a specific function: the artist-as-archivist not only considers and reorders, but also produces materials, and in doing so underscores the nature of all archival materials as "found yet constructed, factual yet fictive, public yet private" (2004, 5). Yvonne Hardt observes about such trends in dance that on European stages "artists have discovered the past as a playground for the present" (2012, 218; see also 2011, 27), a phrase that seems significant. Earlier debates concerning dance reconstructions revolved around questions of fidelity toward certain characteristics of a perceived "original" versus allowing the past to mature (for example, Rubidge 1995). By contrast, the newer set of "re"-performances have tended to be more invested in what can be made in the present, using the past. They posit understandings of history, as Gerald Siegmund puts it, "as production that occurs between the active acquisition of sources and passively allowing oneself to give oneself over or be affected by that which must remain unavailable within them" (2010, 26).

---

[2] An alternative version that Bengt Häger notes is "What You take shall be taken away from You—what You give is Yours for ever" (1976, 6).

[3] For a trailer of *Future Memory*, see https://vimeo.com/81489773.

[4] At the University of Bristol, for example, I taught undergraduate and graduate courses on "Performing the Archive" and "Performing Theatre Histories." In addition to the many essays that have filled the pages of *Dance Research Journal*, a compilation of artists' writings and scholarship from performance can be found in *Perform, Repeat, Record*, ed. Amelia Jones and Adrian Heathfield (2012).

For Foster, the framework of "art" licenses certain potentially erroneous affective investments whose combination of utopia and paranoia suggest failures in larger structures at the same time as they offer new possibilities of order.[5] However, the more time I have spent with *Future Memory*, the more it has clarified the potential, but also the very precarious nature, of working with creative strategies at the intersection of multiple contested legacies. *Dixit Dominus* has often been seen as an addendum that does not fit neatly into the canon of dance history. Although Jooss is cited as central in narratives of twentieth-century dance theater, this solo falls through the cracks. While it is not well recognized within Jooss's ouevre, because it was made for Häger almost ten years after what was considered to be his last choreography, it is also too early in other ways, built out of friendship before contemporary hybrid practices had much visibility in either the Swedish or German dance scenes.[6] Likewise, the intertwined German and Indian dance practices that grounded the *Dixit* collaboration were each reinvented during the twentieth century. One of the challenges of returning to those materials today was how to resist flattening the distinct temporalities that we negotiated, in particular with regard to multiple practices that have their own histories of redoing. *Future Memory* develops an alternative history, in which a "minor" work takes ten years of another artist's life, and where the roles of insider and outsider are more complicated than we might think.

This chapter is not entirely a view from inside, since I consider my role as dramaturg to be in part that of the First Spectator, an acute observer who watches over and over and articulates what she sees. Nor is it, however, entirely from outside, because I have, through this process of observing over eight years, actively taken part in shaping the work about which I now write. In the early stages, my work ranged from tweaking Nair's performance qualities to change the effect of a particular moment, or suggesting an alternative way to sequence or layer materials, through raising more substantive concerns about the overall trajectory of the piece, and offering prompts that generated the material to get there.[7] As *Future Memory* settled in form and began to tour in Europe and Asia, my dramaturgical role shifted, for example, considering how to scale an intimate performance initially made for forty, and later for 150, to a sold out 450-seat theater. This essay is also not meant to substitute explanation or documentation for an experience

---

[5] This proposition of failure is what André Lepecki responds to in suggesting that such work should be seen not to originate from loss, but from a more excessive impulse to explore the abundant immanent possibilities (2010).

[6] While *Dixit* was made in 1975, it did not premiere until later. Jooss made dances consistently through 1966 and then stopped. He continued to do some choreography for theatrical productions through 1972. See the full register of works in Stöckemann (2001). Even in the United Kingdom, where contemporary South Asian Dance is most prominent today, Akademi was not founded as a center until 1979.

[7] Just as my thoughts take part in shaping the work that Nair performs on stage and even in the letters themselves, what is here on paper owes so much to our conversations, as well as those with others that she has recounted to me, all of which are an ongoing part of her inheritance. Because my participation was first as a dramaturg and historian for the project, but only years later as also a writer, I treat exchanges from within our collaboration in a practice-based, rather than ethnographic, manner.

of viewing the performance, or even to provide a cohesive process report. Rather, the chapter's shifts from the anecdotal to the critical mark an experiment in "writing along-side," an attempt to give written form to a series of thoughts that have developed with, through, and sometimes even against the dialogical process of making *Future Memory*, in a manner that combines multiple registers of research.

I start this essay in close proximity to the studio and stage, with decisions we made about handling the archival materials to create a performance that dealt less with the choreographic movement of *Dixit Dominus*, than with movement in the sense of the dance's circulation among multiple protagonists. From there, I work my way outward, toward some of larger questions that have arisen regarding how contemporary performance can rework the past, in particular the stakes of balancing the historical specificity of contested legacies with the global nature of their interconnections. I have kept Rani's letters in chronological order, which follow in their own way a similar, outwardly spiral-ing path that is at once intimate and critical, historical and practical.

## FROM *DIXIT DOMINUS* TO *FUTURE MEMORY*

Kurt Jooss's last dance, *Dixit Dominus*, was made over a period of five weeks in 1975 as a solo for Lilavati Häger, a friend who had always wished she could dance the role of the guerrilla or partisan woman in his famous *Green Table* (Figure 9.2). That *Dixit* itself already began as a kind of reworking of time is suggested by a conversation in which Häger proposes to Jooss that she would have been one of his dancers, had they met ear-lier (Sjögren 1975). Learned from film and coached by Bengt Häger, Nair's reconstruc-tion toured extensively between 2003 and 2006, and was presented, among other places, at the Centre National de la Danse in Paris and at the Hanoi Opera House. The early 2000s reconstruction was relatively faithful to the shapes and timing of the older move-ment, with controlled doses of intentional and unintentional anachronism. Bengt not only gave Nair his wife's costumes, but also traveled to Malmö during the rehearsal per-iod in order to give his approval, and eventually left a request that Nair dance it at his funeral.

That said, it is worth pointing out that even this version of *Dixit Dominus* involved sig-nificant decision-making. Writing about the reconstruction, Lena Hammergren suggests that "[i]n Nair's performance, both vocabularies are given equal weight, and she performs the solo as a dialogue between aspects of two worlds that are never fully joined together—as if addressing the issues of multiculturalism versus integration, which were hotly debated in Swedish politics and media at the time" (2009, 27). Nair had experimented with how much to smooth over the multiple logics of time in reconstructing the unforgiving move-ment. For example, the 1970s tension of Häger's body in the floor sections was something Nair attempted to update by adding more weighted qualities, and yet she did not want to fully commit to the release-based relationship to the floor that may be read as "better" in more recent dance contexts. Because Nair was much younger than Häger at the time she

FIGURE 9.2. Lilavati Häger in *Dixit Dominus*. Photo by Studio Liseg, Paris. Courtesy Rani Nair.

undertook the reconstruction, there were also questions regarding whether to perform *Dixit Dominus* as it was created for a dancer past her prime who was never entirely happy with her own performance of it, or whether to perform the dance that Lilavati Häger would have wanted to dance.

Nair and I were first introduced by a mutual friend in 2008 because she was unsatisfied with the "successful" reconstruction, and wanted help thinking about other ways to keep working with this gift.[8] I fell in love with the potential of the nascent project at a moment when she was struggling to locate it in a way that would generate interest and funding. We conversed intermittently though various showings and lulls between 2009 and 2011 in Belgrade, Hamburg, and Stockholm, among other places. In the early stages of *Future Memory*, one of the most difficult things for Nair was separating herself from Häger. I eventually proposed that she try establishing a different relationship by writing letters to Häger, which she did in Swedish and English. The letters confided things and asked questions not only about Jooss and the dance, but also about living

[8] Although it is beyond the scope of this chapter, this core question of inheritance could also be considered by comparison to discussions of the master-disciple relationship (*guru-shishya parampara*) in Indian cultural practices, as Cynthia Ling Lee has pointed out to me.

with mixed heritage, about Häger's love life, and even what she liked to eat.[9] Through the letters, Nair started to develop a sense of compassionate distance from the older dancer. She also began to stage herself as various other figures who might bridge the gaps she identified between herself and the many protagonists of *Dixit Dominus*, filling my inbox with images of herself as the English–Sri Lankan rapper M.I.A., as Scheherazade next to Bengt Häger (Figure 9.3), and, my favorite, one with a wig and moustache that arrived under the subject "Went lookin for Kurt Jooss, found Frank Zappa." Although none of these alter egos made it as such into the final version of *Future Memory*, traces of them remain in the wig that Nair wears for the middle of the piece, a prop that allows her the flexibility of going into a "not-not" persona at times, because of the way it makes her appear both more artificial and more like Häger. The personas and letters showed what had been missing from the earlier reconstruction: the complex network that the piece engendered not only between the two women, but also with Jooss, Bengt Häger, and others, relationships that had been overwhelmed when Nair actually dressed up as Lilavati Häger or tried to take on her movements too perfectly.

After working with these ideas off and on in various forms, in 2011–2012 we received generous funding from Konstnärsnämnden and Kulturrådet to develop *Future Memory* as an evening-length piece that would play in a smaller gallery-type space.[10] By this time, we understood the need to return to *Dixit Dominus* differently. To extend *Dixit's* circulation as gift—to receive the inheritance in a manner that does not simply take, but rather continues toward passing on—*Future Memory* needed to be not about the dance as movement in itself, but rather about the movement of the dance. In this sense, although I call it a second-order performance, it might be understood to waver between second- and third-order, because it is not only about the 1975 piece or even the 2003 reconstruction. While the choreography and performance remain important threads, at the core of the new piece is the relationships that occurred through the work: between different traditions of dance that have their own contested legacies; between the chore-ographer and first solo performer, as well as her husband, who passed the dance along; between the various artifacts that remain and those who encounter them today and, like Nair and myself, even build new relationships through them. A critic from *Svenska Dagbladet* wrote, "It is a gift to inherit something significant, but it can also mean a lot of pressure. You may even need to distance yourself and revolt [ . . . ]. And capture the time elapsed between the generations [ . . . ]. The dancer Rani Nair does all this in the

[9]  As well as being published in *Ful* (2010) and presented on their own as readings, some of these letters also appear as part of *Future Memory*, read aloud by Nair as well as audience members. The translations here are from the selection that are given out at the end of the show.

[10]  After its December 2012 premiere in Malmö, *Future Memory* has since appeared elsewhere in Sweden, including being chosen for the Scenkonstbiennalen in Jönköping. It was reworked for its first run in a larger theater at Dansens Hus (House of Dance) in Stockholm in March 2014, where it was programmed alongside Olga de Soto's *An Introduction*. Since then, it has also appeared among other places at the Salzburg Experimental Academy of Dance, the IGNITE! Festival of Contemporary Dance in New Delhi, ImPulsTanz—Vienna International Dance Festival, and the Singapore International Festival of Arts.

FIGURE 9.3. Webcam shot of Nair and Bengt Häger in Häger's apartment, ca. 2009.

solo 'Future Memory,' a wonderful, soul-searching, smart, funny and deeply personal act" (Angström 2014, n.p.). This balance of what a preview called "humor warmth, and intellectual sharpness, all in one" is something Nair and I have worked to maintain. We looked for a register that resonates with the intimate nature of the stories surrounding *Dixit Dominus*, while still keeping some of their secrets, as well as our own.

Just before the premiere, an interviewer asked whether I thought Kurt Jooss would be pleased with *Future Memory*. My answer was that I suspected no choreographer could help but appreciate when someone spends so long caring for a single one of their dances, particularly one like *Dixit Dominus*. Jooss's biographer Patricia Stöckemann gives his last dance only a few lines in an immaculate book, dismissing *Dixit Dominus* as something that Jooss was cajoled into doing "out of friendship," resulting in "a 1976 dance with a touch of Indianness [that] remained in its unadorned simplicity nothing more than marginalia in Jooss's creations" (2001, 397).[11] When I pointed this out, Nair told me that, in 2005, when she toured *Dixit* in Germany, she was confused because people would tell her afterward, "this is not the real Jooss." We also initially ran into issues finding funding for *Future Memory*, until we could articulate that there was something important about the piece's relative obscurity. Whereas Nair had struggled earlier with

---

[11] In addition, neither the piece nor Lilavati Häger herself appears in the index of names and works, although Bengt Häger does (Stöckemann 2001, 463–476).

*Dixit Dominus*'s ambiguous place outside the canon, *Future Memory* embraces that position. And yet that erodes a little more each time Nair performs it, each time a new audience spends an hour with the dance's traces.

Narvik, Norway March 18, 2010

Dear Lilavati!

Today I'm wearing your snakeskin belt. I wish you were here so we could talk some things over. It's a bit boring being here by myself.

I think I should write to you in English. It's strange. Already a lot slower. Makes me think of the language of this work. Should I have a working language? Reminds me of the time when I had just performed Dixit Dominus in Stockholm and I bumped into some dance critics. They commended me for the performance and my interpretation, which made me super happy. And I remember I dared to say something like: "Maybe I could perform it internationally . . ." and they told me off saying that they didn't think anyone outside Sweden would be interested.

I found this passage in my diary from the premiere of that performance in autumn 2003: "When I stand on the stage and hear the music begin to come through the speakers, I try to imagine that I am a goddess; generous and radiant, my breast open and ready to give. But deep inside I feel my fear. I have probably always felt nervous whenever I stand completely alone, in the middle of the stage, as the lights slowly, slowly go up in time with the music. But this time I really am scared. Scared of disappointing Lila and scared of being compared to her. And scared of what everyone will say; that little nobody me is dancing Kurt Jooss, that I can never do the piece justice or measure up to the man and the woman that created it. I am afraid of exposing all my weaknesses as a dancer, that my legs aren't strong enough to execute a decent plié, that I have trouble keeping my balance, that I can't round my spine while keeping control in my pelvis. The solo is so simple that it highlights any imperfection. And the tempo is difficult to follow with those speeding rhythms that change several times and syncopations and some of those traditional Indian dance steps that have been adapted so much that they are transformed into something new. It is really hard to understand what was intended and even harder to do it. And hard to keep those arm movements in line and to know if it should be Indian movements, higher with straight lines or the flowing arms of contemporary dance—and so hard to switch from one to the other."

Imagine that I was so afraid? It sounds really terrible. These days I think it had as much to do with the context, the huge empty stage at The House of Culture, the distance to the audience, the piece's formal choreography. It has elements that we don't see on the stage anymore these days. Aside from the lifted breast, the feet close together and arms out like a cross. It's in the qualities of movement, the almost trembling especially noticeable in the sections on the floor. It's also in the pirouettes, the spinning on the heel. And the audible beats of the feet on the floor, syncopated in rhythm with the music. It's interesting that Kate and I have talked about how the feeling of not keeping up with the music was an effect that Kurt Jooss intended, and was produced by setting certain sets of steps in a faster tempo, forcing the dancer to chase the music. I never needed to feel ashamed that I wasn't keeping up, that was the feeling he wanted to create. Maybe he wanted to give that kinesthetic experience to the audience as well?

Did you feel alien when you spoke Swedish? I remember when the two of us spoke we used a mixture of the two languages. Just like the first time we met. I was doing the end of the tour performance with the Shobana Jeyasingh Dance Company at the Queen Elisabeth Hall in London. My father was visiting and I went to the foyer looking for him, to sort him out with free tickets. Since we were in England we used the possibility to talk freely in our secret language, Swedish. When you approached us: —Who is this that is talking in Swedish?

I was struck by how you at the same time seemed to radiate energy and of how much older you'd become, compared to the picture in your book, which I kept in my shelf back home. Your long hair was still as black, just like the picture. I told you this, that I have your book on my shelf, and that I was going to be in the performance that you had tickets for. It felt nice. Strange and kind of huge.

I didn't see you after the performance that evening. Next time we met was later that fall at the Museum of Dance in Stockholm. It was almost like a cliché meeting from a movie or something, two artists from different generations meeting, representing different aesthetics, styles and tastes, but with a mutual respect for each other. It felt like you could see me for who I was and for what I was interested in, in my work, but at the same time you would easily admit that you didn't like all of "the new" and couldn't even understand it all. But you had the curiosity to ask. You wanted to understand. You commended me for my performance and told me you thought I was a great dancer. You also mentioned something about my quality, something about my jumps, that I had great technique, that I could so easily shift between the different dance forms. And that I possessed great charisma. But towards the end of the conversation you revealed that you actually didn't like the Shobana Jeyasingh performance after all. You thought the choreography was too out of synch and you didn't like the music. You said you were too traditional. I was kind of happy to hear that, both the way you said it, but also since I had decided to leave the company. You must have been very critical. You didn't even like your own performance of Dixit.

I fantasize about the life you had when you travelled around the world with Ram Gopal. I think you were a principal dancer, sometimes his dance partner but mainly a soloist. The Ram Gopal Dance Company, which had the longest running dance performance at the London West End until Adventures in Motion Pictures beat that record in the '90s, with their all male version of Swan Lake.

What colorful fancy dresses did you wear at your performative press conferences? What stories did you tell? Which were your strategies to manipulate the journalists? Did you also use a heightened language or emphasize the Indian accent?

How did it feel to travel the world at that time? What people did you meet, kings, queens, fans? Did you have any fans? Did you feel lonely in the hotel rooms? What did you do to keep fit? Was it possible to stick to a vegetarian diet? Were you able to enjoy the bland food of Europe?

I had a hamburger yesterday at a local bistro. I spent the night in a floating hotel, Hurtigruten's boat, Richard With. The room is small and claustrophobic. It's cold and as always I had a bad first night's sleep.

I'd better go and get ready now, breakfast, shopping, rigging at the theatre. "Verdensteatret." There's a performance tonight!

Rani

PS. I feel a little tired of myself as I am writing this. I want to get working on the production. But the way things are looking—this is turning out to be an eternity project—a thing that never, ever ends. What curse have you laid on me? I accept it!

# STAGING INHERITANCE

It is October 2012 and Nair and I are deliberating how to redo the last scene of *Future Memory*, which will premiere in just over a month at Danstationen in Malmö, Sweden. Having just watched a full run of the work in progress, I am troubled that, no matter how far the previous sections go in constructing a constellation of new scenarios from costumes, music, memories, and documentation associated with *Dixit Dominus*, the current ending fetishizes those traces: the stage empty, other than a microphone that sits on a tape recorder, amplifying a rehearsal tape from which Jooss's elegant, accented voice counts and sings over the Händel cantata. We love the effect of that tape, are enchanted by how it can fill the white space with a score of ever-changing numbers and instructions: "one and two and three, four; *one*, two, three, four [ . . . ] swim, two, three, four, five, six, seven, eight [ . . . ] da-da-da, step, two, three [ . . . ]." But my concern is that to play it alone risks privileging the past at the last minute. Instead, our task is to work with the tape un-elegiacally; rather than finishing on loss, we need to reframe the scene in a way that allows audiences to see the tape and all of the objects as we do—a trace of an overlooked past experiment in hybrid dance practice brought into coexistence with the present through another such experiment, one that locates the multiple times and places that it brings together, at the same time as it allows something new to be "re-membered" in the empty space.

One of the through lines to *Future Memory* is a series of memory tasks that stage Nair's intimacy with the material in a manner that is at once authoritative and eccentric. The evening begins with her absorbed in an iPhone video of herself performing the reconstruction of *Dixit* in Paris. We only see hints of the recording as she walks in and sits upstage; we mostly hear her "singing the score" of the full-length piece, counting off the timing of the movements in a combination of vocalizations that call

FIGURE 9.4  *Future Memory*: "Singing the Score."
Photo by Kevin Lee at Singapore International Festival of Arts, 2015.

toward Indian dance practices ("dit-dit-dey, dit-dit–dey, takadehmi . . .") and her own, more idiosyncratic locutions (Figure 9.4). Later, she balances in a headstand to recite the text of a letter she received from the Carina Ari Library years ago, loaning her the now deteriorating videotape, commenting on the condition, and asking her to please return it when she is done. In a section called "Memory of Lila," Nair sits cross-legged on top of an old television, describing without seeing exactly what is happening on the screen below as Lilavati Häger performs *Dixit Dominus* (Figure 9.5). Nair's spoken text fuses different times and places of the dance and its documentation. She demonstrates her favorite mudra (hand gesture) as Häger does it; remarks on the effect of Vaseline on the camera lens in another; and jokes that she thinks of a particular moment as a kind of Indian disco dance. We watch Häger's *Dixit* through Nair's words in a manner that integrates and differentiates their respective performances of the dance, for example: "I imagine that I pick flowers and give them to the audience. But Lila's eyes are a little higher so she might give them to the gods?" When Nair gets down, toward the end of Häger's dance, she blocks the television, preventing the audience from seeing as she explains that the choreography does not actually end in the way the filmed version suggests. Yet another exercise in remembering comes with a verbatim section in which Nair voices an interview with Jooss about *Dixit*. Although we hear his words only as she receives them through headphones, her face, head, and hands duplicate the small gestures that we see Jooss making on the television behind her.

**FIGURE 9.5.** *Future Memory*: "Memory of Lila."

Photo by Kevin Lee at Singapore International Festival of Arts, 2015.

Each of these memory tasks involves a form of documentation that is remediated through Nair's familiarity with it, drawing attention to the materiality of the archival artifacts through, rather than despite, her performance. One of the luxuries of a long rehearsal process was the time it afforded to keep clarifying the terms of such interactions until the performance of inheritance developed a covert virtuosity. The "Memory of Lila" section, for example, was developed in several stages: initially, Nair was experimenting with watching the film and articulating in different registers what she saw; when I realized she could likely play the film in her head without seeing it, I suggested she move from facing the television to standing behind it, so that the familiarity would be more legible; and she then shifted herself from behind to atop the television. Even after the premiere, however, this section has continued to evolve: in addition to adding memories (recently, a place where

Nair notes "she's late" because Häger's timing does not match the one she has internalized from her earlier reconstruction), Nair now begins watching the film along with the audience, and only gradually transitions to commenting without seeing. Rather than simply representing familiarity, however, the precision required from these tasks also opened up new levels in our understanding of the documentation material in the process. For example, Nair used to think Jooss was lying at points in the interview, because of how difficult she found it to perform the conversational body language that did not match the spoken text timing-wise. We had to rehearse the pattern of the physical gestures as a parallel but distinct track that tended to punctuate the speech in pauses or on unaccented syllables. But more recently Nair realized that, because Jooss is translating his thoughts into English, his body reacts to what he has decided to say before he actually does so. Her observation regarding the out-of-timeness of the translation underscored our sense of Jooss's strange out-of-placeness by the time of the interview, something we never mark explicitly, but which is nonetheless reinforced when a native Swedish speaker takes on his German-accented English.

This casual intimacy extends to Nair's work with the other, more tangible things that she also inherited (Figure 9.6). The collection of Lilavati Häger's photographs, costumes, jewelry, and rehearsal tapes that Bengt Häger gave to her over the years are so familiar that when Nair's baby, crawling in the studio, began to teethe on Häger's snakeskin belt, friends joked that she would grow up with history inside of her. While these seemed too isolated when confined to Nair's private apartment or studio, that changed overwhelmingly once *Future Memory* began to be shown. Initially this collection did not have a physical place in the performance itself—Nair considered simply leaving the objects as an installation on the edges of the space—and yet their centrality to Nair's personal relationship with caring for *Dixit Dominus* made it important to include them. Eventually we developed a bazaar-type exhibition scene in which she brings items out individually, displaying some from afar, stopping by small clusters of audience members to tell short stories about others.[12] She comes out wearing a wig, holding Häger's clutch purse under her armpit, while she puts on first the snakeskin belt, and then Häger's favorite perfume, which wafts as she walks back and forth. And later she shows someone in the second row the sweat pads under the armpits or the misspelled name tag of the two-piece costume Häger wore when filming *Dixit Dominus* for Swedish television, before leaving it with the audience member, returning ten minutes and two sections later to retrieve it. Later in the piece, instead of talking about the costumes, she simply holds each in turn before relating the history of the one she puts on, if necessary asking for assistance with the back zipper. While an intimate performance facilitates such tactile strategies, Nair jokes that the version for a larger-scale venue should involve a scent capable of being blown over the entire theater.

---

[12] In addition, the entire performance is structured around accumulation. It begins with only a letter hanging from a single thread, as well as the chair on which Nair sits with her iPhone, after which all but one of the subsequent sections adds at least one item to the full stage installation.

FIGURE 9.6. *Future Memory*: Nair's onstage collection of Häger's *Dixit Dominus* costumes, bells, performance jewelry, and other items.

Performance photo by Kat Reynolds at ImPulsTanz in Vienna, 2015.

The use of these objects underscores some of the issues at stake in how *Future Memory* at times works against more traditional muséal principles of preservation.[13] There are a limited number of performances in which the perfume can be used. The liquid line in the Tabu bottle goes down each time Nair uses it, or she could spill it. But then again, it will likely eventually go stale or evaporate The fabric of the costume is that fragile polyester of the late 1970s, which will corrode on its own, but this process is accelerated by the oils of audience members' hands. They grow careless after a while. One leans his forearms on the leotard that lies across his lap as he leans forward to watch the videotape in which Häger wears it. The perfume and the costume pose two different but related

---

[13] Critiques regarding hierarchies of transmission have often been grounded in non-Western or disenfranchised perspectives, catalyzing around questions of who controls the archive and the more mutable ways in which memory is understood to be stored, transformed, and passed on. To name just a few of many possible examples: Diana Taylor builds her distinction between the "archive" and the "repertoire" through an argument that, exploring the transmission of knowledge in the form of embodied action, "decenters the historic role of writing introduced by the Conquest" (2003, 17); Priya Srinivasan argues for the need to use "kinesthetic history" in order to show the interactions of multiple laboring bodies and thus complicate binary judgments regarding orientalism (2012, 72); and David Román suggests that instances of "archival drag" exceed the static capacities of more traditional archival systems such as museums or libraries when "embodied archival systems" based in queer communities pass and transform the work through affect and interest (2005, 165, 174).

problems: first, if preservation only prolongs degradation, why police these items, in other words, why not share them with the largest possible number of people before they are gone? And second, what happens if you trust people, even temporarily, with the costume or with the diamond ring that Nair leaves in the space as well—a gift from Bengt Häger for her first *Dixit Dominus* performance? Clearly, objects like the costume and the bottle, unlike the sensory impressions or even the perfume, will (hopefully) return to Nair by the end of the evening, albeit with a bit more wear and tear. Yet what happens with them counters any presumption that caring for these things would mean squirreling them away in a protected location, held for registered users in numbered boxes to be handled only while wearing white gloves. If the work of the piece is about inheritance, then this suggests an archive that is kept in circulation by entrusting it to others, even if that risks the possibility of change.

Stockholm, April 13th, 2010

Dear Lila,

I wonder if you were happy with the character Jooss and you worked with? Your role as the performer, was it satisfying? Did you get what you wanted from the collaboration?

I imagine what you would be dancing if you and Jooss worked now. I fantasize about you making a performance, like a solo. Working with a lot of details in the costumes, exaggerated Indian style costumes. Possibly red as the base, perhaps like a red overall trouser suit. And with army boots, perhaps Dr. Martins. And a lot of belts, gold belts and ammunition belts going across your chest and your waist, mixed with flowers and medallions. And makeup brushes, a mix between an Indian goddess figure and a guerilla woman, just like you said you wanted, but more hardcore and exaggerated. Like an installation. And yes, you would share more of the process, so you would do photo shoots all the time and invite audiences during the rehearsals. And include elements from the Boy Scout cabin where you started working. And the music would be . . . M.I.A!

I don't think you would work with nudity. That would be too mediocre and lame, at least for performances in central Europe where they get their clothes off all the time. Maybe in Sweden it could shock a few people or point at queer-politics or make sense to use the skin and its different colors?

Did you give up on the fusion of western contemporary dance and traditional Indian forms? I remember Bengt saying something about you feeling you had failed in challenging the traditional form or finding a new approach to Indian dance. Maybe I should continue along that road. Forging a modern dance with Indian elements. Switching between different expressions, not being so bound to one form. Deconstructing Indian dance to the degree where it becomes unrecognizable. Adding a touch of flamenco, the footwork, the arms, the rhythm! Dancing in a blonde wig with my face painted white, or sometimes with long, dark hair and lots of paint around the eyes, with dark skin and the traditional blue and yellow folk dress of Sweden. I might even do a face dance right into the camera.

In a notebook, I was reflecting on an exhibition at the Tate Modern curated by Bourriaud. It was called Altermodern. Among other things I wrote about heterochronia. It is a way of relating to time, not like the modern linear time or the postmodern spiral, but more as if time occurred in groups or clusters. What if artists were to use symbols that weren't current in the western dictionary, if they could allow themselves to borrow from the vocabularies of other times and relate to a global context.

You dreamed that you would dance this all over the world and even perform it at the United Nations. I am trying to find different ways to share it. More and more, I see that my work will compose several different works. One will be a lecture performance and I will be the interpreter of history, the master, one who maps tendencies, maps attempts to create a modern Indian dance, hybrid forms and inspiration from other cultures. I'll talk about Pavlova and tell the story of her foot bells, I'll tell about Nijinsky when he danced the blue god, the first Indian choreography that Kurt Jooss ever did, Martha Graham's entire floor piece, where she sat on the floor in lotus position, and I'll show how India inspired all this work. Some of it will materialize into dance productions—and hopefully some will turn into photography.

Maybe I don't have to make a pretty performance?

Take care, Rani

p.s. Today my father came up to Stockholm. He is going to apply for a PIO from the Indian Embassy, you know, a Person of Indian Origin card, it's a kind of permanent visa. Strange that he, Dr Baboo Monibhoshanen Nair, needs to apply for permission to visit the country where he was born and raised. And that he has to provide proof in his application. I used him as a reference when I needed proof myself.

## REWORKING CONTESTED LEGACIES

*Future Memory* joins many other performances on contemporary European stages that draw on German dance, which itself has a particularly problematic legacy of rewriting and forgetting over the past hundred years. One of the terms still most common with regard to German modern dance history, *Ausdruckstanz*, did not come into regular usage until the late 1940s and early 1950s, at which time it was meant to reimagine a set of practices from the early twentieth century.[14] More than a terminological technicality,

---

[14] This term and our understandings of the practices to which it refers have been revised substantially over the past few decades, beginning with the conference that led to the edited collection *Ausdruckstanz: eine mitteleuropäische Bewegung der ersten Hälfte des 20 Jahrhunderts* (Oberzaucher-Schüller 1992), and continuing with discussions including the relationships between *Ausdruckstanz* and *Tanztheater*, its relationships to German fascism, and its transnational connections. On the historicization and reinvention of *Ausdruckstanz*, see Franco (2007) and Elswit (2014). For a general overview of German dance in the immediate aftermath of World War II, see Müller, Stabel, and Stöckemann (2003).

this renaming also involved designating a story of inclusion and exclusion. As I have argued elsewhere, Jooss is a critical figure to historicizing the connections between earlier twentieth-century German modern dance and *Tanztheater*. He is often taken up as both a central and yet simultaneously exceptional figure, because his absence from Germany for nineteen years has been foundational to various narratives of continuity that short-circuit dance's development under the Third Reich. Whereas in the late 1940s and early 1950s, Jooss's work was described by many critics as an unfinished form of late *Ausdruckstanz*, by the 1970s and 1980s, his place as a precursor to *Tanztheater* was ensured by an argument that the political charge of his work distinguished him from the alleged naïveté of those bracketed as *Ausdruckstanz* practitioners.[15]

Susan Manning recently pointed out that German dance has spent so much time dealing with its relationships to fascism that it seems to now be acceptable to once again overlook them altogether in favor of other questions deemed to be more pressing and urgent. For her, the current disinterest in the connections between *Ausdruckstanz* and National Socialism is less a disavowal than a consensus that has closed the topic until future researchers return to the archive to ask new questions in new ways (Manning 2012). Such inquiries do not have to be separated. Seen differently, archive-based experimental dance practices might themselves not only function as aesthetic exploration but also provide new ways for considering such contested legacies.[16] Each time that they revisit the past, they have the potential not only to play within what they consider to be a commonly accepted narrative of the dance historical canon, but also to expose its gaps and discontinuities through their labor of redoing.

The three projects that have garnered the most attention in recent years for reworking the materials of German dance history on contemporary concert stages are Martin Nachbar's *affects/rework* and *Urheben Aufheben*, both based on Dore Hoyer's 1962 *Affectos Humanos*; Fabián Barba's *A Mary Wigman Dance Evening*, based on Wigman's first US tour in 1930–1931; and Olga de Soto's *An Introduction* and *Débords: Reflections on the Green Table*, both based on Jooss's most famous piece from 1932.[17] Even as I collect them under their German referents, I want to mark the internationalism in how the majority of these choreographers encountered their practices in other places. Nachbar is German. De Soto is Spanish, trained in France, but working in Belgium. Barba is Ecuadorian but began his project while studying in Belgium. And Nair is Swedish but met Häger while working in England. A key framing element of their works is how each artist foregrounds the labor of engaging with these past practices. For example, de

---

[15] On Jooss's return, see the chapter on "Watching after Weimar: Dance's Intellectual Property and the Protection of Memory" in Elswit (2014), and also Elswit (2017). On the problem of exiles being out of time, see Elswit (2017) and also Elswit (2012).

[16] Beyond concert stages, there are examples of this in terms of artful social justice work, for example Petra Kuppers's writing on the Olimpias's Anarcha Project, which makes the case for how "the response to the archive can help create a shared repertoire of political action" (2011, 166).

[17] Because so much has been articulated about these performances by scholars, as well as by the artists themselves, in both German and English, I limit my commentary to the details that are most salient to framing some of the issues that have arisen through *Future Memory*.

Soto makes visible the usually hidden work of dance history by discussing onstage her research process or using her performers to stage the projection of "testimonies" about *The Green Table* that she has collected from former dancers and spectators. Likewise, Nachbar not only recounts the ordeal of learning Hoyer's work from Waltraud Luley, but also sets up performances that highlight what it takes to inhabit the foreignness of an older physical technique. Barba's work is the most naturalized—his effort of performing Wigman becomes most apparent when an audience member takes one of the many candelabra-lit interludes to reflect on how uncannily effortless his performance is.

While all three engage with a family of works from within the same half-century, their projects use practice to propose different relationships to that history. Nachbar has written about his collaborators' interest in Hoyer's *Affectos Humanos* as coming from an investment in *Ausdruckstanz*: "Besides Pina Bausch, we hardly knew anything about German Ausdruckstanz and its influences, and we were curious to find out how choreographers of this tradition had worked, and had approached the body as a tool of expression" (2012, 8). Likewise, Fabián Barba proposes that his reenactment work with Mary Wigman should "find its place among other attempts to analyze the tradition of Ausdruckstanz" (2011, 86). At the same time, their actual approaches to that "tradition" are quite different. Barba informs his reconstructions through the Ecuadorian dance practices already available in his body, in the process using their affinities to *Ausdruckstanz* to propose alternative linkages between then and now (2011, 84, 87–89). By contrast, Nachbar's process of learning what he identifies as *Ausdruckstanz* material in a body trained for release technique has to do with exploring the possibilities and limits of citation. There are also a few moments in which dance history is more explicitly revised. For example, when Barba appears in de Soto's *Débords*, our identification of him with Wigman as a performer in "Jooss's" piece brings together the two opposed progeny of Rudolph Laban's teaching.

The danger in such projects that draw upon twentieth-century German dance, *Future Memory* included, is that their creative return to a problematic past risks strengthening, rather than mitigating, dominant narratives. The creative work in the present may ultimately take an ahistorical turn by flattening certain temporal economies that should remain destabilized, even as it disrupts others. This concern is raised by Jens Giersdorf, who uses the celebration of Nachbar's work by West German dance scholars to point toward the ways in which such reconstructions reinforce the erasure of East German dance practices from the dance historical canon (2013, 86). Giersdorf points out that Nachbar and those who discuss his work tend to cite only the previous 1988 reconstruction by West German choreographer Susanne Linke, not that by East German Arila Siegert, which was done in the same year. Referring to Nachbar's lecture performances as "a poststructuralist scholar's dream (or nightmare)" because of their inward focus (106), Giersdorf calls for the need to go beyond an aesthetic and methodological analytic frame in order to understand the ideological ramifications of such projects of redoing. At the same time, he suggests that the artistic work itself prohibits accounting for larger ideological structures, since it is in fact supported by them; Giersdorf suspects that Nachbar cannot reference Siegert as "it would force him to leave the confines of his own aesthetic and his notion of dance history, because Siegert does not appear in it. Siegert seemingly fails on an aesthetic level and does not exist in historical terms" (107).

While addressing the precariousness of reworking contested legacies, it is important to mark that it is not only the German but also the Indian strands of *Dixit Dominus* that have their own histories of reconstruction, with the invention of "classical Indian dance" forms starting in the early twentieth century. As Pallabi Chakravorty puts it, Indian classical dance must itself be seen as a "revivalist and reconstructive movement," one that extends the discourses of "East" and "West" that were foundational for Indian national ideology (2000/2001, 110). Avanthi Meduri further argues for the inadequate binaries of any tradition/change model, because all "traditional practitioners" should themselves be seen as "inside-outsiders" negotiating the "burden of the reinvented past" (2004, 21). Häger herself was raised amid this history; in an interview, she describes names critical to remaking Indian dance as regular visitors in her childhood home because her father brought Anna Pavlova to India, whose story intertwines with such figures as Uday Shankar (Häger and Ulvenstam 1984).

These histories matter in particular in the context of European performances working with the past where, as Hardt points out, ethnographic tradition tends to be aligned with the past, versus the avant-garde with the new (2011). Whereas the distinction between, for example, art and heritage may tend, as Hardt suggests, to mean one thing in the context of a concert stage, in the twentieth-century construction of the "tradition" of classical Indian dance, the hereditary performers were those displaced.[18] The project of interweaving Western and non-Western practices, both past and present, within the implicitly uneven power structures of the contemporary European theatrical milieu[19] can be further destabilized by thinking in terms of reconstructions of reconstructions in order to keep in play the slipperiness of referents once multiple invented traditions are taken into account, each of which was itself developed through a layered process.

Such complexity is also necessary for understanding the collaboration between Häger and Jooss (Figure 9.7). Häger was famous in Sweden by the time of *Dixit Dominus*, with countless photos depicting her in high society, including alongside the king, while ladies' magazines published features on her domestic life that, as Nair points out, were probably the only time she held a kitchen implement. The qualifications of the phrase that often comes up—" 'our' Lilavati" or "our Indian Lilavati" (for example, Sjögren 1975, and Westerberg in Jooss and Westerbeg 1977)—are telling; no matter how well known she

---

[18] This in turn was reflected in how Indian practice appeared in diasporic communities and how its relationship to other art practices was negotiated in a manner that supported multiple nationalist projects at once. On the ways in which the negotiation of "traditional" and "modern" played out in American diasporic communities, see Srinivasan (2012), and in British communities, see Lopez y Royo (2004). On the displacement of hereditary performers, see Peterson and Soneji (2008, 7, 20).

[19] Recall the case Savigliano makes for recognizing the encounters of multiple structures when she argues that the term "World Dance" is itself always fusion because "[s]taging, regardless of format, introduces a context that excises the impetus for, and nature of, mobilisation (the 'how these dances came to be') by installing a performer/audience structure in a venue or space charged with differing significations and established requirements" (2009, 177).

FIGURE 9.7.  Kurt Jooss and Lilavati Häger, after a performance by Häger, likely 1970s.

Courtesy Rani Nair.

was, her status as a non-white foreigner meant that she was excluded from the position of being unquestionably "ours." At the same time, Häger both capitalized on and renegotiated the mythology of her identity onstage and off. It is important to mark that Häger's interest in Jooss making a dance for her was part of her larger trajectory of experimentation between Indian and European forms. Newspaper clippings from the period before *Dixit* show a range of activities, including choreographing a *Scheherazade* in Malmö in 1969—a performance with strange racial politics that was described as "the first time an Indian dancer uses her own technique for a great Western ballet" (Ståhle 1969)—and participating in an "East Meets West" concert tour in 1972, in which she shared a bill with Jean Cebron and Pina Bausch.[20] Hammergren describes the tension between Häger's performances that relied "on a 'cosmopolitan' consciousness typical of the time" and the solo work "in which she kept more strictly to Indian dance forms, usually a combination of Bharatanatyam, Manipuri, and Kathak dances." And yet, despite the lack of closure that Häger maintained about her own background, Hammergren points out that

[20]  A review from this concert tour produces a fascinating observation in retrospect: at the time, Häger was better known to Swedish audiences than Cebron and Bausch (Ståhle 1972).

she never articulated the more Westernized elements of her work in terms of diasporic identity (2009, 24–26).[21]

However, early on, I had to convince Nair that it was too easy to place Jooss as the patriarchal foil for Häger, because both collaborators were outsiders in their own ways, verbally included in their respective "homes," but always as Other. Despite Jooss's privileged place in German dance history, once Jooss returned to Germany from exile in England, the company he had been promised, which only had its first performance in 1951, lost funding in 1953. Speaking with Bengt Häger around the time of *Dixit*, Jooss described hopes and promises being repeatedly "dissolved into nothing" on his return, until he was too old. He explained that he did what he could, but "[a]fter the war, when I came back to Germany I thought I would have become a sort of artistic leader in questions of ballets. But that did not happen because I was a refugee. I came as a stranger and remained a stranger. Nothing doing" (Jooss and Häger 1975, tape 15b, 21:26).[22] In the interview that Nair voices—the one in which his body and speech are out of time—Jooss says that he wanted to "withdraw" as a choreographer for various reasons, a carefully chosen and emphasized word (1977). He broke this withdrawal to make *Dixit* with Häger. The piece was conceived while listening to music in a car and made over a short time in a Boy Scout building in the Swedish seaside resort town of Tylösand on the body of a friend whose training was very different from his and who was, in her own way, also simultaneously central and exceptional. While *Dixit Dominus* has been seen as far from pivotal to Jooss's legacy, it seems significant to ask why this was the work that allowed him to return briefly to choreography after his role as a historical figure rendered him out of place in the present. At the same time, understanding how such a piece came to be written off as "minor" may reveal certain biases that support dance's histories. What myths of continuity would be disrupted by giving more weight to Jooss's legacy beyond *Green Table*, not just as a pedagogue but as a choreographer? Could doing so draw attention to the way in which his centrality in German dance history required situating him as exceptional in a manner that ultimately displaced him from the very canon he supported? How would this story change, were *Dixit* not to be seen within modernism's ubiquitous orientalism, but rather as part of a collaboration that could only have happened between two artists who understood what it meant to be insiders and outsiders at the same time?

Something that comes up for us often is how to contextualize this project theatrically, because audience members will likely come with no prior knowledge of *Dixit Dominus* itself, although some may recognize Häger or Jooss. As the performance artist Janez Janša writes, "In reconstructions, one first needs to prove that the object of a reconstruction actually existed" (2012, 368). If the potential of reperformance strategies depends in part on the gaps between multiple temporalities even as they intersect, there always remains the question of how that might be marked, as opposed

---

[21] Hammergren also historicizes Häger's later career, pointing out that the intercultural projects were subsequently overshadowed by a return to a more mythologized India-as-origin.

[22] I deal with this quote and more material from the extensive 1975 interviews in Elswit (2017).

**FIGURE 9.8.** *Future Memory*: Nair with the haute couture costume that Häger never wore on stage.

Performance photo by Kat Reynolds at ImPulsTanz in Vienna, 2015.

to simply absorbed. One of the things we are careful with in *Future Memory* is not to show photographs or film clearly until two-thirds of the way through the piece. Were the images to appear too soon, they would serve as a container for audience imaginations, whereas we challenge those watching to construct new images from the pieces we give them. We also wait until post-show to project a layered film of Nair and Häger both dancing *Dixit*. In addition, even when working with what is already a "minor" work, *Future Memory* explores paths not taken. For example, there is the moment when Nair creates a ghost dance using a hairdryer on the silk haute couture costume that was made for Häger by a famous designer, but never worn in performance (Figure 9.8). *Future Memory*, then, is a chance to both question old stories and tell new ones.

Berlin April 20th, 2010

Dear Lila!

It was so wonderful the other day, after I had written that letter to you, I really felt that I wanted to dance. A little hesitant at first. It was as if I needed to write all these letters to you before I could start moving and find the dance. I tried to confuse myself so that I wouldn't end up just in my head. It's so easy to fall into vnegative thoughts. So now I try to find the desire first of all, to figure out how to wake up my body. A relay system between head and body, shifting back and forth, going back into my body to see how it feels inside and then see myself from the outside, try and imagine how it looks, what would look cool, exciting, with contrasts. I let things take their time, I follow the body, look to see where it wants to go and what it can do.

Last time it was at home in my living room, which isn't so big. So there were loads of turns and change of directions. But sometimes I followed a movement all the way and danced into the hallway, out into the kitchen, bumping into walls and ceilings and floors. It felt like a Deborah Hay choreography, without composition. So then I went and found the manuscript to her solo, "Market." I started reading it and it seemed kind of cool, just hard to remember it all . . . but that might be why I should do it? It might be just the thing?

I listened to Kurt Jooss counting, too. Yes, Bengt and I found the tape you recorded for the rehearsals. It was difficult to transfer the original music, which is for the first part protected by copyright and also only recorded on old reel-to-reel tapes. He sounds extremely bossy. I imagine you dancing in front of him as he is talking. He is sometimes counting with the music and other times with the movements. Sometimes he counts to ten, other times to eight and sometimes he sings to seven, eight, arms, arms, swim, swim. It gave us some keys to the movement material and some parameters for how much freedom we could take in interpretation.

Rani—from an airport in Berlin, delayed on account of an erupting volcano on Iceland that sent up a huge cloud of ashes that covered most of the European sky.

p.s. I might call it "Dixit Jooss."

p.s. 2 . I need to tell you—from talking to Kate: ". . . We also particularize the historical encounter through the specific bodily relationship of re-enactment, and the ways in which it both depends upon borrowing identity and yet can never wholly succeed in that impersonation." I will tell you more, later.


St. Isidoro, Italy July 25th, 2010

Dear Lila!

I showed some pictures of our work to my friend "J" and this is what he said:

R: Who do you see?

J: He seems quite sober, maybe a bit ehh . . . like very sharp, and very precise in his ideas. Maybe he had a lot of ideas also. He looks like someone extremely clever. He definitely looks like a choreographer and not a dancer, someone behind the stage?

R: Why?

J: I don't know. He has this like, look of someone, who likes to work with ideas, more than with his body. And also he's a bit old, so I am just supposing that right now.

R: Do you think he was a dancer before?

J: Probably, they all were. But maybe not, maybe he was just a writer and decided to make some dance.

R: Yes, that is Kurt Jooss. And this is Lilavati, they made a choreography together.

J: Well, he was in love with her. She is very pretty. Maybe he met her in India and she was just a dancer, probably would have had a very difficult career in India. He probably thought that she was very talented, and he thought he could help her. "I can make a solo for her, and since I am still a name, people would come and watch it." Probably, because he's very talented anyway, he made a good solo instead of just an excuse.

It makes me think of the material ways in which we can access dance history, faded old black and white photos or videos with people you hardly can see, moving too fast and very staccato, like in silent movies. In fact it is very often exactly that, a silent movie or very annoying buzzing sound. How does this affect the way we look at dance and artists from before? How can we understand the aesthetics, get a feel of the movement quality, the musicality? How can we understand the dance?

Or the fact that nobody can find sufficient information when they Google you. How can anyone understand what kind of an artist you were? It's so strange to have to explain who you are all the time, what you've done, where you've performed, who you collaborated with.

Slowly, they are forgetting who you were, or nobody cares any more. Nobody knows you travelled all over the world, performed at all major theatre stages and dance festivals. Your exchange with Pina Bausch, composers who wrote compositions for you, your work at the Royal Opera Ballet. That you were the head of the Dance Museum in Stockholm!

Lots of work to be done . . . I will now take a break and buy new batteries for my headphones. They are amazing, with built in noise control. I don't hear anything disturbing!

Rani

# On Tangling with Histories: Reconstructing Reconstructions on a Global Stage

In the letter from April 13, 2010, that she reads onstage, Nair asks Häger: "Did you give up the fusion of Western contemporary dance and traditional Indian forms? I remember Bengt saying something about you feeling that you'd failed in challenging the traditional form or finding a new approach to Indian dance." Later, during the verbatim interview, Nair gives voice to Jooss's explanation of *Dixit Dominus* as an attempt to make "something which was modern European but at the same time did not neglect or contradict Indian traditional ideas of movement." He described Häger as a "Hindu dancer with lots of European leanings," yet when pushed by the interviewer to articulate how Häger's background as an Indian dancer fit his choreographic style, he refused to draw finite distinctions between the practices, explaining that "it fits into my choreography because my choreography fits into her" (1977). One of Nair's goals for *Future Memory* was to realize what that kind of fusion might look like today. There are two explicit dance sections in which Nair experiments with contemporary forms of *Dixit Dominus*. One takes its starting point from particular moments of *Dixit*, such as the slicing arms that she thinks might have been Häger's favorite movement ("I picture her cutting the heads off demons," Nair explains during "Memory of Lila"), the gesture's articulation of the ribs and shoulder girdle gradually developing into a broader range of tested possibilities, performed in silence for the length of the first section of the music. The other section is set to the counted rehearsal tape, but draws on *Dixit*'s movement material only in fits and starts. However, it would be a mistake to locate hybridity in those moments alone, rather than seeing the piece in its entirety as a container for larger questions of conjunction and dislocation, one that not only comments on such concerns but also absorbs them into its own project. Creating such a space that preserves difference, while allowing for shades of Indianness, Swedishness, and Germanness, is particularly important for us in working with *Dixit Dominus* and its many protagonists, times, and places.

In a recent article on the contemporary "global stage," Ananya Chatterjea posits that the power dynamics of hybrid forms are often disguised by the erasure of difference. She writes that "[w]hat seems to be increasingly popular in the sphere of Asian 'contemporary' dance is a kind of ventriloquism, where contemporary Asia finds its voice through signifiers of the Euro-American modern/postmodern, the latter passing once again as the neutral universal, which is able to contain all difference" (2013, 11). By contrast, one of Nair's starting points had to do with too much difference; she wanted to know whether anything she could do would always be marked as "Indian" within Swedish dance, or whether there were ways to push the limits of movement or embodiment toward a more ambiguous legibility, in which multiple practices interrelate without either entirely revealing themselves as such or dissolving into one another.[23] Hammergren has written about the difficulty of classifying Europe and India separately in *Dixit Dominus*, because of their status as lived geographies (2011). Such undoing of presumed monocultures is something that Sandra Chatterjee is now extending through research that places both *Dixit* and *Future Memory* within a larger project on "kinesthetic entanglements" between Indian and Northern European practices on contemporary dance stages.[24] However, I think that one of the key elements of marking and thus exposing the kind of "difference" to which Ananya Chatterjea refers is crossing the geopolitical with the temporal dimension. In *Future Memory*, what Nair calls the "classical Indian dance" is a loose mixture of physical practices including Kathak, Bharatanatyam,

---

[23] This project follows several of Nair's earlier works, including *Pepparkakeland* (2007), which more explicitly took up such questions regarding the legibility of racialized bodies in a contemporary Swedish cultural context.

[24] Chatterjee's work is ongoing as part of the FWF Project "Traversing the Contemporary (pl.): Choreographic Articulations between European and Indian Dance" (P24190), conducted at the Department of Music and Dance Studies, Paris Lodron University, Salzburg, Austria.

and various yogas in which she has trained and performed in Sweden, the United Kingdom, and India in the past two decades.[25] By contrast, pressing beyond the twenty-first-century European experimental performance strategies that structure the piece, it is actually Nair's referent for "contemporary dance" (*Dixit*) that is tied to a specific time and place that appears anachronistic in the present, a dance by an aging modernist choreographer in a postmodern age.

Nair and I talk a lot about how to present a dance that is out of time without being nostalgic or a museum piece, on the one hand, while also not erasing its difference, on the other. If "classical Indian dance" is for Nair a more universal signifier than the already-then-out-of-date particularities of a 1975 "contemporary" dance collaboration (which already aimed to bring together the two), then it seems there might be a way for the future promise of the piece to fix and release ideas of tradition—both Indian and European—by understanding both to be deeply unstable, and working into those instabilities. When Nair started trying to place *Dixit Dominus*, one of the things that troubled her was how it stood outside the progress narrative of dance history as she had learned it. Yvonne Rainer's 1966 Judson classic *Trio A*, for example, preceded *Dixit* by a decade and yet felt more familiar. Nair also began by articulating the power structures of who choreographed whom; but the longer she worked with the piece, the more her assumptions were undone. The footwork, for example, that she initially presumed was a contribution from Häger, started to feel more Joossian. Around the time of a showing in Hamburg at Kampnagel's P1 space in 2010 as part of Treffen Total, she was still reaching for the Western dance history canon to anchor this difference, for example transitioning from flat-footed stamps—that fall somewhere between a Bharata Natyam solo and role of Death in *The Green Table*—into the toe-taps of *Trio A*.

It was not until 2012 that Nair began to play with the mixture of practices that coexisted within her own body, neither flattening nor smoothing them to a continuous whole, nor allowing clear distinctions to emerge. The improvisational process that she calls "contemporary Indian dance" ultimately developed as a container that allows for abrupt shifts between the performance registers accessible within her corporeal archive: a lunge that hops up and down to a gesture in which the hands each make small circles with two fingers pointed out, as she leans into a hip; a neck circle becomes a full-body gyration. The purpose of the practice is to disrupt flow, using the body to hijack messages sent from the brain and vice versa (Figures 9.9 a and b).[26] This is what ended up helping to solve the problem of the rehearsal tape at the end of *Future Memory*. By now, Nair's multicolored jumpsuit is covered by the version of the red costume that she had commissioned to dance *Dixit Dominus* again while pregnant at Bengt's funeral. She listens to a mixed playlist through wireless headphones, while the audience hears

---

[25] In some senses, this is not so distant from Häger, who worked in a more pan-stylistic Indian mode like Ram Gopal, with whose company she first came to Sweden.

[26] Because a full "contemporary Indian Dance" performance for Nair would need to be at least half an hour (more like the length of a conventional ballet), she sees the improvisation at the end of *Future Memory* to be a form of placeholder for that possibility, rather than a fully realized version.

the *Dixit* rehearsal tape with Jooss's elegant voice counting and singing over the music that comes from the miked tape recorder. The television is paused on the title "Dixit Dominus." Nair's dance sometimes meets up with the rehearsal tape, at times the timing between the two is syncopated, at others they are simply in parallel worlds altogether. Nair takes the microphone with her when she leaves the stage after the first section of the music, but leaves the cassette playing. By the time the sound returns from the theater's speakers to the tape recorder to finish out the second part, I can only hear it in conjunction with the different ways that Nair had inhabited the now-empty stage.

This historical dimension—thinking through the temporal other in relation to racial or spatial complications of otherness—is crucial to the "future" potential of the piece. Early on in making *Future Memory*, Nair was taken by the "Altermodern Manifesto" (2009a), Nicholas Bourriaud's proposition for a global form of recycling and reuse that she references in the letter from April 13, 2010. The "altermodern" articulates a "concept of wandering—in time, space and mediums" (Bourriaud in Ryan 2009, n.p.), a response to "a new globalised perception" in which "the artist becomes 'homo viator,' the prototype of the contemporary traveller whose passage through signs and formats refers to a contemporary experience of mobility, travel and transpassing" (Bourriaud 2009a, n.p.). In this sense, it speaks to *Future Memory*'s promiscuous use of performance registers, its investment in translation, as well as the multiple times and places that overlap within it in a manner that does not strictly reinforce a narrative of the colonial West. However, there is an extreme presentism to Bourriaud's insistence that the cultural and social structures in which we live are nothing more than information to be translated, transcoded, and reassembled. By contrast, *Future Memory* not only "produces a singular itinerary within different knowledge streams" (Bourriaud in Ryan 2009, n.p.), but also, in so doing, reveals the ways in which those streams as already "entangled," as Göran Therborn would put it, in a manner that not only coexists in the present, but also draws on more durational historical relationships (2003).[27] It is by revealing such entanglements that its wanderings suggest new paths, routes between and beyond the more familiar canon in which *Dixit Dominus* has little place. To wander into this piece in isolation and then back out again would be to miss the opportunities it offers to reflect back and, in so doing, ahead.

While Bourriaud's perspective comes from a view that the "postmodern" notion of cultural hybridity is too invested in identity politics to deal with any meaningful sense of singularity (2009b, 13), other scholars have shown the potential in approaching global memory with a sense of historical specificity. This is particularly important in a German context, where memory has itself been so contested in relation to German materials as to become, as Andreas Huyssen puts it, a "particularly ubiquitous cipher for memories of the twentieth century," an "international prism" that focuses local discourses around the world (2003, 18, 98).[28] Michael Rothberg, for

---

[27] For a useful overview of discussions on alternative, hybrid, multiple modernities, and what they each offer up to scholarly thought, see Grossberg (2010).

[28] In addition to demonstrating how the Holocaust and other key moments of twentieth-century German history have come to frame more international discussions of memory, several of the essays in Huyssen's anthology deal with Germany's multiple moments of rewriting its own past in various media.

**FIGURE 9.9 A, B.** In the final section, Nair places a microphone on the tape recorder, amid the larger stage installation that has accumulated (a), and then begins the "contemporary Indian dance," illuminated by a sodium lamp (b).

Performance photos by author at Dansens Hus in Stockholm, 2014.

example, argues for the need to recognize the borrowing and cross-referencing process of "multidirectional memory," a "convoluted, sometimes historically unjustified, back-and-forth movement of seemingly distant collective memories in and out of public consciousness," whose imaginative links have the potential to produce new objects and perspectives (2009, 17–19). Likewise, Huyssen argues that, while memory discourses may appear global, they are at their core still tied to the histories of specific nation-states, and can thus also help develop new forms of grounding in an increasingly globalized world. However, in order for them to do so, he cautions that we need to recognize what is happening and how, rather than simply celebrating instability and in-betweenness: "Memory as re-presentation, as making present, is always in danger of collapsing the constitutive tension between past and present [ . . . ]. Thus we need to discriminate among memory practices in order to strengthen those that counteract the tendencies in our culture to foster uncreative forgetting, the bliss of amnesia, and what the German philosopher Peter Sloterdijk once called 'enlightened false consciousness' " (2003, 10).[29] Both Huyssen and Rothberg ultimately suggest that new paths for the future come from understanding how multiple pasts continue to be asked to work in the present, often in unexpectedly intersecting ways that may help to articulate one another.

Coming full circle, Huyssen's imperative to distinguish is crucial for Hardt's suggestion that what is happening on European stages is a performative means of "doing history" in the playground of the past (2012, 218, 230), a way to ask not only what kinds of history are being done, but also what that doing does or can do. One of the things we have struggled with most in *Future Memory* is how far we can go in pushing toward something "new" when the referent exists in so few people's consciousnesses. Huyssen prompts us to think more specifically about what creative practices do when they do history. Are they telling stories about the constructedness of historical materials, which are ultimately rooted in the present? Or might even those belong to a set of formative stories of place and thus speak to more durational and specific entanglements? If so, how can we still deal with the ways in which multiple othernesses—temporal, racial, and spatial—may help to articulate one another? The thing that I am coming to terms with through *Future Memory* is how to think in a manner that is at once global and historically specific—the stakes of reinserting temporal and geopolitical groundings even as boundaries are crossed in creative ways that help us to remember alternative histories and, through them, other futures.

Cosgrove and Fuchs describe such "memory contests" in the German context as a reaction to earlier collective coming to terms with the past (*Vergangenheitsbewältigung*), instead emphasizing "a pluralistic memory culture which does not enshrine a particular normative understanding of the past but embraces the idea that individuals and groups advance and edit competing stories about themselves that forge their changing sense of identity" (2006, 4).

[29] The timing noted in other fields for the turn from "history" to "memory" also coincides with the first round of modern dance's reconstructions (see Franko 1989).

London, November 27th 2010

Lila!

I just found out that you are not born in India! That's fantastic. It changes a lot! You, the object, created the myth about yourself! You were not the victim of media's perception; you simply manipulated them and exaggerated the exotic interest already existing. It all makes sense. Of course you had to talk about India all the time, it was part of your plan.

Maybe we have more in common than I first thought? But then it's partly your fault that I am left with those exoticizing questions. Or did you also realize that this strategy wouldn't ever be the solution, or that it might even invert itself and become, well, more like a trap?

Did you use the work with Jooss as your escape from the exotic gaze? I sense this is in the choices you made, rejecting the extravagant set design and costume proposal and instead going for a very simple costume. In the dance I see a lot of modernistic dance steps, many known from the dance vocabulary of Jooss, but since it is your body performing them, we mainly see them as deriving from traditional Indian dance. We fail to see the dance beyond your body. We don't even see your body.

R


Malmö 3 December 2010

Hello again!

I am trying to imagine what will happen after all these letters I've written for *Ful* have been published. Things will be different then. The text is the dance. I am so used to dance, which disappears and is gone in the same instant it is performed or shared, but text is always there, even after the reader has put the paper down, the text is still right there on the page. It will be there as long as the book itself. It can't be changed, adapted for different audiences, explained or delineated or corrected by me. I will paint pictures of the dance in the text, but only so that the reader can catch a glimpse of it, the same as in my work with Dixit, that I reveal only a glimpse.

And yesterday, when I was with Bengt (and he seemed a lot better than the last time), we found loads of interesting things that I never saw before; pictures, photographs and press clippings. Super cool! Until now I'd only seen the articles that The Dance Museum decided to archive, and every one of those just talks about how Indian you are and at the same time sophisticated and cultured. You were variously referred to as Lilavati or Lilavati Devi or sometimes Lilavati Devi Häger, as if you had several aliases and could switch identities. (And Devi means Goddess!)

Something important changed for me there, at Bengt's house. I felt that I understood you better and could finally grasp the complexity in your work. You haven't only involved yourself in "fine" art with performances at The Royal Dramatic Theatre. You've sought out other situations and contexts, danced in front of the camera, created choreography for musicals, explored nudity on stage. You even performed for the troops during World War Two and were given the rank of Captain. When I thought of you, I only pictured you in a sari, but in the photographs I saw at Bengt's place you wore modern clothes; tight white bellbottom jeans, boots with wedge heels, china slippers, fake furs. I could feel my picture of you changing. You weren't as traditional as you made yourself out to be. You were no longer untouchable. I had gone for so long feeling too much respect for you, afraid to destroy that pretty picture (sweet, kind, cute, holy, mystical, beautiful) that I had created, based on our meetings but also on newspaper articles and books. Suddenly, after seeing these "new" pictures I felt it was easier to relate to you and perhaps I could understand your fascination with the character called Guerilla Woman in Kurt's The Green Table. It reminds me of an embarrassing project I tried to bring about. I wanted to explore power, violence and terrorism, perhaps even in connection to my own background. I had a military costume tailored to fit me. I stood in front of the mirror and took photographs of myself. I remember how sad I looked. I never got any farther since some of my colleagues stopped me, calling my experiment provokingly banal. I also saw an interview column in an old newspaper. When asked what attribute you wished you had, you answered, "I wish that I could write." I hadn't previously understood that you wanted me to write.

I also found an article that states that you really *were* born in India. So now I don't know what to think. But at the same time I think that it doesn't make any difference at all, either way. I understand how easily one can be misunderstood and I myself try to avoid discussing nationality as far as I can, in order not to reproduce what I myself criticize. So if I publish these letters, nationality is one little detail I might forget to mention.

Rani

## WORKS CITED

Angström, Anna. 2014. "Rani Nair skapar laddad dialog om att ärva ett danssolo." *Svenska Dagbladet*. March 15. http://www.svd.se/kultur/scen/rani-nair-laddar-solo-med-smarta-perspektivbyten_3367538.svd.

Barba, Fabián. 2011. "Research into Corporeality." *Dance Research Journal* 43(1): 82–89.

Bourriaud, Nicolas. 2009a. "Altermodern Explained: Manifesto." *Tate Britain*. http://www.tate. org.uk/whats-on/tate-britain/exhibition/altermodern/explain-altermodern/altermodern-explainedmanifesto. (accessed January 13, 2009).

Bourriaud, Nicolas. 2009b. *The Radicant*. Translated by James Gussen and Lili Porten. New York: Lukas & Sternberg.

Chakravorty, Pallabi. 2000/01. "From Interculturalism to Historicism: Reflections on Classical Indian Dance." *Dance Research Journal* 32(2): 108–119.

Chatterjea, Ananya. 2013. "On the Value of Mistranslations and Contaminations: The Category of 'Contemporary Choreography' in Asian Dance." *Dance Research Journal* 45(1): 7–20.

Cosgrove, Mary, and Anne Fuchs. 2006. "Introduction." *German Life and Letters* 59(2): 3–10.

de Soto, Olga. 2012. "Olga de Soto about 'Débords. Reflections on The Green Table'" [Interview with Andrea Keiz]. http://vimeo.com/49506237. (accessed June 16, 2013).

Elswit, Kate. 2012. "Back Again? Valeska Gert's Exiles." In *New German Dance Studies*, edited by Susan Manning and Lucia Ruprecht, 113–129. Champaign: University of Illinois Press.

Elswit, Kate. 2014. *Watching Weimar Dance*. New York: Oxford University Press.

Elswit, Kate. 2017. "The Micropolitics of Exchange: Exile and Otherness after the Nation." In *The Oxford Handbook of Dance and Politics*, edited by Rebekah Kowal, Randy Martin, and Gerald Siegmund, 417–438. New York: Oxford University Press.

Foster, Hal. 2004 "An Archival Impulse." *October* 110 (Fall): 3–22.

Franco, Susanne. 2007. "Ausdruckstanz: Traditions, Translations, Transmission." In *Dance Discourses: Keywords in Dance Research*, edited by Susanne Franco and Marina Nordera, 80–98. London: Routledge.

Franko, Mark. 1989. "Repeatability, Reconstruction and Beyond." *Theatre Journal* 41(1): 56–74.

Giersdorf, Jens Richard. 2013. *The Body of the People: East German Dance since 1945*. Madison: University of Wisconsin Press.

Grossberg, Lawrence. 2010. *Cultural Studies in the Future Tense*. Durham, NC: Duke University Press.

Häger, Bengt. 1976. "Homage à Kurt Jooss." *Dans* 11: 1–6.

Häger, Lilavati, and Lars Ulvenstam. 1984. Filmed Television Interview for "Nyfiken på" series. ID# 30131. Sveriges Television AB.

Hammergren, Lena. 2009. "The Power of Classification." In *Worlding Dance*, edited by Susan Leigh Foster, 14–31. New York: Palgrave Macmillan.

Hardt, Yvonne. 2011. "Staging the Ethnographic of Dance History: Contemporary Dance and Its Play with Tradition." *Dance Research Journal* 43(1): 27–43.

Hardt, Yvonne. 2012. "Engagements with the Past in Contemporary Dance." In *New German Dance Studies*, edited by Susan Manning and Lucia Ruprecht, 217–231. Champaign: University of Illinois Press.

Huyssen, Andreas. 2003. *Present Pasts: Urban Palimpsests and the Politics of Memory*. Stanford, CA: Stanford University Press.

Janša, Janez. 2012. "Reconstruction2: On the Reconstuctions of Pupilija, papa Pupilo and the Pupilceks." In *Perform, Repeat, Record: Live Art in History*, edited by Amelia Jones and Adrian Heathfield, 367–383. Bristol: Intellect Books.

Jones, Amelia, and Adrian Heathfield, eds. 2012. *Perform, Repeat, Record: Live Art in History*. Bristol: Intellect Books.

Jooss, Kurt, and Bengt Häger. 1975. [unpublished interview tapes]. Carina Ari Library, Stockholm.

Jooss, Kurt, and Stig Westerberg. 1977. "Dixit Dominus" [filmed television interview]. Sveriges Television AB, December.

Kuppers, Petra. 2011. *Disability Culture and Community Performance: Find a Strange and Twisted Shape*. New York: Palgrave Macmillan.

Lepecki, André. 2010. "The Body as Archive: Will to Re-Enact and the Afterlives of Dances." *Dance Research Journal* 42(2): 28–48.

Lopez y Royo, Alessandra. 2004. "Dance in the British South Asian Diaspora: Redefining Classicism." *Postcolonial Text* 1(1). http://postcolonial.org/index.php/pct/article/viewArticle/367/809.

Manning, Susan. 2012. "Looking Back Again, and Again" [unpublished lecture]. Journée d'Étude: Autour de l'historiographie de la danse moderne allemande: état de lieux et perspectivesm, University of Nice Sophia Antipolis, March 29.

Meduri, Avanthi. 2004. "Bharatanatyam as Global Dance: Some Issues in Research, Teaching, and Practice." *Dance Research Journal* 36(2):11–29.

Müller, Hedwig, Ralf Stabel, and Patricia Stöckemann, eds. 2003. *Krokodil im Schwanensee: Tanz in Deutschland seit 1945*. Frankfurt am Main: Anabas-Verlag.

Nachbar, Martin. 2012. "Training Remembering." *Dance Research Journal* 44(2): 5–12.

Nair, Rani. 2010. "RANI <3 LILAVATI FRÅN 1975 TILL 2020." *Ful* 2. http://www.tidskriftenful.se/mag.php?m=ful&issid=1292059906&text=1339153154.

Oberzaucher-Schüller, Gunhild, ed. 1992. *Ausdruckstanz: eine mitteleuropäische Bewegung der ersten Hälfte des 20 Jahrhunderts*. Wilhelmshaven: Florian Noetzel Verlag.

Peterson, Indira Viswanathan, and Davesh Soneji. 2008. "Introduction." In *Performing Pasts: Reinventing the Arts in Modern South India*, edited by Indira Viswanathan Peterson and Davesh Soneji, 1–42. New York: Oxford University Press.

Pikula, Joan. 1981. "Kurt Jooss's Dixit Dominus for Lilavati." *Dance Magazine* (August): 54–56.

Román, David. 2005. *Performance in America: Contemporary U.S. Culture and the Performing Arts*. Durham, NC: Duke University Press.

Rothberg, Michael. 2009. *Multidirectional Memory: Remembering the Holocaust in the Age of Decolonization*. Stanford, CA: Stanford University Press.

Rubidge, Sarah. 1995. "Reconstruction and Its Problems." *Dance Theatre Journal* 12(1): 31–33.

Ryan, Bartholomew, and Nicholas Bourriaud. 2009. "Altermodern: A Conversation with Nicolas Bourriaud." *Art in America*. March 17. www.artinamericamagazine.com/news-features/interviews/altermodern-a-conversation-with-nicolas-bourriaud/ (accessed October 30, 2013).

Savigliano, Marta. 2009. "Worlding Dance and Dancing Out There in the World." In *Worlding Dance*, edited by Susan Leigh Foster, 163–190. New York: Palgrave Macmillan.

Siegmund, Gerald. 2010. "Affekt, Technik, Diskurs: Aktiv Passiv Sein im Angesicht der Geschichte." *Original und Revival: Geschichts-Schreibung im Tanz*, edited by Christina Thurner and Julia Wehren, 15–26. Zürich: Chronos.

Sjögren, Margarete. 1975. "En ny Balett av Kurt Jooss." *Svenska Dagbladet*. October 18.

Srinivasan, Priya. 2012. *Sweating Saris: Indian Dance as Transnational Labor*. Philadelphia: Temple University Press.

Ståhle, Anna Greta. 1969. "Exotiskt balettmöte I Malmö." *Dagens Nyheter*. February 1.

Ståhle, Anna Greta. 1972. "Öst och väst dansar på Scala." *Dagens Nyheter*. April 19.

Stöckemann, Patricia. 2001. *Etwas ganz Neues muß nun entstehen: Kurt Jooss und das Tanztheater*. München: K. Kieser Verlag.

Taylor, Diana. 2003. *The Archive and the Repertoire: Performing Cultural Memory in the Americas*. Durham, NC: Duke University Press.

Therborn, Göran. 2003. "Entangled Modernities." *European Journal of Social Theory*. 6(3): 293–305.

# PART IV

INVESTIGATIVE
REENACTMENT

*Transmission as Heuristic Device*

CHAPTER 10

........................................................................

# (RE)ENACTING THINKING
# IN MOVEMENT

........................................................................

MAAIKE BLEEKER

In *The Idea of History*, Robin Collingwood proposes that reenactment is fundamental to how we think, and in particular to the possibility of sharing thoughts. One of his examples is Archimedes and his insight into the law of special gravity. Getting the idea of gravity, Collingwood explains, involves grasping the relationships observed by Archimedes between mass and volume of an object, an insight that history tells us occurred to Archimedes while taking a bath (Collingwood 1993, 287, 444–446). Understanding the idea of gravity involves a kind of reenactment of grasping this set of connections perceived by Archimedes, and as a result we "get" the same idea. Collingwood was not thinking of the kind of reenactments created by dance and performance makers today, nor of the actual redoing of historical events like battles, voyages, practices of daily life, or the historical event of Archimedes' discovery. Reenacting Archimedes' idea of special gravity, as Collingwood sees it, does not require taking a bath, nor is it about gaining a better understanding of the historical person Archimedes and his situation. Rather, it is a matter of grasping the logic perceived by Archimedes and, in this sense, thinking the same thought. Precisely for this reason, I will argue, Collingwood's conceptualization of reenactment offers a most useful perspective on the material and embodied practices of reenactment in dance. This perspective gains new actuality with the emergence of embodied, embedded, and enactive approaches to cognition, as well as with transformations in ways of engaging with information characteristic of pervasive mediatization and the rise of digital culture.

Digital culture has altered our modes of investigating and understanding history, and our modes of relating to historical documents, events, and creations. "Our sense of history—of facticity in relation to the past—is inextricable from our experience of inscription, or writing, print, photography, sound recording, cinema, and now (one must wonder) digital media that save text, image, and sound," Lisa Gitelman observes in *Always Already New: Media, History and the Data of Culture* (2008, 20–21). This is not only a matter of how media represent history, or capture and transmit traces of historical events, but also of how they afford different ways of engaging with what is captured and stored: different ways of finding, searching, investigating, and interpreting. Exploring the implications of Gitelman's observations for our understanding of performance history, Sarah Bay-Cheng points out that "[d]igital access to documentation via computers (searching library databases, viewing digitized documents, scanning photographs, and most significant, sharing these within digital networks) affects the ways in which we approach and organize performance history" (2012, 32). Digitalization foregrounds how historical research is not merely a matter of (re)discovering the past as if somehow stored in the archive, but of producing an understanding of the past based on active engagement with traces from the past. Bay-Cheng observes that "[a]s archives and libraries digitize their historical documents, the traditional paths and processes of scholarship inevitably shift from discovery to creation—the reperformance of documentation" (32). In this context, reenactments by dance, theater, and performance makers appear as staged versions of new modes of approaching history, brought about by the emergence of new, digital media.

The transformations brought about by digitalization and pervasive mediatization bring to the fore how our engagement with information is itself a performance, while at the same time understanding that what is performed here requires us to think of performance less as a discrete event and more as a mode of proceeding. Bay-Cheng refers to the *Oxford English Dictionary* definition of performance as "[a] way or manner in which something is done or takes place; a method of proceeding on any activity, business, etc." (Bay-Cheng 2012, 35). This means that "[r]ather than framing a phenomenon *as* performance, it proposes to adopt performance *as the mode* through which we assess phenomena, including digital documentation" (35). Thus understood, "performance itself functions [ . . . ] as a network of interrelated components, both on- and offline, both overtly mediated and immediate to various and dispersed recipients. What we encounter in performance (and what we may seek to historicize later) is a network of constitutive parts" (35). Elsewhere I have elaborated an understanding of reenactment as the tracing and rethinking of the logic of this network of interrelated parts (Bleeker, 2012). Specifically, I considered how we might conceive of such rethinking as a reenactment in Collingwood's sense, namely as the grasping (or attempt at grasping) of the artistic thought proposed by the logic that brings together the constitutive parts of an artistic creation. In the following, I will return to Collingwood's understanding of reenactment as a perspective on how we perform our engagement with information.

This brings me to an understanding of the relationship between reenactment and thinking that differs from how Collingwood's ideas can, and have been, applied in approaches to reenactment as a means to gain access to the psychology and the experiences of historical agents. This possibility is indeed suggested by Collingwood, for example when he discusses the Codex of Emperor Theodosius. This Codex was an attempt to install a formalized form of law in the Roman empire. In order to understand what this codex was and what it meant within the historical situation, Collingwood argues, a historian must envision the situation with which the emperor was trying to deal, and "then he must see for himself just as if the emperor's situation were his own, how such a situation might be dealt with" (Collingwood 1993, 283). He must imagine "the reasons for choosing one [course of action] rather than another and thus he must go through the process which the emperor went through in deciding on this particular course" (283). Examples like this one suggest that reenactment would provide access to the psychology of a historical agent. In this sense, they are quite different from the example of Archimedes discussed before, where reenactment describes enacting the grasping of a logic of connections also grasped by the historical agent, but does not offer insight into the psychology or experiences of this agent. I share the critique expressed by others before me of the understanding of reenactment suggested by Collingwood's elaboration of (among others) the case of Emperor Theodosius. However, I will nevertheless argue that Collingwood's explanation of the possibility of sharing thoughts in terms of reenactment, exemplified in his discussion of Archimedes, is most useful as part of an enactive, embodied, and embedded approach to thinking. This approach gains new actuality in relation to transformations in modes of engaging with information made possible by the affordances of new media technology.

The notion of *affordance* was first introduced by James J. Gibson to describe the ways in which environments hold the potential for actions. Some environments afford things like walking, picking berries, or growing plants, whereas others afford climbing in trees, hunting animals, or catching fish. What people will do in certain environments will depend not only on what they are capable of, but also on the affordances of the environment and how such affordances will invite them to use their capacities in certain ways rather than others. Gibson also demonstrates the potential of affordance for understanding how we perceive and make sense of things. In his book *The Ecological Approach to Visual Perception*, he uses the idea of affordances to elaborate an understanding of perception. This perception is not a matter of an autonomous perceiver simply taking in what is there through the senses as passive channels that connect the perceiver to the outside world, but of the senses as what he calls active perceptual systems that explore and try to grasp what they encounter. How they do so, and how as a result we come to perceive what we encounter, including a sense of self in relation to it, will depend on how the world we encounter affords to be grasped by our perceptual systems. Our perception of the world and our sense of self as agent of these perceptions emerge from our interactions with and are afforded by the environment. Our capacity for doing things and making choices takes shape within these interactions.

Gibson's ideas about affordances would become very important to today's embodied, embedded, and enactive approaches to perception and cognition that set out to explain our cognitive perceptual engagement with what we encounter as the result of the interaction between our cognitive perceptual capacities and how what we encounter affords to be grasped by these capacities. Gibson's ideas also found their way into theories of design and media. Design and media literally shape the world we encounter. They afford perceptions and actions as the potential for engagement. In this context, reenactment gains new actuality as a perspective on the transmission of information through media, not in terms of how media represent content, but how they afford modes of enacting our engagement with them, and in doing so grasp the ideas embodied in their very (digital) materiality. In this context, I argue, Collingwood's work becomes interesting not as an empirical approach to the experience of historical agents, but as a speculative approach to how ideas and thoughts can be shared. This involves an understanding of Collingwood in line with Guiseppina D'Oro's (2000) observation that the potential of Collingwood's ideas about reenactment might be less in how they are part of his philosophy of history and more in how they can be read as a theory of mind. Approaching his ideas as a theory of mind will involve acknowledging that some of the ways in which Collingwood applies his ideas to the practice of historical research are not (or are no longer) tenable or necessary, and perhaps even impede an understanding of the full consequences of his speculative approach to thinking.

This speculative approach, I will show, proves most useful as a perspective on modes of performing our engagement with information afforded by current media developments, specifically how these media draw attention to perception and thinking as a result of how we enact our encounters with the world through media. From this perspective, reenactments in dance appear as both symptom of and reflection on what Mark Hansen, Katherine Hayles, and others have termed *techogenesis*: our coevolution with technology (Hansen 2000, 2006, 2015; Hayles 2012). Human intelligence and modes of thinking, they argue, cannot be understood separately from the technology through which humans interact with and relate to their environments. What we conceive of as human—as human modes of doing, thinking, and experiencing—is actually the result of the coevolution of humans with technology, and how this coevolution has shaped our modes of doing, thinking, and experiencing. Furthermore, this evolution in interaction with technology is not a matter of increased alienation from our bodies, but of ever new couplings of our bodies with technology. As a result, new developments in media technology may highlight aspects of our corporeal performance of engaging with information that previously went unnoticed. Reenactments in dance provide a perspective on what is involved in performing these modes of engaging with information brought to us by media, while also gesturing toward implications in relation to our understanding of what it means to share thoughts, to grasp an idea, and to transmit knowledge.

## DANCING IN DIALOGUE WITH THE HISTORICAL IMAGINARY

In dance, works that are referred to (by their makers or others) as reenactments involve redoing of (aspects of) works by other makers. Such redoing often involves an explicit *relating to* this earlier work that highlights both the reaching out to the past from the present and the historical distance separating the two. In this respect, reenactments differ from reconstructions, repertoire, or reinterpretations (although sometimes the exact difference can be hard to determine). Often, the aim of reenactments is not to make present what was once there (which is usually the aim of reconstructing a historical performance), to revive a work (as in performing repertoire), or to offer a new inter-pretation of it (for example, Mats Ek's or Matthew Bourne's versions of *Swan Lake*), but rather to engage with work created in the past from the perspective of the present. Nicole Beutler's *Les Sylphides* (2007) is not an interpretation of Mikhail Fokine's creation, but an exploration that directs attention to choreographic principles deployed by Fokine. She takes the audience along in looking at aspects of his work through her reworking of (parts of) it (see Bleeker 2012). Similarly, one might argue, Fabian Barba's *A Mary Wigman Dance Evening* (2009) shows us his engagement with Wigman's work. The fact that his male body is performing her dances is not an interpretation of her dances, nor does he attempt to erase the differences between her body and his. Rather, he evokes her dances while also remaining very much present himself as the one engaging with parts of her creations. Martin Nachbar's *Urheben/Aufheben* (2008) very explicitly frames his redoing of parts of Dore Hoyer's work with reflections about what he discovered about the logic of her ways of moving. Being trained mostly in release techniques and contact improvisation, he found it difficult to embody and actualize Hoyer's expressive style of moving.[1] The performance thus constantly stages and highlights the distance (and the difference) between Hoyer's original and Nachbar's redoing of the work.

Reenactments like these demonstrate Alexander Cook's point that actually "projects of reenactment are not in any direct sense about the period or the events being reen-acted. Rather they are about a modern set of activities that are inspired by an interest in the past. They are about placing modern individuals in dialogue with a historical imag-inary" (Cook 2004, 494). Cook is a historian writing about his own experiences as par-ticipant in the BBC series *The Ship*, in which a crew of fifty "experts" and volunteers sailed a replica of Captain James Cook's ship *Endeavour* from Australia to Indonesia along the path it sailed in 1770. In such television programs, Cook observes, reenact-ment is both a narrative strategy and a research tool. The aim is "not to dramatize a past that is already known, but to learn something new about the past through the activity of reenactment itself and to communicate those findings to a wider audience" (487–488). Although Cook is sympathetic toward the potential of reenactment as an investigative strategy, he also observes three key problem areas of the genre. The first is the risk of mapping the subjective experience of participants, or their behavior as observed by a third party, directly onto an original historical situation. The second is the result of the demands imposed by the television genre:

> On the one hand, it wants to tell a story about a group of modern individuals, stripped of the protective layer of their normal routine and thrown together in adver-sity. [ . . . ] On the other hand, it wants to tell a story about a particular period in his-tory or a particular series of historical events that may or may not be amenable to treatment in the aforementioned terms. (489)

---

[1] These reflections are part of the performance (a recording of which can be found online at https://vimeo.com/74015952). See also Bleeker (2012).

The director will have to negotiate a balance between these two demands and in such a way that it becomes interesting television. The third risk observed by Cook is the "persistent tendency to privilege a visceral, emotional engagement with the past at the expense of a more analytical treatment" (490). The challenge, Cook observes, is to find a way of illustrating critical engagement with the past in a manner that captures the imagination of a lay audience.

Although reenactments in the field of dance do not usually aim to satisfy a mass audience, as is the case with popular television, they are also an investigative practice, created with the aim to be staged for an audience. This is usually a much smaller and more specialized audience, yet nevertheless an audience that needs to be accounted for. The way in which Nachbar frames his redoing of Hoyer's work with reflection is informative about what he learned in redoing Hoyer's work, but is also a way of relating to his audience and of capturing their imagination. His anecdotes about his initial failure to perform Hoyer's movements and his encounters with Waltraud Luley, the official custodian of Hoyer's legacy, are instrumental in drawing the audience into his project and his fascinations. These reflections function as acts of focalization that mediate closeness to Nachbar as the audience's contemporary, while at same time highlighting the distance between this shared point of view and the past he attempts to relate to. Anouk van Dijk deployed a similar strategy in her redoing (2007) of Hans van Manen's *Situation* (1970), in which she included a voice-over of one of the dancers who performs in the remake, attempting to describe to us what he sees in a video recording of the original piece.

These strategies of focalization that capture the imagination of the audience, while at the same time mediating a certain distance to the historical material being reenacted, evoke a disjunction that, according to Cook, is essential for reenactments to be productive as a mode of research. For, despite their obvious inauthenticity as a replication of historical experience, Cook also observes that there may be an important value in investigative reenactment, namely as a means to improve our understanding of the past as a world that differs from ours. Although reenactment cannot give access to the experiences and thoughts of historical agents, it can make experiential the disjunction between the outlook of modern reenactors and the recorded or imagined perspective of their historical predecessors, and thus can alert us to differences between our contemporary modes of experiencing and thinking and those of the historical actor. This disjunction is an important component of the dramatic presentation of the television genre described by Cook. It is also a recurring dramaturgical principle in reenactments in dance.

The ways in which these reperformances evoke such disjunction also draws attention to an aspect of reenactment not addressed by Cook. This is the relationship between reenactment and transformations in reorganizations of knowledge-making brought about by mediatization. These pieces reflect not only on the past works, and the thinking embodied in them, but also on how the new makers came to know the work of previous makers through media. Van Dijk's performance includes the description of the video through which she got to know the choreography. In his redoing (and in the text he wrote about it), Nachbar describes how he learned about Hoyer's work through his archival encounter with the filmic images (Nachbar 2012, 6–8). Beutler shows a recording of *Les Sylphides* to the audience waiting to see her redoing of it. In an interview (in Dutch, available on YouTube https://www.youtube.com/watch?v=wO4CZ4_lPao), Beutler explains how she started creating two other redoings—of Lucinda Child's *Radial Courses* (1976) and *Interior Drama* (1977) (presented together under the title *Dialogue with Lucinda*, 2010)—from having her dancers learn the movements from video recordings of the works. In the reenactment of Child's work, one of the dancers reflects on the differences between what can be seen in the video recordings and their take on the work. Another very interesting example is Daniel AlmgrenRecén's remake (*I Live*, 2009) of Hans van Manen's *Live* (1979). AlmgrenRecén's remake starts from an attempt at reconstructing the first part of the work from a video recording made during a performance of the original work and a sound recording of an interview with one of the dancers who performed it. The original is also about media and mediatization. Created in 1979, it explored the possibilities of live video projection at the moment this became technically possible. The choreography begins with a duet between a dancer and a cameraman holding a big video camera and shooting the dancer while moving with and around her. These recordings are the ones used by AlmgrenRecén. This means that AlmgrenRecén had to reconstruct where the dancer and the cameraman were relative to each other and to the audience from the images showing the dancer as seen from the constantly changing point of view of the cameraman. In the first part of his redoing, the audience sees AlmgrenRecén marking positions in space while they hear a sound recording of him and one of the dancers who once performed the part. Together, they try to work out the spatial relationships between the dancer in the recordings, the cameraman, and the audience at each moment of the recording. His performance presents a literal illustration of Bay-Cheng's observation (referred to at the beginning of this chapter) that our engagement with mediatized information is itself a performance and shows this performance to be an embodied enacting of the spatial logic of the work.

# (RE) ENACTING MOVEMENT

Like Collingwood's reader trying to grasp the logic of Archimedes' insights, these dance makers attempt to grasp (aspects of) the artistic thought embodied in the creations of others. Reenacting these thoughts is not a matter of (or an attempt at) redoing the thinking process of the choreographers who created these dances, but rather of grasping the logic of thought embodied in the dance. This distinction between thinking and thought is important to Collingwood's theory for the way it explains how different people can have the same thought, and how thought can be shared. In sharing thoughts, we grasp the internal consistency of someone else's thought and mentally reenact this logic. Reenactments in dance present an image of such grasping of the internal consistency of a thought as an embodied practice. They demonstrate how this involves relating to the thoughts embodied in an artistic creation from (the framework of) one's own body.

In these reenactments, the movements of the reenactor are a means of engaging with works from the past as they have come to us through recordings. Movement becomes a way of exploring historical creations and coming to an understanding of the artistic thinking embodied in them. These works continue a line of thinking about and practicing dance as a way of investigating and exploring movement, particularly as it has been important to the (self)understanding of modern dance as it emerged from the resistance to ballet in the late nineteenth and early twentieth centuries. The idea that movement plays a crucial role in how we make sense and understand is central to John Martin's (in)famous theory of dance, *metakinesis*, developed in response to the development of modern dance in the 1920s and 1930s (Martin 1965). Movement, he argues, is central to perception. In watching dance, we mimic the movements of bodies seen on stage and "dance along" with them. This does not mean that the body will actually perform all these actions. Many motor responses are registered but not carried out. Yet, as motor impulse, they still play an important part in our experience of what we see. These motor responses connect what is seen to previous experiences and thus awaken earlier sense perceptions and the feelings, emotions, and expectations related to them.

In the further elaboration of his ideas, the centrality of movement becomes part of an explanation of how the new (at that time) modern dance of Martha Graham and others evokes feelings that are universally shared and recognized because of a (supposedly) natural connection between movement and feeling. Notwithstanding this claimed universality, however, not all moving bodies appear to be equally able to make this connection happen. It is in particular in the bodies and dances of his white American contemporaries that Martin recognizes this ability, while other bodies are considered too specific to evoke the universal. Yet, leaving aside these problematic claims for universality, his ideas make sense as a theory about the centrality of movement to perception and thinking. Actually, without these claims for universality, his ideas become all the more interesting precisely for how Martin, in dialogue with a culturally and historically specific development in dance practice, develops a theory that is not only a theory about dance, but also a theory about perception that, like more recent theories of embodied cognition, explains how we perceive from how we enact our encounter with the world, and how movement plays a central role in this. In this respect, connections can be perceived as well with Maurice Merleau-Ponty's (2012) phenomenological approach to embodied perception, originally published in 1945, one year prior to when Collingwood's *The Idea of History* first appeared. Merleau-Ponty's work was to become an important source of inspiration for embodied and enactive approaches to perception and cognition.

The premise of enactive approaches to cognition is the insight that perceiving something is not merely a matter of receiving sensory stimulation but requires an active process of making sense of sensory stimulation. Doing so involves enacting the logic that connects the various stimulations. We do so by means of what Alva Noë terms "sensory-motor skills," that is, our practical experience with movement (Noë 2004). Human bodies have a great number of sensors through which they are capable of receiving stimuli. The possibility of receiving stimuli itself, however, cannot explain how we perceive a world filled with objects and inhabited by moving bodies. Noë gives the example of perceiving the shape of a rectangular box in the dark. With our fingers we can feel different sides of the box. The impression of the surface of the box on our fingers, however, cannot explain how we are capable of grasping from these various simultaneous and successive impressions that what we are touching is a rectangular box. To do so involves our practical experience with movement. Perception, Noë points out, is not an activity in the brain, but rather a skillful activity on the part of the organism as a whole. And the basis of perception is implicit practical knowledge of the ways in which movement gives rise to changes in sensory stimulation—implicit knowledge, for example, that movement of the eyes to the left produces rightward movement across the visual field. But it also includes the kind of implicit knowledge that, when looking at one side of a tomato, makes us see a tomato. We see not the surface of one side of the tomato, but the presence of a three-dimensional object in space. Perceiving is not merely to have sensory impressions, but rather to *make sense of* sensory impressions and this happens through our sensorimotor skills. "[M]ere sensory stimulation *becomes* experience with world-presenting content *thanks to* the perceiver's possession of sensorimotor skills" (Noë 2004, 183). Furthermore, such understanding is constitutive of not only our experience of the world we encounter, but also the root of our ability to think about it. Experience presents things, the world, as being such and such. It is about the world. What he means is that our perceptions are not reflections of a world existing independently of us, but are our way of understanding what the world out there might be like. Experience is about the world in the sense that we do not experience the world as it is, but as a result of how our bodies make sense of what they encounter from the perspective of the organism. To have an experience is "to be confronted with a possible way the world is (189)." Perception, therefore, is bound up with our broader capacities to think about and understand the world.

Enactive approaches to perception like Noë's reactualize Martin's observations about the centrality of movement. They also clarify that this centrality of movement is not a matter of mimicking (as Martin would have it), but of enacting. Bringing to bear our sensorimotor skills in perception is not a matter of mimicking something (a movement) seen, but of grasping what we encounter from the perspective of own body. It is enacting our sense of it. This is in line with what Nachbar describes in his reflections on redoing Hoyer's work. His reenactment of Hoyer's work is not a matter of copying (an image of) her moving body (mimicking what he sees), but of grasping its logic from the perspective of his own embodiment. This is also what produces a sense of disjunction, an awareness of difference. AlmgrenRecén's reenactment of *Live* also shows that such a process of grasping from the body is not matter of mimicking a body seen moving. AlmgrenRecén does not even use a recording that shows him how the dancer moves through space. How the dancer moves is precisely what he tries to understand through his reenactment.

# TOOLS TO THINK THROUGH

AlmgrenRecén was born in 1979, the year that *Live* was created. He grew up with the technologies that were still new in 1979, as well as with technological developments since then. These technologies are part of his modes of thinking, including his modes of thinking dance. His reenactment may be called exemplary for how a new generation of dance makers relates to the work of previous generations through recordings that are now widely available in archives and on the Internet. These recordings have become increasingly important in not only how knowledge about dance and choreographies is transmitted, but also how dance is (re)created. More than ever before, understanding of dance today is informed by the ubiquitous presence of recordings, as well as of recording technology and the possibility of instant playback, cut and montage. That is, the ubiquitous presence of media is a matter of not only what is available through recordings, but also of new modes of engaging with media and new ways in which media have become part of all kinds of other behaviors. Today's media users are not passive consumers, but active users capturing images, cutting and pasting, and sharing them. These new media technologies afford new modes of performing with and through them. Again, AlmgrenRecén's remake of van Manen's *Live* is an interesting example.

In van Manen's original, the female dancer is the object of the camera eye, an eye that is literally gazing at her from a male point of view. The cameraman is the voyeur who looks at her while he himself remains largely outside the circle of light surrounding her. He is placed in the dark, dressed in black coveralls, and carries a big camera on his shoulders, which hides his face; meanwhile, all attention is directed toward the female dancer and her image. She is excessively visible, both onstage and in the greatly enlarged projected image on a huge screen at the back of the stage. While he is looking through the camera at her, we see her as an object being looked at, both onstage and in the projection. In AlmgrenRecén's reenactment, it is a male dancer (AlmgrenRecén himself) who is the object of the eye of the camera, and it is a female cameraperson holding this camera. Instead of the large apparatus carried by the cameraman on his shoulder in *Live*, she uses a small handheld camera, which she holds away from her face. Not only is her face not hidden behind the camera, the camera turns into an object featuring in a triangular relationship. Unlike the situation in *Live*, the camerawoman does not look at the dancer through the camera. Instead, she looks directly at him and at the little screen on the camera she is holding. The dancer looks equally at the camera and directly at the camerawoman. Together and through their interaction, they produce images of the dancer that, as we will see later, are the spatial equivalent of those produced by the cameraman in *Live*.

The result is a different portrayal of gender and is also illustrative for technological developments since the creation of *Live* in 1979. In particular, it illustrates how mobile media and the distribution of computers in everyday life have inaugurated changes that are not merely a matter of the swapping of bigger machines for smaller ones. More important than these material technical changes, media theorist Mark Hansen observes, are the social and cultural developments with which they are connected. Mobile media are exemplary for the rise of the mixed reality paradigm and how the virtual dimensions to which media provide access are no longer a separate realm distinct from physical reality (a world "in a mirror"), but become an integral part of our modes of accessing reality. "Our mobile technologies are currently in the process of transforming the function of recording," Hansen observes, "no longer solely or primarily a technical process for memorizing human experience, as it largely was in the cinematic age, recording now typically operates in the service of connection" (2015, 39). Media become ways of connecting and ways of navigating. More than tools to archive, media become tools to create. When incorporated in practices of exploring dance, they become tools to think through.

The modes of interacting afforded by these technological developments foreground Gibson's point that how we make sense of what we encounter is not a matter of passive reception of stimuli, but an active exploration through what he terms "perceptual systems" (Gibson 1966). With this approach he argues against an understanding of seeing, hearing, tasting, and so on, as happening independently from one another and as each related to a separate set of sensors. Rather, how the world appears to us as audible, tangible, visible, taste-able, and so forth, is the result of how sensors for receiving stimuli function as part of systems for grasping the world encountered. How bodies are capable of grasping and making sense of what they encounter will depend on the possibilities given in the structure of their embodiment, how they have learned from experience, and on the affordances of what they encounter.

This role of the body is foregrounded by technological developments that afford new modes of enacting our engagement with information. These new modes of enacting sense-making and thinking are the subject of Katie King's *Networked Reenactments: Stories Transdisciplinary Knowledges Tell*. In this book, King proposes reenactment as a perspective on newly emerging modes of distributed, embedded, and embodied cognition. The kind of televisualized reenactments discussed by Cook, she argues, actually mark the beginning of transformations in practices of sharing and producing knowledge that would later be taken further by digital and networked technologies (King 2011). Reenactments on television demonstrate the emergence of new practices of knowing that result from how media (in this case, television) afford users to navigate between what she terms "knowledge worlds." One of her examples is the television program *Leonardo's Dream Machines*, in which two teams attempt to reconstruct two of Leonardo da Vinci's inventions (a flying machine and a giant crossbow). The program is not merely a documentary showing the attempt at redoing. Rather, it is a montage of highly diverse materials that takes the viewer along from documenting the attempt at reconstructing, to reenactments of historical scenes by actors ("Leonardo in his studio"), to interviews with participants, to scenes that combine different realities (like a voice-over of actors narrating a historical situation, combined with images of the historical site as it looks today, documentation of historical objects in museums and libraries, animations, and computer simulations). Reenactments, King argues, are experiments across knowledge worlds. They are *pastpresents*, in the way that past and present mutually construct each other. In the reenactment, this produces what King describes as *cognitive sensations*, experiences that result from a kind of grasping that is not only rational but also compositional, affective, and associative. This logic, King points out, foreshadows the kind of navigating that is now structurally part of practices of gathering knowledge and producing understanding using the Web. This involves a shift from knowledge as given and represented, to a situation in which we experience knowledge in the making as a result of modes of navigating through knowledge worlds.

Reenactments created by dance makers reflect (aspects of) these broader cultural transformations, while at the same time they show how dance and dance knowledge provide a context and a history of knowledge-in-practice for reflection about and further development of the implications and potential of these transformations. The reflections of Nachbar, for example, are telling about practices of getting to know and of grasping knowledge practiced by these makers. In Nachbar's performance, this attempt at reaching out to the historical imaginary also involves navigating across "knowledge worlds." His reenactment of Hoyer's work not only shows him redoing the choreography, but also includes very different scenes, like his dialogues with Waltraud Luley, his investigations in the library, his attempts in the studio to grasp the logic of Hoyer's movements, and many more. And although in *Urheben/Aufheben* we do not actually see Nachbar in the library, in the studio, on the telephone with Waltraud Luley, and so on, his monologue cum dance performance brings together moments in which he performs part of Hoyer's dances with scenes in which he evokes other moments from his voyage of discovery. The performance shows him navigating through these knowledge worlds and inviting us to navigate with him. By showing (parts of) the actual reenactment of Hoyer's performance with many instances of attempting to enact his relationship to what she is doing, his performance presents a fleshing out of what it means to navigate through knowledge worlds. This navigation involves not only different ways of combining and connecting information about the work he attempts to understand (or, to invoke Bay-Cheng, new modes of performing our modes of processing information) but also invites a different understanding of what it is that one "gets" when one "gets" what this work is.

## WORKS CITED

Bay-Cheng, Sarah. 2012. "Theater Is Media: Some Principles for a Digital History of Performance." *Theater* 42(2): 27–41.

Bleeker, Maaike. 2012. "(Un)covering Artistic Thought Unfolding." *Dance Research Journal* 44(2): 13–26.

Collingwood, Robin G. 1993. *The Idea of History*. Oxford: Oxford University Press.

Cook, Alexander. 2004. "The Use and Abuse of Historical Reenactment: Thoughts on Recent Trends in Public History." *Criticism* 46(3): 487–496.

D'Oro, Guiseppina. 2000. "Collingwood on Reenactment and the Identity of Thought." *Journal of the History of Philosophy* 38(1): 87–101.

Gibson, James J. 1979. *The Ecological Approach to Visual Perception*. Boston, MA: Houghton Mifflin.

Gibson, James J. 1966. *The Senses Considered as Perceptual Systems*. Boston: Houghton Mifflin.

Gitelman, Lisa. 2008. *Always Already New: Media, History and the Data of Culture*. Cambridge, MA: MIT Press.

Hayles, N. Katherine. 2012. *How We Think: Digital Media and Contemporary Technogenesis*. Chicago and London: Chicago University Press.

Hansen, Mark. 2000. *Embodying Technesis: Technology beyond Writing*. Ann Arbor: University of Michigan Press.

Hansen, Mark. 2006. *Bodies in Code: Interfaces with Digital Media*. New York and London: Routledge.

Hansen, Mark. 2015. *Feed-Forward: On the Future of 21st Century Media*. Chicago: University of Chicago Press.

King, Katie. 2011. *Networked Reenactments: Stories Transdisciplinary Knowledges Tell*. Durham, NC, and London: Duke University Press.

Martin, John. 1965 [1939]. *Introduction to the Dance*. A Dance Horizons republication. New York: W. W. Norton.

Merleau-Ponty, Maurice. 2012. *Phenomenology of Perception*. New York and London: Routledge.

Nachbar, Martin. 2012. "Training Remembering." *Dance Research Journal* 44(2): 3–12.

Noë, Alva. 2004. *Action in Perception*. Cambridge, MA: MIT Press.

# CHAPTER 11

# NOT MADE BY HAND, OR ARM, OR LEG

## *The Acheiropoietics of Performance*

BRANISLAV JAKOVLJEVIĆ

## PHANTOM PERFORMANCES

"HERMANN Nitsch's OM Theatre slaughter 100 sheep in castle grounds in art ritual, selected crowd of art and social élite guests watching, mid-summer day. High on blood" (Christopherson 1976, 44). This is one of the performances described in "Annihilating Reality," an article signed by Genesis P-Orridge and Peter Christopherson, in the July–August 1976 issue of *Studio International*, dedicated to performance and guest edited by RoseLee Goldberg. Published alongside articles on Joan Jonas, Laurie Anderson, Adrian Piper, Joseph Beuys, and other leading performance artists of the mid-1970s, "Annihilating Reality" is a print-performance in its own right. Each of its four pages is divided into four columns: the ones positioned on the extreme left and right contain a series of four photographs with captions, while the inner two columns consist of short paragraphs on performance. Most statements in the inner left column are prefaced with the word "hearsay"; some statements in the inner right column begin with the word "heresy."

Part montage of documents, part manifesto, "Annihilating Reality" argues for a new and radical form of performance that eludes spectatorship and is reduced to the intentions and perceptions of the performance maker. "Heresy: A lot of the best, youngest, performance artists have an incredibly sophisticated perception of art media, galleries, socialities [ . . . ] . The basic tenet is that art is the perception of the moment. And in the perception of the moment, all things are art" (48). Drawing from sources that range from art publications to artist books, police reports, zines, and pornographic publications, Christopherson has put together a mosaic of stunning "actions" that erode the boundary between the aesthetic, the pathological, and the criminal. The "hearsay" paragraph that contains the brief depiction of Neitsch's performance begins with references to Mayan and Aztec blood sacrifices, then turns to Texas serial killer Dean Corll, and then to OM Theater's slaughter of sheep. It ends with the question: "Is it only legality that prevents the artist from slaughter of human beings as performance?" (44). This is an intriguing question. However, its "documentary" support does not hold, since most likely the "art ritual" of mass sheep slaughter never happened. Neitsch kept meticulous records of his actions, which he published in the 1980s. In the volume *Das Orgien Mysterien Theater: die partituren aller aufgeführten aktionen 1960–1979* (The Orgien Mysterien Theater: Partituren and Listings of All Actions 1960–1979), there is no mention of the slaughter of sheep during any actions he organized at Prinzendorf castle. The record for an action staged in 1975 mentions the slaughter of a bull, but again not a single sheep, and the killing was done by a local butcher, not by blood-thirsty happeners (see Nitsch 1986, 331).[1] Christopherson's article-manifesto is a catalog of carefully selected documents of performances that were usually witnessed by just a few people and, at best, perceived as artworks only by the performers themselves. The only evidence of their existence is found in scattered documents in various media, which Christopherson exaggerates to make his point. So, in his rendering of Gina Pane's *Escalade non Anesthesiée* (Unanaesthetized Climb, 1971), the artist climbs up and down a ladder with sharp nails on the rungs "until she reaches the limits of her endurance"; and, again according to Christopherson, during Marina Abramović's action *Rhythm 0* (1974), "two men stabbed her in the throat" (47, 48).[2] Christopherson's article is a glaring example of the danger in establishing a metonymic relation between a performance event and its documentation: the latter may produce phantom performances that exist only in and as documentation. Once they enter performance history, they are indistinguishable from "legitimate" performances that can prove their "live" pedigree.[3]

This assembling of remnants to conjure a lost act—not necessarily an act that has been lost for a long time, but an act that has been lost for as long as it has not been perceived as art—is neither new nor "incredibly sophisticated." More than anything else, it resembles the nineteenth-century art-historical procedure known as *Kopeinkritik*, whose methods it unwittingly follows. Following German eighteenth-century art historian and archaeologist Johann Joachim Winckelmann's arguments for the centrality of the Greek "golden age" to the development of the arts of antiquity, *Kopienkritik* developed in the course of the nineteenth century as an attempt to retrieve lost Greek masterpieces through careful study of their Roman copies. As Elaine K. Gazda explains, *Kopienkritik*

---

[1] Malcolm Green, who in his introduction to *The Writings of Vienna Actionists* raised the possibility of Christopherson's false reporting about Neitsch's Prinzendorf action, went by pure logic: "100 sheep? Neitsch could never have afforded them. And who would have eaten them? The fridge in Prinzendorf isn't big enough to keep them, either" (personal email to the author, February 11, 2013).

[2] Compare this with other descriptions of Pane's and Abramović's performances, such as Anne Tronche in the case of Pane (1997), and the artist herself in the case of Abramović (1998).

[3] Another instance of such a performance is VALLIE EXPORT's *Genital Panic*. See Mechtild Widrich's exemplary work of performance historiography "Can Photographs Make It So? Repeated Outbreaks of VALIE EXPORT's Genital Panic since 1969" (2012).

was modeled on methodology developed by philologists who attempted to "reconstruct the stemma of a lost manuscript in an effort to recover the Ur-text" (1995, 127). According to her, the fundamental premises of *Kopienkritik* included a need for copies that emerged after Roman war bounty in Greece was exhausted. As this hypothesis goes, Roman patrons developed a "desire for *exact* copies," and Roman copiers advanced their technological capability to produce such replicas. Once they successfully hypothesized these material conditions for the production of statuary copies, *Kopien*-critics were able to argue for and prove the possibility of reconstructing lost works of art using evidence provided by the copies; further, they could safely assume that the sheer number of copies of the same figure served as proof that they derived from a "famous Classical masterpiece" (Gazda 2002, 6).[4] Two unstated premises of *Kopienkritik* are easily recognizable, even in this cursory survey of its basic assumptions. First, it naturalizes and universalizes the capitalist logic of its own time, and following this logic, it establishes a hierarchical order between the original and the copy. This relationship is not limited to art, and is in fact the basis for an economy based on scarcity, production of needs, and their fulfillment through the industrial production of commodities that come in seemingly endless series. From this follows the second premise, which is that the recognition of artistic value is closely tied to the separation of the aesthetic realm from the culture in general and the professionalization of knowledge that pertains to this realm.

In the conceptual pair "extant Roman replicas" / "lost Greek masterpieces," neither the original nor the copy is fully present. The copy is transparent: it has no inherent value other than its reference to the thing it imitates. It is a document deprived of that which it is documenting, a phantom performance like the one from the pages of *Studio International*. In short, it is pure medium. Principles of the uniqueness and distinctiveness of different media were established in nineteenth-century artistic and scholarly practices such as *Kopienkritik*. The first concern of the media, like that of commodities, is to sustain themselves as distinct entities and to prove their own existence. In the words of the "young" and "brave" performance artist who authored the "Annihilating Reality" manifesto, "nothing is real except the medium" (1976, 48). Not surprisingly, the main critique of *Kopienkritik* was that it reduced Roman sculpture to a repetition without an original. Numerous preserved sculptures are but a series of echoes of a distant, albeit irrevocably lost, originary act, and as such they fully replace what they copy.[5] *Kopienkritik* opens up the possibility for an additional relationship between performance and document, exemplified in Christopherson's restatement of Nitsch's Prinzendorf action: the performative power of the document as proof of a "lost"

---

[4] Miranda Meriwn cites "programmatic hypothesis" as one of the possible alternatives to "copy hypothesis," which "explains the existence of the replica series as a tribute to the usefulness of its base type in Roman contexts and its dependence on an original Greek work as true for some series but not for all" (Marvin 1989, 40). The "usefulness" here pertains to the use of sculpture not just as aesthetic objects but as public markers, as certain types of sculptures were regularly found in public baths, theaters, etc.

[5] For an outline of the main objections to *Kopienkritik*, see Eliane K. Gazda's "Roman Sculpture and the Ethos of Emulation: Reconsidering Repetition" (1995).

performance and its continuation in another medium overwhelms its own source and replaces it to such a degree that the performance becomes redundant. In fact, as we have seen, the performance needs not be made at all if there is an object (a sculpture, a text, or even a photograph) to document it.

As a method that introduced a distinction between the work of art and the document, *Kopienkritik* anticipated late twentieth- and early twenty-first-century art criticism's interest in questions of reconstruction and repetition. Like appropriation art of the 1980s and reperformance of the 2000s, *Kopienkritik* was in no small part initiated and driven by the emergence of new technologies that made possible the collection, comparison, and presentation of a vast amount of data. In the case of nineteenth-century *Kopienkritik*, these technologies were forensic archaeology and photography. If the former was used to produce new evidence, the latter was instrumental for its interpretation. By the end of the nineteenth century, Heinrich Brunn published a vast compendium of photographs, *Denkmäler der griechischer und römicher Skulptur* (Munich, 1888), and a few years later his student Adolf Furtwängler set the standard with his *Greek and Roman Sculpture* (*Denkmäler griechischer und römischer skulptur*, 1898). In order to validate its own premises, the method must project its own principles onto the very object of investigation. In *Kopienkritik*, this validating assumption was that ancient sculpture, like modern photography, was mechanically reproducible. Kopien-critics presumed that in order to produce faithful replicas of Greek masterpieces, Roman sculptural copyists employed a mechanical device similar to the pointing machine, used in the late eighteenth and early nineteenth centuries, even though there was no convincing historical or archaeological evidence to support this claim. The modernist logic of *Kopienkritik* dictates that it is precisely the inimitability of the original that calls for the establishment of the method of preservation and multiplication. *Kopienkritik* ends up casting onto ancient Rome not only nineteenth-century art tastes, but, even more important, a dynamic of newness and repetition typical for industrial capitalism. Even more than reproducibility, general repeatability is the mode of capitalist production that undergirds all of its transformations, from Fordist production lines to recent high-tech genetic re-engineering of extinct species.[6] If only in its title, Michael Kirby's Happening *The First and Second Wilderness* outlines the happeners' understanding of nature as something that is man-made, and it also anticipates the twenty-first-century attempts by radical conservationists to (re)turn the course of history and bring back that which has been lost.

Wedged between the antiquity of Athens and Rome and the modernity of the *Kopienkritik* is an economy of art production that seems completely at odds with the latter. It is best exemplified in acheiropoietic images, the form of icons that emerged in the Byzantine early Middle Ages, which, as some theologians claimed, "human hands have

---

[6] For the concept of "rewilding" as a radical form of nature conservationism, see Dave Foreman, *Rewilding North America: A Vision for Conservation in the 21st Century* (2004), and Richard Manning, *Rewilding the West: Restoration in a Prairie Landscape* (2009); for genetic de-extinction of lost species, see Jacob Sherkow and Henry Greely's article "What if Extinction Is Not Forever?"

not made."[7] In his study of these kinds of icons, Ernst Kitzinger notes that "acheiropoi-etai are of two kinds: Either they are images believed to have been made by hands other than those of ordinary mortals or else they are claimed to be mechanical, though mirac-ulous, impressions of the original" (1954, 113). The former were holy icons that appeared like other artistically produced works but with no "human" origin, and as such they as a rule became models to be reproduced; the former were "imprints" of Christ's body, such as that on the column of flagellation. In its sudden leaps, modernity has produced artis-tic phenomena that, while thoroughly de-sacralized, display a similar not-made nature.

# ART OUT OF BOUNDS

The life cycle of Happenings, both as individual works and as a form, was unusually short, even when measured by the standards of mid-century avant-garde trends. Happenings exploded on the New York art scene in the early 1960s, spread through other art cen-ters in the United States, Europe, and beyond, and by the end of that decade they were almost an extinct art form. From *18 Happenings in 6 Parts*, performed at the Reuben Gallery on October 4–10, 1959, to Jean-Jacques Lebel's political Happenings of the late 1960s, most individual works were conceived and performed as one-off events. Whereas critics and artists quickly noted and amply celebrated the "birth" of Happenings, there were no eulogies to mourn the death of the form. Happenings seem to have simply wilted away. Perhaps the biggest reason for their disappearance in the early 1970s was the appropriation of their main tenet—liveness—into new art forms such as body art, performance art, and conceptual art, but also into popular culture: writing in 1970, at the very moment of Happenings' expiration, Barbara Rose casually noted that this cele-brated new art form had its "denouement in the multimedia discotheques" ([1970] 2012, 130). After a decade of experimentation, the novelty of this live art form simply wore off. Toward the end of the 1960s, Peter Brook quipped that "the sadness of a bad happening must be seen to be believed" (1968, 54).

By necessity, the study of Happenings misses the works to become a study of the discourse about Happenings. The special issue of *Tulane Drama Review* published in 1965 became an early primer for the historiography and theory of Happenings. Here, the discourse of Happenings builds on three kinds of documents: first, an explana-tory apparatus that situates the new art form in relation to the past and present; sec-ond, artists' statements and synopses of their works; and finally, visual documentation such as drawings, photographs, and films. Missing, without exception, are the objects used in Happenings. All early happeners were visual artists, and they conceived of Happenings as a spatial and temporal expansion of a painting. The de-reification of

---

[7] This is Ernst Kitzinger's quote from the sixth-century monk Eugarius's text about the famous icon of Christ from Edessa in upper Mesopotamia (1954, 114).

the art object was an inherent part of this change in painting's dimensions. But no less important than the use of living bodies was the use of *things* in Happenings: an inherent aspect of the "theatricalization" of visual art was the transformation of the art object into a prop that then became obsolete as soon as the performance was over. Here, the exchange value of the work of art is completely repudiated in favor of its use value. One of the first to acknowledge this material ephemerality of Happenings was the Fluxus artist Robert Filliou who, in *Teaching and Learning as Performance Arts*, wrote of "Audito-Destroyed Art (art being destroyed by the spectator without his being told or helped to do so)":

> The 1st principle is psychological: the spectator will destroy (physically, or through the written or spoken word) any work that challenges too much his esthetics or ethics. The 2nd principle is financial: the spectator will destroy an artwork if the material in which it is made, or the space it occupies, is more valuable to him than the final product. (1970, 66)

Happenings belong to the last category. The reception of Happenings was inseparable from their physical destruction. Since they were never touched by the magic of the art market's fetishism and transformed into "artworks," objects used in Happenings were never elevated from their status as props. In that sense, they shared with trash the status of anti-commodities par excellence.

Happenings criticism from the 1960s stands witness to critics' and artists' attempts to comprehend and valorize the new form of live art that staked its claim of newness on the rejection of traditional forms of writing for performance such as script, score, and libretto. In this way, artists' statements, descriptions, and drawings emerged not as pretexts for performance, but post-texts or rather post-performance documents, in the same way that photographs constitute the most trustworthy record of these ephemeral artworks. As a result, the archive of Happenings consists of an excess of documents positioned metonymically in relation to the works themselves. In that, they are paradigmatic of the situation of all live performance forms that emerged in their wake. As Amelia Jones argues in "'Presence' in Absentia: Experiencing Performance as Documentation," it is precisely this visual and textual record that helped performance "to attain its symbolic status within the realm of culture" (1997, 13). The perception we have of Happenings today has been shaped not by the Happenings themselves, but by this documentation. In that sense, the study of Happenings shares a great deal with *Kopienkritik*. The documents substituted for "works" engage in symbolic circuits quite different from the live events that they purport to preserve. These circuits start at the place of a Happening and continue, as Jones argues, following Derrida, in a "sequence of supplements" consisting of "video, film, photograph, and text documenting it for posterity," thus multiplying "supplementary mediations that produce the sense of the very thing they defer" (1997, 14). These supplementary mediations are neither linear nor pure. They join with other mediations in a process of give and take, of analogy and metaphor, of similarity and difference, all of which in the end produces a highly contingent and ambiguous idea of an originary "Happening." This is the "document" that every attempt at restaging Happenings engages with.

The reperformance of Happenings is not only a transfer of performance in time and space, but also an institutional translation. This translation is multiple, and it involves not only a displacement from a non- or low-art space to a high-art museum, but also a conceptual transfer from an institution of teaching and learning to an institution of display and commerce. Popular histories of Happenings prefer to overlook evidence that pushes Happenings' beginning from the Reuben Gallery to Rutgers University. In her research on Kaprow's early work, Joan Marter shows that he presented his first public Happening on April 22, 1958, in the Voorhees Chapel at Douglas College, Rutgers University. This nameless event "featured no characters or plot" and, according to Kaprow's recollections, his aim was to create a "formal, ceremonial effect because the event was staged in a chapel" (Marter 1999, 9). However, instead of the faithful, the audience of this ceremony consisted of students and faculty (8).[8] To a certain degree, any restaging of Happenings in a university setting necessarily recalls their place of origin.

The first time I presented Happenings to my students in the Theater Studies program at the Tisch School of the Arts, they responded by searching, instinctively, for ways to relate this live art form to their preexisting ideas of theater. Most of them were coming from the Experimental Theater Wing studio at Tisch. Not being art historians, they approached documents of Happenings not as post-texts and artifacts, but as pre-texts for performance. While some students wanted no part of Happenings, others desired, quite literally, to put their hands on them. In the spring of 1999, Will Daddario and Ben Branson, then enrolled in my class on the neo-avant-garde, suggested that we stage 18 Happenings in 6 Parts. They went as far as contacting Kaprow, but at that point he was still strictly opposed to the idea of repeating past Happenings.[9] In subsequent iterations of the class, I recognized a similar impatience among students with the substitution of critical discourse for the work itself. Their highly evolved mechanisms for the visualization of theatrical performance regularly stumbled over Happenings' ambiguities and loose ends. At one point, I asked them to create their own Happenings. Unmistakably, they latched on to the perceived absence of a plan or score in Happenings, which led to a reductive way of understanding them as an art form in which anything goes. Instead of making Happenings, they ended up staging their misconceptions about them, based on artists' mis-stated intentions and critics' vague descriptions.

This misreading of Happenings is almost inevitable. It is caused not by the works themselves, but by the ideological discourse in which they were—and still are—steeped.

---

[8]   Kaprow readily acknowledges that his idea of Happenings emerged in a similar educational setting. In the winter and spring of 1958, he attended John Cage's class on Experimental Composition at the New School, where he did his first actions (Marter 1999, 6).

[9]   Several years later, Kaprow agreed to have his Happenings restaged for the exhibit *Allan Kaprow. Kunst Als Leven/Art as Life* in Haus der Kunst, Munich. On this occasion, André Lepecki recreated Kaprow's landmark *18 Happenings in 6 Parts*. See *Allan Kaprow: 18/6: 18 Happenings In 6 Parts, November 9/10/11 2006*.

In her influential 1962 article "Happenings: An Art of Radical Juxtapositions," Susan Sontag describes this kind of performance, as it were, *via negativa*: "They don't take place on a stage conventionally understood [ . . . ] In this setting a number of participants, *not* actors, perform movements and handle objects [ . . . ] . The Happening has no plot [ . . . ] It also shuns continuous rational discourse [ . . . ]" (1966, 264). Three years later, in the special Happenings issue of *TDR*, Richard Schechner wrote that "those few who have seen or participated in a Happening have undergone the beginning of a perceptual re-education. Accustomed to 'packages' of every kind in every walk of life (from A&P commodities to political theories), *the receiver now confronts a freedom* which is difficult to avoid once presented, and is equally risky to accept" (1965, 231; emphasis added). Surely enough, Kaprow himself argued in *Environments, Assemblages, and Happenings* for a radical unframing of Happenings—from a room, to a building, to a city block, to one or more cities, and "finally all around the globe"—that presumably ends with the disappearance of a Happening as a discrete event or artwork (1966, 190). If early in the twentieth century Soviet constructivists asked for art to organize itself in order to become a part of life, some forty years later, happeners asked art to do precisely the opposite in order to achieve the same goal. It seems that what defined Happenings was not their form, but a perceived lack thereof. In other words, the discourse of Happenings proclaimed freedom as the main property of this new live art, and by extension of all variations of live art that emerged in its wake. I contend that it is precisely this forced freedom that produced the bad Happenings that had to be "seen to be believed."

## Rigor of the Form

Filliou's 1970 book/compendium *Teaching and Learning as Performance Arts* is one of the earliest texts I know in which "Happenings" have been replaced with "performance art." It seems that he started thinking in this direction a decade earlier, as Pierre Tilman reports that Filliou first used the word "performance" in 1960 (1998, 40). This is not only a question of semantics. For Filliou, Happenings represented just one of many forms of participatory, non-text-based, and non-commercial performance.[10] While subsuming Happenings into a broad genre of performance, he elaborated on the pedagogical process as one of the central properties of Happenings. Embedded deeply within the experience of Happenings, this process continued long after Happenings left their birthplace in Rutgers University halls, studios, and classrooms. In his notes for the Happening *Moveyhouse*, performed on December 1–3 and 16–17, 1965, in the Cinematheque movie theater on 41st Street in Manhattan, Claes Oldenburg wrote that " 'teaching' today is

---

[10]   After earning a master's degree in economics from UCLA and working in South Korea for three years on an economic reconstruction program, he left his job and lived an itinerant life that led him through Egypt, Spain, Denmark, Britain, his native France, back to the US, and to Germany. He wrote poems and did street theater wherever he could.

more shaping of 'perception' happenings in that way didactic"; "audience is not passively watching a spectacle;" and "a 'teaching' period could be a series of happenings or
series of happenings could be a 'teaching' period" (Oldenburg 1973, 85). If the Rutgers
group (Kaprow, George Segal, Lucas Samaras, Robert Whitman, Robert Watts, Geoffrey
Hendricks) was the "first generation" of happeners, then Oldenburg, who started working on Happenings only a few years later, already belonged to a second generation
(together with Jim Dine and Red Grooms). The year in which he staged his *Moveyhouse*
(which belonged to his third series of Happenings, the first being a group of actions he
did in The Store and Ray Gun Theater from 1960 to 1962, and the second the ones he
staged outside of New York between 1963 and 1965) was the same year *TDR* published its
special issue on Happenings. Oldenburg's remarks seem to echo Schechner's reflections
on Happenings. In his notes for the Happening *Washes*, published in the same issue of
*TDR*, Oldenburg explains that his procedure for working on a Happening begins with
collecting urban images and experiences (Oldenburg 1965, 108). Indeed, his notes for
*Moveyhouse* resemble a sound poem more than a plan for a live art project:

- SKISS UNO
- ice cream cone
- burlesque
- blow up screen. Let air out.
- Mattresses all over audience
- SKINNY MOO TEX
- SKANNY MAWTECH
- CHINGA CHOTEX OKEX.

    (Oldenburg 1973, 54)

This list continues for pages. Eventually, notes become more elaborate and turn into
outlines for images, actions, and situations. Some words and images are invoked and
then dropped, and some, such as "ice cream cone," come back. My students and I understood why Oldenburg retained the "ice cream cone" after Reed Anderson, an MFA student in art practice, together with a group of students from my class on Happenings,
staged *Moveyhouse* in the winter of 2008. This site-specific Happening takes place in
an empty movie theater and, not surprisingly, its main visual element is a beam of light
from a film projector, streaming through the thick smoke enveloping the theater seats
and hitting an empty film screen. Oldenburg started working with ice cream cone soft
sculptures as early as 1962. By 1965, the cone was more than soft: it was barely material. "To physicalize—by which I mean make material—the cone (Ice Cream—Illinois
Central cone) of light," wrote Oldenburg in his notes for this Happening: "Light comes
in cones, like ice cream. To physicalize, realize, actualize . . . this cone, proceeding from
the projector" (1973, 81). We came to understand the distance between the cones in
Alberti's fifteenth-century writings on single-point perspective and the light cones projected through the multifocal space of this and most other Happenings. And we came

to observe the major difference between these two cardinal points in the history of Western art: whereas the old masters established not only a style in their painting, but also a method for the transfer of knowledge on perspective and other painterly tricks, and in doing so provided a basis for the institutionalization of art, happeners intentionally rejected these skills and positioned themselves outside of these institutions.

In their brief lifespan on the art scene, Happenings were extremely successful in redefining the very idea of the art*work*. While producing a number of more or less successful art events and provoking a lively corpus of critical responses, Happenings did not establish a method for the transmission of knowledge and skills that would secure the survival of the form. This absence of method was, in fact, one of the central conceptual tenets of Happenings. Oldenburg, again: "The original happenings were non-professional, in that they required no special skill. Only one skillful person necessarily involved, who obtains, organizes, but especially *perceives*. Concept of my hap[ennin]gs 1961 was as a way of showing How I see. That is, the professionalism (if offhand) of Artist. But dancers actors not necessary. In fact *not wanted*. What was wanted: the suggestiveness of raw action" (1973, 85).[11] Oldenburg wanted a conspicuous absence of method and instead sought "raw action." What Jake Haskell, an undergraduate who spearheaded the restaging of Robert Whitman's *Water* that same winter of 2008, uncovered was not a lost meaning of this Happening that was performed only once in 1961 in a Los Angeles driveway, but the "raw action" that Nicole Demby, also an undergraduate, had to perform in order to push her slender body through a column of stacked automobile inner tubes. The discovery made in the restaging of *Water* was not accomplished by realizing spectacular visual effects or revealing the conceptual profundity of this work, but through these vigorous movements which were dictated by a very specific set of objects and a unique way in which a body is invited to engage with them. The crucial segment of this Happening was not the environment made of wooden rafters covered with plastic sheets and its visual, aural, and even tactile properties, but the gestures Demby produced in her encounter with stacked automobile inner tubes. Demby learned how to negotiate her way through slippery tubes right then and there in front of us, and any of the spectators could do what she did.

While being "free" from the kind of rules that constrain traditional art forms, and from any prescribed method, the performance of Happenings is never completely random. In Happenings, the rigor of the form does not come from an adherence to art decrees, and even less from improvisation, spontaneity, or the employment of aleatory techniques, but from precision inscribed in the encounter of the body, the object(s), and the circumstances that bring them together. At best, a happener outlines an event and, at best, a poorly rehearsed performer guesses what that outline is. The Happening is contained neither in this vague outline nor in the naïve performance. Instead, it materializes, as from the thin air, from the space between them. In that sense, it can be seen as a late-twentieth-century variant of acheiropoietic images. Here, I am not arguing for the medievalism of Happenings or their ritual or spiritual value, but rather for their status

---

[11]  I have preserved syntax and punctuation from the original.

as not being authored in the modern(ist) sense of the word, by the employment of skills acquired though repetition.

The Happenings restagings that my students did in the winter of 2008 and again in the winter of 2012 were not, nor were they intended to be, a theater of instruction; they were most definitely not class projects produced in workshops on art practice or performance making. Instead, they were staged within seminars dedicated to the critical investigation of performance, and as such they were exercises in the reading of primary documents. The first thing that this kind of reading reveals is the nature of the discourse it is engaging. In writings on Happenings, formal description replaces interpretation. Critics' choice of ethnographic over art-historical procedures was dictated by the very object of their study. In his 1964 interview, Oldenburg insisted on the experiential nature of Happenings: "maybe it's more important that it's a certain kind of experience: simply sitting and watching in an isolated way something that's very familiar" ([1964] 2012, 120). In her article published at the twilight of the era of Happenings, Barbara Rose took seriously Oldenburg's rejection of meaning: "Happenings are not meant to be interpreted, but to be experienced directly" ([1970] 2012, 132). And performance of the post-Happening era retained this focus on experience, as evidenced in Christopherson's art magazine performance: "Performance art is investigation, a learning situation, actual and direct. People have to be able to emotionally touch art, to feel it allows them to exist" (1976, 45). In formal descriptions of Happenings, the question of quality, ubiquitous in critical and historiographic discussions of traditional performance genres such as opera and ballet, was replaced by questions of quantity. This is nowhere demonstrated as clearly as in Kirby's essay "On Acting and Not-Acting" (1972). Focus on quantity in performance indicates the shift from "how" to "what." Further, in Happenings, the absence of narrative relieves performers from the heavy burden of communicating a "message" and, in that sense, they are unconcerned with virtuosity and failure. Since the quality of performance has been replaced by quantity, there is nothing to be perfected—hence the rejection of professional performers of any kind. No "system," no "method," just *doing*. Here, the task, not the text, becomes the enabling limit of performance. Instead of preserving and fetishizing the artist's outline that always has a potential of becoming an archival document, performance destroys it by wrestling itself free from this symbolic chain.

Most artists who made Happenings in the 1960s, such as Claes Oldenburg, Jim Dine, and Red Grooms, moved back to object art in the 1970s and beyond. Kaprow, who was already teaching when he started making Happenings, moved forward toward an increased dematerialization of art. Even those who have never given up Happenings, such as Robert Whitman, cannot be said to have established a professional Happenings practice, and certainly not a pedagogy of Happenings. Probably the biggest realization my students had when Whitman came to Stanford in the winter of 2012 to help us remount *The American Moon* was that he knew only slightly more about this Happening than they did. It was clear that for him, the (re)staging of his Happening was not about expertise, or authority, or even memory, but the experience of the unforeseen in performance. It would be too much to expect from happeners to teach Happenings the way nineteenth-century studio art teachers taught drawing and painting.

Faced with this performance that requires no skill and no training, we are all laymen. In remaking *Water, Moveyhouse,* and *The American Moon,* my students and I discovered that equality, not freedom, is the central artistic and ideological principle of Happenings. There is no such thing as a "history" of Happenings, just a certain symbolic chain made of documents. And there is no archive proper, but instead an *anarchive* that vigorously resists all institutional frameworks. In his reflections on the experience of restaging *The American Moon,* theater and performance studies graduate student Ryan Tacata commented on Whitman's "cavalier attitude," which impressed him as "more innocent than anything, childlike almost" (Tacata 2012); and Barbara Greene, a graduate student in the art history department, wrote that "Whitman's presence at our reperformance, as helpful as it was, also created potentially the largest challenges to work through, because it only highlighted the disconnect between our iteration and his own" (2012). The institutional translation proved more difficult than transfer across time and space: some of the things that were normal and permissible in Reuben Gallery in 1960 were unthinkable in an institution of higher learning forty-two years later. At times, the San Mateo County fire marshal seemed to be a force more powerful in shaping the 2012 restaging than the original work, its author, and all of his latter-day collaborators.

## POETICAL ECONOMY OF HAPPENINGS

> I've been kind of in contact with some people who are working for a large industrial laboratory and the attitude there is that if they succeed more than ten percent of the time in an experiment they're considered bad scientists because it means they're not really doing anything that's hard to do or interesting. So I think it's just a fantastic idea, to think that a giant industry that's involved in producing failures. You know, just absolutely, and I don't see why artists can't undertake the same kind of responsibility. (*Film Culture* 1966, 2)

This is Robert Whitman, speaking at the Expanded Cinema Symposium that took place in conjunction with the Fourth New York Film Festival's Independent Cinema Series. Whitman's was one of the most provocative statements of the evening. The audience members and other panelists engaged in a vigorous debate that steered this discussion on expanded cinema to an economy of expansion. Stan Vanderbeek, the inventor of Cenemadrome, a dome-like, multiple-projector movie theater, concluded, "the whole culture is going that way, and mixing up artists with money and the opportunity to try out ideas is where it's all going to go" (2). These words were spoken in September 1966, on the stage of the East Village's Film Makers' Cinematheque, located, as one of the panelists put it, in "the darkest Lafayette street" (1). The "industry" harbors the assumption that the scientific experiment should not produce something that is ordinary and predictable, but rather should uncover something that is unforeseen. This presumption is driven by profit, not by scientific rigor. One of the highest values of capitalist production is that only the new and the unpredictable merit endless reproduction. The "mixing up of artists and money" was one direction for artistic experimentation. The second direction is harder to trace because it adopted an economic model completely foreign to the capitalist mode of production.

The transcript of the symposium was published in a special issue of the journal *Film Culture* on expanded cinema, published in the winter of 1966. What made this issue "special" was not only the topic, but also its format (a newspaper), layout, illustrations, and a number of contributions on a recent Fluxfest. Essentially, it was a Fluxus publication. Before Gene Youngblood adopted it for the title of his book, "expanded cinema" was part and parcel of a larger Fluxus interest in the intermediality of the arts. This crossing of disciplinary boundaries was not limited to traditional artistic media, such as painting, theater, music, or film, but "expanded" to include everyday activities, such as cooking, eating, sleeping, walking, learning, and teaching. The latter two were taken up with particular vigor by the author of *Teaching and Learning as Performance Arts*. This compendium summarizes Filliou's work from the 1960s, and picks up on projects such as the Non-school of Villefranche in La Cédille qui Sourit, a store he ran together with George Brecht from 1965 to 1968 in the small city of Villefranche in the south of France: "We have said that the Non-école de Villefranche never got further than just being a letter-head, conceived for all useful and useless ends. The whole programme was under the letterhead—I still stick to it—I am doing it now," recounts Filliou in a transcript of a videotape he made in 1977: "it's a carefree exchange of information and experience. No students, no teachers" (in Sava 1995, 78). Another project that is closely related to both La Cédille and *Teaching and Learning* is what he called *The Territory of the Genial Republic* (*La Territoire de la République Géniale*, 1971), which presents research as an ignorance-driven enterprise: "Research [ . . . ] is not the privilege of people who know—on the contrary it is the domain of people who do not know. Every time we are turning our attention to something that we do not know—we are doing research" (82).

Filliou's projects on performance and pedagogy are grouped around the turn of the seventh decade of the twentieth century: the dates of the non-school of Villefnache are 1965–1968, and the conceptual work, *The Territory of the Genial Republic*, is dated 1971. Between them came *Teaching and Learning as Performance Arts*. In a disclaimer at the opening pages of the book, Filliou notes that during the interval between the completion of the book in the winter of 1967 and its publication in 1970, the 1968 student protests happened, but he felt no need to change anything. "The students' unrest was already mine, their revolution my revolution" (Filliou 1970, 12). That puts *Teaching and Learning as Performance Arts* at the very center of post-1968 debates about education in France, which also informed Jacques Rancière's *The Ignorant Schoolmaster*, even though, as Kristin Ross suggests in her introduction to the English translation, this might not have been "immediately apparent to most of the book's readers when it appeared in 1987" (in Rancière 1991, vii). In *Artificial Hells*, Claire Bishop dedicates an entire chapter to art projects by a new generation of artists at the turn of the twenty-first century that borrow the pedagogical situation as their basic structure. She remarks that Rancière's book "has been frequently cited in recent discussions of art and pedagogy," and, paying no heed to Ross's warning, she notes that "it is striking that his polemic makes no reference to the emergence of critical pedagogy in the late 1960s" (2012, 266). While she sidelines Rancière, she completely omits Filliou, thus reducing post-1968 critical pedagogy to Paulo Freire's *Pedagogy of the Oppressed*. The reason for this might be the relative invisibility of Filliou's work, especially if observed from within art institutions, which is the main frame of reference for most recent artists who claim experimentation as the main property of their art.

For Filliou, performance is not a discrete action. Like teaching and learning, it is not framed by time, space, or institutional support. "If there is no fiction then art is the same as life: many people have tried to look upon art this way and have made attempts to arrive at it, except that we are always doing a performance. What I am doing now, although it's life, *is* a performance," spoke Filliou into a microphone in his 1977 video performance *Porta Filliou* (in Sava 1995, 84). This approach to performance is indicative of his notion of Permanent Creation:

> [ . . . ] I use this word frequently rather than using the word art, because I practice art as creativeness, and often I have defined anti-art as the diffusion of the works coming out of that creativeness, and non-art as being creative without caring whether one's works are diffused or not. Anyway, for me the idea of creation came very soon to imply that creation should be permanent and I should practice the idea and the ideal of Permanent Creation. (Filliou and Erlhoff 1984, 52)

Needless to say, Permanent Creation abolishes distinctions between traditional artistic genres. Its most striking and concise manifestation is probably *Permanent Creation Toolbox #1* (1969), an ordinary blue toolbox that contains the words "imagination" and "innocence," fashioned out of fluorescent tubes. Imagination and innocence are the main tools for stripping art of its aesthetic properties and turning it into Permanent Creation. In his 1977 performance for the camera, Filliou referenced his 1965 performance at the Café au Go Go in New York, in which he identified this principle as the Filliou Ideal: "not choosing, not wanting, wide awake, sitting quietly doing nothing. Another way I have presented Permanent Creation as a practice is what I have called 'work as play' and 'art as thought,' because I consider myself as an entertainer of thoughts, and art works as exchange of foodstuffs" (in Sava 1995, 85). What sets apart Filliou's approach to teaching and learning from other "discussions of art and pedagogy" in the 1960s is that he sets it squarely within that second direction of "mixing up of money and artists," which in *Teaching and Learning as Performance Arts* he identifies as "poetical economy." He explains this by setting up a counterexample that he calls the Economics of Prostitution:

I have called art a form of organized leisure. It can be a full time or a part time activity. It may or may not enter the normal economic circuit. For instance, a sudden realization that each and every moment of one's life is art does not imply that one will engage in other activities than those previously engaged in. Yet, even so, the emphasis will change, and will have bearings on the normal economic process. In general I will include these artistic activities (including my own) that enter the normal economic circuit in the study of the Economics of Prostitution. What escapes the normal economic circuit, I will analyze in Poetical Economy. (77)

In *Teaching and Learning*, Filliou cites innocence, imagination, freedom, and integrity as its four main principles (1970, 45). In a statement "The Principles of Poetic Economy," he identifies it with his project " 'Dessins sans Voir, Desseins sans Savoir'—drawing without seeing, deigns without knowing" (1984, 131). These drawings, which he made with his eyes closed, are intimately related to another series, *Portraits Not Made*, from around 1970, which instead of a painting or a drawing contain just the subject's name, or often nothing at all: they are just pieces of blank paper. These two series are brought together by that which they lack—sight, image—rather than by their contents. As such, they both illustrate the Principle of Equivalence, the central tenet of Filliou's Poetic Economy:

> In December 1968, Herr Schmela proposed me to have an exhibition in his Düseldorf Gallery. I took this opportunity to develop visually what I consider an important element of Permanent Creation: the Principle of Equivalence:
>
> WELL MADE
> BADLY MADE
> NOT MADE
>
> In terms of Permanent Creation, I suggest that these possibilities are equivalent. I began applying the Principle of Equivalence to a 10cm x 12cm object (a red sock in a yellow box). The 5th object I arrived at attained the dimension of 2m x 6m. There I stopped because of lack of space. I figured out, tho' [*sic*], that if I made a series of 100 objects, instead of 5, the dimension of the 100th object would have been: 5 times around the earth in length 60 000 000 000 000 000 000 000 000 000 000 km in height. Remembering that the speed of light is 180 000 km a second, I wondered: "isn't it conceivable that the initial gesture of the Creator has consisted as it were, in merely 'putting a red sock in a yellow box,' the principle of equivalence being responsible since then for the permanent creation of the universe?" (1984, 58)

Filliou, the ignorant schoolmaster of performance, understood that the only way for art to save itself without resorting to preservationist instincts is by stepping out from the institution of art altogether. Confined within art institutions, performance furnishes the market with scarce commodities of originals and authentic experiences. Once they exit the highly charged space of art economy, these performances enter circuits of exchange and dissemination in which the original–copy binary is just as irrelevant as it was to the Roman "art patrons." The models of Roman copies were not made, nor was the OM Theater cited in Christopherson's *Studio International* piece. Both of them, in their own way, belong to the category of repetition without an original. Conversely, the repetition of non-art comes from its never having been made. In their best moments, *which don't have to be seen to be believed*, Happenings *enacted* this (acheiro)poietic economy.

The crossing from Rutgers to Reuben, this expulsion from the safety of institutions to the wilderness of the (art) market, represents the defining moment in the history of Happenings. That is because poetic economy undergirds the higher learning of Happenings. Here, performance does not play the role of a mnemonic, but of a heuristic device. The discovery that happens in Happenings comes from its method of ignorance-driven research.[12] Equality, not freedom, is the main pedagogical principle of Happenings. It is because of the inherent equality of everyone involved in the production and reception of Happenings that this form of live art resists all forms of traditional teaching and remains impermissible in institutionalized forms of education. Each return of Happenings into institutions of higher education is also a reopening of the wound made by their radical displacement. And the further we go in space and time, the more significant this dislocation appears to be.

## WORKS CITED

Abramović, Marina, and Dobrila Denegri. 1998. *Marina Abramović: Performing Body*. Milano: Charta.

Bishop, Claire. 2012. *Artificial Hells: Participatory Art and the Politics of Spectatorship*. London: Verso.

Brook, Peter. 1968. *The Empty Space*. New York: Atheneum.

Christopherson, Peter. 1976. "Annihilating Reality." *Studio International* 192(982) (July–August): 44–48.

Filliou, Robert. 1970. *Teaching and Learning as Performance Arts*. Köln: Verlag Gebr.

Filliou, Robert, and Michael Erlhoff. 1984. *Das immerwährende Ereignis zeigt Robert Fillliou [sic] = the Eternal Network presents Robert Fillliou [sic] = la Fête permanente présente Robert Fillliou [sic]*. Hannover: Sprengel-Museum.

Film Culture. 1966. "Expanded Cinema: A Symposium N.Y. Film Festival 1966." *Film Culture— Expanded Arts* 43 (Winter): 1–3.

Foreman, Dave. 2004. *Rewilding North America: A Vision for Conservation in the 21st Century*. Washington, DC: Island Press.

Gazda, Elaine K. 1995. "Roman Sculpture and the Ethos of Emulation: Reconsidering Repetition." *Harvard Studies in Classical Philology* 97: 121–156.

Gazda, Elaine K. 2002. "Beyond Copying: Artistic Originality and Tradition." In *The Ancient Art of Emulation: Studies in Artistic Originality and Tradition from the Present to Classical Antiquity*, edited by Elaine K. Gazda, 1–24. Ann Arbor: University of Michigan Press.

Green, Malcolm. 2013. Personal email correspondence with the author, February 11.

Green, Malcolm, ed. 1999. *Writings of Vienna Actionists*. London: Atlas Press.

---

[12] The equality of the ignorant is at the very center of Filliou's performance pedagogy of teaching and learning: "While people sleep, they are equal. Roughly one third of the day, equality exists. Art should have the same effect as sleep. It should make everybody equal" (1970, 78).

Greene, Barbara. 2012. "Bacon Tubes and Fire Codes: Our American Moon and the Material Perspectives of Reperformance and Reconstruction." Unpublished manuscript.

Jones, Amelia. 1997. "'Presence' in Absentia." *Art Journal* 56(4) (Winter): 11–18.

Kaprow, Allan. 1966. *Assemblages, Environments, Happenings.* New York: H. N. Abrams.

Kaprow, Allan., Eva Meyer-Hermann, Stephanie Rosenthal, and André Lepecki. 2007. *Allan Kaprow: 18/6: 18 Happenings In 6 Parts, November 9/10/11 2006.* Göttingen: Steidl.

Kirby, Michael. 1972. "On Acting and Not-Acting." *The Drama Review* 16(1) (T53): 3–15.

Kitzinger, Ernst. 1954. "The Cult of Images in the Age before Iconoclasm." *Dumbarton Oaks Papers* 8: 83–150.

Manning, Richard. 2009. *Rewilding the West: Restoration in a Prairie Landscape.* Berkeley: University of California Press.

Marter, Joan. 1999. "The Forgotten Legacy: Happenings, Pop Art, and Fluxus at Rutgers University." In *Off Limits: Rutgers University and the Avant-Garde 1957–1963,* edited by Joan Marter, 1–47. Newark, NJ: Newark Museum.

Marvin, Miranda. 1989. "Copying in Roman Sculpture: The Replica Series." In *Retaining the Original: Multiple Originals, Copes, and Reproductions. Studies in the History of Art,* Vol. 20, 29–40. Washington, DC: National Gallery of Art.

Nitsch, Hermann. 1986. *Das Orgien Mysterien Theater: Die Partituren aller aufgeführten Aktionen 1960–1979.* Wien: Edition Freibord.

Oldenburg, Claes. 1965. "Washes." *TDR* 10:2 (T30): 108–118.

Oldenburg, Claes. 1973. *Raw Notes.* Halifax: Press of the Nova Scotia College of Art and Design.

Rancière, Jacques. 1991. *The Ignorant Schoolmaster,* translated by Kristin Ross. Stanford, CA: Stanford University Press.

Rose, Barbara. [1970] 2012. "Theater of Action (1970)." In *Claes Oldenburg,* edited by Nadja Rottner, 129–148. Cambridge, MA: MIT Press.

Sava, Sharla, ed. 1995. *Robert Filliou: From Political to Poetical Economy.* Vancouver: Morris and Helen Belkin Art Gallery.

Schechner, Richard. 1965. "Happenings." *TDR* 10:2 (T30): 229–233.

Sherkow, Jacob, and Henry Greely. 2013. "What if Extinction Is Not Forever?" *Science* 340(6128): 32–33.

Sontag, Susan. 1966. *Against Interpretation and Other Essays.* New York: Farrar, Strauss and Giroux.

Tacata, Ryan. 2012. "Fireproof the Moon." Unpublished manuscript.

Tilman, Pierre. 1998. "The Four Lives of Robert Filliou." *Art Press* 233 (March): 38–43.

Tronche, Anne. 1997. *Gina Pane: Actions.* Paris: Fall édition.

Widrich, Mechtild. 2012. "Can Photographs Make It So?: Repeated Outbreaks of VALIE EXPORT's Genital Panic since 1969." In *Perform Repeat Record: Live Art in History,* edited by Amelia Jones and Adrian Heathfiled, 89–104. Bristol: Intellect Books.

# CHAPTER 12

# PEDAGOGIC IN(TER)VENTIONS

## On the Potential of (Re)enacting Yvonne Rainer's Continuous Project/Altered Daily in a Dance Education Context

### YVONNE HARDT

IN 1989, Mark Franko made a strong argument for a critical form of working with the past in dance (1989, 133). Taking Susanne Linke's reconstruction of Dore Hoyer's *Affectos Humanos* as a positive example, he lamented that her mode of distancing herself from the dance she reconstructed was, itself, a rare form of critical historical presentation. The last two decades have witnessed a formidable interest among contemporary artists in the questions of the past and its critical appropriation. Jérôme Bel's *Véronique Doisneau* (2004), Martin Nachbar's *Urheben-Aufheben* (2004), Boris Charmatz's idea of a center of choreography as a museum, Fabián Barba's imaginative (re)construction of a full evening work of Mary Wigman, and Olga de Soto's performative intervention based on interviews of those who watched dances seen decades ago as a basis for her performances are exemplary of the reappropriation of dance history from a critical standpoint.[1] In the wake of this development, the spectrum of what reconstruction or reenactment encompasses has considerably broadened. Working with the past is no longer considered a field for highly specialized dance historians who try to reconstruct old dances based on rare and fragmentary archival sources to render the past of dance as closely as possible to an ostensible original. Rather, with the insight that this will never be possible, the critical potential of reconstruction became apparent, as the constructing

[1] See, for further information, http://www.museedeladanse.org/fr (accessed September 9, 2016); Fabián Barba's *A Mary Wigman Dance Evening* (2009); and Olga de Soto's *histoire(s)* (2004) and *Débords. Reflections on the Green Table* (2012).

(and therefore revision of the term as "reconstruction") and artistic acts implied in this process were foregrounded (e.g., de Laet 2010; Franko 2015; Hardt 2011, 2012a; Thurner and Wehren 2010).

In this context, reconstruction is also perceived as an ideal field for combining the seemingly incompatible realms of academia and practice quite easily (Franko 2015; Hardt 2005; Siegmund 2010). In both fields, the past is no longer conceptualized as something static that could be retrieved from the archives; rather, remembering in itself comes to be considered as a performative process, "which establishes, stages, restages, and constantly modifies its object while simultaneously creating new models and media of commemorating" (Fischer-Lichte 2000, 14; author's translation).

In this context, however, the practice of dance transmission and the effects and purpose of reconstruction in the field of dance education are rarely discussed. This is surprising because many of the contemporary appropriations are combined with a pedagogical impulse. Dancers or choreographers frequently explain the processes of appropriation onstage in the course of the performance in such a way as to document and reflect the learning process involved in the endeavor to reconstruct an earlier work while simultaneously providing information to the audience on the pieces they reconstruct.[2] In addition, artists have ventured into university and teaching contexts (e.g., Boris Charmatz, LIGNA, Martin Nachbar, Olga de Soto, etc.) to produce and research their work with students or lay dancers. These developments can be linked to a long history that working with reconstruction has had in the university context—especially in the United States, where an institutional and financial framework has been provided for such projects. Subsequently, the institutionalization of this artistic-reflexive appropriation of dance history not only is visible at festivals, and through substantial funding programs, but also has found access to dance educational programs in Germany.[3] Nevertheless, reflection on historical appropriation in pedagogical settings has received only marginal attention in academic discourse, and is undertaken mostly by teachers and artists who teach dance in the studio (Hermes 2010). Thus, the academic discussion of innovative forms of historical appropriation might unwillingly be accused of maintaining a hierarchy between contemporary (or avant-garde) art (which is heavily theorized and interlinked with aesthetic and philosophical discourses) and education (which is treated, for the most part, outside these discourses, in the field of physical education).

By examining the appropriation of Yvonne Rainer's *Continuous Project/Altered Daily* (1969)—a piece based on improvisation scores—in a university educational setting, I

---

[2] This can happen in the format of the lecture performance or through the framing of the presentation in program notes, documentation, or inclusion of film footage.

[3] The "Biennale Tanzausbildung" (Dance Education Biennale) is a platform in which German institutions of higher education offering professional dance training meet every two years to exchange the latest trends in dance education. Since 2010 it has been funded by the highest level of German government (The Federal Ministry of Education and Research [BMBF]). The same year, in its second iteration, the Biennale dedicated itself to reconstruction as a topic. In this context, students of the University of Music and Dance Cologne worked on Yvonne Rainer's *CP-AD*.

seek to elucidate the potentials of reflecting on dance transmission for a further the-orization of historical reenactment.[4] I want to propose that this gears the attention to contexts and group constellations as a crucial part of artistic work, as well as to the diver-sity of performative skills. As such, I seek to discuss jointly aspects of dance appropri-ation, improvisation, and hierarchies within the artistic field, the critical potential of working with this historical score, and evolving perspectives on what constitutes dance education.

From a methodological perspective, focusing on the participatory moments of reen-acting seems here also to be a productive framework for illuminating the ideological operations that structure what is considered a valued artistic as well as pedagogical practice in a given moment. Reflecting on the practice of reenactment more generally in the context of higher education and dance training helps us to recognize that what is considered canonical is bound to specific individual and artistic standpoints, discursive power, and/or a shared understanding and knowledge about dance history in a given context. From which perspective does dance material appear historical? How can one gain access at this remove to material that was formed with quite different ideological underpinnings and interests? Such questions provoke one not only to pay attention to the movements, forms, and aesthetic principles, but also to focus on the contexts, and interactions between the dancers, as well as with the audience, as part of the production of meaning and the sense of a given piece or score.

Mark Franko has convincingly argued that the restaging of historical dance works is not merely about the movement material; rather, restaging also needs to ques-tion the principles and effects that guided the creation and reception of the works. In reconstructing or reenacting a piece while disregarding this crucial contextual compo-nent—the reaction of the audience at a given time—is to neglect the effect a piece of "the original impact of the choreography" (Franko 2015, 134).

Thus, in an educational setting, the question of "effect" and context become even more urgent, and constitute a twofold problem: neither will the participants share an overarching artistic goal or group experience—even if the educational frame seeks to achieve this—nor will the audience be similarly affected, especially when perceiving it as student work. However, from an educational perspective, these problems mark an interesting challenge for exploration and provide the basis for a differentiated learning experience. Reenactments with students allow the participants to reflect on the implicit rules and skills invisibly grounding the practice. Reciprocally, as I shall argue, such a

---

[4] The project was introduced for the first time by Matthieu Doze in December 2009 with ten students. Presentations at the Second Dance Education Biennale at Essen in March 2010 and in the framework of the Fourth Choreografie Tagung at ZZT/HfMT Cologne followed. This theoretical reflection is based on my collaboration in the process. Observations and experiences from the process are necessarily selective/personal. Still, I do consider experiences and practical involvement in the process, as well as reflecting on one's own teaching practice, as steps toward a reflective research practice that respects dance education and physical formation on the threshold between theory and practice, which is as central to understanding dance and historical reenactments as the so-called artistic product; this helps to theorize production processes as complex scenarios.

historical appropriation with and by students also generates insights, in this case, into the theoretical investigation of Rainer's work. This is possible because working with students brings to the forefront aspects of skill, and group know-how, which are sometimes missed in the discussion of Judson's task-based and apparently casual performance style. As such, it seems also highly important to speak here of an appropriation of the historical material. It is not per se given as a material or score that can simply be reenacted; rather, it must be created with a body and a group, it must be learned and worked with. Subsequently, I would like to suggest that reflecting on questions of learning, technical requirements, and group constellations also helps in theorizing historical reenactments of the dance avant-garde more generally. In short, the pedagogical context is an appropriate one within which to unearth neglected aspects of the "original work," seen as the result of processes of movement development and performance practice.

## YVONNE RAINER: REENACTMENT AND INSTITUTIONAL CRITIQUE

Yvonne Rainer is considered one of the central figures of avant-garde or postmodern dance practice as it developed in the 1960s and 1970s, to the point that she has become an icon for institutional critique in the field.[5] As a member of the Judson Dance Theater, Rainer distanced herself from an expressive and emotional understanding of dance as it was associated for her and others of her generation with dancers like Martha Graham. More generally, she re-conceptualized and broadened what dance could be by working with everyday movement, rejecting the ostensible form of virtuosity, and opting instead for a matter-of-fact performance style induced by work with tasks, and eclectically selected movement material that resisted what might be called an "organic" movement flow. Rainer—along with her collaborators of the Judson Dance Theater—avoided conventional sites of performance and instead showed their work in old churches, community houses, museums, streets, and even on the rooftops of New York, or along the walls of buildings. At the same time, they developed new forms of collaboration and presentation of their work.[6] These characteristics are highly present in *Continuous Project/Altered Daily* (*CP-AD*), which was first performed in 1969 and then evolved "continuously." Along with Rainer's seminal *Trio A* (1965), *CP-AD* is one of the projects that have contributed to a renaissance in reconstruction or reenactment (Siegmund 2010).

[5] For the enormous attention and influence Rainer has gained in the dance studies field, see, for instance, McDonagh (1970), Banes (1987, 1993), Huschka (2002), Burt (2005), Hardt (2006), and many more.
[6] While these elements are usually considered characteristic, more recent studies also demonstrate a more heterogeneous image of the Judson Dance Theater. See Burt (2005); Lambert-Beatty (2008); Hardt (2006).

Various questions arise about the historical appropriation of Yvonne Rainer's *CP-AD* regarding the relationship between dance and its institutional framework, improvisation, and reconstruction: How can one reconstruct an improvisation? What happens with the impetus of institutional critique, which is central to the conceptualization of Rainer's project, in the process of "appropriation," especially if this reenactment takes place in the highly institutionalized setting of a university and the sphere of dance education? What does such an "institutionalized" appropriation of the historical avant-garde reveal about the possible meanings, significations, and dimensions of credibility and power of reconstruction or reenactment? What kind of repercussions for the institution does the integration of art have if it is an art considered to be critical of institutions? Moreover, what does the appropriation of such critical art reveal about the changing self-understanding and self-reflectiveness of contemporary institutions? Conventionally, neither reconstruction nor education is aligned with institutional critique. Rather, they symbolize canons, or the development of specific learning standards, usually within a clear hierarchical structure. As such, institutional critique appears to be a paradox in this context. Yet, this paradox simultaneously demonstrates that the goals of education have been reformulated, as well as those of reconstruction; and in the meantime, the avant-garde itself has become an institution.[7]

The dance avant-garde of the 1960s, which was once considered highly critical of institutions, has been institutionalized paradoxically through this critical endeavor by a discourse and by arts institutions that have, conversely, started to cherish the notion of criticality. Through the prominent attention and position that the Judson Dance Theater had, and still has, in the Anglo-American dance studies discourse (Anderson 1997; Banes 1987, 1993; Burt 2005; Lambert-Beatty 2008; McDonagh 1970; Wood 2007) through presentations in well-known festivals, or reconstructions and appropriations of their work by legendary dancers—for instance, by Mikhail Barishnikov in the context of the *White Oak Project* (1999)—it becomes apparent that the dance avant-garde has found its way into the "dance establishment." Dorothea von Hantelmann has described this paradoxical phenomenon more generally for the art avant-garde: "At the moment when the avant-gardes became historical, they failed due to the integrating and reintegrating power of exactly those conventions which they had tried to overcome" (von Hantelmann 2007, 8; author's translation).

In the context of reappropriating the dance avant-garde, the term "reenactment" rather than "reconstruction" is often used to signify the alternative and critical potential of working with historical material (Backoefer, Haitzinger, and Jeschke 2009). For instance, Krassimira Kruschkova speaks of an understanding of reenactment in dance that is captured by the notion of "again and against" (*wieder und wider*) (Kruschkova 2010). Accordingly, with this notion she understands reenactment as ideally doing both: working with the past and also re-evaluating it, rereading it against the

---

[7] See the newly established study programs, for instance at the HZT (Berlin) or ZZT (Cologne), and the accompanying theoretical discussions in Melzwig et al. (2007) and Albrecht and Cramer (2006).

conventional grain of historiographical understanding. However, such a critical and alternative understanding of the term "reenactment" has not always been common, as it is used in more classical historical research outside the contemporary dance scene with a more affirmative—or one might say, positivistic—connotation.

Nonetheless, there are also aspects of reenactment that make it very plausible to speak of it in the context of the dance avant-garde and improvisation of the 1960s. Here I wish to emphasize the stem of *enact* and the action it involves. It is this interest in action and tasks that were preoccupations in the working process of the Judson Dance Theater. Structured improvisations, or the solving of tasks, defined postmodern dance more than content or narration. In the word "enactment" one hears also a reference to "direct action," a central term that the Judson performers used to describe their scores in the 1960s (Banes 1993, 27).

Moreover, reflecting on the different fields in which the term "reenactment" is used leads one to recognize that historical reappropriation often deals with improvisation. Thus, dealing with improvisation does not automatically allow for a perspective that would be critical of institutions. Moreover, looking at reenacting improvisation scores within an educational setting will also demand a shift in perspective from simple action toward an appropriation and learning that is prefiguring the execution of scores and often is omitted in discussions of reenactment. Focusing on improvisation (and more generally on actions that constitute all historical events) not only gears one's attention to the physical archives and helps to complicate notions of classical historiography and archiving, but also demands that one places the discussion of improvisation and its potential impetus of being anti-institutional in the specific context of the dance avant-garde.

## IMPROVISATION AND THE INSTITUTION

By the 1960s, improvisation was well received as an accepted form of generating movement material in modern dance. However, it was not yet established as a form of dance performance.[8] As such, when Rainer started working with improvisation as part of her pieces, it still marked a breakaway from stage conventions. Up to this point, Rainer's work had been clearly set and composed. This was linked to her aesthetic goals and principles, because overcoming what she believed to be an expressive and organic tendency called for clear compositional devices or scores. Rainer had experimented with improvisation in performance before—for instance, in *Terrain* (1963) and in *Carriage Discreteness* (1966), which was her contribution to the *9 Evenings: theater & engineering*. However, these were more restricted in regard to the individual choices they granted the

---

[8]  For an overview on dance improvisation, see Lampert (2007) or Foster (2002). For a different perspective, see also Goldman (2010).

performers.[9] In comparison to this approach, *CP-AD* marked a clear change in perspective around the function and potential of improvisation as part of performance. While there are elements of set movement materials and sequences (e.g., "Couples," "Pillows and Chairs," and "Group Hoist"), the dancers decided when to show them, how long to take, and in which order they would be done in performance. Accordingly, there was a need to negotiate the procedures with each other. Furthermore, the material could be further developed and altered in the process as part of the negotiation.

Rainer's *CP-AD* thus continued and expanded her critique of the "dance establishment"—as it dealt, on the one hand, with the forms of presentation in a self-reflexive manner by aiming to withstand legible narration (although the audience might read one into it, and Rainer was aware of this); on the other hand, it challenged notions that pieces must be clearly rehearsed and set, consequently championing improvisation as a valid form of performance.

Linking improvisation theoretically to institutional critique has been quite an established discourse for some time. According to Peggy Phelan's legendary, yet also highly challenged perspective, improvisation and performance art withstand, through their inherent ephemerality and non-repeatability, economic calculations—that is, by not providing a stable product (Phelan 1993). In this line, Lambert-Beatty argues, regarding Rainer's work, "its [improvisation's] constant vanishing, makes it always at least potentially resistant to the operations of power in a visually oriented social, cultural, and economic order" (2008, 50). Phelan's once euphoric ontological definition of dance and performance as disappearance belongs to a wider re-evaluation of the ephemeral.[10] Ephemerality is no longer considered a deficit of dance, which it was for a long time in history, but rather has become considered the quality that allows dance to be critical of conventional forms of knowledge and grants it a political status (Brandstetter 2007; Klein 2007). In this line of thought, improvisation, spontaneity, and chance procedure were the central aspects that led Sally Banes to name her seminal research on the Judson Dance Theater *Democracy's Body* (Banes 1993).

Describing improvisation as ephemeral, as experimental, and as part of an alternative dance scene has remained an influential perspective in the dance field, despite being challenged from several quarters. First, Guy Debord in the *Society of Spectacle* saw the striving after the new and the valuing of things vanishing as part of a society that followed a capitalistic logic (Debord 1995). Also in this vein, more recent interpretations see the tendency to fluidity and flexibility as a characteristic of neoliberal capitalist thinking (Boltanski and Chiapello 2007). Second, those working and reflecting on improvisation in different artistic fields have demonstrated quite clearly that improvisation is not as clearly linked to freedom or ephemerality as one might have imagined, but

[9]  In *Carriage Discreteness* Rainer had planned to give instructions via walkie-talkies. Even if technical problems restricted Rainer's ability to do this in the actual performance, the original concept did not provide the dancers with a feeling of freedom, but rather with the experience of being instructed and given the challenge to act instantaneously without much preparation.

[10]  For a longer discussion on the re-evaluation of the ephemeral in dance, see Siegmund (2006).

instead evokes or relates to established forms (Goldman 2010; Hardt 2012b). Moreover, from a critical dance studies perspective that tries to re-evaluate different hierarchies and borders between dance practices and genres, seeing improvisation as challenging established forms of dancing is revealed as being primarily based on Western stage dance practices (Foster 2002). Outside this context, improvisation—in social dancing as well as in other cultural contexts—is a rather traditional or conventional part of dancing. Accordingly, the potential of critiquing the institution of dance by integrating dance improvisation on the stage can only be understood in the specific context of a "dance-establishment" and as a specific set of "doings" of improvisations linked to a specific practice (Schatzki 2002, 73). This is also a highly pertinent restriction if one understands the institution not as a static formation (like a theater or school), but as a rule-based figuration that requires improvisation in order to enact and re-establish continuously its own norms (Hardt and Stern 2011, 11). Such a performative understanding of the institution also requires detecting the institutional critique of Rainer's work not as operating outside of institutions, but as working with them in order to expose their working methods. Improvisation, ephemerality, and institutional critique are then not so mutually linked as it sometimes appeared in discussions of the dance avant-garde.

In this vein, Lambert-Beatty argues convincingly that ephemerality was neither practically nor theoretically at the center of Rainer's concerns because Rainer was interested in reworking material and in documentation. Working with slow motion and repetition not only inhibited an organic flow of movement, but also brought to the fore moments of remembering, and of sensing a past (Lambert-Beatty 2008, 49). The extensive use of (new) media (at that time, photography and film) to both document rehearsal processes and stage practice of many of the pieces of the Judson Dance Theater raises central questions in regard to the notion of instantaneousness and vanishing that is associated with postmodern improvisation practices. More so, this tendency toward a constant documentary practice can be found in almost all of Rainer's work—for instance, in the detailed descriptions, notations, photography, and films that she actively produced with her pieces. As such, the reconstruciton of her work was also encouraged by the fact that early on she published her documentation and reflected in theater journals about her work.[11] In addition to her extensive program notes, Rainer published a collection of her pieces in her book *Works* as early as 1974. All this documentation established a basis for reconstructing or appropriating her work,[12] and provokes us to look at Rainer's work

[11] See, for example, "Some Retrospective Notes on a Dance for 10 People and 12 Mattresses Called 'Parts of Some Sextets' Performed at the Wadsworth Atheneum, Hartford, Connecticut and Judson Memorial Church, New York, in March 1965." *Tulane Drama Review* 10 (Winter 1965): 168–178. Reprinted in Rainer (1974, 45–51).
[12] This documentation should also be analyzed for how it formed a specific image of these works shaped by specific media practices and, as such, cannot be simply understood as documentation. Lambert-Beatty argues for the generative power of the photos that were taken from the Judson Group, when she describes the function of the photographer Peter Moore in this context: "Moore participated in a reaction against the cult of personality in post-war artistic culture. In this way, also, his images share in the direct, factual, or tasklike mode we associate with the art of Rainer and her peers. And in this way, it must also now be acknowledged, the images he created actively *produced* what we now understand that

along the lines of a documentary practice that allows conceptualizing her institutional critique as a productive rather than simply a resistant force. Institutional critique is here not situated at the level of ephemerality, or spontaneity, but rather at the level of chore-ographic strategy, mode of presentation, and forms of collaboration. As such, improv-isation is here neither opposed to a documentary practice nor a simple antidote to the institution; rather, with improvisation it is possible to use and reflect on the modes of rule-based practices and figurations that are constitutive of institutions. With this in mind, we can re-conceptualize the purpose of its appropriation in an educational setting more in regard to reflecting on the norms of improvisation and its standing within an educational curriculum, instead of focusing on the vanishing quality of improvisation and the presumed subversive potentials of its aesthetic, which have been absorbed and neutralized within the dance establishment. Both the challenges for such an appropria-tion in an educational setting and the potentials become clear if one looks at the details of the score for *CP-AD*.

## THE CHALLENGES OF THE
## PERFORMANCE SCORE

What began as a rather informal, thirty-minute event at the Pratt Institute in 1969 soon took on a structured form, as within a year from its first showing Rainer systemized the rules and introduced them to the audience in a five-page program for the performance at the Whitney Museum in 1970 (Rainer 1974), which is usually considered the premiere of the project. Here she named three different levels (one may also think of them as modes) at which the material could be engaged: It could be performed in the original form with a personal style; one could try to perform the material of somebody else as close as pos-sible to the original or in a known "style" or genre; or, one could show the material in a form that was alien or even inappropriate for the material (Rainer 1974, 130).

   With this score, Rainer not only extended her questioning of the representational codes that shaped the dance field in this period, but also went even further in her goal to reflect on and dissolve the boundaries between rehearsal and performance. This can be placed within the wider context of the challenging of those boundaries by theater and performance art at the end of the 1960s. However, the dance field still considered a well-rehearsed piece as the standard. Moreover, there was the problem that true rehears-ing might not take place. In order to find a solution to this problem, Rainer considered seven modes for *CP-AD*, which could influence the way the material was performed or open it up for reflection while working with it: 1) rehearsal mode, where material could be worked on or taught to others; 2) run-through mode in which material could

mode—and that art—to have been" (Lambert-Beatty 2008: 16). Nonetheless, they have inspired many appropriations and re/constructions of Rainer's work.

be shown in the mode of performance, meaning rehearsed and polished by the dancers; 3) new material could be generated; 4) material could be marked. Furthermore there was element 5), which was called „surprise", where objects and actions could be introduced without the knowledge of others. A sixth element was that of teaching: Here new material could be taught to other dancers or those not familiar with material of the project could learn it.

These instructions granted the performers of *CP-AD* an enormous freedom of decision-making; at the same time, it required them to make these decisions. And Rainer still retained her right to veto decisions that the dancers took with the material. This indicated the difficulty of relinquishing control as a choreographer but also pointed to the preciseness of her ideas. This collection of modes and elements of performance can be considered pathbreaking for the development of score-based improvisation as a performance practice. Not surprisingly, *CP-AD* also marked the beginning of "Grand Union," a collective that grew out of the Judson Dance Theater and which performed and toured improvised dances. This group included the original cast of *CP-AD*: Becky Arnold, Douglas Dunn, David Gordon, Barbara Lloyd, Steve Paxton, and Yvonne Rainer. Improvisation and group formation require, then, special attention in reconstruction contexts. For the context of appropriating *CP-AD* with students in an educational setting, it is important to understand not only the score, but also the common ground of knowledge that a group of performers might have shared in executing the score. Scores can be executed—despite their preciseness—in very different manners and can change substantially with the performative impetus and skills that performers bring to the improvisation. To understand the specificity of Rainer's score, it is thus important to identify the challenges for its reenactment in an educational setting.

The many rules that characterize *CP-AD* indicate that improvisation is here not to be understood as something personal or expressive. The rules were needed in order to challenge older norms of presentation, as well as bodily anchored movement conventions that would more easily surface in other forms of improvisation. The proponents, as well as the critics, of the Judson Dance Theater have always emphasized the everyday task-oriented performance style, which was highly significant, as it spelled adherence to a specific artistic understanding in which *CP-AD* operated. However, while it was casual it was not arbitrary, and it is nothing that happens easily or "naturally." There is probably nothing more difficult than acting "casually" on stage while simultaneously being reflective and creative with the rules of the score. Such a mode of performance was the outcome of several projects that Rainer and the Judson protagonists had undertaken. Rainer commented in her autobiography that her comportment in her earlier works had been criticized for an expressiveness she wanted to resist (Rainer 2006). So it seems not to suffice if the aesthetic ideal was to execute movements casually; this also requires skill and practice. It is a mode of experience and trust—as one easily recognizes if one works with students. To stage the everyday and casual behavior on stage, to dissolve borders between rehearsal and performance modes, requires extensive work and abilities on the part of performers. Moreover, to keep a variety of rules and choices in mind while performing sometimes rather basic yet highly structured movement material is a challenge, even for more experienced performers. For instance, Lucinda Childs remarked about performing in Rainer's piece *We Shall Run* (1963):

> We all came out, and I remember worrying that I was going to forget it. The piece was very complex. You had to go over here and make a little circle, and come back here and make a big circle. It was hard to keep it in my head. But we did it. You broke off from the group here and there, but you always had to remember where you splintered out to. You couldn't just drift, and if you got in the wrong group you wouldn't know what they were doing. (Childs, cited in Banes 1987, 87)

Despite the simplicity of the movement material—an everyday action like running—the structural complexity that needs to be memorized makes this kind of work difficult to perform. As with *CP-AD*, the performers needed to consider not only the material, but also a reflective stance and active choices about the different possible qualities it could be performed with. This requires performance experience and a well-developed responsiveness toward the other performers. At the end of the 1960s, when *CP-AD* was staged, one can presume that the group had exactly this sort of experience, as they had worked in very different situations for several years with each other. *CP-AD* was developed and performed by a group that not only knew each other well, but also shared a similar vision about aesthetic and choreographic principles. They wanted to redefine what is considered dance; they challenged the excessive, expressive, and openly virtuosic display of dance. Even though they worked very differently in their use of simple or casual movements, they shared an interest in compositional devices and structures that were needed in order to withhold conventional narrative structures or emotional movement sequencing. As such, the structural principle became paramount in many (although certainly not all) of the works of the Judson Dance Theater: Their pieces are marked by moments of repetition and an aesthetic of the extreme (e.g., very slow, never looking at the audience, no variation in phrasing, emotion according to a timer) (Lambert-Beatty 2008). Through their common experience of working together, they built the basis of a compositional knowledge and understanding of each other, which they could then build on in their improvisations.

This constitutes a practical and embodied knowledge, as well as a performative know-how that needs to be considered when opting for appropriating *CP-AD*. Oscillating between bodily and theoretical reflection in their shared work, they established a reflexive-body-compositional-knowledge, which could also be described, in Susan Foster's sense, as a "body-of-ideas" (Foster 1997, 235). Based on Michel Foucault and Marcel Mauss, Foster seeks to capture with this term the process of the materialization of dance training, which forms the body in conjunction with aesthetic, pedagogical, (anti-)hierarchical, and cultural discourses. This also can be understood in the sense of Pierre Bourdieu's concept of habitus, where modes of knowing, acting, sensing, and feeling are tightly interlinked with the physical routines that accompany these norms. Bourdieu also articulates a concept of time layers that are present in habitus, when he says that the habitus secures the "active presence of past experiences" (1990, 54). As such, the physical art of dance, which is usually considered so ephemeral, and its past, which consequently seems inaccessible, might be already more diversified in its co-presence of both past and present. In her essay "Rests in Pieces," Myriam van Imschoot has described performers as "mobile body-archives. They are not merely domiciled containers, but metabolic ecologies that compose the living traces of experience" (2005, 7).

The question then becomes how to replicate the physical know-how that grounds these processes in a reconstruction. In such a framework, the context needs to be considered more than the time at which the scores were created, with their aesthetic and ideological implications. Additionally, I propose that one needs to look at the embodied and shared artistic knowledge and experience of the performers of *CP-AD* as a significant component in understanding the context of Rainer's work. This allows for seeing the significant group-dynamic and productive aspects of these works, which are usually not considered in discussions of the Judson Dance Theater. Instead, research has focused on the negation of older aesthetics and hence anti-institutional impetus. These discourses, which focus primarily on the "subversive, disturbing, withholding" characteristics of Rainer's work (Banes 1987, 1993; Burt 2005; Siegmund 2006), might ideally correspond to pedagogical concepts that see stumbling blocks and reworking of the known as essential in altering perception modes and thus as crucial for aesthetic education (Ahrens 2014; Stern 2011). To consider "failure" as almost ontologically definitive for reenactments, as well as the basis for educational development, misses the potential of understanding them in regard to shared knowledge and support. Working with the past—critically in an educational setting—brings these aspects to the forefront and into conversation. What, then, are the constructive and embodied forms of knowledge, and the reflective and creative potentials of enacting *CP-AD* with students?

## REENACTING: WHAT ARE SKILLS?

To begin, one starts from the perspective that in reenacting a work that is improvised, the goal is less to recreate an ostensibly historical object by realizing the score, than it is to work with and through the score as a field of potentials. This perspective allows one to search for the explicit and implicit structures and embodied knowledge of dance and improvisation practice. In such a sense, then, it is more appropriate to speak of appropriation than simply reenacting. It must be made one's own in a physical and performative sense. The work with the score thus becomes or requires a training of performative competencies: the sensibilities for different compositional elements and attitudes of performance can be rehearsed. They not only furnish a possible basis for recovering such an improvisational work of the past, but also gear the attention toward a specific form of virtuosity that needs to be studied. The competencies that constitute virtuosity are not as visibly transparent in improvisational art as they are in more classical understandings of skill and technique. What constitutes the virtuosity of the performance? What are the skills and know-how needed or embodied by a group of performers? These questions mark a specific challenge in working with reconstructions of improvisation-based choreography. Thus, reenacting *CP-AD* with students in an educational context may gear the attention toward the (technical) requirements beyond simple movement capacity, and toward the diverse concepts of improvisation, which exist at any given time.

## Case Study

First, learning the movement material "Couples," students faced the difficulty of appropriating a movement material that appeared at odds with their acquired movement preferences and skills. "Couples" is part of the set movement sequences that then can be reworked and performed with different qualities, or can be taught to others on stage during the performance. It is a partnering material that moves in a straight line through the space, where one partner supports a position and then by removing the support, the partner will fall into the next position, which is seemingly found again through the support of the partner. It is a duet of consistent stop and go, with sometimes twisted positions or "poses" (in order to stay in line) and off-balance leg stances with always altering (sometimes awkward) points of support by the partner. From a technical perspective, students needed to be willing to be precise, because they easily found a version of the poses, which they could hold on their own and then would not surely fall once the support was released. However, what made working on the material more difficult for them, at first, was not the issue of technical ability, but an apparent disjunction between principles and terms associated with the piece, on the one hand, and forms of movement, on the other hand, for which students had specific interpretations that could not be aligned easily with each other. The notion of letting go and partnering that are at the core of the "Couples" material provoked concepts of ease and organicity for the students that did not function well in this appropriation. To create this material with a partner required a rethinking of how hold and flow are to be conceived and executed, and what training can be devised for partnering. While there is a constant play between holding and letting go that is based on the interaction of two partners, this has little to do with the effortless and smooth flow that many students initially like, or even with more historic forms of fall and recovery, although the reference to these practices is clearly visible. Moreover, the rehearsal process and the feedback with students revealed that the seemingly static and quite formal poses that were not flowing and relaxed were linked for them with quite a different aesthetic (usually not associated with the Judson but rather with historical modern dance, to which they have a more distanced stance). This inhibited the performance of them as simple or casual tasks. In appropriating this material, in addition to finding a precision in movement forms and modes that students had not anticipated, a discussion was needed to reflect on potential prejudices that the students brought to certain forms of dancing. Throughout this appropriation, they were asked to consider that not necessarily the forms (poses and movement patterns) but the modes of working, contextualizing, and repeating made for the contemporary quality and the interestingly challenging aspects of the material.

Reworking one's own perception of the material was also granted with another choreographic element, "Pillow and Chair," which allowed the students to experience how seemingly everyday movement can be difficult to remember and may entail more detail and complexity than one might suspect. What appeared as very easy when watching—picking up a pillow, turning around with it, placing it on the floor, and then placing one's head on it, and so on—became challenging. It was difficult to remember the arbitrary order of the tasks, as the movement itself had no logic. Learning this choreographic material also geared the attention to the meticulous details of timing of the sequence that were not rhythmically in tune with a casual appearance or comportment—for instance, granting relatively little time for placing the head on the pillow, or running around the chair and putting emphasis on counts like seven.

Once they were mastered, the students came to like these movement materials, but what remained difficult for them was how to choose when and in which mode and quality to perform them. They felt vulnerable in regard to this improvisational aspect of the performance, sensing that their compositional abilities were yet not fully developed, and also because there was no obvious shield of virtuosity in the movement that would demonstrate the scope of their skills. Others felt that the score was rather simplistic.

Subsequently, the historicity of certain forms of improvisation and of the scores also became a point of discussion. While some might not be able to discover at first sight the complexity of the improvisational structure, the historically shaped notion of improvisation became apparent to others, who had been trained in the follow-up of the influence of the postmodern dance era. Improvisational techniques and scores also have a history and require that one consider the context of their genesis. For instance, many improvisation competencies in partnering today are influenced by the development of contact improvisation. "Couples" and, even more so, the element of "Group Hoist" were clearly predecessors of contact improvisation; however, these movement materials were neither aesthetically nor formally as clearly shaped as they might be today. They seem, from an aesthetic of flow, ease, and sharing of weight (that for many mark contact improvisation today), rather stiff, awkward, and unexciting. Seeing this shift allows for a reflection on how rules and competencies in improvisation are also historically and aesthetically shaped, and a rediscovery of how improvisation is based on different forms of training, experience, and attitudes. As such, interrogating the rules and modes in which one could perform and rework the material became necessary in order not only to make an appropriation nuanced, but also to allow for a transfer into the present. What does it mean, for instance, to perform the material in a rehearsal mode? Exploring this question led to a reflection of one's own daily practice, the inherent, often implicit rules of the dance field. And in this we finally saw a correspondence between Rainer's interest and the potential it brought to the contemporary practice of the students. Thus in the last section of this chapter, I want to argue that *CP-AD* as and in reenactment can lead to a self-reflexive approach to one's own dance practice as it brings attention to how rule-based it is in its ostensible training of individuality.

# REENACTING AS A REFLEXIVE FORM OF INVESTIGATING THE IMPLICIT RULES OF IMPROVISATION

The rehearsal mode was extremely difficult for the students to perform. Preventing students from simply "playing rehearsal" instead of actually rehearsing forced us to consider the rules according to which rehearsals are usually held. Such self-reflection provoked various questions: How is movement material taught and learned? How is it developed? How often is it repeated, how often are sections repeated, or variations of it? How is feedback given? Is it always given in the same mode? It is of course not possible to know how consistent the rehearsal mode might have been in Rainer's performance of *CP-AD*, as rules and scores do not equal performances. Nonetheless, it was Rainer's concept to take seriously the notion of the rehearsal process as being part of performance. She actively advocated, in fact, for the dissolution of the boundaries between performance and rehearsal. While this endeavor might be considered both theoretically and practically futile, it should nonetheless be considered as a serious maneuver to recapture the concept of the project in reenacting it. And it is quite a challenge for students who do not have the years of rehearsal experience that the performance group around Rainer had. Accordingly, one needs to ask, what are the strategies that allow the recreation of aspects of rehearsal on stage such as they appeared in Rainer's work? One possibility is to conceive new—even very extreme—rules, based on a reflection on rehearsal practices. For instance, it seemed helpful in the work with students (who usually do not like repeating something or working on one element for a long time) to establish the rule that "Group Hoist" in rehearsal mode would need always to be taken from the top, once somebody found or called out that a mistake was done. The sequence of "Group Hoist" could not be stopped and abandoned before it was danced through in its entirety. This led students to stick to the material for a very long time; it allowed them to be precise and fully present. Subsequently, it also loaded the material with a certain group dynamic and power (some wanted to get done with it, others simply enjoyed calling out a mistake, even if one was not visible). The group needed to negotiate this. Such a procedure in a reenactment is only considered problematic if one does not always believe reconstruction to be a construction. Mark Franko has called this procedure simply a construction—in contrast to a reconstruction—of the past, one that opens a dialogue "between forms and periods on the basis of style, vocabulary, and theory, rather than history alone" (Franko 2015, 135).

Setting new rules created a group awareness and dynamics that were also part of the "original" project. The group continued to work on the project in its own spirit, as the invention of rules was already part of *CP-AD*. And they were sometimes paradoxical. For instance, there was the rule of the "surprise," which Rainer "authorized." One could initiate something surprising or bring a surprising object. The surprise (often associated with spontaneity and an unplanned action) worked, despite the fact that it was grounded in a rule. Educational theories have recently become very entangled in such paradoxical situations, where, in a rule-based setting, experiments and contingency are sought instead. The experiment—according to Sönke Ahrens—is a space where the already known is (re)discovered and the new is found within already familiar terrain (in contrast to exploration, which ventures into yet unknown fields, the blank spots on the map) (Ahrens 2014). It is this chance of reenacting dance that provides the basis for an educational potential, in which rules and contingency, the learning of new skills and the reworking of embodied and habitual practices, can go hand in hand.

# CONCLUSION

While it is not possible for students to reenact the political context, discussing it nonetheless allowed them to reflect on the production framing and their expectations in regard to group processes and how theses processes shaped not only the choreography, but also its performative quality. Focusing on group constellations also brings a more productive and supportive note into the historical discourse, as many scholars see the main focus of dance's critical potential as consisting in notions of disruption, halting and arresting of movement, representation, and meaning.

As such, the piece also continues to exist in its affect, its potential to make dancers reflective or bored. Appropriating *CP-AD* opens up the possibility to reveal our explicit or implicit value systems and standards around improvisation. More so, if one sees the score as a safe space where experience can happen, more might be saved of the exciting aspect of the piece than if an interesting performance was created through it. If one considers discussion (as it also took place within Rainer's group) as an essential part of reconstruction or reenacting, the original impetus of the piece might stay alive, despite the fact that it has become an icon of avant-garde art and a part of dance education. With such a pedagogical perspective, the anti-institutional impetus of the piece might be fruitful for the use of dance education.

## WORKS CITED

Ahrens, Sönke. 2014. *Experiment and Exploration: Forms of World-Disclosure. From Epistemology to Bildung. Contemporary Philosophies and Theories of Education*, translated by Andrew Rossiter. Amsterdam: Springer.

Albrecht, Cornelia, and Franz Anton Cramer, eds. 2006: *Tanz(Aus)Bildung: Reviewing Bodies of Knowledge*. München: Epodium.

Anderson, Jack. 1997. *Art without Boundaries: The World of Modern Dance*. Iowa City: University of Iowa Press.

Backoefer Andreas, Nicole Haitzinger, and Claudia Jeschke, eds. 2009. *Tanz & Archiv. Reenactment*, H. 1. München: Epodium.

Banes, Sally. 1987. *Terpsichore in Sneakers: Postmodern Dance*. Middletown, CT: Wesleyan University Press.

Banes, Sally. 1993. *Democracy's Body: Judson Dance Theater 1962–1964*. Durham, NC, and London: Duke University Press.

Boltanski, Luc, and Eve Chiapello. 2007. *The New Spirit of Capitalism*. Translated by Gregory Elliott. London: Verso.

Bourdieu, Pierre. 1990. *The Logic of Practice*. Translated by Richard Nice. Stanford: Stanford University Press.

Brandstetter, Gabriele. 2007. "Dance as Culture of Knowledge. Body Memory and the Challenge of Theoretical Knowledge." In *Knowledge in Motion: Perspectives of Artistic and Scientific Research in Dance*, edited by Sabine Gehm, Pirkko Husemann, and Katharina von Wilcke, 37–48. Bielefeld: Transcript.

Burt, Ramsay. 2005. *Judson Dance Theater: Performative Traces*. New York and London: Routledge.

Debord, Guy. 1995. *Society of the Spectacle*. New York: Zone Books.

Fischer-Lichte, Erika, and Gertrude Lehnert. 2000. "Einleitung." *Inszenierungen des Erinnerns, Paragrana. Internationale Zeitschrift für Historische Anthropologie*, 9(2): 9–17.

Foster, Susan. 1997. "Dancing Bodies." In *Meaning in Motion: New Cultural Studies of Dance*, edited by Jane C. Desmond, 235–258. Durham, NC: Duke University Press.

Foster, Susan. 2002. *Dances That Describe Themselves*. Middleton, CT: Wesleyan University Press.

Franko, Mark. 1989. "Repeatability, Reconstruction and Beyond." *Theatre Journal* 41(1) (March): 56–74.

Franko, Mark [1993] 2015. "Epilogue: Repeatability, Reconstruction, and Beyond." In *Dance as Text: Ideologies of the Baroque Body*, Cambridge: Cambridge University Press: 131–151.

Franko, Mark, and Annette Richards. 2000. "Actualizing Absence. The Pastness of Performance." In *Acting on the Past: Historical Performance Across the Disciplines* edited by Mark Franko and Annette Richards, 1–9. Hanover, NH: Wesleyan University Press.

Goldman, Danielle. 2010. *I Want to Be Ready: A Conceptual Framework for Understanding the Development of Improvised Dance in Late 20th-Century America*. Ann Arbor: Universtity of Michigan Press.

Hantelmann, Dorothea von. 2007. *Zur Bedeutsamkeit der Performativität von Kunst*. Zürich/ Berlin: Diaphanes. (Also available now in translation: *How to Do Things with Art: The Meaning of Art's Performativity*. Zürich: JRP Ringier and les presses du réel, 2010).

Hardt, Yvonne. 2005. "Prozessuale Archive. Wie Tanzgeschichte von Tänzern geschrieben wird." In *Tanz.de. Zeitgenössischer Tanz in Deutschland—Strukturen im Wandel—Eine neue Wissenschaft Theater der Zeit Arbeitsbuch 2005*, edited by Johannes Odenthal, 34–39. Hamburg: Theater der Zeit.

Hardt, Yvonne. 2006. "Reading Emotions: Lesearten des Emotionalen am Beispiel des modernen Tanzes in den USA." In *e-motion. Jahrbuch der Gesellschaft für Tanzforschung*, Bd. 16, edited by Margit Bischof, Claudia Feest, and Claudia Rosiny, 139–155. Münster: Lit. Verlag.

Hardt, Yvonne. 2011. "Staging the Ethnographic of Dance History: Contemporary Dance and Its Play with Tradition." *Dance Research Journal* 43(1) (Summer): 27–42.

Hardt, Yvonne. 2012a. "Engagement with the Past in Contemporary Dance." In *New German Dance Studies*, edited by Susan Manning and Lucia Ruprecht, 217–231. Chicago: University of Illinois Press.

Hardt, Yvonne. 2012b. "Pushing Borders of Thinking and Moving: On Theoretical Framing." In *Crossover 55/2—Internationally Mixed: Reflections, Tasks and (F)acts*, edited by Yvonne Hardt and Katarina Kleinschmidt, 26–37. Köln: ZZT.

Hardt, Yvonne, and Martin Stern. 2011. "Choreografie und Institution. Eine Einleitung." In *Choreographie und Institution. Zeitgenössischer Tanz zwischen Ästhetik, Produktion und Vermittlung*, edited by Yvonne Hardt, Martin Stern, 1–32. Bielefeld: Transcript.

Hermes, Karin. 2010. "Choreographie im hermeneutischen Prozess. Reflexionen zu künstlerischen-methodischen Rechereche an Hand von Beispielen." In *Original und Revival: Geschichts-Schreibung im Tanz*, edited by Christina Thurner and Julia Wehren, 169–180. Zürich: Chronos.

Huschka, Sabine. 2002. *Moderner Tanz. Konzepte—Stile—Utopien.* Reinbek bei Hamburg: Rowohlt.

Klein, Gabriele. 2007. "Dance in a Knowledge Society." In *Knowledge in Motion: Perspectives of Artistic and Scientific Research in Dance*, edited by Sabine Gehm, Pirkko Husemann, and Katharina von Wilcke, 25–34. Bielefeld: Transcript 2007.

Kruschkova, Krassimira. 2010. "Tanzgeschichte(n): wieder und wider. Reenactment, Referenz, révérence." In *Original und Revival: Geschichts-Schreibung im Tanz*, edited by Christina Thurner and Julia Wehren, 39–45. Zürich: Chronos.

Laet, Timmy de. 2010. "Wühlen in Archiven." *Tanz* 2: 54–59.

Lambert-Beatty, Carrie. 2008. *Being Watched: Yvonne Rainer and the 1960s.* Cambridge, MA: MIT Press.

Lampert, Friederike. 2007. *Tanzimprovisation. Geschichte—Theorie—Verfahren—Vermittlung.* Bielefeld: Transcript.

McDonagh, Don. 1970. *The Rise and Fall and Rise of Modern Dance.* New York: Outerbridge & Dienstfrey.

Phelan, Peggy. 1993. *Unmarked: The Politics of Performance.* London: Routledge.

Rainer, Yvonne. 1974. *Work (1961–73).* Halifax: Press of Nova Scotia College of Art and Design.

Rainer, Yvonne. 2006. *Feelings Are Facts: A Life.* Cambridge, MA: MIT Press.

Siegmund, Gerald. *Abwesenheit. Eine performative Ästhetik des Tanzes. William Forsythe, Jérôme Bel, Xavier Le Roy, Meg Stuart.* Bielefeld: Transcript.

Siegmund, Gerald. 2010. "Affekt, Technik, Diskurs. Aktiv passiv sein im Angesicht der Geschichte." In *Original und Revival: Geschichts-Schreibung im Tanz*, edited by Christina Thurner and Julia Wehren, 15–26. Zürich: Chronos.

Schatzki, Theodore. 2002. *The Site of the Social: A Philosophical Account of the Constitution of Social Life and Change.* University Park: University of Pennsylvania Press.

Stern, Martin. 2011. "Tanz als Möglichkeit ästhetischer Bildung in der Schule." In *Choreographie und Institution. Zeitgenössischer Tanz zwischen Ästhetik, Produktion und Vermittlung*, edited by Yvonne Hardt und Maritn Stern, 209–232. Bielefeld: Transcript.

Thurner, Christina, and Julia Wehren, eds. 2010. *Original und Revival. Geschichts Schreibung im Tanz. Original und Revival. Geschichts-Schreibung im Tanz.* Zürich: Chronos.

Van Imschoot, Myriam. "Rests in Pieces: On Scores, Notation and the Trace in Dance." http://www.make-up-productions.net/media/materials/RestsInPieces_Myriam%20 VanImschoot.pdf (accessed September 20, 2015).

Wood, Catherine. 2007. *Yvonne Rainer: The Mind Is a Muscle*. London: Afterall.

# PART V

..................................................

# ENACTING TESTIMONY/ PERFORMING CULTURAL MEMORY/ SPECTATORSHIP AS PRACTICE

..................................................

# CHAPTER 13

..................................................................

# WHAT REMAINS OF THE WITNESS? TESTIMONY AS EPISTEMOLOGICAL CATEGORY

*Schlepping the Trace*

..................................................................

## SUSANNE FOELLMER

"I once danced in a piece by Kurt Jooss," says Reinhild Hoffmann during an audience talkback on the occasion of a performance of Christina Ciupke and Anna Till's *undo, redo and repeat*. "I couldn't describe it to you today if I tried. Take, for example, my role as the cat in Peter and the Wolf. I can't for the life of me remember how it goes" (Ciupke et al. 2015).

Consulting with contemporary witnesses of pivotal past dance is a common key component for many working on reperforming such pieces, as they pursue approximations of material that is already history. At first blush, these witnesses seem to affirm the possibility of "authentic" revival with respect to the re-practicing of choreographies, their movement sequences, and their spatial coordination or their bodily alignment or texture. This status of "having been present" supposedly wins out over any lingering uncertainty regarding the capacity of photos, video, sketches, or written documents to provide robust and faithful insight.

Audience talkbacks, a unifying hallmark of the otherwise varied projects made possible by the German subsidy program *Tanzfonds Erbe* (Dance Heritage Fund),[1] evidence

---

[1] *Tanzfonds Erbe* is a program of the German Federal Cultural Foundation that is planned from 2012 until 2018; it is devoted to contemporary artistic approaches to dance history. The objective is to create an improved visibility of dance in the canon of the established arts—this is to be reached by an "access to a lively dance history." Choreographers can apply with suitable projects on an annual basis. http://www.tanzfonds.de/en.

the tenuousness, if not the outright failure, of the "faithful" transfer that living witnesses are supposed to secure. Emma Lewis Thomas, for example, finds herself unable to report anything specific on the movements or spatial orientation of Dore Hoyer's role of The Chosen One in Mary Wigman's *The Rite of Spring* ([1957] 2013) because, at the time, the choreography in the critical scene placed her with her back to the protagonist (Barnett et al. 2013).[2]

In *undo, redo and repeat* (2014–2015), former Wigman student Irene Sieben could relay basically nothing about her work as a dancer despite having reprocessed it in her capacity as a teacher, and Reinhild Hoffmann finally shared her own piece inspired by Kurt Jooss's signature technique, rather than the choreography from a role she danced in one of his works, which she could no longer recall.

Whatever testimony these "guarantors" may have cognitive access to, it seems not to survive the transmission process, arriving full of gaps and holes. Consequently, what the witness conveys is compromised by his or her personal experience in the moment of remembering and repeating, and it seems impossible to tell one from the other. What reward, then, does the appeal to the witness promise to bestow? And what depredations is knowledge subject to by virtue of inaction?

In what follows, I will weigh the (im)possibilities for dance that arise from the notion of the living witness. If the passage of decades so compromises memories and their transfer, it must be asked just what witnesses are capable of passing on. What do witnesses' oral and corporeal accounts of past dance knowledge count for? And how might the notion of the witness in a philosophical and art-historical setting prove advantageous for reflection on reconstruction and reenactment in dance?

# HANDING IT DOWN

In Ciupke and Till's aforementioned project, the focus rests on the diverse methods that exist for transferring dancerly and/or choreographic knowledge. The work surveys several of these methods by appeal to a selection of five personalities—Mary Wigman, Kurt Jooss, Dore Hoyer, William Forsythe, and Pina Bausch—that collectively comprise the "major protagonists of German dance history" and indeed draw

> from the perspective of their living witnesses: their friends, students, collaborators, and audience in whose memories they live on. Consciously or unconsciously, these witnesses harbor a living memory in which they broaden the scope of choreographic legacies through new interpretations and reconstructions as well as doctrines and lessons, and which contain the potential for various kinds of transfers. (Ciupke and Till 2014, 2)

---

[2] Thomas was involved in the reconstruction of the piece as an eyewitness.

At the project's inception, Ciupke and Till asked a group of people who had sustained contact with these choreographers for a scene or fragment of their choreography that they remembered and that they might wish to pass on, along with a written testimony of their choice. Participating in the project were Irene Sieben, one of Mary Wigman's last students, and Martin Nachbar, a Berlin-based choreographer well-versed in the reenactment of Dore Hoyer's *Affectos Humanos* (1962) from his piece *Urheben Aufheben* (2008). In addition, Thomas McManus, a longtime dancer and member of the Forsythe Company, and Reinhild Hoffmann, who was originally asked for a fragment of Joossean choreography before she decided to pass on a part of one of her pieces, were contributors, as were former audience members who were able to speak to their experience of attending works by Pina Bausch.

The outcomes of these attempts at transmission exist in three distinct but comparable forms: as an exhibition shown in the Heidelberger Kunstverein (May 16–August 3, 2014)[3]; as the link connecting a collection of rehearsal stills, audio instructions, and videos about working with the "witness"; and as information on their respective artistic processes, which not only conveys a sense of the transmission experience, but promotes its dancerly mode (www.undo-redo-repeat.de/ausstellung.html). Apart from two performance series (2014 and 2015) presenting the passed-down, corpo-realized excerpts, Ciupke and Till created a website for the project, which serves as an "enduring" portal to material such as interviews with the witnesses themselves (www.undo-redo-repeat.de).

Even this short description of the project inspires a wealth of questions, the most pressing of which arguably concerns how "living" memory can actually function if, for instance, as in the case of Reinhild Hoffmann, there is barely anything there. How are we to understand "living," or animation, as a model for memory, and how does it affect current discourse on reenactment and reconstruction? It is, moreover, apparent that although the "witnesses" are all experts, the sort of expertise they embody can vary widely between them: at first glance, the witness role seems to fit the cases of Jooss dancer Reinhild Hoffmann and Wigman student Irene Sieben, with the caveat that Hoffmann was ultimately only able to account for her own choreography. Respective excerpts from the chosen choreography reveal, furthermore, exactly those difficulties, tensions, and inconsistencies that body-to-body transfer opens up, owing to the temporal gap and to the substantial differences in how they transmitted their technique to dancers who were trained differently than themselves.

Personal acquaintance is equally important to Thomas McManus, who can report on a surviving choreographer with ease. Does this, then, broaden the concept of witnessing, which to date has seemed limited only to historical events?[4] On the other hand,

---

[3] In the context of the reopening of *undo, redo and repeat* (April 16–19, 2015), parts of the exhibition were on show in the Sophiensæle's foyer.

[4] According to Sigrid Weigel, the concept of witnessing should be understood especially in terms of its function of giving an account in the sense of a procedure of historiography. Citing Alexander García Düttmann, she emphasizes: "Thus you are only a witness when you can no longer rely on any knowledge [ . . . ]" (Weigel, 2000: 132, 117).

Martin Nachbar (who was born in 1971), never having known Dore Hoyer, appropriated her work through filmed documentation as well as yet another witness (Waltraud Luley; see Nachbar, Chapter 2 in this volume).[5] A different format was assigned to those attesting to the performances of Pina Bausch's work. They offered no choreography, but rather accounts of their individual, aesthetic experiences (statements that were subsequently projected onto screens as part of Ciupke and Till's performance).

This brief rundown of participants and their contributions should already leave an impression of how manifold and diffuse the concept of the witness can be. The theory and modalities underpinning witnesses and witness-hood should be more precisely construed to begin with, yet it stands here askew at the very heart of the project.

# The Epistemological Model of Witnessing

Debate on the nature of the witness has accelerated in the past few decades, spreading through disciplines and igniting debate in the realms of both philosophy and cultural theory. While witnessing itself is considered a fragile model for knowledge in philosophy (cf. Lackey and Sosa 2006), more historical discussions, especially those about the Holocaust, and in particular theories put forward by Giorgio Agamben ([1998] 2005), focus on the (im)possibility of accounting for events that exceed the limits of the human.[6] Certain key antagonisms have long guided discussions in philosophy of knowledge at the level of epistemology: dating back to David Hume, so-called reductionists have accepted the witness only as a secondary source of knowledge, which, affirmative only of the subject's individual experience, is no replacement for knowledge generated according to the principal foundation of empiricism (Lackey 2006, 5). The "anti-reductionists," who oppose this understanding, appeal instead to Hume's contemporary, Thomas Reid, according to whom "testimony [ . . . ] is *just as basic* a source of justification [ . . . ] as sense perception memory, inference, and the like" (Lackey 2006, 4; emphasis in original). Philosopher Sybille Krämer opposes the reductionist proclamation of "know it yourself"—which, in my view, lives or dies entirely on the question of how one might understand the individual as an "experiencing entity" in a sense satisfactory to postmodernity and even more so to dance—pleading instead for a "social epistemology" (Krämer 2011, 129). She cites literary scholar Sigrid Weigel, who stresses that it is from precisely this tension that testimony confirms its existence "because it is about

[5] Luley was Hoyer's partner for many years and the designated custodian of Hoyer's works until her death.
[6] Sibylle Schmidt establishes that authors such as Giorgio Agamben, Jacques Derrida, and François Lyotard particularly focus on the "extreme case of survival witnesses" for questions relating to what can actually be said or witnessed (Schmidt 2011: 51).

testifying to an experience that is not available to another [person]" (Weigel 2000, 116; Krämer 2011, 130). Perception, as Krämer has it, is not some pre-conscious operation of reflex, but rather still "bound up in discursive thought," which leads her to conclude that "[k]nowledge granted from the words of others is inevitable and neither is it reducible to knowledge certified by a sole individual" (Krämer 2011, 130).

The fields of dance, reconstruction, and reenactment are interested in the previously mentioned modes of knowledge because of the challenge of defining these operations as distinct categories without leaving behind a gaping chasm. We can observe this in how "knowledge we derive from the words of others" on dancerly and/or choreographic experiences generally line up with the gestures, such as hand signs, that accompany their verbal descriptions. This comes to life in Ciupke and Till's project, which features a sequence from William Forsythe's piece *Die Befragung des Robert Scott* (1986): Witness Thomas McManus details a specific swaying motion not only by affecting it physically, but by verbally narrating his own demonstration. Take, for example, the use of the word "bounce," with its correspondingly dynamized pronunciation and to some degree drawn-out articulation (Ciupke and Till 2014b). Accordingly, in most cases, learning a new dance style or movement protocol requires a verbal mode of instruction. At the very least, it is unusual to attempt a transmission of this kind using nothing but the body. Irene Sieben alludes to this fact while discussing her time as a student of Mary Wigman.[7] *Sui generis* perception, generated without the aid of language, does not necessarily hold a place in the schema of dance knowledge.

The act of receiving the testimony not only includes what the witness says, but also the physical interpretation (indeed itself a kind of reenactment) of the material, as seen in Ciupke and Till's reconstructive approach to the choreographic excerpt submitted by Thomas McManus. Cognition and perception, as the gathering of shared information in dance, always already belong in the realm of physical and oral transfer,[8] between one's own comprehension of that which one has not experienced and a "second person" communication. Epistemology's empirical approach becomes less stable when we realize that language and perception are too interdependent to be dichotomized.

According to Aleida Assmann, witnessing is always already a "*performative* act." (2007, 34; emphasis in original) Without such action there can be no witness. "It is generally the interlocutor who turns memory into testimony" (34). Thus, there remain even

---

[7] Sieben describes the teaching sessions in an interview with Ciupke and Till. Although "the movement was in the foreground," a subject of movement was generally quickly introduced verbally at the beginning; the exercises were then accompanied by comments and discussed again at the end (Sieben et al. 2013). The influence of language, also with Wigman's increasing age, was not unimportant, as Sieben explains: "Depending on her form on that particular day, she sat in a chair and celebrated wonderful word constructs, or she led a diagonal in a long, slim flared skirt and black high-neck sweater or white blouse." (Sieben 2003: 8).

[8] See also Edward C. Warburton's thoughts on the matter; he postulates an interrelation between a "simple" embodiment and more difficult cognitive processes that include thinking and remembered experience in a constitutive way—as, for example, in the case of marking in dance as a mode of "physical re-languaging" (Warburton 2011, 76).

more cracks in an understanding of the witness based on a dichotomous model of perception. Such a witnessing depends not only on incorporations of perception (adaptations), but also on further, secondary acts of corroboration, which go beyond mere perception. Those acts of witness corroboration have the capacity to, I would argue, locate talk of *re*enactment (understood here as a genuine act of recollection) already before the actual carrying out of a redoing or reperforming, and specifically as acts of testimony-giving and testimony-taking. This is a process, which, before the *redo* begins, I understand as *re-construction already*,[9] as reproduction, and which, with respect to personal changes and temporal gaps, always must be understood as doing something new or in a new way (Willeit 2010, 48).

# CONTEMPORARY WITNESSES

Witnesses and their addressees in the framework of a reconstructive process in dance (and also performance) find themselves always in an intermediate corporeal space of both primary and secondary (verbally accessed) perceptions, between reproduction and uptake. We cannot help but wonder at the status of the witness and the actor in this particular situation. This question becomes manifest when one takes into account the quite divergent backgrounds from which the witnesses in *undo, redo and repeat* emerge; for it is interesting that there is no clear-cut case here of an eyewitness. As previously described, Irene Sieben experienced Mary Wigman only as a student, not as a dancer, and Reinhild Hoffmann's memory of working with Kurt Jooss does not extend to the specific roles she danced. Martin Nachbar never knew Dore Hoyer personally, and those attesting to the Pina Bausch performances drew exclusively on visual knowledge, with no physical knowledge to appeal to. Only Thomas McManus was directly involved in the work of his protagonist; however, William Forsythe is still alive, and so he could, in principle, be his own witness.

These details become crucial in view of Ciupke and Till's intentions, which were, as they set it up, to learn a sequence of movement from each respective choreographer. In the case of the Bausch witnesses, it was simply not on the table, as they could only expect to receive an overall atmospheric tableau of what it was like to attend one of her performances. There is no attempt here at the transfer of precise 'movement material'. These witnesses would, realistically, have fallen under the category of the oral reporter, who is involved with the relevant event, but is distanced from its physical reality, the ramifications of which, in this case, only a professional dancer would appreciate.[10] To this extent,

---

[9]   This idea of re-construction is based on Mark Franko's understanding of a redoing as "construction" that adds the notion of invention to the redone event (Franko 1989, 58). In my case I would suggest that the construction however is preceded by an act of re-constructing an event by testifying to it.

[10]   Though in this case, the idea of "neutral observation" should not be propagated. Instead, it is about distance in respect to the profession of dance that is not (usually) pursued by the person in question.

the closest analog to these types of witnesses is the legal witness: following Assmann (2007, 36), the legal witness is meant to be impartial, to speak selflessly—in the case of the Bausch witness, we would have to make yet another caveat, since the spectators did not themselves dance it, yet indeed had an aesthetic experience, but hardly one that can be labeled "objective."

However, the juridical comparison highlights the *faktum* of the *having-been-there* as "immediate sensory experience" (Ibid.) The stressing of a particular time span as a necessary precondition for the witness itself results from a being-present that nevertheless precludes personal involvement in the proceedings in question. Here, too, one can easily spin out of control when theorizing the category of the theater experience—after all, an aesthetic experience can hardly be separated from a being-touched or being-moved. But the aspect of presentness is, at any rate, relevant to all of Ciupke and Till's witnesses at any point even if the level of experience among them differs, depending whether or not they remain in personal dancing contact with their respective choreographers.

Those interviewed are thus distinguishable from one another by their witness-hood. Assmann recalls the notion of the witness as flourishing in the wake of a growing amount of work on the Holocaust. In what she calls the category of "historical witness(es)" (*historische[r] Zeuge*), which here, especially, connotes the status of the survivor capable of "reporting to posterity" (*den Bericht an die Nachwelt weiter[]geben*) (Assmann 2007, 39), it is above all "living testimony" (*zeitnahe[s] Zeugnis*) (41) which is decisive in the authentification of what is transmitted.[11] *Undo, redo and repeat* does not abide by these temporal concepts. On the one hand, the interviewees are not witnesses in the strictest sense—Irene Sieben was only present for a fraction of Wigman's career, and Martin Nachbar was simply 'born too late'. On the other hand, they are witnesses, 'close' enough to the happenings such as the Bausch dances, just not (as a general rule) involved professionally. Again, witness Reinhild Hoffmann's memories are fragmentary, the historical distance evidently too vast. And McManus is indeed not just temporally close but 'up close', yet the fact that his memories could be perpetually subject to verification or falsification by Forsythe himself completely torpedoes the idea of the witness as having irrevocable authority over the narrative of a deceased person's past life.

The models of witness-hood introduced thus far prove inadequate to address work with witnesses in the context of reconstruction in dance and performance, owing both to a problematic focus on epistemology as well as a tension with the existing definitional proposals for witness-hood. The witness should thus subsequently be evaluated as a medium-specific model and amended with an eye toward the research objects that are relevant here.

---

[11] "Accounts of the Holocaust that were recorded up to 1946 are judged differently than accounts that were recorded 50 years after the events. The witness [ . . . ] is 'an endangered species'" (Assmann 2007: 41).

# DANCE MESSENGERS

Sybille Krämer (2011) addresses this state of dependence on certain people as information carriers and transmitters through the lens of her own medium/message model. For Krämer, witnesses can be understood as messengers, as middlemen and middlewomen for happenings affected by large gaps of time (Krämer 2007, 126). The defining characteristics are the removal of the self in the presentation of the message, the bridging of a "spatial or temporal gap," as well as "the involuntary messaging of the vestigial trace" (127). The second attribute already hints at the third, for the messenger is "a part of the past in a material continuum, [ ... ] given that the message itself is inscribed in his or her corporeal memory" (126).

This is to set aside for the moment that body memory does not represent—as we saw in the case of Reinhild Hoffmann—an, as it were, frictionless record-taking process. It must, then, be remarked that a mode of (corporeal, perceptual) involvement is inherent to any similarly construed concept of witness-hood. The model continues to function even without the neutral third party that the idea of the gap seems to necessitate. Furthermore, witnesses are always, then, "schlepping" these traces around with them, bringing us to Krämer's third proposition that the interpretation of the "residue" of that which, for example, has gone unsaid, which was uttered outside of the realm of the verbal, falls on the recipient—the "decipherer of traces" (Krämer 2007, 128). According to Krämer, witnesses are thus doubly marked as such: simultaneously "recording device" and "trustworthy, credible person." She continues: "The figure of the witness is the site of a conflation between the personal and the depersonalized. They must conduct themselves as material artifact and authentic human being at the same time" (128).

Thus this relation is a productive problem to work through in the context of dance, as it also promises to hone our understanding of the nexus of being involved in and bearing testimony to choreographic events. As Sabine Huschka notes, dance has always conflated the material plane with the authorial plane: "Dance consistently operates on this double, paradoxical structure that renders subject and object one and the same [ ... ]." The principle of each of these respective moments "is determined," thus, "by precise bodily knowledge on the one hand and modes of perception on the other" (2002, 26). Aside from (most of) the Bausch witnesses, it is now certainly the circumstance of the "doing-oneself" or the "having-done-oneself" that becomes relevant to the witness's role in the reconstruction of dance and performance. And yet it is not just the mode of the witness that is always determined by this subject-object relation. Even that which is produced by witnessing is shot through with this doubleness.

In terms of Irene Sieben's status as Mary Wigman's contemporary witness, we can now make the provisional inference that, in a certain sense, she executed the legal witness's stipulation: As a student no longer dancing with Wigman, she brings knowledge of a certain historical interval to the table, and at the same time, through her status as a former student, as knowledgeable, she is confirmed to be—in Krämer's sense—a "trustworthy" person adequately close to the happenings in question. Sieben is and was, however, involved with the physically achieved experience of Wigman's movement principles (and surely, too, in the frequently tumultuous relationship between teacher and student) and can consequently function as a historical witness and messenger of pertinent bypassed events (*entzogene Ereignisse*) as "living testament" and messenger alike. These events leave quite literal traces, such as Sieben's memory of Wigman "spinning through space," which she can attest to because of how the memory itself "clings" to her body (Ciupke and Till 2014c). How might we say that this stipulation behaves in the cases of Reinhild Hoffmann and Martin Nachbar?

The admitted gaps in Reinhild Hoffmann's memories of dancing in Kurt Jooss's piece initially confronted Ciupke and Till with an omission that would eventually fly in the face of their very premise. Interested not in passing on a sequence from another choreographer, but rather in passing down a segment of her own solo piece (*VOR ORT* 1997), Hoffmann suggested the following compromise: she would use her piece to demonstrate and analyze principles that she first learned from Jooss. The Hoffmann case complicates the witness-hood model in more ways than one. First, Hoffman is, like Sieben, a former student and thus should be able to transmit certain techniques and movement qualities. However,

> I can't exactly describe where Kurt Jooss's influence on my work is overtly visible. [All I] can say is that I have an eye for qualities of movement. [ . . . ] One should always be making decisions not only about which movements are to be made, but also which qualities those movements take on. That's really the one thing for which I can say with confidence: Yes, I got that from Jooss. (Ciupke and Till 2014, 11)

Unlike Sieben, Hoffmann is unable to pass on any concrete movement principles of learned processes,[12] denying Ciupke and Till their desired (proof of) concept of written records for past dances:

> The thing I was trying to describe becomes quite different once the body has processed it. The body can read even if you maybe can't put it into words. [ . . . ] I get the feeling that no description can really get anywhere near doing it justice. Part of it has to come from the physical experience, not just the intellectual—something else— that's crucial to understanding it, that isn't verbal. (2014, 11)

It is worth briefly mentioning here that as she worked through her transfers of selected works on a subsequent generation of dancers, Hoffmann actually did verbalize certain moments of her demonstration when she felt that further explanation or commentary was needed (Ciupke and Till 2014d). Nevertheless, we must not sidestep the fact that

---

[12] To what extent this is related to the fact that Irene Sieben had already decided to become a journalist and complete an education as a Feldenkrais teacher at the end of the 1960s, but in the case of Hoffmann what she learned may be overlapped by decades of her own choreographic practice and the development of her own movements, can only be speculated upon here.

there are multiple ways to understand both verbal and physical transfer. It is vital for our construal of the witness here to recognize that Hoffmann, so to speak, *writes off* language and verbal description as potential means of transmission. In so doing, she instantly, too, blots out the witness's dual role as "living testament" and messenger (if not also in the subsequent practice of transmission itself). Only physical transfer could produce evidence from the work, but this obviously can only take place in the passing on of one's own work.

Having negated not only the possibility of testifying to Kurt Jooss but also certain dimensions of testimony-giving in general, Hoffman's next move, the shift toward becoming her own witness, complicates our model even further: one can only gather that she was so close to the events that she cannot also occupy the position of the third party. This circumvents the moment of self-withdrawal observed by Krämer (2011). What kind of witness-hood, then, can we say Hoffmann is offering? The piece she wished to quote from in her transmission to Ciupke and Till has indeed been performed, and so she is eligible to be classified as a historical witness of this past event. Herein, however, lies the paradox of being one's own witness: Such a figure would negate testimony's fundamental qualification of "having-been-present" (Krämer 2011, 120), which itself implies not-being-self.

If Hoffmann represented an extreme case of the (at bottom, impossible) witness who collapses testimony and event together, then Martin Nachbar, in turn, finds himself at the other end of the spectrum: Testifying to events he never saw live, he lacks the "eye" that implicitly prefixes "witness." What would it mean to be a witness without the benefit of co-presence? The answer is, perhaps—adding a layer to the basic method of appropriation—to bear witness to a reconstructive process already completed and guided by prior witnesses such as Waltraud Luley, thus doubling the idea of reconstruction: A testimony-giving and a reconstructive furthering thereof, it is knowledge that has been gathered and appropriated by means of documents and witnesses. Nachbar is fittingly not motivated by an interest in the most precise transfer of movement sequences or patterns as possible. He is given, rather, to a self-referential style, focused on the (im)possibilities of transmitting past dance events, informed primarily (if not deliberately) by media such as films and accounts from witnessing colleagues. Based also on his search for an affective center of the negotiative act in his own reconstruction of Hoyer's *Affectos Humanos*, we can conclude that Nachbar's focus is on the character of the transmission itself.[13]

---

[13]  However, such affectedness already begins with getting to know Dore Hoyer's dances, as Gerald Siegmund illustrates: "For Nachbar, it is precisely this difference between two bodies—how Hoyer's dances affect him, move him, and in their repetition, change him—that interests him." (Siegmund, Chapter 23 in this volume, page 476). In the process, affects should always already be understood in relation to accompanying techniques and the surrounding and intersecting discourses, as Siegmund emphasizes: "Discourse enables the production of historically faithful technical bodies, like those of classical ballet, which are conducive to affect's demonstrability, communicability, and tangibility." (Ibid.: 474)

In *undo, redo and repeat*, he characterized his work with Waltraud Luley, among others, mainly through the example of the dance *Angst*, remarking that his reconstructive attempts never stirred any recognition of the original dance in Luley's eyes, except a particular moment in the final sequence of the dance. The exception led to a remarkable final moment: A trembling Nachbar slowly made it up to his feet from lying down and, after a turn, "thrust my arms up in a desperate gesture that my gaze followed upward: [at the moment] she was touched" (Ciupke and Till 2014, 15). Without getting bogged down here in a complex debate regarding what exactly can be imported from a historical dance into the present and whether it must be near (or opposed) to the most precise possible reconstruction of movements and spatial setups (which, as Hoffmann points out, are not available in written form), it is worth noting that Luley's memory and her appraisal of the "felicitous" moments of the reconstruction in this case happen to transpire in an affective register. Nachbar consequently chose to fulfill Ciupke and Till's assignment by forwarding them a written score in view of the moment of becoming-moved: "[Please] [r]econstruct the final moments of the dance 'Angst.' Sought to experience through it the final stages of anxiety and helplessness, shortly before giving up" (2014, 15).

With his score, Nachbar once again singles out a process of perception and testimony: the final moment of *Angst* should be danced by one dancer while another observes her—then they switch (Ciupke, Till 2014, 15). In the performance, however, a few moments of "being-moved" showed themselves possible *ex negativo*: Nachbar may have chosen this choreographic sequence due to its affective content, but the moment at which the second dancer prompts her repetition of the sequence, which sometimes interrupts the first dancer before she is finished, is notably devoid of affect.

Nachbar's understanding of transfer, which articulates the model of witness-hood in terms of media, unfolds in three steps: first, Nachbar passes on his own reconstructive situation; second, Ciupke and Till receive his situation as witnesses; third, they testify to the moment of affective transmission they find within it. This interlacing serves to break through the conventional constitution of the witness-hood model's modes of nearness and distance. Distance from events, no longer valued in Nachbar's version of the historical witness, is put forth as a basic modality and establishes the threefold testimony as the very possibility of transmission. This occasions itself in a now reversed configuration of proximity induced not by the having-been-there, but rather created with reference to being-moved—whether this is visible in the performance of *undo, redo and repeat*, it remains unacknowledged, along with a fourth and final level of witness-hood: that which belongs to the audience, which is present throughout the process of negotiation, and in some cases, even has an affective experience of it.

All of this cannot but leave us asking what, absolutely, can we say the witness is able to transmit about a past event. Just what are witnesses able to show when the case calls for something outside the realm of the factual? Are they not always already removed from the event as such?[14] Before I address these gaps  which do represent a sort of

---

[14]  Siegmund also pleads for a critical view of witnessing in art: it cannot be limited to a "totalizing gesture" as it is always far from the artistic event (Siegmund 2013: 47/375).

impossibility for the practice of giving testimony—I would first like to consider those gaps in relation to the question of the reliability of the witness.

# Trusting and Believing

In her interview with Ciupke and Till, Irene Sieben concedes that there are some aspects of Wigman's work on movement that she is not passing on. For that matter, neither was this fully explicated in her, Sieben's, teaching.

> [ . . . ] regarding the hands. [ . . . ] The hands were for her a kind of a fetish. [ . . . ] I don't know how I would go about teaching it because there's nothing more to it than I can account for. It isn't something that I myself have an authentic experience of it. Hands were very important to her, but I just have to leave that out for now, as I have no access to it. (2013)

Sieben evinces here a certain understanding of witnessing that is already inherent in the process of testimony as Sybille Schmidt stresses: namely, that she concertedly omits certain, indeed important, aspects of Wigman's movement language. Yet in its juridical sense, the witness stands as an "unreliable narrator." (Schmidt 2011, 49) The ideal of the eyewitness as an "objective and reliable transmitter of information" has always been fallible; there is no eyewitness who is not an exception to the rule (48). Research in the field of oral history has touched on this, particularly in its anti-reductionist line: "[Oral history] doesn't regard the testimony just as historical source, but as expression of subjective experiences and memories, too" (49). Such subjective experiences are precisely what, in Martin Nachbar's reconstruction, became more important than the rendering of precise movement sequences, as well as what Reinhild Hoffmann ran into in her attempt to synthesize the quality of Jooss's movement.

However, Sieben emphasizes that she may be missing knowledge on some key aspects of her subject. Nonetheless, she is brought forth as a witness. Joining the ranks of the factors of (juridical) witness-hood laid out by Krämer such as "evidence," or "perception" *qua* "physical co-presence," we now see "believability" leap to the foreground (Krämer 2011, 120–121): "The reliability, authenticity, and believability of the witness [are] *conditio sine qua non* of the persuasiveness of their testimony" (121; emphasis in original). For our purposes here, the "credibility" of testimony is certainly not a matter of his or her facticity being verifiable or corroborated through evidence. Yet, from this angle, another epistemological plane enters into view: something that would like to be known, but that one could not be present at. Along with "epistemic competence," it is especially the register of belief that lends authority to the witness (Schmidt and Voges 2011, 11–12). Philosopher Martin Hartmann explains:

> We believe that our neighbor went to the theater yesterday without having seen him go ourselves, because he told us so. We voluntarily believe things only if we take the source of information to be a believable and competent one. (2011, 126)

Philosopher Elizabeth Fricker also suggests that belief is a necessary condition of epistemological processes, speaking about "belief-formation" and its basis in the "trustworthiness of the speaker" (Fricker 2004, 117). The "worthiness" in "trustworthiness," which Krämer also underlines as vital to certifying testimony, seems especially key for understanding what we expect from witnesses. Witnesses have been favored as sources in many of the reconstructions and reenactments produced in recent years, because they seem to offer the possibility of closing the gap between visible evidence (like video, photography, or text) and what happened in live performance. As mentioned before, it is hard to imagine this even being possible in court.

Irene Sieben expands, rather than closes, the gaps, inasmuch as she willfully refuses to pass on certain aspects of Wigman's creation, which she simply cannot capture the meaning of:

> To pulsate and to subside . . . it was the pathos embodied here that inflamed my resistance. My relationship with my teacher was tense, ambivalent, and uncertain from the start, since I didn't come to her as a blank slate, as she would have preferred. (2003, 10)

Although we can now definitely count Sieben among the trustworthy—she did learn dance technique from Wigman, and now embodies that movement experience—nevertheless, an essential element on the expressive spectrum of Wigman's dance escapes her.[15] Sieben frequently problematizes this, and in so doing points to two further dimensions of the witness; the first is expressed in how Sieben's act of omission upends Krämer's idea of the "involuntary messaging of the trace." Rather than the unspoken or the (still) to-be-interpreted, what comes through in Sieben's messaging is its wholesale inseparability from Wigman's movement technique. While it may be difficult to isolate specific moves from Wigman in Sieben, every one of Sieben's moves is, to a certain extent, "weighed down" by Wigman's influence. One must be cautious when dealing with this "blending" and with traces in general, as they mark the self-negated, the disowned, and the problematically communicated (for how would something be relayed if averse to the body and to motivation?). In treating these, Sieben teases out the consequence of her selective form of transmission. This is, in effect, the articulation of yet another dimension of the witness, which Sigrid Weigel outlines as a differential model in her thoughts on testimony, subjecting the idea of the witness to the critical question

---

[15]   Instead, Sieben limits herself to the transfer of formal principles of movement to Christina Ciupke and Anna Till in the form of "circles without a change in the front" that are characterized by flowing movement (i.e. Ciupke and Till 2014, 7).

of its "facts" (*Zeugnis*), as distinct from a form of "manu-facture" (*Erzeugnis*), and thus a construction. The differences between the two are immediately evident in work on the Holocaust, which gives the idea of a belief in the lack of adulteration, and with it, the "purity of the survivor's testimony," as well as the ahistorical referentiality Paul Celan has been accused of dealing in and which is responsible for the alleged manufactured quality of his work (Weigel 2000, 127). So, for Weigel,

> It makes all the difference whether we are talking about a construct (*Erzeugnis*), such as a text, or testimony (*Zeugnis*). It's just that there is no proof for this distinction. It is much more a question of how the listener or reader will read it. (2000, 127)

Yet again we are dealing here with the necessity for belief and trust, on which the field of dance reconstruction and reenactment is left to remark that witnesses do not simply exist, but are created. The same goes for reconstruction, which, as Willeit says, is always a new formulation of that which has been, and to that extent cannot substantiate a claim to authenticity—I would argue that the testimony is rather marked by its reproductive character, its ability to make new, to recreate for the first time. Yet often invitations and opportunities for witnesses still entreat them as guarantors of the afterlife of a "that-which-has-been." I propose that to understand the true dilemma of witness-hood, we must consider the product character that testimony represents, as well as acknowledge what it means for the self in this context to be inextractible: a modality that Irene Sieben explores and exposes purposefully, and in so doing discloses the antagonism of witness-hood.

## In Conclusion: Dance-Testimonies

I have shown the extent to which the model of the witness as guarantor of 'objective' knowledge is already articulated as a weakness of its juridical and philosophical analogs. Dance does not downplay ruptures in this way, but holds them up for all to see; the testimony of past events is always already characterized by the gaps it emerges from. One commonality between the differing construals of witness-hood, which can depart drastically in how they treat closeness and distance, body as messenger, and objective fact as object of manufacture, is that, in moments of omission, of unsayability or untransferability in Agamben's sense ([1998] 2005, 142),[16] testimony of dance (as conveyance of the past) first authorizes and then, too, refers to the impossible 'complete' transfer.

In most cases, one comes to be a dance witness because of trustworthiness and authority as former contemporaries and eyewitnesses of those figures or events being

---

[16] That is to say "How can a subject give an account of its own ruins? [ . . . ] between the sayable and the unsayable" (Agamben 2005: 145).

reconstructed or reenacted. At the same time, it certainly seems that the dance witness could be reducible to nothing more than yet another document to be decoded since their ability to transfer knowledge, like any source, has its limits. However, this is not about lamenting the loss of movement, space, or atmosphere in the records of dance, as much as it is about the witnesses's failure to "deliver" the "full" event. Moreover, the paradoxical figure of the witness points to a possible impossibility of speaking (and showing) built into the foundation of (contemporary) dance, which, I would argue, is in a state of constant flux between embodied memory and recreation. Before the actions of dance took place, the experiences traversing the body always already awaken the "re-". As "subject and object" of these representations, at once actor and document, witnesses of dance *schlep* the traces of the past around with them, unable to fully rid themselves of them or to fully access them. Hence, we can argue for reconstruction in dance on the basis of its genuinely constructive character.

Translated by Alessio Franko and Mark Franko

## WORKS CITED

Agamben, Giorgio. [1998] 2005. *Remnants of Auschwitz: The Witness and the Archive*. New York: Zone Books.

Assmann, Aleida. 2007. "Vier Grundtypen von Zeugenschaft." In *Zeugenschaft des Holocaust. Zwischen Trauma, Tradierung und Ermittlung*, edited by Michael Helm and Gottfried Kößler, on behalf of Fritz Bauer Institute, 33–51. Frankfurt am Main and New York: Campus.

Franko, Mark. 1989. "Repeatability, Reconstruction and Beyond." *Theatre Journal* 41(1): 56–74.

Fricker, Elizabeth. 2004. "Testimony: Knowing Through Being Told." In *Handbook of Epistemology*, edited by Ilkka Niiniluoto, Matti Sintonen, and Jan Wolenski, 109–130. Dordrecht, Boston, and London: Kluwer Academic Publishers.

Hartmann, Martin. 2011. *Die Praxis des Vertrauens*. Frankfurt am Main: Suhrkamp.

Huschka, Sabine. 2002. *Moderner Tanz. Konzepte, Stile, Utopien*. Reinbek b. Hamburg: Rowohlt.

Krämer, Sybille. 2011. "Vertrauen schenken. Über Ambivalenzen der Zeugenschaft." In *Politik der Zeugenschaft. Zur Kritik einer Wissenspraxis*, edited by Sibylle Schmidt, Sybille Krämer and Ramon Voges, 117–139. Bielefeld: transcript.

Lackey, Jennifer. 2006. "Introduction." In *The Epistemology of Testimony*, edited by Jennifer Lackey and Ernest Sosa, 1–21. Oxford: Oxford University Press.

Lackey, Jennifer, and Ernest Sosa, eds. 2006. *The Epistemology of Testimony*. Oxford: Oxford University Press.

Schmidt, Sibylle. 2011. "Wissensquelle oder ethisch-politische Figur? Zur Synthese zweier Forschungsdiskurse über Zeugenschaft." In *Politik der Zeugenschaft. Zur Kritik einer Wissenspraxis*, edited by Sibylle Schmidt, Sybille Krämer and Ramon Voges, 47–66. Bielefeld: transcript.

Schmidt, Sibylle, and Ramon Voges. 2011. "Einleitung." In *Politik der Zeugenschaft. Zur Kritik einer Wissenspraxis*, edited by Sibylle Schmidt, Sybille Krämer, and Ramon Voges, 7–20. Bielefeld: transcript.

Sieben, Irene. 2003. "Die Liebe der Gärtnerin. Irene Sieben erinnert an Mary Wigmans letzte Jahre." *Tanzjournal* 5: 7–13.

Siegmund, Gerald. 2013. "Zeugen: Vom Zeigen des Nicht-zeigen-Könnens" (Witnesses: On Showing the State of Not-Being-Able-to-Show). In *Moments. Eine Geschichte der Performance in 10 Akten*, edited by Sigrid Gareis, Georg Schöllhammer, and Peter Weibel, 41–52 (English translation, 372–379). Cologne: Walther König.

Warburton, Edward C. 2011. "Of Meaning and Movement. Re-Languaging Embodiment in Dance Phenomenology and Cognition." *Dance Research Journal* 43(2): 65–83.

Weigel, Sigrid. 2000. "Zeugnis und Zeugenschaft, Klage und Anklage. Die Geste des Bezeugens in der Differenz von 'identity politics', juristischem und historiographischem Diskurs." In *Zeugnis und Zeugenschaft*, edited by Einstein Forum, Yearbook 1999, 111–135. Berlin: Akademie Verlag.

Willeit, Simone. 2010. "Stolpern und Unzulänglichkeiten. Interferenzen in Tanz-Rekonstruktionen." In *Original und Revival. Geschichts-Schreibung im Tanz*, edited by Christina Thurner and Julia Wehren, 47–58. Zürich: Chronos.

## Websites

Ciupke, Christina, and Anna Till. 2014a. *undo, redo and repeat*. Website of the performance. Berlin: Sophiensaele, http://www.undo-redo-repeat.de (accessed August 26, 2016).

Ciupke, Christina, and Anna Till. 2014b. "We aim for learning the phrase 'tuna' from 'Die Befragung des Robert Scott' (1986, William Forsythe). Part 3." http://www.undo-redo-repeat.de/aspekte-der-weitergabe/weitergabepraxis.html?page_n29=2 (accessed March 9, 2015).

Ciupke, Christina, and Anna Till. 2014c. "Irene Sieben und Martin Nachbar sprechen über ihre Erfahrung mit Rekonstruktionsarbeit und Weitergabe im Tanz." http://www.undo-redo-repeat.de/wege-der-weitergabe/die-zeitzeuginnen/irene-sieben/medien.html?page_n32=6 (accessed March 9, 2015).

Ciupke, Christina, and Anna Till. 2014d. "Reinhild Hoffmann gibt ihr Solo 'Vier' (UA 1992) an die Tänzerin Héloise Fournier weiter." http://www.undo-redo-repeat.de/aspekte-der-weitergabe/interpretation.html (accessed March 9, 2015).

Sieben, Irene. 2013. "Autorisation und Rekonstruktion der Tänze von Mary Wigman. Anna Till und Christina Ciupke im Gespräch mit Irene Sieben." http://www.undo-redo-repeat.de/files/undo-redo-and-repeat/PDF/130816_ISieben_Interview_02_PDF.pdf (accessed July 9, 2015).

Sieben, Irene, Christina Ciupke, and Anna Till. 2013. "Wie war das Verhältnis zwischen Sprache und Bewegung im Unterricht von Mary Wigman?" (interview). http://www.undo-redo-repeat.de/wege-der-weitergabe/die-zeitzeuginnen/irene-sieben/medien.html?page_n32=4 (accessed March 9, 2015).

## Miscellaneous

Barnett, Susan, Henrietta Horn, Madeline Ritter, and Patricia Stöckemann. 2013, November 14. "Frühlingsopfer rekonstruieren?" Audience talk on the occasion of the reconstruction of Mary Wigman's *Le Sacre du Printemps* by Theater Osnabrück and Theater Bielefeld. Moderation: Claudia Henne. Berlin: Radialsystem.

Ciupke, Christina, Anna Till, Reinhild Hoffmann, Thomas MacManus, Irene Sieben, and Katrin Schoof. 2015, April 17. "Erinnerung mit Zukunft." Audience talk with the participating artists on the occasion of the reopening of *undo, redo and repeat*. Moderation: Eva-Maria Hoerster. Berlin: Sophiensaele.

Ciupke, Christina, and Anna Till. 2014, May 2–4. *undo, redo and repeat*. Program of the performance. Berlin: Sophiensaele.

CHAPTER 14

# BAROQUE RELATIONS

*Performing Silver and Gold in Daniel Rabel's*
Ballets of the Americas

VK PRESTON

## QUALIA: THE SEEMING OF SILVER

SITTING in the second floor *Cabinet des dessins* (Cabinet of Drawings) in Paris with the album open at my desk, Daniel Rabel's exquisite, seventeenth-century drawings of dancers create unexpected illusions. Due to the drawings' fragility, I have been told that I may see these images at the Louvre only once in my lifetime. Touching their binding makes my heart beat faster, especially once the curator and room supervisor reproach me for handling its leather incorrectly. Laid open and covering much of a large table, this album seems too large for the tenderness of touch it requires, and turning its fragile pages manifests itself in an awkward care as I lumber over the book, gently lifting its images, as if enchanted, for six hours.[1]

Turning the album's enormous pages, touch draws my attention to research as embodied rather than archival, disclosing the risk and possible destruction of documents. As I glean the violence reflected in the archive before me, my presence, against my wishes, troubles this book's survival. Page after page catches my curiosity, impelling an active theorization. Something of the order of light passes between us, as if set in movement, entangling the seventeenth-century artist's hand and my twenty-first-century spectatorship, in a reorientation of the drawings' scope toward spectacle rather than record.

Unpredictable casts of light, falling on the pages at just the right angle, create perceptions that resist reproduction and photographic capture. These "raw feels"[2] (or qualia)

[1] My thanks to the Louvre's Department of Graphic Arts for generous access to the drawings. In *Album Daniel Rabel* of the *Fonds des dessins et miniatures, Réserve des grands albums*, INV 32602, recto–32693, recto (folios 1–93).

[2] See Zemach (1966) on perception, "raw feels," and shared experience.

**FIGURE 14.1.** "First entry of the Americans, six figures" (*Première entrée des americains, six figures*), INV 32620, Recto.

With the courtesy of the Département des Arts graphiques, Musée du Louvre. Photo: VK Preston.

seem to plunge or lift lines off the paper, gleaming as if in three-dimensional relief. These glints hail from event into memory, offering a felt relation to history, like a *punctum* (Barthes 1985), that only appears when revealed to the viewer at a certain angle, in certain conditions, or out of the corner of the eye.

These images are of costumes for Rabel's drawings for *Ballets of the Americas*, and I find their sources in Andean danced protest and published European chronicles of processions in the city of Cuzco (Qosqo or Qusqu), the former capital of the Inca Empire. Drawn to what appears in photographs as an ill-defined grey-green smudge, I realize, turning to Rabel's drawings of costumes for *Ameriquains* ("Americans") that the elusive non-colors are silver and gold. Drawn as faux tattoos, these lines gleam with ground metals, as if rippling in folding designs painted onto fabric skins (Figure 14.1).

Spectating dovetails with politics and substance in this phenomenologically charged experience of the image, tracing unexpected histories of the Andes in the often bawdy, burlesque ballets of 1620s France.[3] Hands clad in electric blue latex gloves, and surrounded by research paraphernalia—from LED-lit magnifying glasses to velvet book supports—I liken my dance with the drawings to a critical practice of embodied reenactment.

---

[3] See Franko's reflections on periodicity, reenactment, and dissent in "Political Erotics of Burlesque Ballet, 1624–27" (1993, 63–107) and in Chapter 24 in this volume.

Through the visual trick of precious metals, figures seem to alight from the paper. Like the "beings of fiction" of Bruno Latour's *Inquiry into Modes of Existence*, Rabel's drawings of dancers are both of and not of the page, gleaming for an instant as if pulling away from their material conditions of existence. Here, "[m]aking room for the beings of fiction" amounts, paradoxically, "to authorizing ourselves to be materialists at last" (Latour 2013, 252). As Rabel's lines flatten and fold, offering a virtual field of ungraspable, represented dimensions, their unexpected *éblouissements* (dazzlings) draw my attention to the images' materials: to the temporal experience of seeing dancing, to acts of looking, and to the invasive conditions of my gaze.[4]

What, in a physical and embodied sense, is reenacted in such an experience of performance records? Rabel's *Ameriquains* dance silver's early modern provenance, performing critical imaginaries of Spanish and Castilian economies of Andean plunder. These mercantile ventures fueled fantasies of accumulation and infinite growth, based on the colonial extraction of precious metals in conditions, Nicholas A. Robins writes, that were "in a literal sense genocidal" (2011, 193). The ballet depicted in these French drawings both participates in and parodies these transformations, performing a gender-crossing ethnomasquerade that overtly comments—notably in its staging of slavery—on the notorious mines of Huancavelica and Potosí (see Moore 2007; Robins 2011). Details of the scenes explicitly evoke nearly a century of published accounts of the Andes, suggesting both written and unwritten narratives of Peru. These likely served as the ballet's sources, and they are fueled with criticism, notably that of Bartolomé de las Casas, challenging the mines' legality, the treatment of Andeans, the plunder of Peru, and the legality of its invasion.[5]

In what follows, I unpack Rabel's use of metals in relationship to the roles and characters identified in the ballet's visual and textual documentation.[6] This approach investigates silver and gold in these drawings, and perhaps staged in the dance's burlesques,

[4] See Reuell (2010) on restoring Rabel's drawings at Harvard Library, after water damage, and on the fragility of these gold and silver paints.

[5] Bartolomé de Las Casas's writings on the Andes were repeatedly translated, and they circulated widely at a time when Peru's mines were synonymous in European imaginaries with wealth. In *Brevísima relación de la destrucción de las Indias* (*A Short Account of the Destruction of the Indes*, 1552) and *De Thesauris in Peru* (*The Treasures of Peru*, 1563), he published challenges to Iberian claims on Peru's treasure, condemning mass deaths and the looting of precious objects from graves. The work's translations took an explicit, anti-Spanish turn in the French-language version of *Brevísima relación*, betraying the Protestant leanings of its translator and the propagandistic uses of Las Casas's writings by Spain's opponents. See *Tyrannies et cruautez des Espagnols perpétrées ès Indes occidentales, qu'on dit le Nouveau Monde, brièvement descrites en langue castillane par l'évesque Dom Frère Barthélemy de Las Casas ou Casaus* (1579).

[6] Confusingly, there are multiple texts for this ballet, with similar titles, published by four identified authors working in differing degrees of collaboration. See René Bordier's *Grand Bal de la douairière de Billebahaut, ballet dansé par le Roy au mois de février 1626*. Paris: Henault, 1626a, BnF 8-YTH-8021(A), *Grand bal de la douairière de Billebahaut, Ballet dansé par le Roy au mois de Fevrier 1626. Vers dudit ballet par le sieur Bordier, ayant charge de la Poësie pres [sic] de sa Majesté*. Paris: impr. du Louvre, 1626b, BnF, YF-814; and Bordier, Imbert, and Sorel, *Grand bal de la Douairère de Billebahaut* [ . . . ] n.p., [16 . .] BnF, YF-815; l'Estoile, *Maistre Galimathias, pour le grand bal de la douairère* [ . . . ] [n.p.], 1626, BnF, YF-1158.

of dancers with faux tattoos, the Inca emperor Atahualpa (*Atabalipa*, in hispanicized spelling), dancing "ANDROGINES," and "parrots." The envelope-like structure of my approach reflects the intervals between these images and texts, in a study of the construction, sequence, and content of the performance's (dis)ordered archive, as well as its relationships to procession practices in Peru.

# REENACTMENT

The reenactment I address in this chapter is not a matter of remounting or restaging works, as theater—but rather of a spectator's heuristical shaping of time, performance, and records. This approach to examining the experience of "research-spectatorship" seeks to bring dance, visual art, and performance studies into a dialogue with new materialism, foregrounding proto-globalized histories of capitalism, as well as the "physico-chemical strata" of images (Kontturi 2013, 24). My focus on reenactment here addresses the baroque meeting of French ballet and Incaic procession,[7] investigating metals, and especially gold and silver, as embodied archives. Precious metals are living things in Andean cosmologies,[8] entwining a baroque "Age of Spectatorship" with the "Age of Discovery," as witnesses of histories of cultural, physical, and epistemological violence.[9]

Rabel's drawings glitter with sensory invitation; substances, movements, dances, and instruments offer not just a visual "reconstruction" of Andean procession, but a raucous imaginary of Peru—performing far-flung, imaginatively global spectacles of dances', instruments', and materials' provenance.[10] The images I take up here offer a sequence of eight drawings for *Ballets of the Americas* (*Ballets des Amériques*)[11]—a subset of the album depicting musicians, a llama, and a solo lutanist, tattooed groups of *Amériquains*,

[7] "The Baroque is far from being the first intercultural aesthetic," writes Leo Cabranes-Grant, "but because of its emphasis on transitions, kinesis, and liminality, it allows an unprecedented degree of legibility with respect to intercultural exchange" (2010, 468). See also Zamora (2006) and Zamora and Kaup, eds. 2010.

[8] On living objects, see Taylor (2004, 368). I am also indebted to two compelling talks, Jill Lane's analysis of procession, Cuzco school paintings, and the "The Potosí Principle" exhibition, delivered at the American Society for Theatre Research (2012), as well as to Tomson Highway's keynote address, and Cree conceptions of the live, at *Encuentro* in Montreal (2014).

[9] See Lois Parkinson Zamora on the idea that silver altars in baroque Europe silently continue to witness the labor of the *indios* in the mines (Zamora 2006, xv–xvi).

[10] On the display of objects of foreign provenance in baroque paintings, as well as a debate over methodology and materials, see Byron Ellsworth Hamann (2010) and the special issue of *Art Bulletin* on "New World" materials in Diego Rodríguez de Silva y Velásquez's *Las Meñinas* (Powell, ed., 2010), with respondents Adam Herring, Walter Mignolo, Suzanne L. Stratton-Pruitt, et al.

[11] See *Grand bal de la douairière de Billebahaut* at the *Bibliothèque nationale de France* (BnF); 8-YTH-8021(A), 5.

the Inca emperor Atahualpa,[12] slaves in manacles, collars, and fetters, a quartet of (human-sized) dancing parrots, and a trio of "ANDROGINES."[13]

These scenes of "Andean" music, dances, instruments, and animals were imagined by French artists who had almost certainly never been to Peru. Like the game of "broken telephone" (Scolieri 2013), they imagine detail from what were claimed to be eyewitness accounts recorded in early modern travel publications, or "relations"—as well, quite possibly, as stories from such travelers themselves. In this sense, the ballets' burlesques are already founded within a practice of reperformance, staging imagined world cultures from the archives of conquest.

These scenes are archives of perception as well as of movement, combining interiorities of felt perception and exteriorities that, as Jacques Derrida writes, displace memory (1993, 26). The exteriorization of memory (into drawings as media) and the heuristics of the album converge here in felt experience, in a baroque attention to perception that intensifies proprioceptive gradations. Like an early modern hologram, the drawings lure viewers into subtle movement, diagramming spectatorship in an "inseparability of body and milieu" (Thain 2010, 56). Such an approach might take the collection of Rabel's drawings not as an inaccessible, antiquarian book, but as a flexible, nonlinear, and relational thing—a thing in movement that remixes and folds temporalities reimagined in the ballet's danced geographies. This form of the archive escapes the conceit of the archive as an exterior only, as memory's supplement, as if binding these images together remixed and reinvented dramaturgical forms—transmuting spectatorship into a critical practice of witnessing. Alanna Thain (2010) terms such relation the *anarchival* because it is inventive, gathering and remixing a multiplicity of lived experience, media, and materials activated in motion—in the folding of perception. This notion of spectatorship, which Jill Lane elsewhere terms a "portal," slips and slides transversally in the traumatic legacy of conquest in the Americas (Lane 2010, 116–117).[14] The elegant disorder of these drawings, sewn meticulously together out of sequence, both disrupts and points toward what Lane has described as "colonial serialization" (Lane 2010, 120). Invoking a hierarchy of the so-called parts of the world, forged through danced comparison, this "ballet of nations" (Franko 1993, 189) begins in the Americas, moves on

---

[12] Held captive by the *conquistadores*, Atahualpa was ransomed for vast volumes of gold and silver objects soon before his 1533 execution. The subsequent circulations of these objects, many of which were sacred, often remain unknown. International efforts led, in recent years, to the return of a number of works taken over centuries of colonization. Many gold and silver objects, however, were melted down. On early accounts published in France, see Gohory and Bowen (1938).

[13] See INV 32618, recto to 32624[r], and INV 32692[r] in *Album Daniel Rabel*. I retain this capitalization of "ANDROGINES" as it appears in both the album and *livrets*.

[14] Zamora (2006) writes of Inca and Andean mnemonic forms that records, maps, and codexes were not objects presumed to stand on their own. The task of a live speaker was to perform a cultural practice of historiography, interpreting documents and materials, in a notion of historical account rich in acknowledging creation and relation.

to Africa and Asia, and concludes its tacitly teleological trajectory with the *Ballets of Europe*.[15]

To address this dance's leapfrogging between continents and its episodic documentation, I follow an enveloped sequence of scenes through this chapter, drawing attention to repertoires within archives and archives within repertoires.[16] This approach situates key features of the drawings in a circum-Atlantic performance context (see Roach 1995, 1996), addressing spectatorship and reenactment in the context of compelling recent scholarship on art, performance, and historiography in the Americas (Cabranes-Grant 2010 and 2016; Cusicanqui 2014; Hamann 2010; Guss 2000; Lane 1998 and 2010; Mignolo 2014; Roach 1995; Scolieri 2013; Taylor 2003, 2004, 2006; Ybarra 2009), and turning to Diana Taylor to examine "how performed, embodied practices make the 'past' available" (2006, 68) or "*make* history" (2006, 73).

# ALBUM

Puzzling these drawings into sequences engages a structure of critical reenactment, drawing attention to the tasks of organization and of "putting-in-order" at stake in the fashioning of the ballet's sequences. Picking out these details sets forth an ethico-aesthetic task—one that is tacitly historiographical yet fantastical—reimagining space, time, and geography.[17] The dance of Rabel's metallic *rehauts* (highlights) leads the viewer's attention through this parade-like archive (or archive-like parade)—imbuing the drawings of this paper theater with subtle, though strangely nonhuman, effects of dance-like motion.

While some pages and characters in this album are numbered, in a way that possibly reflects their relationships before their binding together, no cipher has been provided. They appear out of order—as if in a wildly visual theater that exceeds any known performance. Gender-crossing fairies (*Fées*) parade through stagings of Africa, the Americas, Asia, and Europe—as do images of animals, musicians, phantoms, and pimps (Leconte 2012). Drawings from at least three different works over a seven-year period—*Le Ballet des Fées des forêts de Saint Germain* (1625), the *Ballet de la douairière de Billebahaut*

---

[15]  Louis XIII, then king of France, danced in the entry for the *Ballets of Europe*, following the performance of his younger brother, "Monsieur," in blackened skin, for the *Ballets of Africa* (see YF -8201-A).

[16]  See Schneider (2011, 20); Taylor (2003, 2006). Taylor describes this distinction in her terminology, writing that the "rift, I submit, does not lie between the written and spoken word, but between the *archive* of supposedly enduring materials (i.e., texts, documents, buildings, bones) and the so-called ephemeral *repertoire* of embodied practice/knowledge (i.e., spoken language, dance, sports, ritual) (2003, 19).

[17]  See Franko on these works' "anti-Aristotelian qualities" (1993, 2) and Mignolo on "[r]ituals and ceremonies that are no mimicry and "do not fulfill the expectation of the fictional" (2014). For critical analyses of nonlinear historiography and temporality, see Schneider (2011, [2001] 2012), Lane (2010), and Traub (2013).

(1626), and *Le Ballet du château de Bissestre* (1632)—were sewn together out of sequence in the making of the album. Though this task is specifically not theatrical here, it remains performative. It infers staging possibilities from concordances between prose, poetry, and images, and it uses the ballet's multiple, polyvocal print accounts to posit an analysis of a "lost dance" dramaturgy (see Pakes, Chapter 5 in this volume).

## LUMINOUS TIME

In *Dance as Text: Ideologies of the Baroque Body*, Mark Franko investigates the "spirit of dissidence" (1993, 69) of baroque ballets of the early seventeenth century as a "real theater of ideological tensions [ . . . ] less consistently responsive to the dominant ideology than is commonly supposed" (1993, 2). Tension between sung texts and visual spectacle played out in these dance-theaters as political allegories and visual articulations of dissent. Such burlesques, routinely involving gendered and racialized disguises, performed aesthetics of eroticized subjection that stand in contrast to the significantly later idealization of the sovereign in ballets of the second half of the seventeenth century. These burlesque performances, moreover, significantly predate the birth of the myth-historical patriarch of the medium, Louis XIV. Franko claims the *Ballet* (or *Grand bal*) *de la douairière de Billebahaut* among the three most prominent works of the burlesque era, offering a grotesque, gender-crossing "travesty of theatrical ostentation as a tool of foreign policy" (1993, 189).[18] He dates the height of these danced burlesques in France to 1624–1627, a moment that parallels early French efforts to expand settlement and trade in the Americas, as well as the Caribbean, in share and company-based colonial ventures that would officially begin, months after this ballet, in 1627 (Boucher 2010, 60). On this cusp of entering into such investments in conquest and proto-colonization, Rabel's Gallic drawings parody Spanish expansion and profiteering as a grotesque, even inept dance of plunder.[19]

## PERFORMING HISTORY, DANCING VALUE

Directly at the heart of early modern authors' criticisms of Spanish conquest (Guamán Poma de Ayala 1615; Las Casas 1579), the silver on Rabel's pages shimmers with paradox.

---

[18] Certainly the *Ballet de la douairière de Billebahaut* is among the best documented of the early seventeenth-century burlesque works, offering not just visual records, but also the names of the ballet's (all-male, European) cast members, poetry for the entries, and published descriptions of the dance.

[19] Later, in the second half of the seventeenth century, France would become a major force in the triangular trade (of human beings, resources, and materials traded between the Americas, Europe, and Africa).

It reflects early modern controversies over the ethics and legality of conquest, of forced labor, and of the plunder of precious metals.[20] These drawings' one-sided transculturations glitter with the very material of this controversy, overtly staging an imagined Peru in kinetic articulations of a new economic precarity. Tracing sixteenth-century market and currency instabilities to the massive influx of metals from the Andes, the French author Jean Bodin first identified this so-called paradox of value in 1568,[21] addressing what were perhaps the world's first transnational economic bubbles—cascades of economic crises marked by spiraling prices, which we would today term inflation. These effects, most recently, have been studied by historians, artists, and activists as a leading edge of global capitalism, with Nicholas Robins writing that this "unprecedented flow of New World silver" catalyzed "the development of a global economy [ . . . ] spurring inflation in the regions through which it passed, [and creating] the milieu and networks from which the industrial revolution, and modern global capitalism would ultimately emerge" (2011, 6). The scandal of the faux "Indigenous" bodies in the ballet thus edges into a complex imaginary of satirical and transnational forces, parodying Spain in a spectacle of newly unmoored, pinwheeling concepts of value and wealth, spinning across theatricalized geographies. In this light, the "tattooing" of precious metals on the fabric skins worn by these French dancers figures an emblem of a changing world—a politics of movement, crisis, and excess linked to economic and mercantile transformations—fantasies of the Andes unfolding, *in medias res*, in an emerging "global economic vortex" (Robins 2011, 39) of catastrophe.

In the Andes this boom mentality came at a toxic and terrible cost, driving Andean tribute labor, environmental devastation, mass displacement, and trans-Atlantic slavery—along with the industrialization of mining processes using mercury that poisoned minds, bodies, and ecologies (Moore 2007; Robins 2011). Along with multiple concurrent epidemics, the fatalities of sixteenth- and seventeenth-century Peru are of a scale that "almost defies the imagination" (Robins 2011, 15).[22] Nicholas Robins turns to movement as a metaphor to describe this mining's local and global effects, "spinning fastest as it drew in goods and people in the Andes, yet casting its current as far away as Africa, the Middle East, and China, while showering the globe with a deluge of silver" (2011, 39–40). This global vortex echoes the ballet's continent-leaping dramaturgy as a burlesque "ballet of nations" linked through dance and movement.

---

[20] The tattoos in Rabel's drawings share certain formal details with pre-Columbian Andean objects, including Chimú burial gloves. For photographs, see Pimentel, ed. (2013).

[21] The sixteenth-century French theorist of sovereignty, Jean Bodin, was among the first to show that mass influxes of precious metals destabilized European economies. His sixteenth-century analysis of inflation, currency devaluation, and a quantity theory of money conceive this as a "paradox of silver" (Bodin 1568).

[22] Addressing this as the "greatest catastrophe in human history," Robins describes mortality in the Andes that exceeded eight million persons (2011, 15): "[i]n the region of present-day Peru, the total population fell from approximately 9,000,000 people in 1520 to about 1,000,000 in 1580, reaching a nadir of only 600,000 in 1620" (15). In 1608 the colonial government was officially granted permission by Spain to import slaves from Africa to work in these mines.

# ENTRIES AND CROSSINGS

The ballet begins with a noisy, imagined staging of an Andean procession, with the entry of Atahualpa, playing music on a hurdy gurdy (*vielle*), as its centerpiece.[23] Carried on a litter, on the shoulders of pale-skinned slaves, Rabel's use of silver for fetters, manacles, and collars, imagines temporarily absent chains (Figure 14.2). Identified as an effigy in the ballet's printed texts, the scene evokes procession practices preserving Andean cultural memory of Inca leadership for centuries after Atahualpa's death. Rabel's drawing for the emperor's arrival at the Louvre (in a performance of February 1626) enacts this scene nearly a century after the *Sapa Inca*'s execution by the Spanish, in 1533, emphasizing the pale-eyed stare and outsized head of this "inanimate" "King of Cusco" (8-YTH-8021(A), 4).

Atahualpa's execution at the hands of the Spanish was itself a long-running, Andean theatrical genre (Cummins 2013; Millones 2013). His death was a recurring theme of Indigenous theater cycles, writes Luis Millones, in "Andean *takis*" (*thakis*) or "choreographed spectacles," whose form as danced theaters of the king's execution may appear as early as 1555, within living memory of the *conquistadores*' arrival.[24] These cycles were not, Millones writes, derived from practices "imported from across the Atlantic," however, but rather from "a whole corpus of *fiestas* that came into contact with the native corpus" (2013, 197). Dancers, as well as "[s]ilversmiths, painters, sculptors, actors, and musicians [ . . . ] carried on traditions that they had inherited from the Inca" (2013, 193), writes Thomas B. Cummins, which participants "creatively adapted [ . . . ] to a different reality," to keep "the memory of the Inca very much alive throughout the Andes" in a legacy that continues "until today."[25]

In one account of recurring festivities marking the day of the Virgin's birth, the eighteenth-century French spy Amédée-François Frézier describes Indigenous cycles reenacting Atahualpa's death at the hands of the Spanish as a staple of Peruvian "Tragedy." Andeans in "the great Towns up the Country [ . . . ] revive [this] Memory [ . . . ] by a Sort of Tragedy they act in the Streets on the day of the Nativity of the Virgin" (Frézier in Cummins 2013, 188), he continues.[26] Dressed "after the ancient Manner, and [carrying] the Images of the Sun their deity [and] of the Moon," these celebrants

---

[23] My thanks to colleague Alexis Risler, doctoral student and lutanist at McGill's music conservatory, for identifying the instrument and its relationship to non-noble popular music and dance, and in particular that of the peasantry. Significantly, and by no means an Andean instrument, it is also associated with dancing, blindness, and dispossession. On instrumentation, see Durosoir (1995).

[24] On the sixteenth-century Andean *Taki Onqoy*, the impact of Luis Millones, as well as Peruvian scholarship and sources, see Mumford (1998) and Stern (1993, 50–71, 223).

[25] Regarding ceremonies, dances, processions, and effigies in the Andes, see Bradley and Cahill (2000); Cahill (2002); Cusicanqui (2014); Dean (1999); Jouve Martín (2007); Osorio (2004, 2008); Pimentel, ed. (2013); Scolieri (2013); and Seed (1991). On methodology and the embedding of stories within larger *fiesta* cycles, see Taylor (2006, 76).

[26] For a more critical view of tragedy, mimesis, and coloniality, see Mignolo (2014).

**FIGURE 14.2.** "Entry of King Atabalipa" in *Ballet de la douairière de Billebahaut.* INV 32622, recto.

With the courtesy of Département des Arts graphiques, Musée du Louvre. Photo: VK Preston.

wore "Garments of Feathers with Wings, so well fitted, that at a distance they look like Birds" (188).

As these festivities continued, Frézier writes, the Spanish in Peru would "shut themselves up in their Houses, because the Conclusion of those Festivals is always fatal to some of them"—as celebrants slung stones with deadly efficacy. "Endeavours [were] constantly used to suppress those Festivals," Frézier reports, writing that the Spanish "have of late Years debarr'd [Indigenous performers] from the Use of the stage, on which they represented the Death of the Inca [Atahualpa]" (188).

Andean participants performing these scenes, Cummins continues, divined (or prognosticated) the emperor's mythic return. Though the *conquistadores* strangled Atahualpa, rather than decapitating him, he explains, Indigenous iterations of this execution enacted it with a critical difference, separating the effigy's head from its body in a decapitation that in Andean cosmologies anticipated rebirth and "resurrection" (Cummins 2013, 189).[27] Such death and return, anticipated and enacted cyclically year

---

[27] This eighteenth-century account of cycles performing Atahualpa's execution is not an isolated record. Cummins and Millones address drawings of Atahualpa's death scene in Guamán Poma's 1615 illustrated history of Peru and Jaime Martínez Compañon's codex (Pimentel 2013, 196). Claude

after year, constituted a live account of Andean history that resists European epistemologies of life and death. It enfolds Christological resonance of divine living and dying marked on the putative day of Mary's birth, but it also asserts a politics of Inca religiosity and resistance, expressed in peripatetic practices and processions, bearing silver and gold as well as effigies and remains, asserting the return of Inca leadership and divinity.

Metals, however, were living things and divine remains in Andean cosmologies: the tears of the moon (silver) and the sweat of the sun (gold) (Fraresso 2013, 146).[28] Objects fashioned from these substances could record history as well as genealogies, expressed in relationships of silver and gold. Their destruction could thus violate ontologies of the living and the dead, since metals were living beings "endowed with a soul or a mystic spirit and subject to the same life cycle as men, animals, and plants" (Fraresso 2013, 146).[29] Andean metals therefore raise complex, transcultural questions. As living metals, silver and gold breach Western European and settler distinctions of the live and the archive, and indeed of the "live" in performance as well as in archives and objects, documents, and works of art.[30] Turning now from Atahualpa's effigy to the network of roles that surrounds him, the next sections of this chapter investigate the dances of parrots and "ANDROGINES" in the ballet's archives as similar borrowings and transculturations from Andean dance-theater, protest movements, and cosmology.

## *BALLETS OF THE AMERICAS*: PARROTS AND "ANDROGINES"

The most conspicuous (and witty) of Rabel's drawings for the *Ballet de la douairière* offers "a troupe" of parrots (Figure 14.3) "showing their beaks at the doors of the theater" (see 8-YTH-8021 (A), 4–5). Playfully ambivalent about whether this dance was "good or bad," the anonymous author of its performance description recounts arrestingly strange music that mesmerized the parrots or set them into flight, as hunters, wearing parrot-feather capes, captured them with nets and curved mirrors.[31] Poetry corresponding to these drawings maintains a sense of levity—albeit in an obscure register—and yet it also

de l'Estoile's verse for "Atabalipa [ . . . ] King of Cusco" comments metatheatrically on the size of the character's head, suggesting it held rooms for madness and the moon (YF-1158, 1).

   [28]  Pre-Columbian Andean metalworking, writes Carole Fraresso, involved intensive religious training. Those who worked with metals were "[o]ften isolated from the rest of the community [ . . . ] perceived as intermediaries between the gods and men—magicians able to transform natural elements into brilliant, sonorous, eternal objects in the likeness of the gods" (Fraresso 2011; 2013, 146).
   [29]  These metals "were born, grew, and died; and they were regenerated in the earth, where they took on sacred value (Fraresso in Pimentel, 146; citing Salazar, Carcedero, and Parodi).
   [30]  On the blurred and entangled epistemologies of liveness and things, see Schneider (2001, 2011) and Taylor (2004).
   [31]  See Album Rabel INV 32623 -INV 32624 at the Louvre's *Cabinet des dessins* and 8-YTH-8021 (A), 4–5 at the *BnF*.

**FIGURE 14.3.** "Entry of the Parrots" (*Entrée de quatre perroquets*), INV 32624, Recto.
With the courtesy of the Département des Arts graphiques, Musée du Louvre. Photo: VK Preston.

offers oblique, political commentary voiced by a bird "who speaks incessantly and yet never offends."[32]

In *Pour les Perroquets, Aux Dames* (*For the Parrots to the Ladies*), a bird addresses the women (*dames*) in the audience on the "ravishing" of liberty, appealing against this hunt with the alarm that "it must be that we die" (Imbert in YF-815, n.d., 10). These roles, I suggest, explicitly resonate with accounts of avian protest in Peru, as cited earlier,[33] in processions associated with the birth of the Virgin and the cycle of Atahualpa's murder, culminating in Frézier's eighteenth-century account with nights of stone throwing, Indigenous resistance, and Spanish deaths. The French dancers put on their birdlike costumes, therefore, within a network of roles anchored in Andean repertoires, yet associating these in the ballet's verse with the crafty Daedalus—a classical Mediterranean association with *mimesis* and uncannily lifelike appearance—donning wings to escape from prison. Mignolo links such impositions of the mimetic to the very "logic of coloniality" in which "art is mimesis, representation, a fiction, a fake, a simulacra of the real"

---

[32] Bordier, Imbert, Sorel, *Grand Bal* (YF-815), 1626, 10.

[33] Searching "*Danza* [or *Baile*] *de los Guacamayos*" on Youtube, for example, returns vast media archives of present-day parrot dances and choreographies in Peru and Guatemala. Bird dancers, related to the sun, also appear in an eighteenth-century watercolor from the collection of Bishop Baltasar Jaime Compañón at the *Real Biblioteca de Madrid*. See a "Dance of the Macaws" (*Danza de los Huacamaios*), depicting Andean festival celebrants disguised as birds in brilliant green and red masks and wings (Cummins 2013, 188–191; see Pimentel 2013, 191).

**FIGURE 14.4.** "Entry of the Androgines" (*Entrée des androgynes, trois figures*), INV 32692, Recto.
With the courtesy of the Département des Arts graphiques, Musée du Louvre. Photo: VK Preston.

(2014b). This trans-Atlantic slip between the active protest of *fiestas* and Western theatrical dance slides right through ontological and epistemological fault lines here, even as the man inside the parrot costume decries injustice and death.[34]

Conflating love and politics once again, dual-gendered "ANDROGINES" appear in the ballet's next scene, performing both Atlantic and gendered crossings. These homologous figures appear in Rabel's drawings, split vertically between male and female halves, that both suggest theatrical practice and abstraction, exposing a costumed *coup-de-théâtre* to the viewer. Echoing Andean practice—and yet delinked from any sacred associations—the costumes again testify to Andean sources, unquestionably mistranslated in performance and seemingly peppered with a sexual overture. This occasion for spectacle, however, seems to remix, and even transculturate, ballet's gendered codes, deploying this imagined dance of androgynes to bypass France's censors.

Set well apart from the other images for *Ballets of the Americas* in Rabel's album, the drawing for the "Entry of the ANDROGINES" (Figure 14.4) appears nearly at its end,

[34] Allusions to a classical world, and in particular to Greek Antiquity, are explicit in the text, commenting meta-theatrically on Daedalus's escape from prison disguised as a bird.

set among changeable and fantastical figures.[35] Raising a golden distaff (*quenoüille*), for spinning (in one hand), and a silver ceremonial club (*massuë*) as a weapon (in the other), these "two spirit," dual-gendered *travesti(e)s*[36] split the body as if in a vertical line. The costumes' conceit offers a congenial range of play for the performers: either alternating "male" and "female" profiles, or, as in Rabel's drawing, directly facing the audience to perform both genders at once.

Each figure wears an exposed, idealized, prosthetic "female" breast, striped Andean fabrics, and flowing, blonde locks (on one side of the body) and a curled moustache, feather regalia, and cropped hair (on the other).[37] Additionally, these male-and-female costumed halves echo and reverse the masculine and feminine associations of gold and silver in Andean cosmologies.

Like Atahualpa's effigy and the dancing parrots, the roles again take root in accounts and chronicles of the Americas, in a rhetorical tradition deeply steeped in animosity, in which speculation on gender and sexuality in the so-called New World regularly played a role in justifying its invasion. The ballet's "ANDROGINES" thus mix both European and Andean gender associations.[38] The ballet, it would seem, performs these "ANDROGINES"[39] as a retort to Spanish acts of conquest, parodying sacred roles that in Cuzco, Michael J. Horswell writes, bore the task of interpreting and attending to cultural memory in moments of cataclysmic change (2005, 1–2).

In *Decolonizing the Sodomite*, Horswell suggests that accounts of dual-gendered Andeans put Spanish orthodox gender representations in crisis, enacting a "complementarity" between the sexes as well as power of androgynous forms. Labeling these non-binary genders both "diabolical and deviant" (Horswell 2005, 2), an arsenal of Spanish "historiography, civil law, ecclesiastical literature, and religious art and performance" unleashed a "near erasure and eventual transculturation" of third-gender ceremonial roles and subjectivities (2005, 4)—an elimination, he argues, that aimed at destroying not just a "part of the people's memory," but an Andean "understanding of the cosmos" (2005, 4).

---

[35] See Bordier, Sorel, et al. (16 . ., 4) [in YF-815]: "As women they bore the distaff (spindle), & as men the club, for weaving on one hand and for hitting on the other" (*Elles portent comme femmes la quenoüille, & comme hommes la massuë, pour filer d'un coster & assommer de l'autre*). See *Album Rabel*, INV 32692, recto; folio 92.

[36] I adapt "*travesti(e)s*" from French-language grammatical gender usage as a written signifier of neutrality that paradoxically pluralizes grammatical gender.

[37] Natalie Zemon Davis reminds readers that gendered and racialized disguise offered reactionary impulses that paradoxically instantiated the power and potency of subaltern and women's speech. See the "Woman on Top" and traditions of gender-crossing and blackened as signifiers of political disorder in early modern French iconography and popular protest traditions (Davis 1965).

[38] These *travesti(e)s* cannot in good faith be mapped onto Andean gender roles, though their trans-cultural appearance in ballet and indications of transforming its vocabulary present major, understudied records of transculturation in early modern theatrical dance.

[39] For an account of this sequence in performance, see *Grand Bal de la douairière* (n.d.), 8-YTH-8021 (A), 4–5, at the BnF.

Mixing "male" and "female" movement codes in ballet (Franko 1993, 67), and performing roles associated with sodomy in conquest rhetoric, the French elites who danced these faux "Andean" figures challenged the gendered limits of acceptable movement in France—to the extent that the ballet's archives repeatedly point toward censorship, revision, and displacement of this scene. The seams of this transculturation appear on the vertical threshold of the dancers' costumes, fashioning visible distinctions between male and female and carrying gold and silver attributes that reverse Andean associations of silver with female divinity and the moon, *Mama Quilla*, and gold with the "male" sun deity, *Inti* (a figure also associated with birds). This mixing, set in movement through dance, blends the codes of French dance with Inca cosmology, about which there seems to have been a vogue in this period, bilaterally marking the body with Incaic gold and silver to perform theatrical metamorphoses between female and male roles.[40]

# Censors

An extremely rare mention of censorship appears in published accounts of this entry (8-YTH-8021 (A), 5), and it is especially glaring because it is also the most overt reference to such restrictions in the entire published corpus of early French ballets. Its narrator insists that the dancers playing "ANDROGINES" kept their legs and leaps low throughout the entry, guaranteeing the expectations of "our Censors" ("pour garantir leur Ballet des atteintes de nos Censeurs"). Entering after the parrots' hunters as the last of the *Ballets of the Americas*, this scene ended, according to the same account, with a sustained note on a violin, launching a transition from the "Americas" to "Asia" and an entry of the prophet "MAHOMMET" and his scribes.[41]

Nor is this the only evidence of modification to records of this scene in the ballet's archives. A technique used in the early modern period to revise or censor print works obscures verse for these "ANDROGINES," here termed *les Eunuques*, penned by Claude de l'Estoile (a founding member of the French Academy) (YF-1158, 4).[42] This instance of revision, after printing, is the only example I have yet seen of a *carton* (printed text glued over printed text) in the published corpus of verse for court ballets. It indicates, if not censorship, the compulsion to revise the ballet's records even after publication.

---

[40] "Metamorphosis is analogy set in motion," writes Leo Cabranes-Grant, "for a moment, an either-or relation is presented as a dynamic both-and creature" (2010, 475).

[41] See 8-YTH-8021 (A), 5–6, and the entry of "MAHOMMET" (6).

[42] "ANDROGINES" are termed "eunuchs" (*Eunuques*) in Claude de l'Estoile, and spectators are encouraged to eroticize these dancers: "What do I see here, are these bodies/[ . . . ] living as we are [ . . . ] Until we know / Whether they are men, beasts, or women / They are everything that would please you" (de l'Estoile 1626, 4). See "*Pour des Eunuques*": *Que vois-je icy, sont-ce des corps/Qui soient vivans comme nous sommes, Ou des souches que par ressors/On fait danser en habit d'hommes. [ . . . ] En attendant que l'on sçaura/Silz sont hommes, bestes, ou femmes/Ils sont tout ce quil vous plaira.*" In BnF, YF 1158, 4.

Moreover, Rabel's album also distances the drawings of the "ANDROGINES" from the rest of the costume images for the "Americas." The gold and silver drawings of the male-and-female "ANDROGINES" have been sewn into the album well apart from the other drawings for the *Ballets of the Americas*—including Atahualpa, the tattooed dancers, and parrots. The "ANDROGINES" instead appear among the last images of the album, bound among *fantasques*—"fantasticals" or "fantasies"—signifying mutable and irrational impulses.

If the dual-gendered "ANDROGINES" of this ballet indeed incited censorship in baroque Paris, as I suggest, more than the height of the dancers' leaps was in question. As spectacularly visible targets of the *conquistadores*,[43] "two-spirit" or "third sex" Andeans regularly appeared, as Jonathan Goldberg offers in *Sodometries*, as rhetorical tropes deployed to justify the invasion of the Americas. The most famous of such scenes of gendered and sexual violence in the visual archive is undoubtedly that from Theodor de Bry's *Americae IV* (1594), in which Vasco Nuñez de Balboa sets his dogs on Andean "sodomites" to maul them to death. French nobles performing "ANDROGINES" in this danced satire of Spain, therefore, seem to serve as a political denunciation of Spanish acts of conquest and to publish, through dance, a spectacular identification with the Andes, even as France overtly competed with its southern neighbor to claim land and resources in the Americas.[44]

Indications of censorship, modification, and reorganization of the European performance's archives, however, pale in contrast with the silencing of Indigenous protest against Spanish invasion, among these texts by Andean authors withheld from printing presses in Europe. Felipe Guamán Poma de Ayala, for example, a Quecha noble, sent a nearly twelve-hundred-page illustrated manuscript, *Nueva corónica y buen gobierno (New Chronicle and Treatise on Government)*, to the king of Spain about a decade before the ballet in 1615/1616. Denouncing the mines, the *mita* system of forced labor, and Peru's colonial government, Guamán Poma also pointedly defended Andean dance and festival cycles (Guamán Poma 1615, 317–329) from censure, illustrating both dances and a scene of Atahualpa's decapitation *in medias res* (Cummins 2013; Millones 2013). This substantive manuscript "disappeared," however, into the archives of royal collections, and it was not published until after it was identified in the royal library of Denmark in the early twentieth century, nearly four centuries after it first arrived in Spain (see Adorno [1986] 2000).

Poma's accounts of dance and ceremony remain underexamined in dance historiography outside the Andes, where the history of a sixteenth-century danced protest against Spain—the *Taki Onquy*, or "disease of the dance," described by Luis Millones

---

[43] Queer studies approaches to early modern and baroque France have proposed an emergence of a self-consciously queer subjectivity in this era. On Theodor de Bry's *Americae IV*, see Gaudio (2008), Goldberg ([1992] 2010, 179–222), and Horswell (2005, 71–73).

[44] De Bry, a Protestant, has also been interpreted as producing anti-Spanish propaganda, presenting colonial violence in the "new world" as a politicized extension of the violence of European wars over religion. See also Wiesner-Hanks 2014.

as a political movement sweeping the Andes—has played a major role, since the 1960s, in aligning Andean "national identity not to the Spanish conquerors but to the Andean conquered" (Mumford 1998, 150).

Addressing Andean dance and festival as avowal in "The Potosí Principle: Another View of Totality" (2014, n.p.), Silvia Rivera Cusicanqui defines the "*Thaki* . . . [as] a polysemic Aymara word that connotes the itineraries of ritual libations, dances, and chants in the routes that connect the *wak'as* [sacred objects and locations] with the centers of [Andean and cosmological] power in successive historical horizons." Challenging the binary of Western mercantile capitalism and Indian rebellion as a "Manichean" construct, Cusicanqui fiercely explores dance ontologies that both persisted and persist in the Andes as corporeal experiences that shared in the "loving *tinku* (encounter) of dance" (2014). Cusicanqui writes of "songs and paths of the present" as interweavings of "pierced" nets and "territorial fabrics," revealed in the multiple trajectories of processions and dances, rendering these through the Andean cosmological metaphor of woven fabric as a semantically dense landscape danced and traversed over centuries.

This movement exceeds the individual "I," she writes, summoning subjectivities "configured in and through displacement." As "circulation and interconnection," Cusicanqui proposes the *thaki* as a pattern of intellectual engagement as well as embodiment: "an intellectual *thaki* that would not succumb to the truculence and horror vacuum of the Spanish baroque, neither to the irresistible disorder of postmodern cultural plazas." Such a *thaki* "would enable us to think in reverse," she continues, singing-dancing along multiple roads of cultural memory, "from the *jayamara* (ancient times) to the *qhipnayra* (future-past) through the *amuyt'awi* (reflexive thinking)" (2014).

# COLLECTION, RECEPTION, AND "REFUSING TO REDO"

The first sheaf of papers in Rabel's leather-bound album is an act of appraisal: a page of spidery, handwritten commentary penned by the renowned collector Pierre-Jean Mariette. While Mariette praises Rabel's artistry, he suggests that the roles in Rabel's album are too "base" and too "grotesque" for the eighteenth-century stage.[45] His observation emphasizes reception's changeability in time and the drawings' offense to the "politeness" of eighteenth-century baroque theatricality in France. In doing so, Mariette underscores a major shift in the perception of dance in Western Europe between the

---

[45] "On ne souffriroit certainement point sur scène certaines figures trop grotesques et trop indécentes dont on s'amusoit alors. Les mœurs ne sont certainement pas meilleures, mais il y a plus de politesse." In "*Dessins français de la collection Mariette*" (2011). See also Astington (2001). On politics and figuration in European baroque performances and on maps, see Arcangeli (2010); Christout (1948); Franko (1989, 1996, 2003, 2007); McGowan (1963, 2012); Meglin (2000); Moureau (2004, 2005); Orgel (1965); Orgel and Strong (1973); Ravelhofer (2006); and Traub (2010).

seventeenth and eighteenth centuries (see Franko 1993), marking an effort to govern the medium of ballet that both produced its canon and obscured its archives.

This chapter redoubles Mariette's observation, problematizing the archive's rhetorics of conquest and ethno-masquerade and offering these as sites at which to resist reperforming this "lost dance" (Pakes, Chapter 5 in this volume). Any reperformance of the *Ballet de la douairière* today could not but evoke blackface, minstrelsy, and "playing Indian" (Deloria 1998). To embark upon reconstruction in this context is to repeat histories of abuse without hearing their legacies. My approach instead delves into the cultural politics of reconstruction and reperformance by way of spectatorship, beginning with an argument for eschewing redoing. Turning away from reconstruction and toward an "anarchival" critical research praxis that I link to the tricky glints of Rabel's album, this approach actively resists mimetic repetitions, concentrating instead on pluralizing danced epistemologies and the medium's transnational histories. Investigating spectatorship as a scene of reenactment, rather than of bodies dancing on a stage, this approach takes up "the archive *as another kind of performance*" (Schneider 2011, 108), and even spectacle, foregrounding material qualities of records as sites of critical reenactment that are politically compromised and compromising. Like Rabel's precious metal highlights, these position and reposition spectators at varying angles of approach, making and unmaking themselves in shifting dimensions and illusions. This approach to a notion of an unrepeatable relation to images and documents also seeks a way of decentering ballet genealogies, particularly at a dramaturgical or heuristic level, rather than iconography. It turns to sensory and material intersections of bodies and things, performance and media—of which Tavia Nyong'o proposes that our senses are "theoreticians of the possible," creating worlds through which we both co-investigate and co-invent "so-called bodies of evidence" (2011, n.p.)—affording the senses the capacity to theorize and, indeed, perform.

Reconstructing such a dance surely raises red flags, especially within contexts of "settler reenactment" (Lamb, Agnew, and Spoth 2009; Agnew 2004).[46] My preference is to withhold or interrupt such repetition, or else to refract it in the (meta-)critical interplay Jill Lane terms "re-enactments of [ . . . ] (re-)enactments" (2010, 111), speculative and critical reimaginings that reveal its fissures and exclusions and set the past askew. Rather than seeking to render past dances like the *Ballet de la douairière* as dance-theaters today, my approach to materials, perception, and reception as changeable and in flux interrogates their conceptual foundations and performance genealogies. Delaying or abstaining from reconstruction, this approach unsettles ballet historiography through the performative labor of a dancer as an archivist (see Skantze, Chapter 16, and Franko, Chapter 24, in this volume) who refuses to redo. The approach holds back—interrogating, as an organizing heuristic, the dancerly politics of felicitous repetition.

---

[46] The images and texts offer differing forms of evidence and forgetting. In the performance's written account, for instance, we would not know that characters, including the slaves in Rabel's drawings, appeared at all in these ballets' *mises en scène* (see Figure 14.4).

# (AN) ARCHIVAL PRACTICE

Rabel's paintings of *Ameriquains* lead the viewer in a subtle dance of reflected light, inviting embodied and affective response. Turning the pages of the album, like drawing, translates the hand as well as the eye, transforming acts of spectatorship (Skantze, Chapter 16 in this volume) in mobile, transitive relations with materials and sources. This attention emphasizes the records' temporal and tactile qualities, as well as their capacity for illusions, while honing in on their continuum of relationships to plundered objects and stolen metals.[47]

This approach to handling archives is performative: it participates in history-making, and yet it asserts that researchers' always "impure reconstruction[s]" (Phelan 2004, 14) are organizing acts to which research brings embodied criticism into ethical account. Moving with these images illuminates histories of plunder and extraction, as well as speculative movements with and toward performance. This materialist approach to (an)archival reenactment involves transversal research, interrogating heuristics and drawing from performance studies, as well as critical historiography.[48] Here, the dramaturgical task of historiography begins with a "dance of perception" (Manning, 142)[49] in which raw feels of light and color provide powerful insight into the entanglements of performances and things. This immanent approach to archival work does not limit itself to a "fun," bottom-up, or "accessible" method of public history (Agnew 2004, 327, 330). Rather, it approaches archival research as processual and embodied, attending to the "task of perception" (Deleuze [1993] 2006, 99) as an ontologically, historically, and culturally troubled site—crossing and recrossing categories and temporalities as it traces an imperial historiography and aesthetics of this dance.

Jill Lane, writing on hemispheric temporalities, describes this slide into witnessing through artworks as a movement in time or "portal" (2010, 123), and I glimpse something of this quality, or perhaps its obverse, in the ballet's staging of nested and telescopic pasts. Glimpses of these defy the attempt to bind these drawings into "a rationalized

---

[47] Peruvian metals and their complex relationships to performance have recently spurred controversy over the display and return of Andean artworks and objects (Cusicanqui 2014; Lane 2012; Pimentel 2013).

[48] This approach investigates what Gins and Arakawa, in the *Architectural Body*, term "tactile-imaging," "kinesthetic-*imaging*," and "seeing touching" as "world-constituting procedures" (2002). See also Keane (2013).

[49] "A dance of attention has its own technicity," writes Erin Manning. "For each work [ . . . ] a rigorous setting into place of conditions is necessary. These conditions are always specific to the event but never completely stable across its iterations [ . . . ]. No movement can be cued, aligned to, or performed in exactly the same way twice [ . . . ]. What emerges as a dance of attention cannot be replicated [ . . . ]. We feel attention's dance, but it is not of us or even for us. It is *with*, in the milieu [ . . . ]. It is how we feel the work working. For when attention dances, the ground begins to move, and in the moving, we are moved" (Manning 2013, 142). On perception and place, see Morris (2013).

European temporal logic" (Lane 2010, 117), seeming to invent another dance in binding them together.[50]

Sitting with the drawings and learning to turn the album's fragile pages investigate these hermeneutics corporeally. Thain, writing on the anarchive, describes this immanent approach as a "loss of a space that provides a singular external orientation for a spectator" (2010, 53), setting spectatorship into movement. She imagines this as the anarchive, because it is inventive, co-creating perception with a surround. As ethico-aesthetic experience, moreover, this is "[n]o longer a question of a perceiving subject and a perceived object, [but an] intensive extension [that] makes relation felt as a resonant reserve of potential" (Thain 2010, 57). This potential for the creative entails an ethics of research and performance, even as it discloses fantasies of accumulation and objection nested in the archive.

Instead of approaching reenactment as an "end," this chapter investigates (an)archival possibilities, observing and suspending the politics of reperformance in a call that Lane describes as "temporal without being historical; that is about history [ . . . ] without being reducible to it" (Lane 2010, 123), and that nonetheless anchors itself in relations, in archival work, and critical historiographical approaches. Future studies of the album will almost certainly further and complicate Rabel's geographic fantasies, teasing out the album's syntaxes and appropriations—not only in relation to the Americas but also to Africa, Asia, and Europe.[51] Here, I have argued that these histories inhere in the drawings' materials, as substances and figures inter(in)animated with Indigenous theologies, dances, and sacred substances.[52]

Performance and spectatorial perception, writes Walter Mignolo in *The Darker Side of the Renaissance*, offer opportunities to "rethink the hermeneutical legacy" of cultural traditions and research, embracing performance as a critical method of interrogating culturally different systems of thought ([1995] 2014, vi, 15). A critical approach to reenactment, here, moves conceptually between enormously different heuristics and ontologies, remembering, as Mignolo writes, that "[e]nacting is performing," that constructing order is performative, and that reflection culturally embedded in heuristics is often largely invisible to the researcher ([1995] 2014, 20). In so doing, he reminds readers and spectators that as "participants . . . we are already observers" (23), encouraging the "shak[ing] up [of] the patterns of understanding" inherited from the era of conquest, which I argue can and must include those of dance. Silver's legacies—its toxicities of extraction, displacement, and dispossession—expose fraught tensions between Indigenous and European conceptions of the live, of the (embodied) archive, and of

---

[50] The logic of this album is neither rational nor of the Enlightenment, I contend; it slips in and through breaches, presenting multiplicities sewn together and folded across disjunctions.

[51] Rabel's drawings of *Ameriquain* figures are a subset of the album's images. The larger task to be taken up, which exceeds the focus of this chapter, is to theorize the heuristics of other "parts of the world," and their relationships and transitions, as structures of this ballet's globalist orientation.

[52] On "inter(in)animation" see Schneider (2011, 1, 31, 108). My thanks to Rebecca Schneider for co-instructing a graduate seminar on this concept with me, at Brown University's Theatre and Performance Studies program, in 2016.

accumulation. Deployed as emblems of baroque-world transformation, Rabel's drawings evoke renewal as well as return, as seen in the example of Atahualpa's beheading in effigy, even if this reiteration in these baroque ballets and drawings is partial and unwitting. Where these drawings transpose iconographical details from European travel chronicles and oral relations, torn out of context from Cuzco's festival culture and translated into Parisian burlesque and ballet festival traditions, these feed a spirit of largely unexamined dissent and transculturation generally unsuspected in ballet's hegemonic historiography. I believe the dances these images provoke offer a far more nuanced and complex politics, not only of appropriation and extraction, but also of fabulation and cultural memory—a forgetting of the impact of what Roach terms circum-Atlantic performance on the shaping of ballet's early archives and repertoires.

Rabel's drawings reveal the surprisingly "global" and understudied reach of baroque archives on dance and performance, notably with regard to the Americas (Scolieri 2013). These, as Paul Scolieri writes, "reflected back [the chroniclers'] own experiences, fantasies, or interpretations: as acts of historiography, as emblems of conversion, and even as symbols of death and extinction" (2013, 55). In doing so, these traces nonetheless testify to the mnemonic resiliency and wide circulation of danced repertoires from the Americas, complicating notions of the live and the archive, insinuating themselves in transcultural performance media, and exposing the proto-globalizing logic of some of early ballet's most beautiful, as well as perhaps least studied, records.

## WORKS CITED

Adorno, Rolena. [1986] 2000. *Guaman Poma: Writing and Resistance in Colonial Peru.* Austin: University of Texas Press.

Agnew, Vanessa. 2004. "Introduction: What Is Reenactment?" *Criticism.* 46(3): 327–339.

Arcangeli, Alessandro. 2010. "Dancing Savages: Stereotypes and Cultural Encounters across the Atlantic in the Age of European Expansion." In *Exploring Cultural History: Essays in Honour of Peter Burke,* edited by Melissa Calaresu, Filippo de Vivo, and Joan-Pau Rubiés, 289–308. London: Ashgate.

Astington, John H. 2001. "Daniel Rabel and the Grotesque." *Early Theatre* 4(1): 101–109.

Barthes, Roland. [1981] 1985. *Camera Lucida: Reflections on Photography.* Translated by Richard Howard. New York: Hill and Wang.

Bodin, Jean. 1568. *Responses aux paradoxes du sieur de Malestroict* [ . . . ]. In *Les paradoxes du seigneur de Malestroict,* [ . . . ] *sur le faict des monnoyes, présentez à Sa Majesté au mois de mars 1566, avec la response de M. Jean Bodin ausdicts paradoxes.* Paris: M. Le Jeune. BnF E*-535 and Gallica NUMM-80089.

Bordier, René. 1626a. *Grand Bal de la douairière de Billebahaut, ballet dansé par le Roy au mois de février 1626.* Paris: Mathurin Henault. BnF 8-YTH-8021 (A).

Bordier, René. 1626b. *Grand Bal de la douairière de Billebahaut, ballet dansé par le Roy au mois de février 1626. Vers dudit ballet par le sieur Bordier.* Paris: L'Imprimerie du Louvre. BnF YF-814.

Bordier, René, Imbert, and Charles Sorel. 16[. .]. *Grand bal de la douairière de Billebahaut. Ballet dansé par Sa Majesté.* [n.p.]. BnF YF-815 and Gallica NUMM-5507411.

Boucher, Philip. [2008] 2010. *France and the American Tropics to 1700: Tropics of Discontent?* Baltimore, MD: Johns Hopkins.

Bradley, Peter T., and David Cahill. 2000. *Hapsburg Peru: Images, Imagination and Memory.* Liverpool: Liverpool University Press.

Cabranes-Grant, Leo. 2010. "The Fold of Difference: Performing Baroque and Neobaroque Mexican Identities." In *Baroque New Worlds: Representation, Transculturation, Counterconquest,* edited by Lois Parkinson Zamora and Monika Kaup, 467–486. Durham, NC: Duke University Press.

Cabranes-Grant, Leo. 2016. *From Scenarios to Networks: Performing the Intercultural in Colonial Mexico.* Evanston: Northwestern University Press.

Cahill, David Patrick. 2002. "The Virgin and the Inca: An Incaic Procession in the City of Cuzco in 1692." *Ethnohistory* 49(3): 611–649.

Christout, Marie-Françoise. [1948] 1961. "Les ballets-mascarades des Fées de la foret de Saint-Germain et de la douairière de Billebahaut et l'oeuvre de Daniel Rabel." *Revue d'Histoire du Théâtre* 13(1): 7–29.

Cummins, Thomas B. F. 2013. "Inca Heritage in Peruvian Colonial Art." In *Peru: Kingdoms of the Sun and the Moon,* edited by Victor Pimentel, 188–193. Montreal: 5 Continents.

Cusicanqui, Silvia Rivera. 2014. "The Potosí Principle: Another View of Totality." In *E-Misférica* 11.1: *Decolonial Gesture.* http://hemisphericinstitute.org/hemi/en/emisferica-111-decolonial-gesture/e111-essay-the-potosi-principle-another-view-of-totality (accessed September 29, 2014).

Davis, Natalie Zemon. 1965. *Society and Culture in Early Modern France: Eight Essays.* Stanford, CA: Stanford University Press.

Dean, Carolyn. 1999. *Inka Bodies and the Body of Christ: Corpus Christi in Colonial Cuzco, Peru.* Durham, NC: Duke University Press.

Deleuze, Gilles. [1993] 2006. *The Fold: Leibniz and the Baroque.* Foreword by Tom Conley. New York: Continuum Press.

Deloria, Philip Joseph. 1998. *Playing Indian.* New Haven, CT: Yale University Press.

Derrida, Jacques. 1993. *Mal d'archive: une impression Freudienne.* Paris: Galilée.

Durosoir, Georgie. 1995. "Traces de la musique instrumentale dans les ballets de cour (c. 1600–1630)." In *Le concert des voix et des instruments à la Renaissance: colloque [ . . . ] Tours 1991: actes,* edited by Jean-Michel Vaccaro, 579–585. Paris: CNRS.

Franko, Mark. 1989. "Repeatability, Reconstruction and Beyond." *Theatre Journal* 41(1): 56–74.

Franko, Mark. 1993. *Dance as Text: Ideologies of the Baroque Body.* New York: Cambridge University Press.

Franko, Mark. 1996. "The King Cross-Dressed: Power and Force in Royal Ballets." In *From the Royal to the Republican Body: Incorporating the Political in Seventeenth and Eighteenth Century France,* edited by Sara E. Melzer and Kathryn Norberg, 64–84. Berkeley and Los Angeles: University of California Press.

Franko, Mark. 2003. "Majestic Drag: Monarchical Performativity and the King's Body Theatrical." *TDR/The Drama Review* 47(2): 71–87.

Franko, Mark. 2007. "Fragment of the Sovereign as Hermaphrodite: Time, History and the Exception in *Le Ballet de Madame.*" *Dance Research* 25(2): 119–133.

Fraresso, Carole. 2011. "Ancient Peruvian Gold and Silver Jewelry: Fashion and Religion." In *Berg Fashion Library Encyclopedia of World Dress and Fashion,* vol. 2, edited by Margot Blum Schevill, Blenda Femenías, and Lynn Meisch, 1–8. Oxford: Berg Publishers.

Fraresso, Carole. 2013. "The Sweat of the Sun and the Tears of the Moon: Gold and Silver in Ancient Peru." In *Peru: Kingdoms of the Sun and the Moon*, edited by Victor Pimentel, 142–150. Montreal: 5 Continents.

Gaudio, Michael. 2008. *Engraving the Savage: The New World and Techniques of Civilization.* Minneapolis: University of Minnesota Press.

Gins, Madeline, and Shusaku Arakawa. 2002. *Architectural Body.* Tuscaloosa: University of Alabama Press.

Gohory, Jacques, and W. H. Bowen. 1938. "L'histoire de la Terre Neuve du Peru." *Isis* 28(2): 330–340.

Goldberg, Jonathan. [1992] 2010. *Sodometries: Renaissance Texts, Modern Sexualities.* New York: Fordham University Press.

*Grand Bal de la douairière de Billebahaut, ballet dansé par le Roy au mois de février 1626.* Paris: Henault, 1626, BnF 8-YTH-8021(A).

Guamán Poma de Ayala, Felipe. 1615. *Nueva corónica y buen gobierno (The First New Chronicle and Good Government).* Det Kongelige Bibliotek, GKS 2232 4°. http://www.kb.dk/permalink/2006/poma/info/en/frontpage.htm (accessed July 1, 2014).

Guss, David M. 2000. *The Festive State: Race, Ethnicity, and Nationalism as Cultural Performance.* Berkeley: University of California Press.

Hamann, Byron Ellsworth. 2010. "Interventions. The Mirrors of *Las Meninas*: Cochineal, Silver, and Clay." *Art Bulletin* 92(1–2): 6–35, 57–60.

Horswell, Michael J. 2005. *Decolonizing the Sodomite: Queer Tropes of Sexuality in Colonial Andean Culture.* Austin: University of Texas Press.

Jouve Martín, José R. 2007. "Public Ceremonies and Mulatto Identity in Viceregal Lima: A Colonial Reenactment of the Fall of Troy." *Colonial Latin American Review* 16(2): 179–201.

Keane, Jondi. 2013. "Æffect: Initiating Heuristic Life." In *Carnal Knowledge: Towards a 'New Materialism' through the Arts*, edited by Estelle Barrett and Barbara Bolt, 41–63. London: Tauris.

Kontturi, Katve-Kaisa. 2013. "From Double Navel to Particle-Sign: Towards the A-Signifying Work of Painting." In *Carnal Knowledge: Towards a 'New Materialism' through the Arts*, edited by Estelle Barrett and Barbara Bolt, 17–28. London: Tauris.

Lamb, Jonathan, Vanessa Agnew, and Daniel Spoth. 2009. *Settler and Creole Reenactment.* Basingstoke, UK: Palgrave MacMillan.

Lane, Jill. 1998. "On Colonial Forgetting: The Conquest of New Mexico and Its *Historia*." In *The Ends of Performance*, edited by Peggy Phelan and Jill Lane, 52–69. New York: New York University Press.

Lane, Jill. 2010. "Hemispheric America in Deep Time." *Theatre Research International* 35(2): 111–125.

Lane, Jill. 2012. "Potosí Principle: Savage Capitalism." Plenary paper presented at the American Society for Theatre Research, Nashville, November 2012.

Lane, Jill, Marcial Godoy-Anativia, and Macarena Gómez Barris. 2014. In *E-Misférica 11.1: Decolonial Gesture.* http://hemisphericinstitute.org/hemi/en/emisferica-111-decolonial-gesture (accessed October 1, 2014).

Las Casas, Bartolomé de. 1579 [French edition]. *Tyrannies et cruautez des Espagnols perpétrées ès Indes occidentales, qu'on dit le Nouveau Monde, brièvement descrites en langue castillane par l'évesque Dom Frère Barthélemy de Las Casas ou Casaus [ . . . ]* Trans. Jaques de Miggrode. Anvers: F. de Ravelenghien.

Latour, Bruno. 2013. *An Inquiry into Modes of Existence: An Anthropology of the Moderns.* Translated by Catherine Porter. Cambridge, MA: Harvard University Press.

Leconte, T. 2012. *Les fées des forêts de Saint-Germain, 1625: un ballet royal de "bouffonesque humeur."* Turnout: Brepols.

l'Estoile, Claude de. 1626. *Maistre Galimathias, pour le grand bal de la douairière & de son fanfan de Sotte-Villle, dansé par le Roi au mois de février* [n.p.]. BnF, YF-1158.

Louvre. 2011. "Dessins français de la collection Mariette: Exposition du 10 novembre 2011 au 6 février 2012." Press release. http://www.louvre.fr/sites/default/files/medias/medias_fichiers/fichiers/pdf/louvre-dossier-presse-mariette.pdf (accessed July 9, 2014).

Manning, Erin. 2013. *Always More Than One: Individuation's Dance.* Prelude by Brian Massumi. Durham, NC: Duke University Press.

McGowan, Margaret. 1963. *L'art du ballet de cour en France, 1581–1643.* Paris: Éditions du centre national de la recherche scientifique.

McGowan, Margaret. 2012. *La danse à la Renaissance: sources livresques et albums d'images.* Conference held at the BnF, March 7 and 8, 2012. Paris: Bibliothèque nationale de France.

Meglin, Joellen A. 2000. "Sauvages, Sex Roles, and Semiotics: Representations of Native Americans in the French Ballet, 1736–1837, Part One: The Eighteenth Century." *Dance Chronicle* 23(2): 87–132.

Mignolo, Walter D. [2005] 2014a. *The Darker Side of the Renaissance: Literacy, Territoriality, and Colonization.* Ann Arbor: University of Michigan Press.

Mignolo, Walter D. 2014b. "Looking for the Meaning of 'Decolonial Gesture.'" In *E-Misférica* 11.1: *Decolonial Gesture.* http://hemisphericinstitute.org/hemi/en/emisferica-111-decolonial-gesture/e111-essay-the-potosi-principle-another-view-of-totality (accessed September 29, 2014).

Millones, Luis. 2013. "Colonial Theater in the Andes." In *Peru: Kingdoms of the Sun and the Moon*, edited by Victor Pimentel, 195–198. Montreal: 5 Continents.

Moore, Jason W. 2007. "Silver, Ecology, and the Origins of the Modern World, 1450–1640." In *Rethinking Environmental History: World-System History and Global Environmental Change*, edited by Alf Hornborg, J. R. McNeill, and Joan Martinez-Alier, 123–142. Plymouth: Altamira Press.

Morris, David. 2013. "Casey's Subliminal Phenomenology: On Edging Things Back into Place." In *Exploring the Work of Edward S. Casey: Giving Voice to Place, Memory, and Imagination*, edited by Donald A. Landes and Azucena Cruz-Pierre, 53–61. New York: Bloomsbury.

Moureau, François. 2004. "American Aboriginals in the *Ballets de Cour* in Champlain's Time." In *Champlain: The Birth of French America*, edited by Raymonde Litalien and Denis Vaugeois, translated by Käthe Roth, 43–50. Montreal and Kingston: McGill-Queen's University Press and Septentrion.

Moureau, François. 2005. "Danses amérindiennes à la cour." In *Le théâtre des voyages: une scénographie de l'âge classique.* Paris: Presses de l'Université Paris-Sorbonne.

Mumford, Jeremy. 1998. "The Taki Onqoy and the Andean Nation: Sources and Interpretations." *Latin American Research Review* 33(1): 150–165.

Nora, Pierre. 1989. "Between Memory and History: Les Lieux de Mémoire." Translated by Marc Roudbush. *Representations* 26: 7–24.

Nyong'o, Tavia. 2011. In "Public Feelings Salon with Lauren Berlant." http://vimeo.com/22854077 (accessed May 1, 2014).

Orgel, Stephen. 1965. *The Jonsonian Masque.* Cambridge, MA: Harvard University Press.

Orgel, Stephen, and Roy Strong. 1973. *Inigo Jones: The Theatre of the Stuart Court.* London: Sotheby Parke Bernet.

Osorio, Alejandria B. 2004. "The King in Lima: Simulacra, Ritual, and Rule in Seventeenth-Century Peru." *Hispanic American Historical Review* 4(3): 447–474.

Osorio, Alejandria B. 2008. *Inventing Lima: Baroque Modernity in Peru's South Sea Metropolis*. New York: Palgrave Macmillan.

Phelan, Peggy. 2004. "Trisha Brown's *Orfeo*: Two Takes on Double Endings." In *Of the Presence of the Body: Essays on Dance and Performance Theory*, edited by André Lepecki, 13–28. Middletown, CT: Wesleyan University Press.

Pimentel, Victor, ed. 2013. *Peru: Kingdoms of the Sun and Moon*. Exhibition catalog. Montreal: Musée des Beaux Arts de Montréal.

Powell, Richard J., ed. 2010. [Special Issue]. *Art Bulletin* 92(1–2).

Ravelhofer, Barbara. 2006. *The Early Stuart Masque: Dance, Costume, and Music*. Oxford: Oxford University Press.

Reuell, Peter. October 2010. "Water Damage Leads to Revelation." In *Library Notes, Harvard College Library Communications*. 1356. http://hul.harvard.edu/publications/ln1356/01.html (accessed July 1, 2014).

Roach, Joseph. 1995. "Culture and Performance in the Circum-Atlantic World." In *Performativity and Performance*, edited and with an introduction by Andrew Parker and Eve Kosofsky Sedgwick, 45–63. New York: Routledge.

Roach, Joseph. 1996. *Cities of the Dead: Circum-Atlantic Performance*. New York: Columbia University Press.

Robins, Nicholas A. 2011. *Mercury, Mining, and Empire: the Ecological Cost of Colonial Silver Mining in the Andes*. Bloomington, Indiana University Press.

Schneider, Rebecca. [2001] 2012. "Performance Remains." In *Perform, Repeat, Record*, edited by Amelia Jones and Adrian Heathfield, 137–150. Bristol: Intellect and the University of Chicago Press.

Schneider, Rebecca. 2011. *Performing Remains: Art and War in Times of Theatrical Reenactment*. New York: Routledge.

Scolieri, Paul. 2013. *Dancing the New World: Aztecs, Spaniards, and the Choreography of Conquest*. Austin: University of Texas Press.

Seed, Patricia. 1991. "'Failing to Marvel': Atahualpa's Encounter with the Word." *Latin American Research Review* 26(1): 7–32.

Stern, Steve J. [1982] 1993. *Peru's Indian Peoples and the Challenge of Spanish Conquest: Huamanga to 1640*. Madison: University of Wisconsin Press.

Taylor, Diana. 2003. *The Archive and the Repertoire: Performing Cultural Memory in the Americas*. Durham, NC: Duke University Press.

Taylor, Diana. 2004. "Scenes of Cognition: Performance and Conquest." *Theatre Journal* 56(3): 353–372.

Taylor, Diana. 2006. "Performance and/as History." *TDR* 50(1): 67–86.

Thain, Alanna. 2010. "Anarchival Cinemas." *Inflexions* 4, "Transversal Fields of Experience," 48–68. www.inflexions.org (accessed July 1, 2014).

Traub, Valerie. 2000. "Mapping the Global Body." In *Early Modern Visual Culture*, edited by Peter Erickson and Clark Hulse, 44–97. Philadelphia: University of Pennsylvania Press.

Traub, Valerie. 2013. "The New Unhistoricism in Queer Studies." *PMLA* 128(1): 21–39.

Wiesner-Hanks, Merry. 2014. "Latin America." In *Christianity and Sexuality in the Early Modern World: Regulating Desire, Reforming Practice*, edited by Wiesner-Hanks, 140–177. New York: Routledge.

Ybarra, Patricia A. 2009. *Performing Conquest: Five Centuries of Theater, History, and Identity in Tlaxcala, Mexico.* Ann Arbor: University of Michigan Press.

Zamora, Lois Parkinson. 2006. *The Inordinate Eye: New World Baroque and Latin American Fiction.* Chicago: University of Chicago Press.

Zamora, Lois Parkinson, and Monika Kaup, eds. 2010. *Baroque New Worlds: Representation, Transculturation, Counterconquest.* Durham, NC: Duke University Press.

Zemach, E. M. 1966. "Sensations, Raw Feels, and Other Minds." *The Review of Metaphysics* 20(2): 317–340.

# CHAPTER 15

.................................................

# REENACTING *KAISIKA NATAKAM*

## *Ritual Dance-Theater of India*

.................................................

### KETU H. KATRAK WITH ANITA RATNAM

The ritual importance of *Kaisika Natakam* resides in its story that explodes the caste system and that also glorifies the power of devotional music.

In the original source story of *Kaisika Natakam*, from the *Varaha Purana* (Hindu scriptural text), Lord Vishnu tells his wife Goddess Lakshmi that of all the modes of worship directed towards Him, the paths of music and dance are what please him the most. Vishnu has over 1,000 names but in Tirukurungudi [the village that is the custodian of this ritual dance-theater], he is also known as Nambi, translated as "belief" (hence Nambi is the One who can be believed in), and as Nada Vinodana, translated as the one who loves music.

—Anita Ratnam[1]

The effort to find "that was then" inside "this is now"—the tangle of then is now . . . [haunts] reenactment as a practice that like all representational practice . . . is composed in reiteration . . . what Richard Schechner has termed "restored" or "twice-behaved behavior."

—Rebecca Schneider 2011, 10

[1] Anita Ratnam (email correspondence to Katrak, May 28, 2014) is a prominent performing artist and scholar based in Chennai, whose family has ancestral roots in the temple village of Tirukurungudi in Tamil Nadu, South India.

Please see details on Ratnam's creative activities at: http://www.arangham.com/anita/anita.html. See also Katrak (2011) for a discussion of Ratnam's contemporary Indian dance (especially Chapter 4).

In November 2005, on an overnight train journey, we are comfortably lulled to sleep by the rhythmic sound of the wheels in a two-tier sleeper compartment, from Chennai to our destination of Tirukurungudi, Anita Ratnam's ancestral village in Tamil Nadu, South India.[2] From the train station in Tirunelveli, we travel by car to the village, looking forward to witnessing *Kaisika Natakam* (Figure 15.1), the thirteenth-century ritual dance-theater performance, inside the village's main Vishnu temple that night.[3] It is Ekadesi, a significant day in the Tamil lunar calendar, associated traditionally with fasting, rest, and meditation that represent one's faith and humility. Ekadesi means "eleventh day" on both the waxing and waning cycles of the moon. Ratnam comments, "families from the village and the surrounding areas including little children and sometimes babes in arms are brought in for the blessing of being witness to the play during this sacred night of Ekadasi that is marked by fasting and wakefulness. To watch this story unfold while being in contemplation of the Lord is one of the sacred tenets of Hinduism" (email to Katrak, May 23, 2014).

By 9 p.m., a large audience of nearly the entire village—youth, children, babies, and the elderly—gather inside the *Kaisika Mandapam* (hall), used solely for this much-anticipated ritual dance-theater that has been performed annually since 1999.[4] The audience is lively, interactive, and participatory, greeting the main characters with applause, laughter, and theatricalized fear as they respond to the *rakshahsa*'s (demon's) dramatic entrance and brandishing of prop swords. The "show" inside the temple integrally blends dance, dialogue, song, and musical interludes that all convey the story of *Kaisika Natakam*, gripping the spectators until around 2 a.m.

This chapter analyzes the process of reconstructing *Kaisika Natakam* over four years from 1996 to 1999, and then reenacting this ritual dance-theater that had fallen into abeyance since 1955, especially with the passing away of T. V. Sundaram Iyengar and

[2] Ratnam had invited Katrak, who was on a Fulbright Research Award (2005–2006) in Chennai, working on her book on contemporary Indian dance, to accompany her to Tirukurungudi. This chapter continues our transnational scholarly collaboration over the years—Ratnam is based in Chennai, India, and Katrak in the United States, at the University of California, Irvine.

[3] Vishnu, along with Brahma and Shiva, form the major male trinity of gods in Hinduism. In general terms, Brahma is considered the Creator, Vishnu the Preserver, and Shiva the Destroyer, although Shiva is both creative and destructive. Shiva is also considered the God of Dance.

[4] *Kaisika Natakam* is performed at the special theater called *Kaisika Mandapan* (hall), constructed within the larger structure of the Azhagiya Nambi temple in Tirukurungudi, and is used only for that one event in the year. However, the temple itself has over sixty-five festivals and ritual celebrations that are observed throughout the year. Bringing the deities out into the streets for public worship, pulling the large temple chariot through the streets, folk dancing and singing, and sacred chanting by priests and other groups are just some of the observances. *Panguni Utsavam*—the ten-day festival during the lunar month of February 15 to March 15—is especially significant for this temple. There are performances of classical and folk dance and music. On a special day at the *Mattaidi Mandapam*, a mock play is enacted—the Lord goes outside the temple to meet his secret girlfriend and is found out by the goddess. The doors of the temple are blocked for his return, and the *devadasis* step forward to argue on the goddess's behalf, while the male priests, called Arayers, speak for the Lord. After much persuasion, the goddess relents, but not before the *devadasis* strike each of the male priests (*matta adi*) with a long bamboo cane as punishment for straying!

**FIGURE 15.1.** *Kaisika Natakam* opens with Vishnu Nambi in procession. Actor-dancers (left to right): Selvam, Balaji, Girija, Aruna, Raja.

Photographer: Chella Video (© Anita Ratnam/Arangham Trust).

his key patronage. As Ratnam remarks, "the play seemed to have lost its appeal, content and audience" (2000, 49). We argue that this reenacted ritual dance-theater, performed every year since 1999 in Tirukurungudi, needs critical attention for its unique features, namely, for its story that challenges the rigid caste system (that still remains problematic) in India, for its gender reversals whereby women play the roles of the lead male characters, for its deployment of what Rebecca Schneider calls a "syncopated time of reenactment, where *then* and *now* punctuate each other" (Schneider 2011, 1). For our discussion, Schneider's analysis of the temporal dimension (developed later in the chapter) involved in reenactment, namely the past and present, the "then and now" that are evoked in reenactment, is useful. Temporal notions are involved in reenactments, which can either "imitate" a past event as closely as possible, recreating its original costumes and stage presentation, or can deconstruct such imagined simultaneity of past and present by demonstrating the lags of time between what took place in the past with our present time. Here, we also rely on Mark Franko's formative contribution in his essay, "Repeatability, Reconstruction, and Beyond" on how time functions in the repetition (and reenactment) of historical events in performance (1989, 56–74).

We distinguish between our use of the words "reconstruction" and "reenactment," and do not use them interchangeably.[5] Reconstruction involves the scholarly tasks of

---

[5] Mark Franko, editor of this *Oxford Handbook of Dance and Reenactment*, provided astute comments that enabled us to think further about the differences in these words, as we discuss in the chapter.

excavating material, often in archives, of deciphering and interpreting original materials. As Susan Leigh Foster discusses usefully in her Introduction to *Choreographing History*, "Historians' bodies amble down the corridors of documentation inclining toward certain discursive domains and veering away from others. Yes, the production of history is a physical endeavor. It requires a high tolerance for sitting and for reading . . . staring alternately at the archival evidence and the fantasies it generates" (1995, 6). As in the case of *Kaisika Natakam*, it was a major scholarly undertaking involving the labor of historians, musicologists, artists, and living descendants' memory-contributions to reconstruct this ritual dance-theater whose original story was found on palm-leaf manuscript in the Tamil language. Reconstruction involves a methodology of operating with particular kinds of archival material and their interpretation. The collaborators who worked on *Kaisika Natakam* agreed on the method being pursued and its ultimate goal of reenacting this ritual dance-theater that fulfills a ritual purpose for onlookers/participants. In Hindu worship, it is considered auspicious simply to be present and to witness a ritual dance-theater such as *Kaisika Natakam*.

Reenactment is a different activity from reconstruction. Reenactment, according to Mark Franko (see Franko, Chapter 1 in this volume) involves theatrical tools of presenting a ritual or a historical event from the past. The reenactment of *Kaisika Natakam* restores the ritual dance-theater to the village temple of Tirukurungudi, its original repository. With respect to the site of performance, their reenactment is in situ, to borrow a term from art history. The live bodies of the dancers and actors animate the reenactment of this ritual dance-theater. On stage, they use various performance forms of movement, music, gesture, dialogue, costumes, and stagecraft. In the Indian aesthetic-philosophical tradition, the categories of movement, music, and nonverbal gestural language (*abhinaya*) are connected integrally.

# THE GENRE OF DANCE-THEATER IN INDIA

The ancient (second–fifth centuries CE) Sanskrit text, *The Natyasastra*, the oldest compendium or treatise (*sastra*) of all aspects of drama (natya) including dramaturgy, acting, gesture language, the navarasas (nine primary human emotions) is a cornerstone of India's aesthetic and philosophical thought-system. *The Natyasastra* posits that *natya* (translated literally as "drama") includes dance, music, gesture, theatrical story-telling, expression via the physical body and facial expression, along with different architectural structures of the stage (oblong, square), and the overall stagecraft. There is no separation of the forms of drama from dance, or of poetry from music. Another key concept in Indian aesthetic and religious belief is the integral connection of the sensual, the sexual, and the spiritual in Indian thought, wherein the body is the vehicle (as in yoga) to reach the higher realms of spirituality. The spiritual itself is not located *only* in ritual worship or temple ceremonies, but in the highest aesthetic experience (for performer and audience), which, for the tenth-century CE Indian philosopher Abhinavagupta, is akin to a spiritual experience. In *Kaisika Natakam*, the singing of the low-caste protagonist, Nambudavan, an aesthetic experience, creates a miracle—it transforms the demon from his distorted physique back to his human form. The aesthetic joy of devotional singing is the same as an uplifting feeling of spiritual transcendence. The ritualistic base of this dance-theater reenacts artistic cum religious goals. The reenactment enables audiences in the village itself and, increasingly, spectators from across India and abroad to gain the ritual benefits of viewing, witnessing, and participating in this event. Enaction is to practice as reenactment is to theory.

## REENACTING THE STORY OF *KAISIKA NATAKAM* IN DANCE AND DRAMA

The storyline of this ritual dance-theater engages with significant ethical values that the reenactment portrays to contemporary audiences. First, the story challenges the caste system among Hindus, still prevalent today, that asserts a hierarchy in which birth determines one's status and opportunities in life. *Brahmins* (priests) belong to the highest caste, followed by *kshatriyas* (warrior caste), next *vaishyas* (merchant caste), and the lowest caste, the *shudras*, who perform menial and "unclean" tasks such as cleaning latrines. This lowest caste continues to suffer much prejudice in the social hierarchy, even in India today. The *shudras* were renamed by Mahatma Gandhi as *harijans*, namely, children of God. Today, *harijans* call themselves *Dalits* (the oppressed).[6]

In *Kaisika Natakam*, the protagonist is the lowborn male devotee, Nambudavan (played by a woman), who is elevated to a status even higher than the *brahmins* when his music and devotion transform the demon back to his human shape. In other words, Nambudavan is the agent of a miracle. The story recounts that this humble man, Nambudavan, was on his way on Ekadesi to the Vishnu temple. Although as a *shudra* he cannot enter the temple, he can sing outside its physical precincts in adoration of the Lord. His journey is intercepted by a *rakshasa* (demon) that threatens to devour him (Figure 15.2).

Nambudavan pleads with the demon to allow him time to go to the temple and perform his singing ritual, after which he promises to return to the demon to be

---

[6] Violent incidents against the lowest caste in India continue today, especially in rural areas. For instance, on May 27, 2014, in Katra village (North India), a horrifying incident of two teenage girls of the lowest caste who were raped and hung by their *dupattas* (scarfs) on a tree sent shock waves across the world.

**FIGURE 15.2.** *Rakshasa* (demon). Actor-dancer: Gopika.

Photographer: Chella Video (© Anita Ratnam/Arangham Trust).

devoured. Nambudavan gives his word. The demon relents, allowing Nambudavan to go to the temple. After completing his musical worship, Nambudavan is on his way back to the demon when he encounters an old man (Lord Vishnu in disguise, played by a woman), who tries to warn Nambudavan to avoid the road where the *rakshasa* is waiting to eat his next victim. But Nambudavan insists on following that road since he had given his word to the demon to return in order to be devoured (Figure 15.3). Here again, the story raises Nambudavan to exemplary height as someone who keeps his word even at the expense of his life. It is, after all, Nambudavan's intense love for Lord Vishnu, conveyed via his devotional singing, that makes the Lord himself intervene to help him.

The story enacted in *Kaisika Natakam* "has an unusual element," remarks Lalitha Venkat, "in that it points to the special place music and dance have in religious worship in temple societies of ancient times" (2001, n.p.). These qualities of the expressive arts of music and dance are uniquely important in the reenactment efforts, which involved contemporary musicians and musicologists in recreating the rhythms, lyrics, and songs of this ritual dance-theater. These qualities have, as it were, a double import as both historically documentary and narratively substantive. Venkat continues:

FIGURE 15.3. *Rakshasa* and Nambudavan in conversation. Actor-dancer: Gopika (as demon) and Rajeswari (as Nambudavan).

Photographer: Chella Video (© Anita Ratnam/Arangham Trust).

The divisions of caste and class were blurred when it came to the purity of a devotee's intent. Similar to the practice connected with Vaikunta Ekadesi, devotees would fast and stay awake during the night of the Kaisika Ekadesi and listen to music and dance in praise of Nambi Perumal (the name given to Lord Vishnu in Thirukurungudi in Tirunelveli district of Tamilnadu). This was an act of great piety (2001, n.p.).

Moreover, the significance of music and dance in the worship of Hindu deities is a distinctive aspect of this religion's ritual practices. Hence these art forms not only entertain human beings, but also delight the deities who *require* the devotees to express their artistic abilities as part of their worship.[7] The tradition of female saint-poets, such as Andal, Akka Mahadevi, and Meera, and male devotees, such as Tyagaraja, Kabir, and Tukaram, among others, is significant in Hindu lore. These human figures attain divine status in their single-minded devotion to the Lord, expressed via ecstatic, even erotic, poems and songs; note here the connection between the physical and the spiritual in Indian aesthetic and philosophical thought discussed earlier. Andal's poems express her yearning for Lord Vishnu in explicitly physical terms.

[7] A personal note from Katrak, whose daughter, Roshni, studies classical Carnatic vocal music (of South India) in the Los Angeles area with a teacher, Shubha Narayan, from India. At one event held at the Hindu Temple in Malibu, California, celebrating a major composer-saint, Tyagaraja, of the Carnatic tradition, by singing his many compositions, Shubha asked Roshni and some of her other students to sing in front of the deity, Lord Venkateswara, as their offering, and to seek His blessings.

*Silapaddikaram* (*The Ankle Bracelet*), the second-century CE Tamil epic, dramatizes the origin of dancing. Movement and music, with gesture, dramatic dialogue, lyrical songs, and incantations, are a part of *Kaisika Natakam* that originated during the rule of the Chola dynasty (late ninth–thirteenth centuries CE). This dynasty comprised avid patrons of the arts, who built magnificent temples with stone sculptures. Chola bronzes of the Hindu gods, especially of Lord Shiva, are legendary. The Hindu religious traditions of worship reach back even further into ancient times. For instance, during the sixth–ninth centuries CE, Tamil literature included Alwar saint-poets (*alvar* translates as "immersed in divine devotion") such as the woman poet Andal, who wrote passionate love poems (describing, for instance, how her breasts long for the Lord's touch), desiring nothing short of physical union with her beloved Lord Vishnu. The key use of literary imagery and poetic expression, along with dance, for religious purposes is a significant aspect also of ritual dance-theater such as *Kaisika Natakam*. The work has, therefore, an overdetermined relation to both aesthetic and religious belief, one that demands of any enactment of its score a corresponding reenactment of this entwinement. Hence, we conceive the difference between reconstruction and reenactment to lie chiefly in this distinction.

During the same time period of *Kaisika Natakam*, the thirteenth century, one finds ecstatic poems inspired by religious devotion by practitioners of different religions, such as Rumi who wrote during what is described as the golden age of Sufi poetry. Christian mystics of the same period include Saint Francis of Assisi (1181–1226). The additional element of such religious devotional poetry in the Indian tradition is that during worship, or ritual enactments in the Hindu temples, the arts of music and dance are profoundly significant. For instance, particular songs and chanted *slokas* (religious verses) "awaken" the deities in the morning, followed by ritual offerings. In the afternoons, which are usually very hot in India, the gods "go to sleep." They are reawakened with music and dance as the sun tilts and the weather cools in the evening.

It is significant that a ritual dance-theater tradition did not suffer from the historical campaign during the 1930s by British colonizers and native Indian elites to ban the *devadasi* tradition from the temples (a complex history, told from many points of view) since such ritual dance-theaters were not part of what was considered "the great tradition."[8] Such restrictions did not apply to dance-theater rituals such as *Kaisika Natakam*, and other forms such as *Bhagavata Mela, Annan Maar Koothu, Angala Parameswari Koothu*, and *Kaatavarayan Koothu*, since they were all considered part of the "little tradition" known broadly as *koothu*, or ecstatic theater. They were not connected directly to temples, but were related to villages and specific families from whom one male actor played one of the significant roles through generations. *Koothu* traditions did not involve the *devadasis* or their families.

---

[8] There are several scholarly studies of the *devadasi* tradition and its eradication. See works cited: Peterson and Soneji (2008); Srinivasan (1985), O'Shea (2007), and Katrak (2011).

## GENDER DIMENSIONS OF *KAISIKA NATAKAM*

The contemporary reenactment of *Kaisika Natakam* features the unique gender dimensions of the original thirteenth-century ritual in which the roles of the male devotee Nambudavan and Lord Vishnu (in disguise as the old man) are played by females. This gender reversal differs from other ritual theater practices in India, such as *Kathakali, Yakshagana, Bhagvata Mela*, or *Therukoothu*, where males played female roles. In *Kaisika Natakam*, in medieval times, women playing both the human male protagonist, as well as the divine Lord Vishnu, gave the female temple artists pride of place and worship, right next to the male deity. This is an accepted practice, honored by the male priests and the assembled crowd.

One reason for this gender reversal was that the royal families of Kerala, who abided by matriarchal supremacy as the hallmark of their society, governed the temple town of Tirukurungudi for three centuries. Another possible reason could be that the devotee Nambudavan actually could have been a woman since in Tamil and South Indian society there are several historical references to female saints and poets, such as Andal and Akka Mahadevi, who were devoted to the divine.

## THE PROCESS OF RECONSTRUCTION LEADING TO REENACTMENT OF *KAISIKA NATAKAM*

A team of Tamil scholars, including Professor S. Ramanujan, musicologist Srinivasan, and dance artists such as Dr. Anita Ratnam (whose doctoral dissertation from Madras University is on the many dance and drama dimensions of *Kaisika Natakam*), dedicated four years (1996–1999) to reconstructing *Kaisika Natakam*. They painstakingly transliterated the script discovered on palm-leaf manuscript, conducted interviews with aging performers—actors, dancers—including Ramanuji Amma and Doraima, among others. This scholarly team attempted to recreate the music, songs, rhythmic patterns for the movement, and the entire affect of this performance.

Along with reconstructing the script of this ritual theater, the creative team of Tamil scholars also relied on musicians to recreate the sounds of a bygone era with instruments such as the *nagaswaram* (used in ritual practices in temples in Southern India), *irattai chinnam, shudda maddalam, kombu, damaaram, tavil*, interviews with the surviving artists (accessing memory stored in the body), theater specialists, and dancers. They all bring research, scholarship and artistic activity together in this reenactment.

Ratnam, a performing artist of contemporary Indian dance (based in *bharatanatyam*, along with her style of contemporary Indian dance that she names Neo-Bharatam—a hybrid of modern dance, theater tools, martial arts, storytelling) redefines the sacred in her choreography on parallel mythologies and goddess traditions. As a scholar, and a native speaker of Tamil, Ratnam's interest in the sacred provides a base for her work in reviving *Kaisika Natakam* in Tirukurungudi, her ancestral village.

Multiple challenges faced Ratnam and Ramanujam in their efforts to reconstruct the ritual dance-theater. "There were very few traces of the script, music, movement and style," remarks Ratnam in her article in *Sruti* (2000). "Prof. Ramanujam had extensive discussions with musicologist Vaithialingam in Chennai," continues Ratnam, with "natyacharya Herabanathan of Tanjavur and musicians of the Melattur Bhagvata Mela. Out of these discussions emerged a framework" (50). The selected artists from Tanjavur were taken to Tirukurungudi village, continues Ratnam, "to meet the traditional performers of Kaisiki Natakam at the Nambi temple" (*Sruti*, 51). This meeting was highly productive and "many new discoveries about the dance, music, and dialogue were made during casual conversations with the traditional artists and local residents" (51).

After this initial meeting, "a prototype of the reconstructed *Kaisiki Natakam*" remarks Ratnam, "was revealed to a group of writers, theater directors, musicians and dramatists from Chennai, Tanjavur, and Madurai on 15 September 1999 at the Venkatesa Perumal sannidhi in Tanjavur. It was accepted by everyone and it was agreed that the artists would work towards a full-length performance in Tirukurungudi on Kaisiki Ekadasi on 19 November 1999" (Ratnam 2000, 51). Nearly 3,000 people gathered at the main temple to see this historic reenactment with twenty-two actors and musicians from Tanjavur and five traditional Tirukurungudi performers. The latter included seventy-two-year-old Kurungadi Amma, and eighty-four-year-old Ramanuji Ammal, who used to play the role of Nambi Perumal (Lord Vishnu) disguised as an old man. Ratnam notes that although this first phase of the reconstruction was a successful three hour and fifteen minute performance, the "full revitalization is still in progress .... Specialists in music and movement are being enlisted to work with the artists to reconstruct the entire five-hour ritual drama" (2000, 50).

The 1999 performance triggered—after a long break in time—memories in the elderly residents of Tirukurungudi, who made "invaluable inputs," remarks Ratnam in her article in *Sruti*. "Several women have come forward and offered their earlier memories of how the actors would move or speak, their tone and their mannerisms. All the suggestions have been recorded and noted for implementation" in future reenactments of this ritual dance-theater. The original length of the play was about six hours—we decided that this length would not work for today's audiences. Hence, we have edited it down to a four hour version that starts around ten p.m. and ends around two a.m." (2000, 51).

Current reenactments of *Kaisika Natakam* are not simply mimetic in terms of recreating a replica of what occurred in the past. Rather, such reenactments, based on tools of scholarly textual materials and orally recorded memories of surviving elderly artists who sang and danced in this ritual, offer a present-ness of the past, albeit "preserving" it on one level as a significant part of the community's history, but also breathing new life into it as appropriate for today's audiences. This reenactment involves a creative balancing act between the textual archival materials and oral "texts" in recorded interviews and in recreating movement and music via these sources. Such material is now part of the archive for this ritual dance-theater form. Diana Taylor's formative book, *The Archive and the Repertoire* (2003), reminds us that recorded materials—in history books, as well as in the muscle memory of live bodies, the "embodied memory" of past performers— are crucial components of reenacted art.

The challenge in finding records of Indian dance movement styles from medieval times lies in the fact that this remains basically an oral transmission of knowledge from teacher to student (even today with the use of recordings, or learning via Skype). There is no recognized form of notation for Indian dance—different teachers and students evolve their own "written" memory banks for their embodied learning process. The reenactment of the ritual dance-theater (which also undergoes change from one year to the next) involves interpretation and reinterpretation of the materials. Here, to use Mark Franko's evocative phrase, there is a "trend to quote choreography" (In Franko's Proposal for this volume). In the Indian context, "dance composition" with *abhinaya* (gesture language) may be more appropriate than the word "choreography." What traditional gurus in India term "dance composition" refers mainly to using traditionally codified dance technique and putting different segments of movement together in order to make a whole. Although dance composition certainly involves creativity, it is of a different kind from what one understands by "choreography" in the Western world. "Choreography" is not a word native to Indian languages. It is derived from the Greek *khoreia* (dance) and *graphia* (to write). Recall the earlier comment that the transmission of dance training and composition in the Indian context is oral, with no system of written dance notation. Choreography, on the other hand, is a field of study in which artists train and attain skills to deploy and combine different movement techniques with the option to have written records, along with the consideration of overall effect, which may include input from lighting, sound, and costume designers, as well as the use of stage space.

# The Temporal Dimension
# in Reenactment

> To witness a reenactment is to be a bystander, a passer-by, possibly out of step in the leak of another time, or in a syncopated temporal relationship to the event that (some) participants hope will *touch the actual past* at least in a partial or incomplete or fragmented manner.
>
> Schneider 2011, 9; emphasis in original

Rebecca Schneider's formative work on the subject of reenactment includes a nuanced analysis of the *temporal dimension* of how the past is brought into focus in the present in the remounting of past historical events, or artworks that may have fallen into oblivion. Re-enactors, witnesses, and bystanders are all involved "in a knotty and porous relationship to time" (Schneider 2011, 10). In *Kaisika Natakam*, the memories of elderly artists who once performed in this ritual dance-theater raise the complex intermediations of time in reenactment. As Schneider remarks,

> The temporality of reenactment and the inter(in)animation . . . of intermedia, of syncopated time, and of theatrical acts [make] the experience of reenactment (whether in replayed art or in replayed war) an intense, embodied inquiry into temporal repetition, temporal recurrence. As such, an exploration of affect *as* inquiry . . . and the promises and pitfalls of such investigations [are] at the edges of every example of reenactment. (Schneider 2011, 1–2; emphasis in original)

As with any reenactment, "the political stakes," remarks Schneider, are significant in replaying "apparent beginnings and apparent endings of events, performances, and modern art to theatre stages" via the tools of "repetitions, doublings, and the call and response of cross- and inter-authorships" (2011, 11). Schneider recognizes the increased popularity in present times of recreating "living history" via restaging past historical events such as the Civil War. The reenactment acts, notes Schneider, are part of an "academic 'memory industry' . . . [that] attempt[s] to literally touch time through the residue of the gesture or the cross-temporality of the pose" (2011, 2). Schneider asks provocatively, "what if time (re)turns? What does it take along with it?" In the effort to replicate, recreate, or reenact an art form, there is a citational dimension—of the past, and also of the "before, during and after of any action *taking place* in or as re-action: the affected effects and the after-affects of art/events posed as relative to origin(al)s" (2011, 2; emphasis in original). The coming together of the past with the present is as significant in our analysis of *Kaisika Natakam* as are the historical, critical, and theoretical implications of what Mark Franko describes as "the return of past work" (Franko's Proposal for this volume).

*Kaisika Natakam*'s reenactment is both faithful to its historical reconstruction and simultaneously is not frozen in time; indeed, it is reinterpreted by contemporary artists. As Schneider remarks in *Performance Remains*,

> The experience of reenactment . . . is an intense, embodied inquiry into temporal repetition, temporal recurrence . . . . Reenactors in art . . . try to bring that time—that prior moment—to the very fingertips of the present . . . I am interested in repetitions, doublings, and the call and response of cross- and inter-authorships. (2011, 1–2)

Our discussion of this ritual dance-theater relies on the reenactment of movement and music, enabled through the reconstruction of historical documentation by the scholarly labor of historians, artists, and musicologists interpreting the original text. Issues of translation certainly confront not only non-Tamil-language speakers; even Tamil speakers need to decipher the text from medieval Tamil into modern-day patterns of speech. After all, the reenactment of a thirteenth-century ritual dance-theater work needs to speak to a contemporary audience that is used to today's speech patterns, not to mention modern elements of stagecraft, lighting, and technology, even in a village in India. *Kaisika Natakam*'s reenactment brings today's audiences into a connection with its ritual dimensions.

The news of this ritual dance-theater's successful reenactment has spread far and wide as more and more spectators make the journey to Tirukurungudi to witness it. Ratnam comments on the growing audiences for this event:

> Audiences have grown immensely. Crowds now number up to 3000 with close[d] circuit giant TV screens that are being planned for this year (2014). Music and theatre scholars have attended from France and Norway and several CEOs and top corporates have begun attending from around India. The age group is still largely over 45 years but the numbers have expanded considerably since I saw the performance in 1996 when 4 artistes were on stage and 3 people watching. (email May 23, 2014)

The local and global audiences traveling to this remote village in order to experience this ritual dance-theater live also encountered technology via closed-circuit giant TV screens in 2014 in order to reach more spectators. As Schneider remarks,

> "Live" and "liveness" are words that sometimes attend, like difficult cousins, to reenactment, for reenactment as a performance practice appears to "take place" in time, live, even as the times that take place are given to be multiple, layered, or crossed. (2011, 90)

The theoretical distinctions between "live" and "recorded" are complex. Is "live" to be interpreted as happening in the now (and hence its temporal aspect is its most defining feature), as opposed to a "live recording" that can be viewed at any time long after the event/performance? Performance studies scholars Philip Auslander and Peggy Phelan hold different positions on the phenomenon of "liveness." According to Auslander, "live performance is always already inscribed with traces of the possibility of technical mediation (i.e. mediatization) that defines it as live" (1999, 53). For Phelan, live performance indicates "representation without reproduction." She asserts that "performance's independence from mass reproduction, technologically, economically, and linguistically, is its greatest strength" (1993, 146). I agree with Phelan's position that live performance is different from any kind of reproduction. This distinction of live bodies on stage holds true, even with Auslander's argument that "traces of technical mediation" are present in live performance. In our increasingly media-saturated world, we may well have to contend with different forms of "liveness"—the kind that Phelan upholds, the flesh-and-blood human actor or dancer, as well as the reproduction of breathing human beings on video, film, smartphone cameras, and so on.

In the case of audiences of *Kaisika Natakam*, the introduction of closed-circuit large TV screens as the mediated form through which they experienced this ritual dance-theater in November 2014 was a significant watershed moment. How satisfactory will TV mediation be to audiences, rural or global, who today are used to media images? Television came to India only in the 1970s. Will they miss the "liveness" of dramatic characters of the story, such as the lively demon, threatening to eat the protagonist Nambudavan and extending his threat to squealing children in the audience? Or, will his "likeness" on the screen be adequately affective in replacing the live human actor/dancer? What is at stake here is that the cultural context in twenty-first-century India has shifted from the 1980s onward with the proliferation of new media. Now, technology via giant TV screens enables the simultaneous presentation of the live performance to audiences inside the temple, and to many more spectators outside, since they cannot be accommodated inside the temple hall. Today, villagers and cosmopolitan onlookers visiting from metropolitan urban locations in India or from abroad are increasingly media savvy. But are the ritual gains from viewing this reenactment the same for those viewing the projection on TV screens as for those sitting on the floor of the temple, witnessing live performers? The initial 2014 audience viewing the performance on giant TV screens found the experience as vital as witnessing a live program. Although a TV reproduction does not substitute or supersede the live performance, it is simply strategic in accommodating more viewers who, in today's world, are familiar with digital technology. I personally would not wish to give up the liveness of seeing the performance, sitting close together with many villagers and their families on the temple floor and savoring the textures, the smells, the live music, along with the breathing and sweating actors/dancers and the overall participatory nature of the event.

This chapter has traced the process of reconstructing *Kaisika Natakam*, which remains valuable to its custodian community and is now a lasting part of Tirukurungudi village's heritage. Its reconstruction has resulted in successful theatrical reenactments of its performance each year, and has generated interest beyond the borders of the village to include audiences from across India and beyond. Although challenges of "translation" remain in terms of making this ritual dance-theater accessible to audiences from across India and transnationally, this key dance-theater ritual of India is of significant scholarly interest to dance, ritual, and theater scholars across the world.

In conclusion, *Kaisika Natakam* is a successful reenactment in terms of performative and affective dimensions, strong characterization of archetypal roles of a humble devotee who gains the Lord's intervention in saving his life, or the demon that through the power of devotional music regains his human form. This unique artistic form, when reenacted on the auspicious day of Ekadesi each year, fulfills the community's religious goals. The attendees, as spectators/participants, believe that they receive Lord Vishnu's blessings by simply being present physically at this ritual dance-theater.

Ultimately, the ritual base of this dance-theater form remains most significant, as Hindu devotees believe that their very physical presence at the ritual dance-theater, viewing the simple story that challenges caste and gender boundaries, will bring them divine blessings. *Kaisika Natakam* reaches across historical time to speak to us today, from medieval to contemporary times.

## WORKS CITED

Auslander, Philip. 2009. *Liveness: Performance in a Mediatized Culture.* London and New York: Routledge.

Elswit, Kate. 2014. "Inheriting Dance's Alternative Histories." *Dance Research Journal* 46(1) (April): 23–40.

Foster, Susan Leigh. 1995. "Choreographing History: Manifesto for Dead and Moving Bodies." In *Choreographing History*, edited by Susan Leigh Foster, 3–21. Bloomington and Indianapolis: Indiana University Press.

Franko, Mark. 1989. "Repeatability, Reconstruction, and Beyond," *Theater Journal* 41(1): 56–74.

Katrak, Ketu H. 2011. (2014, paperback). *Contemporary Indian Dance: New Creative Choreography in India and the Diaspora.* Basingstoke, UK: Palgrave Macmillan.

O'Shea, Janet. 2007. *At Home in the World: Bharata Natyam on the Global Stage.* Middletown, CT: Wesleyan University Press.

Peterson Viswanathan, Indira, and Davesh Soneji. 2008, eds. *Performing Pasts: Reinventing the Arts in Modern South Asia.* New Delhi: Oxford University Press.

Phelan, Peggy. 1993. *Unmarked: The Politics of Performance.* London and New York: Routledge.

Ratnam, Anita. 2000. "Kaisiki Natakam: A Report on a Revival Project." *Sruti: A Monthly Magazine on Indian Performing Arts* (July, Chennai): 49–51.

Schneider, Rebecca. 2011. *Performance Remains: Art and War in Times of Theatrical Reenactment.* London and New York: Routledge.

Srinivasan, Amrit. 1985. "Reform and Revival: The Devadasi and Her Dance." *Economic and Political Weekly* 20(44) (November 2): 1869–1876.

Taylor, Diana. 2003. *The Archive and the Repertoire.* Durham, NC: Duke University Press.

Venkat, Lalitha. 2001. "Reconstructing and Reviving an Ancient Temple Theater Ritual." Interview with Professor Ramanujam. (December) www.nathaki.com.

# CHAPTER 16

# GLORIOUSLY INEPT AND SATISFYINGLY TRUE

## Reenactment and the Practice of Spectating

### P. A. SKANTZE

Animal Noises, not necessarily authentic.

—Stage direction, *All That Fall*, Samuel Beckett

## THE PRACTICE OF SPECTATING

"IT is characteristic" of the practice of spectating "that it must continually confront the question of representation" (Benjamin 1998, 27).[1] Borrowing Walter Benjamin's opening line in his "Epistemo-Critical Prologue" to *The Origin of German Tragic Drama* (1928), I have taken the liberty of replacing Benjamin's words "philosophical writing" with "the practice of spectating." Benjamin, in his lively and dramatic sense of philosophy, illustrates how the demands on the writer and the writing must follow "tirelessly" the process of thinking as it "makes new beginnings" and returns in "a roundabout way" (28). Questioning the common understanding of philosophy as a "guide to the acquisition of knowledge," Benjamin advises instead an "exercise" of the form, the action of doing philosophy, rather than settling for a collection of safe axioms. In order to confront the problem of representation, Benjamin names his method for this paradoxically active contemplation as "essentially representation" (28). The "exercise" in Benjamin's

---

[1] I would like to thank Mark Franko, without whose vibrant research seminar on Walter Benjamin's *The Origin of German Tragic Drama* in London (May 2014) I would not have made what now seems to me a rich connection between Benjamin's exploration of method and the epistemology of practice, particularly the practice of spectating. See Franko 2017.

complicated challenge to German philosophy and literary culture, I would suggest, translates to the "practice" in spectating: the experience both of being an audience member and the demands made on the writing driven by the necessity to communicate, indeed to represent what one has heard and seen.

As I have suggested throughout *Itinerant Spectator/Itinerant Spectacle* (2013), a spectator who is in the midst of a practice when spectating becomes an active partner in the making of performance. While careful and interesting analysis of the audience has long been a feature of writing about dance, theater, and performance in the field, this work has focused mainly on the conditions and quality of being an audience in general, or has emanated from the perspective of the writer who recounts a performance in something like a review or who studies it in something like semiotic analysis. The potential in exploring the spectator as practitioner shifts not only how we write as scholars/critics about performance itself, but also how we manifest in our writing and our showing not only what we have seen and heard when we are spectators, but also what we have made of what we have seen and heard. It is no accident that Benjamin's topic in his extraordinary thesis on method is drama. And no accident that he further develops the section on method as essentially representation: "Method is a digression. Representation as digression" (1998, 28).

If the spectator embarks upon a practice, then like the philosopher, he or she begins with the question of method, and the method itself, as Benjamin argues, depends upon motion and patience, a willingness to digress, and a belief that the digression, while itself perhaps not immediately comprehensible, solicits an apprehension, a sensual understanding:

> A methodology of suggestion rather than argument, an invitation to look together rather than a flat rendering of the afterimage, the leftover surface of the remembered performance. A methodology, I might name it and indeed hope to replicate it, of narrative care, tenderly lifting the boiling beaker from the Bunsen burner to place it on the countertop, infinitesimal movements necessary for the discoveries small and grand. W. G. Sebald practices such a methodology in his work . . . [Sebald] models a kind of observing that facilitates reflection on, in his case, observing and history, in mine, being a spectator . . . [his]method a kind of staging of memory, a reanimation with intent, choosing where to exaggerate, where to indicate with a faint nod what those of us reading his hypnotic prose might want to give more attention to for ourselves. (Skantze 2013, vii)

A reader of this *Handbook* on danced reenactment will by now already have noted the recurrence of terms used in the discussion of any reenactment: memory, history, reflection, reanimation. The conscious remaking of a dance, of a performance, awakens a responsibility in the makers, but often we overlook the call and response embedded in the act of reenactment: the receivers knowing that they are witnessing something "done again"—notwithstanding the mixed motives on the part of the makers—collect the information of their watching and their hearing, and construct meaning.

# REENACTMENT

> Once an occasional spectator of dance I soon became an impassioned
> one. So much of the training in the itinerant practice of spectating hap-
> pens by accumulation, by the first curious move towards something . . . .
> The *flâneuring* becomes richer with an accumulated collection of experi-
> ences, my growing recognition that the performances that "spoke" to me
> the strongest spoke through choreography and sound. Yet the spectator/
> collector has no cabinet of curiosities beyond her own memory, more of
> a storage space marked by potential than a box to open in order to see
> an object, moments come alive again in reprise by the effect of what I am
> seeing or any of the coercive conjunctions that reignite memory. (Skantze
> 2013, 166–167)

Metaphorically speaking, a practicing spectator enters the archive at the performance
of a reenactment.[2] She does not enter the archive as a visitor at a distance; she enters the
archive as a *spectator* at a distance, into whose purview come bits of a collection performed before her, a collection of received gestures, a collection of duets, solos, ensembles redone, reconstructed. To read in a program or hear in the announcement of a
narrator that "this is a reenactment of . . ." is to be placed between past and present. Even
if one has no prior model—has not seen the original, does not know the work being
reenacted or the work of the artist/choreographer being invoked—a spectator nevertheless begins to assemble and interpret against an imagined background of past production and present performance.

The "imagined background" supplied by the spectator is what distinguishes thinking about reception as a practice of spectating from the common practice of assuming
a passive receiver of performance or, as commonly, an entity called an audience, whose
responses are accounted for en masse. Spectatorship as a practice collaborates in the
making of work, anticipates, experiences, and reflects in the before, during, and after
of performance. What I develop in *Itinerant Spectator/Itinerant Spectacle*, however, is
not a model of the "participant spectator," a term frequently used in the context of reenactment where certain historical reconfigurations encourage, nay urge, the watcher
to be participator, as Rebecca Schneider describes in *Performance Remains: Art and
War in Times of Theatrical Reenactment* (2011, 14). Too often a choreographer or performer assumes that participation can only be solicited by directly addressing the audience, supposedly making the audience a "part" of the work. Such assumptions forget,
or worse dismiss, the autonomy of the spectator, who can always be a part of the work
by doing his or her part. Jacques Rancière, describing the emancipation of the spectator, insists on a "capacity of the anonymous, the capacity that makes everyone equal to

---

[2]  I am indebted to both Matthew Fink and Flora Pitrolo and their insights in the conversation about
reenactment.

everybody." Paradoxically, the heat of the connection between spectator and dancer can occur "through unpredictable and irreducible distances" (2007, 279). In practice, this can mean that one can be "too close" sitting at the back of a theater, and at a distance while standing beside the performers (2013, 181).

Reenactment then might call for all sorts of responses from a spectator, whether in a traditional space for dance or in a more intimate setting. The distance, the gap between maker and receiver already present in theater and dance performance, underlies the theatricality on which Rebecca Schneider insists in reenactment, as she moves Richard Schechner's theory of "twice-behaved behavior" into the realm of the uncanny: "we might use his insights to explore how the very explicit *twiceness* of reenactment trips the otherwise daily condition of repetition into reflexive hyper-drive, expanding the experience into the uncanny"( Schneider 2011, 14; emphasis in original). Schneider herself writes as one steeped in the culture of every form of reenactment in *Performing Remains*, and the reinstating of the "theatrical" in her study, I would argue, comes in part from her own complex practice as a spectator. The evocation of how reenactment works in all the media she discusses comes through the recounting of her experience as a spectator, indivisible from the complex interdisciplinary theories she brings to bear on reenactment.

Not all spectators engage in a practice, any more than all reiterations of art are reenactments. A "time-based art," the practice of spectating works by accumulation, and as in any art, there is a period of apprenticeship to the medium. As varied as the practice of choreography or dramaturgy and as idiosyncratic, the recognition of spectating as a practice may begin with a consciousness brought on by the confrontation with the "problem of representation" in the practice of writing. However, spectators engaged in a practice do not necessarily turn to the medium of writing to communicate; the practicing spectator might compare, for example, a gesture or move, a directorial choice, and incorporate this knowledge into future creations for performance, or into the studio or classroom in a form of representation as oral transmission. Wherever the practice takes the spectator, the accumulation of performances seen and heard provokes "an intense, embodied inquiry into temporal repetition, temporal recurrence"; the spectator embarks on an exploration of "affect *as* inquiry" (Schneider 2011, 2; emphasis in original). While Schneider employs the terms I have quoted earlier specifically for reenactments historical and theatrical, as I have suggested, her investigation by way of repetition describes as well the repetition made by the body that always recurs in relation to all modes of witnessing and receiving, whether a dance performance or a historical battle reenacted: that of the spectator.

# ULTIMA VEZ, *BOOTY LOOTING*

On a stage prepared for what could be a piece of theater or a piece of music, with an electric guitar, amplifiers, a soundboard to the left of the empty space, a man walks out.

I expect a piece of dance, but I have been a dance spectator long enough to know that "to expect a piece of dance" in 2014 might mean anything from a mass of leotard-clad bodies to a man standing on stage speaking and not moving. This man tonight begins to speak, and his speech immediately falls into the category of narration. Now I am wary: I don't like to be told ahead of time about "what we are going to be doing" or what I as the spectator can expect. Old-fashioned in my love of show, I want it to be the dancers' work, the performers' work, to unfold for me in time the ingredients of a dance or piece of theater and then to swirl them together into meaning, to encourage me to make meaning in the swirl with them.

So I stiffen a little in my seat, but the man—affable, European in that "easy with his feminine side" way—tells us that the company will reenact Joseph Beuys's *I Like America and America Likes Me* 1974 performance in a gallery. I relax a bit. I confess this relaxation is due in part to my admiration for Beuys. Even just the idea of Beuys in the air, as against other performance artists whose work could and has been reenacted a great deal lately, makes me want to see what the company is going to do. Then the narrator, Jerry Killick, continues. He talks to us in the way one does when you assume common knowledge, about the piece with the felt and the fat and the stick and the coyote. In the back of my mind I "remember" pictures of a man who looked a bit like a tepee with a stick or a cane coming out of it, of an animal, of a gallery. These memories are mixed with the work of Beuys I have seen, work always made of rough material tactile even to the eye: scratchy fabric, chalky bricks, gritty dirt.

Then Killick looks out at us, somewhat sheepishly, and says, "We don't have a coyote [pause] but we have dancers who will be the coyote." Most of the audience laugh, simultaneously forgiving the inauthenticity of this part of the reenactment and marking the absurd trade of four dancers for the coyote. Then the figure of Beuys is constructed on stage before me. They have the felt, but for the stick they use a broom with the handle sticking out of the felt at the top, so now the stick of memory comes sharper into my mind: its dark curve in direct contrast to the smooth, blonde, round handle sticking out of felt. The dancers enter, ferocious and fast. They circle the Beuys figure, menace conveyed by jumps and twists, a kind of Animal Planet breakdancing. The energy and the keen interest of the coyote (here the coyotes) comes through the bodily power of the dancers.

The leaps and twirls, their approaches as they grab at the felt, all look animalistic. I well know I am doing the work of translation that is spectating, willingly supplying the context set forth for me by the narrator—the past performance with the coyote and Beuys. But dance itself, as a form of performance that animates space, offers me the gaps in time and talk from which I construct from this, it must be said, meager archive of the narrator's instruction, and some materials that evoke a past performance of a brilliant, politically vital artist. So the work becomes more urgent for its being played out against the storeroom in my memory marked "Josef Beuys." I am in the midst of dwelling in what Mark Franko terms "subjective reminiscence," as I must be in order to practice as a spectator. Franko and Benjamin converge in Franko's vital notion of our work in archives as scholars, but also, I would argue, this is heightened by our practice as spectators when we merge "an imaginary performance practice" with the performance before us, "returning theory"—and with Benjamin, we might say confronting representation to return theory—"to its etymological roots in vision and speculation" (Franko 1993, 152; Franko and Richards 2000, 1).

Everything about this basic description of what happens on stage should convey how "wrong" the reenactment is, how off, how inaccurate. Who is in the room that night at the Queen Elizabeth Hall in November 2013 in London? For how many people does the name Josef Beuys bring to mind the artist's work, the artist's interventions? For how many does the felt and stick remind them of the subsequent debunking of Beuy's wartime story about being discovered after his plane crashed in the Crimea in World War II, when Tartars warmed his freezing body by wrapping him in animal fat and felt? Some, while reading the program notes before the performance, have learned of Beuys for the first time. Some may have seen *I Like America and America Likes Me*, and some may be watching a dance where a man wrapped up in felt with a broomstick sticking out of it makes himself a target for hungry dancers.

How many things go on at a performance, and even more at a performance that marks itself as a reenactment. Here dance visits performance art to reanimate it, and to offer a rich collection for what I described earlier as a kind of spectator's moment in the embodied archive. A reasoned argument, perhaps what Benjamin might place in the category of knowledge as acquisition, would suggest that the inaccuracy, the flaunting of approximations such as dancers substituting for a coyote, would conclude that this reenactment was a failure: a failure of labor and the time it takes to redo with care and precision the original performance. Of course that would be not untrue, to use a Miltonic phrase. In the medium of photography, for example, two photographs set next to one another to be compared, one labeled the original and one scrutinized to see how well the copy holds up against it, might indeed show conclusively the remarkably true or glaringly false. But when put into motion through dance, and with the addition of an audience in the space between the original invoked and the work being made, the mistakes and misprisions awaken the third term: the spectator who is in the midst of her practice of reception and interpretation.

A spectator's experience of original practices in Shakespeare studies, of original instruments in the search for the true sound of Bach, or original moves in the Baroque dance, can prove to the watcher the truth of an odd reception paradox: the more accurate the reproduction, the more boring the reperforming. Of course the arc extending from the accurate of reenactment performances to the wildly inaccurate is much fuller than I can account for here in this chapter. But the general rule of really, really faithful extinguishing the life of the now from the redoing holds. As Schneider theorizes when writing of the Wooster Group's theatrical reenactment of *Poor Theatre*: "watching the *exact* replication from the audience, it seems as though the more they got the reenactment exactly right, the more *uncannily* wrong it began to feel" (2011, 112). Schneider's assessment reminded me of the inexplicable effects of another Wooster Group's production of *Hamlet*. The choreography of that theatrical reenactment of a film with Richard Burton from the 1960s demanded that the performers work to match camera angles, with bodies shifting while speaking the lines in time to the muted voices of the actors on the screen. As an early modern scholar who has worked with the plays and the performance history of Shakespeare productions, I have had several conversations with Shakespeare scholars and directors about how this performance might get us closer to something original in the way the play worked on stage than does the setting of the Globe, the use of the "correct folio," and the insistence on gesture and pronunciation.

Why should this be true? The Wooster Group uses more technology per square inch of stage—not to mention the earphones from which emit directions from Elizabeth LeCompte during the performance itself—than was dreamed of in the philosophy of Horatio. But not unlike the Bullwinkle cartoon episodes of "Fractured Fairytales," the story we may have forgotten, or a performance lodged in a cultural unconscious where, as Joseph Roach suggests, "memory reveals itself as imagination," appears sharper and more distinct for the flaw in the retelling (1996, 3). The flaws or approximations in the reenactment can prompt the spectator to correct by memory, to supply from memory the "original" as best it is lodged there, and to adjust, augment, and realign so that the memory of the past sharpens while the pleasure/intrigue/annoyance of the present heightens a sense of the making—affect *as* inquiry, as Schneider tells us.

Wim Vandekeybus, choreographer and founder of the company Ultima Vez, in *Booty Looting* sets his faux dancing reenactment firmly within the hall of mirrors that is performed memory acting in the performed moment. (The evocation of continuous reenactment was emphasized in the premiere of *Booty Looting* in 2012 on the occasion of the twenty-fifth anniversary of the company, when Vandekeybus paired it with a reperformance of his first piece, tellingly titled *What the Body Does Not Remember*.) Among the dancers and the narrator and the Beuys figure roams a contemporary sign of the always already archived, the photographer. As the photographer moves around the action on stage, his stills are projected onto a screen behind the set. To this stuff of reenactment moving on stage between Beuys, dancer coyotes, and the photographer as predator, Vandekeybus adds a "character" whose name is Birgit Walter. A striking and elegant woman, tall, somewhere in middle age and wearing a white robe, walks to the center of the stage and falls face first in the way that makes the audience flinch in sympathy. She hits the floor: "I am dead." Of course the audience laughs as I do, in the reassurance that someone who says "I am dead" cannot quite be yet. But this gesture, which follows the Beuys, keeps us firmly in the land of reenactment. Walter is "dead" because she will now, by way of the narrator's repetition of her name and descriptions of her brilliance as an actor, be the centrepiece for the group of dancers. The dancers physically embody a response to the memory of the actor Birgit Walter. They move against her as we hear about her extraordinary talent, and as we hear about her less than extraordinary history as a mother, the latter seeming to be the role in reenactment most associated with disappointment.

Walter's career as an actor is evoked by the narrator the way one might hear of great actors such as Lauren Bacall, whose work remains in film memory and whose presence and the sound of her voice are unforgettable. I wonder who she is as I watch this woman, resurrected to then become a kind of not exactly dancing still figure in the fury of her neglected dancer sons and daughter. I am supposed to wonder who she is; this is part of Vandekeybus's collection that he offers me as prompts to memory, or more exactly, as prompts to remind me of the falseness of memory and of the susceptibility to belief a willing spectator might experience. Set alongside the historical fact of an artist named Josef Beuys, Walter takes on the status for me of someone who must be an actor known to Belgians and their European counterparts. Even the program, which lists one of the players as Birgit Walter, doesn't entirely erase the possibility of a real Walter. Meanwhile, I am captivated by this woman on stage and discomfited by the unfolding of a story too familiar even to those of us who are not mothers: how angry—in a heteronormative and, I fear, also in a non-heteronormative world—men and women still are at the perceived flaws of women who cannot assure their sons and daughters enough that they love them more than their own bodies, work, husbands, girlfriends, etc.

In this series of fierce dancing and petty persistent acts of violence narrating the "life" of Birgit Walter, an awkward object completes the triptych of reenactment in *Booty Looting*. A Xerox machine, a large one belonging to an office, with the capacity to make multiple copies, stands center stage. Documentation comes to the fore. Of course a more familiar kind of documentation has been with us in the body of the photographer. But the Xerox machine in its bulk matches the multiplication of the coyote into dancers because it is wrong, unwieldy. And when the dancers press Walter's face down on the glass plate and press "copy," out comes a poster-sized reproduction; the flat piece of paper then gets pinned to a piece of flat scenery, a memento of someone not gone.

Both the copier and the fat/felt/broom offer to the spectator a reflection on past and present. The agile photographer, shooting artfully made stills, which we the spectators see immediately on the scale of a large screen, plays mobile contrast to the bulk of the copier. The bodies of Walter and the dancers, who at some point all get "copied," tell by their strange contortions as they try to match the one-dimensionality of the Xerox plate how copy distorts, how round we are despite the fantasies of a virtual world, where we are as thin and shiny as a screen. The faces scrunch, the cheeks merge with eyes; still the large poster copies are arresting—much more arresting than the photographs taken in the moment before us, the implied proof in the immediate document that what we see is what is happening.

And the Beuys felt sans fat? All of the dance made around this reenactment might for some spectators remind us of the bargains made for authenticity or accuracy. A man, an artist, wrapped in felt with fat, the curve of a cane sticking up from this human huddle, and a coyote, curious, attracted to the smell of fat. Here is an intimacy and a sensuous terrain that belongs not only to the gallery where it occurred and the smallness of scale of that room, but also to the absence of spectators holding iPhones or cameras, circling with perhaps a bit less corporeal interest than the coyote, hungry for proof of having been there, if not hungry for animal fat.

I did not see *I Like America and America Likes Me*, but *Booty Looting* made me remember the context in which it was made, as well as making me move, propelled by the particular kind of musing that dance provides to the spectator—a musing something very much like the philosophical state of contemplation Benjamin describes, where writing (spectating) "must stop and restart with every new sentence" (1998, 29). Sitting relatively still in my seat, I am moving, moving between questions ("Is there really a Birgit Walter?") and desires ("I wish I had seen *I Like America and America Likes Me*"), collecting the instruments, improvised electric guitar, cameras, Xerox machines, brooms, making meaning by setting the past, the imperfectly rendered, approximate past against the present, the impossibly cluttered and yearning present.

## WORKS CITED

Benjamin, Walter. 1998. *The Origin of German Tragic Drama*. Translated by John Osborne. London: Verso Books

Franko, Mark. 1993. *Dance as Text: Ideologies of the Baroque Body*. Cambridge and New York: Cambridge University Press.

Franko, Mark, and Annette Richards, eds. 2000. *Acting on the Past: Historical Performances across Disciplines*. Hanover, NH, and London: Wesleyan University Press.

Franko, Mark. "The Conduct of Contemplation and the Gestural Ethics of Interpretation in Walter Benjamin's 'Epistemo-Critical Prologue.'" *Performance Philosophy* 2(3) (2017): 'Towards an Ethics of Gesture', edited by Lucia Ruprecht, forthcoming.

Rancière, Jacques. 2007. "The Emancipated Spectator." *Artforum* (March): 267–281.

Roach, Joseph. 1996. *Cities of the Dead: Circum-Atlantic Performance*. New York: Columbia University Press.

Schneider, Rebecca. 2011. *Performing Remains: Art and War in Times of Theatrical Reenactment*. London and New York: Routledge.

Skantze, P. A. 2013. *Itinerant Spectator/Itinerant Spectacle*. New York: Punctum.

# PART VI

THE POLITICS OF
REENACTMENT

# CHAPTER 17

# BLASTING OUT OF THE PAST

*The Politics of History and Memory in Janez
Janša's Reconstructions*

RAMSAY BURT

THREE works by the Slovenian director Janez Janša (formerly Emile Hrvatin) during
the 2000s open up significant issues concerning the politics of history and memory in
reconstructions and reenactments. The first of these, in 2006, was a reconstruction and
reenactment of a controversial happening, *Pupilija, papa Pupilo pa Pupilčki* (*Pupilija,
papa Pupilo and the Pupilceks*), created in Ljubljana in 1969 by a group of young concrete
poets and visual artists. The second, in 2007, was a performance *Fake It!* which included
unauthorized versions of famous works by Pina Bausch, Trisha Brown, Tatsumi
Hijikata, and others. For the third, in 2009, Janša worked with Dušan Jovanović, who
had been part of the group that in 1969 had created *Pupilija* and is now a celebrated
Slovenian director; together they created *Spomenik G2 (Monument G2)*, a reconstruction of the latter's early piece of experimental physical theater, *Spomenik G*, from 1972.
Until Janša reconstructed them, *Pupilija* and *Monument G* were largely forgotten and,
for a younger generation, entirely unknown. In neither case, however, was Janša trying
to reconstruct the works authentically as they might have been performed in the mid-
twentieth century. Instead, these two productions, through reenactment, drew attention
to the processes of their reconstruction, revealing their archival sources, and explicitly
posing questions about the meaning of doing so today, both for Slovenians and for the
wider international community. *Fake It!* was in effect a reperformance of famous works
from the canon of recent dance history, but, like the other two, it drew attention to what
it was doing while posing questions about the meaning of doing so in Ljubljana at that
time. All disrupted an approach that tacitly supports normative assumptions about the
history of experimental performance. To put it simply, Yugoslavia during the communist period is not where such work is generally supposed to have taken place, while post-
communist Slovenia is widely assumed to be behind, striving to catch up with what are
supposedly more advanced developments in the West.

Walter Benjamin, in his essay "On the Concept of History" (often referred to as "Thesis on the philosophy of history"), writes about blasting "a specific era out of the homogeneous course of history, blasting a specific life out of the era or a specific work out of the lifework"; when this is done, he suggests, one can recognize "a revolutionary chance in the fight for the oppressed past" (1973, 265). With *Pupilija, Monument G2*, and *Fake It!* Janša chose to make a calculated use of reconstruction and reperformance to present works that were strongly affective and made a powerful intervention within the kind of linear history and notion of progress that Benjamin critiqued in his essay. The normative, linear history of contemporary dance and performance is one that consigns much of the artistic production of communist Eastern European countries like Yugoslavia to what is a forgotten, hidden, or perhaps, following Benjamin, oppressed past. Through a discussion of these three works by Janša, this chapter reflects on the utopian ideas that reconstructions, reenactments, reperformances, and related projects can offer by blasting performances out of the pigeonholes into which normative historical processes have consigned them.

# SLOVENIAN CONTEXTS

It is necessary here briefly to give some contextual information about avant-garde art practices in Yugoslavia during the communist period, and about the intellectual and cultural climate in post-communist Slovenia in which these three works were reconstructed and reperformed. The work in the 1980s by the artists' collective Irwin and the new wave rock group Laibach, both of which were involved with the movement Neue Slowenische Kunst (New Slovenian Art), received some recognition at the time in Western Europe and North America (see Monroe 2005). This is perhaps because they were largely dissidents who exploited the relatively relaxed attitude of the Yugoslavian Communist Party (compared with that of other Warsaw Pact countries) to use avant-garde artistic tactics in a cleverly oppositional manner. From a Western point of view, these artists appeared to be critical of communism and thus fit a Western, Cold War agenda. The earlier work of the OHO group (1966–1972) or the Pupilija Ferkeverk Theatre (which in 1969 created *Pupilija*) did not fit that agenda and had far less impact.[1] Like young people around the Western world in the 1960s, members of these groups rebelled against the conservatism of their parents' generation. For many of these young Yugoslavians, however, this meant disappointment that their parents had not lived up to the implications of the utopian ideals espoused by the communist partisans who freed Yugoslavia from German occupation during World War II.

---

[1] Janša points out that Grotowski's poor theater, with its bleak, gray vision of experience, fit the Western view of communism, whereas *Pupilija*'s happy anarchy did not fit this view (see Janša 2012). A cynic might say that it was necessary to suppress information about the progressive Yugoslavian avant-garde in case this encouraged leftist artists in Western countries.

As Serbian art theorist and conceptual artist Miško Šuvaković (2003) has shown, there has been a long history of avant-garde artistic activity in Yugoslavia, dating back at least to 1918. In the 1920s, for example, the modernist magazine *Maska* was founded in Ljubljana. This title was revived in 1993 by a group of performing artists and theorists, who founded the Maska Institute in the newly independent Slovenia. Maska, which is an independent nongovernmental organization, produced all three of the works by Janez Janša that are discussed in this chapter, and over the years has produced work by a number of progressive Slovenian performing artists. In addition to producing and promoting performances, Maska hosts lectures about contemporary performance and publishes books as well as the journal *Maska*.[2] It has ties with two similar organizations in Croatia and Serbia that both produce performing arts journals—*Frakcija*, founded in 1996 in Zagreb, and *TkH* (Teorija koja hoda, which translates as Walking Theory), which formed in 2000 in Belgrade. Many of those writing for these journals, such as Bojana Kunst and Ana Vujanovic, are trained philosophers. Together, these three groups were involved with the creation of the 2009 conference of the international organization PSi (Performance Studies International) in Zagreb, under the title "MISPERFORMANCE: Misfiring, Misfitting, Misreading." Janša was consulted about parts of the program. Artists and writers associated with these journals mostly grew up under communism and witnessed the dismantling of the web of social support structures of communist Yugoslavia under foreign pressure in the name of neoliberal market reform and economic restructuring. This experience informs the sophisticated theoretical debate about artistic practice that they are developing. Janša's work has been produced within this context.

# HISTORY, MEMORY, AND UTOPIAS

Thus far I have been using the terms "reconstruction," "reenactment," and "reperformance" to describe what Janša and his colleagues were doing in these three pieces. These works can be seen as part of a wider phenomenon that has emerged in Europe and North America over the past decade, in which, in addition to "reconstruction" "reenactment," and "reperformance," words like "reinterpretation," "reactivation," "recreation," and other similar terms beginning with the prefix "re-" have been applied. A central concern running through most of these kinds of works, which I will generically call "reworks," is a concern with history and memory. The specificity of history and memory in theater dance and performance lies in the embodied experience of performing—that is

---

[2]  Maska runs a Performance Studies course accredited by the University of Ljubljana as part of their undergraduate degree (as this is not a subject the University covers). Their book series includes single authored books and edited collections of writings by Slovenian and international writers, some in Slovenian, some in English, and includes Slovenian translations of works by Jacques Rancière, Nicolas Bourriaud, and Hans-Thies Lehmann. See www.maska.si (accessed November 9, 2013).

to say, in sensations of motor actions and associated muscle memories. These sensations often carry affective associations so that histories of dance and performance include the history and memory of the ways of thinking, feeling, and acting that informed their creation and performance. Some dance and performance artists are explicitly interested in the way memory operates, either on a personal level or as collective memories persisting within the world of performers and spectators. Even where this is not the intention, re-works nevertheless invariably reveal the role that memory plays for individuals and communities.

Re-works generally cite pieces from the past that are still within living memory, or that were created by people who have died within living memory. Some of the recent interest in memory among artists and academics is because of its potential as a tool for resisting the effects of globalized capitalism and its pursuit of ever increasing economic growth. Thus Philosopher Simon Critchley, echoing some of Benjamin's concerns in "On the Concept of History," has recently argued that progress is the ideology of capitalism that is directed toward an ideology of the future. "I think what we have to do," he writes, "is refuse the idea of the future. What we should be concerned with is the cultivation of the past, of memory" (2011, 116). There is increasing disenchantment with the modernist belief that technological progress and industrialization will generate ever greater prosperity and thus create the resources with which to solve the world's ills. Susan Buck-Morss (2002) has usefully pointed out that utopian, modernist ideologies of progress not only underlie Western capitalism, but also were present within Russian communism. The collapse of communism in Russia and Eastern Europe in 1989, she points out, should not be seen as the triumph of capitalism, but as symptomatic of problems within the utopian dreams that progress promised to turn into reality. The collapse of these dreams brings with it the danger of falling into nihilism. The cultivation of the past and memory is a way of averting this nihilism and is a first step toward re-evaluating the modernist legacy and valuing it differently. By "utopia" I mean a coming into being of something not yet existing, or nonexistent, which we nevertheless feel as a powerfully present potential. The ability to believe in some sort of utopia is surely a condition of possibility of performance and indeed of all artistic production.

By remembering avant-garde works from the past, it is possible to draw attention toward and celebrate the persistence of utopian artistic projects that trouble normative ways of thinking and resist ideologies of progress. It allows artists, like Janša, to legitimate their own current, oppositional projects, and poses questions about who "owns" the history of dance and performance. Janša and Bojana Kunst, Aldo Milohnič, and Serge Goran Pristaš raise this question in their essay "East-Dance-Academy":

> An urgent issue in dance is to redefine European dance history: to substitute it by one that would not be determined by Western parameters or based on aesthetic evaluation. That approach would be something that we might call political aesthetics (analogous to political economy). (2013, 17–18)

It is the way that this political aesthetics draws on history and memory that I am examining in these three works by Janez Janša.

# "Metis" and Collective Memory

In order to understand the particular role that memory plays in the way re-works create meanings, it is necessary to consider how one responds to live performance. In his book *The Choreographer's Handbook*, Jonathan Burrows notes:

> Let's be honest. When we talk about audience, we're talking about ourselves. I am often an audience member, so anything I think or say about audience has to include me as being a likely candidate. (2010, 159)

What Burrows touches on here is the extent to which one imagines that what one feels while watching a performance is shared with the rest of the audience (and probably also with the performers). This is particularly likely at moments when one finds oneself laughing with others, or applauding strongly at the curtain call. At the same time, of course, it is possible to be swayed at such moments by what appears to be general approval. Within this apparent consensus there may in fact be a range of different ideas and feelings about the performance so that while one may perhaps imagine that everyone is thinking and feeling exactly what one feels oneself, this may not actually be the case. Furthermore, no two audiences are the same; as Janša has observed, "What makes a performance part of its time is not only the performance itself but its audience. In this sense, the only real reconstruction would be the reconstruction of the audience" (2012, 268). However, one cannot reconstruct audiences because one cannot go back to the particular pool of memories that an audience would have brought with them to a particular performance.

One key factor affecting one's responses is the way that one's memories are brought into play while watching performances. As I watch someone dance, I often not only remember others dancing like this, but also remember the people with whom I saw these earlier performances, and the discussions I had with them about it afterward; or I remember hearing from other friends about an artist or company that I didn't see but who I suspect might have danced like this. Or I think of other friends who I am sure would like this performance and wish that they were here to see it themselves. So although I may perhaps be sitting on my own, there are others with whom I share memories that contribute to my response to the present performance.

Michel de Certeau has written of an art of memory that employs what the ancient Greeks called "metis." This is knowledge and experience, and the ability to use this to grasp the right moment. As de Certeau puts it, "metis" involves using one's memories whose attainments are indissociable from the time of their acquisition and bear the marks of its peculiarities. Drawing its knowledge from a multitude of events among which it moves without possessing them (they are all past, each a loss of place but a fragment of time), it also computes and predicts "the multiple paths of the future" by combining antecedent or possible particularities. (1988, 82)

As I watch a dance performance, the memories that I draw on are not preserved images that have an independent existence, but something useful that may come up unexpectedly because of present needs. As de Certeau suggests, this process is not necessarily systematic in a formal way, but can be opportunistic and depends on circumstances:

> Perhaps memory is no more than this "recall" or call on the part of the other, leaving its mark like a kind of overlay on a body that has always already been altered without knowing it. This originary and secret writing "emerges" little by little, in the very spots where memory is touched: memory is played by circumstances, just as a piano is played by a musician and music emerges from it when its keys are touched by the hand. (1988, 87)

The performance I watch can therefore play with my memories, reminding me of things that I might not otherwise have brought to mind. Although I may be skilled and experienced in the way I am able to bring past experiences to mind, my memories are not entirely unique to me. As I have just suggested, they concern things that I have seen with others, or have heard about from them. One of the pleasures of talking about performances with others are moments when there is a flash of shared recognition. Re-works often set out to deliberately touch one's memories and experience to provoke such flashes of recognition. By making them, their creators employ "metis" in grasping the right moment to blast into the present a particular historical set of circumstances.

The sociologist Maurice Halbwachs has argued that most memories are collective. This means that we have very few memories that we do not also share with others. He argued that "our confidence in the accuracy of our impressions increases [ . . . ] if it can be supported by others." It is as if the very same experience were relived by several persons instead of only one (1980, 22). Re-works like *Pupilija* and *Monument G2*, based on works still within living memory, therefore make space in the present in which to keep alive collective memories of a radical or alternative nature, relived by several persons at a time, when such memories still have the potential to challenge normative ways of thinking. As Janša observes, underlying *Pupilija* in 1969 was "resistance to all forms of authority. Pupilija distances itself, mocks and subverts authorities, from the external (state, nation, party, church, market) to the internal (theater, aesthetics)" (Janša 2012, 369). One's confidence in the power of these utopian ways of thinking and feeling increases if it seems to be supported by collective memories. This is the political significance of Simon Critchley's exhortation to refuse the future and to cultivate instead the past and memory.

If Critchley advocates cultivating the past and memory, then *Pupilija* and *Monument G2* do so in a different way from *Fake It!* The first two pieces reactivate the potential of archival traces and scores from the 1960s and 1970s in a way that resonates with the present. *Fake It!* rereads the normative history of the past in a critical way, challenging its Western bias by putting forward a post-communist point of view. The rest of this chapter identifies these two approaches in these three works. Underpinning these reactivations and critical interrogations are physical memories within contemporary dance and performance communities, together with "metis," the ability to use memory to grasp the opportunities of the present moment in creative and resonant ways. The politics of history and memory that these works articulate is grounded in acts of remembrance that challenge the ideology of progress.

## PUPILIJA AND MONUMENT G2

*Pupilija, papa Pupilo and the Pupilceks* was the second piece by the Pupilija Ferkeverk Theatre. The first time the name *Pupilija* was used publicly was in the title *Noble Mould of Pupilija Ferkeverk*, a performance of poetry by members of Group 442, presented on three nights in May 1969 on a small stage in the National Theatre in Ljubljana. The links between concrete poetry and experimental performance are evident when one considers that, in order to perform this kind of work vocally, a reader would need to adopt a manner of declamation radically different from that of character acting in narrative theater. These poets were then joined by visual artists, musicians, and other performers to create *Pupilija, papa Pupilo and the Pupilceks* for the Festival of Ljubljana in October that year (see Milohnić and Svetina 2009). This performance, or Happening, consisted of twenty scenes collaged together, which drew on a wide variety of different forms. Some were drawn from popular media culture and advertising: they included the staging of an advertisement for packaged Swiss cheese and an enactment of scenes from a graphic novel. It also included some contemporary dance movement, children's games, and nudity. There was a scene suggesting same-sex attraction, and another in which a man aggressively mimed intercourse with a school classroom globe (fucking the world). There was also a military drill, a Slovenian folk song, and dancing, which were part of the Communist Party's approved education curriculum. On the first night, October 29, the performance ended with the killing of a chicken. As posters for the event promised, *Pupilija* was a *Šoking gala šov*, a shocking gala show. After the second night, the director of the festival canceled further performances. A member of the central committee of the Yugoslavian Communist Party was called from Belgrade to Llubljana because of the scandal caused by the performance. He recognized that banning the piece altogether would create considerable political fallout. He decided that they should therefore starve it of the oxygen of publicity. It was henceforth shown, without the chicken scene, to students but not to the general public, and over the next eighteen months was occasionally performed within Yugoslavia in university halls of residence and at student arts festivals.

It was filmed in 1969 without an audience in a Slovenian television studio, though the final scene was erased.

The presence in the cast of visual artists who had no performance training or experience meant that some of the material was performed in an everyday, task-like manner. Most of the cast look like typical hippies[3] with long hair, beads, and faded denim jeans, and in many ways the piece can be compared with the kinds of countercultural performances that were happening in other parts of Western Europe and North America around that time.[4] It was also a very early example of experimental performance that combined a wide variety of different modes of performing, including dance, physical theater, and improvisation. It is this innovative approach that Dušan Jovanović explored further in his 1972 production *Monument G.* Janša writes that *Pupilija* "is an iconic event of Slovenian neo-avant-garde and one of the most influential experimental performing works" (2012, 367). This is a big claim. One section recorded in the 1969 film is indeed surprising for its time. It shows the performers rolling over each other on the ground, then standing up to make statuesque poses with angular outstretched arms, then moving their arms in a mechanical way so that they appear to become parts of a large machine. It is an odd moment. The rolling section looks like the sort of things that Simone Forti or Steve Paxton were experimenting with around this time, but no one else in Europe, as far as I know, was exploring this kind of movement. The poses they then take up look a little like momentary tableaux in Martha Graham's work, while the mimed machine resembles experimental French corporeal mime. The way the section morphs from one mode of performance to another is strange, and suggests that the piece created the kind of important transitional moment within experimental performance that Janša describes.

When it was reconstructed in 2006, a lot of material connected with the original production was still available. There were photographs, posters, reviews, and, as already mentioned, about two-thirds of it had been filmed in a television studio. While preparing for the reconstruction, Janša contacted some of the members of the original cast and interviewed them. The reenactment was presented on a stage with a white cyclorama at the back onto which photographs, quotations from reviews and interviews, and footage of the television studio version were projected during the performance. Samo Gosarič and Igor Štromajer worked on this, with the idea of presenting different feeds simultaneously, in the way that MTV or a television news channel might have looked if it had existed in 1969 (Janša 2012, 370). All of the 1969 film was shown in part of this display. Members of the original cast made guest appearances during a special performance in Ljubljana in October 2009, when it formed the centerpiece of the festival *Šoking gala šov: Events Marking the Fortieth Anniversary of the Emergence of the Pupilija Ferkeverk Group.* During this and other performances of *Pupilija*, audiences were made aware of

---

[3] The performers in the reenactment have noticeably shorter hair than the performers in 1969.

[4] One significant difference is the music in *Pupilija.* Three musicians play a double bass, a Spanish guitar, clarinet, and accordion, and the music ranges from jazz to Slavic folk music. In the West at the time, popular music would have been rock, played on electric guitars.

the piece's history and of the material used for the reconstruction. Janša states that the point of reconstructing *Pupilija* "is not just to re-experience a performance from the past but to experience the very relationship to history: what we are watching when we see the reconstruction is our relation to history" (2012, 368). This relation is most evident at the end of the performance, which raises the problem of how to reconstruct the slaughter of the chicken.

I will write here about the end of the performance that I attended in Rijeka, Croatia, in September 2010, which I understand was typical of the piece's run. Before the start, as we entered the auditorium, we had all been given four pieces of paper; each sheet was printed with a large letter (A, B, C, or D). At the end we were told that the first performance, back in 1969, ended with the slaughter of a chicken on stage, and we were asked to vote for one of four options. These were (A) to watch a video of a reconstruction of the chicken being killed; (B) to watch a recorded interview with Junoš Miklavec and Dušan Rogelj, who killed the chicken in the 1969 performance; (C) to hear an extract from the regulations on the protection of animals at the time of slaughter; or (D) to kill a real chicken live on stage. We were asked to hold up the piece of paper with the letter corresponding to our choice. While we were being asked this, images of the four options were projected on the cyclorama, and one of the performers proceeded to sharpen a knife in a coldly sinister way.

I myself didn't vote for the chicken to die on stage, and no one I spoke to afterward admitted to doing so, but this, we were told, was the result of the ballot.[5] A galvanized tin bath was brought forward in which to kill the chicken, and loud, alarmed clucking noises came from a back corner of the stage as a performer captured a chicken from a cage and brought it over to the bath. We were then told that since this is what the audience had chosen, a member of the audience should therefore kill the chicken. No one, however, came forward from the audience.[6] I was not alone in finding this whole scene extremely disturbing, and I was aware of discussions taking place all around me, and at least one person left the auditorium at this point. The performer with the knife then proceeded to reach into the bath and acted as if he was slitting the throat of the now hidden but very noisy chicken. He then covered the bath. Subsequently, I was very relieved when, during the final bow, he took the still living chicken out of the bath and let it

---

[5] Janša tells me that the counting may not always be 100% correct. "It's in performers' hands the way they do it" (email, Janez Janša, September 2013).

[6] Janša tells me that there were three situations in which somebody from the audience came on stage. In Belgrade, Serbia, at the BITEF Festival in September 2007, a young man came on stage and prepared to kill the chicken, but a woman from the audience then ran on stage, taking the chicken out of his hands, to loud applause from the audience. In Cividale in Italy at Mittelfest in July 2007, a woman from the audience ran on stage, took the chicken from the hands of a performer, and was applauded. In Berlin at the Volksbuehne during "The Idea of Communism" festival in June 2010, a young man came on stage, tried to kill the chicken with a knife, but couldn't do it, because the knife was a theatrical prop and was not in fact sharp. The audience was in total shock and silence. The young man insisted on trying to kill the chicken. At the end it is not clear whether the chicken survived or not. The official version from the organizers, Janša says, is that the chicken survived (email, Janez Janša, September 2013).

walk around on stage. This section created an extremely powerful theatrical experience because of the reality of the chicken on stage and the level of audience participation and engagement. Janša (2012) has written that the audience always chooses the option that the chicken should be killed. He suggests that this is because, up until the ending, the performance has a playful, easy-going quality. In his opinion, the audience wants to play a joke on the performers. From my own point of view, the performers played a joke on us in the audience when they challenged us to kill the chicken ourselves.

The reason that, Janša says, the artists in 1969 killed the chicken was "because they were looking for the live on stage [. . . and] it is exactly the confrontation between the real and the performed that creates the real in performance today" (2012, 374). Up until the chicken section, the relation between the live action on stage and the documentation projected behind it reinforced the connection between what the performers were reperforming today and what the artists created in 1969. What the chicken section did, however, was to ask what relation there might be between the audience to which I belonged and the one in 1969, who saw the chicken being slaughtered. I may find folk songs and military drill rather mystifying, and homosexuality is far more acceptable today than it was in 1969. But my shock at the prospect of the slaughter of a chicken begins to put me in touch with the shock that the audience must have felt in 1969. Back then, however, the audience was not given the choice with which I was confronted in Rijeka. In order to begin to put me in touch with the older audience, the reconstruction was therefore not faithful to the original. As Janša proposes, "reconstructions have to 'betray' the original in order for it to even function in the time of the reconstruction" (2012, 268). This issue of betrayal and falsification is a feature of all three of Janša's reconstructions, particularly in *Fake It!* Before turning to this, it is necessary to briefly discuss *Monument G2*.

*Monument G* was adapted from a play by a Yugoslavian playwright and theater director Bojan Štih about a monumental sculpture of a revolutionary partisan who comes to life, gets down off his pedestal, and expresses his opinion about how Yugoslavia has developed in recent years. Dušan Jovanović, who had been one of the Pupilija group, edited this text heavily so that it no longer made narrative sense, but constituted a series of poetic fragments. It had a small cast, one actor with one musician. Like *Pupilija*, the production was partly developed through improvisation and used a broad range of performance techniques. When *Monument G* was presented at the 1972 Bitef festival in Belgrade, it won an award for the best performance in the festival, beating works by Richard Schechner, The Living Theatre, Merce Cunningham, and Peter Brook. Jovanović and Janša reconstructed the 1972 production together, and presented it as *Monument G2*. Like *Pupilija*, *Monument G2* include projections of documents, interviews, and other information about the earlier production. A folder of documents is at one point brought on stage and used by a performer; at another point, a portable DVD player shows video of the original performance; this is then copied live on stage. Jozica Avbelj, who had been the main performer in *Monument G*, worked with Jovanović to reconstruct her role in *Monument G2*, and appeared alongside a younger performer, Teja Reba, who presented another reconstruction of it which she had worked on with Janša. Sometimes one of them performed on their own, sometimes one performed material that was then performed again by the other, or copied by the other, and sometimes the two performed together in unison.

Like *Pupilija, Monument G2* foregrounded the process of its reconstruction as part of its reenactment. Far from trying to be "authentic," both went out of their way to admit any uncertainties about material and problematized any idea that it was possible to perform them exactly as they had been initially. At the beginning, the younger actor counted the number of theater lights hanging in the studio theater and noted it in chalk on the black side wall, together with the number of lights used for the 1972 performance. She then counted the audience and again wrote the number down, alongside the number that had been in the audience in 1972. The audience was made aware of other details. In one section, a projected subtitle informed us that Avbelj was rolling on the floor in the way she remembered, initiating the movement from her hips, while Reba was initiating the movement from her feet and ankles, as is shown in film documenting the 1972 performance. The impossibility of there being a true historical reconstruction was clearly demonstrated. Avbelj is an older and much more experienced performer than she was in 1972, while Reba is from a younger generation with different ideas about performance. I was told that Avbelj is a very well known Slovenian actor on stage, television, and film. Many Slovenians in the audience must have brought to the performance their memories of seeing her in other more recent roles. They may also have brought with them knowledge and memories of Jovanović, who is a celebrated theater director, playwright, and, in recent years, a newspaper columnist. Audiences might not, however, have realized that both had worked in an experimental way earlier in their careers. By evoking memories in this way, *Monument G2* offered opportunities to reflect on some of the origins of today's acting style and the similarities and differences between this and those of the early 1970s. It also drew attention to the gaps in memories, and like the reenactment of *Pupilija*, forgrounded the way the history of artistic experimentation in Slovenia has been marginalized and hidden. What both these reenactments did was to challenge this marginalization while celebrating Slovenian artistic achievements.

## *FAKE IT!*

If *Pupilija* and *Monument G2* remembered pieces that had been marginalized and hidden from history, *Fake It!* focused attention on the kinds of works that normative historiography celebrates and canonizes. In *Fake It!* a group of Slovenian dancers, under the direction of Janša, restaged excerpts of canonical works from recent dance history for a particular event, the 2007 *Exodos Festival* in Ljubljana. Its starting point was the desire to make a performative response to the fact that the government, at that time formed by the Slovene Democratic Party, had cut financial support for the Exodos Festival so that it was no longer in a position to program the kinds of international artists that, for many years, it had presented alongside Slovenian artists. The group of dancers working with Janša drew up a list of artists whom, had money been no problem, they would have liked to program in the festival; they identified Pina Bausch, Trisha Brown, William Forsythe, and Steve Paxton, and Sankai Juku because it was a key company with which Tatsumi Hijikata had been associated. These artists or their administrators were then contacted with invitations to perform in Exodos and were asked what fee they would charge. Because the invitations were extended so late, none of the artists was able to accept, though some fondly recalled previous visits to Ljubljana. During *Fake It!* the email correspondence was projected digitally on a screen, together with contextual information about the works, as well as statistics about the dance scene in Slovenia. Meanwhile, the dancers performed their own "fake" versions to an audience seated in the round. For this they chose excerpts from Steve Paxton's *Goldberg Variations*, Trisha Brown's *Accumulation*, Pina Bausch's *Café Muller*, an improvisation based on those in William Forsythe's CD-rom *Improvisation Technologies*, and a solo choreographed by Tatsumi Hijikata. A piece, *Monument for an Unknown Dancer*, by a forgotten choreographer Guido Carmelich was subsequently added. With the exception of the latter, these pieces are part of the canon of recent dance history. Even if the audience for *Fake It!* had not seen these works, they would have known the names of their choreographers. They are part of the collective memory of dancers and dance audiences.

In the summer of 2007, Emil Hrvatin and two other artists, Davide Grassi and Žiga Kariž, all legally changed their names to Janez Janša—the name of the then prime minister and leader of the Slovene Democratic Party, elected on a conservative, nationalist manifesto.[7] This act was part of an artistic project of works made in the name of the prime minister, although the artists never directly stated this. Although *Fake It!* was not directly part of this project, it was nevertheless presented in the name of the political leader whose government's cultural policies had created the circumstances in which *Fake It!* came to be presented. These policies had made it necessary for Exodos to program only local Slovenian artists. By creating their own versions of extracts from well-known works by leading international dance artists, *Fake It!* both conformed with a policy of, in effect, only supporting Slovenian work, while at the same time corresponding to the stereotypical notion that work from off-regions is merely a derivative imitation. *Fake It!* was performed in the name of the Slovenian prime minister in such a way as to trouble and undermine the processes of national identity formation on which the government's nationalistic policies depended.

By making their own unauthorized versions of works from the canon, *Fake It!* also challenges the ways in which the majority of large, institutionalized dance companies maintain their repertoire. Dancers in large established dance repertory companies develop skills of learning choreographed material by watching it on video. Company video-viewing rooms sometimes include a full length mirror for this purpose. This can be comparatively effective when the choreography being learned is based on one of

---

[7] The politician Janez Janša was prime minister of Slovenia from 2004 to 2008, and then from February 2012 until March 2013. Earlier he had been minister of defense during the Slovenian war for independence from Yugoslavia. In 2013 he was convicted of corruption in connection with an armaments contract.

the standardized movement vocabularies such as ballet. It is less successful when the work has been choreographed using a more individualized movement vocabulary, particularly one based on the kinds of somatic knowledge developed through approaches based on contact improvisation and release work. I have already noted that in preparing the Forsythe section of *Fake It!* dancers referred to the 1994 CD-rom *Improvisation Technologies*. Although Forsythe created this teaching resource primarily for use by the dancers in his company, it was made available for purchase and use by others. Jurij Konjar, the dancer who created the *Goldberg Variations* section of *Fake It!* had, as a student, been taught by Steve Paxton when the latter had been a visiting lecturer at the Brussels dance school, PARTS.[8] While working on *Fake It!* Konjar also used Paxton's 2008 DVD *Material for the Spine* in which Paxton offers movement exercises for developing dancers' somatic awareness. Whereas the majority of institutionalized dance companies seek to create a monopoly for their repertoires, Forsythe and Paxton, and a few others, have sought to share the kinds of underlying somatic knowledges informing their work, which are least accessible through purely visual approaches.

At the end of *Fake It!* the dancers invite the audience to join them in the performance space for a short movement class and learn one of the approaches to movement informing either Bausch, Brown, Forsythe, Hijikata, or Paxton's work. At the performance I attended, I joined a group in which Jurij Konjar taught an exercise from Paxton's *Movement for the Spine*. The dancers, having claimed the right to situate themselves within their own revisionist account of recent dance history, in effect offered everyone in the audience an opportunity to become part of this themselves. By doing so, in Simon Crithley's terms, dancers and audience together involved themselves in the cultivation of the past and memory. On legal advice, *Exodos Festival* decided not to sell tickets to *Fake It!* but to offer free performances so that no one could accuse them of gaining financially from the performance of dance material for which they had not obtained the relevant rights. *Fake It!* has subsequently been performed outside Slovenia. Walter Heun, who programmed it both in Munich and at the Tanzquartier in Vienna, has told me that Matthias Schmiegelt, who had previously been managing director of Pina Bausch's Tanztheater Wuppertal, saw the piece in Vienna. After the performance, when Heun asked him what he thought of the excerpt of *Café Müller*, Schmiegelt said that if he had still been with the company he would have sued. If one manages a company of that size and stature, that is perhaps what one would be expected to do. It also demonstrates that not only is the discipline of historiography responsible for this process of marginalization, but also the institution of the law.

In later performances of *Fake It!* the dancers added a sixth work, *Monument for Unknown Dancer* by Guido Carmelich. This constitutes another more subversive form of the cultivation of the past and memory that Critchley advocated. According to the program, Carmelich, from Trieste but of Slovenian origins, was a colleague of Maurice

[8] Konjar subsequently spent time with Paxton in Vermont and produced his own version, with Paxton's support, of *Goldberg Variations*, which has been performed internationally.

Béjart and created this piece in the same Brussels studio while Béjart was creating his *Le Sacre du Printemps*. They later fell out over the name of their company; Carmelich wanted to call it Ballet of the 21st Century because, in his opinion, "the 20th Century represented the defeat of the humanist idea and he didn't want to associate his art with historical experience of exploitation, wars and catastrophes. An unbridgable conceptual chasm divided Béjart and Carmelich so their collaboration actually ended before it really began."[9] Although not many people who have seen this production realized it, Carmelich is an invention, partly inspired by the fact that one of the lesser known Italian Futurists, Giorgio Carmelich (1907–1929), who created a painting *Ballet* in 1920, was from Trieste. There might indeed have been dance artists of Slovenian origin working in Europe in the 1950s and 1960s whose careers have gone unnoticed.[10] The invention of Guido Carmelich is yet another betrayal, this time of historical truth, in order, as Benjamin puts it, to begin to blast "a specific era out of the homogeneous course of history."

# CONCLUSION

I noted earlier that Janša, together with Bojana Kunst, Aldo Milohnič, and Serge Goran Pristaš, called for an approach to history that was in effect a political aesthetics. Compared with the nationalistic politics of the prime minister, *Pupilija, Monument G2*, and *Fake It!* were all international in their political stance. *Pupilija* and *Monument G2*, which both toured internationally, asserted the significant place of Slovenian avant-garde performance within the wider international context, while *Fake It!* underlined the importance of the international dance scene for Slovenian artists. All three, each in its

---

[9] Email, Janez Janša, August 8, 2010.

[10] In June 2012, Janša did a similar project with Master's students at the Freie Universität, Berlin, called *Performing Document*. For this they imagined an artistic practice that could have existed at the time and created documentary evidence about it. The students invented the Kuche Elf (the Kitchen Eleven), a group of women from West Berlin which in 1966 created several works based on the ordinary everyday life of Berlin housewives. "The core of the group consisted of 6 members who would gather often and discuss matters from their everyday lives. One of the reoccurring themes were ants, who were very common guests in their Berlin homes. Ants became their friends and they could share with them many approaches to the labour. Kuche Elf created 3 works, which are recorded. 1. street action 'Ameisen auf der Straße' ('Ants on the Road'). The action consisted of putting simple posters with that writing on the streets of Berlin. With this action Kuche Elf made street intervention, media performance, and activist message, which got its full sense in their next work. 2. 'Queren' (Ants Crossing the Road)—in this work Kuche Elf made choreography with thousands of ants which they've been collecting in their homes. The choreography was placed on a Berlin street and ants would cross the road back and forth. Their path was made upon sewing patterns as they could be found in the women magazine *Brigitte*, one of the first German magazines for women. 3. "Oper A"—this is the only stage work made by Kuche Elf. The opera was based on sounds of ants they recorded and choreography inspired by movements of ants. The work of Kuche Elf was nearly unnoticed. There were some writings and interviews with some members of the group mainly in marginal press." Email, Janez Janša, June 3, 2012.

own ingenious way, grasped the right moment with what de Certeau called "metis" to blast out of the past a particular performance event or events. By doing so, each reenactment made space in the present for something that no longer existed. Furthermore, when betraying the past or, as with *Monument for Unknown Dancer*, inventing it untruthfully, each made space for something that never existed but that nevertheless exists powerfully as a utopian moment.

## Works Cited

Benjamin, Walter. 1973. *Illuminations*. London: Fontana Press.

Buck-Morss, Susan. 2002. *Dreamworld and Catastrophe: The Passing of Mass Utopia in East and West*. Cambridge, MA: MIT Press.

Burrows, Jonathan. 2010. *A Choreographer's Handbook*. Abingdon, UK: Routledge.

Certeau, Michel de. 1988. *The Practice of Everyday Life*. Berkeley: University of California Press.

Critchley, Simon. 2011. *How to Stop Living and Start Worrying: Conversations with Carl Cederström*. London: Polity.

Janša, Janez. 2012. "Reconstruction2: On the Reconstruction of *Pupilija, papa Pupilo and the Pupilceks*." In *Perform Repeat Record*, edited by Amelia Jones and Adrian Heathefield, 367–384. Bristol: Intellect Books.

Janša, Janez, Bojana Kunst, Aldo Milohnič, and Serge Goran Pristaš. 2013. "East-Dance-Academy." In *Parallel Slalom: A Lexicon of Non-Aligned Poetics*, edited by Bojana Cvević and Serge Goran Pristaš, 16–30. Belgrade and Zagreb: Walking Theory and CDU.

Milohnic, Aldo, and Ivo Svetina, eds. 2009. *The Pupilceks Have Arrived: 40 Years of the Pupilija Ferkeverk Theatre*. Ljubljana: Maska.

Monroe, Alexei. 2005. *Interrogation Machine: Laibach and NSK*. Cambridge, MA: MIT Press.

Šuvaković, Miško. 2003. *Impossible Histories: Historical Avant-Gardes, Neo-Avant-gardes, and Post-Avant-gardes in Yugoslavia, 1918–1991*. Cambridge, MA: The MIT Press.

CHAPTER 18

..............................................................................

# REENACTMENT AS RACIALIZED SCANDAL

..............................................................................

ANTHEA KRAUT

IN the fall of 2011, the pop star Beyoncé released a music video for her single "Countdown."[1] Singing about her steadfast love for her man, Beyoncé appears in a series of quick edits—sometimes in close-up, sometimes in split screen, sometimes in long and medium shots—with a small group of backup dancers. The video is packed with references to icons of the 1950s, 1960s, and 1970s, including Audrey Hepburn, Andy Warhol, and Diana Ross. But, as some were quick to notice, much of the movement vocabulary— floor rolls, head swings, hands running through hair, the sliding of a shirt on and off the shoulder, casual pivot turns, the shifting of positions while seated on a chair—as well as some of the *mise en scène* and camera shots, bore a striking resemblance to two works by the Belgian choreographer Anne Teresa De Keersmaeker: *Rosas danst Rosas* (1983), and *Achterland* (1990), films of both of which are accessible online. More than one YouTube user compiled a side-by-side comparison of the video and these works, highlighting the similarities.[2] Catching wind of the likeness, De Keersmaeker issued a statement alleging plagiarism and threatened legal action against Sony, Beyoncé's music label.

Beyoncé's revisiting of De Keersmaeker's choreography is not included in discussions of the recent phenomenon of contemporary choreographers reenacting earlier dance works. There are some good reasons for this. Beyoncé's use of isolated fragments, rather than the entirety, of De Keersmaeker's choreography is not exactly a "re-playing or re-doing [of] a precedent event, artwork, or act" that, as performance studies scholar Rebecca Schneider writes, propelled the term "reenactment" into "increased circulation in late twentieth- and early twenty-first-century art, theatre, and performance circles" (Schneider 2011, 2). Still, Beyoncé's embodiment of De Keersmaeker's choreography does mark a "return" to the "tracks and steps and bodies and gestures and

---

[1] The video is available here: http://www.beyonce.com/photos-videos (accessed August 21, 2013).
[2] See, for example, http://www.youtube.com/watch?v=3HaWxhbhH4c, and http://www.youtube.com/watch?v=PDTom514TMw (accessed August 21, 2013).

sweat . . . performed by past dancers," which André Lepecki has called "one of the most significant marks of contemporary experimental choreography (Lepecki 2010, 29).[3] As such, "Countdown" participates in what Schneider calls the "syncopated time of reenactment, where *then* and *now* punctuate each another" (2011, 2) and in what Lepecki calls its "particular economy, where bodies intertwine, or intermingle, across time" (2010, 39). Like the artists considered by Schneider and Lepecki, Beyoncé's restaging of De Keersmaeker's choreography raises questions about the relationship between past and present and the original and the copy, about the intersubjectivity of bodies performing at different times, about repetition and reproducibility, and about the afterlives of dances.

Of course, the most conspicuous feature of Beyoncé's reenactment of De Keersmaeker is that it was unauthorized. Beyoncé did not seek permission from De Keersmaeker before recreating her choreography, and the dancing in the music video only became evident *as* reenactment (as a copy of a prior original) after scrupulous viewers called attention to its movement sources. But if this lack of authorization or acknowledgment seems to violate one of the implicit tenets of reenactment art (that its relationship to something prior be visible from the outset), the violation of De Keersmaeker's "authorial authority" is, according to Lepecki, part and parcel of reenactment's politics (2010, 35). "Re-enactments transform all authored objects into fugitives in their own home," he writes, by releasing works from the "arresting" force of an artist's original intent and control (2010, 35). In simultaneous corroboration and contradiction of Lepecki's point, it is the very threat of "fugitiveness" that led acclaimed performance artist Marina Abramović to embark on the project of reperforming her own earlier works. As Schneider (2011) relays, citing Abramović and a *New York Times* interview by art critic Carol Kino, Abramović saw reenactment as a means of ensuring the " 'correct' transmission of 'seminal' works" in the face of younger artists' attempts to restage performance art from the 1960s' and '70s, "often without consulting or crediting the originator" (4).[4]

Whether Abramović's sentiments are widespread or not, her desire to control the afterlife of her performance art suggests a degree of overlap between reenactment and the institution of copyright. As I have written elsewhere (Kraut 2011, 2015), choreographers like early modern dancer Loïe Fuller turned to copyright as a means of curbing unauthorized reproductions of their dances, which threatened to reduce them to the status of exchangeable commodities. Reenactment and copyright, too, share the premise that, rather than disappear, performance recurs. Complicating views of dance as a present-tense medium, both reenactment and copyright underscore dance's ability to persist.[5] Yet, as the reported rationale for Abramović's reenactment series indicates, this ability breeds its own kind of anxiety. Schneider elaborates:

---

[3]  See also Burt (2003).

[4]  See Abramović (2007, 11, 25); and Kino (2010, AR25).

[5]  The argument that disappearance defines dance and performance has been most famously articulated by Siegel (1972) and Phelan (1993). Both Schneider (2011) and Lepecki (2010) discuss reenactment as a challenge to this ontological claim. Schneider's chapter "In the Meantime: Performance Remains" takes up the issue of performance's ephemerality at length (2011, 87–110).

With reperformance, what had been lost to time, returns—but so does a medial anxiety around the temporal gap in performance-based work. If another body performs a performance artist's "original," "pure," time-based act, then body-to-body transmission might threaten to unsettle the singularity of the original, and return that singular act again to the scandal of *unrestricted circulation and exchange* without regard to property and the authorizing arm of legitimizing institutions. (2011, 129; emphasis in original)

In highlighting performance's capacity for return, then, we may dispense with the melancholia that arises from approaching it as a constantly receding art, only to worry over questions about its temporal mobility.

This chapter takes up the "scandal of *unrestricted circulation and exchange*" represented by Beyoncé's embodiment of De Keersmaeker's choreography. Approached as reenactment, Beyoncé's act of alleged copyright infringement brings to the fore certain issues that have been less discussed in other analyses of reperformance. As an unauthorized copy that transposes De Keersmaeker's avant-garde choreography to the mass cultural medium of the music video, Beyoncé's recreation is particularly well-suited for examining the "medial anxiety" that can attend performance's return. Moreover, the fact that avant-garde performance and music video choreography circulate in very different reproductive economies (with the former often assigned a non-reproducibility, and the latter epitomizing the commodity form) accentuates the "temporal gaps" between source and copy. Perhaps most urgently, the Beyoncé–De Keersmaeker example forces attention to the ways in which race structures the anxieties and gaps that reenactment produces. What happens when the body of an African-American female celebrity becomes the site of reenactment? What happens to the "syncopated time of reenactment" when "then" signals the white avant-garde and "now" indexes black popular culture?

In the remainder of this chapter, I explore the ways in which past and present disrupt one another (Schneider 2011, 15) in Beyoncé's reembodiment of De Keersmaeker's choreography, and unpack the racial implications of those disruptions. Turning first to an analysis of the music video itself, I argue that temporal reversal is present not only in the "Countdown" of the song title and in the aesthetic of the video; it also undergirds Beyoncé's ostensible choreographic infringement of De Keersmaeker. When we approach time in a historical sense, that is, Beyoncé's unauthorized reproduction of De Keersmaeker emerges as an inversion of the deeply entrenched pattern of white modern and postmodern artists "borrowing" from non-white movement practices. Yet, lest we be too quick to see this inversion as a sign that, in the age of YouTube, a leveling of racialized hierarchies between protectable works of authorship and the unrestricted public domain has taken place, the response to Beyoncé's use of De Keersmaeker's material forces us to think again. Treated as a scandal by De Keersmaeker and by a range of observers, "Countdown" demonstrates the persistence not just of choreography, but also of racially tinged anxieties about who is authorized to reenact what. As I hope to show, choreography's return simultaneously destabilizes and reifies intersecting racial and artistic hierarchies. In the last section of the chapter, I briefly consider how the shot-for-shot remake of Beyoncé's video by a Vietnamese-American boy, as well as De Keersmaeker's recent decision to take *Rosas danst Rosas* viral, perpetuates and obscures reenactment's racially charged meanings.

# "It ain't nothing that I can't do": Inverting White Privilege

Retro and reversal are at the heart of the three minute and thirty-three second music video for "Countdown," a song featuring "a toothsome mix of hip-hop and dancehall and Afro-beat," which was generally seen as the most experimental track on Beyoncé's fourth solo album, titled *4* (Rosen 2011). The chorus is a literal countdown, itself a sample from the 1990s R&B group Boyz II Men's song "Uhh Ahh," on top of which Beyoncé sings:

My baby is a ten
We dressin' to the nine
He pick me up we eight
Make me feel so lucky seven
He kiss me in his six
We be makin' love in five
Still the one I do this four
I'm tryin' to make us three
From that two
He's still the one.[6]

The video, co-directed by Adria Petty and Beyoncé, plays with the idea of countdown even before we reach this chorus (Battan 2011). Fifteen seconds in, Beyoncé, wearing bangs, a black turtleneck, and cropped pants à la Audrey Hepburn from *Funny Face* (1957), circles her arms counterclockwise like the second hand of a clock. Temporal rewind is also writ large in the video's overall retro aesthetic. Described as "a technicolor dream ride through mod and vintage cinema glories," and an "homage to '60s chic," the video has Beyoncé alternately channeling various black and white female icons—not only Hepburn and Diana Ross, but also the British model Twiggy and the French model and actress Brigitte Bardot (Gayles 2011; Nika 2011). The visual look of the video, meanwhile, alternates between black and white and color blocking.

Beyoncé's resurrection of De Keersmaeker's choreography, which constitutes the most extended dance sequences in "Countdown," is further evidence of Beyoncé's

---

[6] http://rapfix.mtv.com/2011/10/06/beyonces-confusing-countdown-lyric-revealed/ (accessed August 13, 2013).

"affinity for recalling the past in her videos" (Mitchell 2011). De Keersmaeker's movement, first performed by Beyoncé's dancers, who are then joined by Beyoncé, crops up
less than a minute into the video and continues intermittently throughout. That the past
recalled choreographically was not the 1960s but the 1980s (and 1990) did little to disturb the video's aesthetic. In fact, until viewers familiar with De Keersmaeker's work
called attention to the correct sources, most viewers mistakenly identified the 1980s
dance films *Fame* (1980) and *Flashdance* (1983) as the referents for the straight-up dance
segments in "Countdown" ( "Beyoncé 'Countdown' Music Video Look by Look" 2011;
Mitchell 2011). Perhaps not surprising, given the off-the-shoulder shirts and open studio space that appear in "Countdown," this misreading reveals how far off the pop culture radar De Keersmaeker was. While critics later pronounced it "weird" for Beyoncé
and De Keersmaeker to occupy the same sentence (Jennings 2011), the movement qualities of De Keersmaeker's choreography—both the expression-filled, minimalist gestures of *Rosas danst Rosas* and the dramatic falls, rolls, and rippling body isolations of
*Achterland*—seemed to fit right in with the retro chic femininity of "Countdown."[7]

Yet Beyoncé's reenactment of De Keersmaeker's movements, I want to suggest, does
more than recall the past; it also inverts it. In making De Keersmaeker just one more
source for her own creative output, Beyoncé upends the pattern of appropriation that,
as recent dance scholarship has shown, defined much of the Euro-American dance field
in the twentieth century. From Ruth St. Denis's exploitation of Asian Indian "nautch"
dancing, to Helen Tamiris's use of "Negro" spirituals, to Merce Cunningham's reliance
on Asian-inspired chance procedures, the tradition of "experimental" concert dance
has long mined the cultural practices of racialized groups.[8] In the process, white experimental artists have established reputations for themselves as innovators, even as they
treat their (typically uncredited) influences as a kind of free-for-all "raw material."[9] As
Brenda Dixon Gottschild wrote in 1996, while "[t]he 'high' is sanctioned to borrow from
the 'low,' whites from blacks, ballet from folk dance, and so forth . . . the road for the
black artist borrowing from high-culture white forms has been posted with 'no tres-
passing' signs" (28). Beyoncé's choreographic actions flip this script on its head, turning
the white avant-garde into fodder for a black woman's cultural production. The temporal disjuncture between the "then" of De Keersmaeker's originals and the "now" of
Beyoncé's copies is thus also a dislocation of a racialized artistic hierarchy.

In proposing that Beyoncé's unauthorized reproduction of De Keersmaeker's choreography represents a decidedly un-retro about-face to the legacy of white artists'
taking from non-white dancers, I do not mean to equate Beyoncé with the generally

---

[7] In De Keersmaeker and Cvejić (2012), Cvejić refers to *Rosas danst Rosas*'s "pronounced feminine
character" (85), and in her review of *Achterland*, *New York Times* critic Anna Kisselgoff (1991) wrote,
"Before they hurl themselves against the floor and rebound at a tilt, the women practice vamping, Betty
Grable-style" (1991).

[8] See, among others, Srinivasan (2011); Manning (2004); Wong (2010, 51); and Foster (2002, 34–37).

[9] In the field of intellectual property (IP) scholarship, K. G. Greene has compellingly examined the
racial inequities that structure the public domain in the United States. See, for example, Greene (1999).

anonymous and uncompensated dancers of color who have frequently served as inspiration for white choreographers. Beyoncé is hardly what we could call disenfranchised. One of the most popular recording artists of this century, she had an estimated net worth of $350 million in 2012 and was number thirty-two on the *Forbes* list of the world's most powerful women.[10] As others have observed, much of Beyoncé's music is specifically about black female empowerment and material success or, more precisely, female empowerment as material success. Music critic Jody Rosen (2011) notes that "from 'Independent Women' to 'Single Ladies' to 'Run the World (Girls),' Beyoncé's anthems view female self-determination in mercenary terms." In her analysis of Beyoncé's 2006 album *B-day*, scholar Daphne Brooks (2008) likewise notes a "troubling . . . fixation on materialism" coursing through the album (183). But, in a compelling reading that juxtaposes Beyoncé's assertion of black female "socioeconomic autonomy" with black women's massive dislocation and dispossession in New Orleans in the wake of Hurricane Katrina, Brooks argues that the album's focus "on ownership and personal property" represents a provocative refutation of what Brooks calls "the spectacular marginalization of African-American women in American sociopolitical culture" (183).

Following Brooks's lead, I also read Beyoncé's choreographic moves in "Countdown" as an assertion of power and agency. Instead of being about material belongings, however (although she does tell us that "Yup, I buy my own, if he deserve it, buy his shit too"), the video is a testament to a different kind of possessiveness: the right to acquire movement from whatever source Beyoncé sees fit. In asserting this right by borrowing whole chunks of movement from De Keersmaeker, Beyoncé corporeally claims a privilege that has historically belonged to whites. As I argue elsewhere (2015), legal scholar Cheryl Harris's influential argument in "Whiteness as Property" (1993)—that whiteness in the United States has been protected as a kind of property right—helps explain white artists' entitlement "to use and enjoy" racially marked cultural traditions. In "Countdown," however, the white, high art choreographer De Keersmaeker is the object, rather than subject, of this racialized property logic, becoming the thing used, rather than the user.

In response to accusations of plagiarism, Beyoncé issued a statement, explaining:

> Clearly, the ballet "Rosas danst Rosas" was one of many references for my video "Countdown." It was one of the inspirations used to bring the feel and look of the song to life. I was also paying tribute to the film, "Funny Face" with the legendary Audrey Hepburn. My biggest inspirations were the '60s, the '70s, Brigitte Bardot, Andy Warhol, Twiggy and Diana Ross. (Higgins 2011)

Adria Petty likewise told MTV News that she "brought Beyoncé a number of references and we picked some out together. Most were German modern-dance references, believe it or not. But it really evolved" (Vena 2011). Beyoncé reported finding *Rosas danst Rosas* "refreshing, interesting and timeless," adding, "I've always been fascinated by the way

---

[10]   See Said and http://www.forbes.com/profile/beyonce-knowles/ (accessed August 29, 2012).

contemporary art uses different elements and references to produce something unique"
(Higgins 2011).

The inexactitudes here are noteworthy. De Keersmaeker is a Belgian not German
choreographer, and her works date from none of the decades that Beyoncé invokes. Yet
I can't help but be reminded of the long history of mis-recognition of African diasporic
dance—perceptions, for example, of Josephine Baker as an African dancer, and of jazz
dance as the sign of a timeless primitivism. Inaccuracies aside, Beyoncé's point is that
she considered De Keersmaeker not some off-limits realm of high art but, rather, one of
many sources of inspiration, just as available to her as pop culture icons like Twiggy and
Diana Ross. Invoking the freedom that contemporary art enjoys to use "different elements and references to produce something unique," Beyoncé implies that she should
possess this same prerogative.

Again, given her wealth and celebrity status, to advance an argument about Beyoncé's
assertion of possessive individualism may seem redundant. The perception of her power
to police her own work is such that, in the wake of the "Countdown" incident, *Rosas
danst Rosas* filmmaker Thierry De Mey remarked,

> If tomorrow I were to look for the music, the videos by Beyonce or any other pop or
> rock stars and use them in my movies without asking for their authorisation, I think
> Exocet missiles would fall over the Charleroi dance festival and myself. ("Beyoncé
> Plagiarism Claims" 2011)

Hyperbole aside, the fact that Beyoncé's legal team sent cease and desist letters to websites that leaked the "Countdown" music track before its official release date leaves no
ambiguity about her pronounced sense of proprietorship (Kennedy 2011).

Likewise, even before the De Keersmaeker flap, Beyoncé had developed something of
a reputation for taking and using preexisting visual images and choreographic concepts.
The most well-known choreographic example of this tendency was her liberal borrowing of Bob Fosse's "Mexican Breakfast" number for her 2008 video "Single Ladies (Put
a Ring on It)."[11] Beyoncé has even joked about her propensity for appropriation: in a

---

[11] In addition to "borrowing" from Fosse—in both "Single Ladies" and "Get Me Bodied"—Beyoncé
has been accused of ripping off the concept for her performance at the 2011 Billboard Awards from
the Italian singer Lorella Cuccarini. See Perricone (2011). She has also been accused of stealing
choreography from the all-male group New Edition for her video "Love on Top." See http://clatl.com/
cribnotes/archives/2011/10/17/is-beyonce-stealing-love-from-new-edition (accessed September 21,
2012). Reportedly, New Edition was honored rather than peeved by the resemblances, and the video was
generally interpreted as an homage. http://www.sodahead.com/entertainment/watch-beyonces-love-on-
top-video-spawns-more-stealing-accusations-theft-or-homage/question-2228447/ (accessed September
21, 2012).
  There was also briefly some Internet chatter over Beyoncé's appropriation of dance steps by a
Mozambique kwaito group named Tofo Tofo in her music video for "Run the World (Girls)." As it
turns out, Beyoncé found the group on YouTube and tracked them down so they could appear in
the video with her. Interestingly, Beyoncé's choreographer Frank Gatson, Jr., is quoted as saying that
they "had to bring them around to learn that [move]" because "none of us could imitate that" http://
concreteloop.com/2011/05/info-on-tofo-tofo-the-african-dancers-who-inspired-beyonces-run-the-

twenty-four-second video clip that circulated online, she tells her choreographer Frank Gaston, Jr., laughingly, "Nobody going to want us to come to their shows . . . because we going to take everything."[12] (She says this while seated in a dance studio, a playbill for the musical *Chicago* right beside her.) In claiming theft as her M.O., Beyoncé implicitly positions her body as a processor of others' work, a living archive of performances that have come before her. There is, I would hazard, a resemblance between Beyoncé's compulsive recycling and what Lepecki calls the "will to archive" that drives "experimental" choreography's recent fascination with reenactment. The difference is that Beyoncé's black body is more typically regarded as an unoriginal imitator than "an endlessly creative, transformational archive" (Lepecki 2010, 46).[13]

Writing from another perspective, Thomas DeFrantz's 2012 essay "Unchecked Popularity: Neoliberal Circulations of Black Social Dance" critiques the ease with which African-American social dances spread beyond the particular sociohistorical contexts that gave rise to them. A far cry from Lepecki's celebration of dance's ability to "come back around" (2010, 39), DeFrantz focuses instead on the ways in which "[a]ppropriation . . . , the re-purposing of dance to allow its entry into diverse economic markets—reconfigures black physicalities into a place of interchangeability with any who would do the dances, and allows access without concerns of situation or material circumstance of the dancer under scrutiny" (2012, 135). What is so captivating about the "Countdown" video, I want to suggest, is that this is almost exactly what Beyoncé has done, but with a critical difference: she repurposes white experimental dance and, in the process, reconfigures the primarily white physicalities of De Keersmaeker's dancers into a place of interchangeability with her own body and those of her dancers.[14] In a description of how the movement for *Rosas danst Rosas* came into being, De Keersmaeker stated, "We wanted everything to stay close to ourselves . . . it was 'Rosas danst Rosas'— we dance ourselves. So we did what we had to do and expressed what seemed natural

world-choreography#more-737532 (accessed September 20, 2012). In other words, while YouTube makes it possible to assimilate a good deal of choreography, some movements can only be learned in a body-to-body encounter. According to one observer, however, the results are much better when Beyoncé goes the less ethical route: http://www.grantland.com/blog/hollywood-prospectus/post/_/id/35200/lets-all-stop-complaining-when-beyonce-steals-things-from-youtube (accessed September 21, 2012). See also Beyoncé's documentary on the making of the album 4: http://www.drfunkenberry.com/2011/07/05/behind-the-scenes-of-beyonces-making-of-4/ (accessed October 29, 2012). The video shows Beyoncé and her dancers trying to learn the Tofo Tofo moves without success until they fly the men in.

[12] http://perezhilton.com/2011-10-25-beyonce-admits-to-stealing-video#sthash.hvrugT77.dpbs (accessed August 14, 2013).

[13] In fact, as at least a couple of newspaper reports pointed out, De Keersmaeker participated in this will to reenact herself: her 2006 work *D'un soir un jour* contains a fragment of Valav Nijinsky's 1912 *The Afternoon of a Faun*; unlike Beyoncé, De Keersmaeker acknowledges the debt on her website. See http://www.rosas.be/en/production/dun-soir-un-jour (accessed August 20, 2013); Jennings (2011); and Kaufman (2011).

[14] Although Fumiyo Ikeda, one of the founding company members of De Keersmaeker's company Rosas and an original cast member in *Rosas danst Rosas*, is Japanese, the dancers who appeared in the 1997 film version of *Rosas danst Rosas*—the version to which Beyoncé had access—are all white. Ikeda does appear in the 1994 film adaptation of *Achterland*.

and close to us, and not external" (De Keersmaeker and Cvejić 2012, 85). In other words, De Keersmaeker's original choreography was anchored in the individual personalities and corporealities of the dancers with whom she worked. Beyoncé's easy access to this choreography, made possible by the posting of film versions of *Rosas danst Rosas* and *Achterland* on YouTube, allowed her to unmoor it from those bodies without any knowledge of its underlying conditions of production.

None of this is to say that Beyoncé was justified in neglecting to seek permission from De Keersmaeker for using her choreography and neglecting to give her credit before accusations of plagiarism emerged.[15] But it is precisely her failure to do either—along with her leveling of any distinction between her pop culture and high art sources—that signals a usurpation of what has typically been white privilege. Claiming the experimental artist's prerogative, Beyoncé not only reenacts the past in "Countdown;" she also rescripts its racialized norms of authorization, authorship, and ownership, while reversing the dominant direction in which choreographic traffic has historically flowed.

# NEITHER ANGERED NOR HONORED: WHITE AVANT-GARDE ANXIETY

Admittedly, my reading of Beyoncé's choreographic borrowing as a powerful inversion of historical patterns of white appropriation was not the prevailing response to revelations of her work's debt to De Keersmaeker. On the Internet, Beyoncé was widely condemned as a copycat.[16] In the words of one YouTube poster, "[w]ell if it's all just copying then I guess she won't mind if I copy her music off the internet without paying for it—just like she didn't pay these people when she decided to use their moves without permission. I mean hey, it's not like she needs the money!"[17] From the vantage point of this consumer, Beyoncé's economic capital renders her an unsympathetic player in any debate over intellectual property rights.

For De Keersmaeker, too, Beyoncé's position in the global marketplace was a critical factor in assessing the propriety of her reenactments. De Keersmaeker's response to "Countdown" was both legal and rhetorical. A lawyer for her company, Rosas, evidently contacted Sony, maintaining that the music video could not be shown without the prior approval of De Keersmaeker and Thierry De Mey, the filmmaker of *Rosas danst Rosas* (La Rocco 2011). Although little is known about the resulting negotiations, several factors suggest that the parties reached a settlement: first, Beyoncé released an alternate

---

[15]  In an interview with *GQ*, music video co-director Adria Petty claimed that "it was everyone's intention from the get-go" to credit De Keersmaeker and that the failure to do so was "basically an oversight" ("Video Deconstruction" 2011).

[16]  A Google search for "Beyoncé copycat" on August 14, 2013, turned up 263,000 results. See, among them, Ramirez (2013).

[17]  cbatgm on http://www.youtube.com/watch?v=3HaWxhbhH4c (accessed August 30, 2012).

version of the video with De Keersmaeker's choreography excised; second, when the video was nominated for a 2012 MTV Video Music Award for best choreography, De Keersmaeker was listed as co-choreographer (along with Danielle Polanco, Frank Gatson Jr., and herself); and third, the original, unexcised "Countdown" video remains on Beyoncé's website.[18]

Meanwhile, in an interview with the radio station Studio Brussel, De Keersmaeker called Beyoncé's actions outright "stealing." "I'm not mad, but this is plagiarism," she maintained, adding that she found it "rude" that "they don't even bother about hiding it" (McKinley 2011).[19] De Keersmaeker also issued the following public statement, which was posted on Studio Brussel's website:

> Like so many people, I was extremely surprised when I got a message on Facebook about the special appearance of my two choreographies—Rosas danst Rosas (1983) and Achterland (1990) in Beyoncé's new videoclip Countdown. The first question was whether I was now selling out Rosas into the commercial circuit.

She continued:

> People asked me if I'm angry or honored. Neither. On the one hand, I am glad that Rosas danst Rosas can perhaps reach a mass audience which such a dance performance could never achieve, despite its popularity in the dance world since 1980s. And, Beyoncé is not the worst copycat, she sings and dances very well, and she has a good taste! On the other hand, there are protocols and consequences to such actions, and I can't imagine she and her team are not aware of it. To conclude, this event didn't make me angry, on the contrary, it made me think a few things. Like, why does it take popular culture thirty years to recognize an experimental work of dance? A few months ago, I saw on Youtube a clip where schoolgirls in Flanders are dancing Rosas danst Rosas to the music of Like a Virgin by Madonna. And that was touching to see. But with global pop culture it is different, does this mean that thirty years is the time that it takes to recycle non-mainstream experimental performance? And, what does it say about the work of Rosas danst Rosas? In the 1980s, this was seen as a statement of girl power, based on assuming a feminine stance on sexual expression. I was often asked then if it was feminist. Now that I see Beyoncé dancing it, I find it pleasant but I don't see any edge to it. It's seductive in an entertaining consumerist way.[20]

---

[18] The alternate video was released in late November 2011. See "VIDEO: Beyoncé releases Alternate Version of 'Countdown'" (2011). The 2012 VMA nominations are listed here: http://bostinno. streetwise.co/2012/09/06/mtv-vmas-nominees-check-out-the-full-list-of-the-2012-mtv-music-award-nominations/ (accessed August 21, 2013).

[19] It should be noted that plagiarism and copyright infringement are often overlapping but not interchangeable charges. In general, plagiarism is the academic infraction of using another's work without giving credit, while infringement is the legal offense of using another's intellectual property without permission. See, among others, Posner (2007).

[20] http://theperformanceclub.org/2011/10/anne-teresa-de-keersmaeker-responds-to-beyonce-video/ (accessed September 7, 2012).

De Keersmaeker's statement has been variously interpreted as generous and restrained and, conversely, as scathing in its ridicule of Beyoncé.[21] What strikes me are the subtle contradictions it contains. Stating not once, but twice, that she is not angered by Beyoncé's use of her choreography, De Keersmaeker nonetheless betrays an anxiety about the relationship between the avant-garde, historically aligned with whiteness, and "global pop culture," which we might read here as subtly coded "black."[22] Even as she voices concern about the perception that she has "sold out" her choreography to the commercial circuit, she ever-so-slightly grumbles about the three decades it took for her "experimental" performance to register with the mainstream. By this logic, De Keersmaeker's choreography circulates both too much and not enough, both too slowly and too quickly.

It is worth pointing out that, in contrast to some of the avant-garde choreography currently being resurrected in the contemporary dance milieu, De Keersmaeker's works were never really out of circulation. After its 1983 debut, for example, *Rosas danst Rosas* was performed between 1985 and 1987, between 1992 and 1994, between 1995 and 1997, and was revived again in 2009, 2010, and 2011 (De Keersmaeker and Cvejić 2012, 115; Suclas 2011). In 1994, De Keersmaeker made a black-and-white film adaptation of *Achterland*, and in 1997, Thierry de Mey made a film version of *Rosas danst Rosas*, which aired on all of the major European television channels and toured the art house cinema circuit.[23] Both choreographic works, moreover, are listed as part of the repertory curriculum for dancers training at PARTS (Performing Arts Research & Training Studios), the international school for contemporary dance that De Keersmaeker founded in 1994.[24] This means that De Keersmaeker's choreography lives in the bodies of numerous dancers. Yet, within these avant-garde afterlives, the participation of "original" bodies in the transmission process is considered crucial. "Repertory workshops are always taught by dancers who have been in the original creations of the pieces," the PARTS website states, and De Keersmaeker has noted how much more she can transmit to company dancers when she performs in the work herself. Even so, when asked about the revival of *Rosas danst Rosas* with a fourth generation of dancers, De Keersmaeker responded that, because the piece "bears the personal expression of the particular dancers I made it with, of their bodies and movements . . . it is always somewhat delicate whenever we renew it" (De Keersmaeker and Cvejić 2012, 115). In contrast to the "delicacy" of these authorized body-to-body transmissions, and in contrast to the three months that students at PARTS take to "bring the work on a level where it can be performed on professional stages,"[25] sits the transmission process by which Beyoncé presumably learned (portions

---

[21] See, for example, http://www.artinfo.com/news/story/38829/avant-garde-belgian-dancer-ridicules-beyonce-for-stealing-her-moves (accessed September 7, 2012); and Horwitz (2011).

[22] As DeFrantz (2012) writes, "A curiosity with profound economic, social, and representational consequence places African American social dances at the corporeal center of global discourses of the popular" (128).

[23] http://www.rosas.be/en/film/rosas-danst-rosas (accessed August 16, 2013).

[24] http://www.parts.be/en/curriculum-training (accessed August 16, 2013).

[25] http://www.parts.be/en/curriculum-training (accessed August 16, 2013).

of) De Keersmaeker's choreography: mediated by film and video, measured in hours rather than months, and assimilated by a body more proficient in African-American vernacular styles than in ballet and release technique.

De Keersmaeker's singling out of a group of white schoolgirls' reenactment of *Rosas danst Rosas* to a Madonna tune as "touching," however, should give us pause, for it contains the hint that De Keersmaeker's objection was not to unauthorized reenactments per se, nor to the circulation of those reenactments online, nor to having her work sit alongside popular culture (albeit from the 1980s). The fact that the Flanders girls were not poised to profit from their video reenactment, where Beyoncé most certainly was, is of course relevant. We might conclude, then, that the problem for De Keersmaeker was becoming situated *within* "global pop culture," a situating that occurred when her choreography came to reside *within* Beyoncé's body. Although she stops short of calling "Countdown" "an egregious example of the devaluing and exploitation of contemporary performance by mainstream, commercial culture" (Horwitz 2011), as one blog poster did, she damns Beyoncé's rendition as only superficially pleasing and denuded of any critical edge. This is everything to which the avant-garde is opposed.

Beyoncé's reembodiment of De Keersmaeker's choreography thus represents a clash between different types of dance economies—the unhurried reproductive economy of the avant-garde versus the sped-up reproductive economy of popular culture—and a corresponding clash between different types of capital: cultural versus economic. It also, I would argue, engenders a kind of crisis in status and identity for De Keersmaeker. To the extent that Beyoncé's treatment of *Rosas danst Rosas* and *Achterland* as "free" source material amounted to a seizing of what has characteristically been a white appropriative prerogative, that same treatment threatened to have the converse effect for De Keersmaeker: a tacit attenuation of white privilege. While, as De Keersmaeker noted, her choreography stood to gain greater exposure by appearing in "Countdown," this came at the expense of becoming a "fugitive" dance object: displaced from the restricted, authorial economy of the avant-garde, stripped of any special protection against capitalist exchange. For De Keersmaeker, claims of plagiarism and threats of legal action against Beyoncé served as a means of resisting the commodification of her choreography and recouping her privileged status as rights-bearing author and owner.[26]

---

[26] The recent collaboration between the rapper Jay-Z, who is Beyoncé's husband, and Marina Abramović presents an interesting counterpoint to the Beyoncé–De Keersmaeker incident. In July 2013, in a clear nod to Abramović's 2010 performance of immobile endurance in *The Artist Is Present*, Jay-Z performed his song "Picasso Baby" continuously for six hours at the Pace Gallery in Chelsea before an audience that included a number of art world elites, Abramović among them. In the song, Jay-Z raps about his desire to possess famous artworks, name-checking prominent visual artists and comparing himself to a "modern-day" Picasso. While we might read his engagement with Abramović as a response to the furor over Beyoncé's unauthorized use of white avant-garde choreography, Jay-Z generally seems to rank higher on an artistic hierarchy than Beyoncé. And in contrast to De Keersmaeker, Abramović evidently viewed Jay-Z's homage to her as an amplification of her power, rather than a diminishment. She told *New York Magazine's* Vulture.com, "It's really important that I can shift the public from the one field [i.e., pop music] to the arts, which rarely happens. So, this was really very meaningful thing" (Sharpe 2013). See the "performance art piece" (not music video) for Jay-Z's "Picasso Baby," which debuted on

One year after the release of the "Countdown" video, De Keersmaeker and Bojana Cvejić published a book containing extensive documentation and discussion of four early works by De Keersmaeker. Titled *A Choreographer's Score: Fase, Rosas danst Rosas, Elena's Aria, Bartok*, the book is largely a transcription of interviews with De Keersmaeker, in which she recounts in detail the process of creating these choreographies. Alongside the text are sketches, notes, and other ephemera related to each of the choreographic works, and on four accompanying DVDs, we see and hear De Keersmaeker answering questions from Cvejić. Standing before a blackboard, onto which she at times maps the structures and concepts that undergird her dances, occasionally demonstrating bits of movement, De Keersmaeker is very much the choreographer as author and teacher here. Although Cvejić writes in her introduction that the text is "by no means a definitive or authoritative account of the four works," she acknowledges that the book "favor[s] the authorial perspective that reverberates in the title *A Choreographer's Score*" (2012, 18). Calling the documentation a "score" may signal De Keersmaeker's anticipation of future reenactments, and the archiving of her dances may have stemmed from a desire to reach "a broader, more heterogeneous readership" (2012, 7), but the book unequivocally reasserts De Keersmaeker's authorial control and returns her choreography to the more circumscribed economy of the avant-garde.

Or does it?

## Reproductive Bodies and the "Snuggie" De Keersmaeker

If the conflict between De Keersmaeker and Beyoncé was fundamentally about control over the terms of dance's participation in a reproductive, capitalist economy, reproduction of a different sort served as a point of unity between the two dance artists. De Keersmaeker concluded her public comments about Beyoncé by noting what she called "one funny coincidence":

> Everyone told me, she is dancing and she is four months pregnant. In 1996, when De Mey's film was made, I was also pregnant with my second child. So, today, I can only wish her the same joy that my daughter brought me.[27]

Setting aside their differences, at least momentarily, De Keersmaeker finds connection with Beyoncé over their shared identity as mothers-to-be. While De Keersmaeker's

HBO, here: http://pitchfork.com/news/51506-watch-jay-zs-picasso-baby-performance-art-video-featuring-marina-abramovic-judd-apatow-and-more/ (accessed August 27, 2013).

[27] http://theperformanceclub.org/2011/10/anne-teresa-de-keersmaeker-responds-to-beyonce-video/ (accessed September 7, 2012).

pregnancy was, to my knowledge, never spotlighted in performances of *Rosas danst Rosas* or *Achterland* as Beyoncé's baby bump is in "Countdown," biological reproduction collapses the distance between pop culture and the avant-garde and provides a temporary reprieve from the contest over choreographic reproduction.

Yet even the pregnant female body, or at least its image, is not immune to the dynamics of exchange and the circulatory flows of the Internet. In July 2012, a sixteen-year-old Vietnamese-American boy named Ton Do-Nguyen posted to YouTube his own reenactment of Beyoncé's "Countdown" video, matching the original shot for shot, including all of the editing, dancing, and pregnant belly poses.[28] Known as the "Snuggie" version because Do-Nguyen dons a blue Snuggie blanket throughout, the video quickly went viral, receiving hundreds of thousands of views on YouTube. As a reenactment, Do-Nguyen's "Countdown" is remarkable for its fidelity to the original—Beyoncé herself praised Do-Nguyen for performing it better than she had[29]—and for the absurdity that the presence of the Snuggie gives it.

Beyoncé's endorsement of Do-Nguyen's reproduction, a far cry from the legal threats with which she met the online leaking of "Countdown," echoes her response to the proliferation of choreographic imitations of the 2008 video for "Single Ladies (Put a Ring on It)." In that case, Beyoncé sponsored a video contest challenging participants to post videos of themselves that adhered to the "Single Ladies" choreography as faithfully as possible. As Harmony Bench writes, the contest functioned as a way for Beyoncé to retain oversight of the viral phenomenon and thereby preserve her "status as author" (2012, 132). Along similar lines, Beyoncé posted a side-by-side video comparison of the original "Countdown" video and Do-Nguyen's version on her official website—effectively "co-signing" it (Ziegbe 2012).

But if Do-Nguyen's reenactment does not pose a threat to Beyoncé's authorship, what does it do to De Keersmaeker's? There is an interesting parallel between the Flanders schoolgirls' reproduction of *Rosas danst Rosas* and Do-Nguyen's reproduction of "Countdown," both of which constitute what Bench (2010) calls "social dance-media," a participatory mode of production that overlaps with, but is not identical to, "global pop culture."[30] One wonders, therefore, whether De Keersmaeker might also find the Snuggie version of her choreography "touching." Yet, to state the obvious, unlike the Flanders girls, Do-Nguyen's referent is Beyoncé, not De Keersmaeker. As far as I can tell, no mention of De Keersmaeker appeared in the flurry of overwhelmingly favorable responses to the Snuggie "Countdown."

Do-Nguyen's reproduction of Beyoncé's video thus represents another turn of the screw for De Keersmaeker's choreography, drawing it into the viral economy of the

---

[28]  See the Snuggie version here: http://www.youtube.com/watch?v=6GohpyK5Y3g (accessed August 21, 2013).

[29]  http://www.beyonce.com/news/brilliant (accessed September 12, 2012).

[30]  According to Bench (2010), "social dance-media" circulate "in internet environments" and "elaborate upon social media's ideologies of participation while remaining in the image-based domain of dance-media."

Internet. Although, unlike the movement from Beyoncé's "Single Ladies," the choreography in "Countdown" has not been re-embodied by hundreds (or thousands) of dancers, the Snuggie version shows how readily one reenactment can beget another. This reproductive chain seems an apt illustration of Rebecca Schneider's (2011) claim that there is

> a certain superabundance to reenactment, like a run-on sentence, as if an event in time, refusing to be fully or finally "over" or "gone" or "complete" pulses with a kind of thriving afterlife in an ecstasy of variables, a million insistent if recalcitrant possibilities for return. (29–30)

Looked at from one angle, this superabundance transforms De Keersmaeker's choreography into a "shared cultural object," a site at which bodies from disparate locations intermingle across time and space (Bench 2012, 133). Reenactment places De Keersmaeker's white female body, Beyoncé's black female body, and Do-Nguyen's Vietnamese-American male body in relation to another and, in the process, releases all kinds of new significations from De Keersmaeker's choreography.[31] But even as we might be tempted to celebrate the cross-temporal, intersubjective minglings and decentralized meanings that reenactment makes possible, we cannot ignore its equally potent capacity to stir up anxiety. Mediated by Beyoncé, De Keersmaeker's choreography moves across bodies and time "as if it [were] communally created and owned and not subject to copyright" (Bench 2010). As surely as the treatment of the avant-garde, first by Beyoncé and then by Do-Nguyen, "as if"—*as if* it were just another fugitive source in the public domain—inverts entrenched racial and artistic hierarchies, it simultaneously generates new attempts to restore them. Depending on your perspective, choreography's return is full of promises or threats.

* * *

And the screw continues to turn. In the fall of 2013, having completed a draft of this chapter, I learned that De Keersmaeker had embarked on "Re: Rosas! The fABULEUS Rosas Remix Project," which invited the public to recreate the chair section of *Rosas danst Rosas*. In an echo of Beyoncé's "Single Ladies" video contest, and as if revisiting the scene of the original crime, De Keersmaeker turned to the Internet to issue the call to the public to learn the *Rosas* choreography and upload videos of themselves performing it. As the site states, "Precisely 30 years ago, dance company Rosas put itself on the map with the production *Rosas danst Rosas*. This choreography has since been staged

---

[31] Do-Nguyen's Snuggie "Countdown" stands in interesting relationship to the phenomenon of male dancers reperforming "Single Ladies," which, as Bench (2012) argues, multiplies the signifying possibilities of the choreography and opens a space for "the performance of a spectrum of masculinities and male femininities" (134). Though Do-Nguyen identifies as straight, he was widely assumed to be gay, and one blogger designated him "the queer icon of tomorrow" for representing "a new coalition of gay, bi, straight, trans, and queer teens who are embracing their fabulous talents in whatever form they take, no matter how they ID." http://tomorrowmag.tumblr.com/post/27698211874/the-queer-icon-of-tomorrow-ton-do-nguyen-of-countdown (accessed August 21, 2013).

all over the world. And now it's your turn."[32] In separate videos posted on the site, De Keersmaeker and Rosas dancer Samantha van Wissen demonstrate a three-and-a-half minute (simplified) segment of the choreography, break down the movements, and discuss their structure. Unlike Beyoncé, De Keersmaeker invited participants to play with the choreography, to "make up your own *Rosas danst Rosas*." According to an article in *The Guardian*, 1,500 responded to De Keersmaeker's call, and, as of this writing, 368 filmed versions of the choreography appear on the remix site, featuring dancers of all ages from around the globe (Mackrell 2013).

Though no mention of Beyoncé is made on the site, it is impossible not to read the *Rosas* remix project through the lens of her earlier, unauthorized recreation. Indeed, *The Guardian* framed De Keersmaeker's public invitation as a way of acting upon her "acid" claim that Flanders schoolgirls performed her choreography better than Beyoncé (Mackrell 2013). It is as if in unleashing *Rosas* to the public, De Keersmaeker seeks to cover over the Beyoncé episode entirely. Turning *Rosas* into "a globally communal project" (Mackrell 2013) becomes a way of removing the taint of its dalliance with "global pop culture" and recuperating its non-commercial potential. Orchestrated as part of a commemoration of *Rosas*'s avant-garde status,[33] De Keersmaeker's decision to take the work viral is, paradoxically, the equivalent of a legal claim of copyright: an attempt to regulate choreography's reproduction and to separate out the right reenactments from the wrong.

## WORKS CITED

Abramović, Marina. 2007. *Seven Easy Pieces*. New York: Charta.

Battan, Carrie. 2011. "Video: Beyoncé: "Countdown." *Pitchfork*, October 6. http://pitchfork.com/news/44223-video-beyonce-countdown/ (accessed July 13, 2013).

Bench, Harmony. 2010. "Screendance 2.0: Social Dance-Media." *Participations: Journal of Audience & Reception Studies* 7(2). http://www.participations.org/Volume%207/Issue%202/special/bench.htm (accessed August 19, 2013).

Bench, Harmony. 2012. "'Single Ladies Is Gay': Queer Performances and Mediated Masculinities on YouTube." In *Dance on Its Own Terms: Histories and Methodologies*, edited by Melanie Bales and Karen Eliot, 127–151. New York: Oxford University Press.

"Beyoncé 'Countdown' Music Video Look by Look." 2011. MTV Style, October 6. http://style.mtv.com/2011/10/06/beyonce-countdown-music-video-look-by-look/#more-64612 (accessed August 14, 2013).

"Beyoncé Plagiarism Claims: Copying Her Videos Would Have Got Me Killed, Says Belgian Director." 2011. *The Telegraph*. October 13. http://www.telegraph.co.uk/culture/music/music-news/8823834/Beyonce-plagiarism-claims-copying-her-videos-would-have-got-me-killed-says-Belgian-director.html (accessed August 19, 2013).

---

[32] http://www.rosasdanstrosas.be/en-home/ (accessed November 22, 2013).

[33] Video entries received by October 1, 2013, were exhibited as part of an installation that accompanied a revival of *Rosas danst Rosas* in Brussels, October 8–12, 2013. http://www.rosasdanstrosas.be/en-home/.

Brooks, Daphne A. 2008. "'All That You Can't Leave Behind': Black Female Soul Singing and the Politics of Surrogation in the Age of Catastrophe." *Meridians: feminism, race, transnationalism* 8(1): 180–204.

Burt, Ramsay. 2003. "Memory, Repetition and Critical Intervention: The Politics of Historical Reference in Recent European Dance Performance." *Performance Research* 8(2): 34–41.

De Keersmaeker, Anne Teresa, and Bojana Cvejić. 2012. *A Choreographer's Score: Fase, Rosas danst Rosas, Elena's Aria, Bartók*. Brussels: Mercartorfonds—Rosas.

DeFrantz, Thomas. 2012. "Unchecked Popularity: Neoliberal Circulations of Black Social Dance." In *Neoliberalism and Global Theatres: Performance Permutations*, edited by Lara Nielsen and Patricia Ybarra, 128–142. New York: Palgrave Macmillan.

Foster, Susan Leigh. 2002. *Dances That Describe Themselves: The Improvised Choreography of Richard Bull*. Middletown, CT: Wesleyan University Press.

Gayles, Contessa. 2011. "Beyonce Flaunts Baby Bump in Retro 'Countdown' Video Clip." The Boombox, October 3. http://theboombox.com/beyonce-countdown-video-preview/ (accessed August 13, 2013).

Gottschild, Brenda Dixon. 1996. *Digging the Africanist Presence in American Performance: Dance and Other Contexts*. Westport, CT: Greenwood Press.

Greene, K. J. 1999. "Copyright, Culture & Black Music: A Legacy of Unequal Protection." *Hastings Communication & Entertainment Law Journal* 21: 339–392.

Harris, Cheryl I. 1993. "Whiteness as Property." *Harvard Law Review* 106(8): 1707–1791.

Higgins, Charlotte. 2011. "Beyoncé Pleasant but Consumerist, Says Plagiarism Row Choreographer." *The Guardian*, October 11. http://www.theguardian.com/music/2011/oct/11/beyonce-pleasant-consumerist-plagiarism-row (accessed August 21, 2013).

Horwitz, Andy. 2011. "Anne Teresa De Keersmaeker vs. Beyonce." Culturebot. http://www.culturebot.org/2011/10/11496/anne-teresa-de-keersmaeker-vs-beyonce/ (accessed August 16, 2013).

Jennings, Luke. 2011. "Beyoncé v De Keersmaeker: Can You Copyright a Dance Move?" *The Guardian*, October 11. http://www.theguardian.com/stage/theatreblog/2011/oct/11/beyonce-de-keersmaeker-dance-move?newsfeed=true (accessed August 14, 2013).

Kaufman, Sarah. 2011. "Beyoncé: 'Countdown' Video and the Art of Stealing." *Washington Post*, November 18. http://articles.washingtonpost.com/2011-11-18/lifestyle/35281728_1_rosas-danst-rosas-beyonce-marcel-duchamp (accessed August 20, 2013).

Kennedy, Gerrick D. 2011. "Beyoncé's '4' Leaks Online, Three Weeks before Release." *Los Angeles Times* Music Blog, June 7. http://latimesblogs.latimes.com/music_blog/2011/06/beyonc%C3%A9s-4-pops-up-online-three-weeks-before-release.html (accessed August 28, 2013).

Kino, Carol. 2010. "A Rebel Form Gains Favor. Fights Ensue." *New York Times*, March 10, AR25.

Kisselgoff, Anna. 1991. "Review/Dance: Belgians Go Beyond Minimalism." *New York Times*, September 28. http://www.nytimes.com/1991/09/28/arts/review-dance-belgians-go-beyond-minimalism.html?pagewanted=2 (accessed August 14, 2013).

Kraut, Anthea. 2011. "White Womanhood, Property Rights, and the Campaign for Choreographic Copyright: Loïe Fuller's Serpentine Dance." *Dance Research Journal* 43(1): 3–26.

Kraut, Anthea. 2015. *Choreographing Copyright: Race, Gender, and Intellectual Property Rights in American Dance*. New York: Oxford University Press.

La Rocco, Claudia. 2011. "Anne Teresa De Keersmaeker Responds to Beyonce Video." *The Performance Club* blog. http://theperformanceclub.org/2011/10/anne-teresa-de-keersmaeker-responds-to-beyonce-video/ (accessed September 7, 2012).

Lepecki, Andre. 2010. "The Body as Archive: Will to Re-enact and the Afterlives of Dances." *Dance Research Journal* 42(2): 28–48.

Mackrell, Judith. 2013. "Beyoncé, De Keersmaeker, and a Dance Reinvented by Everyone." *The Guardian*, Oct. 9. http://www.theguardian.com/stage/2013/oct/09/beyonce-de-keersmaeker-technology-dance (accessed November 22, 2013).

Manning, Susan. 2004. *Modern Dance, Negro Dance: Race in Motion*. Minneapolis: University of Minnesota Press.

McKinley, James C., Jr. 2011. "Beyoncé Accused of Plagiarism over Video." *New York Times*, October 10. http://artsbeat.blogs.nytimes.com/2011/10/10/beyonce-accused-of-plagiarism-over-video/ (accessed August 15, 2013).

Mitchell, John. 2011. "Beyonce Flaunts Baby Bump in 'Countdown' Video." *MTV News*, October 6. http://www.mtv.com/news/articles/1672134/beyonce-countdown-video.jhtml (accessed August 13, 2013).

Nika, Colleen. 2011. "Beyonce Takes a Fashionable Trip through Retro Cinema in 'Countdown' Video." *Rolling Stone*, October 7. http://www.rollingstone.com/music/blogs/thread-count/beyonce-takes-a-fashionable-trip-through-retro-cinema-in-countdown-video-20111007 (accessed August 13, 2013).

Perricone, Kathleen. 2011. "Beyoncé on Controversy She Ripped Off Italian Pop Star: Lorella Cuccarini 'Inspired Me So Much.'" *New York Daily News*, May 25. http://www.nydailynews.com/entertainment/music-arts/beyonce-controversy-ripped-italian-pop-star-lorella-cuccarini-inspired-article-1.142895#ixzz2cdAjXQ9m (accessed August 21, 2013).

Phelan, Peggy. 1993. *Unmarked: The Politics of Performance*. London: Routledge.

Posner, Richard A. 2007. *The Little Book of Plagiarism*. New York: Random House.

Ramirez, Erika. 2013. "Op-Ed: When Beyoncé's Inspiration Turns into Imitation." *Billboard*, May 1. http://www.billboard.com/articles/columns/the-juice/1560092/op-ed-when-beyonces-inspiration-turns-into-imitation (accessed August 14, 2013).

Rosen, Jody. 2011. "Beyonce Gets Intimate in First of '4' Roseland Ballroom Shows." *Rolling Stone*, August 15. http://www.rollingstone.com/music/news/beyonce-gets-intimate-in-first-of-4-roseland-ballroom-shows-20110815 (accessed August 21, 2013).

Said, Sammy. "Beyonce Net Worth." http://www.therichest.org/celebnetworth/celeb/singer/beyonce-net-worth/ (accessed August 29, 2012).

Schneider, Rebecca. 2011. *Performing Remains: Art and War in Times of Theatrical Reenactment*. New York: Routledge.

Sharpe, Jamie. 2013. "Marina Abramovic Wants the Rap Community to Google 'Performance Art.'" *Vulture*, July 30. http://www.vulture.com/2013/07/marina-abramovic-jay-z-performance-art.html (accessed August 27, 2013).

Siegel, Marcia B. 1972. *At the Vanishing Point*. New York: Saturday Review Press.

Srinivasan, Priya. 2011. *Sweating Saris: Indian Dance as Transnational Labor*. Philadelphia: Temple University Press.

Suclas, Roslyn. 2011. "Repetitions Build Drama with Rhythm and Gesture." *New York Times*, June 14. http://www.nytimes.com/2011/06/15/arts/dance/reviving-de-keersmaekers-rosas-danst-rosas-dance-review.html?_r=1 (accessed August 15, 2013).

Vena, Jocelyn. 2011. "Beyonce's 'Countdown' Video Shoot Was 'Evolving, Spontaneous.'" *MTV News*, October 7. http://www.mtv.com/news/articles/1672200/beyonce-countdown-video-shoot.jhtml (accessed August 29, 2012).

"VIDEO: Beyoncé Releases Alternate Version of 'Countdown.'" 2011. *Pop Culture Major Blog*, November 27. http://www.popculturemajor.com/2011/11/27/video-beyonce-releases-alternate-version-of-countdown/ (accessed September 7, 2012).

"Video Deconstruction: Director Adria Petty on Beyoncé's 'Countdown.'" 2011. *The GQ Eye*, October 10. http://www.gq.com/style/blogs/the-gq-eye/2011/10/video-deconstruction-director-adria-petty-on-beyoncs-countdown.html (accessed August 15, 2013).

Wong, Yutian. 2010. *Choreographing Asian America*. Middletown, CT: Wesleyan University Press.

Ziegbe, Mawuse. 2012. "Beyonce Co-Signs 'Snuggie' Version of Her 'Countdown' Video." *Pop Radar*. http://www.boston.com/ae/celebrity/blog/popradar/2012/07/beyonce_co-signs_snuggie_version_of_her_countdown_video.html (accessed August 19, 2013).

CHAPTER 19

# REENACTING MODERNIST TIME

## *William Kentridge's* The Refusal of Time

CHRISTEL STALPAERT

In his multimedia installations, South African artist William Kentridge (Johannesburg, 1955) works with a variety of media: soundscapes, (animation) films, charcoal drawings, printmaking, and sculpture. Kentridge combines archival material and found footage referring to the violent history of South Africa, with his own stop-motion animated films, often erasing as well as adding lines and forms to his drawings. In this ambiguous, dense material, Kentridge provides a powerful comment on the charged history of colonialism and Apartheid in his homeland, and on racism in the world at large. The son of two prominent anti-Apartheid lawyers, it is no surprise that Kentridge's oeuvre is engaged with social conflict and inequality. As Kentridge himself observes, "I have never tried to make illustrations of Apartheid, but the drawings and films are certainly spawned by and feed off the brutalized society left in its wake. I am interested in a political art, that is to say an art of ambiguity, contradiction, uncompleted gestures and uncertain endings" (2015, n.p.).

Art historians have studied the political dimension of Kentridge's work extensively, referring mostly to the (animation) films and the charcoal drawings (Stewart 2005; Hennlich 2015). Less attention has been paid, however, to the particular function of movement and dance in his installations. This is surprising, as dance seems to have a modest, but nevertheless recurrent and significant place in them. *I Am Not Me, the Horse Is Not Mine* (2008) and also his latest installation, *More Sweetly Play the Dance* (2015), feature a ballerina dancing *en pointe*. In the performance *Refuse the Hour* (2012),[1] Dada Masilo is standing on a rotating platform with a costume that is very much reminiscent

---

[1] This performance was originally created and premiered in June 2012 in Cape Town, South Africa, at the Cape Town City Hall in February 2015.

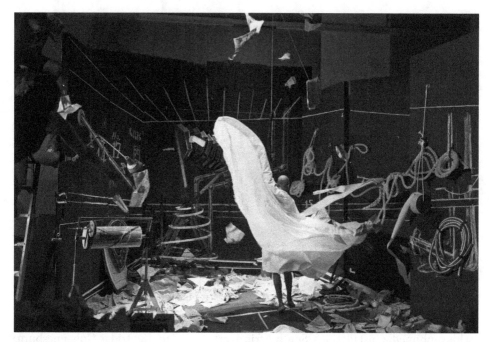

**FIGURE 19.1.** Dada Masilo performing Loïe Fuller's *Serpentine Dance* in a projected film sequence in William Kentridge's multimedia installation *The Refusal of Time* (2012).

Courtesy of the artist and Marian Goodman Gallery.

of Oskar Schlemmer's *Figurine* in *The Triadic Ballet* (1922). Dancing figures also frequently appear in the parades projected in his installations. *More Sweetly Play the Dance* (2015), for example, features a dancing ballerina in a cage, pulled forward on a cart. One of the most remarkable references to dance history, however, is the reenactment of a modern dance sequence by choreographer and dancer Dada Masilo in the five-channel video in the multimedia installation *The Refusal of Time* (2012) (Figure 19.1).

During *The Refusal of Time*, a film sequence is projected on one of the museum walls, displaying Dada Masilo's reenactment of Loïe Fuller's *Serpentine Dance*. The contemporaneous art critic Arsène Alexandre described the American pioneer of modern dance as "the marvelous dream-creature you see dancing madly in a vision swirling among her dappled veils which change ten thousand times a minute" (1900, 24). Masilo performs Fuller's typical free-flowing movements in the iconic silk costume, animated by long baton-like wands, which prolong her arm movements. The similarities are striking: the contour of the dancer's body disappears in the billowing folds of transparent silk, while the wavy folds in the soft texture of the silk accentuate her swirling movements.

However, this is not a mere reconstruction of the *Serpentine Dance* that was originally created toward the end of the nineteenth century, and an imitation of which was said to be recorded by the Lumière brothers in 1896. Three striking differences give the reenactment a deconstructive potential. First, the serpentine dance is performed by a dancer of color. Second, the dance sequence is part of a multimedia installation that questions "the ready-made, simultaneous, and quickly consumed facility of photographic imagery" (Stewart 2005, 52). Third, the film sequence of the dance is shown backward, that is, it is time reversed. Using the age-old cinematic trick of reversed footage, Kentridge makes sheets of paper fly through the air, as if they were pushed upward by Masilo's dance.

With this special effect, however, Kentridge does not seek to enchant the viewer. In fact, the visual trickery functions as a reminder of the constructed nature of our mental and perceptual processes. Kentridge not only questions the white supremacy in the official history of dance by having Fuller's iconic serpentine dance reenacted by a dancer of color. The time-reversed quality of the images also challenges our habitual way of seeing things in a linear and chronological order, including the chronological linearity of dance history. This reenactment in *The Refusal of Time* thus exceeds mere reconstruction. It becomes an artistic strategy with a particular potential to "rethink relations among memory, history, archive, time and performance" (De Laet 2013, 150). According to the modern conception of time, history was understood as "a succession of singular, autonomous moments that were unique and repeatable" (Le Roy 2012, 82). With this particular reenactment of an iconic modern dance, *The Refusal of Time* questions time regimes that support a chronological, modernist conception of time and (dance) history. Kentridge's dancing figures in the closing parade of *The Refusal of Time* likewise differ from the usual actors in the historical parade. The actors reenact historical events, and incorporate mythological figures or exemplary heroes. However, as I will observe, Kentridge's parade reveals the modernist desire to reenact history along a chronological timeline, instead of merely supporting "the theatrical experience of historicist historiography" (Le Roy 2012, 85).

The Western notion of chronological and linear time is considered a central tenet of modernity, capitalism, and colonialism (Bal 2015; Osborne 2015). Connecting Kentridge's *The Refusal of Time* with Deleuze's onto-aesthetics, this chapter seeks to examine the Western time regime and to reflect on how reenactment can be political in the sense that it articulates an ontological politics of time and movement. In other words, this chapter provides a philosophical-historical perspective on the notion of reenactment in the installation *The Refusal of Time* and examines "the relationship of danced reenactment to historiography, periodization, center-periphery, and non-synchronicity," as Mark Franko outlined in the call for papers of this book. I will observe how *The Refusal of Time* dismantles the Western time regime through four concepts that are related to time: time as Chronos or clock-time; time as Aeon or duration; time as protocol or networks and systems; and time as Kairos or the revolutionary aspect of time. *The Refusal of Time* reveals how clocks regulate time, but also how Western time machines such as metronomes turn rhythm into a standard tempo, and dances into unique and repeatable moments in a (chronological) history. The unconventional reenactment of Loïe Fuller's *Serpentine Dance* in *The Refusal of Time* in this regard inaugurates time as Kairos, touching upon the revolutionary aspect of time, blowing up our habitual way of perceiving time and history.

# TIME AS CHRONOS

*The Refusal of Time* was commissioned for the thirteenth dOCUMENTA in Kassel, in 2012,[2] and was erected in one of the storage spaces of the *Hauptbahnhof*. The main function of most of these annexes is now an exhibition space of contemporary art, but the central building of the *Hauptbahnhof* is still operating as a train station. Thus, before entering the venue, one has to find one's way through the main entrance of the railway station, along the platforms and the railways, to the storage room turned into exhibition space. First encountering those nervous people, hurrying in their everyday life, rushing to catch their train, and then having to wait for almost half an hour to be able to attend Kentridge's *The Refusal of Time* gives the visitor two different time experiences. Seeking to enjoy some time off in an art exhibition, one is first confronted with the tyranny of clock time in everyday life, with "the mechanization of human activity in work environments, made most obviously visible by the appearance of clocks in train stations, factories, and offices" (Smith 2015, 12). This particular time experience was indeed Kentridge's intention, and he therefore collaborated with time-expert Peter Galison:

> Since Newton's time, that ordinary, all-too-measurable clock time has appeared everywhere. It wired up school and factories, and was installed for public display all around the cities, inside government buildings and on our wrists. Throughout *Refusal*, we wanted to disrupt that coordinated ubiquity. (Galison 2012, 312–313)

It is no coincidence, then, that references to time machines are abundantly present in *The Refusal of Time*. From the very first minute one enters the darkened exhibition space where the artwork is installed, the visitor is confronted with the pressure of clock time that is imposed on human beings. On three of the four museum walls, a film sequence of lofty metronomes is projected, producing the loud, clicking sound of regular, metrical ticks (Figure 19.2). These mechanical rhythmic beats constitute a mechanized standard tempo. Invented at the beginning of the nineteenth century as a tool for musicians to produce a standard tempo reference, this machine was celebrated for its perfect sense of timing and its consistent tempo. However, it was also heavily criticized for its mechanical and hence inhuman character. Opponents criticized the metronome for making rhythm mechanical; no human being would ever be able to create such a perfect tempo. Metronomes, for that matter, were reproached for undoing all musically expressive qualities in a musical performance. They were said to render music sterile, expressionless, and inhuman (Jones 2014, 659–660).

In *The Refusal of Time* the ticking of the metronomes gets louder and louder, and this does not fail to affect the visitor, who becomes annoyed and agitated by the loud,

---

[2] I visited the installation *The Refusal of Time* for the first time during the dOCUMENTA biennial in Kassel and saw it again in the Iziko South African National Gallery in Cape Town in February 2015.

**FIGURE 19.2.** The ticking metronomes in William Kentridge's *The Refusal of Time* (2012).

Courtesy of the artist and Marian Goodman Gallery.

regular beats. In a very e/affective way, Kentridge confronts the visitor here with the tyranny of measured time. In *The Logic of Sense*, Gilles Deleuze calls this the tempo of time as Chronos: it is "the regulated movement of vast and profound presents" (1990, 163). In *A Thousand Plateaus*, Deleuze and Guattari link their notion of Chronos with Pierre Boulez's notion of pulsed, metrical time in music (and dance). "Pulsed, metrical Chronos" is in that sense the time of "regular repeated intervals" (Bogue 2012, 42). It is controlled by "conventional meters and regular beats" (Bogue 2012, 42) and inaugurates "a formal and functional music based on values" (Deleuze 1990, 289). Dancers absorbing regulated beats without variation or limit are in that sense said to be "mickey-mousing" the music. They dance "the rhythm of [ . . . ] correct time" (Galison, 2012, 30).

After some considerable time, the metronomes fail to keep up with the perfect synchronicity of mechanically controlled time. Pulsed time goes into overdrive. Chronos gets out of joint. The steady beats of the metronomes gradually turn into an overwhelming soundscape, composed by Philip Miller. Pulsed time or tempo becomes non-pulsed time here, or—in musical terms—"rhythmic Aeon" (Bogue 2012, 42), inaugurating "floating music, both floating *and* machinic, which has nothing but speeds or differences in dynamic" (Deleuze and Guattari 2007, 289). It is the time of "irregular, incommensurable intervals" (Bogue 2012, 42).

Kentridge not only reveals how clocks regulate time, and how time machines such as metronomes turn rhythm into a standard tempo. He also reveals how time as

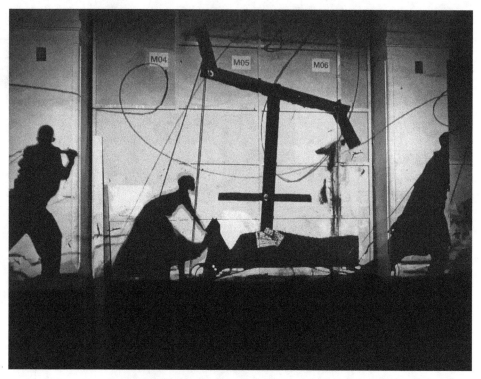

**FIGURE 19.3.**  An optical telegraph featured in the parade of William Kentridge's *The Refusal of Time* (2012).

Courtesy of the artist and Marian Goodman Gallery.

Chronos is imposed on bodies, regulating their (dance) movements and daily activities. Having perceived ordinary people in their daily activity of rushing against clock-time at the railway station before entering the installation, the visitor is well aware of "how time registers in people" (Galison 2012, 160), of how we all have become "temporal beings" (Rosse 2012, 7). Indeed, clock time is presented as a form of control and measurement that percolates in our bodies and regulates human behavior. In *A Thousand Plateaus* Deleuze and Guattari defined this clock-mode of temporality as "the time of measure that situates things and persons, develops a form, and determines a subject" (2007, 289). Marquard Smith reformulates this thought more specifically as follows:

> Clock time has infiltrated every aspect of our lives and beings to the point where, as temporal beings, we are ourselves subjects of and subject to it: we may still clock on and clock off, but even when we are not at work, we are never off the clock. There is no "free" time, much like there is no such thing as a free lunch. (2015, 12)

Suddenly, a drawing of an optical telegraph is projected on the museum walls (Figure 19.3). The projected drawing is reminiscent of an archival document in the exhibition catalogue,[3] referring to Claude Chappe's invention in the nineteenth century. This pendulum system was an important step in the Western control of time and space. Located on a hill, the operators of optical telegraphs could read each other's codes through telescopes, and transmit the signal swiftly to the next optical telegraph down the line. The optical telegraph was celebrated for its transmission speed, which was said to cover 760 kilometers in a few minutes (Moran 2010, 149). The optical telegraph was used for transmitting information over a long distance in the shortest possible time span, overcoming the time-space limitations of printing and writing messages. The arms of the pendulum system could move into different positions, meaning different codes. Kentridge's hand-drawn image of the optical telegraph is animated on a black surface. The stop-motion animation, in a dominant palette of black and white, is full of erasures, revisions, and transformations of lines and forms. The drawn object seems to have a life of its own, and repeatedly shape shifts into a gallows. Later, a shadow-transformation of this object, lingering between an optical telegraph sending signals and a gallows waiting for the moment of execution, haunts the shadowy figures dancing, laboring, and moving along the museum walls. This is but one of the startling examples where a seemingly "harmless" or "innocent" time machine obtains a threatening dimension.

Triggered by these historical references, the visitor is invited to draw conclusions about the function of these seemingly harmless time machines in relation to history in general and to colonialism in particular. Time seems to be measured out not only in beats, meters, seconds, minutes, and hours, but also in centuries, eras, and histories.

Kentridge delivers a political message in a very particular way here. He is not seeking to uncover the "truth" from the folds of history. Kentridge does not want to convince the viewer of a truth behind a historical event. As opposed to the documentary style that sides with a positivist historiography, Kentridge is more interested in truth functions than in the truth itself; he is mostly investigating "the conditions of its creation."[4] His art of ambiguity, contradiction, uncompleted gestures, and uncertain endings explores—to paraphrase Deleuze—from where time as Chronos draws its measure.[5]

## TIME AS PROTOCOL

Time as Chronos draws its measure from time protocols and networks. Optical telegraphs, time zones, calendars, travel system schedules, speed reading systems, and so

[3] The exhibition catalog reveals what time machines from the nineteenth century and the beginning of the twentieth inspired Kentridge: an optical telegraph (1803), a pneumatic clock (1879), the pneumatic mother clock by Charles Bourdon (1885), the Neuchâtel Master Clock (1924), a photo of the clock at the Porter's Lodge at the Greenwich Observatory (1900), a drawing of the Great Equatorial Telescope at the Greenwich Observatory (1877), a metronome, among others.

[4] The "truth" is called truth function in Deleuze's thinking: "[A] concept always has the truth that falls to it as a function of the conditions of its creation" (Patton 1997, 5).

[5] "But from where exactly does it (time as Chronos) draw its measure?" (Deleuze 1990, 163).

on, are such protocol-constituting elements. These time protocols and network systems connect people and infiltrate bodies, aligning them to the Western time regime (Smith 2015, 16). Kentridge works with and against the logic of such systems and interrogates them critically throughout *The Refusal of Time*.

It is no coincidence that the invention of most of the time machines that Kentridge evokes in the installation—such as the metronome and the optical telegraph—date from the nineteenth century. Clock time is a central tenet of modernity and capitalism, and its universal value has a particular relation to colonialism. Mieke Bal put it clearly and starkly: "clock time, dating from the colonization period, is fundamentally in the interest of capitalism" (2015, 38). As philosopher Peter Osborne argues in his *Notes on the Dialectics of Differential Historical Time*, under colonialism, time was transformed from a neutral medium into a historical force. In the late eighteenth century, the concepts of "progress" and "development" form the basis of "modernity" and provide the perfect alibi to "develop" the colonies—albeit for the main profit of the colonizer.

> It is the idea of the *non-contemporaneousness of geographically diverse* but *chronologically simultaneous* times which thus develops that, in the context of colonial experience, becomes the basis for universal histories with a cosmopolitan intent. Once the practice of such comparisons was established in colonial discourse, it was easily transferable to the relations between particular social spheres and practices within different European countries themselves, and thereafter, once again, globally. (Osborne 2015, 63)

As Kentridge grew up in South Africa, his oeuvre also reflects the complex colonial history of his native country. When the British gained permanent control over the Cape Colony in the beginning of the nineteenth century, they not only colonized the land and its raw materials, they also colonized time. The parallels between what is considered as the "milestones" of colonization—the construction of a railway network and the introduction of a Western time regime in South Africa—are striking and are referred to in *The Refusal of Time*.[6] The episode *Give Us Back Our Sun* indicates how the colonization and transportation of raw materials coincides with imposing a Western time regime on a community that hitherto had the natural time span of the sun to guide them through their days and years. When colonization reaches its peak, the American system of electrical time announces a universal, standardized time, and the British system of undersea cables announces the transcontinental arrival of European time. This

---

[6] In 1859, Cape Town's first industrial site was erected, the railway workshops at Salt River. In the 1860s, the first telegraph line was drawn between Cape Town and Simon's Town. In that same year, the New Harbor plans started with the construction of breakwater and Alfred Basin. In 1862, the Cape Town Railway and Dock Company railway line was erected to Eerste River. In 1863, the railway reached Wellington, and by that time also, Cape Town was linked to Grahamstown by telegraph. In 1864, the railway line reached Wynberg. In 1867, diamonds were discovered in Kimberly, and in 1886, gold was discovered in Witwatersrand. These raw materials were transported, via the railway network, to the colonizer's homeland. In 1885, a submarine cable connected Cape Town with Europe.

**FIGURE 19.4.** The Clock Room in William Kentridge's *The Refusal of* Time (2012), referring to the Royal Observatory in Greenwich, 1894.

Courtesy of the artist and Marian Goodman Gallery.

is "time synchronized to the globe's zero point, the Royal Observatory in Greenwich" (Galison 2012, 30). As such, telegraphy also "promised to increase the control of great empires by their central government, something rulers of empires had always yearned for" (Headrick 2012, 67).

Moving through the history of science and colonialism in different projected rooms or *chambers*, *The Refusal of Time* reveals the darkest side of time as protocol. Each of the chambers has a clear indication of time and space and refers to a specific entanglement of the history of science and colonial rule.

The first chamber that is projected on the museum walls is the Clock Room, referring to the Royal Observatory in Greenwich, 1894 (Figure 19.4). This observatory is situated on a hill in Greenwich Park, London, and was commissioned in 1675 by King Charles II for perfecting navigation charts and maps. In 1851, however, it became the center of world time, as the prime meridian was located in the observatory. The Clock Room, full of clocks, features a man and his assistants struggling to synchronize time, making it pulsed, standardized, and universal. *The Refusal of Time* thus represents the European sense of order imposed by cables and time zones. Eventually, the Royal Observatory also became the base of British astronomy, mapping the seas and the stars. This chamber hence also houses a telescope, "a planetary machine that would bring the world under one ticking clock" (Galison 2012, 31) (Figure 19.5). This chamber in *The Refusal of Time* represents Western control over time and space on a global scale, strengthening colonial rule and removing the local people from their natural time span.

**FIGURE 19.5.** The Clock Room with the telescope in William Kentridge's *The Refusal of Time* (2012), referring to the Royal Observatory in Greenwich, 1894.

Courtesy of the artist and Marian Goodman Gallery.

These strings of cables, these birds nests of copper, turned the world into a giant switchboard, for commerce and control. The world was covered by a huge dented bird cage of time zones, of lines of agreement of control, all sent out by the clock rooms of Europe. Local suns were shifted further and further from local zeniths. (Kentridge 2012, xiv)

A second chamber is the Engine Room, referring to the Colonial War Office, 1919 (Figure 19.6). This chamber points to the controversial topic of the British colonial development policy and its role in the so-called "Scramble for Africa" during the period of New Imperialism. Following the General Act of the Berlin Conference of 1885, summoned by Bismarck, Africa was to be divided among five European nations (Harlow 2003, 1). It was the beginning of a blunt invasion, occupation, division, colonization, and annexation of African territory by European powers. The main task of the Colonial War Office was to "increase colonial production and ease the process of trade between the colonies and the outside world" (Constantine 2005, 9). Hence, it facilitated the construction of railways, roads, harbors, and so on, that would benefit the economic infrastructure. Under the guise of enlightened aid for colonial development, progress was primarily made for the British Empire, culminating in the late nineteenth and early twentieth centuries.

The Map Room, referring to the London Telegraph Office, 1902, reveals how colonial expansion sided with transatlantic cable enterprises.[7] Time is also geography:

---

[7] The telegraph was an important tool in British colonial development policy. It is no surprise then, that also in the nineteenth century, electric telegraph companies were busy connecting London with the

**FIGURE 19.6.** The different rooms (chambers) in William Kentridge's *The Refusal of Time* (2012).

Courtesy of the artist and Marian Goodman Gallery.

Time is distance, but it is also geography. The 19th century coordination of clocks was undertaken to synchronise the clocks with stations in Europe. [ . . . ] The perfection of chronometers had long been the aim of geographers, to fix more precisely the positions of islands and continents in relation to Europe. With the spread of cables under sea and over land, that followed the development of electric telegraphy, time was taken from the master clocks of London and Paris and sent to the colonies. The lines on maps were miniature renderings of the real lines of cables that snaked round continents [ . . . ]. The clock and the colonial observatory completed the mapping of the world. (Kentridge 2012, xiii)

The scientist in the Map Room, measuring the world with the help of globes, maps, and measures, displays the "arrogance of British control of the word" (Galison and Kentridge 2012a,158). In the exhibition catalog, Kentridge further illustrates this arrogance by including a photograph of the Time Desk at the Greenwich Observatory

rest of the (colonized) world. Colonial governors of the time considered the telegraph an important tool for exerting power and control over South African territories. The governor of Victoria, Lord Brassey, called the telegraph "a great Imperial binding force" (in Headrick [1991] 2012, 68). As historian Daniel R. Headrick points out: "control operated through the telegraph wires and cables" in the colonies (68). He even calls the telegraph an invisible weapon in the hands of the colonizers.

in 1900. Seated at a table, one white man is put in control of the time of the rest of the world.

Being located at the Kassel *Hauptbahnhof*, the site-specificity of *The Refusal of Time* also resonates with the entanglement of the history of science and colonialism in Germany. The construction of the central railway station of Kassel was one of the high-prestige projects of the German government. It originally started between 1851 and 1856 and eventually played an important part in the relatively short, but nevertheless important colonial history of Germany (1884–1919), as economic colonial success depended on reliable transportation facilities. Bismarck's "Scramble for Africa" (Taylor, qtd. in Frierichsmeyer et al. 2001, 9) actually started in South Africa. What was called a "protective" measure to fend off threats from other colonizing forces[8] soon became a colonial politics with flourishing mercantile tactics. By 1885, Germany had acquired, next to other territories in the Pacific, four African territories: Southwest Africa, Togo, Cameroon, and German East Africa (Frierichsmeyer et al. 2001, 9). These African territories were used as trading colonies, with an impressive railway network at its service. It was the German government that had control over the construction of the railway network, a project essential to the expansion of trade relations between Germany and Africa. These investments were portrayed by the Germans as contributions to the development of the colonies, but the objectives of these investments were mainly for the benefit of the German economy. The railways, penetrating further into the interior of Africa, were constructed to link areas of "agricultural cultivation" with the harbors of the coast and served mainly to facilitate the export of raw materials and agricultural products. The railway network in fact supported the large European-run rubber and cocoa plantations in which Africans were forced to work (Friedrichsmeyer et al. 2001, 12). The local people were confined to cheap labor in the plantations or were, like the Herero, even removed from their land and expelled to the Kahahari Desert, where many of them starved to death, or were exterminated. Some historians therefore term this part of German history "genocidal" (Friedrichsmeyer et al. 2001, 13). The European-led plantations, of course, mainly served German economic interest, and although the official discourse testified to model colonies "where major military efforts to suppress indigenous uprisings were unnecessary," there were harsh military campaigns by the colonial forces, forced labor that often lead to death, and many violent incidents of suppression of the indigenous peoples (Friedrichsmeyer et al. 2001, 11).[9]

---

[8] On April 24, 1884, he sent a telegram to the German consul of Cape Town, "proclaiming that the areas of Southwest Africa granted to tobacco merchant Adolf Lüderitz by local chiefs were now under the protection of the German government" (Friedrichsmeyer et al. 2001, 9).

[9] Germany's state-sponsored colonial ventures took place between 1884 and 1919, but the country exhibited a longer history of imperialist attitudes. As Heinrich Schmitthenner points out, "There are colonies which are territorially contiguous with the Mother Country, and there are colonial activities without the flag. Colonization does not emanate from the State alone but from the colonizing activities of the race" (qtd. in Friedrichsmeyer et al. 2001, 8). Sara Friedrichsmeyer concludes, "From this point of view the Germans are colonizing people with centuries of experience. They have traditions of settlement, missionary work and commercial activity which go back far more beyond the short-lived colonial empire of 1884–1919" (2001, 9).

The site-specificity of Kentridge's *The Refusal of Time*, together with striking projected sentences such as "Those who could travel and those who stayed home," reminds the viewer of the colonial history of violence that the Germans inflicted on non-European peoples. There were German people who could travel to Africa, starting from the main central station in Kassel to a harbor, where a boat brought them overseas to Africa, and from there, further inland, to the countryside, where they could run prosperous plantations of tobacco and cocoa.And there were indigenous people who stayed "home": they were confined to hard labor in the plantations, or had to flee to less fertile fields, where they lived a much less fortunate life.

# TIME AS AEON

An important motif in *The Refusal of Time* is "trying to resist the imposed order that time supposed" (Galison and Kentridge 2012a, 157). Kentridge refuses to accept Chronos as a "cold quantification of the world," as "the dead circulation of geometry" (Galison 2012, 312). Instead, he is looking for "particular collisions," for human measures against time and its entanglement with the history of colonialism. Kentridge returns to the human measure of time again and again in *The Refusal of Time*, treating "bodies as breathing, ticking, yet all-too fragile clocks" (Galison 2012, 312). He seeks to revalue corporeal measurements, to free Aeon from Chronos, duration from clock-time, and rhythm from tempo, believing that people can still retain "their own private time" from "the universally audible tick-tock" (Galison 2012, 312).

Philosopher Giorgio Agamben observed that the "task of a genuine revolution is to change time" (2005, 99).[10] But what could a decimal clock and a revolutionary explosion have in common? In *Blowing up the Meridian*, time specialist Peter Galison tells the story of a young French anarchist, Martial Bourdin, who in February 1984 planned to blow up the Royal Observatory in Greenwich. He wanted to destroy the first meridian: time zero. Kentridge interprets this anarchistic idea as a particular collision in the history of time, as an act of resistance against mechanical modern time. He recalls the resistance to colonial rule, which was to him in fact also an attempt to resist the time regime of the European clock.

> The Chilembwe revolt of 1915, the Herero revolt of 1906, the movement and actions against Europe, [ . . . ] were all attempts to resist the weight and control of Europe.

---

[10] Every conception of history is invariably accompanied by a certain experience of time that is implicit to it, conditions it, and thereby has to be elucidated. Similarly, every culture is first and foremost a particular experience of time, and no new culture is possible without an alteration in this experience. The original task of a genuine revolution, therefore, is never merely to "change the world," but also—and above all—to "change time" (Agamben 2005, 99).

Give us back our Sun. As if blowing up a train line could blow up the pendulum of the European clock, which swung over every head. (Kentridge 2012, xiv)

Inspired by Bourdin's anarchistic plans, Kentridge has all the chambers exploded in *The Refusal of Time*. It means the end of measuring time and space in the Clock Room (Royal Observatory Greenwich, 1894) and the Engine Room (Colonial War Office, 1919). It also interrupts the chronological logic, the rhythm, and the ubiquity of Western time protocols. Of course this is more than a reference to Bourdin's revolutionary plans. Kentridge's particular collisions not only question the global use of these standardized clock times, but also all knowledge that is gathered through these systems: the archival, the knowable, the searchable, and the historical.

When the established time machine collapses in the Engine Room, representing the Colonial War Office, sheets of paper are blown through the room and performer Dada Masilo is dancing around them, reenacting Loïe Fuller's *Serpentine Dance*. It is striking, however, that Kentridge is showing the dance backward, with reversed footage. Instead of merely recognizing a reconstruction of an iconic modern dance, we perceive bizarre movements, with swirling sheets of paper flying up in the air (Figure 19.7).

Kentridge himself was struck by the power emanating from the movements in reverse: "Maybe what we remember most are these wonderful and bizarre backward dances and the paper going up in the air; and the dislocation of how one expects a rather

**FIGURE 19.7.** Dada Masilo in William Kentridge's *The Refusal of Time* (2012), her dancing "pushing the paper up into the air."

Courtesy of the artist and Marian Goodman Gallery.

ordinary world to turn" (Galison and Kentridge 2012b, 250). This dislocation prevents the viewer from being immersed in the past that is being represented in the reenactment. Rather, Kentridge inaugurates a particular collision; the reversed movement generates an "energy that comes from the refusal itself" [ . . . ] the sense that her dancing is pushing the paper up into the air" (Galison and Kentridge 2012b, 250).

In showing the dance sequence backward, that is *time*-reversed, Kentridge in fact disrupts our habitual way of perceiving time in a linear, progressive, and chronological order. Together with the non-pulsed, floating music of the soundscape, this dance sequence unfolds time as Aeon, or duration. Instead of being encapsulated by motivated action or measured beats, Masilo's dance movements generate a particular rhythm, rather then merely following a steady tempo. One could say that her dance movements are liberated from time as Chronos in the sense that they can no longer be explained in terms of "actions" or "tempos"; they remain notions of energy, slowness, and speed.

In Deleuze and Guattari's words, Masilo's dance movements give "time a new rhythm" (2007, 393) and are in that sense reminiscent of Heinrich von Kleist's notion of movement as developed in his essay *On the Marionette Theater* (1810). In this essay, the movements of the marionette are estimated above human dancers' movements, because they do not obey pulsed time or measured beats. They only obey one law: that of gravity, and they even have the power to transgress this law:

> The span of their movements is quite limited, but those movements of which they are capable are accomplished with a composure, lightness, and grace that would amaze any sensitive observer. [ . . . ] Like elves, the puppets need only to touch upon the ground, and the soaring of their limbs is newly animated through this momentary hesitation; we dancers need the ground to rest upon and recover from the exertion of the dance; a moment that is certainly no kind of dance in itself and with which nothing further can be done except to at least make it seem to not exist. (von Kleist 1972, 23, 24)

Deleuze and Guattari link Heinrich von Kleist's notion of movement with the notion of time as Aeon, or duration. They refer to Kleist's *On the Marionette Theater* in order to point to another way of understanding the relationship between time and movement, which is a different way of understanding the concept of speed. Whereas pulsed time has bodies "mickey-mousing" the tempo, that is, along "conventional meters and regular beats" (Bogue 2012, 42), Dada Masilo moves within the floating, unmarked time of non-pulsed, rhythmic Aeon. In this time as Aeon, Ronald Bogue argues, "performers freely execute motifs within a given duration [ . . . ] at their own pace, with no pulse provided by the conductor" (Bogue 2012, 42). Meter generates movements as motivated action; rhythm creates affects of qualitative speed. By presenting the dance reenactment backward in a multimedia constellation, Kentridge avoids harmonic movements and any "developmental organization of sectional units" (Bogue 2012, 43). The endless repetition of gestures generates a "hypnotic, trance-like drone" (43). There is no logical relation between sections; it is "a series of self-contained, intensely pulsed rhythmic units punctuated by a sequence of erratic, spasmodic jolts, fits and starts" (43). Masilo's dance reenactment of Fuller's *Serpentine Dance* hence unfolds in the present, as a moment of speed and rest. In disrupting the coordinated ubiquity of time as Chronos, the dance sequence affects the viewer with disjointed time. Masilo's dance works against "any kind of interpretation" and marks "the absolute state of movement" (Deleuze and Guattari 2007, 294–295). This present of the Aeon "is the present of the pure operation, not of the incorporation" (Deleuze 1990, 168).

In *The Refusal of Time*, rhythm is regained from tempo, Aeon from Chronos. But there is more. Dada Masilo is a dancer of color. In presenting pure operation, Masilo is not merely incorporating Loïe Fuller to represent a truthful reenactment of her *Serpentine Dance*. She performs a deliberate similarity in dance movements and costumes, but there is no attempt at exactitude in the reenactment. In her reenactment, there is no claim of authenticity, and *The Refusal of Time* is full of anachronisms, being "an art of ambiguity, contradiction, uncompleted gestures and uncertain endings" (Kentridge 2015).

Following the modern, chronological conception of time and history, a reality effect is needed in order for reenactment to revive history in a convincing manner: "the historical representation had to convince the receiver that what was being shown also took place as such" (Le Roy 2012, 82). In other words, the modern historicist regime had to be both a truthful and an authentic representation. The truth represented in the reenactment therefore also makes a claim on authenticity regarding the course of history. Rebecca Schneider observed how reenactors are usually eager "to touch an absolute and transcendent historical 'authentic' through a repetition of acts as divided of anachronisms and temporal error as humanly possible" (2011, 13). Masilo's critical mode of reenactment provides an interruption of the linear, chronological, and progressive time of modernity. This particular reenactment of modern dance questions time regimes that support a linear, chronological, progressive modernist conception of time and (dance) history. In Masilo's reenactment, we not only read traces of the history of modern dance. We are also and at the same time reminded of the constructed nature of that history, and of how some (white people's) dances are considered as singular, autonomous moments in that history, and others—of colored people—are not.

A similarly deconstructive mode of reenactment is at work in the final episode of *The Refusal of Time*, where a parade of dancing, laboring, and moving shadow figures is projected on three of the museum walls (Figure 19.8). These shadow figures do not incorporate mythological figures or exemplary heroes, as is the case in the historical parade, reenacting historical events. Instead of supporting "the theatrical experience of historicist historiography" (Le Roy 2012, 85), Kentridge's parade in fact reveals the modernist desire to reenact history along a chronological timeline.

## Historical Parade

Following Kosseleck and Osborne, Frederik Le Roy points to the modernist time regime at work in the reenactment practice in the popular spectacle of the historical parade at the beginning of the nineteenth century. It is a striking example of the modernist desire

FIGURE 19.8.   A parade of dancing, laboring, and moving shadow figures in William Kentridge's *The Refusal of Time* (2012).

Courtesy of the artist and Marian Goodman Gallery.

to reenact history along a chronological timeline (Le Roy 2012, 80). In reenacting historical events, the historical parade pretended to render a "lifelike reproduction of the past" (Le Roy 2012, 82). The performers were dressed up in costumes of the time, reenacted moments of history, and carried along artifacts of the time (or reproductions of them) to convince the spectator of the truthful representation of the past. Leaflets were distributed with a clear explanation of the scenes depicted, giving the whole spectacle an official aura of scientific knowledge. Functioning as an antidote against the sense of loss that comes with the passing of time, the historical parade created the comfortable illusion of having a grip on the "lost" past. Being a live event, it sustained the illusion in an almost literal way; it sustained "the illusion of the proximity of the past" (Le Roy 2012, 83). Rosen calls this "the transparent re-creation of a pre-existing referent" (Rosen 2001, 57; see also Le Roy 2012, 85).

The past, however, is not only rendered palpable through reenactment, but also ordered alongside modernist timetables. It therefore construes time as protocol. It is embedded in the construction of a cultural memory that guarantees the continuity and identity of a community gathered in and around the historical parade. It anchors cultural memory (again) in a (re)constructed past. Le Roy aptly calls the historical parade "the theatrical experience of historicist historiography" (2012, 85). It is, to use Lütticken's words, "historicism in action" (2005, 31; see also Le Roy 2012, 85). Not only does the linear format of the historical parade provide a chronological arrangement of historical events, it also selects those heroic episodes that are most suitable for building a coherent national identity. Well-chosen heroes feature in the carefully selected, glorious episodes of national or local history, hence functioning as examples for those watching. The heroic events they represent and the heroic actions they reenact had to "strengthen the sense of community [ . . . ] the spectators were invited to identify themselves with *their* nation and *their* history" (Le Roy 2012, 86). The historical parade, for that matter, constitutes a master narrative that is supportive of a heroic national identity. It enabled a community to make meaning out of past events and connected individuals in a community. Reenactment in historical parades founds tradition, safeguards (historical) continuity, and constitutes a national identity.

This master narrative works in an imperative way, as the historical parade is designed with the desire to impose a certain narrative upon the spectators, who are commemorating the past, witnessing at a remove, and observing the spectacle passing through in the streets. The "strategic memory" (Thompson 2009, 98) at work in the historical parade is a structuring device that maintains a group's homogeneous and coherent identity. It is therefore not only inclusive, in the sense that it connects people into a community, but also exclusive. These exclusive mechanisms are not to be underestimated. They operate at the cost of what Franz Fanon termed the "wretched of the earth" ([1961] 2007). One could say that parades in a colonial context support "colonialist attitudes" (Berman 2001, 53): they lay the foundation for an imperialist national identity, reinforce and sustain white supremacy, and hence consolidate power relations between Europe and Africa.

The final episode of Kentridge's *The Refusal of Time* restages the historical parade in a multimedia environment. A long parade of shadow-figures are dancing, laboring, and moving slowly but steadily from left to right, along three of the four museum walls. The film sequences are projected as communicating vessels; when a shadow-figure moves to the right, and eventually off-screen, it soon appears again, from the left, in the film sequence projected on the second wall, and so on, along the three museum walls. The result is a visually and auditory stunning succession of passing people. The movements are accompanied by a remarkable soundtrack by Philip Miller, using mechanical sounds, breathing tubas, brass tunes by the African Immanuel Essemblies Brass Band, the hisses and pops of old phonographs, and the voice of Ann Masina singing, using the typical click sounds of the indigenous South African people.

However, this parade does not feature mythological figures (as in religious processions), or recognizable historical figures (as in the historical parade), but shadow figures. This is not a lifelike, historically accurate representation, even though these shadow figures do have recognizable attributes, such as an iron tub, a headscarf, an overall, a cart. This parade does not envisage a "magnificent or grand representation of the past" (Le Roy 2012, 89). The parade features the "wretched of the earth" (Fanon [1961] 2007), with a clear reference to the labor of Africans in plantations. The parade has no chronological development, but unfolds in an almost never-ending stream of passersby. They are not the masses, but an ever-progressing queue of shadow figures. They bow their head slightly, but they do not appear to be desperate. An immense power emanates from them. Their persistent attitude fills us with awe and respect. Ann Masina's voice underscores the parade as an act of resistance. She repeatedly utters an emphatic and breathy "uh uh!," which Miller calls a vocal gesture meaning a strong and persistent "no," having "a particular resonance to a South African ear" (Miller and Kentridge 2012, 199).

# TIME AS KAIROS

Mieke Bal has noted that the medium of video installation is a particular art form that "enables reflection in, and subsequently, the development of strategies for, the struggle against the tyranny of clock time. In this sense, video installation is a time machine [ . . . ] for shifting priorities in experiencing time socially" (2012, 37). Bal calls the creative appeals to the spectator's imagination by the use of film and video in multimedia installations such as in William Kentridge's *The Refusal of Time* a form of political art. She links the *readiness to act* with the potential of film and video installation to get time as Chronos out of joint:

> This Bergsonian movement, the *readiness to act*, lies at the heart of the political potential of the (figurative) image, film, and video installation [ . . . ]. Multiple movement as the basis of the (moving) image as interacting with viewers who suspend their haste and their suspicion, and as they are relaxing their bodies, they relax their minds. This opens them up to an experience of all those movements, in a time of duration that is, temporarily, relieved of relentless clock time. Suspension, in terms of time, when actively done, is stalling.
>
> Stalling is a bit like resistance, but not quite as negative. (Bal 2015, 48)

Kentridge invites the visitor to rethink time; not only to reflect on its oppressive measuring and conditions, but also—through his particular collisions and disruptions of time—to regain our vital, own, private time from the universally audible tick-tock, to revalue our individual heterochronological experience of time.

Bal refers to how Kentridge's particular collisions and disruptions of time create opportunities to experience the different time experiences as a heterochrony, to experience time as Aeon. I would take this political aspect in Kentridge's *The Refusal of Time* one step further. With the particular use of reenactment in his multimedia installations, Kentridge turns the museum space into a place of resistance against the modernist conception of (dance) history. *The Refusal of Time* reveals the conditions of time in our contemporary late capitalist society, tracing back those conditions through modernity and colonial times. I would say that these moments also entail the revolutionary aspect of time as Kairos, which is the qualitative account of time, meaning "the right or opportune moment."

> Kairos is the instant, that is to say, the quality of the time of the instant, the moment of rupture and opening of temporality. It is the present, but a singular and open present. (Negri 2003, 156)

While Chronos is trapped in the linear, unidirectional chronological ordering of time, Kairos is untimely. The logic of the possible that emanates from the Chronos mode of temporality is stuck in a container-thinking of the plausible: the actions in the future can only take place if they are extensions of certain actions in the present, which are, in turn, connected with a certain logic of actions in the past. In this mode of temporality, a revolution is trapped in the past, constituting dead matter in history. Kairos, on the other hand, adopts the logic of potentiality. It is the eruption of an opportune moment, acting against any transcendental logic of time. Kairos is in that sense untimely; it does not need past or future to erupt. "It's a moment of time lapse, a moment of indeterminate time, an intervention in time" (Smith 2015, 19).[11] Deleuze's hope for Kairos is, in that context, the "expectations of occasions favorable to an 'event' as unforeseeable as it will be explosive" (Mengue 2008, 238).

In his book *Time for Revolution*, Antonio Negri understands Kairos as an alternative for the total subsumption of time by capitalism. Building on Deleuze's and Guattari's concept of the war machine, Negri also considers this intervention in time as a revolutionary act. Kairos is "the to-come"; it is "ontological constitution in action" (2003, 167).

> Kairos is the power to observe the fullness of temporality at the moment it opens itself onto the void of being, and of seizing this opening as innovation. (Negri 2003, 161–162)

In his particular reenactments, Kentridge does not fix time along a historical timeline, "according to a cemetery-like order" (Negri 2003, 168). He does not reconstruct the past in the present. Instead, he "tests" the archive of the past in the present, as Negri would call it, in order to inaugurate particular collisions in a "kairological" revolution. In *The Refusal of Time*, the universal clock-time is dispersed with potentialities for heterochronical experiences in time and (dance) history. The viewer who is seized in the kairological moment in *The Refusal of Time* might become intoxicated by the potentialities it emanates. This is not a rational act. One does not seek to seize the opportune moment, one is seized by it, but one must be open and receptive in affirming the ethical gesture in the moment. Only then can the promise of the new unfold.

## WORKS CITED

Agamben, Giorgio. 2005. *The Time That Remains: A Commentary on the Letter to the Romans*. Translated by Patricia Dailey. Stanford, CA: Stanford University Press.
Alexandre, Arsène. 1900. "Le theater de la Loie Fuller." *Le Théâtre* (August 11): 24.
Bal, Mieke. 2015. "The Time It Takes." In *How To Construct a Time Machine*, edited by Marquard Smith, 34–50. Milton Keynes: MK Gallery, January 23–March 22.

[11]  See also on Kairos, in relation to Chronos, Agamben (2005). Kentridge's heteroaesthetics is supported by visual cultural scholar Mieke Bal, who observes that no homogenized clock can regulate heterochrony away. A heterochrony, "by its very nature, is multiple and cannot be equalized" (2015, 37).

Berman, Nina. [1998] 2001. "Orientalism, Imperialism, and Nationalism. Karl May's *Orientzyklus.*" In *The Imperialist Imagination: German Colonialism and Its Legacy*, editied by Sara Friedrichsmeier, Sara Lennox, and Susanne Zantop, 51–68. Ann Arbor: University of Michigan Press.

Bogue, Ronald. 2012. *Deleuze's Way: Essays in Transverse Ethics and Aesthetics*. Surrey, UK: Ashgate.

Constantine. Stephen. [1984] 2005. *The Making of British Colonial Development Policy 1914– 1940*. London: Routledge.

De Laet, Timmy. 2013. "Bodies With(out) Memories: Strategies of Re-enactment in Contemporary Dance." In *Performing Memory in Art and Popular Culture*, edited by Liedeke Plate and Anneke Smelik, 135–154. London: Routledge.

Deleuze, Gilles. 1990. *The Logic of Sense*. Translated by Mark Lester and Constantin V. Boundas. New York: Columbia University Press.

Deleuze, Gilles, and Félix Guattari. 2007. *A Thousand Plateaus*. Translated by Brian Massumi. London: Continuum.

Fanon, Frantz. [1961] 2007. *The Wretched of the Earth*. New York: Grove Press.

Friedrichsmeier, Sara, Sara Lennox, and Susanne Zantop. [1998] 2001. *The Imperialist Imagination: German Colonialism and Its Legacy*. Ann Arbor: University of Michigan Press.

Galison, Peter. 2012. "Time, Art, and Science." In William Kentridge, *The Refusal of Time*, 311– 318. Paris: Éditions Xavier Barral.

Galison, Peter, and William Kentridge. 2012a. "Give us Back Our Sun." In William Kentridge, *The Refusal of Time*, 157–164. Paris: Éditions Xavier Barral.

Galison, Peter, and William Kentridge. 2012b. "Blowing Up the Meridian." In William Kentridge, *The Refusal of Time*, 249–250. Paris: Éditions Xavier Barral.

Harlow, Barbara, and Mia Carter. 2003. *Archives of Empire*, Vol. II: *The Scramble for Africa*. Durham, NC: Duke University Press.

Headrick, Daniel R. [1991] 2012. *The Invisible Weapon: Telecommunications and International Politics, 1851–1945*. Oxford: Oxford University Press.

Hennlich, Andrew J. 2015. "Amnesty with a Movie Camera." In *Film, History and Memory*, edited by Jennie M. Carlsten and Fearghal McGarry, 101–117. New York: Palgrave MacMillan.

Jones, Barrie. 2014. *The Hutchinson Concise Dictionary of Music*. New York: Routledge.

Kentridge, William. 2012. *Refuse the Hour*. Lecture, delivered during the performance *Refuse the Hour*.

Kentridge, William. 2015. *If We Ever Get to Heaven*. Amsterdam, EYE Filmmuseum, April 24–August 30.

Le Roy, Frederik. 2012. *Verknoopte tijd, verfrommelde geschiedenis. Een theaterwetenschappelijk en geschiedfilosofisch onderzoek naar theater en performance als politiek van de herinnering in het modern en presentistisch historiciteitsregime*. Gent: Universiteit Gent.

Lütticken, Sven. 2005. "An Arena in Which to Reenact." In *Life, Once More: Forms of Re- enactment in Contemporary Art*, edited by Sven Lütticken, 17–60. Rotterdam: Witte De With.

Mengue, Philippe. 2008. "People and Fabulation." In *Deleuze and Politics*, edited by Ian Buchanan and Nicholas Thobum, 218–239. Edinburgh: Edinburgh University Press.

Miller, Philip, and William Kentridge. 2012. "Gathering Sounds and Making the Object Breathe." In William Kentridge, *The Refusal of Time*, 197–212. Paris: Éditions Xavier Barral.

Moran, Terence P. 2010. *Introduction to the History of Communication: Evolutions and Revolutions*. New York: Peter Lang.

Negri, Antonio. 2003. *Time for Revolution*. Translated by Matteo Mandarini. London: Bloomsbury.

Osborne, Peter. 2015. "Modernity Is a Qualitative, Not a Chronological Category." In *How To Construct a Time Machine*, edited by Marquard Smith, 52–73. Milton Keynes: MK Gallery, January 23–March 22.

Patton, Paul. 1997. "Introduction." In *Deleuze: A Critical Reader*, edited by Paul Patton, 1–17. Oxford: Blackwell.

Rosen, Philip. 2001. *Change Mummified: Cinema, Historicity, Theory*. Minneapolis: University of Minnesota Press.

Rosse, Christine. 2012. *The Past Is the Present. It's the Future Too. The Temporal Turn in Contemporary Art*. London: Bloomsbury.

Schneider, Rebecca. 2011. *Performing Remains. Art and War in Times of Historical Reenactment*. New York: Routledge.

Smith, Marquard. 2015. "How To Construct a Time Machine." In *How To Construct a Time Machine*, edited by Marquard Smith, 5–21. Milton Keynes: MK Gallery, January 23–March 22.

Stewart, Susan. 2005. "William Kentridge." In *The Open Studio: Essays on Art and Aesthetics*, 51–65. Chicago: University of Chicago Press.

Thompson, James. 2009. *Performance Affects. Applied Theatre and the End of Effect*. Hampshire, Palgrave Macmillan.

Von Kleist, Heinrich. 1972. "On the Marionette Theater." Translated by Thomas G. Neumiller. *The Drama Review* 16(3): 22–26.

# PART VII

## REDISTRIBUTIONS OF TIME IN GEOGRAPHY, ARCHITECTURE, AND MODERNIST NARRATIVE

CHAPTER 20

QUITO-BRUSSELS

*A Dancer's Cultural Geography*

FABIÁN BARBA

## *A MARY WIGMAN DANCE EVENING* AND A PERSONAL YET COLLECTIVE HISTORY

WHEN I was working on the creation of *A Mary Wigman Dance Evening* (*AMWDE*, 2009),[1] I encountered for the first time a rather a curious phenomenon: certain dances could be said to look old-fashioned.[2] When those dances were created several decades ago, this kind of observation doesn't seem to pose any major problem. However, it can become a rather thorny situation when those dances have been made recently, but outside of what could be considered the centers of the so-called contemporary dance scene. I am unable to approach this problem without considering my own personal story. Through my dance education in two different places—Quito from 2000 to 2004; Brussels from 2004 to 2008—I came in contact with two different dance scenes in which this perception—of one of them looking old-fashioned in relation to the other—has come clearly to the fore.[3]

I started to study dance in Quito with Kléver Viera, one of the modern dance pioneers in the city. While I was studying with him, I took him as a model that embodied for me

---

[1] See my "Research into Corporeality" (2011).

[2] I want to thank Mark Franko for encouraging me to write this text and for all his help in its preparation.

[3] I would like to make clear that when I talk about the dance scene in Quito I'm mainly talking about my experience and memory of that dance scene. My relation with that dance scene cannot represent that of other dancers. Therefore, I would like us to keep in mind that everything I am going to say about the dance scene in Quito is necessarily a partial and subjective view. The same applies for what I will say about the dance scene in Brussels. When I talk about the dance scene in Brussels, I will actually be talking about my experience and the relation I've come to establish with that dance scene.

an image/idea of dance and of a good dancer; taking him as a model, I strove to embody those ideals in myself. At least in an initial formative moment, I could say that *that* was the kind of dance I wanted to do and *he* was the kind of dancer I wanted to become.[4] A similar process took place while I was in PARTS[5] The main difference was that instead of having one teacher to look at, I had several, all of them with their different bodies, different exercises, different skills, all of them actualizing differing ideas of dance and what a good dancer could be.

This entanglement of (embodied) images, ideals, and ideas made me think that an education in dance is not only a technical education, but also an education in the ideas and ideals that a technical training seeks to attain/embody. When I went to PARTS I thought I would be taught to do a proper grand plié and kick my legs up high, and that then I would be able to go back to Quito to keep on dancing as before, but better. It took a while before I realized that I could not improve my Quito-acquired technique in Brussels. We can say that something is better only when comparing two things within the same paradigm. Traveling from Quito to Brussels, I actually changed paradigms: I invested myself in a different kind of technical training, I was initiated into commerce with other ideas, and I started pursuing and negotiating other ideals. I didn't improve my previously acquired technique; I put it on hold to focus on acquiring a new one. Thinking retrospectively about this, I've become convinced that an education in dance implies not only a technical education, but also an education in a way of thinking, a way of appreciating work (a way of enjoying or disliking dances), a way of interacting with the network in which one is educated: *a dance education is a way of inscribing oneself within a dance culture.*

To recognize the existence of different dance cultures and one's inscription in them through training and education doesn't pose a problem. The problem appears when the contemporaneity of one of those dance cultures is denied and thus is relegated to the past—or when, complementarily, we think that if the past still exists, it must exist elsewhere, exiled into another geographical location, so to speak[6] (I will return to this in what follows). After *AMWDE* I tried to approach these questions through the creation of another performance, *a personal yet collective history* (*apych*, 2012), which also followed the logic of a dance recital. It combined eight short solo dances created in different contexts: the United Kingdom (1976), Brazil (2003), and Ecuador (2003), to name a few. This compilation didn't aim to present different decades or periods, or to give a concise, complete, and systematic account of history; it simply looked for dances that could refer me to a different milieu than the one I was inhabiting at the time. I wanted these dances to allow me to infer—however phantasmagorically or vaguely—an idea or

---

[4] At age nineteen, I saw *Vista de Ojos*, a group choreography by Klever. I remember thinking to myself, "that's what I want to do, that's where I want to be," hence my coming back to dance, and studying with him.

[5] PARTS (Performing Arts Research and Training Studios) is a dance school based in Brussels and directed by Anne Teresa de Keersmaeker.

[6] I thank Mark Franko for helping me formulate this perception.

image of the context in which they were created, a context historically or geographically different from my actual, present one. *apych* sought to consider dance history as a plurality of voices that overlap, contradict, and resonate with one another; it was conceived as a resonance box in which the public was invited to listen to the mixing of some of those voices.

One of the dances I was considering for this dance evening was a short solo created by Kléver Viera for my colleague Yolanda Endara (*Yoli's solo*, 2003.) That solo was part of the evening-length performance *Yo, otro eco*, in the creation of which I participated. As I was coming to Europe to visit different dance schools, I asked Yoli to teach me that solo so I could present it during my auditions. I asked her to teach me that solo specifically because I thought it was a most beautiful dance and that it was the best I could offer as my calling card. Nine years later, during the rehearsals for *apych,* my affinity for this dance remained undiminished; the pleasure of dancing this solo as I retrieved it from the video surfaced to my skin. Nevertheless, I noticed a gap between this dance and my present situation as a dancer in Brussels. Notwithstanding the familiar pleasure and enjoyment, there was a distance that had installed itself; Yoli's solo seemed out of place, or old-fashioned. It was as if traveling outside of what I had come to recognize as a center for contemporary dance (Brussels) could be perceived as traveling back in time.

Is it so? Can traveling geographically be perceived as traveling back and forth in time? Even my experience with *Yoli's solo* seemed to indicate so: I had learned to recognize that dance as belonging to the past, even though I had fully identified with it only nine years earlier. Is nine years time enough for something to become part of the past? No, I don't think that the time marked in the calendar can account for this transformation from "present" to "past"; rather, it was the travel from Quito to Brussels, the change from one dance world to another, that evoked the paradigm shift. The dance tradition into which I was inscribed through schooling in Brussels now constituted my present. But did it have to necessarily transform my previous experience as a dancer into "the past"? Did it have the right to deny the contemporaneity of the dance world I had come to know in Quito and with which I still entertain affective and professional relations?

To complicate things a bit more, there was another solo haunting the creation process of *apych: La mujer de los fermentos*. This is a dance I learned from my teacher Klever Viera, who had created it for himself in Quito at the end of 2002. As far as I know, he has rarely taught his dances to other people. To learn this dance was a very special experience for me. It was a transmission that didn't have anything to do with the teaching of a repertory; it felt rather like a bestowal—something was being passed from one body to the other, from one person to the other, with extreme generosity and care. *Me gustaría decir que con mucho cariño.* Learning this dance created a strong bond with Klever, with that specific dance, and with that dance world.

Ramsay Burt (who was assisting in the creation of *apych*) asked me why I didn't include *La mujer de los fermentos* in the performance. The immediate answer was that with this dance I didn't have the detachment I experienced with the other dances, a detachment or distance I experienced even with *Yoli's solo*. I was afraid that my affective ties to this dance would dissolve any kind of critical distance, which was very important to me. However, my initial resistance to performing this solo might have been due to my unuttered fear that a dance that I had come to recognize as part of the past (as in the case of *Yoli's solo*) could have the power to forcefully invade the present. I was perhaps afraid that I could suddenly discover myself turning my back on the future and walking to the past right in front of me.

How can I define the present that I felt I had to protect from invasion? As that which was happening in 2012, in opposition to what had happened in 2002? No, this present is not defined by chronological time only. The present I was guarding had to do with my current inscription within a dance network based in Brussels. It is precisely this inscription that was being challenged by performing *La mujer de los fermentos* in Europe. Had I been invited to dance this solo in Quito, I would have accepted gladly, as it would have reaffirmed my inscription within that dance scene. Why did I perceive my concurrent inscription into two different dance traditions as a struggle between that which belonged to "the present" and that which belonged to "the past"? Why is it difficult to recognize two simultaneous dance scenes as contemporary with each other?

# HISTORICISM

We can observe how the frontiers between what properly belongs to "the past" and what belongs to "the present" are also being policed in situations other than the one under discussion here. In Hamburg in 2009 I attended the presentation of a dance performance by a choreographer working in Colombia. At the end of the performance I overheard an important curator saying "that looked very 80s." We don't need to discuss the quality of that specific work; what is important to my argument is that a recently made work was relocated to another moment in time. Also in Hamburg I was told about an Eastern European theater festival that took place in that city before my arrival. Apparently the festival "looked 80s" and was not very successful. They explained to me that "they were dealing with questions and concerns that we (in Hamburg) were not busy with *anymore.*" Dance scholar Bojana Kunst, in her article "Politics of Affection and Uneasiness" (2003), talks extensively about this by critically describing the (deceptive) reception of Eastern European performance art as something *already seen* from the viewpoint of Western European art programmers.

To say that something that is taking place in the now looks as though it belongs to the past is a clear example of the denial of coevalness as described by Johannes Fabian in his book *Time and the Other: How Anthropology Makes Its Object* ([1983] 2002). Fabian derives this concept from anthropological praxis. He explains that when an ethnographer is doing field work, he or she enters into dialogue with an "other" with whom he or she shares a present. However, when that encounter is translated into an anthropological text, that "other" is placed into another historical time, a former period. The denial of coevalness places into a historical past someone with whom we actually could establish a relation in the now.

This denial of coevalness is enacted from a locus of enunciation, which benefits from a relative hegemonic position. Even though this locus of enunciation is not directly rooted in a well-defined geographical space, it is grounded in a specific culture, which, at least at an initial moment, was not global, but locally circumscribed. Thus, the denial of coevalness is enacted from a hegemonic geo-cultural location (Mignolo 2012), and consequently one way of conceiving historical time, as embedded in European modernity, has spread into other geographies, subsuming their temporalities within the temporality of the dominant one. As we will see in the following, this has had as a consequence the spatialization of historical time, which pictures excentric geo-cultural locations as "the past."

These concerns invaded most of the creation of *apych*, turning it into a thorny and uncomfortable affair. I noticed that I had come to recognize *Yoli's solo* as part of the past because I was thinking of history as a *single linear progression* with a past that is gone, a present that is singular, and a future to which we are all heading. At this moment I came upon Dipesh Chakrabarty's book *Provincializing Europe: Postcolonial Thought and Historical Difference* (2000), which deals with the mythical image of Europe as the cradle of modernity, the formation of political modernity and capitalism in South Asia, and the subsequent postcolonial encounter of different worlds with their distinct thought-categories. Even if this book is not concerned with dance or with South America, from the very first pages I found passages that resonated strongly with my questions, especially in the way Chakrabarty understands historicism:

> Crudely, one might say that [historicism] was one important form that the ideology of progress or "development" took from the nineteenth century on. Historicism is what made modernity or capitalism look not simply global but rather as something that became global *over time*, by originating in one place (Europe) and then spreading outside it. This "first in Europe, then elsewhere" structure of global historical time was historicist; [ . . . ]. It was historicism that allowed Marx to say that the "country that is more developed industrially only shows, to the less developed, the image of its own future." [ . . . ] Historicism thus posited historical time as a measure of the cultural distance (at least in institutional development) that was assumed to exist between the West and the non-West.[7] (2000, 7)

For Chakrabarty, "to critique historicism in all its varieties is to unlearn to think of history as a developmental process in which that which is possible becomes actual by

---

[7] This quote, talking primarily about economic development and political dependency, does set the terms with which to analyze the power relations operating in art production around the world through the notions of development and underdevelopment; after all, the perception of a dance recently made as "old-fashioned" bespeaks some sort of underdevelopment ("being too late," "having to catch up"). As Mark Franko suggested to me, one way of approaching this question would be to consider art as a cultural commodity circulating within a political economy. The dance scenes in Quito and Brussels are also art markets, which are liable to devalue certain dances by anachronizing them. To pursue this question is beyond the scope of this chapter.

tending to a future that is singular" (2000, 249). This race toward the future is related to the "'desire to wipe out whatever came earlier,' so as to achieve 'a radically new departure, a point that could be a true present'" (244) from which to "create 'something that has never existed'" (245). Seen otherwise, to critique historicism "is to learn *to think the present—the 'now' that we inhabit as we speak—as irreducibly not-one*" (249; my emphasis).

It is precisely the historicist understanding of history as a single linear progression that underlines the idea according to which the present of Ecuador could be understood as the past of Europe. If there is only *one* historical development possible, the whole world needs to adhere to it, regardless of the specificities of different local histories. Or, those local histories have to be overlooked in order to make them fit into a global (universal) account of history.

During the creation process of *apych*, I noticed that I didn't need to think of history as something we find in books or archives that throw us back to a time we didn't experience and that is detached from us. The past I was dealing with actually had the capacity to affect/act upon my present, be it through the sensual enjoyment of the dancing or by the capacity and desire to fully inhabit *La mujer de los fermentos*. The past I was dealing with was not something past, but present. In *apych* I wasn't dealing with pasts that have passed (away)—those might be the pasts that are gone and lost: the past of the originals and the origins, perhaps. I was busy with pasts that *are*, that are active and necessary. These pasts do not need to be recuperated; at most, they need to be acknowledged and given a place. The idea of pasts that *are* is also articulated by Chakrabarty:

> Pasts *are* there in taste, in practices of embodiment, in the cultural training the senses have received over generations. They are there in practices I sometimes do not even know I engage in. This is how the archaic comes into the modern, not as a remnant of another time but as something constitutive of the present.[8] (2000, 251)

How can we conceive a present populated by pasts that *are*, a present that is not singular, that is not a complete and closed entity unto itself, a present that doesn't reify and detach us from the past?[9] The historicist notion of history as a single linear progression doesn't allow room for that.

---

[8]  For a more in-depth presentation of this notion, consult the section "Beyond Historicism" in Chakrabarty (2000, 249). Based on the second division of Martin Heidegger's *Being and Time*, Chakrabarty outlines a proposal for thinking of historical time in a non-historicist way, i.e., a way that is not linear and that embraces the "now" as constantly fragmentary and irreducibly not-one; as not-being-a-totality and non-universal. It is within this discussion that Chakrabarty introduces the notions of pasts that are. He also talks about the futures that are understood in terms of "the futurity that humans cannot avoid aligning themselves with" and "that laces every moment of human existence" (2000, 251, 250) and continually modify and challenge the future that "will be," the (historicist future) necessary for the subject of political modernity in the pursuit of (a universalizing project, such as) social justice.

[9]  Is interesting to note how radically different this conception of the present is from the one advanced by C. F. von Weizsäcker: "One could say that the present is the one-ness [Einheit] of time" (Quoted in Fabian, [1983] 2002, 89).

One month before the premiere of *apych*, when I was still struggling with the status of *Yoli's solo* and *La mujer de los fermentos*, I read in *Provincializing Europe* an anecdote about the Indian physicist and Nobel laureate C. V. Raman:

> Raman, it is said, would rush home from his laboratory in Calcutta in the 1930s to "take a ritual bath ahead of a solar eclipse." When questioned about this, the physicist is reported to have simply quipped, "The Nobel Prize? That was science, a solar eclipse is personal." (2000, 254)

How could a scientist, proficient in the use of rational thinking, engage in so-called superstitious practices? How could a scientist, as a modern man, engage in practices that could be deemed to be traditional, as not belonging to modern times? Or more roughly, how could "primitive mentality" and "modern rationality" operate in one and the same person?[10] For Chakrabarty this exemplifies how ". . . practicing Indian scientists [ . . . ] often have not felt any intellectual or social obligation to find one single overarching framework within which to contain the diversity of their own life practices (as distinct from their practices as scientists)" (2000, 253). This and other similar stories, Chakrabarty says, "refer us to the plurality that inheres in the 'now,' the lack of totality, the constant fragmentariness, that constitutes one's present" (243). The proposition "to learn to think the present—the 'now' that we inhabit as we speak—as irreducibly not-one" (249) resonates with the idea of "different temporalities inhabiting the now" articulated by Homi Bhabha (2008).

I had learned to recognize *Yoli's solo* and *La mujer de los fermentos* as belonging to an overcome past, as anachronisms, because they didn't seem to belong to "the true present."

> What is the "true present?" The "'full power of the idea of modernity,'" writes Marshall Berman quoting de Man; "lay in a 'desire to wipe out whatever came earlier,' so as to achieve 'a radically new departure, a point that could be a true present.'" The true present is what is produced when we act as if we could reduce the past to a nullity. It is a kind of a zero point in history—the pastless time, for example, of a *tabula rasa*, the *terra nullius*, or the blueprint. (Chakrabarty 2000, 244)

To undo my own historicist way of thinking meant that I needed to unlearn to think of *La mujer de los fermentos* as belonging to an overcome past, and to acknowledge it as a past that *is*, that affects my present, that inhabits the now; it was to acknowledge the *living* relations that I maintain with this dance.

One of the problems with historicism is that it reifies the past, it turns it into an object of knowledge: a thing we can learn "about," but not "from," something we can

---

[10] This binary opposition is mentioned by Johannes Fabian: ". . . anthropologists have used the term *animism* (which they invented in order to separate primitive mentality from modern rationality) as a means to indicate that an opponent is no longer in the contemporary arena of debate" (2002, 152).

see, but not experience. A couple of years after the creation of *AMWDE*, I noticed that during that creation process I wanted to know how Wigman thought and worked, not in order to learn "from" her, but to learn "about" her; at that time I didn't even consider the possibility of learning something "from" *Ausdruckstanz*. In this I unwittingly subscribed to a detrimental relation to history that turns "the past into an object of knowledge," (Vázquez 2011, n.p.) thus negating "the past as an open realm of experience" (2011, n.p.). This conception of the past relies upon being able to establish a clear distance (schism, abyss) between that past and our observer's place in the present.

After reading Raman's story, I felt encouraged to give a place in my present situation as a "contemporary" dancer working in Brussels to *La mujer de los fermentos*. I understood that I didn't need to relegate this dance to an overcome past, but that I could acknowledge it as a past that *is*.

A shortcoming of this performance was that even though I managed to modify my relation to this dance and to my own past, I didn't manage to involve important segments of the audience in this process. Some people who attended the performance could see in *La mujer de los fermentos* only a part of my past, for they expressed their desire to see how I would dance "now." Their dissatisfaction could be summarized in these words: "You are showing us what you used to dance, but we'd like to see how you would dance now." This proved to me that I didn't manage to share with them the realization that the "now" that I might inhabit as I dance is irreducibly not-one, that the solo Klever taught me is part of my past as much as it is part of my present—a present that is not singular. Is it a present that I cannot share with every audience? Am I facing once again a present that cannot be defined through temporal coordinates only? Is "my present in Quito" different from "my present in Brussels"—presents that I build through the relations I cultivate with those two dance communities?

# HISTORICAL DISTANCES

During the creation of *AMWDE* I was knowingly dealing with a problem of historical distance; I was working with dances made about eighty years ago. So far I had understood this notion of historical distance as a being aware that these dances had emerged in a specific historical context that is not ours, and that their reenactment supposed establishing a critical approach to them and not a coming back to, or a restoration of, the past.

What's more, I worked on these dances with a very clear target audience: my classmates at PARTS, for whom these dances belonged to a dance world alien to the one we shared in Brussels. In this case, the historical distance between our daily activities at school and the Wigman dances was almost an abyss. But I haven't encountered this abyss everywhere. Wherever I have shown this work, it has been well understood that these dances are not from 2010, but from 1930. And yet, I have the impression that for some audiences there is a continuity taking place that was not there with my first target audience in Brussels.

The elements that mark a clear historical distance are the length of the dances (people can say to themselves: "Ah, in the 30s dances were short like this!"); the diva figure appearing after every dance to bow; the scratchy sound of the recorded music I took from the video recordings; the décor, with the front curtains, the chandeliers, and the hand programs; the costumes and overstylized gestures. However, these elements that would seem to ascribe a date to the dances do not always create much of a problem at the moment of their apprehension. Or, this historical distance sometimes seems to exist within a historical continuum and not through the kind of abysmal distance I had sought and somehow achieved while presenting these dances at PARTS. As an example, after I presented *AMWDE* in Quito in November 2011, I met with a small group of dancers and theater makers to talk about the performance. They mentioned their impression that, broadly speaking, most audiences in the city would hardly accept a dance without emotional intensity and without the construction of a character—characteristics that allowed for a familiar reception of *AMWDE*. We even got to say that it might be generally understood that in Quito *this intensity is dance*. If we could say that in Quito this intensity is dance, I could also say that this intensity was banned from (my experience of) PARTS.

Indeed, modern dance in Quito related itself since its inception to the genealogy of modern dance (Wigman, Graham, Limon, Humphrey) with its emphasis on interiority and emotional empathy. My path within PARTS tended to align itself with the legacy of the Judson Dance Theater and its critique of modern dance's reliance on personal expression. Taking these circumstances into account, it might well be said that one of the elements that creates the difference between an "abysmal historical distance" and a "temporal distance within a historical continuum" is the presence of the strong emotional intensity of the Wigman dances.

If the necessary existence or absence of this intensity could mark the difference between different dance traditions, the kind of distance that audiences could experience while viewing *AMWDE* would depend on their familiarity with (and inscription within) one or another dance tradition. To put it otherwise, I would like to propose that the abysmal distance was produced in PARTS because the Wigman dances were linked to a different dance tradition. The abyss was between one dance tradition and another one, and not due to the eighty years in between, which was my first hypothesis.

From this I would like to derive two conclusions. First, the historical distance doesn't need to be abysmal, a schism. It can exist due to a time difference within a same or familiar dance tradition. This is what I have called a "temporal distance within a historical continuum" and it is exemplified in the affinity between modern dance in Quito and *Ausdruckstanz*. Second, the abysmal historical distance does not require a time gap; it can appear between different dance traditions contemporaneous to each other, where contemporaneous is used in the sense of the simultaneous. This is exemplified in the relation between dance in Quito (with its linkage to a genealogy of *modern* dance) and dance in Brussels (linked to a genealogy of so-called postmodern or *contemporary* dance, after the Judson Dance Theater.)

Perhaps I had learned to recognize *Yoli's solo* and *La mujer de los fermentos* as belonging to "the past" due to their emotional intensity and expressive qualities, which contrasted with the pedestrian facticity of the Judson Church legacy with which I became familiar at PARTS. Indeed, *Yoli's solo* and *La mujer de los fermentos* can be catalogued as *modern* dance and, in a naïve and historicist way, I had assumed that *modern* dance was *before* postmodern and *contemporary* dance.

This erroneous reasoning evidences how much my dance education was imbued by a historicist master narrative of dance history. According to this, and echoing Clement Greenberg's theory of aesthetic modernism, dance was progressively seeking the purity of its own medium through a process of formalist purification: *modern* dance rejecting the recourse to narrative and reliance on the music of *romantic ballet*; *postmodern* (or *contemporary* dance) emerging as a reaction and break against the expressionism and codified vocabularies of *modern* dance—a succession of stages that seems to follow a sequential, rather than additive, logic (Burt 1998, 14). This master narrative is indeed historicist insofar as it presents a continuing series of upheavals in a singular, progressive and linear evolution toward a goal of pure abstraction: dance reduced to what constitutes it fundamentally and what could place it as an autonomous art.

This master narrative has been exposed to critical scrutiny by several dance scholars, including Susan Manning, Mark Franko, and Ramsay Burt (to mention just the authors I'm most familiar with).[11] And yet, this narrative seems to remain operative in a surreptitious manner. It is this historicist, stagist account of dance history that creates the conditions of possibility to perceive *modern* dance as an anachronism in relation to *contemporary* dance; as if, in the process of "narrowing [the] range of options that refine away each immediate precursor's stake" (Franko 1995, ix) the latest proposition had to displace all the previous ones, as if they could not exist at the same time.

# REENACTMENT: CREATION OF COEVALNESS AND CULTIVATING RELATIONS WITH THE PAST

> The age of museums has reduced the past into a "proper place"; the past has been objectified within history as institution and as a discipline. The past is thus subsumed under the objectivity of the present. History cancels the experience in the past, the experience of memory, and reduces the past to the space of text or the museum.
>
> —Vázquez (2011, n.p.)

---

[11]  See, respectively, Manning ([1993] 2002), Franko (1995), and Burt (1998).

The critical thinker of time does not want to conquer time, but rather she seeks to rescue, to salvage *our relation* to time, to the past, to memory, to history.

—Vázquez (2011, n.p.; my emphasis)

At the beginning of the work on *AMWDE*, I didn't think thoroughly about the differences implied in the terms "reconstruction" and "reenactment," though I intuitively preferred the latter term. The reason for my lack of attention was that I was busy trying to present the dances of Wigman in such a way that they could bring forth certain initial concerns of mine, that is, the uncanny experience when first viewing the dances on video. Busy with this concern, I wasn't trying to discern if the methodology I was putting in place could be better described as reconstruction or reenactment; I was just trying to make use of a methodological procedure that would serve my purposes, not knowing yet what that procedure would be. However, when I tried to translate the article "Research into Corporeality" (Barba, 2011) into Spanish, I didn't find a correlate term for "reenactment" and I wasn't satisfied with the notion of reconstruction (*reconstrucción*) alone. Trying to understand this dissatisfaction, I noticed that the term "reconstruction" made me think above all of the recuperation of an object, while "reenactment" seemed to propose a possible (re)activation of an act. In that sense, reconstruction seemed to suggest an understanding of history as detachment, loss, reification and recuperation—a history with which I could at best enter into a relation as an external observer. Reenacment, on the other hand, seemed to allow the possibility of diving into a situation that I would have to necessarily experience for myself. Intuitively, I prefered the term "reenactment" insofar as it didn't freeze history into bygone times, but instead attended to history's dynamic way of operating in the moment of the performance of the dances.

Ramsay Burt, discussing *AMWDE*, said, "The word 'convention,' he [Raymond Williams] points out, means a coming together of people, while 'conventional' means conforming to accepted standards; but to say that something is conventional is often a criticism, implying that it is routine or somewhat old fashioned" (2011, n.p.). Fabián Barba's "aim was also to try to re-present these conventions as if they had not yet hardened and become routine—had not yet become conventional" (2011, n.p.). Maybe in reenactment we are invited to become participants, either as dancers or as audience; maybe we are invited to make use of the conventions proposed as a site for experience, rather than becoming spectators to stiffened conventional dances, reified objects deprived of any capacity to affect our reality.

Here is also where the *re* of reenactment acquires its meaning. Based on the work I've done, I could say that reenactment tries to overcome a historical fracture. It tries to reestablish a link with a dance tradition or a dance event that, for historical circumstances, has been drawn to a halt, has been interrupted, or has been silenced. By exchanging conventional reproduction for a *re*activation of the conventions, reenactment allows precisely that: to establish *living* relations with a past that has been damaged (dismissed, invisibilized, anachronized, etc.) This would also mark the difference between reenactment and repertory or restagings: in the two latter cases we find a continuity that has not suffered any major impediment to its ongoing reproduction.

The performance *AMWDE* asks its audience to enter the game: they have to find out when to clap and what to do during the many pauses of the performance. The performance might also ask the audience to establish *living* relations with the dances. Thanks to conversations with spectators after the performance, I've noticed that the relations they establish with the dances and the way they get to appreciate them, or not, is highly mediated by their personal stories as spectators: the kind of dances they have seen prior to this performance, the kind of dances they usually like, the dance culture in which they have, indeed, *cultivated* their spectatorship.

If reenactment actually allows us to put the emphasis on experience, participation, and the creation of *living* relations, this was an effect I did not foresee from the start. I had initially understood my work as a process of translation into and out of different dance traditions, that is, *Ausdruckstanz* presented in the *contemporary* dance scene in Brussels.[12] The specificity of this translational gesture (or displacement) was to try to suspend the immediate subsumption of one into the other, as would have been the case had I tried to make *Ausdruckstanz* more easily assimilable to its new context, had I tried to make it more *contemporary*.[13] My intent was to try to create a confrontation. And yet, because the theater itself is a public space that encourages communication, I encountered the conditions of possibility for a dialogical exchange, an intersubjective relationality, a tuning-in between the audience and the Wigman dances.

Following the propositions that "for human communication to occur, coevalness has to be *created*" (Fabian, [1983] 2002, 30–31) and that "communication is, ultimately, about creating shared Time," (31) I'd like to think that the logic of reenactment can participate in the creation of coevalness necessary for initiating a dialogical relation between different dance traditions. That would be to say that the logic of reenactment engages in an *intersubjective*[14] use of time in which the dismissal of a dance as an anachronism is troubled:

> To recognize *Intersubjective Time* would seem to preclude any sort of distancing almost by definition. After all, phenomenologists tried to demonstrate with their analyses that social interaction presupposes intersubjectivity, which in turn is

---

[12] Where translation is understood as moving something from one place to another.

[13] This would have been translation in the sense of rendering one thing into another, like translating a poem into a different language

[14] "For lack of a better label, I shall speak of it as *intersubjective time*. The term points back to one of its philosophical sources in phenomenological thought, as exemplified in Alfred Schutz's analyses of intersubjective time [ . . . ]. More important, the attribute *intersubjective* signals a current emphasis on the communicative nature of human action and interaction. As soon as culture is no longer primarily conceived as a set of rules to be enacted by individual members of distinct groups, but as the specific way in which actors create and produce beliefs, values, and other means of social life, it has to be recognized that Time is a constitutive dimension of social reality" (Fabian [1983] 2002, 24).

inconceivable without assuming that the participants involved are coeval, i.e. share the same Time. (30)

In the case of *AMWDE*, this creation of coevalness was related to the effort not to turn these dances into museum objects—not to reduce them to their "proper place" in history. Even though signaling its point of emergence in the late 1920s, the performance seems to have made it possible to experience the dances in a dynamic and *living* way without purposely modifying the dances in order to make them more suitable to their new context. This process of translation as displacement (or replacement) that I have signaled in the practice of reenactment in *AMWDE* was present with a clearer intent in the creation of *apych*. Even though the displacements that I was operating in *apych* were geographical rather than temporal, they too were historical: it was about bringing together different contexts, genealogies, and histories. The interest in the creation of coevalness through the intersubjective, shared time of the performance was central. I don't think we can talk of reenactment when discussing *apych*, but I do think that the logic of reenactment is there.

Ultimately reenactment, in the performing arts, challenges predominant ideas of historical time by dismantling the distinctiveness and stable order of past, present, and future; in doing so, it opens up the possibility of questioning that notion of history based on such an exclusively temporal axis, however unsettled and mobile it might become. In so doing, reenactment also has the potential to bring to our consideration the coexistence of heterotemporalities that are geo-culturally enacted (coexistent and divergent among them), and thus it can dismantle the historicist and ethnocentric assumption that the past, if still exists, must exist elsewhere, as if exiled into other geographical locations

These questions, articulated through the performing arts, envision not only a rational, conceptual undertaking: this is not an exclusively intellectual task. It implies an exercise on incorporated modes of being and sensing. To paraphrase Chakrabarty, reenactment in the performing arts asks for an active re-elaboration of the way our taste has been cultivated through practices of embodiment, through the cultural training our senses have received over generations.

## WORKS CITED

Barba, Fabián. 2011. "Research into Corporeality." *Dance Research Journal* 43(1): 81–89.
Bhabha, Homi. 2008. "On Global Memory: Thoughts on the Barbaric Transmission of Culture." Published by UC Berkeley Events. https://youtu.be/5Fp6j9Ozpn4 (accessed April 30, 2017).
Burt, Ramsay. 1998. *Alien Bodies: Representations of Modernity, 'Race' and Nation in Early Modern Dance*. New York: Routledge.
Burt, Ramsay. 2011. "Moving Memories: Contemporary Dance in Dialogue with Memory and History." Symposium presentation with Timmy de Laet and Fabián Barba. Unpublished.
Chakrabarty, Dipesh. 2000. *Provincializing Europe: Postcolonial Thought and Historical Difference*. Princeton, NJ: Princeton University Press.

Fabian, Johannes. [1983] 2002. *Time and the Other: How Anthropology Makes Its Object*. New York: Columbia University Press.

Franko, Mark. 1995. *Dancing Modernism/Performing Politics*. Bloomington: Indiana University Press.

Kunst, Bojana. 2003. "Politics of Affection and Uneasiness." *Maska* 5–6: 23–26.

Manning, Susan. [1993] 2006. *Ecstasy and the Demon: The Dances of Mary Wigman*. Minneapolis: University of Minnesota Press.

Mignolo, Walter. 2012. *Local Histories/Global Designs: Coloniality, Subaltern Knowledges and Border Thinking*. Princeton, NJ: Princeton University Press.

Vázquez, Rolando. 2011. "Modernity Coloniality and Visibility—The Politics of Time." In *Asking We Walk*, edited by Corinne Kumar. Bangalore: Streelekha Publications.

CHAPTER 21

..................................................................................

# DANCE AND THE
# DISTRIBUTED BODY

*Odissi and* Mahari *Performance*

..................................................................................

ANURIMA BANERJI

Can a different history of the dancer's body be written, one that does not glorify dance history for the needs of the present, but unveils instead the life-and-death stakes of its performance in the there-and-then?

—Mark Franko, *Dance as Text* (1993)

REENACTMENT is a central ideal in many of the Indian classical dance forms moored principally or partially in ritual practice, and in myriad ways. Reenactment not only serves as a key predicate of Indian classical dance, but is also its power and promise. This is especially true in a form like Odissi dance, a classical style rooted in the eastern Indian state of Odisha, which transparently invokes a history of ritual traditions like *mahari naach*—the dance of female ritual specialists attached to the Jagannath temple—in its aesthetics.[1] Arguably, the very foundation of classical Odissi is attached to the imperative of iterability: reenactment of a ritual past, made possible by absorbing a

---

[1] *Mahari* is the term for Hindu female ritual specialists in Odisha. The term *mahari* is often used interchangeably with *devadasi*, a title that denotes a similar ritual function for women dedicated to Hindu temples in South India and broadly on a pan-Indian basis. *Mahari* performance was once an important part of ritual life at the Jagannath-Puri temple in Odisha, but declined in postcolonial India. Today, only one *mahari*, Parashmoni Devi, survives from the group of women last inducted into the Puri temple in the 1950s. For an excellent ethnography on the Puri *maharis*, see Frédérique Apffel Marglin's *Wives of the God-King* (1985). There is by now a vast literature on the history and context of *devadasi* performances across India; see, for example, Allen (1997), Chatterjee (1945), Gaston (1992), Goswami (2000), Jordan (2003), Kersenboom (1998), Meduri (1996), Neville (1996), O'Shea (2007), Parker (1998),

dance repertoire in the body and reperforming it—a repertoire transcending the time and space of its creation, handed down through the repetition of its gestures and techniques, pedagogies and philosophies.

The assumption guiding this conventional approach to reenactment is that dance is purely visible in the mining and display of physical vocabularies and expressions; defined as such, it presumes that a seemingly intact dance repertoire is easily portable from one setting to another—for instance, from the Hindu temple to the concert stage. Yet, to focus on dance as a set of movement practices alone ignores the whole complex sphere within which the choreographic takes place. Classical dance is more than a suite of performed products, or a set of bodily tactics; it is also a discourse, the revelation of a historical process. As such, its successful reenactment might require the illumination of these historical circumstances and their implications.

Dance scholar Mark Franko's perceptive critique in *Dance as Text* (1993) is illustrative and relevant here for thinking through issues of reenactment in Odissi. Speaking of attempts to reconstitute French court dance in the twentieth century, Franko repudiates the very idea of "reconstructive" choreographic projects on the grounds that revisiting the past is only relevant if the new event reproduces the *effects* that were created in the original performance. This is not a passive mode of "reconstruction," but an active mode of "construction" that implies "a move towards the creation of a choreography that actively rethinks historical sources" (Franko 1993, 167)

In this chapter, my aim is to apprehend the unique effects of *mahari naach*, the "stakes of its performance in the there-and-then," and critically contemplate the ways it has been called into service for "the needs of the present" (Franko 1993, 137). I will argue that the attempt to fuse *mahari naach* with Odissi represents a failed reenactment, based as it is on the teleological premise that *mahari naach* is solely a set of corporeal techniques that can be merged with other sources to produce a refined classical dance. This failure cannot be attributed solely to the interpretation that Odissi "inauthentically" replicates *mahari naach*. Rather, the distinction between *mahari naach* and Odissi lies in the different kinesthetic and theoretical resonances they propose and produce. The major effect of *mahari naach*, I suggest, is that it indexically generates the ideation of a "distributed body" and thus promulgates a unique intersubjective model of reenactment—an important effect that is obscured in Odissi today. Indeed, Odissi cannot hope to integrate *mahari naach* unless it fully recuperates its philosophical, spatial, and performative ecology. It is not enough for Odissi to claim the movement sources or the mystical aura of *mahari naach*; the choreographic imperative demands a more substantial, sustained, and sophisticated encounter with its radiant effects, which entails constructing the distributed body—a feat that cannot be realized in contemporary Odissi.

Prasad (1991), Ramberg (2009), Roy ([2002] 2004, 2006, 2007, 2009), S. Anandhi (1991), Soneji (2012), Srinivasan (1985, 1990), Thielemann (2002), Vijaisri (2004), and Whitehead (1998, 2001).

# ODISSI AND *MAHARI* DANCE

As noted, *mahari* performance is aesthetically and ideologically linked to Odissi; for many, the *mahari* tradition is the source of an authentic Odissi, and the culture of the Jagannath temple and its presiding deity are equally prominent in the dance's history.[2] To understand the formation of contemporary Odissi, then, we need to analyze its relationship to *mahari* ritual dance (among other forms). Here, I explore the discourses of embodiment and the hermeneutics of the corporeal subject subtending and surrounding *mahari* dance. To excavate the body of dance in this sense involves looking simultaneously at the spaces surrounding it, as well as viewing its relationship to divinity. With this in mind, I mine three layers of the body illuminated in the history of *mahari naach*: the body of the deity, the body of the temple, and the body of the dancer.[3] I explore the relationship between the bodies of dancers, the deity, and the architectures within which they were conceived, framed, and culturally comprehended, as well as reflecting on the ways in which concepts of the body are generated and perpetuated by spatial, sacred, and artistic forms in this context. For in Odishan cultural logics, the temple and the deity constituted "bodies" in themselves. I argue that *mahari* dance represents an intersubjective encounter between the ritual performer, the material space, and the religious icon, producing a "distributed body." As I will discuss, the distributed body thus emerges in between these performative entities.

The value of the distributed body lies in hinting at a parallel economy of the subject that lies at the center of *mahari* dance. The idea of the distributed body contests dominant ideas of liberal subjectivity, which have come to serve as the harbingers and hallmarks of the ethos of modernity, and which are apparent today in Odissi dance. The distributed body, in contrast, shows how ritual practices contain and articulate— essentially reenact—the perspectives of a regional epistemology, opening up new possibilities for imagining notions of the subject on grounds different from those offered by the conventional narratives of Western modernity or dominant Indian paradigms. The distributed body of ritual dance thus generates and reenacts a voluptuous history that is otherwise lost to what Michel Foucault calls "subjugated knowledge" (1980, 81).

Odissi belongs to the canon of Indian classical dance, along with Bharatanatyam, Kathak, Kuchipudi, Manipuri, Kathakali, Mohini Attam, and Sattriya. Individually, each dance signifies a specific regional ethos; together, these dances perform the "unity in diversity" of the Indian nation-state. As part of this dual aesthetic and political mapping, Odissi represents the cultural heritage of Odisha.

---

[2]  The Jagannath temple in the city of Puri is a renowned religious center, within and beyond the borders of Odisha. The presiding deity is Jagannath, or "supreme lord of the world." I discuss the ritual activity of the temple later in this chapter. See Eschmann et al. (2005) for more on the Jagannath cult.

[3]  I pursue this analysis in the context of the ascent of mahari dancing at Puri's Jagannath temple by the twelfth century CE, and its continuity into the 1950s.

Odissi is often called the oldest classical dance form in India, based on claims of its consonance with an ancient style called Odra-Magadhi, which finds mention in the *Natyashastra*—a venerable Sanskrit treatise on performance, which was instrumental to the revival of several classical art forms in the twentieth century.[4] Noted scholars have also analyzed sculptural images in Odisha's Udaygiri caves, dating to the first century BCE and commissioned by the Jain monarch Kharavela; these relics, in concert with the *Natyashastra* references, they claim, serve as the earliest known evidence of the Odra-Magadhi form.[5]

Representations of dance in Odisha are difficult to trace after this historical moment. There is some sculptural evidence early in the first millennium which allows us to speculate that a form of Odra-Magadhi, or some of its traces and variations, continued to thrive in the region (Patnaik 2006). Dance rose to prominence again in early medieval Odisha, between the sixth and tenth centuries CE with the emergence of four historical changes: the popularization of Vaishnavism through the Jagannath cult, the origination of stone temples, the advent of the *mahari* system, and the development of new state formations.[6] The position of dance continued to shift under subsequent regional, colonial, and national regimes, and underwent significant transformations in the twentieth century.

The appellation "Odissi" emerged in the 1950s, when a group of scholars, critics, artists, dancers, and choreographers based in Odisha began to define a new dance form, inspired by cultural pioneers in South India who had successfully revived and reconstructed classical dances like Bharatanatyam, Kathakali, Kathak, and Manipuri.[7] Advocates argued that Odisha, too, had a distinctive dance history. Given that Odisha

[4] The *Natyashastra* is an ancient manual on dance and dramatic arts, its authorship attributed to the sage Bharatmuni. Its precise date is unknown, but it is thought to have been written between the second century BCE and the second century CE. Odra Magadha, one of the historical names of Odisha, is mentioned in the text as the place where the graceful, or *kaishiki,* style of Odra-Magadhi flourished. See Bharatmuni/Ghosh ([1967] 2007), Natyashastra XIV: 43–46).

[5] See, for instance, Kapila Vatsyayan (2007), Sunil Kothari (1990), and D. N. Patnaik (1990, 2006), three of the best-known commentators on Odissi dance. See also Ragini Devi (2002). In my research, I have suggested that the Odra-Magadhi dance belonged to a multiplicity of spaces, functioning as a political symbol of royal power as well as public entertainment. I discuss this in the first chapter of my dissertation (Banerji 2010). For more on the Udaygiri inscriptions, see Banerji and Jayaswal (1933), Barua (1938), Kant (2000), and Mishra (2006).

[6] Diverse religions coexisted in ancient and early medieval Odisha, including Buddhism, Jainism, and Hinduism. "Hinduism" is/was also known as Sanaatana Dharma, or "the eternal way." While the label "Hindu" is a fairly recent one (see Sharma 2002), it refers to a group of religious communities and cults that were once quite discrete as devotional movements: Vedic religions, based on the philosophies of the Vedas; Shaivism, the cult of Shiva; Shakti and Tantra, the goddess cults, with the latter incorporating esoteric rituals; Vaishnavism, the cult of Vishnu and Krishna; and Bhakti, the mystical movements usually dedicated to Shiva or Vishnu. Jagannath is a cognate of Krishna, who in turn is considered an incarnation of Vishnu in Hindu thought. For more, see Eschmann et al. (2005). On changing state regimes in Odisha, see Panigrahi (2008) and Kulke (2006).

[7] See Gandharva Mahavidyala (1985) and *Marg: A Magazine for the Arts* (March 1960) for a collection of documents that discuss Odissi's position as a classical form. See also Coorlawala (2005) and Pathy (2007) on the Sanskritized discourse of classical dance.

had just achieved official recognition as an autonomous state in 1936, and given its relative economic and political marginalization within the national Indian landscape, dance arguably became a form of cultural capital that was integral to Odisha's project of asserting a strong regional identity in post-independence India. The Sangeet Natak Akademi—the central government body charged with the task of rejuvenating and promoting Indian culture in the postcolonial era—finally initiated granting Odissi "classical" status on April 5, 1958, after a prolonged lobby by the dance's architects and proponents.[8]

What we know as "Odissi dance" in the contemporary sense is a (re)construction and amalgamation of four prominent sources. Texts such as the *Natyashastra, Abhinaya Darpanam, Abhinaya Chandrika, Abhinavabharati*, and Jayadeva's twelfth-century Sanskrit poem, the *Geeta Govinda*, among others, collectively form a repository for the dance's content, choreographic principles, presentation philosophies, body techniques, and ideal aesthetic modes, both formalist and narrative. The visual and tactile archive of relics, temple sculptures, drawings, paintings, and palm-leaf manuscripts in Odisha offered a lexicon of static dance movements to be interpreted and mobilized by the live dancer (Kothari 1990). The *gotipua* tradition was a major contributor to the formal Odissi repertoire; indeed, in dominant historiographies, virtually all the personalities cast as founding gurus of Odissi trained as *gotipuas* in their youth. *Gotipua* means "single boy," and the associated dance appears to have emerged out of a Bhakti tradition in which young male dancers feminized their appearance to pay homage to the deity Krishna-Jagannath, considered the supreme masculine force.[9] *Gotipua* repertoire consisted of spectacular performances set to vernacular poetry and songs (Patnaik 2008). The dance served the twin purposes of ritual and entertainment, as it was also designed to propagate the message of Bhakti.[10] Finally, Odissi revivalists drew upon the dances of the *maharis*, the female ritual specialists of the Jagannath temple in Puri. *Mahari* dances were tied exclusively to the goal of religious propitiation of the presiding deity,

[8]  Kavichandra Kalicharan Pattanaik, also a member, is credited as the scholar who named the new dance "Odissi," which means an entity that belongs to Odisha. Pattanaik's presentation at the April 1958 National Dance Seminar in New Delhi, along with Indrani Rehman's concurrent performance, convinced the Sangeet Natak Akademi to begin the process of giving Odissi classical status. Accounts of this history can be found in Patnaik (2006), Pathy (2007), Mohanty Hejmadi (1990, 2008), Gandhi (2009), and "The Dance Seminar in Retrospect," a cultural report in the April 8, 1958, edition of *The Statesman* (p. 5). See also Pattanaik et.al. 1958. Many of the details of Odissi's classicization process were confirmed in my interview with D. N. Patnaik (2008), a key scholar and member of the Jayantika group, involved in Odissi's revival.

[9]  Bhakti was a popular devotional movement that emerged in the sixth century CE in South India and subsequently spread all over the subcontinent. Initiated by mystics and poets, Bhakti rhetorically rejected caste and other forms of social hierarchy, repudiated Brahmin authority, and preached a direct relationship between deity and devotee. Bhakti reached its zenith in Odisha in the sixteenth century CE through the influence of the Gaudya Vaishnava movement, lead by the revered saint Sri Chaitanya Mahaprabhu. For more on Sri Chaitanya and his Bhakti philosophy, see his disciple Krishna Das Kaviraj's sixteenth-century biography, *Chaitanya Charitamrita* (translated by Dimock and Stewart, 2000).

[10]  On the *gotipua* tradition and its links to Odissi, see Coorlawala (1996), Kanungo (2006–2007), Khokar (1998), Kothari (1967, 1990), Mohanty Hejmadi (2008), and Roy (2009).

Jagannath. The *mahari* dance, like other *devadasi* dances in India, was disciplined for its alleged immorality under British colonial rule; stigmatized as prostitutes, *maharis* faced social opprobrium, and the system declined until it was finally outlawed in post-independence India (Jordan 2003; Parker 1998). The last *maharis* were inducted into the Jagannath temple in the 1950s—their dance tradition ironically dissipating and dissolving into Odissi, just as the nascent classical form appeared on the horizon.

The rise of Odissi dance at this important historical juncture produced significant effects in terms of its link to its root traditions and antecedents. While Odissi clearly had myriad genealogies, its new organization as a seamless and coherent entity depended on collapsing these multiple points of origin and absorbing them into a single discourse—its internal heterogeneity thus was abruptly homogenized. This reconfiguration had the further effect of placing Odissi, and the practices that influenced it, in a simultaneously synonymous and metonymic relationship: its constitutive traditions became Odissi, and Odissi became those traditions. Previously independent arts thus lost their autonomous character upon their absorption into the Odissi framework. And so forms as temporally and ideologically diverse as Odra-Magadhi dance, *mahari* ritual, and *gotipua* performance could be cast as part of the changing same of Odissi.

In the new discourse, certain sources were selectively and retroactively highlighted as emblematic of the dance's very essence. Initially, the *Natyashastra* and the Hindu temple enjoyed special prominence; the *maharis* were marginalized during the revival process (Roy 2006, 2007). Later, however, as the *mahari* tradition faced its demise in the 1950s, and the historical contribution of pan-Indian *devadasis* came to be re-examined—even glorified—in the narratives of allied classical dances, the *mahari* role in Odissi's formation was recast and valorized. Dance scholar Alessandra Lopez y Royo has argued that "Odissi was being created anew as a re-imagined mahari ritual" even as the link between the two styles "remains open to controversy" (2008, 11–12). Consequently, "Odissi as the-dance-of-the-mahari-of-Lord-Jagannath continues to play on the ambiguity and ambivalence of a ritual and exotic spectacle" (2008, 15). This is largely because Odissi's reconfiguration as a "classical" dance was heavily predicated on its identification with precolonial religious tradition.[11]

---

[11]  Starting in the 1950s, Guru Pankaj Charan Das, who was adopted by a *mahari*, developed a style of Odissi based on his intimate knowledge of the ritual practice—a style he imparted to his well-known disciples, Ritha Devi and Ratna Roy (Roy 2006; Ritha Devi 2003a, 2003b). Indrani Rehman, who popularized Odissi on the international stage, met with *maharis* early on in her Odissi training to understand their dance techniques (Rehman [1975] 1976). Special publications by Kala Vikash Kendra (1958) and *Marg* (1960) explored the nexus between *maharis* and Odissi. By the 1980s, *mahari* dance came to hold a privileged position as a precursor of Odissi, and efforts were underway to acknowledge this history through its recuperation in Odissi literature, performance, and pedagogy. The famous dancer Sanjukta Panigrahi even applied to dance in the Jagannath-Puri, with some falsely reporting her intention to become a *devadasi*, but her request was rejected by the temple committee (Panigrahi [1995] 1997). Frédérique Apffel Marglin's *Wives of the God-King* (1985) was the first in-depth study of *mahari* rituals. Ratna Roy (2004, 2006, 2007, 2009), Ileana Citarasti (1987), Sunil Kothari (1990), and Sharmila Biswas (2003–2004, 2008) have conducted extensive research on *mahari* practices, and the latter developed a project to re-present several items from the *mahari* repertoire (see Sangeet Natak

Dominant narratives of Odissi tend to emphasize its past position as a temple dance to validate its long lineage and sacred status. Indeed, several scholars, artists, critics, and members of the viewing public locate the authentic identity of Odissi in *mahari naach*.[12] This premise organizes the story of Odissi's temple-to-stage trajectory, suppressing the form's eclectic influences in favor of an exclusive identification with Hindu temple ritual. It promotes the reinterpretation of Odissi as a purely devotional dance, problematically positing texts and practices appropriated in its historical telling—like the *Natyashastra* and Odra-Magadhi—as religious in nature, despite their contested status. The move further connects the dance to other classical forms that claim to trace their genesis to the temple order, like Bharatanatyam and Kathakali, and magnifies the links between dance and religiosity to elevate and authorize Odissi's special position among Odisha's myriad performing arts.

Yet, at the same time, we cannot overlook the role of Hindu praxis as a vital force in Odissi's formation. *Mahari* performance, the Jagannath cult that supported its growth, and the Puri temple were all essential components in shaping the history and aesthetics of the dance style (though not exclusively so). The temple's centrality in Odishan culture and the significance of its iconography and ritual system absolutely account for the privileged position of *mahari naach* in Odissi's narrative. The strength and preeminence of the dance/temple nexus thus merits close attention.

# THE CITY OF JAGANNATH-PURI AND THE BODY OF THE DEITY

The *maharis* are significant figures as purveyors and protectors of a cultural tradition that thrived within the precincts of the Jagannath temple in Puri, publicly embraced as the hallowed ancestral site of Odissi dance (Figure 21.1). A place that combines both pleasure and pilgrimage, the city of Puri is a magnet for pilgrims and seekers, *sadhus* and *sants*, tourists and devotees, those in search of the healing waters of the Bay of Bengal, and those coming to be blessed by Jagannath, lord of the universe, and his sister and brother, Subhadra and Balaram (Figure 21.2).[13] Puri is one of the *char dham*—that

---

Akademi 2003). Sarat Das, the son of Guru Pankaj Charan Das, has taken on the mission of preserving the choreographer's repertoire through his eponymous Odissi Research Foundation (GPCDORF 2012). Rupashree Mohapatra, who studied with Guru Pankaj Charan Das and Haripriya Devadasi, has established Kala Mandir, her Puri-based institute dedicated to presenting *mahari* dances in concert form (Mohapatra 2012; see also *The Hindu,* August 29, 2009, and N. Panda, *The Telegraph,* May 19, 2011). Alessandra Lopez y Royo (2007, 2008) and Ananya Chatterjea (2004) have written critical accounts of the *mahari*-Odissi linkage.

[12]  See, for example, Khokar (1984), Kothari (1990, 2001), and Vatsyayan (1997, 2007).

[13]  *Sadhus* and *sants* are holy mendicants and saints who have left worldly life to wander in search of spiritual liberation.

**FIGURE 21.1.** The eastern gate of the Jagannath temple. Puri, March 7, 2008.

Photo by Anurima Banerji.

quartet of supremely holy places in India, where Hindu pilgrims flock for a vision of the deity and a blessing. Each of these four *kshetras*, or revered places, corresponds to one of the four directions: Badrinath to the north, Rameshwaram to the south, Dwarka to the west, and Puri to the east.[14] Traveling to the *char dham* within one's lifetime is considered to be the sacred duty of every faithful Hindu.

A connection between spatiality and corporeality is embedded in the very name *Puri*: etymologically it is linked to the Hindu concept of *purusha*, indicating a place where the soul has taken root. The concept is also linked to a sense of fullness, abundance, and plenitude, as both the human body and the home are called *pura* (Babaji 2008). Puri thus represents a place of sacred wholeness.

Puri is also considered the spiritual home of Odissi dance, as the site of the Jagannath temple where *mahari* service was formalized. The temple plays an important role in the cultural life of the region. Built in the twelfth century CE by King Anantavarman Chodaganga Deva of the Ganga dynasty, it became a significant space

---

[14] The list of *char dhams* may vary, depending on the perspectives of specific Hindu sects. For instance, other formulations of *char dham* include Benares and Vrindaban instead of Dwarka or Badrinath.

FIGURE 21.2. (From right to left) The trinity of Jagannath, Subhadra, and Balaram, placed on the main stage of the Konark Dance Festival. Konark, Odisha, December 2010.

Photo by Anurima Banerji.

of power and worship (Eschmann et al. 2005). The king formalized three institutions long identified with the culture of the temple—the association of the royal ruler as an embodiment of Jagannath, and the god's reciprocal position as the "king of the kingdom of Odisha"; Rath Yatra, the annual Chariot Festival; and *mahari* service, based on preexisting traditions of dancing girls performing at Odisha's temples (P. Kanungo 2003).

The Jagannath cult developed in Odisha with the rise of Vaishnavism in the region. The deity is an unusual figure in the Hindu pantheon. He is considered to be a living entity. Thus all the rituals of the temple are designed to attend to him and his family's needs. Every day, Jagannath is awakened from sleep; he is bathed, dressed, and offered food. Before the evening prayer, he takes a siesta and so will not meet his worshippers. He grants *darshan* to his followers at specified times of the day, and at night he falls into a restful sleep; the next day, the cycle begins all over again. His consort, Lakshmi, lives in the same temple complex, but Jagannath is always depicted as part of a trio of siblings. The gods leave the temple precincts to meet the faithful at special festivals, most famously the Rath Yatra. They even ritually fall ill once a year after the Snana Yatra (Bathing Festival), when they are sequestered from their devotees. At auspicious intervals, in the years when two full moons appear in the month of *Ashadha*,[15] they are said to die. On the occasion of Nabakalebar the gods are then given new bodies, resurrected in refashioned images made of neem wood, at the center of which is placed a secret substance, which purportedly gives them life; and the old idols are buried in a courtyard in the temple complex. These elaborate daily and ceremonial rituals, it is said, mark a thousand-year-old tradition, and are carried out by local servitors assigned to their specific tasks on a hereditary basis (Mishra 1984; Jagannath Temple 2011).

# THE BODY OF THE TEMPLE

To enter the great temple is to enter an exalted space, as well as an exalted religious and aesthetic history, for Jagannath-Puri is a magnificent exemplar and embodiment of Kalingan temple design. Kalingan temples are marked by a set of traits—conceptual and architectural—that differentiate them from other Indian architectural forms.[16] Famous for their bold and intricate style, Kalingan monuments can be immediately identified by the *rekha* (curved tower), *bhadra* or *pila* (horizontal courses), and *khakara* (spherical shape) structures (Bose 1932; Linda 1990, 87; see Figure 21.3). Once installed as stark and simple single-edifice shrines, they gradually developed into compounds featuring the *deul* (main shrine), the *jagmohan* (audience hall), the *bhoga-mandap* (dining hall), and the *nata-mandap* (dance hall) (Donaldson 1981; see Figures 21.4 and 21.5).

The outer walls of Kalingan temples tend to be exquisitely embellished with images of gods and goddesses, their symbols and vehicles, semi-celestial beings like *yakshas* and *yakshis* (protectors of nature), *nagas* and *naginis* (human-serpent hybrids), *apsaras* and *gandharvas* (heavenly dancers and musicians), legendary creatures (often lions, elephants, and birds), as well as *mithuna* (erotic couples), *nayikas* and *kanyas* (young women), yogis and yoginis, and royal figures. The carvings are placed in a stunning

---

[15]  This is June–July in the Gregorian calendar, according to Puri's ritual calendar.

[16]  Stone temples began to emerge in the fifth century CE in India, proliferating under the auspices of the Gupta dynasty (ca. 320–550 CE) during what is typically regarded as the birth of the classical age in India (Desai 1990). Starting from this time, temples were broadly categorized into three general types—the northern *Nagara*, the Deccan *Vesara*, and the southern *Dravida* varieties. The Odisha temples constitutes a fourth kind, known as the Kalinga style, which achieved recognition between the sixth and sixteenth centuries CE, showcasing "a continuous series of monuments spanning nearly a thousand years of architectural activity" (Donaldson 1985, ix). Often, Kalingan architecture combines elements of the first three dominant types as well as artistic motifs from neighboring regions, exhibiting the hybrid impulse so evident in several of Odisha's cultural forms. Odishan shrines are basically derived from the northern pattern but exemplify one of the most "distinct variations of the *Nagara* style of temple construction" (Donaldson 1985, ix). The Kalingan style was first isolated by scholars in a temple inscription from Karnataka and in Sanskrit texts such as the twelfth-century CE *Kamikagama* (Dhaky 1977, 1; Linda 1990, 87; see also Bose 1932).

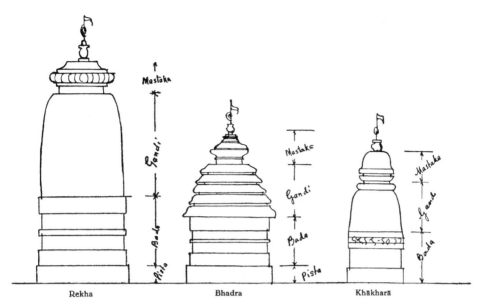

FIGURE 21.3. The three types of Kalingan temple spires. The Jagannath temple incorporates the *rekha* and *bhadra* (also known as *pidha*) styles.

From N. K. Bose, *Canons of Orissan Architecture* (1932; illustration opposite page 20).

FIGURE 21.4. The *deul* (main shrine) of the Konark temple in *bhadra* (also known as *pidha*) style. Ganga period, 13th century CE. Konark, Odisha, February 2008.

Photo by Anurima Banerji.

**FIGURE 21.5.** The *nata-mandira*, or *nata-mandap* (dance pavilion), of the Konark temple, Odisha, is decorated with elaborate sculptures. Ganga period, 13th century CE. Konark, February 2008.

Photo by Anurima Banerji.

aesthetic universe, where every surface is richly adorned with abstract patterns accented by *jali*, or filigree work (see Figure 21.6).[17]

Most important, the Kalingan temple has a specific foundational philosophy, illuminated in its form (Figure 21.7). In standard Hindu architectural works, the earth's surface is represented as a *mandala*—a square diagram signifying cosmic order, infused with sacred meaning—permeated by the male principle of *purusha*. (In Hindu philosophy, the square is the emblem of perfection.) A potent sign, the *purusha mandala* is used as the basis of architectural planning and positioning to maximize the circulation of positive energies in a space and to impede negative forces (Muralidhar Rao 1995). Thus the *purusha mandala* is used to construct and orient the *devalaya* (literally, "home of the gods"), serving as the abstract anchor of its architecture. With the mandala as its model, the sacred space ultimately signifies the universe over which an all-powerful

---

[17]  Soma Chand (2005) points out this type of embellishment is another feature distinguishing Kalingan architecture. According to her, the decorative programs can be classified into three types—the constructive, representative, and ornamental—in conformance with the *Shilpa Shastra*. For more, see Dehejia (1979), Donaldson (1981), and Goswami (1950).

FIGURE 21.6. A pair of dancers in *tribhangi* (three-bends posture), where the body is curved at the knee, torso, and head. This is a signature stance in contemporary Odissi dance. Konark temple *nata-mandira*, Orissa. Ganga period, 13th century CE. Konark, Odisha, February 2008.

Photo by Anurima Banerji.

deity reigns. Axioms of Odishan architecture align closely with the precepts of the *Shilpa Shastra* (a Sanskrit architectural treatise), with a unique twist: the Kalingan temple is specially designed so that its contours and silhouettes correspond to parts of the human body (Figure 21.8) (D. C. Panda 2000, 2003, 2006 and personal communication [2008, 2010]).[18] In this sense, it enacts and enlivens the concept of *sharira yantra* (body diagram). While other Hindu temple styles are based on *principles* of the human body, the Kalingan style moves toward the architectural *personification* of that body.

The Odishan temple's metaphorical and metonymic transformation into a corporeal entity is directly evinced in the naming of each segment. Soma Chand affirms, "architects

---

[18] D. C. Panda, a renowned scholar of Odishan architecture, first explained to me how the Kalingan temple is conceived in terms of a human body. In March 2008 and December 2010, he was my guide on a tour of the Mahamaya temple in Hirapur, the Udaygiri caves, and eighteen Bhubaneshwar temples: Ananta-Vasudev, Brahmeshwar, Bharateshwar, Bhaskareshwar, Jameshwar, Kedar-Gauri, Lingaraj, Markandeshwar, Megheshwar, Mukteshwar, Parashurameshwar, Paschimeshwar, Rajarani, Shatrughaneshwar, Shishireshwar, Siddheshwar, Swarnajaleshwar, and Vaitul Deul. I am deeply indebted to him for sharing his knowledge with me.

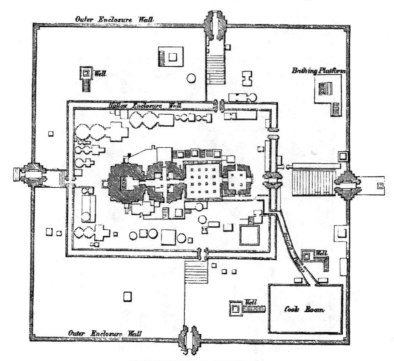

PLAN OF TEMPLE OF JUGGERNAUT.

**FIGURE 21.7.** Plan of the Jagannath Temple.

From Harper's New Monthly Magazine (1878: 226).

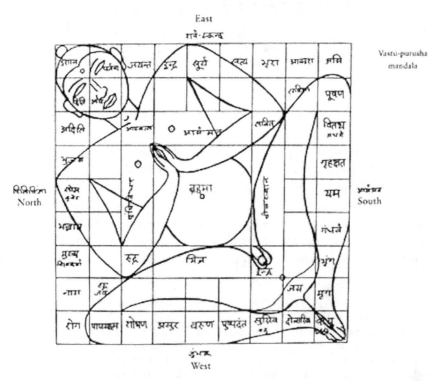

**FIGURE 21.8.** *Purusha-mandala*, according to the *Vastu Shastra*. The plan of the Jagannath temple follows this model and accordingly faces east (*purab*), considered the most auspicious direction.

Public domain image.

perceived the temple in the form of a human male figure or *Purusha*. Like human phys-ical divisions of leg, thigh, waist, chest, neck, and head, the temple had similar shapes and structures" (2005, 50). In this physicalization, the base moldings and plinth are known as *pabhaga*, or foot division. The vertical portion of the wall is called *jangha*, or legs (further split into *tala* and *upar jangha*, or calf and thigh, linked by another class of mouldings called *bandhana*, which means "binding" or "tying together"). The *bada*, or perpendicular wall, constitutes the rest of the body. The *baranda* (lower torso, or "belt region") are upper mouldings that separate the *bada* from the *gandi*, the latter signify-ing the main torso, the curvilinear spine. Above this portion, the structure proceeds on a gradual upward gradient, so that the four walls slope inward, pyramid-like, meeting at a point known as the *mastaka*—the crowning element, or head—which consists of the *beki* (neck), *amala* (top of the neck), and *khapuri* (skull), capped by the *kalasa*, a decora-tive element (Chand 2005; Panda 2008, 2010). All in all, the temple is conceived, visual-ized, and structured as a human body (see Figures 21.9 and 21.10).

D. K. Ganguly elaborates on this association:

> The temple has always been conceived in India as the "visible outer encasement of the invisible deity, a visible image which is installed in it as an emblem of the invisible spirit" which pervades all nature. It is, like the human body, the outer visible shape of the shapeless. This explains why the various parts of a temple in Odisha or elsewhere in India are designated by names which correspond to various parts or limbs of the human body. (1984, 56)

The spatial relationship between the human body and the divine is immediately and irrevocably established in this schema. Importantly, the temple ceases being an inan-imate object. It is refashioned as a religious agent, underscored by the idea that the five organic elements that make up the human body and the temple are one and the same: *bhumi* (earth), *jal* (water), *vayu* (wind), *agni* (fire), and *akash* (space). In this perspective, the essence and substance of each personified entity is indistinguishable from the other. The Kalingan temple acts as both body and abode. Thus the temple exceeds its role as a dwelling or site of representation, housing the deity and bear-ing sculptural depictions of human, celestial, and otherwordly beings. Instead, the temple *becomes* a body. It attains a kind of cosmic corporeality, anointed and ani-mated with the energy of the *purusha* principle. Layers and layers of embodiment reveal themselves, blurring and coalescing together: the temple is a body; the body of the deity lives here; sculpted bodies adorn the larger body of the temple; all wit-ness the migration of flesh-and-blood bodies coming in and out of the vivified place. In a relational cycle, bodies of human devotees pass through the body of the temple for a glimpse of the body of the deity, surrounded by bodies carved in stone. In a mutual manifestation, the human figure is newly spatialized in the bones and scaf-folds of the religious structure. The architecture of the temple and the anatomy of the human body dissolve into a single harmonious entity, bound together within a sacred geography.

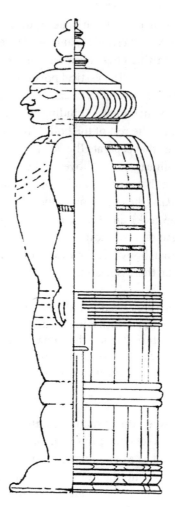

FIGURE 21.9. An illustration of the correspondence between the parts of the human body and linked sections of the temple in Kalingan architecture.

Image courtesy of D. C. Panda. Reproduced with permission.

## THE DANCING BODY: *MAHARI* RITUALS

The concern with corporeality, and the relation between the human and the divine body, are key tropes of foundational Hindu myths. *Maharis* and other *devadasis* are regarded as the descendants of *apsaras*, celestial beings who danced in the heavenly courts to entertain gods and mesmerize mortals.[19] Historically, there is proof of the *mahari*

---

[19] In Puranic legend, the apsaras were born during the *samudra manthan*, the great churning of the ocean that created the universe.

FIGURE 21.10. The *bada* (body), *beki* (neck), *mastaka* (crown), *and khapuri* (head) are visible on the main *deul* in Kalingan architecture. The Jagannath temple spire shares these characteristics, but since photography is prohibited on its premises, a direct view of the *deul* is not available. This is a close-up of a similar type of *deul* at the Ananta-Vasudeva temple. Ganga period, 13th century CE. Bhubaneshwar, Odisha, December 2010.

Photo by Anurima Banerji.

tradition's existence in Odisha as far back as the eleventh century CE, with its formal esablishment at the Jagannath temple dated to the twelfthth century CE, after the temple's inauguration by royal authority.[20] The *mahari* role may have been based on preexisting

[20]  Historical records show that an incipient form of the *mahari* system emerged in Odisha under the Somavamsi-Kesari regime (see Donaldson 1981). Of this there is ample proof in the form of inscriptions and images at the Brahmeshwar temple (ca. 1058 CE), which confirm the dedication of dancing girls by Queen Kolavati at the site.

traditions of dancing girls performing at Odisha's shrines, and until the 1950s, *mahari* performance was the only category of ritual service taken up exclusively by women.[21]

While accounts of *mahari* ritual preceding the twentieth century cannot be fully verified, the extant epigraphic, ethnographic, and textual evidence offers a glimpse of a past tradition that suggests at least some resonance with the recent forms, if not absolute consonance. It is, of course, impossible to tell definitively.[22]

It appears that the *mahari* system was identified with cultivating extraordinary expressions of gender. The young girls, usually nine years of age when they joined the order, were often dedicated by their families to the temple, usually as a sign of gratitude for receiving divine blessings, or as a mode of appeasing the deity in fulfillment of a wish (to avoid a calamity or seek a good marriage alliance in the family, for instance). A girl could also be chosen independently by a *mahari* for adoption. Although her social background held relatively little importance, the girl's beauty, bodily proportions, devotional intensity, and artistic aptitude were all appraised before she could be accepted into the system.[23]

The emphasis on a girl's outward appearance and (potential) talents were just as important as her inner spiritual leanings (see Figure 21.11). The construction of an ideal body in these circumstances was contingent on both of these factors, rather than being mutually exclusive: the cultivation of art and the cultivation of religious character held

[21] My discussion here is based on an analysis of the ethnographic literature (especially Marglin 1985), documentation of *mahari* rituals (such as in Ron Hess's 1985 film, *Given to Dance*) and the related repertoire (Biswas 2003, 2008; Ritha Devi 1987, 1988, 2003 a, 2003b; Guru Pankaj Charan Das Odissi Research Foundation 2012), watching *mahari* or *mahari*-inspired dances, and my interviews with specialists in the field, including Shashimoni Devadasi (2008), Parashmoni Devadasi (2012), Babaji (2008), Raja Panda (2012), and Rupashree Mohapatra (2012). My hypothesis is that *mahari* dance appropriated elements and traces of the preceding Odra-Magadhi style (or its variations), sanctified it, institutionalized it, and redefined it through its transformation in a ritual context. Much of the literature on the rituals associated with the Jagannath cult emphasizes the appropriation of local forms as the basis of temple ritual. For instance, Jagannath himself was once a Sabara tribal deity called Nilmadhava, later assimilated into the Hindu pantheon (see Eschmann et al. 2005). I suggest that, in line with this pattern, existing dance practices could have also been absorbed into the Jagannath temple's services and adapted to meet new ritual requirements.

[22] *Mahari* rituals have been well documented by several scholars, and so I do not dwell on them at length here. In addition to those listed in note 1, see the accounts by Citarasti (1987), Mishra (1984), Mubayi (2005), and Patnaik (2006). For a background on the rituals of Jagannath-Puri, see Kulke (1981) and Eschmann et al. (2005). Since the 1980s, there has been an ongoing debate as to whether the *mahari* order (and *devadasi* expressions in general) can be viewed from a feminist lens as a mode of women's empowerment, or, oppositionally, as a symptom of patriachal exploitation and violence. This debate, while extremely important, is outside the scope of this chapter and I do not address it here; references in note 1 do take up the debate in detail.

[23] Historically, the *maharis* became "casteless" when they entered temple service and achieved equivalence in status, since they received a new identity through their profession. However, the girls chosen for adoption had to belong to "water-giving" castes, which included most caste groups except the Dalits, or untouchables, and tribals, who existed outside the caste system but whose presence in the temple was nevertheless considered polluting. Shashimoni Devadasi states in an interview with dancer/ scholar Rahul Acharya that at the time of her dedication in the early twentieth century, "it was a norm to choose either Brahmin, Karana, or Khandayat girls" for the service (2003).

**FIGURE 21.11.** Group shot of Suhasini Mahari (in full dance regalia for ceremonial perfor-mances) with other *maharis* at Jagannath temple—including Shashimoni Devadasi at far right. Circa 1960s, Puri, Orissa.

Photo courtesy of the Sangeet Natak Akademi, New Delhi.

equal import within a worldview that regarded beauty as inextricably linked to the moral and the good (Dehejia 2009, 65). Beauty was taken as a symbol of the *devadasi's* innate, essential nature, and the presence of the *devadasis* in the temples both beautified and beatified the surrounds.[24]

The *sari-bandhan* or *gopa sari* ritual, marking the girl's dedication to the temple, mir-rored the marriage ceremony. First, her outer body was purified with turmeric and her inner body cleansed through fasting. Freshly bathed and dressed in a new sari, bedecked with jewels, she was taken to the temple by her female relatives and the elder *maharis*

---

[24] Temple inscriptions illustrate the premium placed on the *mahari's* attractiveness; at Megheshwar (ca. 1195–1198 CE), the poet Udayan praised the dancing girls "whose eye-lashes constitute the very essence of captivating the whole world, whose very gait brings about a complete stillness in the activities of the three worlds, whose bangles bejewelled with precious stones serve as unarranged candles during the dance; those deer-eyed maidens are offered in devotion to Him—Lord Shiva" (cited in Patnaik 2006, 32). See also the inscriptions at the Shobhaneshwar and Ananta Basudeva temples, in which similar language is used to describe the dancers and the role of the arts in ritual service (Patnaik 2006, 32–34, Rajguru 1992, 335–346).

for the momentous occasion. Receiving *dikshya* (instruction) from the principal guru signaled her official entry into the *mahari* order. She then was taken to see the deity. A special sari was tied around her head; she received a fragrant flower garland, signifying eternal union with Jagannath; and the part of her hair was marked with *sindoor*, vermilion, the red paste symbolizing her newly married status. After performing circumambulations around the temple, the consecrated *devadasi* celebrated the occasion with a gathering of her family and friends, where she was welcomed with *arati*[25] and given the gift of a special silk sari, reserved for performance. All at the event received *mahaprashad* from the temple.[26] The presence and very sight of the *devadasi* promised auspiciousness to all who congregated at this transformative event (Citarasti 1987; Marglin 1985).

At dusk, the new *devadasi* was taken to visit the king. As part of the *palanka-seva* (bed rituals), she symbolically touched his bed (*sheja meda*) and the two met each other's gaze (*chakshyu milan*). D. N. Patnaik notes the palace ritual "is observed as the Raja of Puri is venerated as the moving image of Vishnu or Jagannath" (2006, 56). The *mahari* became his female counterpart and consort and was herself known as "Chalanti Devi," or "walking goddess" (Marglin 1985, 1990). Disturbingly, there are also firsthand reports provided in Marglin's ethnography suggesting that the touching was more than symbolic, and actually was carnal in nature: some kings sexually exploited even very young *maharis* in the early twentieth century, reflecting social mores regarding the age of consent at the time. Indeed, many progressive activists highlighted the sexual abuse of women and girls in their campaigns to abolish *devadasi* systems all across India; though this was not a uniform experience, it was sufficiently embedded in the system to elicit urgent calls for social and moral reform.[27]

After her initiation, the acolyte lived with her compatriots in quarters close to the temple and began a life of religious service. Along with her new status came the privileges of property ownership, education, artistic training, access to royalty, and elevated ritual status. As a novice, she was given training in dance and music—depending on her particular skill—by the other *devadasis* and their guru, and she was instructed in religious and political protocols by the *rajguru* (the head priest, representing the king). Following this period of immersion in aesthetic and religious disciplines, she could make her debut as part of a formal temple ritual.

Although the *mahari* enjoyed a high status compared to ordinary women, she was still required to conform to a disciplinary regime full of rules specific to the religious habitus. These binding regulations governed the full continuum of her social conduct

[25] *Arati* refers to an act of worship in which the devotee venerates the deity using the purifying element of fire, usually by waving oil lamps in front of the image.

[26] *Mahaprashad* is the food prepared under the supervision of Lakshmi and consecrated by Jagannath and Vimala Devi at the Puri temple, then distributed to devotees. Partaking of *mahaprashad* leads to the expiation of all sins in Hindu thought.

[27] On this, see Reddy (1935) and the in-depth discussions by A. Srinivasan (1990), Meduri (1996), Whitehead (2001), and Chandrikha (2009).

outside the temple and bodily comportment inside it. On the days that she was to perform at the temple, she was forbidden from speaking to any man. She bathed and dressed in her special sari. Typically, once she reached the age of consent, she would be seen as sexually available to the king as well as temple priests. These were unconventional sexual mores and relations, outside everyday social norms, but they were regarded as a part of ritual life to reinforce the special status of the *mahari*, the deity, and the king as intermediaries between the celestial and terrestrial. At the same time, to protect her privileged status, a *mina nayak* (guard) accompanied the *mahari* to and from the temple. This regulation precluded the possibility of the *mahari* entering into contact with ordinary men and thus risking her status by mingling with them socially or sexually. Certainly this was intended as a form of patriarchal control, but it was also imposed in recognition of the *mahari*'s extraordinary status, to guard against public contaminations when she was summoned for ritual occasions and was required to manifest a state of purity, as defined by the moral and social protocols outlined by temple authorities.[28]

The regulation of *mahari* movements occurred both inside and outside the temple, and by the fifteenth century CE, the royal authorities issued a legal proclamation setting the choreographic limits of the *devadasi* repertoire. In recognition of its beauty, its *rasa* (taste, flavor, essence), its *shringara* (eros), and as a sign of his own allegiance to Vaishnavism, the king Prataparudradeva (r. 1497–1540) made it mandatory to use Jayadeva's poetic masterpiece, the *Geeta Govinda*, as the source of all *mahari* performance. Anything other than this was a violation. Dance became a powerful sign of the state, and the integration of the *Geeta Govinda* in the repertoire both represented and reinforced the auspiciousness of the *maharis* and the god-king. Later in time (at least in the mid-twentieth century) the *maharis* were able to experiment with vernacular musical and poetic forms for their dance compositions (Shashimoni Devadasi, 2008).

## DANCE AS PUJA, DANCE AS GIFT

When I met her in 2008, Shashimoni Devadasi was one of two surviving *maharis*, along with Parashmoni Devadasi (Figure 21.12). Sadly, she has since passed away (see E. Barry, *New York Times*, March 23, 2015). She learned dance (*naacha-bhava*) from her adoptive *mahari* mothers and Shri Mohan Mohapatra, one of the last gurus affiliated with the Jagannath temple (interview with author 2008). The training emphasized the qualities of *bhava*, or feeling: "We never had any strict grammar for dance. All lessons were quite spontaneous and we were supposed to feel the dance rather than doing it mechanically" (Shashimoni Devadasi 2003). Although the learning style was flexible, there were still set

---

[28]  See Marglin (1985), Citarasti (1987), and Buli Mahari, cited in Patnaik (2006).

**FIGURE 21.12.** Shashimoni Devadasi performing an *abhinaya* sequence. Puri, Odisha, March 7, 2008.

Photo by Anurima Banerji.

pieces to memorize in the *mahari* dance routine. For her inaugural temple performance at the morning service, *Sakal Dhupa*, she

> performed to the accompaniment of mardala (percussion) and gini (cymbals), quite oblivious of the surrounding. [ . . . ] The dance was a Nritta (pure dance) without any song accompanying it. The second performance took place during *Bada Singara* (the god's bedtime) and this was performed under closed doors. During this time the dance was supposed to be expressional and the songs accompanying the dance were from the *Geeta Govinda* alone. (2003)

Shashimoni Devadasi became a *mahari* at the age of eight. From what she remembered, she conducted her ritual service every day for forty years after the *sari-bandhan*, and "enjoyed performing for the Lord. Each day was a divine experience for me and I used to become ecstatic during my performances" (2003).[29]

---

[29]  It is interesting to note that when some Odissi revivalists and dancers speak of reconstructing the dance, they downplay or disavow the role of the *maharis*, claiming the women simply embellished their songs with mudras and *bhava* (see, for instance, the discussion by Lopez y Royo 2008, 12–13). Yet, from *mahari* descriptions, demonstrations, and existing documentation, it appears there was, in fact, a strong

For those of us who have not witnessed *mahari* rituals firsthand, we can only imagine what the dances must have been like in the atmosphere of the temple. The *mahari* service was qualitatively set apart from the other modes of prayer. Its origination in the female body, its immersion in *rasa*, and the affective dimension of the offering made it a spiritual offering unparalleled by any other kind of worship. Babaji, a *mahant* (spiritual leader) at a local monastery, elaborates eloquently on the singularity of dance as *puja*:

> I believe that [ . . . ] among all the kinds of [temple] services performed [ . . . ] the devadasi's service [was] the most important. [It] is a soul service, an emotional service, a service from the inside; there is nothing superficial about it. The service that devadasi offers god, god recognizes and appreciates. Other things like food, flowers, jewelry, clothes, whatever we have given—we cannot know whether or not god receives them, though we bring them to him anyway. But whatever the devadasi offers—god fully takes this gift, and no one else can conjure it again. This is a great service[.] (Babaji 2008; translated from Bengali by author)

Dance here is envisioned as an ineffable gift. It represents a pure act of giving, mingling devotion with pleasure. In Babaji's view, *mahari* dance was a form of private, sensuous exchange with the deity, contingent upon the presence of the body. Further, dance was a renewable gift, something that could be offered again and again, precisely because it was inalienable from the body of the person producing it.

The dance symbolized the sexual and spiritual union of the *mahari* with her deity-consort, while presenting a separate enactment of puja. The position of dance as a ritual service crystallized the non-reciprocal nature of the gift. Dance is both a highly material activity, located in the intimate milieu of the dancer's body, and highly intangible, in that it cannot be fully captured outside the boundaries of those bodies. Lose the dancers and you lose the dance, which is why performance—cast as a unilateral offering in the ritual setting—was a singular kind of gift to the gods. As Babaji and the *maharis* argue, the nature of the dance is such that it cannot be commodified in the same way as other material goods in the ritual context. As *puja*, it has a specific quality that demarcates it: dance is an offering of the body, of passions that lie in the body, and all that transcends the body, at once. While

---

*nritta* component in *mahari* dance (see, for instance, the descriptions of *devadasi* performance in the *Chaitanya Charitamrita*, colonial reports and travelogues from the seventeenth to the twentieth centuries CE, footage of *mahari* performances in *Given to Dance* (1985), and the lecture-demonstration by Sharmila Biswas in the 2003 SNA colloquium). Rather than doing interpretive dances set to songs and poems, it seems that *maharis* drew upon a repository of rich compositions, combining body technique with expressive *abhinaya* traditions. The alleged lack of a "real" *mahari* dance is often cited as the reason for the peripheralization of maharis from Odissi's revival process (see Lopez y Royo 2008). Many of the dancers and gurus whom I informally spoke to in the course of my fieldwork (but who would not necessarily go on record) said the *maharis* primarily performed basic *abhinayas*, rather than complex dances as the *gotipuas* did; they also alleged *maharis* had been tutored in dance only recently by Odissi gurus, which is why their movements resembled elements of Odissi technique. Others even denied the *maharis* the status of dancers, saying that they were "just" singers who enhanced the lyrics using hand gestures and facial expressions.

presents of food, clothing, money, and other items used for worship can circulate among devotees, none—except those who actually embody it—can "give" the ritual dance.

Because dance performance cannot be divided from the body, it is different in character from those commodities that circulate in the world as autonomous objects and which symbolically stand in place of the donors. While in the religious context these gifts acquire a holy aura, in an extra-religious context, they simply serve as human forms of sustenance: rice and ghee are everyday nourishment, not *mahaprashad*; clothes and jewels cover the body for the sake of social modesty; money is used for worldly transactions. These ordinary things, placed in extraordinary settings, are transformed; they lack innate and fixed signifying powers. *Mahari* dance, and the *mahari* identity, in contrast, were always already holy. Once consecrated to the temple, *maharis* achieved an eternally auspicious status. Unlike objects and practices that could change meaning outside of a religious context, the *maharis* retained their elevated position after entering a sanctified state, accomplished through their marriage to Jagannath. The *mahari* presence brought devotees into the realm of the spiritual while heightening the devotional atmosphere of the temple.

Dance served as a potent emblem of spiritualized eros at Jagannath-Puri. At Sakaldhupa, the Nachuni's dance was instrumental for intensifying the emotional experience of the devotees; and at Sandhyadhupa, the Bhitare Gauni's performance for the deity became an erotic encounter infused with *shringar rasa*. The *devadasi's* body became a site of sensual power, as she channeled religious sentiment and mediated encounters between the worlds of the mortal and the divine; her dance emblematized the intertwining of the sensual and the sacred. By day, her ritual was made public; by night, it was privatized, secluded to the inner chambers of the deity (Shashimoni Devadasi 2003 and 2008).

## RITUAL DANCE AND THE DISTRIBUTED BODY

In the social order of things, the *devadasi* institution was unusual, even exceptional. It was one of the only systems designed to integrate women into ritual service in the temple hierarchy, in a context where religious authority was usually considered the purview of caste-privileged men. Historically, the *devadasi* role existed as one in a range of social roles available to women in medieval and colonial India: as reproductive agent and moral guardian of the family (daughter, wife, mother); as peasant or laborer (usually women in the service class, from lower-caste and working-class groups); as artist (courtesans, poets, public entertainers); as ruler (queens, princesses); and spiritual agent (philosophers, ascetics, mystics), to name a few.[30] *Devadasis*, as the perpetually auspicious brides of Jagannath, enjoyed social authority predicated on their superior

---

[30]  Upon first glance, while the social repertoire was indeed limited, and women's public roles were severely diminished in comparison to men's, the interplay of gender and caste presented a more complex picture. Certain feminist readings of the *devadasi* practice often emphasize the dancer's position as part of a patriarchal order in which women's bodies are controlled by male agents—kings, priests, and even the

status: they had access to wealth, property, education, and ritual praxis; they could never be widowed, and thus were never subject to the stigmatization and exclusion that status entailed. Simultaneously mortal and divine, their proximity to the deity endowed them with extraordinary eminence. Their position was unmatched by any other service group, since they were the deity's exclusive intimates, intermediaries between the celestial and terrestrial worlds, the very embodiment of the goddess Lakshmi, Jagannath's wife.

Thus the *devadasis* inhabited an exotic milieu: the contours of their world were altogether estranged from that of ordinary women. This was particularly palpable in the concept of women as reproductive agents. For *devadasis*, the idea of reproduction reiterated their special standing—they were expected to engage in sexual relations with an approved class of men, especially the king-as-Jagannath. But this ritual/sexual service had no procreative duty or significance attached to it.[31]

Yet the absence of a responsibility for bearing children in no way suggested that the *devadasis* could shed responsibility for reproduction in a larger sense—the reproduction of a *body of ritual knowledge*. With the *devadasis*, reproduction was still a feminine act, but instead of implying direct procreation (as it would under quotidian norms), it implied *cultural* reproduction through the *dancing* female body. That is, the devadasi's power lay in her creative capacities, not her procreative propensities, as was the case with ordinary women. Indeed, the transmission and reenactment of cultural capital in bodily terms became the *devadasi's* special assignment. In both the everyday (social) and exceptional (religious) instances of reproduction, the instrument was the same—the female body—but her labor and somatic significations were qualitatively different. In the context of the *devadasi* order, there was a move away from the domestic arena of family labor and social reproduction to the religious arena of ritual service and animation of cultural heritage.

Rituals are primarily embodied acts, endowed with social power and partitioned from normative routines and conventions, conducted by authorized agents (Bell 1992, 1997; Hobsbawm 1983). They are highly performative, relying on a repertoire of citational gestures, often framed as part of traditions with mystical beginnings, traditions cast as timeless and unalloyed. Most significant, they create a world parallel to the

---

deity himself—and configured as the object of their gaze (see, for instance, Hanna 1998). However, looking at the *devadasis* in the context of their local social networks and values demands a reorientation of such a reading. Compared to conventional gendered modes, the *devadasi* order functioned as a matrilineal community within a larger patriarchal system, giving women a limited avenue for accruing material and religious power. While *maharis* never enjoyed absolute freedom, given the constraints and rules that governed their lives, relative to other women their position was undoubtedly a privileged one.

[31] Indeed, procreation was discouraged, and there was no direct need for it to sustain the *mahari* system, since adoption perpetuated the order. Having children would in fact diminish the *devadasi's* status, blurring the line between her position and that of an ordinary woman. For *maharis* who did become biological mothers, the children's affiliation to the temple was an important way of keeping the rituals alive, and perhaps also a way of keeping the temple's property and wealth intact—girls generally became *maharis*, and boys were trained as musicians. The situation changed in the mid-twentieth century, and the children of *maharis* gradually entered mainstream life. For more, see the interviews with surviving *maharis* in *Given to Dance* (1985); their perspectives are recorded as well in Marglin's 1985 ethnography.

quotidian—a world which, though temporary and transient, is nevertheless transformative and registers real effects.

As a ritual form that relies on mimesis and co-creation with the embodied forms of the deity and the temple, *mahari* dance produces a kinesthetic theory of the subject that, I argue, resonates with eminent anthropologist Alfred Gell's concept of "distributed self." In *Art and Agency*, Gell defines *distributed personhood* as "personhood distributed in the milieu, beyond the body boundary" (1998, 104). Discussing idol worship and the agentic qualities of iconic images of the divine, Gell theorizes the art object as a mediating force in cultural life, dwelling on the forms of social power it generates and the circuits it is embedded within, critiquing the semiotic approach in which the art object is positioned as a passive text to be "read." What Gell proposes, in short, is a theory of the art object as performance.

Analyzing religious idols and their specific identities as "not portraits, not depictions, but (artefactual) *bodies*," (1998, 98; italics in original), Gell speaks of representations and what he calls their original or authentic essences as virtually indivisible. He argues that the image *extends* rather than *substitutes* the entity in question, and "forges a direct link between the image as an index of the prototype, and the index as a (detached) *part* of the prototype" (104). In other words, if the image is an index rather than a sign, its substance can be immediately conflated with it, as the index is a symptom rather than symbol of the thing represented. "We are not accustomed to think of images [ . . . ] as parts of persons, *limbs*, as it were" (Gell 1998, 104; italics mine). This indexical relationship repudiates a semiotic approach in which the signifier and the signified retain their separate coherences, and posits a relationship of synechdoche in its place:[32]

> [I]f the "appearances" of things are material parts of things, then the kind of leverage which one obtains over a person or a thing by having access to their image is comparable, or really identical, to the leverage which can be obtained by having access to some physical part of them; especially if we introduce the notion that persons may be "distributed," i.e. all their "parts" are not physically attached, but are distributed around their ambience. (Gell 1998, 105–106)

This indexical relation allows Gell to speak of an object's emanations as its material ambassadors, as "flying simulacras" and "limbs" that elongate the presence of the thing, expanding its reach into other spaces and times (1998, 105).

Gell's idea of the art object as anaphoric embodiment—as performance—is a particularly productive insight that relates to reenactments of dance and other somatic practices as interventions in the world.[33] Substitute "dance" for "art object," and imagine the

---

[32] Gell, drawing on Charles Sanders Peirce's semiotic theory and his delineations of the icon, index, and sign, uses the well-known example of smoke and fire to illustrate his point about framing the index as part of the entity in question (1998, 104). Likewise, Gell refuses the distinctions made between iconic and aniconic idols (1998, 97–98).

[33] In my view, the traditional idea of the sign in the semiotic framework also has value. Instead of abandoning either one, then, we can arrive at a more textured approach to dance theory by embracing both sign and index, meaning *and* mediation, as modes of analysis.

*mahari's* moving body as "flying simulacra" that touches, with its "limbs," the space of the temple and the icon of the deity, vivifying both—and receiving, in turn, their consecrating force. Then picture the body of the deity, his vibrant stillness engendering space and transforming it, returning the gaze of the dancer and empowering her through the indexical experience of *darshan*, of sight-as-touch.[34] And conjure the body of the temple, activated and anthropomorphized through its relation to the rejuvenating relations with dancer and deity. In this continual cycle, the three elements—the body of the temple, deity, and dancer—disperse among themselves, mutually incorporate each other, reenact each other, co-constituted in a triangle of corporeal power.

In speaking of a distributed body as it related to *devadasi* performance at the Jagannath temple, I am arguing that dance had a diffuse property—dispensed across bodies, spaces, and objects—even as it coalesced in the *mahari's* body, granting its bearer a complex intersubjectivity. Further, ritual dance mobilized the concept of the distributed body in perpetuating itself as tradition. For ritualization created a principle of embodiment that is neither just singular nor plural, neither just one nor many, neither partible nor complete—it was one constructed liminally in between these states as a trans-individual force.[35] The distributed body was no fragmented body, however; there was a wholeness and auspiciousness ascribed to it, and its sacredness derives precisely from its distributed capacity—its ability to enact, reenact, translate, and propagate customs associated with religiosity. In the *mahari* context, the singular dancing body became porous and fractal, regarded as auspicious, infused with spiritual properties; through the ritual activity, the body became sanctified, part of a sacred lineage with complex religious and ideological attachments. In thinking of the distributed body, we can think of an intangible heritage made tangible; the materialization of the abstract in a multiplicity of forms; the corporeal conjuring the ethereal.

Through ritualization, the distributed body was collapsed not only into other bodies, but also into the space surrounding it. The temple acted reciprocally as an archive of corporeal relations. It was architecturally conceived as a body and contained manifestations of that body. It was itself a distributed body that housed other bodies, both still (in the form of sculpture), animated (in the form of the deity), and moving (in the form of pilgrims, pandits, and performers). The aura of auspiciousness was magnified through mimesis. As it carried out its ritual functions, the dancing body affirmed the sacred status of the temple and the deity through its intense exaltation in performance. Dance became a form of divining the body—of the dancer, the deity, and the temple.

---

[34]  Diana Eck's classic 1998 book on the subject offers a nuanced discussion of the *darshan* concept.

[35]  These are insights borrowed from Marilyn Strathern (1988) and Roy Wagner (1991) in their theorizations of "dividual personhood" and "fractal persons," respectively. Strathern argues, based on her fieldwork in Melanesia, that "[f]ar from being regarded as unique entities, Melanesian persons are as dividually as individually conceived. They contain a generalized sociality within" and develop through "the plural and composite site of the relationships that produce them. The singular person can be imagined as a social microcosm" (1988, 13). Wagner pursues the related idea that "a *fractal person* is never a unit standing in relation to an aggregate, or an aggregate standing in relation to a unit, but always an entity with relationship integrally implied" (1991, 163; italics mine).

The distributed body was one expression of the subject that lived among a range of other conceptions in Hindu thought. It distributed spiritual properties into the live dancing body, and animated the still body of the deity and temple, allowing the spiritual presence to materialize in the world: and it distributed itself across different bodies through the "restored behavior" of transmitting and replicating movement and gesture—and through reenactment (Schechner 2004; Schneider 2011).

The construct of the distributed body offers a strong counterpoint to the trope often promulgated in Western dance and performance theory, of the dancing subject as eternally vanishing. Supposedly elusive and ephemeral, dance signals the "disappearing" ontology of performance, ungraspable, elusive, and ephemeral, as it moves fleetingly at the edges of the "vanishing point" (Phelan 1993; Siegel 1973). Yet, this fallible discourse of dance's impermanence conceals the actual evidence that dance *does* leave behind, evidence of its substantive qualities, its resonance, its effects—the "inscriptions of gesture" it leaves in sculpture and scripture, in scaffolds of flesh, and memorializes in muscle and bone (Ness 2008). These indexical traces allow for the continual reenactment of a given dance performance.

The notion of the disappearing subject of dance is a potent myth, governing much of the discourse in which the temporal presence of dance is twinned ineluctably with its purported and palpable absence (Foster 1995; Lepecki 2004). But that idea is predicated upon the privileging of the *individual* body, and holds weight principally in discourses in which the singular self acts as imprimatur. In systems like *mahari* dance, where the self was decentered in place of distributed personhood, the question of "vanishing" was elided. While the impermanence of the singular body was acknowledged, it did not hold absolute import. This is not to suggest that *mahari* ritual practice promoted the notion of the interchangeability of dancing bodies. Far from it. Rather, the idea of a trans-individual subject surfaces powerfully in such ritual thought. Sacrificing the pure agency and temporality of the "one" allowed for the possibility of producing "many" dancing bodies through acts of transmission in the ritual concatenation, leading to the continuity of dance *in* time rather than its constant interruption *by* time. Strikingly, the reenactments performed by the dancers mirrored that of the deities to whom they were dedicated—even those divine bodies were not considered singular, but plural and continually reproducible in the cycle of rebirth, as witnessed in the Nabakalebar ceremony.

The distributed body, simultaneously a sign and index of the dance, became larger than the individual self; in its trans-individual framing, it suggested a practice of renewal, a constant re-emergence through multiplication and re-embodiment, through what Diana Taylor calls "acts of transfer" (2003). *Mahari* dance refused the cult of the individual *and* the cult of the collective, mediating between these two tendencies. The distributed body transmitted dance across multiple subjects—subjects who receive their knowledge of dance through direct transmission from another, as gift—offering an alternative for imagining the implicit fragility of danced knowledge, and posing a new opening: dance as an abiding material act, translated from body to body. These successive bodies indexed each other, embedded in a diffuse set of relations, revealing the continuity and the permanence of the dance in all its migrations, resonating beyond the corporeal boundary of a single subject, beyond the finite limits of skeleton and skin. And in moving to intersubjectivity, the dancing body reverberated in the performative bodies of the deity and the temple, connecting the three entities in a dispersed, distributed corporeality.

The idea of the distributed self in *mahari* dance stands as something of an intervention into, and interruption of, normative models of personhood. One of the popular (if reductive) truisms about Indian identity in the standard scholarship centers on the absence of an individualist theory—the notion being that the individual is subsumed to the idea of collective notions of belonging (see, for instance, Dumont 1986; for critiques, see Kasulis et.al., 1993). Indian personhood in this schema is posited as relational and hierarchical and appears to be coercively determined by superseding institutions and powers. This dichotomized and Orientalized idea of the subject organizes much of the discourse of Indian cultural practices, especially ritual. But these neat categorizations fall apart when we test these claims against actual performed repertoires. What these dominant and totalizing narratives fail to consider are contesting notions of the subject, which, though marginal and misapprehended, still radiate a powerful presence. As Richard G. Fox reminds us, "even if the [dominant] Indian cultural conception of the person is based on the effacement of individuality, it is not wholly constitutive of all self-identities" (in Dissanayake 1996, 106).

The importance of the distributed body, as a concept, goes well beyond the interrogation of abstract theories of subjectivity. Additionally, it challenges the tenets and tenor of contemporary Odissi performance. As argued, *mahari* dance animated and vitalized its surrounds, and was in turn vitalized by its surrounds; the dance, temple, and deity were interdependent and mutually constituting corporeal agents. By appropriating *mahari* dance in its fold, Odissi dancers today often claim to propagate what they posit as the devotional essence of the *mahari* performance. Yet, as developed for the proscenium stage, Odissi presents an acontextual, dehistoricized, and atemporal version of *mahari* ritual. Aesthetic strategies such as using ancient temples as a performance backdrop for public Odissi performances, placing images of Jagannath on stage, and rhetorically identifying Odissi as a devotional dance because of its partial alliance with *mahari* tradition are all gestures designed to bring the atmosphere and interiors of ritual space outside the physical parameters of the temple. These are attempts to recreate *mahari* dance, or at least to approximate its feel. Such Odissi performances gesture toward a complex history that it both invokes and erases in the same moment.

What cannot be replicated today is the tradition or philosophy that produced *mahari* dance, even if its elements are now preserved in Odissi's repertoire. Under the rubric of Odissi, *mahari* ritual was excised from the ritual process, and exhibited as its analeptic relic. The content was partitioned from its past context. Dance, of course, involves much more than simply importing a set of movements and transposing them onto new bodies; habitus matters as much as technique. Odissi is ideologically committed to propagating *mahari* dance, but fails in the appropriative maneuver precisely because what it seeks is ungraspable. In the absence of the spatial and iconographic relationships that shaped the *mahari* dance, Odissi in its concert form loses the potential of producing and mobilizing the distributed body, installing a fully modern subject in its place.

I do not mean to lament the loss of *mahari* ritual in the present and, concomitantly, its discursive and aesthetic knowledges; for Odissi produces its own spatial and spectatorial relations. Rather, my aim here has been to recognize the different paradigm in which *mahari* ritual operated and to acknowledge its conceptual significance, while deconstructing a narrative in Odissi that suggests a total identification between the two. The crux of the difference, I have argued, lies in the concept of the distributed body. The potential of *mahari* dance to posit an alternative subject is, however, diminished by postcolonial movements that deny the importance of ritual dance, either by stigmatizing or sanitizing it. The attempt to replicate the aura of *mahari* dance in Odissi represents both futility and impossibility: a failed reenactment. And so perhaps the potential of the distributed body lies not in the present or future, but only in disparate gestures of history, in the recesses of the past.

## ACKNOWLEDGMENTS

This chapter reworks material from an earlier essay, which appeared as "Dance and the Distributed Body: Odissi, Ritual Practice, and Mahari Performance," in the journal *About Performance* no. 11, special issue, In-Between Moves, co-edited by Amanda Card and Justine Shih Pearson (2012): 7–39.

## REFERENCES

Allen, Matthew Harp. 1997. "Rewriting the Script for South Indian Dance." *TDR* 41(3): 63–100.
Anandhi, S. 1991. "Representing Devadasis: 'Dasigal Mosavalai' as a Radical Text." *Economic and Political Weekly* 26 (11–12), March: 739–741, 743, 745–746.
Babaji, Sachidanda Das. 2008. Interview with author. Jnan Pitha Math, Puri, Odisha, March 7.
Banerji, Anurima. 2008. Field notes from Odissi research. Puri, Odisha, March 7.
Banerji, Anurima. 2010. *Odissi Dance: Paratopic Performances of Gender, State, and Nation*. PhD dissertation, New York University.
Banerji, R. D., and K. P. Jayaswal. 1933. "The Hathigumpha Inscription of Kharavela." In *Epigraphia Indica* XX (1929–1930), 71–89. Delhi: Manager of Publications. Reprinted in 1983 by Archaeological Society of India (ASI).
Barry, Ellen. 2015. "Sashimani Devi, Last of India's Jagannath Temple Dancers, Dies at 92." *New York Times*, March 23. https://www.nytimes.com/2015/03/24/world/asia/sashimani-devi-last-of-indias-jagannath-temple-ritual-dancers-dies-at-92.html (accessed March 28, 2015).
Barua, B. M. 1938. "Hathigumpha Inscription of Kharavela." *Indian Historical Quarterly* XIV, article no. 25: 459–485.
Bell, Catherine. 1992. *Ritual Theory, Ritual Practice*. Oxford: Oxford University Press.
Bell, Catherine. 1997. *Ritual: Perspectives and Dimensions*. Oxford: Oxford University Press.
Bharatmuni/Ghosh, Manmohan. [1967] 2007. *Natyashastra, Ascribed to Bharata-Muni (A Treatise on Ancient Indian Dramaturgy and Histrionics)*, vols. I–IV. Translated from Sanskrit and edited by Manmohan Ghosh. Varanasi: Chowkhamba Sanskrit Series Office.

Biswas, Sharmila. 2003–2004. "The Maharis of Odisha." In *Attendance: The Dance Annual of India 2003–04*, edited by Shanta Serbjeet Singh, 58–65. New Delhi: Ekah-Printways.

Biswas, Sharmila. 2008. Interview with author. Kolkata, West Bengal, February 14.

Bose, Nirmal Kumar. 1932. *Canons of Orissan Architecture*. Calcutta: Prabasi Press.

Chandrikha, G. 2009. "Of Men, Women, and Morals: Gender, Politics and Social Reform in Colonial South India." *Intersections: Gender and Sexuality in Asia and the Pacific* 22 (October 2009). http://intersections.anu.edu.au/issue22/ganapathy.htm/ (accessed December 4, 2011.

Chand, Soma. 2005. "Orissan Temple Architecture." *Orissa Review* (July): 49–51.

Chatterjea, Ananya. 2004. "Contestations." In *Rethinking Dance History*, edited by Alexandra Carter, 143–156. London: Routledge.

Chatterjee, Santosh Kumar. 1945. *Devadasi (Temple Dancer)*. Calcutta: Book House.

Citarasti, Ileana. 1987. "Devadasis of the Jagannath Temple: Precursors of Odissi Music and Dance." *Sruti* 33–34 (June–July): 51–57.

Coorlawala, Uttara. 1996. "Darshan and Abhinaya: An Alternative to the Male Gaze." *Dance Research Journal* 28(1): 19–27.

Coorlawala, Uttara. 2005. "The Birth of Bharatanatyam and the Sanskritized Body." In *Rukmini Devi Arundale (1904–1986): A Visionary Architect of Indian Culture and the Performing Arts*, edited by Avanthi Meduri, 173–194. New Delhi: Motilal Banarsidass.

Dehejia, Vidya. 1979. *Early Stone Temples of Odisha*. New Delhi: Vikas Publishing House.

Dehejia, Vidya _. 2009. *The Body Adorned: Dissolving Boundaries between Sacred and Profane in India's Art*. New York: Columbia University Press.

Desai, Devangana. 1990. "Social Dimensions of Art in Early India." *Social Scientist* 18(3): 3–32.

Dhaky, Madhusudhan A. 1977. *The Indian Temple Forms in Karnata Inscriptions and Architecture*. New Delhi: Abhinav Publications.

Donaldson, Thomas Eugene. 1981. "Development of the Nata-Mandira in Odishan Temple Architecture." In *Kaladarsana: American Studies in the Art of India*, edited by Joanna G. Williams, 35–46. Leiden: E.J. Brill.

Donaldson, Thomas Eugene. 1985. *Hindu Temple Art of Orissa*, vols. I–III. Leiden: E. J. Brill.

Dumont, Louis. 1986. *Essays on Individualism: Modern Ideology in Anthropological Perspective*. Chicago: University of Chicago Press.

Eck, Diana. *Darsana: Seeing the Divine Image in India*, 3rd ed. 1998. New York: Columbia University Press.

Eschmann, Anncharlott, Hermann Kulke, and Gaya Charan Tripathi, eds. 2005. *The Cult of Jagannath and the Regional Tradition of Orissa*. New Delhi: Manohar.

Foster, Susan Leigh. 1995. "Choreographing History." In *Choreographing History*, edited by Susan L. Foster, 3–21. Bloomington: Indiana University Press.

Foucault, Michel. 1980. *Power/Knowledge: Selected Interviews and Other Writings, 1972–1977*. Translated from French by Colin Gordon, Leo Marshall, John Mepham, and Kate Sopher; edited by Colin Gordon. New York: Pantheon.

Fox, Richard G. 1996. "Self-Made." In *Narratives of Agency: Self-Making in China, India, and Japan*, edited by Wimal Dissanayake, 104–116. Minneapolis: University of Minnesota Press.

Franko, Mark. 1993. *Dance as Text: Ideologies of the Baroque Body*. Cambridge: Cambridge University Press.

Gandharva, Mahavidyalaya. 1985. *Angahar Festival of Odissi Dance Souvenir*, March 7–10, Kamani Auditorium, New Delhi. New Delhi: Gandharva Mahavidyalaya.

Gandhi, Aastha. 2009. "Who Frames the Dance? Writing and Performing the Trinity of Odissi." In *Dance Dialogues: Conversations across Cultures, Artforms, and Practices: Proceedings of the World Dance Alliance Global Summit, Brisbane, Australia, 13–18 July 2008*, edited by

Cheryl Stock, 1–11. Queensland: Australian Dance Council, Ausdance, and Queensland University of Technology, Faculty of Creative Industries. http://www.ausdance.org.au/. (accessed December 4, 2011).

Ganguly, Dilip Kumar. 1984. *History and Historians in Ancient India.* New Delhi: Abhinav Publications.

Gaston, Anne-Marie. 1992. "Dance and the Hindu Woman: Bharatanatyam Re- ritualized." In *Roles and Rituals for Hindu Women,* edited by Julia Leslie, 149–171. Delhi: Motilal Banarsidass.

Gell, Alfred. 1988. *Art and Agency: An Anthropological Theory.* Oxford: Clarendon Press.

Goswami, A., ed. 1950. *Designs from Odishan Temples: An Album of Photographs.* Introduction by Kim Christen. Text by D. P. Ghosh, Nirmal Kumar Bose, and Y. D. Sharma. Calcutta: Thacker's Press and Directories.

Goswami, Kali Prasad. 2000. *Devadasi: Dancing Damsel.* New Delhi: A.P.H. Publishing.

Hanna, Judith Lynne. 1998. "Feminist Perspectives on Classical Indian Dance: Divine Sexuality, Prostitution, and Erotic Fantasy." In *Dance of India,* edited by David Waterhouse, 193–231. Mumbai: Popular Prakashan.

Guru Pankaj Charan Das Odissi Research Foundation (GPCDORF). 2012. Site visit and personal communications with Mr. Sarat Das. Bhubaneshwar, Odisha, December.

Hess, Ron. 1985. *Given to Dance.* USA, 57 min, color, DVD.

*The Hindu.com.* 2009. "Mahari Dance Show on August 31." August 29. http://www.thehindu.com/todays-paper/tp-national/tp-otherstates/mahari-dance-show-on-august-31/article215332.ece (accessed May 11, 2014).

Hobsbawm, Eric. 1983. "Introduction: Inventing Traditions." In *The Invention of Tradition,* edited by Eric Hobsbawm and Terence Ranger, 1–14. New York: Cambridge University Press.

Jagannath Temple. 2011. Website of Jagannath temple, Puri, Odisha. http://www.jagannath-templepuri.com/ (accessed December 4, 2012).

Jordan, Kay K. 2003. *From Sacred Servant to Profane Prostitute: A Study of the Changing Legal Status of the Devadasis, 1857–1947.* New Delhi: Manohar.

Kanungo, Aloka. 2006–2007. "Bandha Nritya." *Attendance: The Dance Annual of India 2006–07,* Traditions of East: 70–85.

Kanungo, Pralay. 2003. "Hindutva's Entry into a Hindu Province: Early Years of RSS in Orissa." *Economic and Political Weekly* 38 (31) (August 2–8): 3293–3303.

Kant, Shashi. 2000. *The Hathigumpha Inscription of Kharavela and the Bhabru Edict of Asoka.* New Delhi: D. K. Printworld.

Kasulis, Thomas P., Roger Ames, and Wimal Dissanayake, eds. 1993. *Self as Body in Asian Theory and Practice.* Albany: State University of New York Press.

Kersenboom, Saskia. 1998. *Nityasumangali: Devadasi Tradition in South India.* Delhi: Motilal Banarsidass.

Khokar, Mohan. 1984. *Traditions of Indian Classical Dance,* 2nd ed. Delhi: Clarion Books.

Khokar, Mohan. 1998. "The Tradition of Goti Pua." *The Hindu* folio, special issue with *Sunday Magazine,* Dance (December 27, 2010). http://hinduonnet.com/folio/f09812/98120320.htm/ (accessed May 15, 2009).

Kothari, Sunil. 1967. "The Gotipua Dancers of Odisha." *Illustrated Weekly of India* 88(45) (December 10): 19–21.

Kothari, Sunil. 1990. *Odissi: Indian Classical Dance Art.* Bombay: Marg Publications.

Kothari, Sunil. 2001. "Odissi: From Devasabha to Janasabha." In *Odisha Revisited,* edited by Pratapaditya Pal, 93–104. Bombay: Marg Publications.

Krishna Das Kaviraj/Dimock, Edward C., and Tony Stewart. [1575–1595] 2000. *Caitanya Caritamrita of Krsnadas Kaviraja*. Translated from Bengali and Sanskrit by Dimock; edited by Stewart. Cambridge, MA: Harvard University Press.

Kulke, Hermann. 1981. "King Anangabhima III, the Veritable Founder of the Gajapati Kingship and of the Jagannatha Trinity at Puri." *Journal of the Royal Asiatic Society of Great Britain and Ireland* 1: 26–39.

Kulke, Hermann. 2006. "The Integrative Model of State Formation in Early Medieval India: Some Historiographic Remarks." In *The State in India: Past and Present*, edited by Masaaki Kimura and Akio Tanabe, 59–81. New Delhi: Oxford University Press.

Lepecki, André. 2004. "Inscribing Dance." In *Of the Presence of the Body: Essays on Dance and Performance Theory*, edited by A. Lepecki, 124–139. Middletown, CT: Wesleyan University Press.

Linda, Mary F. 1990. "The Kalinga Temple Form." *Ars Orientalis* 20: 87–111.

Lopez y Royo, Alessandra. 2007. "The Reinvention of Odissi Classical Dance as a Temple Ritual." In *The Archeology of Ritual*, edited by Evangelos Kyriakidis, 155–181. Los Angeles: Cotsen Institute of Archaeology, UCLA.

Lopez y Royo, Alessandra. 2008. "Odissi, Temple Rituals, and Temple Sculptures." *ReConstructing and RePresenting Dance: Exploring the Dance/Archaeology Conjunction*. Online publication. Palo Alto, CA: Stanford Humanities Lab. http://humanitieslab.stanford.edu/117/Home/. (accessed December 4, 2011).

*Marg: A Magazine for the Arts*. 1960. Volume XIII, no. 2 (March), Orissi Dance.

Marglin, Frédérique Apffel. 1985. *Wives of the God-King: The Rituals of the Devadasis of Puri*. New Delhi: Oxford University Press.

Marglin, Frédérique Apffel. 1990. "Refining the Body: Transformative Emotion in Ritual Dance." In *Divine Passions: The Social Construction of Emotion in India*, edited by Owen Lynch, 212–236. Berkeley: University of California Press.

Meduri, Avanti. 1996. *Nation, Woman, Representation: The Sutured History of the Devadasi and Her Dance*. PhD dissertation, New York University.

Mishra, D. B. 2006. "Glimpses of Performing Art Heritage in Orissan Inscriptions." *Orissa Review* (May): 23–29. http://Orissagov.nic.in/e- magazine/Orissareview/may2006/engpdf/22-29.pdf/ (accessed November 3, 2009).

Mishra, K. C. 1984. *Cult of Jagannath*. Calcutta: Firma KLM.

Mohanty Hejmadi, Priyambada. 1990. "The Trinity of Odissi." *Sangeet Natak* 96 (April–June): 3–18.

Mohanty Hejmadi, Priyambada, and Ahalya Hejmadi Patnaik. 2008. *Odissi: An Indian Classical Form*. New Delhi: Aryan Books International.

Mohapatra, Rupashree. 2012. Interview with author. Puri, Odisha, December.

Mubayi, Yamini. 2005. *Altar of Power: The Temple and the State in the Land of Jagannath, Sixteenth to Nineteenth Century*. New Delhi: Manohar.

Muralidhar Rao, D. 1995. *Vaastu Shilpa Shastra*. Bangalore: SBS Publishers.

Ness, Sally Ann. 2008. "The Inscription of Gesture: Inward Migrations in Dance." In *Migrations of Gesture*, edited by Carrie Noland and Sally Ann Ness, 1–30. Minneapolis: University of Minnesota Press.

Neville, Pran. 1996. *Nautch Girls of India: Dancers, Singers, Playmates*. New Delhi: Variety Book Depot.

O'Shea, Janet. 2007. *At Home in the World: Bharatanatyam on the Global Stage*. Middletown, CT: Wesleyan University Press.

Panda, D. C. 2000. *Kalingara Mandira Sthapatya* [Odia]. Buhbaneswar: Art Centre.

Panda, D. C. 2003. *Bharatiya Samskruti O Murtikalare: Hindu Devadevi* [Odia]. Bhubaneswar: Art Centre.

Panda, D. C. 2006. *Kalingara Mandira Gatrare: Devadevi Murti* [Odia]. Bhubaneswar: Art Centre.

Panda, Namita. 2011. "Danseuse Steps in to Revive Mahari." *Telegraph*, May 19. http://www. telegraphindia.com/1110519/jsp/orissa/story_13997791.jsp (accessed May 11, 2014).

Panigrahi, K. C. 2008. *History of Orissa (Hindu Period)*. Cuttack: Kitab Mahal.

Panigrahi, Sanjukta. [1995] 1997. *The Rediff Special/Sanjukta Panigrahi*. Interview with *Savvy Magazine*, originally published in 1995 and reprinted on Rediff.com. http://www.rediff.com/ news/jun/24sanju3.htm (accessed June 3, 2014).

Parashmoni Devadasi. 2012. Interview with author. Puri, Odisha, December.

Parker, Kunal. 1998. "'A Corporation of Superior Prostitutes': Anglo-Indian Legal Conceptions of Temple Dancing Girls, 1800–1914." *Modern Asian Studies* 32(3): 559–633.

Pathy, Dinanath. 2007. *Rethinking Odissi*. New Delhi: Harman Publishing House.

Patnaik, D. N. 1990. *Odissi Dance*, 2nd ed. Bhubaneshwar: Odisha Sangeet Natak Akademi.

Patnaik, D. N. 2006. *Odissi Dance*, 3rd ed. Bhubaneswar: Odisha Sangeet Natak Akademi.

Patnaik, D. N. 2008. Interview with author. Cuttack, Odisha, March 4.

Pattanaik, Kavichandra Kalicharan, Upendra Mitra, Gorachand Misra, and Nilmadhab Bose, eds. 1958. *Dance and Music of Odisha Souvenir*. Cuttack: Kala Vikash Vendra.

Phelan, Peggy. 1993. "The Ontology of Performance: Representation Without Reproduction." In *Unmarked: The Politics of Performance*, 146–166. London: Routledge.

Prasad, A. K. 1991. *The Devadasi System in Ancient India: A Study of Temple Dancing Girls in India*. Delhi: H. K. Publishers.

Ragini Devi. 2002. "The Dance in Ancient Orissa" and "Orissi Dance—Plastic Movements and Repertoires." In *Dance Dialects of India*, 3rd ed., 138–157. New Delhi: Motilal Banarssidas.

Raja Panda. Interview with author. Puri, Odisha, June 29 and 30, 2012.

Rajguru, S. N. 1992. *Inscriptions of the Temples of Puri and Origin of Sri Purusottama Jagannatha*, vol. I, part I. Puri: Shri Jagannath Sanskrit Vidyalaya.

Ramberg, Lucinda. 2009. "Magical Hair as Dirt: Ecstatic Bodies and Postcolonial Reform in South India." *Culture, Medicine and Psychiatry* 33(4): 501–522.

Reddy, Muthulakshmi. 1935. "The Peril in Our Streets." *Indian Social Reformer* (February): 23–25.

Rehman, Indrani. [1975] 1976. "Indrani Interview." Interview by Genevieve Oswald, December 11, 1975; transcript dated May 9, 1976. Item no. *MGZMT 5-391, Oral History Archives, Special Collections, Jerome Robbins Dance Division, New York Public Library for the Performing Arts, Lincoln Center.

Ritha Devi. 1987. *Vibrant Sculpture/Frozen Dance*. USA, color, 29 mins, video. Produced by Ritham Chhanda (Eternal Rhythm) Dance Academy. Jerome Robbins Dance Division, New York Public Library for the Performing Arts, Lincoln Center.

Ritha Devi. 1988. *Satvam Rajas Tamas*. USA, color, 123 mins, video. Jerome Robbins Dance Division, New York Public Library for the Performing Arts, Lincoln Center.

Ritha Devi. 2003a. Lecture-Demonstration on Mahari Dance. Sundaram Tagore Gallery, New York City, New York, June 28.

Ritha Devi. 2003b. Interview with author. New York, August 19.

Roy, Ratna. [2002] 2004. "Mahari Dance—An Alternative Narrative in Orissi. A Feminist Analysis." In *Dance in South Asia: New Approaches, Politics and Aesthetics, Proceedings,*

*March 3, 2002*, edited by Pallabi Chakravorty, 55–59. Swarthmore, PA: Swarthmore College.

Roy, Ratna. 2006. "Politics of Representation: The Portrayal of the Female in Guru Pankaj Charan Das's Pancha Kanya Dance Dramas." *Manushi* 153: 34–41.

Roy, Ratna. 2007. "The Mahari Tradition." *Ragavani: Ragamala's Quarterly Journal of South Asian Music and Dance* (Spring, June 22). http://ragavani.org/AR_MahariTradition_070621. aspx/ (accessed May 15, 2009).

Roy, Ratna. 2009. *Neo Classical Odissi Dance*. New Delhi: Harman Publishing House.

Sangeet Natak Akademi (SNA). 2003. "Proceedings of Symposium and Workshop on Performing Art Tradition of Odisha with Reference to Odissi Dance, 11–14 May 2003, Toshali Sands, Puri (Odisha)." VHS videocassettes, total time 34:12 hours, English/Odia/ Hindi, reference nos. V-6874 to V-6886, Documentation Unit, SNA, New Delhi.

Schechner, Richard. 2004. "Restoration of Behaviour." in *Over, Under, and Around*, 101–186. Calcutta: Seagull Books.

Schneider, Rebecca. 2011. *Performing Remains: Art and War in Times of Theatrical Reenactment*. New York: Routledge.

Sharma, Arvind. 2002. "On Hindu, Hindustan, Hinduism and Hindutva." *Numen* 49(1): 1–36.

Shashimoni Devadasi. 2003. "From the Mouth of a Mahari." Interview with Rahul Acharya; translated from Odia by Rahul Acharya, December 24. *Narthaki.com* and http://rahu-lacharyaodissi.wordpress.com/articles-by-rahul-acharya/from-the-mouth-of-a-mahari/ (accessed December 4, 2011).

Shashimoni Devadasi. 2008. Interview with author. Puri, Odisha, March 7.

Siegel, Marcia. 1973. *At the Vanishing Point: A Critic Looks at Dance*. New York: Saturday Review Press.

Soneji, Davesh. 2012. *Unfinished Gestures: Devadasis, Memory, and Modernity in South India*. Chicago: University of Chicago Press.

Srinivasan, Amrit. 1985. "Reform and Revival: The Devadasi and Her Dance." *Economic and Political Weekly* 20(44): 1869–1876.

Srinivasan, Amrit. 1990. "Reform or Conformity? Temple 'Prostitution' and the Community in the Madras Presidency." In *Structures of Patriarchy*, edited by Bina Agarwal, 175–198. New Delhi: Kali for Women.

*The Statesman*. 1958. "The Dance Seminar in Retrospect," April 8 cultural report, p. 5.

Strathern, Marilyn. 1988. *The Gender of the Gift: Problems with Women and Problems with Society in Melanesia*. Berkeley: University of California Press.

Taylor, Diana. 2003. *The Archive and the Repertoire: Performing Cultural Memory in the Americas*. Durham, NC: Duke University Press.

Thielemann, Selina. 2002. *Divine Service and the Performing Arts in India*. New Delhi: A.P.H. Publishing.

Vatsyayan, Kapila . 1997. *Indian Classical Dance*, 3rd ed. New Delhi: Publications Division, Ministry of Information and Broadcasting, Government of India.

Vatsyayan, Kapila. 2007. *Classical Indian Dance in Literature and the Arts*, 3rd ed. New Delhi: Sangeet Natak Akademi.

Vijaisri, Priyadarshini. 2004. *Recasting the Devadasi: Patterns of Sacred Prostitution in Colonial South India*. New Delhi: Kanishka Publishers.

Wagner, Roy. 1991. "The Fractal Person." In *Big Men and Great Men: Personifications of Power in Melanesia*, edited by Marilyn Strathern and Maurice Godelier, 159–173. Cambridge: Cambridge University Press.

Whitehead, Judith. 1998. "Community Honor/Sexual Boundaries: A Discursive Analysis of Devadasi Criminalization in Madras, India, 1920–1947." In *Prostitution: On Whores, Hustlers, and Johns,* edited by James E. Elias et al., 91–106. New York: Prometheus Books.

Whitehead, Judith. 2001. "Measuring Women's Value: Continuity and Change in the Regulation of Prostitution in Madras Presidency, 1860–1947." In *Of Property and Propriety: The Role of Gender and Class in Imperialism and Nationalism,* edited by Himani Bannerji, Shahrzad Mojab, and Judith Whitehead, 153–181. Toronto: University of Toronto Press.

CHAPTER 22

CHOREOGRAPHIC
RE-EMBODIMENT BETWEEN
TEXT AND DANCE

SUSAN JONES

CRITICS of literary modernism have identified a prevailing skepticism in fictional treatments of sequence, time, and narrative gesture in which the complex disposition of narrators and voices undermines or complicates sequential ordering of event to disrupt the epistemological process. Writers including Conrad, Proust, Woolf, Joyce, Beckett, and Kafka questioned conventional generic forms, the status of closure, and the relationship between authorial and narratorial voice. This kind of narratological skepticism in the modernist period constituted a suspension of judgment on the part of the author and narrator that may be associated historically with sixteenth-century Montaignean skepticism, but which extends doubt in the possibility of ever communicating certain knowledge. Thus the onus of interpretation of the text falls increasingly on the reader. In addition, literary aesthetics identified a skepticism about language, frequently expressed in poetry—as T. S. Eliot put it in "Burnt Norton" (1935), "Words strain, / Crack and sometimes break, under the burden" (Eliot 1963, 194)—in which the very status of language as an adequate means of communication was brought into question. Such inquiries have rarely been associated with a corresponding questioning of conventional narrative modes in choreography of the period, as in the work of Loïe Fuller, Isadora Duncan, Ruth St. Denis, and exponents of expressionist dance who frequently rejected the traditional teleology of balletic storytelling. Yet writers often turned to the metaphor of dance to suggest ways in which a text may, paradoxically, "speak" non-linguistically, as in Stéphane Mallarmé's account of Loïe Fuller's solo dance in Paris in 1893 as a model for poetic practice, when Mallarmé claimed that Fuller's dance encapsulated "la forme théâtrale de poésie par excellence" (Mallarmé 2003, 207).

However, this chapter argues that dance does not appear in the modernist text exclusively as a metaphor or intertextual reference at the service of literary modernism's critique of language. By examining the narrative strategies of two notable novellas,

Conrad's *Heart of Darkness* (1899/1902), and Beckett's *Ill Seen Ill Said* (1981), we find a neglected correspondence in these authors' evocation of movement and gesture, in which a movement phrase in each case questions narrative sequence and the relationship between the bodily experience of time and its representation. Such movement phrases appear as brief "quotations," yet without reference to any historically acknowledged "original" dance. Instead, these writers re-embody phrases, or visual flashes of movement, as a chimera or ghostly repetition of an original, divorced from the context of a dance to which the sequence may once have belonged. These writers introduce a form of choreographed re-embodiment across dance and text in which they utilize the very skepticism about narrative that dance itself explored at this time. Taken out of context, such movement phrases offer these writers a way of translating, through the medium of visual imagery, that which is represented elsewhere in the text as incommunicable: the very silences and gaps that exist beyond language itself.

But this form of translation across dance and text also tells us something about the narrative skepticism of new forms of dance that claimed autonomy for the choreographic act as a form in and of itself, operating apart from any narrative function, and the way in which they were reenacted or re-embodied in literature in the twentieth century. As Mark Franko observes in the Introduction (Chapter 1) to this volume, ideas of reenactment treated throughout this book include "dance beyond dance history per se." The narratological innovations treated in the following, showing how modernist writers examined the tensions inherent in a skeptical treatment of narrative time, inform a wider debate about danced reenactments in the twentieth century.

Before turning to the texts themselves, it is useful to explore the context in which an intriguing correspondence reveals the tensions about narrative time appearing in both literature and dance of this period. These may be examined by considering the use of dance in the two short stories with reference to Gabriele Brandstetter's important study of the visual and literary representation of "body-image" in the *Poetics of Dance* and Paul Ricoeur's account of narratology in *Time and Narrative*.[1] An emphasis on the *spatialization* of time in both accounts shows how non-narrative physical gestures re-embodied in the text may be identified as a corollary for the disruption of narrative closure by the

---

[1] Ricoeur (1984, 32–37), where Ricoeur harnesses Aristotle's dramatic theory to a notion of narrative in general. He looks at the relationship of *muthos* or *mythos* and *mimesis* (emplotment and representation), in which a tension occurs in Aristotle's expression of temporality as a "unity" and the *activity* of emplotment in the representation: "imitating or representing is a mimetic activity inasmuch as it produces something, namely the organization of events by emplotment" (Ricoeur 1984, 34). Ricoeur argues that Aristotle uses the term *mimesis*, not in the Platonic sense of a "redoubling of presence," but rather "the break that opens the space for fiction" (45). Note the distinction from Platonic mimesis, where, Ricoeur observes, "the metaphysical sense of mimesis . . . by which things imitate ideas, and works of art imitate things. Platonic mimesis thereby distances the work of art twice over from the ideal model which is its ultimate basis. Aristotle's mimesis has just a single space wherein it is unfolded—[by] human making [*faire*], [in] the arts of composition" (34). Ricoeur identifies a gap in Aristotle's account of the unity of time and place in the *Poetics* in which Aristotle leaves a silence concerning how the human experience of time is felt and how the spatial activity or movement of plot occurs.

aesthetic act, insofar as the "choreographic" becomes the reeanactment of time in and by space.

Crucially for this discussion, Brandstetter observes a turn-of-the-century burgeoning of aesthetic innovation around 1900, exploring how figural representations of dance were absorbed into painting and literature as symptomatic of a crisis of perception and of language in the period. She draws her theoretical framework from Aby Warburg's *Mnemosyne* project, begun in 1924, which aimed to map pathways of an afterlife of antiquity, reanimated in the art of later times through the reproduction of gestures of great symbolic, intellectual, or emotional power (Brandstetter 2015, 15). Using Warburg's categories of gesture in the *Mnemosyne Atlas*, Brandstetter analyzes how such specific figural representations of movement have particular currency around 1900, when they stand in for a general cultural crisis during the period of modernist innovation, revealing "a moment of aporia between the 'now' of movement and the history of representation" (Brandstetter 2015, 2). Yet narrative theory has also raised similar questions in relation to the nature of fictional representation. Paul Ricoeur strikingly identifies a corresponding tension occurring in literary narrative between the "presentness" of the human experience of time and the historicity of its representation. By identifying a "concordant discordance" in classical accounts of poetic activity—a phenomenon that will be outlined later—Ricoeur refers to the "aporia" within narrative itself that illustrates a gap between present lived experience and its representation in the retelling or performing. Brandstetter and Ricoeur offer a framework through which to explore the distinctive strategies of Conrad and Beckett's skeptical treatment of gesture in their fiction, and open up questions about the nature of reenactment across text and dance.

Brandstetter argues that a period of innovation in modernist aesthetics invoked, among the many cross-disciplinary interactions at this time, the visual and literary citation of contemporary dance and movement practices as a symptom and sign of a crisis of perception concerning "the nature-culture divide, with the duality of dance on the one hand as a transitory art of the body, which is subject to mortality, and on the other hand as a culturally stable set of techniques for symbolic representation exercised by visual images and in literary discourse" (2015, 2). She outlines her routing of the argument through Warburg, describing his "atlas of emphatic gestures" as one that can tell us how contemporary dance to some degree reanimated the gestures of the "ancient" and the "primitive" and how these gestures were used in art at the turn of the twentieth century to embrace and denote the memory of a "gamut of expressions in the grip of emotions"—recovering an ancient "primal instinct" that is transformed anew in modern art. This catalog of Warburg's "pathos formulae" is a repertoire of the history of gesture, "the mimetic human" in corporeal images belonging to cultural memory or symbolic formulations that are "hidden under and transformed by the self-interpretations of the modern subject" (Brandstetter 2015, 13). We shall see in the following that Conrad's use of "primitive" gesture corresponds to this use of the affective mode of twentieth-century dance (as in Ruth St. Denis's or Isadora Duncan's work) to illustrate his critique of the hidden primitive within the Western colonialist subject.

On the other hand, Brandstetter identifies a concomitant sense of the deconstruction of the individual subject in the period that is also present in modernist dance innovations. Drawing on a separate set of Warburgian formulae that focus on "figurations in space" (Brandstetter 2015, 6), Brandstetter shows how dance explorations (of artists like Fuller, Rudolf Laban, or Oskar Schlemmer) also conform to this subset of Warburgian categories, revealing underlying spatial patterns of bodily movement in time, rather than focusing on the expressivist power of the individual. Brandstetter cites the dissolution of the subject in the patterning of spiral (as in Fuller's dance, where the body disappears in the swirling movement of extended material[2]), or in the spatial configurations of abstraction and geometric patterns (as in Schlemmer's 1926 *Bauhaus Dances*). Beckett's non-affective treatment of movement in his late work emphasizes the same kind of spatialization of time in a way that looks back to early twentieth-century dance experimentations.

With these two sets of choreographic innovation in mind, Brandstetter explores "the meeting of spatial figures of a topographical nature and body-images in motion" (2015, 3), and shows how a form of reenactment (or rather re-presentation) of both these kinds of dance gestures in visual or literary aesthetics reveals the importance of modern dance's appearance at a moment of cultural crisis in defining the relationship of time and space. Tellingly, she notes the "fleeting quality of unrepeatable dance moments and the transcendence of the model of presentness in dance performance by situations that transgress this immediacy" (3). The significance of these moments is that the focus on the "unrepeatability" of the movements of what Brandstetter calls "free dance" (in the work of St. Denis, Fuller, Duncan, and others) raises questions about their apparent re-embodiment in literary text.

In order to show how Conrad and Beckett exploited these properties of "presentness" and "unrepeatability" in modernist dance to disrupt the teleology of their narratives and undermine the status of language as dominant mode of communication, we should first consider how these writers' narratological skepticism (i.e., their undermining of narrative time as teleological) arises in part from the tensions inherent in narrative itself. In this respect, Ricoeur's well-known phenomenological study of the relationship between time and narrative offers a provocative framework for examining the representation of the female protagonists of Conrad's and Beckett's narratives as an aestheticizing device for structuring their skeptical reception. Ricoeur explores an interplay between Aristotle's account of dramatic representation in his most famous work of literary criticism, the *Poetics* (the earliest surviving work of dramatic theory, ca. 335 BCE), which emphasizes the unity of time and place, and Augustine's analysis of the human experience of time in the *Confessions* (written between 397 and 400 CE), which spatializes the idea of time as it is imagined in the mind. In both accounts, a gap or *aporia* opens up between accounts of the human experience of time and the historicity of its

---

[2] See Jones (2013, 13–43) for an account of Fuller's solo dancing and its relationship to Stéphane Mallarmé's work.

representation. But the most important aspect of Ricoeur's account for this treatment of dance appears in his discussion of Augustine.

Ricoeur's addition of the "temporal" (found in Augustine), which he reads back into Aristotle's spatial theory of poetry/drama, is helpful in understanding the choreographic re-embodiment of dance in the text. Where Aristotle sees a spatial structure, with beginning, middle, and end as parts of a simultaneous whole, Ricoeur identifies a structure that is both spatial and temporal, or, as William Dowling explains, "a chain of causal implication that must be traversed in time, and in a state of partial or imperfect knowledge, before there dawns any intimation that these same events might also be seen as a unity of action" (2011, 8). For the purposes of understanding the translations of movement across dance and these texts, Ricoeur's reading of Augustine is useful because it enables us to think about the bodily *experience* of time as spatialized, just as Ricoeur finds activity or movement as the key term that is missing from Aristotle's account of spatial "unity" of the poetic act.

Ricoeur introduces Augustine's idea of the "three-fold present" in order to bring this temporal element into Aristotle's spatial structure of beginning, middle, and end. When Augustine questioned himself about how to explain the experience of time, he identified the notion of a distension of the mind or soul (*distentio animi*) as a movement of the mind forward and back between tenses set against the present moment of experience. Ricoeur opens out Augustine's idea to focus on the activity of storytelling—with an emphasis on the temporalities of storytelling, which he sees also as an aspect of the human condition (the way we experience time in the world is narrativized in our own consciousness). At its most fundamental, Ricoeur's account envisages a narrator who tells the story in the present moment, but who uses grammatical tense to gesture to the past, perceive the present, and anticipate the future through an imaginative act (three parts of time folded into one present moment). The distension of the mind by time is for Ricoeur a way of explaining the spatializazation of temporality, our actual experience of time. Augustine's *distentio animi* is crucial for Ricoeur in the fact that the "impression is in the soul only as much as the mind acts, that is, expects, attends, remembers" (Ricoeur 1984, 19). Ricoeur sees discordance emerge again and again out of the very concordance of narratorial intentions, in that a tension is created between the events that happened in the past, or that are anticipated in the future, and the activity of retelling, or anticipating them, in the present moment of narration. Thus the idea of unity or wholeness of a story is always undermined by that which is a characteristic of narrative itself—the potentiality for temporal fracture in the process of retelling.

However, in thinking about the "three-fold present" in relation to dance, which is also encountered in the present moment and engages in complex temporalties, this is not to suggest that the business of dance is narrative per se, nor that dance's gestures point necessarily to the past or to the future, but rather that the authors treated here found in the choreographed phrase a useful expression of the embodied experience of time across space, an experience that frequently disrupts a linear sequence of storytelling. Such authors imagine the movement phrase as a "flash," experienced bodily, in which historicity is the impact of a past on the present, but not a teleological force (something closer to a Benjaminian "jetzt-Zeit" effect [Benjamin 1968, 261]). But these movement phrases (themselves suggesting their disruptive temporality) are used by both authors to structure the *experience* of narrative time (of both the narrator of the tale and the reader) as non-teleological.

Yet we might also think of the way in which we experience the gesture of dance or movement in the now of the present moment, and the ways in which dance activity spatializes time as a counterpart to the disruption of narrative by the aesthetic act in fiction. Such focus on this phenomenon arises throughout Brandstetter's study as she discusses the gestural activity of modernist dance practices that draw attention to their presentness and their *spatialization* of time, but disrupt the notion of a linear narrative by an aesthetic act. But this phenomenon is complicated by the fact that the choreographic act itself becomes the reenactment of time in and by space. We shall see how both Conrad and Beckett utilize this kind of focus on choreographed re-embodiment in their foregrounding of the *aporia* of narrative and how it is that the choreographed gesture and movement phrase enable them to visualize this phenomenon (somewhat paradoxically through the medium of words) in the texts themselves.

# Conrad

Conrad's presentation of movement phrases illustrates metaphorically and ironically the "discordant concordance" that Ricoeur associates with the activity of the mind in relation to the experience of time and its recreation in poetic or narrative activity. Conrad's narrator Marlow, in retelling his tale, sets up three interrelated visions of movement phrases throughout the narrative. Marlow's skeptical treatment of the expressivism of the African woman's movement in *Heart of Darkness* may be read against the impeded progress of the chain gang described earlier in the narrative, and the later despairing gestures of the Intended, following Kurtz's death. These illustrate what Elleke Boehmer has remarked as characterizing Conrad's work, when she suggests that he belongs to postcolonial criticism—"that which critically scrutinizes" rather than merely "coming after" Empire.[3]

But we shall also see that Conrad (to some extent unconsciously, but in the manner of Brandstetter's use of Warburg's "pathos formulae" to represent the anxieties of "primitivism" lying behind the construction of the modern subject) draws on the contemporary currency of innovations in dance at the time of writing to set up a parallel between the treatment of narrative in movement practices of the period and narrative's skeptical treatment of language and narrative closure. Conrad's narrator describes images of

---

[3] Boehmer (1995, 3).

movement through gestural flashes that open up or spatialize the temporalities of the story in a single present moment but disrupt the possibility of closure. These scenes are neither reenactments in themselves, nor intertextual resonances, but "textually" choreographed re-embodiments of remembered gestures.

It is of course a critical commonplace to refer to the literal and metaphorical resonances of Conrad's focus on the movement of travel throughout his fiction. However, Conrad also draws attention to the localized movement phrases, gestures, and postures of individuals, complementing the geographical movements of the narrative with a sense of the physicality of characters' intimate actions (and non-actions) within the larger framework. For example, he punctuates the geographical shifts of *Lord Jim* (1900) with the protagonist's active "leaps" from the ship or over the wall of a compound; and, in *Under Western Eyes* (1911), the movements from Russia to Geneva are simultaneously accompanied by the visual image of physical disintegration of one of the protagonists, Mrs. Haldin. The novella *Heart of Darkness* (serialized 1899, published in book form 1902), one of the earliest of Conrad's experiments in narrative framing, offers us the most famous exposition of the journey metaphor as a test case. Conrad here presents the physical dimension of the tale through the rhythmic alternation of scenes of arrested reflection and/or vision on the part of the narrator. The juxtaposition of these moments produces a kind of syncopation in the text, or perhaps what Gérard Genette would call the "effects of rhythm" (Genette 1980, 88). But the narrative situation is constructed in such a way that a skeptical relationship develops between the events of the tale, or its teleology, and the disordered sequence in which it is told. In this respect, the visual "flash" of bodily movement or stillness illustrates throughout the text this very relationship. The reader's experience relies on her or his memory of the account of past events, attentiveness to the present, and expectation of the future. But it also relies on a sense of imagined embodiment of these events (as in drama), in which the significance of each subsequent event creates a dramatic irony that works on the reader to build a spatial pattern in the text that requires a highly skeptical reading.

*Heart of Darkness* relates the story of a British seaman, Marlow, hired by a European trading company to travel into Africa to find a company employer (Kurtz) who, it transpires, in colonialist terminology has "gone native." An anonymous first-person frame-narrator introduces Marlow and invites him to tell the story of his journey upriver in command of a steamboat. At one point, Marlow suddenly apprehends an African woman striding along the riverbank through the jungle. The woman stops, turns, and fixes her eyes on the men in the boat, returning their gaze, and flings her arms up in a sublime gesture before proceeding as before:

> She walked with measured steps . . . treading the earth proudly, with a slight jingle and flash of barbarous ornaments . . . savage and superb, wild-eyed and magnificent; there was something ominous and stately in her deliberate progress . . . . She came abreast of the steamer, stood still and faced us . . . looked at us all as if her life had depended upon the unswerving steadiness of her glance. Suddenly she opened her bared arms and threw them up rigid above her head, as though in an uncontrollable

desire to touch the sky . . . . She turned away slowly, walked on, following the bank, and passed into the bushes to the left. (Conrad 1988, 60)[4]

On the one hand, the African woman's dehistoricized gestures contribute to a familiar rhetoric of Western European representations of the Other as mysterious and indecipherable. But with this movement phrase, Conrad associates the presentation of the primitive with the atavistic movement of the body and a form of kinetic communication beyond language. The woman's physical confidence and expressivity do not simply inspire anxiety in the Western onlooker—they engender admiration. Conrad presents the action of the African woman both as a manifestation of savagery *and* an expression of grace, illustrating ambivalence running throughout modernist accounts of primitivism in both literature and dance, where the reader/viewer is invited, in her or his encounter with alterity, to experience wonder, awe, erotic desire, but also approbation and fear.

Conrad's famous image provides an arresting vision of expressive movement while conforming to *fin de siècle* tropes of female primitivism. We may be reminded here of Brandstetter's reading of Warburg's gestural inventory, in which she observes how the "corporeal memory" is absorbed into the representations of art and literature, re-expressed in the "free dance" of St. Denis or Isadora Duncan, whose work relives traces of Dionysian frenzy, or passional expressions of grief and awe. Conrad makes no overt reference to the kind of orientalist dance presentations to be seen in the contemporary music hall, which he himself attended (and evidence of which appears in his drawings of "1890s dancers"),[5] but the woman's dramatic gesture and "deliberate progress" nevertheless convey an exaggerated, performative quality, conflicting with the verisimilitude of the dramatized narrator's representation of his experiences elsewhere in the novella. Thus with the actions of the African woman, who is both "ominous and stately," "savage and superb," Conrad stages primitive movement at this moment in the novella as an important signifier of Western anxieties about the Other.

But his representation of visual flashes of movement, in part re-embodied in the text from a primitivist lexicon of late nineteenth-century dance practice, emerges as a device through which to construct the skeptical delivery of the narrative. Throughout the novella, Marlow repeatedly emphasizes the immediacy of expression through the action of the body by pointing out the naturalism of the physical movement of the natives who display "an intense energy of movement that was as natural and true as the surf along the coast" (Conrad 1988, 17). This sentiment is echoed in choreographic terms in the period by Isadora Duncan, whose theory of movement, as Mark Franko shows, reveals no

---

[4] *Heart of Darkness* was initially serialized in *Blackwood's Magazine* in 1899. For a full discussion of narrative and physical movement in this novella see Susan Jones (2008, 100–117).

[5] For Conrad's perception of music-hall exoticism see Karl (1979, 412–413), where he reproduces Conrad's pen-and-ink drawings of a "Woman with a Serpent" (1892–1894) and "The Three Ballet Dancers" (1896). In 1903 the first black revue "In Dahomey" reached the Shaftesbury Theatre in London, introducing "The Cakewalk," which became the latest dance craze.

expressional *product* emanating from her body—hers is a dance of feeling as embodied sensation, not of expressive reaction to sensation (Franko 1995, 15–20). A famous image of Isadora captures this feeling as, dressed in a "Greek" tunic, she raises her arms above her head in a gesture not dissimilar to that of Conrad's African woman. In Conrad we perceive a pull, a tension, between the intuitive body and the rational mind, where the movement is superb, but also savage, and where the dramatized narrator of *Heart of Darkness* nevertheless aestheticizes the Africans' actions, both in the sense of positioning himself as voyeur, and in his aestheticizing practices in the retelling of his story.

This extraordinary moment is often referred to as "the image of the African woman." Yet it is important to remember that its delivery is closer to film than still image. It originates in the dramatized narrator's perception, and is a recounting of present, embodied, living movement. As such, it functions to bring into being the voice of narration in a relationship between the subject who observes/recounts and the subject/object observed/addressed. By focusing on the notion of "image" and assuming a punctual, photographic framing of the body, we lose the significance of what Marlow in fact represents as a far more sustained movement phrase (Crary 1990, 3).[6] The African woman strides along the bank; stops; changes direction and faces the men on the boat; thrusts her arms skyward; continues in her original trajectory; looks back. The even rhythm of her "measured steps" is syncopated by a wild upward gesture. The operatic movement simultaneously fractures the reading process. Interrupting the narrative flow, it nevertheless synchronizes the actual time of the story with reading time. Yet paradoxically the effect is to dehistoricize the textual moment (emphasizing the presentness of the dancing body, as in Brandstetter's account of "free dance"). This a-temporal effect accounts partly for the ease with which we may critique Conrad's method, as he solidifies the image of the African woman into a recognizable stereotype. Its stylized nature, echoing the primitive memory of atavistic movement, also raises questions about the choreographic as a reenactment of time.[7]

Conventionalizing her subject position, Conrad nevertheless makes a political point in relation to an earlier episode. For the African woman's movement is in fact anticipated by another famous "image" of movement in Marlow's apprehension of the chain gang:

> A slight clinking behind me made me turn my head. Six African men advanced in a file toiling up the path. They walked erect and slow, balancing small baskets full of earth on their heads, and the clink kept time with their footsteps. African rags were wound round their loins and the short ends behind waggled to and fro like tails. I could see every rib, the joints of their limbs were like knots in a rope, each had an iron collar on his neck and all were connected together with a chain whose bights swung between them, rhythmically clinking. (Conrad 1988, 19)

---

[6] Crary explains how older models of vision, "loosely definable as Renaissance, perspectival, or normative" are reconfirmed in the nineteenth and twentieth centuries by the new technological inventions of photography and, later, film.

[7] See also Gilman (1985, 15–35). The repetition of well-known gestures might in some cases create a "solidification" of time, a dehistoricizing of the moment through its re-embodiment.

Marlow sets up the visual and aural images of the African woman with her jingling garments and fierce vitality, analeptically and ironically against the earlier image of physical degradation of the "clinking" chain gang. But the moment also points forward proleptically to the Intended's reaching out across the window during her interview with Marlow.

When Marlow visits Kurtz's fiancée after his death, he observes her repetition of the African woman's movement.[8] The Intended "put out her arms, as if after a retreating figure, stretching them black and with clasped hands across the fading and narrow sheen of the window" (Conrad 1988, 75), just as Kurtz's African mistress reached out after the boat as it left the Inner Station with the dying Kurtz aboard: "The barbarous and superb woman did not so much as flinch and stretched tragically her bare arms after us over the sombre and glittering river" (Conrad 1988, 67). On this occasion, Conrad explicitly refers to the chimeric repetition of the silent gesture, the Intended reminding Marlow of "a tragic and familiar Shade resembling in this gesture another one, tragic also and bedecked with powerless charms, stretching bare brown arms over the glitter of the infernal stream, the stream of darkness" (Conrad 1988, 75).[9] Again we are reminded of the gestures of an expressivist dance (of Duncan, perhaps), when the internal movement within the body directly determines the external movement expressed.

These moments, encapsulating the moving images of the chain gang, the African woman, and the Intended, share a structural purpose in unifying the literal and epistemological aspects of Marlow's experience. Thus Conrad presents the physical dimension of the tale through the rhythmic alternation of scenes of "measured" movement. The juxtaposition of these moments produces Genette's "effects of rhythm." But the narrative situation is constructed in such a way, through the silence of gesture, that the narrator Marlow presents aesthetically a relationship between the tale and the way it is told that is skeptical of language. Meaning is illuminated (but never fully defined) through the movement of the body, as much as through the utterance of the words.

Ricoeur is helpful here in the way he explores an interplay between Aristotle's account of "narrative" time in the *Poetics* and Augustine's analysis of time in the *Confessions*, drawing attention to the emphasis on *activity* in both accounts, and on the creative, the making new by the effort of the mind; he shows the potential for reading Augustine's *distentio animi* in relation to the discordance or *aporia* inherent in narrative itself. Conrad's symbolic configurations of physical events—the movement phrases outlined in the preceding—within the narrative as a whole, unify, in an Aristotelian sense, the beginning, middle, and end of Marlow's tale, but they also suggest the discordance "inherent in narrative itself" by building on the reader's ironic association of each event (experienced each time anew by an effort of mental activity) both proleptically and

---

[8]  See Hawthorn (1990, 185–192). Hawthorn has rightly emphasized Conrad's ironic use of parallelism in positing the African woman's role as a symbolic double for the Intended.

[9]  The Shades who stretch out their arms, reaching across the Charyon, appear in Virgil's Aenaed Book 6. See also Thomas R. Cleary and Terry G. Sherwood, "Women in Conrad's Ironical Epic: Virgil, Dante, and *Heart of Darkness*," *Conradiana* 16(3) (1984): 183–194.

analeptically. These phrases offer descriptive pauses, markers, or discrete interludes that punctuate the narrative, but they also provide a chimeric overlaying, or as J. Hillis Miller discussed, the operation of a form of Deleuzian repetition, a "repetition with difference" in Conrad (Hillis Miller 1982, 5–6), symbolically synthesizing Marlow's journey of disillusionment and disintegration of identity. Yet the presentness of each movement phrase also draws attention to the "aporia" that Brandstetter identifies between the moment of dancing and the historicity of its representation. This structuring of the tale effectively metaphorizes the mental activity suggested by Augustine's *distentio animi*, which shows how we experience temporal reality by a movement of the mind forward and backward in the threefold present. But the choreographic re-embodiment of the movement in the text itself leaves a question open about the way in which Conrad exploits dance as an aesthetic form and opens up the question of danced reenactment in the literary text.

In *Heart of Darkness*, Conrad seems to treat movement as always possessing certain properties of language.[10] The ghostly repetition of the rhythmic phrases and gestures of the chain gang, the African woman and the Intended provide a metaphoric aid to interpretation of Marlow's tale, and in this respect Conrad's narrative strategy anticipates certain contemporary choreographic theories and practices that have developed an understanding of dance either as semiotics or as drawing on aspects of semiotics, and have provided material for cognitive and neurological studies of vision, spectatorship, and the extent of visual memory.[11]

Conrad's attitude toward the body, however, remains skeptical of its autonomy as a means of expression in itself. The Intended's unfinished gesture anticipates the open-endedness of Marlow's narrative, which, trailing into dots, mirrors her physical reaching beyond the parameters of the narrative, and points to the inadequacy of any verbal expression of his disillusionment. Nevertheless, Conrad has placed Marlow in control of the aesthetic realm, where the action of the body has been transferred to the objective domain of the controlling artist. Marlow, at the last minute, doubts the alternative potential for expression offered by the body. Marlow's evocation of these three symbolic moments form a kinetic "triptych." Given his critique of language (and Western iconography) elsewhere in the novella, the "natural" language of the body (as in Brandstetter's

[10]  Conrad often characterizes the women of his novels in terms of bodily movement and stillness: Aïssa's defiant gestures in *An Outcast of the Islands* (1896); *Falk*'s lover, silent and statuesque throughout (1903); the women gliding between rooms of the Geneva apartment in *Under Western Eyes* (1911).

[11]  See, for example, Dee Reynolds et al., "Watching Dance and Kinesthetic Empathy," a multidisciplinary project, involving collaboration across four institutions (University of Manchester, University of Glasgow, York St. John University and Imperial College London), http://www. watchingdance.org/. See also Maurice Merleau-Ponty, *The Phenomenology of Perception*, trans. by Colin Smith (1945; London: Routledge, 1962), who uses Husserl's terminology to suggest that the *aspect*'s "invitation to perceive beyond it" is a dynamic aid to interpretation, allowing the viewer to uncover potentialities delimited by the horizon of the view (233); Gaston Bachelard, *The Poetics of Space* (1969); discussions of Virginia Woolf's modernism in both Erich Auerbach's *Mimesis* (1946); space and narrative in Michel de Certeau (1984) and Ricoeur in a later volume of *Time and Narrative*. All these texts owe much to a phenomenological account of the physical experience of time and movement of the body.

account of what modernist aesthetics absorb from modern dance forms) seems at first to offer him an alternative form of expression. Yet the vibrant movement of the African woman is finally absorbed into classical European drama as the gesture of a "tragic and familiar Shade." In presenting Marlow's disaffiliation from Europe and his discomfort in lying to the Intended at the close of *Heart of Darkness*, we sense Conrad's critique of Western European literary and visual traditions *and* his anxiety about that culture's tendency to confine the movement of the body to the realm of the aesthetic. But the open-ended gestures he chooses nevertheless reenact dance's own skepticism about narrative at this time.

# BECKETT

Beckett's prose follows intriguingly, and with even greater skepticism, from Conrad's exploration of the relationship between physical and psychological movement in *Heart of Darkness*. Beckett's focus, however, is not so much trained on ironizing the frame of representation as on ironizing the production of narrative voice as lived experience—showing it to be at once "lived" and an experience of "nothing," a "figure of the inexpressible Nothing that is being in action" (Birkett 2014, 90). Beckett developed, in his re-embodiment of movement in prose and in drama, an abstract aesthetics that was more compatible with his preoccupations with musical form. As S. E. Gontarski observes in his study of Beckett's drama, Beckett also favored the abstraction of music, because, as Nietzsche argued, it resembles "geometric figures and numbers, which are universal forms of all possible objects of experience" (1985, 184).

But if Beckett privileged the abstraction of music, he also understood that the human body produced its own music through movement design and the body's creation of rhythm. He explored this conundrum in the late prose as well as in the drama, especially as he was consolidating his thinking about the relationship between self-consciousness and human movement, and his increasingly minimalist treatment of movement in part reflects his ongoing philosophical interest in the relationship between stillness and mobility. In the prose works it especially illustrates the way in which, for him, narrative voice is re-embodied in the text as an abstract, non-expressivist choreography in which the rhythm, tonal coloring, and physical pattern produce a kind of "music" of their own that patterns and structures the text in ways often compatible with Conrad's use of temporal disjunction or, as Ricoeur suggested in his treatment of narrative, *distentio animi*.

When Beckett began writing for the stage, he frequently revisited in dramatic form the dialogic and "open-ended" closure of his novel *L'Innommable*: "you must go on, I can't go on, I go on" (Beckett 2010, 134). Beckett's decision to dramatize the human condition retains the same sense of the dependence of the construction of identity on observation of, and response to, the Other (Clov in *Endgame*, Winnie in *Happy Days*, etc.), often presented through dialogic engagement and through the characters' finely poised equilibrium between moving and cessation of movement (as in the final stage direction of *Waiting for Godot*, when Vladimir and Estragon do not move). The stage directions' insistence on the precision of rhythm and temporal measure in the delivery of gesture in Beckett's plays helps to place the drama in the realm of the choreographic. To envision the human figure on stage, governed by spatial confinement, performing precise repetitions of speech or action, suggests that the plays to some extent represent a physical reenactment of a verbal imperative to "go on." But Beckett's preoccupation with the motivations and mechanics of human gesture grounded in time and space also holds particular implications for narrative itself, and throughout his life he continued to explore the way in which the narrative voice is produced by lived experience and is re-embodied in the text. In Beckett's carefully calibrated gestures and movement phrases throughout the prose, he raises implications for the theoretical role of choreography in literary experimentation. In this respect, Beckett's prose experimentation provides a complex re-embodiment in literature of the theoretical potential of gesture. Like Conrad, Beckett is alert to Augustine's idea of the threefold present, which Ricoeur uses in *Time and Narrative* to show the *aporia* in narrative; yet critics have not come to terms with the way that bodily movement creates an anxiety for modernist authors in that they wish to acknowledge an extra-linguistic importance to understanding "being," but on the other hand are loath to relinquish the supremacy of the "word" (even Giles Deleuze, who focuses on Beckett's *trois langues* [of names, voice, image], never enunciates fully the fundamental language of movement in the plays [Deleuze 1998, 173]).[12]

Beckett's preoccupation with movement arose initially in his early prose in the 1930s when he was exploring the work of Arnold Geulincx, a seventeenth-century Occasionalist philosopher and follower of Descartes whose meditations on movement as mechanized prompted an inquiry into the causation of human movement. Beckett likewise questions the origins of movement in his representation of *Murphy* (1938) as a quasi-Petrouchkan figure,[13] a preoccupation that continued to run through his later prose right up to the meditations on stillness, the compulsion to breathe and make one last move. In the 1970s his reading of Heinrich von Kleist's 1810 essay on the marionette theater had profound influence on his direction and staging of the late work and his encouragement of a non-affective mode of acting. One could argue that Beckett's later mode of "choreographing" the body on stage and in his late prose looks back to what Brandstetter identified in the early twentieth century as the "figurations of space" that shaped the foundations of a non-affective emphasis in some forms of modern dance—in Beckett's case, particularly relevant is Oskar Schlemmer's exploitation of geometric patterning to explore dance's spatializing of temporalities.[14]

---

[12] See also Shane Weller, *A Taste for the Negative: Beckett and Nihilism* (Oxford: Legenda, 2005), 17. According to Weller, Deleuze identifies the language of images as "the 'specificity'" of Beckett's late work for television in which the playwright overcomes "the inferiority of words."

[13] For a discussion of Beckett's interest in *Petrouchka* see Jones (2013, 282–291).

[14] See Franko (1993). Franko's discussion of Oskar Schlemmer is valuable for this context. Franko looks at Schlemmer's work in relation to Heinrich von Kleist and Edward Gordon Craig's Kleistian theories. Craig's idea of the "Ueber-Marionette" (1908) drew directly on Kleist's essay, "Über Das Marionettentheater" (1810) and Craig wrote: "If you could make your body into a machine . . . and *if*

Yet a number of Beckett's prose works throughout his career also echo Conrad's emphasis in *Heart of Darkness* on the temporal as well as visual possibilities of "tryp-tych" as structural device, and his emphasis on bodily movement and presence as a means of articulating the "gaps" and "silences," the unsayable that Ricoeur had identified as the *aporia* of narrative. In the introduction to Beckett's "Echo's Bones," an early short story composed in 1933, but rejected at that time for publication, Mark Nixon observes how the story "self-referentially calls itself a 'triptych' and it is indeed a piece in three movements, but whose panels barely make up a whole" (2014, xv). In this observation we identify an early example of how Beckett would over and again dramatize (as move-ments) the inexplicable (dis)unity of human conditions and activity. As Nixon also observes in his note to Beckett's use of the word "intermissions" in this story, this was "part of a larger concern with pauses and gaps and silences" (2014, 60).

Much later, in 1961, *How It Is* (*Comment c'est*) displays a further correspondence with Conrad's *Heart of Darkness* in that both texts re-enact the premise of Augustine's "three-fold present." The narrating voice objectifies the subject in the present tense as a speak-ing subject (in the retelling), but what gives that voice apparent credibility is to place narrative form (a fictional illusion) in the *activity* of the mind, imagining the past and the future through the gestural flash of present movement of figures in the text. Once again, time becomes spatialized in the movement of the body. In *Heart of Darkness*, the narrator Marlow's retrospective tale is reconstructed through flashes of physical phrases throughout the text; Beckett's text, *How It Is*, creates a tripartite structure where, accord-ing to Birkett, "The first two parts must already have been completed for the voice to emerge, but without the voice the journey could not have been narrated. Time must be folded back, and what is represented is the illusory present in which all subject being is lived" (2014, 92). What Birkett does not take into account is the way Beckett *embod-ies* fully and gesturally the narratorial function (somewhat in the manner of Conrad's Marlow—the narrator who "steps back from the abyss") to show the human condition as always being both present and not-present—poised between being and non-being, yet moving still, "towards death."

Beckett constantly rehearses the "staging" of the human condition in his prose work, and it is of great interest to dance studies that a group of works suggesting the mys-tery of human movement toward that "last breath" emerged almost simultaneously with his production of *Quadrat I and II* (1981)—his one dance play for German television. As I have explored elsewhere (Jones 2013, 296–300), this play is an important work to

---

it could obey you in every movement for the entire space of time it was before the audience . . . you would be able to make a work of art out of that which is in you" (Edward Gordon Craig, "The Actor and the Ueber Marionette," *The Mask* [1908], 8); Franko also alludes to French theories that are absorbed by Schlemmer through Montaigne and Diderot. Most striking for this discussion is Franko's remark that Diderot's "description of movement . . . is inconceivable without a concept of passion as itself a physiological event," one that "presupposes an internal movement within the body that dictates a response in the form of external movement. Kleist's is merely an extrapolation of the idea of expressivity" (Franko 1993, 147). Beckett's movements, on the other hand, have no impulse or internal movement preceding them.

consider in light of the inspiration it took from early twentieth-century dance experimentation in Oskar Schlemmer's *Bauhaus Dances*. In Schlemmer's 1926 *Space Dance* (*Raumtanz*), three figures move around a grid that has been outlined on the stage, dividing the space into quadrants and triangles, with lines intersecting at the center. The figures are encased in padded all-over suits, color-coded red, blue, and yellow, the face covered by circular masks with two eyeholes. The figures traverse the lines of the grid in mathematically precise divisions of movement—one striding, one walking, one running, always following the triangular patterns of the grid. They never meet at the center, always narrowly missing each other. Schlemmer explores the notion of human encounters and the relationship between the human body and the stage space in terms of mathematical design, and the mechanical and rhythmical workings of the physical body. He interrogates the way in which generic distinctions are created physically in drama as comedy, pathos, and anger, and examines how they are produced, not only through the quality of movement on the grid and the appearance of the figures—which are sometimes disturbing, at other times endearing—but also through the mathematical precision of the figures' movement, which creates either the tragic isolation or the comic near-collision of the figures in space. As Schlemmer himself observed, "human consciousness lies behind the mechanical figure" (quoted in Franko 1993, 150).[15] Behind the abstraction of the presentation lies the unavoidable humanity of the protagonist.

But as Beckett explored the use of the dynamic interpolation of movement phrase in a late prose narrative such as *Ill Seen Ill Said* (1981), he was simultaneously developing his one dance play, *Quadrat I and II* (initially named *Quad*). This piece for German TV might be considered as a form of reenactment of Schlemmer in the light of Mark Franko's discussion in the Introduction to this volume and in his Chapter 24 on Dore Hoyer and Martin Nachbar, of the relationship between reconstructor and re-enactor, "where the reconstructor assumed closeness to the past through witness-hood, the re-enactor assumes distance from the past through temporal estrangement" (Franko, Chapter 1 in this volume).

We can only speculate on Beckett's witness-hood of Schlemmer's *Space Dance*, but the circumstantial evidence is convincing. He could have seen Margaret Hastings's film of a reconstruction of Schlemmer's work in 1968 (she worked in Stuttgart and the film was televised for German TV) at the time of a visit to Berlin to direct *Endgame*. Furthermore, *Quadrat I and II* was commissioned for Suddeutsche Rundfunk in Stuttgart, where Schlemmer initially trained, and where part of his archive is held. In any case, Schlemmer and Beckett both shared the influence of Kleist's marionette theater, and similarities between Schlemmer and Beckett's work are clear from viewing the two. It would be hard not to categorize Beckett's dance play as a reenactment of Schlemmer's

---

[15] See Franko (1993). In the "Epilogue" (133–152), Franko outlines the development of theories of mime and pantomime in the work of Montaigne, Noverre, and Diderot. See also Angelica Gooden, *Actio and Persuasion: Dramatic Performance in Eighteenth-Century France* (Oxford: Oxford University Press, 1986). Beckett's responses to the French traditions and theories of mime are also important in tracing the antecedents of his choreographic method in the plays.

*Space Dance* in the terms of Franko's discussion of Hoyer and Nachbar. The marked-out grid only appears in Beckett's work as a diagram in manuscript notes, and on the TV screen the lines are not drawn on the stage as in *Space Dance*. But within the frame of the TV screen, the unblemished quad appears suspended in space and the protagonists move along imaginary straight lines intersecting at the center. Each figure completes a prescribed trajectory, always appearing and disappearing at the limits or corners of the quad. But rather than following the triadic geometry of Schlemmer's *Space Dance*, in which three figures appear and move around the triangles drawn on the floor, Beckett explores in *Quad* the figural relationships associated with placing the triangular paths of four figures within the spatial patterning of the quad. Four slightly hunched figures dressed in robes with cowls covering their head, suggesting the hypocrites in canto 23 of Dante's *Inferno* (each in a different color—red, blue, yellow, white), shuffle around the grid, each step following a precise mathematical and rhythmic division of pace. The figures move, like Schlemmer's, in triangular paths that traverse the square, each appearing successively until four occupy the space, then one by one moving off the quad at one of the corners into darkness. Each figure turns left at the center (like the occupants of the *Inferno* as they spiral downward) and, as in *Space Dance*, near collisions ensue as the numbers of moving figures on the grid increase and then diminish. But unlike Schlemmer, human consciousness does not "lie behind the mask" in Beckett's dance play; instead, the figures act as if motivated by an outside force, pre-programmed to carry out endless repetitions of the movement along the same geometrically organized pathways.

Nevertheless, the affectless propulsion of the figure has already been explored by Beckett in several prose works, and the formal experiments of this play are already to some extent present in prose pieces between 1979 and 1981—all of which reveal common preoccupations with the mechanics of "going on," sustained from the early prose interrogations of subjectivity and being. But because these later pieces focus on the voice of narration, the important role of re-embodiment of movement in the text and these works' relationship to *Quad*'s rhythmic exactitudes sometimes get neglected in accounts of the late work. Before starting work on *Quad*, Beckett began translating *Mal vu mal dit* in December 1980, even as the French original was being written and revised between 1979 and January 1981. *Ill Seen Ill Said* was published in *The New Yorker* in 1981. Beckett was writing this piece just before he created *Quad*. In fact, we might look at the short prose text "The Way" as most proximate to *Quad* (it was written in mid-May 1981 between two trips to Stuttgart to help with the TV production). *Quad*'s geometrical quincunx can be seen as combining the two signs that announce the two paragraphs of "The Way" (8 and infinity; Beckett draws on Dante again, as well as the Presocratic Heraclitus: "the way up and the way down [are] one and the same" [quoted by van Hulle in Beckett 2009, xi]).

In *Ill Seen Ill Said* we already find something of Beckett's reference to non-affective movement that makes his "ballet" for television so close to the early twentieth-century experiments of Schlemmer. But this novella also looks back to the position of the Intended at the close of *Heart of Darkness*. Beckett's protagonist and main character in

*Ill Seen Ill Said* is an old woman, and the story is narrated in the third person. On the first page of the English manuscript the text was provisionally titled "The Evening or the Night." The emphasis is on the "present" of the narratorial moment: "All this in the present as had she the misfortune to be still of this world" (Beckett 2009, 42) throughout the tale the opposition of dark/light repeats the familiar symbolism of Conrad's tale. The woman moves in and out of a bleak landscape and interior room of monochrome darkness and light (the black and white of *Quadrat II*), and throughout the text "tense" is suggested elliptically by the movement phrases of the woman punctuating the narrative. Her initial pose echoes Conrad's figure, the Intended's position when she was being interviewed at dusk by Marlow, dressed in mourning, stretching out her arms, "with clasped pale hands across the fading and narrow sheen of the window." Beckett's figure, on the other hand, is motionless, having darted between windows of her enclosed cabin, now "[r]igid with face and hands against the pane she stands and marvels long" (Beckett 2009, 46). But Beckett communicates the problem of narrative voice, the narratorial conundrum of representing tense (past, present, future that can only be related in the present) through the woman's choreographed movement phrase, interrupted by dramatic gesture (as with the rhythmic interpolation of the movement of Conrad's African woman, analeptically and proleptically poised at the central moment of the story). Beckett's woman likewise interrupts the textual flow, but the quality of the interpolation is affectless (much as his stage directions indicate movement in the plays) and functions primarily to situate the observing narrator in relation to the woman's position as she emerges into the bleak landscape "in the zone of stones": "she could be seen crossing the threshold both ways and closing the door behind her" (Beckett 2009, 49). Later she moves back and forth inside her dwelling, and again the repetitions are choreographed precisely (rather like May's pacing in *Footfalls*), but here the movement phrase is syncopated: "for long pacing to and fro in the gloom. Suddenly in a single gesture she snatches aside the coat and to again on a sky as black as it" (Beckett 2009, 70). This "endless present" in fact enacts, through rhythmic gestures, the narrator's retelling of a story of the move toward death—the closing of the tale anticipating the desire to finish the gesture—"Grace to breathe that void"—in a way that Beckett continues to envision all his late prose: *Company* (1980), *Worstward Ho* (1983), *Stirrings Still* (1989).

Beckett deflates further the Conradian gesture (often histrionic) by eliminating the expressivist force of its dynamic—but he nevertheless draws on the skeptical move that Conrad had made in order to foreground the ironic retelling of a tale, as Ricoeur understood the *aporia* of narrative itself. Beckett's extreme skepticism focuses on the presentness of lived experience as a function of the narrative, paradoxically engaging the reader in a movement toward closure (nothing) but never reaching it.

Beckett's text, appearing nearly a century after Conrad's, seems at times to incorporate a *critique* of Conrad's very use of the sublime, expressive gesture in *Heart of Darkness*. What is more intriguing is that *Ill Seen Ill Said* was composed at a time when Beckett was preparing his "dance play," *Quadrat I and II* (1981), a play that bears close reminders of the highly stylized, non-affective movement of the early twentieth-century work of the Bauhaus artist and director Oskar Schlemmer. This case of the probable influence of Schlemmer on Beckett might lead us to categorize Beckett's dance play as choreographic reenactment of Schlemmer, rather than the translations across dance and text of movement phrases by the author of the prose. In the prose, two kinds of choreographic re-embodiment across dance and text emerge that correspond to Brandstetter's identification of Warburg's theories of the "body-image": first in the manner of Conrad's expressivist forms; and second, the "figurations in space" that relate more closely to Beckett's exploration of non-affective forms of twentieth-century dance, focusing on the spatialization of time.

But an important issue arises here: the "original" dance also possessed its own skeptical strategies, which in the case of contemporary dance forms undermines the idea of linear duration. The movement phrases thus described in the text generate the kind of suspension of judgment (on the part of the mover herself or the viewer) that literary skepticism invokes in its disrupted representations of time and disruption of narrative closure. But these *kinds* of movements in their original context also possessed their own skeptical strategies in that their very aesthetic activity focuses on the disruption of linear narrative—as the dancing body spatializes time in the "present" moment (in Fuller's or Duncan's work, or Schlemmer's interrogations of spatial activity), it undermines the linear concept of story and proposes the choreographic act as a reenactment of time in and by space.

Both Conrad and Beckett display in their fictional texts a corresponding understanding of the "choreographed" phrase as an aesthetic aid to narratological disruption—a structuring device that gives them a way to incorporate rhythmic disjunctions of conventional narrative time. The description of gesture and movement phrase also focuses on the non-linguistic element of the narrational act: one that generates the dialogic relation between speaking subject and subject/object observed as lived, embodied experience. The modern dance innovations identified by Brandstetter frequently deny narrative modes altogether, but it seems that the modernist writer "choreographs" the movement phrase or gesture in the text in order to communicate the physical or embodied connection of two temporal points without recourse to language. The use of this device does not aid logical sequencing. Somewhat counterintuitively, the imagined gestures in these texts disrupt the teleology and conventional understanding of narrative, introducing into the reading experience modernism's skeptical mode, its focus on the slipperiness and inadequacy of language itself, a sense of the impossibility of (or gap introduced by) grammatical tense.

However, these writers' introduction of gestures associated with innovations in dance at the turn of the twentieth century in itself offers a parallel with dance's deconstuction of narrative form in the early twentieth century. As time becomes spatialized by the movements of the body described in the texts, the spatialization of dance (in its presentness) is the counterpart to the linguistic disruption by an aesthetic act. But these moments leave unanswered questions about "choreographic" reenactment itself, if the choreographic becomes the reenactment of time in and by space. These experiments in narration spanning the twentieth century suggest an intriguing continuity of interest in questioning the production of the narrative voice. But in the movement between dance and text, they also produce an often unacknowledged anxiety about the re-embodiment of the choreographic in twentieth-century modernism.

## WORKS CITED

Bachelard, Gaston. 1969. *The Poetics of Space*. Translated by Maria Jolas. Boston: Beacon Press.

Beckett, Samuel. 2009. *Company, Ill Seen Ill Said, Worstward Ho, Stirrings Still*. Edited by Dirk van Hulle. London: Faber and Faber.

Beckett, Samuel. 2010. *The Unnamable*. Edited by Stephen Connor. First published in French as *L'Innomable* 1953; London: Faber and Faber.

Benjamin, Walter. 1968. *Illuminations*. Edited and with an introduction by Hannah Arendt; translated by Harry Zohn. New York: Schocken Books.

Birkett, Jennifer. 2014. *Undoing Time: The Life and Work of Samuel Beckett*. Newbridge, Co. Kildare, Ireland: Irish Academic Press.

Boehmer, Elleke 1995. *Colonial and Postcolonial Literature*. Oxford: Oxford University Press.

Brandstetter, Gabriele. 2015. *The Poetics of Dance: Body, Space, and Image in the Historical Avant-Gardes*. First published 1995 in German. Oxford: Oxford University Press.

Conrad, Joseph. 1988. *Heart of Darkness* (1902). New York: Norton.

Crary, Jonathan. 1990. *Techniques of the Observer: On Vision and Modernity in the Nineteenth Century*. Cambridge, MA: MIT Press.

Deleuze, Gilles. 1998. *Essays Critical and Clinical*. Translated by Daniel W. Smith and Michael A. Greco. London: Verso.

Dowling, William. 2011. *Ricoeur on Time and Narrative: An Introduction to Temps et récit*. Notre Dame, IN: University of Notre Dame Press.

Eliot, T. S. 1963. *The Collected Poems 1909–1962*. London: Faber.

Franko, Mark. 1993. *Dance as Text: Ideologies of the Baroque Body*. Cambridge: Cambridge University Press.

Franko, Mark. 1995. *Dancing Modernism/Performing Politics*. Bloomington: Indiana University Press.

Genette, Gérard. 1980. *Narrative Discourse: An Essay in Method*. Translated by Jane E. Lewin. Ithaca, NY: Cornell University Press.

Gilman, Sander L. 1985. *Difference and Pathology: Stereotypes of Sexuality, Race, and Madness*. Ithaca, NY: Cornell University Press.

Gontarski, S. E. 1985. *The Intent of Undoing in Samuel Beckett's Dramatic Texts* Bloomington: Indiana University Press.

Hawthorn, Jeremy. 1990. *Joseph Conrad: Narrative Technique and Ideological Commitment*. London: Edward Arnold.

Hillis Miller, J. 1982. *Fiction and Repetition: Seven English Novels*. Cambridge, MA: Harvard University Press.

Jones, Susan. 2013. *Literature, Modernism, and Dance*. Oxford: Oxford University Press.

Jones, Susan. 2008. "'She walked with measured steps': Physical and Narrative Movement in *Heart of Darkness*." In *Joseph Conrad: Voice, Sequence, History, Genre*, edited by Jeremy Hawthorn, Jakob Lothe, and Jim Phelan, 100–117. Columbus, OH: Ohio State University Press.

Karl, Frederick R. 1979. *Joseph Conrad: The Three Lives*. New York: Farrar, Straus and Giroux.

Mallarmé, Stéphane. 2003. "Autre étude de danse (1893–6)." In *Igitur, Divagations, Un coup de dés*, edited and translated by Bertrand Marchal, 206–211. Paris: Gallimard.

Nixon, Mark. 2014. Introduction and Notes to Samuel Beckett, *Echo's Bones* (1933). London: Faber.

Ricoeur, Paul. 1984. *Time and Narrative*, Vol. 1. Chicago: University of Chicago Press.

# PART VIII

# EPISTEMOLOGIES OF INTER-TEMPORALITY

# CHAPTER 23

# AFFECT, TECHNIQUE, AND DISCOURSE

## Being Actively Passive in the Face of History: Reconstruction of Reconstruction

### GERALD SIEGMUND

SOMETHING unheard of seems to have taken place in 1998. A young Frenchman coming from the booming postmodern dance scene of the late 1980s and early 1990s quotes the beginning of a dance by German dancer Susanne Linke in his own piece. Linke, as a former pupil of Mary Wigman, worked in the expressionist dance tradition. Jérôme Bel's *Le Dernier spectacle (The Last Performance)*, the endgame of dance in the final days of the twentieth century, consisted almost entirely of borrowed material. People asked if his practice of borrowing was permissible, and if so, how can a movement be recognized as a quotation? And if all movements are decidedly quotations, then to whom does choreography, let alone dance itself, belong? Who may claim it as their intellectual property? Is it, above all else, a piece by Jérôme Bel, or does it remain Susanne Linke's *Wandlung*? Bel has men and women do the solo, and repeats it four times, and in this way builds a play of identities into it, a construction that is both produced as performed but also left open to question. *The Last Performance* brings to light how identity results from the constant repetition of cultural and societal practices, which means that it is governed by memory.[1]

Many ballet and contemporary dance companies, including that of Pina Bausch, are anchored in institutional support systems (such as the structure of German city theaters) devoted to preserving dance's history and keeping their own repertories intact. But this becomes problematic for independent choreographers, the heirs of free dance (*Freie Tanz*) and modern dance's legacy. In this tradition, each solo dancer is also effectively the author of his or her own work. Performer and choreographer in tandem, each

---

[1] For a detailed analysis of the piece, see Siegmund (2006) and Brandstetter and Peters (2002).

dancer thus embodies the autonomous creator-subject that grasps the inherent element of recreation in his or her movement. But how can this legacy sustain itself once there is discontinuity between the movement and its originating producer (see Schneider 2005)? As for group works, dance companies today often consist of freelance dancers. They get together for one particular production and, due to lack of financial support, simply do not stay together long enough to sustain a repertoire.

In the late 1990s, on the contemporary scene, Alice Chauchat and Thomas Plischke (both alumni of PARTS, a school based in Brussels and run by Anne Teresa de Keersmaeker) were dabbling in Stravinsky and Nijinsky's *The Rite of Spring*, developing their own take on it at the behest of Utrecht's Springdance Festival. In their short piece they reconsidered *Rite* as a strict, rhythmic progression, mediated through the mundane act of eating. This work would later be incorporated into the Thomas Plischke/B.D.C.'s first large-scale production *Events for Television (again)* (1999) and constituted a critical reevaluation of the entire modern tradition. Tino Sehgal's 2000 piece *Untitled* fills an empty space with an abbreviated tour through the history of modern dance, stringing together key moments and tropes that the trained eye will immediately identify as iconic within the modern dance canon, from Isadora Duncan to Kurt Jooss, all the way to Xavier Le Roy. Sehgal notably does not reconstruct any piece in its entirety, but thanks to a wealth of media from which the kinetic and choreographic vocabularies of each respective artist can be reverse-engineered (such as Duncan's drawings and William Forsythe's "Improvisation Technologies" CD), he instead constructs scenes from "memory" that never existed as such.

*Untitled* cites dance history from memory, and in this way opens up new perspectives on that history. Sehgal's choreography was again taken up by Boris Chamatz's *Musée de la danse* in Rennes in 2013.[2] Unlike Sehgal's own version, which was a solo danced by Sehgal himself, the reenactment of the choreography is now danced three consecutive times by three different dancers (Andrew Hardwidge, Frank Willens, and Boris Charmatz), thus underlining the production of difference through repetition beyond the single body of a dancer. Rather than being an integral solo work, the production now takes on the character of an ongoing process of deferral of danced material, which loses its (historical) identity. In the summer of 2000, the *Wiener Festwochen*, together with the Festival Impuls Tanz, dedicated the dance program it assembled to the body as a site of memory. As with the title of the event, *Re-Membering the Body*, it served as a reminder both of the analytical dissection at work and of the imperative to represent a newly historicized body.[3] As exemplified by the Group Lux Flux's staging of Nijinsky's *Rite of Spring*, Nijinsky's seminal modernist work served as a bone of contention for many contemporary choreographers during the festival. Thanks to the critical impetus behind the work, as well as its break with tradition, both of which stand among shifting societal and artistic considerations, the excitement around its untapped potential for a

---

[2] Sehgal's piece now is called *(Untitled)* (2000).
[3] The program was accompanied by the publication of a book with the same title (Brandstetter and Völckers 2000).

critical legacy of dance was high. As dance celebrity Mikhail Barishnikov and his White Oak Dance Project assembled reconstructions of an array of Judson Dance Theater's material from the 1960s under the title *Past/Forward* in 2001, he popularized a seminal reference point for the young artists of the day to reconsider and experiment with.[4]

These were the epicenters from which a lasting preoccupation with the dance history of the twentieth century in particular radiated. This pivotal moment coincided with a prevalent interest in memory as a topic in literary and cultural studies in the 1990s.[5] With the turn of the new millennium came an inexorable sense of the dawning of a new era, a time to look back and take stock of what has been, or is being, lost to time. My first assessment identified an impulse to recall and recollect evidence throughout an entire generation of choreographers, and in the following terms:

> When choreographers of the past ten years, such as Meg Stuart, Jérôme Bel, Xavier Le Roy, Thomas Plischke and Thomas Lehmen, deliberately drew from the experiments of the sixties, they were acting on the impulse to make movement precisely more than just movement. Their goal is rather to bring these experiments out of the framework of theater and conceive of them as cultural as well as artistic productions based on decisions made over and over again. Hence do they turn against the increasingly mannered dances of the same period, which masterfully juggle so many techniques and styles, and so produce pieces that are more and more conformist. What could be the role of dance in a world so altered? What does my body represent when the massive presence of sexualized, monetized, and fabricated bodies turns the body into a commodity? Historical controversy today is not bound up with the museum, but rather with questions of the ethnic, cultural, and historical identity of the dancing body. And these, again, are questions that ring with even more urgency in a globalized world. (Siegmund 2003, 43; author's translation)

As I reconstruct my own thinking and writing on dance, which date back roughly to that same period, three major points assert themselves as crucial to reflecting on this dance history. First, contemporary dance stages a rejection of the very modern paradigm of originality, as well as of the idea of the authentic original. The Internet age has redefined our cultural memory by affording us a new sort of access to it. The historical is now generally at our disposal and eminently citable. Second, it is time for producers to become aware of the territory they occupy as dancers and choreographers in an increasingly mediated and media-oriented society. A moment of pause and reflection is imperative to ensure that the space of action and critical intervention remains open and free. Third, contemporary dance deals with history as a means of emancipation for the dancers themselves. They give themselves a (their) history. In the practice of reenactment, the notorious ephemerality of dance restricting its life span to the present moment gives way to a more conflicting notion of dance's temporalities. Part of the strategy of

---

[4] For further discussion of this performance, see Houston and Tobey (2001).

[5] In the 1990s in Germany, the work of Jan and Aleida Assmann was instrumental in bringing the topic of memory into the domain of cultural studies; see J. Assmann (2011) and A. Assmann (2012).

contemporary danced reenactments is to attain social and cultural meaning by inscribing themselves within collective memory.

We remain sensitive to these issues today—if anything, these questions have become even more infectious. A decade later, we may only have become more pragmatic in our approach to the work of past generations, as is the case with the Dutch *Cover-Project* (2008), where young choreographers are occupied with the work of their predecessors to create an exchange between generations. Think of Annouk van Dijk and company rehearsing Hans van Manen's *Situations*, or Nicole Beutler deconstructing the ballet classic *La Sylphide* by setting it in the round and making the audience vulnerable through an almost unbearable physical proximity to the three dancers (Bleeker 2012).

I put forward the three rubrics that follow as valuable ways to frame the practice of writing historically about dance. The three examples I have chosen all come out of the same circle of colleagues and collaborators I have already introduced. These include Martin Nachbar's reconstruction of Dore Hoyer's dance cycle *Affectos Humanos* (1962), which was originally part of B.D.C.'s production *Affect* (2000); William Forsythe's work on ballet; and the French company Albrecht Knust Quartet, which is deliberate about notation and understands the writing of dance to be an essential component of its work. Looming over these three negotiations with dance history is the fact that they all must come to terms with the unattainable dimension inherent in their specific approach to history. In fact, the three examples I have chosen deliberately and consciously base their work on this unattainable dimension of the past. In their productions they confront the actual dancing bodies with something that may never be fully realized.

This unattainable dimension, set in perennial contrast to the actual dancing body, remains an open concept that is represented in a variety of different ways in the three dance productions discussed here. It is both a working hypothesis and a specific reality for the dancers to set themselves in motion, dealing with history and their own claims in it. In my first example, it is the imagined body of Hoyer that is unattainable for the dancer Martin Nachbar, who can only ever approach it without being able to embody it. In my second example, it is the "code" of ballet itself that remains elusive once it is embodied by the dancers of Forsythe's Frankfurt Ballet. In yet another example, it is Nijinsky's 1915 notation of his choreography *The Afternoon of a Faun* that, despite its presumed clarity as a written text, figures as the elusive element in the Albrecht Kunst Quartet's reconstruction work. I designate these three aspects of the historically ungraspable as affect, technique, and discourse, respectively. For none of these three approaches is reconstruction a more or less successful imitation of a given work according to any dichotomy of mimesis versus original. I argue that these positions are better understood as affective, technical, or discursive responses to specific historical positions. As such, affect, technique, and discourse transmit the past. They make it operable, while at the same time inscribing an impossible element within each effort to reconstruct it. Thus affect, technique, and discourse share a special relationship. Discourse enables the production of historically faithful technical bodies, like those of classical ballet, which are conducive to affect's demonstrability, communicability, and tangibility. Taken together, these three act as guarantors of tradition, which they mutually determine, sustain, and, above all, produce. In that sense, none of the three phenomena is accessible without appeal to the other two. They need one another as general, abstract principles specifying the laws of movement/production. But they also need the individual body as it actualizes, produces, and repeats these principles through performance, which by necessity submits them to change. Yet we must also note that the relationship between the three elements can also have the opposite effect, as the prioritization of one over the others can be a means of setting new types of production into motion.

# AFFECT

With the help of the Dore Hoyer's now deceased heir Waltraud Luley, choreographer Martin Nachbar, a Dusseldorf native living in Berlin, meticulously reconstructed three of five dances of her cycle (namely, *Desire, Hate,* and *Anxiety*) in 2000.[6] Eight years later, he combined his work on the remaining two affects, *Love* and *Vanity*, with the initial three to form a piece entitled *Urheben Aufheben* (*Create Revoke*). The final version consisted of more than simply a presentation of dance; it was framed as a simultaneously performative and discursive reconstruction of Nachbar's own process of reconstruction, beginning with his discovery of the original works in footage at the PARTS film archive in Brussels.[7] Hoyer's trademark was extreme tension in her body as she moved. She danced through her joints, making her slim build, tapering in at the extremities, as well as the flow of her movement itself, seem fragmented. Nachbar's body, on the other hand, is extremely relaxed and fluid, his moderate muscle tone in particular giving his movement a certain smoothness. He blurs the entire kinetic paradigm, changing the movement in ways that extend beyond the joints. Here, again, is where we get the impression that Nachbar has, in a sense, "picked up" Hoyer's body (one of the meanings of *Aufheben* in the work's title), dancing as if moving along with her. In interpreting her movements through his body, he both does her dance and a totally new dance of his own, revealing the tension implicit in the performance of movements developed specifically for someone else's body. What was touted by many as a critical failure fell to the advantage of the reconstructive project because it demonstrated not only the profound implications of reconstruction, but also its very conditions of possibility.

These conditions cannot lie in the embodied present, the here and now of the performance situation. Nachbar calls to mind, rather, a doubled absence—the absence of Dore Hoyer's body, but also the absence of his own body, which, in pursuing the image of Hoyer's, is transformed as if through an unavoidable cut. Nachbar's body is now neither hers nor his, but something else entirely: something formless, a third thing that

---

[6]  For more on Nachbar's work, see the chapters in this volume by Nachbar, Bleeker, and Franko.
[7]  A recording of the five dances was made by the Hessische Rundfunk in Frankfurt in 1967 which, alongside Waltraud Luley's memory and coaching, served as one of the sources for Nachbar's reconstruction.

finds articulation only in the differentiation of the original two poles. Hoyer's phantasmatic body, given to Nachbar only by means of a film recording and Luley's meticulous instructions as she remembered the choreography, is repeated through its very absence. By trying to reconstruct a phantom, Nachbar gains a distance from his own physical shape and form. For Nachbar, it is precisely this difference between two bodies—how Hoyer's dances affect him, move him, and in their repetition, change him—that interests him. Certainly Nachbar rehearsed the choreography according to a specific system of representation to denote the affects at play, but even as he goes through these motions, performing the dance with a different body produces a different result. Nachbar was contemplating just this when he wrote,

> That in all this the AH [*Affectos Humanos*] as interpreted by Dore Hoyer function as an original, that I am gearing my work towards, does not mean that I want to satisfy an ideal. I am much more interested in the transition into an Other that is new to me. And vice-versa, the Other's transition into me. This mutual transitioning makes strangers known to one another. Dances that thematize affects, in turn become affective. It finds mutual affection instead, and memory becomes a kind of viral proliferation. (Nachbar 2003, 95)

A specialized technique designed to help the dancer reinhabit the body of "Dore Hoyer," in other words, is liable to become unmoored from the affect that it was ultimately attempting to engender. Affect takes precedence over technique. Affect cannot be perfectly reconstructed without losing its ability to affect. This said, by being affected, Nachbar nevertheless manages to communicate something in affect's place, insofar as his task is to develop a new vocabulary for his body that can neither draw on Hoyer's example nor forsake it.

In the interest of forwarding this argument as precisely as possible, I look back to Dore Hoyer's original cycle, the title of which refers to Baruch Spinoza's theory of affects in his *Ethics*. First published in 1677, it was one of the works earmarked for posthumous release after the death of the Amsterdam-born philosopher in 1632. It consists of five parts of which the third, *Of the Origin and Nature of Affects*, and the fourth, *Of Human Bondage, or the Power of the Affects*, are particulary relevant to my discussion of affects (Spinoza 1996). At the same time, the notion of "affect" was being revalorized in numerous treatises on dance, as it offered a means of understanding the representation of psychological states through movement. In 1682 Claude-François Ménestrier declared, finally, that ballet was no anomaly in the system of the arts, but was rather, just like all the other arts, based on mimesis. Beyond that, however, dance contained the potential to mimic the hidden in nature, in addition to what we see in nature. "This imitation is indeed an extension of the movements of the body, which are themselves the interpreters of the passions and gut feelings" (Ménestrier 1972, 41; my translation). Spinoza contends that there is a distinction between "affections" (*affectio*) and "affect" (*affectus*), the latter resulting from the former. In both, we come upon the human capacity to be affected, on the one hand, and to affect, on the other. Spinoza defines the affects as different modalties of a holistic and indivisible substance. These affections (*affectio*) are modifications of the substance by which this substance makes itself explicit in the form of affects (*affectus*). As Gilles Deleuze writes in his glossary of Spinoza's terms, "These affections are therefore images or corporeal traces first of all" (Deleuze 1988, 48). "Corporeal traces" must be taken literally here, as they refer to pressure from an outside force. The duration of this continuous transformation of the total substance is called "affect" or "emotion." The affect (*affectio*) now refers not only to the particular condition of the body, but also to the abstract presence of those bodies that affect the body: "The *affectio* refers to a state of the affected body and implies the presence of the affecting body, whereas the *affectus* refers to the passage from one state to another, taking into account the correlative variation of the affecting bodies" (Deleuze 1988, 49). There is something distinctly visual about the *affectio*, which includes a mental image of those bodies that affect the substance, which as *affectus* conversely indicates the movement between bodies that instigates change and production. In this sense, affect is an activity that produces connective relations between bodies, as well as between bodies and their visual representations in the mind. "By affect," as Spinoza's third definition has it, "I understand affections of the body by which the body's power of acting is increased or diminished, aided or restrained, and at the same time, the ideas of these affections" (Spinoza 1996, 70). The consequence of this assertion for Spinoza is the revelation of two types of transformation and thus two types of affect: one is a pleasure (*Lust*), which leads to a heightening of the affected body in the field of action; the other is pain (*Unlust*), that is defined through its tendency to reduce or narrow the sphere of action of the body so affected. The affected body thus *explains* affects, and shows that the body makes affects visible, despite the fact that affects themselves do not belong to the body.

What does this mean for the larger discussion of affect? An affect is unbound energy that brings about what Slavoj Žižek calls "transindividual circulation." As Deleuze later developed it in a Spinozan vein, affects are not something that belong to a subject and are then passed over to another subject; affects function at the pre-individual level, as free-floating intensities that belong to no one and circulate at the level "beneath inter-subjectivity" (Žižek 2012, 31). Put differently, affect is perennially foreign, at once enabling personal change, while remaining a totally impersonal force.

In the psychoanalytic theory of Jacques Lacan, affect emerges as a dislocation, bound up with what is taken for granted as the consistent reality of the subject. Affect, for Lacan, comes from without, to the subject from others. Affect is therefore not the same as a subjective feeling. An affect is a signal triggered by the following question: "How do I figure into the desires of those around me?" This question upsets my standpoint, transfers me to a new space, that of the Other, so that my reality is set in motion. One could almost attribute a transcendental quality to this unfettered, freely circulating affect. It is the condition of possibility for there to be a reality and for a new reality to come into being. It functions as a virtual element that materializes in the body to determine it as a particular body. Inasmuch as affect materializes, however, it awakens the impression that my body is itself the locus of affect. This is a simple yet compelling demonstration of Spinoza's point that affects seem to be explained inasmuch as they are shown in and on the body. It is nonetheless a necessary deception. Affect shatters the cause-and-effect chain in that, as a virtual entity, it enables something real to come into being. One's own body is not the origin or the cause of affects, even though there is an indefatigable, and moreover reasonable, sense that it is. Affect originates elsewhere and finds its way to us. It is therefore always in a relational back and forth, a trading of spaces; that is to say, it is made of movement. The relationship between my body and the mental image of the other body that affect promotes is one that we can only grasp in transit; it is always a changing process, never a fixed object or product.

From this perspective we can gauge Martin Nachbar's distance from the imagined exterior body of Dore Hoyer, the affective representation, the *affectio*, from which develops the affect trigger, the *affectus*, for him. If, for Lacan, reality is that which reappears in the same place, then the affect sets the subject's reality in motion, debunking it by altering Nachbar's own body, which, from now on, will continue to be divided between two identities. From this vantage point, Nachbar reaches no unique and ineluctable embodiment of the body Dore Hoyer crafted for herself in *Affectos Humanos*. For it is no longer his body, but her body that takes on definition through his own. Conversely, Hoyer's body is not being replicated as such. Nachbar is incorporating an absent body, or the idea of her body—a body that makes for the impossibility of embodiment. The question is also not one of the adequacy of the representation of the passions, but of the transformative power of the affect, which, still constituting a relationship, precipitates the production of novel creations and variations. Rather than making Dore Hoyer's presence spectral, Martin Nachbar's choreography *makes her absence visible*, showing it to be a liminal space within which creation is possible. The evidence lies in the transportation of something virtual (the representation of Hoyer's body) into something actual (Nachbar's body).

# TECHNIQUE

The possibility of an adequate and complete representation of the idea of Dore Hoyer's affect-body would, in accordance with Spinoza, result in the perfect embodiment of a preexisting idea, an image of affection, in the dancing body. Thus the potential energy of the subject is transformed. The *passio* the subject is subjected to now becomes the possibility of its *action*, its possibility to move. It is dance technique that makes this accord between *passio* and *actio* possible, since it is geared precisely toward the task of matching the dancing body with its conceptual content: the image that affects it and makes it move. The ballet body and the release body are the products of the rehearsal of specialized practices of holding tension in the body. Through the repetition of certain kinetic procedures, dance technique, on the one hand, literally produces a body memory. On the other hand, it simultaneously allows access to this memory by triggering habitualized movement combinations. In Deleuze's particular reading of Spinoza, there is a productive force (*actio*) available to the passively affected (*passio*) that no longer requires sanction by the original, but in fact makes the original obsolete. In the case of Martin Nachbar as well as that of William Forsythe, whom I will turn to now, the dancer's body in its particular materiality is situated between the image of the body and the materialization of that image which is transformed or (re)moved from its place in the process of physical affection.

Like the presentation of Dore Hoyer's affect-body to Nachbar, the codes of ballet to Forsythe represent an impossibility. The language of ballet as such (i.e., abstract and universal) is unavailable to the dancer, as its instantiations in image and text always fall short of conveying its subject in the material sense. It is this idea that validates Forsythe's famous dictum: "The arabesque does not exist" (quoted in Siegmund 2004, 50). Arabesque is a Platonic idea that immediately becomes stained or imperfect once it is tainted with the individual corporeality of a dancer, however perfect she or he performs it. The codes indeed put forward an ideal of coordination for the arms, legs, torso, hips, and shoulders, and each body will discover its own unique capacity to succeed or fail at obeying it. Strictly speaking, therefore, there are only versions of arabesque, but never "the" arabesque, which is a mere theoretical abstraction. Furthermore, the arabesque as a figure can only ever be an unsustainable intermediacy in the flow of movements, a temporary configuration of extremities, whose essence is ephemerality. The question of the reconstruction of old works is tied up with traditional ballet's demand for unfailing exactness in the remembrance, rehearsal, and performance of the steps and gestures of the past. This demand of perfection remains, although it is self-evident that these seemingly well-documented sources of ballet classics are never sufficiently authenticable because sources are always incomplete. On top of that, although the choreography may remain the same, the movements of the dancers remembering the steps are not.

In lieu of this impossible demand, in his work with Ballet Frankfurt, Forsythe advances a twofold problem as a challenge to the memory of ballet. First, the dancers are confronted with the codes of ballet that they have mastered in training. Throughout the performance, the dancer faces the challenge of tracking and certifying the various motions that moving as a ballet dancer is bound to trigger in the body. In the normal course of events, these residual movements are repressed for the sake of the correct execution of posture or figure. If this awareness, however, is allowed to become productive, it changes bodily coordination and alters the dancer's pacing. Second, the language of ballet, already understood to be in flux, must interface with the complex structure of choreographic technique, which draws from a range of heterogeneous cultural media such as film, architectural drawing, and text. These serve as sources of information for dancers—means of activating movements, which they can then for their part update, adapt, and edit. Ideally, of course, dancers reach the point at which they independently arrive at the decision of what they will dance in the process of dancing it (Siegmund 2012). This sets forth an unmistakable process of reconfiguration within the structure proposed for any piece. Forever changing according to the decisions taken and options realized, it can never be taken as total. Dancers must likewise relinquish the idea of controlling the outcome of their movement and of the choreography. This abandonment, denoted either by activity in a passive state or passivity in an active state, leads to becoming affected by one's own movements, the decisions of others, and the interaction resulting in choreography. This in turn sets into motion a process based in the language of ballet neoclassicism, which results in the overwriting of that language. Mastery thus lies, at least at this stage, not in reproducing the code correctly, which also abolishes the hierarchical system of grading the dancers according to their perfection. Mastery lies in the production of a different kind of awareness, of being Other and becoming Other by letting things happen and by letting them affect you.

We find a good example of this phenomenon in the ballet *The Loss of Small Detail*, the definitive version of which premiered at the Frankfurt Opera House in 1992. The quality of its movement is of an outstanding softness and transparency, fluid and trance-like, oscillating in space. This quality is achieved by a technique that Forsythe calls "disfocus," which dictates that the dancer's eye must not be trained on any one point, despite the typical practice of doing so as a means of keeping the body on an axis. It is instead guided to the back of the dancer's own head, widening their field of perception. Though they perhaps diminish their ability to accurately perceive their surroundings, they do so in favor of a heightened sensitivity to their body's extremities and muscularity, improving the proprioception upon which tension and rapport with the other performers is built. These "internally refracted co-ordinations" (Sulcas 1995, 8) hinder one's ability to dance in the way that would be second nature to any trained and skilled ballet dancer. But holding a soft focus does not change the fact that the dancer is directly facing the audience. "It's not that you destroy the foundations," explains Forsythe, "you just end up in an opposing state of support. The small detail that is lost is your physical orientation. Your body gives up one kind of strength, but another comes into play" (quoted in Sulcas 1995, 8). The dislocation of inner and outer forms of perception can change the balletic body without robbing it of its integrity. The work of both Martin Nachbar and William Forsythe suggest that the dancer's work is ultimately to engage with the unattainable as a limit of what one can do. This enables the dancers to enter into a state of dance through contact with others, the medium of which is affect. This state of dance is completely separate from the choreography that makes it possible to begin with.

# DISCOURSE

The Albrecht Knust Quartet insists upon the difference between dance and choreography. Choreography is a legible series of signs. Dance is the performative act and physical action on the basis of these signs, which gives them their meaning. The group takes this credo into account even in its name, after Albrecht Knust, a Laban collaborator who made singular contributions to the refining and widening of Labanotation and Laban-Kinetography. The group, made up of Dominique Brun, Anne Collod, Simon Hecquet, and Christophe Wavelet, worked with annotated scores for the first time in 1996 when they reconstructed dances by Kurt Jooss and Doris Humphrey.[8]

Between scientific objectification, which lies close to a semiological reading of dance writing, and its breakthrough to the unique and subjective experience of the dancer lies the tension that was the Albrecht Knust Quartet's project. Unfortunately, the group no longer exists. They still work in various configurations among themselves on reconstruction of works from original notation. In 2008, Anne Collod reconstructed Anna Halprin's 1965 *Parades & Changes* for the *Biennale de la danse* in Lyon. She dispensed with certain scenes fairly comfortably and set much of the piece to new music. Notation as a form of writing hence represented for the Albrecht Knust Quartet a friction, which the dancer must negotiate from both a dancerly and choreographic point of view. Because writing is not embodied, there remains a gap between notation and the dancing body. This gap forces decisions that invariably alter the sacrosanct original. The group, moreover, always refers back to discourse, because in a hermeneutic sense it makes the supplementation of cultural material necessary in coming to a decision on how to read the notation.

The third production of the Albrecht Knust Quartet . . . *of a Faun (Fragments)*, which premiered at the Centre Pompidou in Paris in the first decade of the 2000s, took this discourse as a jumping off point for its approach to Nijinsky's *L'Après-midi d'un faune* (*Afternoon of a Faun*). The production caused a controversy after its premiere, two different opinions about its merits and deficits are documented in the reviews by Isabelle Ginot and René Sirvin (2000). Like an archaeologist stripping away the secrets of a rock formation one delicate layer at a time, each turn of their production revealed new possibilities that altered what *Faun* could have been and could be. Nijinsky's notation language was original to him and dates back to 1915. Of particular interest is that Claudia Jeschke and Ann Hutchinson Guest deciphered this language and transposed it into Labanotation. The group came to a preliminary decision about what to treat as "original," namely the Laban transcription, not the Nijinsky notation. Jeschke and Guest for their part certainly had to make choices as they transposed Nijinsky-code into Laban-code, which no doubt had implications for the preservation of the original. Apart from that, there were various stages of development of Stéphane Mallarmé's similarly titled 1867 poem, which served as inspiration for Claude Debussy's score *Prélude à l'après-midi d'un faune* (*Prelude to the Afternoon of a Faun*), just as the sepia-toned photographs from the albums of photographs taken by Adolf de Meyer decidedly impact our memory of Nijinsky's piece (Nectoux and Jeschke 1989). So what did the "real" *Faun* look like?

What the Albrecht Knust Quartet thematizes with its *Faun (Fragments)* is the loss of certainty, along with its flip side, the production of new possibilities. In many ways, the performance stages the dispossession of the original. To underline the composite and fragmented nature of our image of the *Faun*, the Albrecht Knust Quartet makes use of various strategies of withdrawal. The absence of a definitive version of *Faun*, which is not performed in its entirety until the very end of the production, refers to the discourse that

---

[8]  On their work, see Launay (2012).

has instilled this legendary work into our cultural memory. The performance begins with an act of focusing and attention to detail. Four couples enter the empty stage, one after another. One of each pair leaves for a newcomer to take his or her place. Over the course of this relay, we see a specific touch mentioned in the notation four times: the Faun and the Main Nymph touch elbow to underarm. It is in fact the only touch that the notation specifies. Yet we see this movement being performed between four pairs and not one, and between pairs mixed variously according to gender, which the notation does not specify. They all wear everyday clothing and black boots. At the end of the scene, a row of lights blinds the audience while the curtain falls over the dark stage. The voice of a woman, Nijinsky's wife Romola, can be heard, speaking of her late husband. The widow laments that the vestiges of the man are not the man. The announcement displayed on the curtain seems empathetic: "For something to take place" (À ce que quelque chose soit). In order for something to appear, the seven dancers withdraw themselves paradoxically from the sight of the audience. With arms raised as if at the final bow, they retreat upstage while excerpts from Mallarmé's sketchbook about the death of his son, Anatole, appear on a gauze curtain. The loss of the original, claimed by the darkness of the theater, where the traces of history are cobbled together, is expressed in the biographical loss of the people who are related to the coming into existence of Nijinsky's historic performance.

After all this, a dancer recounts the proudest moment in his career. Following him, two dancers argue about the proper placement of the arms and legs, during which they remember an exhibition of Greek vases. They seek to reconstruct the poses featured in the illustrations from memory. Films are shown. In a short clip, we see prima ballerina Tamara Karsavina backstage at the Ballets Russes sinking into a couch in exhaustion after a performance. Another clip shows a burlesque take on the *Faun* from a Jean Renoir film, and a third shows sculptor Auguste Rodin's written defense of the piece *The Renewal of Dance*, in response to its scandalous 1912 premiere. This third clip follows the only integration of orchestral music into the piece, achieving the effect of a time jump. It is as if Rodin is defending not the premiere, but the performance that the audience has just witnessed, which seems to have been projected back into the year 1912. Between the film clips, we are seeing fragments of movement, gestures, and poses from the piece, sometimes upstage, sometimes in close-up, sometimes without music, and sometimes with keyboard accompaniment. Thus the monolithic original is pulverized into a series of sequences that move fluidly between then and there, here and now, liberating it from its master and creator and opening it up as a catalyst for innovation. The appeal of the show almost lies in its casual, non-dramatic demeanor, more a condensed node of all the preceding experiences of working on it, a preliminary, tentative outcome, which in no way limits the many opportunities to draw new meaning into the work.

Today it is the audience who is tasked with supplying new perspectives for and perceptions of the work. The three groups and artists I have introduced use affect, technique, and discourse not to guarantee that reconstruction stays faithful to its source material, but rather appeal to an affective relationality to dissolve their traditional framework and rearrange them with relation to one another. They have shown through this project how history can be understood as production, which occurs between the active appropriation of sources and the passive surrender to transformative affect.

# Confronting the Unattainable

At the beginning of this chapter I spoke about reenactment as a confrontation with impossibilities inherent in dealing with dance history. Despite this, reenactment has become an ubiquitous phenomenon. Does this observation suggest that reenactment and the attention it has generated over the past twenty-five years may be read as a symptom of the changing and uncertain position of the artist in contemporary mediated culture? The impossibilities of history thus speak of the impossibilities of today. This hypothesis could lead us in two directions. The first is to reveal a deep-rooted nostalgia for the lost possibilities of dance. The advent of the new contemporary dance scene around the turn of the century, with all its critical impulses, was welcomed as an emancipatory gesture of dance artists. Contemporary dancers realized that with the dance boom of the 1970s came a radical alteration of dance styles and languages that nevertheless left unchanged the hierarchical company structure under the leadership of a choreographer. Thinking about one's own actions, as well as the power structures and mechanisms of exclusion in dance companies, as Xavier Le Roy's lecture performance *Product of Circumstance* (1999) demonstrated, led to a suspension of traditional dance forms. Yet, to acknowledge that to dance as in the 1970s is for political reasons no longer an option for an emancipated dancer does not extinguish the desire to want precisely that impossibility. Jérôme Bel's *Le Dernier spectacle* is an example of how the quotation consigns to the past a desire to dance with the "soul" or "energy" that is articulated within the Linke phrase, a past in which such a dance was still possible. Reenactment becomes a ruse to still be able to engage with lost desires, options, and possibilities.

The second direction correlates with this finding. Dirk Baecker, German sociologist and student of Niklas Luhman, has recently outlined a different variation on this same idea (Baecker 2013). According to him, the digital revolution of the past twenty years, not unlike the printing press earlier in the modern era, represents an epochal turning point in the production and transmission of cultural knowledge. Each new medium— yesterday the book and today the computer—initially brings with it an information overload, which societies or communities fail to retrieve or master. The seemingly endless space for information that the Internet provides, for economic reasons as well, means that no piece of data need ever be lost again, that forgetting is indeed a thing of the past. Against this background emerges art, and in particular theater, as the nominal exception, proving itself a means of reexamining the cluttered accumulations of knowledge in our new mediated circumstances. Dance, and thus theater in general, asks the questions of what ultimately still speaks to us today, how it does so, and what affects it elicits.

> Theater's social function lies in its ability to, unlike any other social form, both demonstrate and challenge second order observation. Performers on stage are allowing the audience to observe them, but as they play out drama, intrigue, and comedy, they are ultimately demonstrating a process of mutual observation with the audience . . . and that Theater, which we name the Theater of Tomorrow to befit the oncoming "next iteration" of society, is no longer populated only with people in

their roles, but bodies, memories, hopes, lights, spaces, and gestures, which themselves engage in observation, are engaged by observation, and induce certain effects. (Baecker 2013, 7)

Reenactment is such an experiment, seeking to create new forms of physical communication. Affect, technique, and discourse offer ways of playfully probing which among the multitude of forms and positions recorded in dance history remain meaningful, and which, on the other hand, we can wistfully allow ourselves to forget.

Translated from the German by Alessio Franko

## WORKS CITED

Assmann, Jan. 2011. *Cultural Memory and Early Civilization: Writing, Remembrance, and Political Imagination*. New York: Cambridge University Press.

Assmann, Aleida. 2012. *Cultural Memory and Western Civilization: Arts of Memory*. New York: Cambridge University Press.

Baecker, Dirk. 2013. *Wozu Theater?* Berlin: Theater der Zeit Verlag.

Bleeker, Maaike. 2012. "(Un)Covering Artistic Thought Unfolding." *Dance Research Journal* 44(2) (Winter): 13–28.

Brandstetter, Gabriele, and Sybille Peters. 2002. *De figura. Rhetorik—Bewegung—Gestalt*, 7–24. München: Wilhelm Fink Verlag.

Brandstetter, Gabriele, and Hortensia Völckers. 2000. *ReMembering the Body. Körperbilder in Bewegung*. Ostfildern: Hatje Cantz Verlag.

Deleuze, Gilles. 1988. *Spinoza: Practical Philosophy*. San Francisco: City Lights Books.

Ginot, Isabelle, and René Sirvin. 2000. "'… d'un faune (éclats)' von Quatuor Albrecht Knust in Paris." In *Ballet International Tanz Aktuell* 4: 46–50. Berlin: Friedrich Verlag.

Houston, Lynn, and Cheryl Tobey. 2001. "Bodies of History and Historical Legacy: Baryshnikov and the Judson Legacy." *Performing Arts Journal* 69: 13–23.

Launay, Isabelle. 2012. "Citational Poetics in Dance: … *of a Faun (Fragments)* by the Albrecht Knust Quartet, before and after 2000." *Dance Research Journal* 44(2) (Winter): 49–70.

Ménestrier, Claude-François. 1972. *Des Ballets anciens et modernes selon les règles du théâtre*. Geneva: Éditions Minkoff Reprint.

Nachbar, Martin. 2003. "ReKonstrukt." In *Moving Thoughts: Tanzen ist Denken*, edited by Janine Schulze and Susanne Traub, pp. 89–97, 95. Berlin: Vorwerk Verlag.

Nectoux, Jean-Michel, and Jeschke Claudia. 1989. *Mallarmé-Debussy-Nijinskij-De Meyer. Nachmittag eines Fauns. Dokumentation einer legendären Choreographie*. München: Schirmer und Moesel.

Schneider, Rebecca. 2005. "Solo Solo Solo." In *After Criticism? New Responses to Contemporary Art*, edited by Gavin Butt, 23–47. Oxford: Blackwell.

Siegmund, Gerald. 2003. "Tanz als Bewegung in der Geschichte." *Die Deutsche Bühne* 74: 42–45.

Siegmund, Gerald. 2004. *William Forsythe—Denken in Bewegung*. Berlin: Henschel Verlag.

Siegmund, Gerald. 2006. *Abwesenheit. Eine performative Ästhetik des Tanzes. William Forsythe. Jérôme Bel, Xavier Le Roy, Meg Stuart*, Bielefeld: Transcript Verlag.

Siegmund, Gerald. 2012. "Negotiating Choreography, Letter, and Law in William Forsythe." In *New German Dance Studies*, edited by Susan Manning and Lucia Ruprecht, 200–216. Urbana, Chicago, and Springfield: University of Illinois Press.

Spinoza, Benedict de. 1996. *Ethics*. Edited and translated by Ewin Curley, with an introduction by Stuart Hampshire. London and New York: Penguin.

Sulcas, Roslyn, 1995. "Kinetic Isometries." *Dance International* 2: 4–9.

Žižek, Slavoj. [2004] 2012. *Organs without Bodies: On Deleuze and Consequences*. New York and London: Routledge.

.......................................................................................

# CHAPTER 24

# EPILOGUE TO AN EPILOGUE

## *Historicizing the Re- in Danced Reenactment*

.......................................................................................

### MARK FRANKO

A movement always seems to condition the production of a space and to associate it with a history.

—Michel de Certeau (*The Practice of Everyday Life*, 118)

I want to ask whether the current phenomenon of danced reenactment is the return *to*, or the return *of*, a phenomenon that emerged between twenty and thirty years ago in the 1980s and early 1990s.[1] In 1989, I called it reinvention or *construction* (purposively opposed to "reconstruction") in "Repeatability, Reconstruction, and Beyond," which later became the "Epilogue" to *Dance as Text*.[2] As I understood it then, reinvention abandoned the quest for historical authenticity by staging multiple temporalities related to disparate historical moments put into dialogue with one other. Between 1984 and 1991, I worked through this idea in performances.[3] My dual identity as scholar and artist at that time was perplexing (if not vexing) to a number of dance critics and academics.[4]

---

[1] I wish to thank Branislav Jacovlevjic for organizing the mini-conference "Regarding Re-: Reconstruction, Reperformance, Research" at the Humanities Center of Stanford University (February 17–18, 2012), which motivated me to return to this theme.

[2] "Repeatability, Reconstruction and Beyond," in *Theatre Journal* 41(1) (March 1989): 56–74. This article was also published in French translation as "Reproduction, reconstruction et par-delà" in *Degrés* 63 (Fall 1990): 1–18. See also "Epilogue" in Mark Franko, *Dance as Text: Ideologies of the Baroque Body* (New York: Oxford University Press, 2015): 131–151.

[3] This work began in 1985 with *Renaissance Constructions* and continued with *Harmony of the Spheres* (1986), *Le Marbre Tremble* (1988), and *Characters of Dance* (1990).

[4] Between 1983 and 1990 I was an assistant professor of French at Princeton University and the director of a professional dance company, NovAntiqua, in New York City.

Acting as both a scholar and a choreographer was viewed as anomalous both by academe and in the dance world.

I draw upon the example of myself as a precursor to what might be called the dancer's *dual emplacement* as practiced today, which has since become an intentional and strategic feature consciously assumed and theatricalized in many danced reenactments. Dual emplacement is noticeable in recent lecture performances in which the dancer playfully but still seriously assumes the role of pedagogue, historian, and theorist speaking outside the academy on stage, or bringing the academy onto the stage. But dual emplacement is also evident in the space of the stage itself when conceived as an "archival" space, that is, a space interwoven with the theatrical interactions of a contemporary dancer's body with historical documents (films, oral history, texts) and memories testifying to the absent presence of a past dancer and/or a past dance work.

Danced reenactment is characterized in part by the staging of the documentary evidence of a dance, which comes to an admission that the past work cannot simply reappear without the research work sharing the space and time of performance with the reconstructed work(s). The dancer's work, in other words, is no longer exclusively that of dancing, but also that of recovering (in its double meaning of unveiling and covering up again) traces (clues), following indications (leads), constituting background (texture). I call it "work" because it is integrated into the performance. These two forms of work— the work of dance and the work of research—constitute together the poetic structure of reenactment. It is to the poetics of space and time that I wish to attend in this chapter. In my case study, Martin Nachbar's *Urheben Aufheben*, it is the search for traces, the idea of tracing, and finally, the trace form that emerges as containing the poetic structure of reenactment.

The idea of movement as the *trace form* of an absent past is resonant with poststructuralist notions of writing and citation,[5] as well as with phenomena of recording from the notation score to film and motion capture, but is actually taken from the terminology of Rudolf Laban, who also referred to it as a "scribble."[6] Contemporary danced reenactment works toward the idea that documented choreography—even fragmentarily documented—can be reanimated in space as a volumetric trace. There is a fundamental difference, however, between the uses of a trace form and citation, properly speaking. Part of the purpose of this chapter is to outline these differences because the trace form is pertinent to what we mean by danced reenactment. It is important to bear in mind that the trace—like a handprint—is an indexical remainder of an absent presence. By

---

[5]  As is well known, Jacques Derrida has assimilated writing to the trace. In *Of Grammatology* (Baltimore: Johns Hopkins University Press, 1976). Derrida designates as "écriture" everything that can give rise to an inscription, including choreography (9). Hence, poststructuralist thinking is relevant not only to a post-humanist dance, but makes a comeback in the context of reenactment where the citation of a past work assumes the shape of the trace rather than the shape of the Mallarméan poetic image. This new reinvestment in the trace suggests a decisive break between the notion of image and that of choreography.

[6]  I borrow the term "trace form" from Rudolf Laban's *Choreutics* annotated and edited by Lisa Ullmann (London: Macdonald and Evans, 1966), 83.

filling it in, reanimating it as if by placing a hand in a glove, which is the trace of a missing outfit, reenactment achieves its strange amalgam of distance and proximity, whole and fragment, recognition and misrecognition.

On the program cover of Nachbar's *Urheben Aufheben* one sees a photo of Nachbar's face as overleaf to a photo of Dore Hoyer, whose work he is reperforming. Regarding the idea of a trace form, one might identify the smile on both faces as the common trace out of which one performer might fill in and occupy the absent presence of the other. Although the faces are quite different, the line traced by smiling lips of both figures is quite similar (Figures 24.1 and 24.2). That is, the trace form indicates the mark of a common identity that, having to do with shape, line, and physiognomy, is analogous to the choreographic trace of a dance based in the elementary notion of a physical analog. It will be developed into an order of choreographic places.[7]

But, back to my first question: What is reenactment as a contemporary dance phenomenon a reenactment of? Rather than argue that history is repeating itself, I ask what relationship contemporary reenactment bears to the cognate activity of the 1980s, a decade that has frequently been associated with the phenomenon of postmodernism in art and architecture, the baroque music revival and its debates over historical performance practice, and deconstruction in philosophy.[8] The contemporary phenomenon of reenactment begs the question of its own historical contextualization.

## SITUATION OF THE 1980S

In the 1980s there were, as far as I can tell, at least three historicizing modes. First, there were reconstructions of early twentieth-century dance modernism (Duncan, Schlemmer, Wigman, Hoyer), which were paradoxically anti-modernist in that they cast the canonical dance modernists in a deliberately historical light by daring to reperform work until then believed to be so unique to the creator as to be unthinkable apart from the creator's body.[9] Reconstructions of early modernists thus violated the ideologically determined identity of the modern artist as inimitable. Still, the specter haunting the reconstruction of modernism was artist impersonation: the tautology, for example, of Duncan's illusory presence emerging fitfully in Annabelle Gamson's performances. Contemporary danced reenactment seems, on the other hand, to reject impersonation. It stages the uncanny return of the dance work. The very fact that reenactment de-personates the artist in the act of performance opens the way for a visualization of *the*

---

[7] I am indebted to Frances Yates (1966) for this terminology.

[8] The locus classicus of this moment was, of course, Charles Jencks, *What Is Postmodernism?* (New York: St. Martin's Press, 1986).

[9] This point was made by Isabelle Launay in her "Citational Poetics in Dance: . . . *of a Faun (Fragments)* by the Albert Knust Quartet, before and after 2000," *Dance Research Journal* 44(2) (Winter): 49–70, and discussed in Chapter 23 in this volume.

**FIGURE 24.1.** Dore Hoyer on the cover of program booklet for *Urheben Aufheben* (Berlin, 2008). Photographer unknown.

**FIGURE 24.2.** Martin Nachbar on the cover of program booklet for *Urheben Aufheben* (Berlin, 2008).

*work*, as distinct from the myth of the artist.[10] To return to the modernists of the earlier twentieth century was also to make new discoveries (for example, Schlemmer, whose contribution to dance was entirely unknown before Debra McCall's reconstruction of the *Bauhaus Dance*) and/or to see work whose presence in history had to be taken on faith (as in the case of Isadora Duncan or Mary Wigman).[11] In all these cases, the effect was to reevaluate and expand upon the canon.

Alongside reconstructions of modernist dance in the 1980s was the revival by dancers and reconstructors of renaissance and baroque dance, which is where the authenticity debate became particularly virulent.[12] Was the reconstruction of dance that had never been filmed a realistic goal or a mirage? Of course, there was a notation system as of 1701, but its code was only effectively cracked in the 1980s by Francine Lancelot, who was working with dancers who quickly became engaged in playing with the historical sources (this was the case with François Raffinot, for example).[13] It is in the baroque arena that the bifurcation between reconstruction and something else—what we could call reinvention or construction—was the most striking. In French postmodern dance during the 1980s, references to the baroque were almost *de rigueur*.

I polemicized my performance work during that period to dramatize the unrecognized modernity of historical movement, and to wrest contemporary dance from the tyranny of the contemporary. Reinvention included a critical reflection on the hegemony of the contemporary and the displacement of invention to a forgotten past, aiming to decenter the grand narratives of dance history. My aim was to deconstruct in choreography itself the idea according to which dance progresses in a linear fashion toward the future. To be against authenticity was not only to be against the idea of progress fundamental to modernism, but also to be against reconstruction as an antiquarian endeavor, that is, against the reproduction of movement as a museum artifact. As the aesthetician Guy Scarpetta wrote in 1985,

> I am not going back to the baroque, I am not turning back toward it, the Baroque is before me (*"je vais au-devant"*), I am entering into it. As if the historical linearity had been turned inside out, redistributed. This is, perhaps, the only possible meaning for me of the postmodern attitude: to realize that invention does not necessarily coincide with the negation of the past, and that the production of the new is not

[10] Maaike Bleeker has related the resistance to dance as object with the resistance to the dance work. She proposes, in lieu of the making present of the artist, the rendering of artistic thought embodied in the work of the artist. See her Chapter 10 in this volume.

[11] Susan Manning made the point, in her *Ecstasy and the Demon*, that Wigman had been written out of twentieth-century dance history as anything more than a footnote. Throughout the 1960s, Isadora Duncan was no longer considered to be a generative force behind contemporary dance, which made the reconstructions of her work in the early 1970s particularly revelatory.

[12] This was initially the case with music for which the context was the baroque music revival. See Laurence Dreyfus, "Early Music Defended against Its Devotees: A Theory of Historical Performance in the Twentieth Century," *The Musical Quarterly* LXIX(3) (Summer 1983): 297–322.

[13] Catherine Turocy's productions for the New York Baroque Dance Company were also influential in France in the early 1980s.

necessarily bereft of memory . . . . It is not about going backwards . . . but about rewriting history, otherwise. (Scarpetta 1985, 358)[14]

Dance studies itself, which also aspires to rewrite history, was launched during what I would like to call the baroque decade of choreography. It is worth noting that many contemporary dance re-enactors belong to a generation for which dance studies and the project to rewrite history are not foreign.

It was the premise of reinvention to posit that there is no original authentic work to reconstruct. This squared well with Derrida's critique of full presence, the voice, and originarity, which he offset with *différance*, writing, and the trace. They were useful in resisting misguided concepts of authenticity (Franko 2014). But more useful today with respect to reenactment is Derrida's *Archive Fever* (1993). The authenticity debate that took place around historical performance practice *then* is not pertinent to reenactment *now*; for it was from such questions that alternatives to reconstruction first arose thirty years ago.[15] Hence, the methodology of reconstruction itself can be salvaged once it has been liberated from the ideological baggage of the repeatability of the original. The question of authenticity has been displaced by the question of the archive.

## BEYOND IMPERSONATION: THE BAROQUE AS ANTI-MODERN

The sensibility of the baroque in a postmodern context was to unmoor movement possibilities from chronological narratives and also to uncover alternatives that had been suppressed or passed over by history, as well as lost to memory. Scarpetta cited Pier Paolo Pasolini, who believed there was a subversive potential in the historical past. "Let us revisit what has been repressed, denied, misrecognized, condemned in the name of 'progress': let us enter the Baroque" (Scarpetta, 359). If one is neither impersonating an earlier artist nor reconstructing a particular work, it is not hard to imagine how this could be the case.

The field of historical dance differed from the reconstruction of modernism in that the starting point could not be the impersonation or refusal to impersonate key personalities. One underlying question, therefore, was how to render historical dance theatrically viable. Within this context, baroque dance in particular expanded beyond apparently arcane concerns and effectively intervened in the contemporary choreographic scene. So, for example, Rudolf Nureyev decided he would like to perform baroque dance in

---

[14] The whole question of the entanglement of postmodernism with the baroque in the 1980s is beyond the scope of this chapter and demands a separate development.

[15] Amelia Jones privileges this question in her recent discussion of Marina Abramović's re-performances. See "'The Artist is Present': Artistic Re-enactments and the Impossibility of Presence," in *TDR: The Drama Review* 55(1) (T209) Spring 2011: 16–45.

1983 after he saw Francine Lancelot's *Rameau l'enchanteur*. This led to a training period with Lancelot, followed by their collaboration on *Bach Suite* (1984), in which they demonstrate certain continuities between baroque dance and modernism.

So, I would consider baroque dance reinvention and its offshoots to be the third emergent trend of the 1980s in which choreographic postmodernism and deconstruction assumed a more overtly postmodern discourse in the work of Forsythe, Morris, Bagouet, Franko, Kilian, Kelly, and others than did reconstruction (Franko 2010). Although this tendency could be dismissed as pastiche, it implies nonetheless that baroque dance reconstruction, in and of itself, was radically different enough from mainstream forms of stage dance to qualify in its own right as subversive (Franko 2007).

Although I dealt primarily with historical dance in the "Epilogue," the first example I cited was actually an example of the first type of activity, the reconstruction of dance modernism. It was Susanne Linke's *Hommage to Dore Hoyer*, which I was fortunate to see in 1988 while attending the Essen conference "Beyond Performance: Dance Scholarship Today," a conference that referenced the first Dancers's Congress held in Essen in 1928. Linke's performance was far from a conventional reconstruction. She was reperforming Dore Hoyer's *Affectos Humanos* cycle (1962), based on the 1967 film shot slightly before the choreographer's death. The Hoyer solos might almost seem today paradigmatic for danced reenactment, not only because, after Linke, they continued to be reperformed by others—Arila Siegert in East Germany[16] and Martin Nachbar in Berlin—but also because Linke was perhaps the first to create a clear distinction between reconstruction and reenactment. She did this by changing costumes for the different solos before the audience (a rack of costumes was on the stage). Hence, she went in and out of the dances in full sight of the audience, which also meant in and out of the historical representation that the reconstruction proposed. With this distancing gesture, Linke prefigured contemporary reenactment. Linke did not impose an illusion of the past; rather, she made us aware that we were with her in the present as she rearticulated the choreography before our eyes. I wrote at the time: "[S]he [Linke] established a distance between herself and the artist whose work was to be reconstructed" (Franko 1989, 56).

# DIFFERENCE/DISTANCE

Distance contains more than a present encountering a past or a representation of the past with a sense of incomprehension. Distance can be used to avoid embarrassment or to disavow deep attraction. As such, distance becomes structured in the multiple temporalities of the failed encounter that constitutes any visit to the archive: it takes the shape of research. *Urheben Aufheben* makes research the material of the reperformance

[16] See the important discussion by Jens Richard Giersdorf of Siegert's work in relation to the other attempts to reconstruct Hoyer's work—notably those of Linke and Nachbar—in his book *The Body of the People: East German Dance since 1945* (Madison: University of Wisconsin Press, 2013), 97–110.

**FIGURE 24.3.** Martin Nachbar before the blackboard in *Urheben Aufheben* (Berlin, 2008).

Photo: Gerhad Ludwig.

by framing the dances themselves with a didactic lecture—taking place quite literally before a blackboard—on the reconstructive process and its circumstances (Figure 24.3). Nachbar subtitles the piece *An Experiment on Myself* (*Ein Selbstversuch*) in the archive. The first traces he works with are those made with chalk on the blackboard, in an attempt to describe his "relationship" with Hoyer through a series of dates and archival encounters. His lecture becomes a labyrinthine description of *hetero-temporalities* marked on the blackboard.[17] He found the film of Hoyer's dances by chance in 1999 in a Brussels library; the film was shot in 1967; the dance was created in 1962; Hoyer was born in 1911, Nachbar in 1971. When he found the tape he was twenty-nine; now he is thirty-nine, and so forth. But, significantly, he concludes these notations by drawing the outline of his own shoulders and head on the blackboard. The trace of the chalk marks thus links self-reference to reference (the reference to the other), links writing to trace form, and links research to self-discovery (an experiment on myself). The self-tracing—Nachbar drawing the outline of his own upper body on the blackboard, imprinting the outline of his body as another archival text or imprint—mediates between his own physical presence and the didactic narrative account of his discovery of Hoyer, allowing for the possibility that self-reference can become reference.

[17]  I borrow the term "hetero-temporal" from Dipesh Chakrabarty, *Provincializing Europe: Postcolonial Thought and Historical Difference* (Princeton, NJ: Princeton University Press, 2000), xvii. I thank Fabián Barba for bringing the book to my attention.

Like Linke before him, Nachbar undertook to reperform the five Hoyer solos from the 1967 film to the music of Dimitri Wiatowitsch.[18] This cycle was the last gasp of postwar *Ausdruckstanz*; Hoyer was a student of Wigman and Gret Palucca, and the only remaining postwar exponent of the form still performing as a soloist in Germany. However, the fact that Wigman herself survived World War II and continued to teach in Germany through the 1950s and 1960s (she lived until 1973) also meant that at the start of the twenty-first century there were aging dancers who were able to transmit Hoyer's (and Wigman's) movement principles to those born after the death of Wigman and Hoyer (the latter committed suicide in 1967). It was not a question of simply copying the film. Nachbar sought out the custodian of Hoyer's work, Waltraud Luley, to coach him on the solos, and something of these sessions is retained—archived, if you will—in *Urheben Aufheben*.

## TRANSLATION AND HISTORY

Reperforming Hoyer in 2008, Nachbar is cognizant that *Affectos Humanos* had no place on the German stage at the time of its premiere in 1962 (although it did continue to be taught in the studio). Like a historian, Nachbar moves through the archive in his own present, while being mindful of the past this archive has thus far failed to authorize. We are put in mind of Susan Leigh Foster's remarks on the relation of the dancer to the historian: "Yes, the historian also has a body, has sex, gender, sexuality, skin color. And this body has a past, more or less privileged, more or less restricted. The historian's body wants to consort with dead bodies" (Foster 1995, 6). This said, the dancer does not necessarily want to consort with the historian. Nachbar has an adversarial relationship to dance history. His point of view is that dancers have a voice and a say in their own history.

The temporalities of the histories of two distinct subjects, of two incommensurable historical subjectivities, become adumbrated. He found the video on a shelf. Nachbar explains that he "had a kind of shelf of his own with him, full of habits, techniques, sensations, experiences, desires, fulfilled and unfulfilled . . . all stored in his body."[19] Yet, reenactment is here the site of an encounter between two dissymmetrical pasts. Again, distance is accentuated: "Hoyer does not equal Nachbar . . . Nachbar . . . always already had a past, with which he met the past in [the] form of the *Affectos Humanos*." We can note the negativity of this statement: Nachbar is not Hoyer. He comes "*nach*" (after). He is belated, but also related: a neighbor (the meaning of the term "Nachbar" in German).

---

[18] For more information on this work, see Hedwig Müller, Frank-Manuel Peter, and Garnet Schuldt, *Dore Hoyer. Tänzerin* (Köln: Hentrich, 1992), 193–216.

[19] I am quoting here from the English version of Nachbar's unpublished script for *Urheben Aufheben* (n.d., n.p.). In the piece, Nachbar speaks of himself in the third person. I wish to thank Martin Nachbar for making this script available to me.

However belated or neighborly, Nachbar nevertheless establishes his own identity on the basis of a negation, as if saying: "I am not she." One history confronts another history, and keeps its distance.

The archive will henceforth be a site of *translation*: translation from one body to another, from the body of one gender to that of another gender, from one technique to another, from one convention of performing to another, from one set of traces to another. Nachbar explains that his training in release technique was wholly inadequate to the interpretation of Hoyer's movement. There are many instances in which he is clearly far from Hoyer's execution, and he does not attempt to conceal this by altering the choreography in any way.

Translation, as Derrida reminds us, is part of the archive's trouble. (The literal translation of *Mal d'archive* is not archive *fever*, but archive *trouble*.) " . . . [T]he archive always holds a problem for translation. With the irreplaceable singularity of a document to interpret, to repeat, to reproduce, but each time in its original uniqueness, an archive ought to be idiomatic, and thus at once offered and unavailable for translation, open to and shielded from technical iteration and reproduction." [20] As Vanessa Agnew has remarked in a different context, "Paradoxically, it is the very a-historicity of reenactment that is the precondition for its engagements with historical subject matter" (Agnew 2010, 328). It is true that danced reenactment asserts the non-correspondence of two times, two histories, two mentalities. It is by insisting on the degree of this difference, carried to the level of negation, that the primacy of space in reenactment comes to the fore.

It is within space that we find the trace form. The use of space particular to choreography as an "order of places" is the activity though which mutually exclusive temporalites can be brought into alignment.[21] As noted in opening quote of this chapter, Michel de Certeau made a similar connection between movement, space, and history: "A movement always seems to condition the production of a space and to associate it with a history" (1984, 118). If we extend movement to choreography—ordered movement—this would suggest that choreography is structured itself as a memory image, that is, as an order of places where memory images can be stored and from which they can be retrieved.

---

[20] "L'archive réserve toujours un problème de traduction. Singularité irremplaçable d'un document à interpréter, à répéter, à reproduire, mais chaque fois dans son unicité originale, une archive se doit d'être idiomatique, et donc à la fois offerte et dérobée à la traduction." Jacques Derrida. *Archive Fever: A Freudian Impression*. Translated by Eric Prenowitz (Chicago and London: University of Chicago Press, 1998), 90; *Mal d'archive. Une impression freudienne* (Paris: Galilée, 1995), 141.

[21] Frances A. Yates (1966) discusses the ancient art of memory or the "mnemonic of places and images" as developed by ancient rhetoric. According to this art, images of things to be remembered were mentally stored in memorized architectural sites, which could be revisited. This suggests that the archive itself, as Nachbar evokes it, is not a storeroom per se but an architectural site, an imagined place with distinct spatial relationships and characteristics. To the degree that choreographic order is also generative of place—is itself architectural—choreography could be understood as a site of memory. While there is much discussion of how dancers remember choreography, it is possible that choreography itself holds certain keys to memory.

# SPACE, PLACE, AND CONTIGUITY

Unlike the reenactment of historical events that depends upon the exact location of the original event, a danced reenactment often does not take place in situ. The vocabulary elements of Hoyer's work as Nachbar's body begins to inhabit them are imagined to preexist in (the) space, always already inscribed there, left there as it were, and thus susceptible of being refound (literally picked up from the ground and put on like clothing) in and thanks to the very exteriority of that space. Dance therefore displays a phenomenon of contiguity, rather than continuity. Nachbar relates "chalk traces on the blackboard" to

> . . . traces in my memory, in my body and maybe even in space. (Nachbar walks into space). And I don't just mean our projected memories, but that the movement has really cut tunnels into the air, which are connecting to the tunnels of the running in the first step and with the tunnels of the rehearsals and with the tunnels of anything that has ever been performed or rehearsed in this space, all engraved upon it, so that space becomes one big memory space. (Nachbar, "Urheben Aufheben," n.d, n.p.)

Movement is, in other words, a manner of inhabiting space, and reciprocally, traces of the space that has been inhabited by movement cling to movement itself. For Henri Lefebvre, space should not be considered as a container and the body as contained: "[E]ach living body *is* space and *has* its space: it produces itself in space and it also produces that space" (Lefebvre 1994, 170). This was further developed by Michel de Certeau, who wrote, "Space occurs as the effect produced by the operations that orient it, situate it, temporalize it . . ." (1984, 117). De Certeau, in fact, distinguished between space (*espace*) and place (*lieu*): "Space is a practiced place" (1984, 117). Danced reenactment is the event of the recalling the presence of a place as a historical reality, contiguous with other absent historical actions.

Of course, what we see in this body-space of historicity never stands monumentally revealed: Nachbar calls it a "fugitive oscillation."[22] As Michel de Certeau wrote, "Places are fragmentary and inward-turning histories, pasts that others are not allowed to read, accumulated times that can be unfolded but like stories held in reserve . . ." (1984, 108). What is historical is not the body itself, but the impressions on the space produced by the body's former actions, which the present body retrieves.

Nachbar reconceptualizes the reconstructive project as an attempt to locate spatial contiguity within two asymmetrical temporal series. Hetero-temporalities coexist through homo-spatialities. Nachbar also acts out the reconstructive process metaphorically as a lifting of movement from the ground (he reminds us that *Aufheben* means not

---

[22] "The expression emerged from in between her body and the space around it—a kind of fugitive oscillation rather than a monumental position." Martin Nachbar, "Training Remembering" in *Dance Research Journal* 44(2) (Winter 2012): 5–11.

only "to suspend" but also "to pick up"). This act of lifting movement from the place of the ground beneath him is significant to the notion of archival space, as opposed to the impressionistic quality of memory, and it iterates in space the conceit of trace marks of the body's outlines on the blackboard. Nachbar progresses from the trace marks on the blackboard to movement traces in three-dimensional space. As there are two types of traces, there are two types of breaking into the archive: the flat space of the board and the voluminous space of the stage. Through this playing between two and three dimensions, as between lecturing and dancing, so-called tunnels between writing, the archive, and action are materially suggested.

The multiple temporalities constituting the non-correspondence of two historical subjects—Hoyer and Nachbar—become transformed into the single quest of one subject—Nachbar—to "enter the archive," which means entering into a precise space that Hoyer first articulated in and as movement. The theater, the stage, stands for that space in which the dance is to be found (logically enough): in other words, the stage stands outside of time, but is poised as such to host the traces of movement deposited in/on itself as if in an archive. The stage may be a magical place, but it is also a theoretical archive, a place in which the act of research will be carried out. Yet, it seems to me that, if we leave aside for a moment the stage as metaphor for the archive, the relation of choreography to memory images and the spatial environments brought into being by those images are where the effective archive resides.

Were we to consider the sort of "time space" that Nachbar's dramaturgy evokes, it might be helpful to think about Bakhtin's notion of the chronotope (Bakhtin 1981).[23] In his "Forms of Time and Chronotope in the Novel," Bakhtin's object of study is literature, but the chronotope can also be directed toward "the process of assimilating real historical time and space" in dance (1981, 83). As we have indicated, Nachbar's lecture performance portrays neither Hoyer nor himself in what Bakhtin would call either biographical or autobiographical time (116). The virtual encounters and parallelism of dates are fragmented and, in this sense, the lecture is mock serious (when I saw the performance, it evoked bemused laughter). Because of the lecture format, *Urheben Aufheben* works through what I should like to call *the research chronotope*, in which time and space are painstakingly aligned so as to make a certain past apprehendable—nominally visible—in a certain present. This occurs through the *mise en scène* of what I evoked earlier as dual emplacement. Thus, two times are present: that of the research encounters noted on the blackboard and the lecture time itself, which comes to stand in for the time of a dance concert. The dances themselves, when he does finally dance them, constitute a third time whose status is precisely at issue here. And, multiple spaces are present: that of the figure at the blackboard, that of the stage, and the space of the archive, which is the most hypothetical space in that it is realized through a complex positioning of the dancer-lecturer in the space of the theater, which obtains an imaginative dimension as archival. Ultimately, the archive as a representational space does not exist: it is a

---

[23] I wish to thank Lior Avizoor for pointing out to me the relevancy of Bakhtin.

space that becomes visible through movements—movements Nachbar describes as a "pushing into":

> Now, what happens, if, I with my shelf life, go to the archive and take something out of it (like a video) and then don't just visit the memory space but try to push my body into it and at the same time, allow the memory to push itself into my body, so that the archive becomes visible through my body that becomes visible through the archive . . . . [24]

This pushing into could also be construed as the overlapping of trace forms in which the forms themselves become filled out, inhabited, in that one body "pushes itself" into the other, completing the trace form with a volumetric corporeality. The stage space thus becomes a virtual space in which the evidences of the lecture are then fed into the abstract space of the black box to engender a third dimension: an enactment of the traces of the past from which a full picture can show forth. This is what I would call the *research chronotope* of danced reenactment, which introduces the conceit that two-dimensional traces can become three-dimensional: writing can become performance, similarities can be "fleshed out," non-simultaneity can become simultaneous.

# THE QUESTION OF "THERE" AND THE PRODUCTION OF DISTANCE

The archive, in the dramaturgical terms that Nachbar's piece sets up, is neither an invisible corporeal site (one at a distance) nor a precise geographical location (one being represented on the stage), but the imaginary manifestation of a set of intersecting temporalities that converge as *place* in and through spatial practice. It is possible the dances themselves are the archives since Nachbar breaks into them with movement (i.e., by running backward). The backward run at the start of the work when he breaks into the archive (note here how space stands in for time in the trope of going backward) provides a double image: one of symbolic advance toward something left behind, and one of movement practice as warm-up for the act of recovery in movement. Nachbar's dramaturgy plays in this way between symbolism and theory, and this is why, as Jens Giersdorf has remarked, it is the dance scholar's dream or nightmare.[25] But his work demonstrates something further. The temporalities of reenactment are not fully congruent; instead, they create a gap, an irreconcilable interval that it is up to us to fill, based on the degree of knowledge we have of Hoyer and her work. This interval itself is the trace form mentioned earlier. How much the trace form can be filled in depends largely on the audience

---

[24]  Martin Nachbar, "*Urheben Aufheben*—English version," unpublished manuscript.

[25]  "Nachbar's lecture performances are a poststructuralist dance scholar's dream (or nightmare) because they hit all the right marks in current academic discourses that focus inward on disciplinary issues and aesthetics." Giersdorf, *The Body of the People*, 106.

and their prior knowledge. Hence, there is always a question of proximity and/or distance in what can become a publicly shared memory image. Here, let us recall Nachbar's negativity as distance, and his attraction as proximity.

Derrida's commentary on the word "distance" à propos of Nietzsche unites "dance" and "woman" in the German term *Distanz* (a word that includes dance, *Tanz*): distance pertains to the mechanism of (feminine) attraction: "A woman seduces from a distance. In fact, distance is the very element of her power." Derrida concludes: "A distance from distance must be maintained."[26] The gap or interval is this phenomenon of distance doubled (distance from distance) that simultaneously constitutes and negates attraction, that evokes an absent person and asserts a self as distinct from that person. In other words, there is something constitutive of dance in its own self-distancing.[27]

If past movement is available to be taken out of storage, as it were, *re-stored*, then reconstruction, which is always methodologically present in the sort of reenactment under discussion, is not a representation of the past, but its reinstitution as interval, its reproduction as simultaneously distance and proximity. It is in the spacing of the re-stored, dis-*tanz*, that place—inasmuch as it is constituted by movement through space but also inasmuch as movement through space constitutes it—bears witness to its own splitting. To restore is both to bring back to life and to put away again: to take out of storage is to actualize an abiding potential of space to restore place, but only as memory image.

Nachbar's pun on reenactment as "re-storing"—taking out and putting away are both meanings of *aufheben*—serves to remind us of another point Derrida makes: there is no such thing as a meta-archive (1998, 108). *Urheben Aufheben* belongs henceforth, and of necessity, to the Hoyer corpus; it thereby becomes part of Hoyer's archive. But, by this very fact, the archive is open to a future. Her choreography undergoes radical renewal in and by its re-storation. But, it is the future of what "will have been," as Slavoj Zizek pointed out in 1989, that reenactment may accomplish:

> The past exists as it is included, as it enters (into) the synchronous net of the signifier—that is, as it is symbolized in the texture of the historical memory—and this is why we are all the time "rewriting history," retroactively giving the elements their symbolic weight by including them in new textures—it is this elaboration which decides retroactively what they "will have been." (Zizek 1989, 56)

What Zizek points to here, or so it seems to me, is the dependency of history on action, the action of its own creation. Hence, it is always a future anterior.

---

[26] Jacques Derrida, *Spurs: Nietzsche's Styles*, translated by Barbara Harlow (Chicago: University of Chicago Press, 1979), 49. See André Lepecki's discussion of this passage in "Inscribing Dance," in *Of the Presence of the Body: Essays on Dance and Performance Theory* (Middletown, CT: Wesleyan University Press, 2004), 135.
[27] See related remarks on Nachbar Chapter 23 by Gerald Siegmund in this volume. If I am correct in following this lead, reenactment may have something important to tell us about dance itself as distancing.

# IN CONCLUSION: THE FUGITIVE
## OSCILLATION

As Nachbar has reflected, "The expression emerged from in between her [Hoyer's] body and the space around it—a kind of fugitive oscillation rather than a monumental position."[28] He provides us with another meaning of the interval as a certain irregularity or intermittency. Hoyer emerges when Nachbar *forgets* that he is Nachbar. This in-betweeness exists in a particular relation to space that is therefore, and somewhat paradoxically, an abiding potential of movement with respect to the space it engenders, inhabits, and is inhabited by. The multiple positionalities of space, time, and the body, as I have attempted to describe them here, are ultimately responsible for the simultaneity and non-simultaneity of pastness.

The dual emplacement of practice and theory with which I began on an autobiographical note is mirrored, but also continued and altered through time, not only in the theatrical setup of the lecture performance, but also in the strange and fitful encounter—riven by memory and forgetting—of two subjectivies in spatial negotiation at the archive. The pertinence of Derrida's question about the archive has perhaps come into new focus through this material. Although Derrida asserted that the archive must be located, he also asked, "How are we to think of *there*?"[29] Is not the question of the "there" the ultimate question of reenactment? And is not the question of reenactment the ultimate question of dance? In the light of the phenomenon of reenactment, the famous ephemerality of dance needs to be reconsidered—indeed, radically reconceptualized—as fitful movements in, with, and through (historical) space and time.

## WORKS CITED

Agnew, Vanessa. 2010. "Introduction: What Is Reenactment?" *Criticism* 46(3) (Summer): 327–339.

Bakhtin, M. M. 1981. "Forms of Time and Chronotope in the Novel." In *The Dialogic Imagination: Four Essays*, 84–258. Translated by Caryl Emerson and Michael Holquist. Austin: University of Texas Press.

Chakrabarty, Dipesh. 2000. *Provincializing Europe: Postcolonial Thought and Historical Difference*. Princeton, NJ: Princeton University Press.

De Certeau, Michel. 1984. *The Practice of Everyday Life*. Translated by Steven Rendall. Berkeley and Los Angeles: University of California Press.

Derrida, Jacques. 1976. *Of Grammatology*. Translated by Gayatri Spivak. Baltimore: Johns Hopkins University Press.

---

[28]  See Martin Nachbar, "Tracing Sense/Reading Sensation," Chapter 2 in this volume.
[29]  "Comment penser là?" Derrida, *Archive Fever*, 1; *Mal d'archive*, 11.

Derrida, Jacques. 1979. *Spurs: Nietzsche's Styles*. Translated by Barbara Harlow. Chicago: University of Chicago Press.

Derrida, Jacques. 1998. *Archive Fever: A Freudian Impression*. Translated by Eric Prenowitz. Chicago and London: University of Chicago Press.

Dreyfus, Laurence. 1983. "Early Music Defended against Its Devotees: A Theory of Historical Performance in the Twentieth Century." *The Musical Quarterly* LXIX(3) (Summer): 297–322.

Foster, Susan Leigh. 1995. "Choreographing History." In *Choreographing History*, 3–21. Bloomington and Indianapolis: University of Indiana Press.

Franko, Mark. 1989. "Repeatability, Reconstruction and Beyond." *Theatre Journal* 41(1) (March): 56–74.

Franko, Mark. [1993] 2015. *Dance as Text: Ideologies of the Baroque Body*. New York: Oxford University Press.

Franko, Mark. 2007. "The Baroque Body." In *The Cambridge Companion to the Ballet*, edited by Marion Kant, 42–50, 296–297. Cambridge: Cambridge University Press.

Franko, Mark. 2010. "Body-Language and Language-Body in William Forsythe's *Artifact*: Michel Foucault and Louis Marin on the Baroque Body." *Ars Aeterna* 2(1): 84–101.

Franko, Mark. 2014. "Authenticity in Dance." In *Encyclopedia of Aesthetics*. Vol. 2, edited by Michael Kelly, 268–271. New York: Oxford University Press.

Giersdorf, Jens Richard. 2013. *The Body of the People: East German Dance since 1945*. Madison: University of Wisconsin Press.

Jencks, Charles. 1986. *What Is Postmodernism?* New York: St. Martin's Press.

Jones, Amelia. 2011. "'The Artist Is Present': Artistic Re-enactments and the Impossibility of Presence." *TDR: The Drama Review* 55(1) (T209) (Spring): 16–45.

Launay, Isabelle. 2012. "Citational Poetics in Dance: . . . *of a Faun (Fragments)* by the Albrecht Knust Quartet, before and after 2000." *Dance Research Journal* 44(2) (Winter): 49–70.

Lefebvre, Henri. 1994. *The Production of Space*. Translated by Donald Nicholson-Smith. Oxford: Blackwell.

Lepecki, André. 2004. "Inscribing Dance." In *Of the Presence of the Body: Essays on Dance and Performance Theory*, 124–139. Middletown, CT: Wesleyan University Press.

Nachbar, Martin. n.d. "Urheben Aufheben – English Version." Unpublished script.

Scarpetta, Guy. 1985. *L'Impureté*. Paris: Grasset.

Yates, Frances A. 1966. *The Art of Memory*. Chicago: University of Chicago Press.

Zizek, Slavoj. 1989. *The Sublime Object of Ideology*. London and New York: Verso.

CHAPTER 25

....................................................................................................

# THE TIME OF REENACTMENT IN *BASSE DANSE* AND *BASSADANZA*

....................................................................................................

## SEETA CHAGANTI

REENACTMENT presents itself as a fraught and complicated enterprise for a number of reasons. But I think that we might organize some of this complexity by considering reenactment as a critical proposition that negotiates several difficult, but related, binaries. One such binary contrasts the literal *reconstruction* of a past performance with what Mark Franko has defined as the *reenactment* of a past performance to allow for the reinvention of the original, the theorization of the reenactment process (Franko 1989, 57–58). A related binary sets Paul Veyne and Michel de Certeau in opposition within the discourse of historical reenactment. This conflict lies between the material specificities or the micro-level of the past event and a broader conceptual understanding of its meaning or impact (Weymans 2004, 164–165). In R. G. Collingwood's much-debated thesis on reenactment and historical inquiry, we find a basis for these other binaries. Collingwood proposes applying a dichotomy of interiority and exteriority to historical reenactment (1977, 213, 298), but this in itself is confusing. In thinking about recreating a past event, how do we understand the relationship between what is internal to the historical subject and what is external? Do these have to do with the actions of the body/ world as opposed to the mind? Is this really an enforceable dichotomy? Where does Collingwood's "activity of thought" (1977, 293) fall within it (Dray 1995, 42)? These concepts of interiority and exteriority underlie the other binaries' terminologies of concept and physical action, and their own elusiveness animates the challenging fluctuations of all these binaries.

In this chapter, I attempt to clarify the dichotomous nature of the reenactment project by analyzing one of the earliest Western opportunities for reenactment: the dance manuals of fifteenth-century *basse danse* and *bassadanza*. These manuals, I argue, articulate the difference between reconstruction and reenactment, between concrete detail and concept, and between physical action and internal perception, as a distinction in temporal experience. Using the manuals as instructions for performance enables a reconstruction focused on bodily action and the micro-level of detail concerning steps. Reading the manuals in this way reveals that the dances are invested in a model of time as anticipatory, always forward-looking. But if we choose to seek instead in this evidence the dancer's perception and the dance's conceptual investments, we uncover another kind of time: one that is recursive and multiple in its trajectories. I will experiment with different ways of reading the evidence to reveal this other temporal dynamic in the reenacted spectacle, a dynamic that allows *basse danse* and *bassadanza* to theorize reenactment. The question around whether or not reenactment ultimately can be an effective "tool for historical understanding" (Agnew 2004, 330) must always remain, in part because of the historical body's particularity in time, the "shap[ing] by historical forces" (Howard 1998, 4) that countermands the possibility of our inhabiting that historical body in the reenactment process. These early dances, however, address these issues by illustrating in a specific way the different layers of experience and understanding that emerged for medieval dancers between the work of the body and the work of cognition. Ultimately, I will suggest that recognizing these temporal experiences, as part of our own and the dances' meditation on reenactment, offers a means to historical understanding that is not negated by the historical body's contingency.

# Reconstruction through Instruction: Anticipatory Time

The fifteenth-century dances that I will discuss enjoy a certain exceptionality relative to other sources for reenactment. They are, for instance, unlike the kinds of events that have often served as the subjects of critical examination in studies of reenactment, such as the recreation of battle scenes (Schneider 2011), or ship voyages (Agnew 2004; see also the essays in McCalman and Pickering 2010). *Basse danse* and *bassadanza* have arrived in our time with what seem like thrillingly specific blueprints for movement and placement. One might thus say that they more closely resemble the choreographic notation used to restore famous dances of the more recent past. But here again, the manuals for fifteenth-century dance are exceptional, occupying a different sphere from the kind of performance reenactment that intends to preserve the legacy of a celebrated, culturally weighty choreographer. While the manuals are not themselves anonymous, their dances do not participate in this dynamic of choreographic *auteur*.

They do, however, share with other apparatuses of reenactment a complex relationship to the historical reality that they attempt to convey. A manual, like any record or chronicle, is equally subject to the kind of mediation and distortion we would suspect in manuscript illustrations or literary depictions of early dance. For example, Ardis Butterfield argues that literary depictions of dance might not have as their main motivation the most objectively accurate or clear rendition of the dance. Rather, they are working through a self-conscious process of description and, more broadly, the "dynamic of oral relations being constructed through, and by means of [performance's] textual representation" (2002, 51–52, 63). Along parallel lines, Sharon Fermor contends that painters who included dance in their paintings often did not do so with the goal of recording dance techniques and practices accurately. Rather, the dance carried symbolic significance (1987, 18–19). We might think that manuals, as chronicle and record, might successfully avoid these entangling mediations; however, such documentary evidence clearly holds the same potential for distortion. Vanessa Agnew argues, in her discussion of a contemporary reenactment of Captain Cook's first voyage, that those historiographic records, and the travelers' self-conceptualizations, have their own filters: "Cook and his fellow voyagers were not entering a discursive tabula rasa at all. They staged their 'first discoveries' according to classical topoi" (2004, 332). Dance manuals are subject to the same caution that we would exercise in dealing with all these other types of source.

And yet, the manual's habitation of a generic category closer to record than to representation and, moreover, its prescriptive tenor contribute to its ability to build confidence in the work of reconstruction. Manuals can contain narrative accounts of how steps are performed, philosophical treatises on the good dancer, and perhaps even notation specifying step sequences; they are later understood to address the problem of dance's constant change (Arena 1986, 24, 11). All these features seem, on the surface, to provide useful opportunities to remake a dance that has been lost in time. The manuals and treatises associated with fifteenth-century *basse danse* and *bassadanza* boast just such features and therefore provide tantalizingly specific glimpses into a performance world otherwise quite obscure. *Basse danse* and *bassadanza* were both characterized by stately, ordered movements, of varying speeds, but appropriate for a courtly setting. French and Burgundian *basse danse* was somewhat processional in character, with dancers advancing, retreating, and moving slightly to the side while facing front. Italian *bassadanza*, meanwhile, has often been understood as a more conceptually sophisticated and livelier development of its counterpart.[1] The Italian form features in particular more elaborate floor patterns, ultimately tending toward a dance that is more explicitly narrative than the abstract patterns of *basse danse*.[2] These related but distinct dance forms represented an important aspect of dance culture in the fifteenth and sixteenth centuries, and the existence of manuals attesting to these traditions has played a valuable role in our understanding of this era.

These instruction manuals also exemplify performance's inevitable basis in what Richard Schechner calls "restored behavior" (1986, 35), and for this reason they are in

(Translations throughout are mine with assistance, where applicable, from cited editions.)

[1] For instance, a *bassadanza* called "Mignotta alla Fila," appearing in both Guglielmo and Cornazano's manuscripts, varies the *bassadanza* step repertoire and thereby creates a more complicated floor pattern than the usual procession (Thomas 1978, 25).

[2] Elsewhere, I examine the relationship between French, Burgundian, and Italian tradition, as well the implication of these geographic traditions within the temporal dynamics of anticipation; I contend that the manuals at once reinforce and complicate scholarly definitions of historical period (Chaganti 2012). See also Payne 2003, 30; and Franko 1985, 55–66.

a sense anticipatory in their entire character. Schechner has argued that performances often require the possibility of "organized sequences of events" existing separately from the performers who enact them (35–36), and that this structure—allowing for repetition, variation, and other kinds of iteration—underlies performance as "twice-behaved" (36). From the moment they appeared in the late Middle Ages to the present, every act of reading of these manuals, to say nothing of each embodied instructional use, represents an impulse toward the repetition of behavior. Their very existence testifies to the need and desire to restore dances, and in recording a dance, they ensure that its continued performance will always be a form of reconstruction from the moment the manual first appears. In this sense they are anticipatory by nature. And indeed, the fifteenth-century manuals' instructional discourse reveals that both within particular manuals and across them, these texts are invested in progression and anticipation.

In this section of the chapter, I will read the manuals in a way that highlights what they would reveal were we to turn to them for instructions in executing their steps. Their treatises on how to dance are noticeably informed by the mechanics of anticipation. The manuals' use of anticipatory temporal structures appears within the context of an evocation of classical memory theory. From Domenico da Piacenza, considered the father of dancing masters, to his pupils Antonio Cornazano and Guglielmo Ebreo, the Italian dancing masters of the fifteenth century all establish the importance of a good memory in dance (Cornazano 1981, 18; Gombosi 1941, 298; Smith 1995, 10–11; Sparti 1993, 93–95). Their manuals conjure a cultural discourse of humanist learning that was deeply preoccupied with its memory of, and relationship to, the past. Exploration of this relationship to the past often coexisted with meditations on humanist principles and the liberal arts. Guglielmo Ebreo, in particular, is seen as wishing to assert dance's place in the liberal arts, drawing upon Leon Battista Alberti's strategies in *On Painting*, and presenting the conventional attributes of the dancer—memory and measure—as related to the liberal humanist tradition of arts and sciences (Sparti 1993, 9–11). The manuals use memory to illuminate dance's connection to learned, humanist, and classical traditions.

As these authors discuss memory in instructing dance, they shape it as an activity of looking back to look forward. In Domenico's manual, memory engenders prudent behavior by allowing one's knowledge of the past to affect judgment in the future. For Domenico, *misura*, prudence, and memory exist in a tightly linked triangle: "non sapiamo noi che la mexura e parte de prudentia et e nele arte liberale. No sapiamo che la memoria e madre dela prudentia . . ." (Smith 1995, vol. 1, 14, ll. 80–82) ("do we not know that measure is part of prudence and of the liberal arts? Do we not know that memory is the mother of prudence?").[3] He implies not only the interdependence of memory and *misura*, but also the role of memory in understanding the structure—beginning, middle, and end—of the dance over time. As prudence always sees past, present, and future, the skilled and temperate dancer at once orients himself toward the beginning,

---

[3] Guglielmo will later make explicit the importance of the connection between memory and the knowledge of beginning, middle, and end: "not remembering what is the beginning, the middle, or the end—will appear absent minded, and his dancing will be imperfect" (Sparti 1993, 95).

middle, and end of the dance.[4] By emphasizing that the dancer must always understand where he is in relation to the temporal points lying ahead, Domenico illustrates that in the fifteenth century, memory in dance always occurred as simultaneous recollection and anticipation.

Indeed, the factor of anticipation played an important role in early memory theory, particularly in connection to acts of composition. The fourth-century Julius Victor, for example, was less interested in memory storage and *loci* than in the uses of memory for future compositional and rhetorical acts. Basing his own words on Quintilian's, Victor argues for the importance of memorization as a source of "models for imitation." The memory of such models helps to avoid "the dangers of chaotic, unplanned movement" (Carruthers 2008, 107). In the sixth century, Boethius also associated memory with composition in describing a "program of mental representation." Images are stored in the mind in order to produce concepts (Copeland and Sluiter 2009, 24). These theories correspond to Domenico's use of memory in dance instruction. Victor and Quintilian use memory to avoid a metaphoric movement that is unstructured and chaotic, and, correspondingly, Domenico shows how memory keeps the formalization of physical movement safe from such disorder.[5] Guglielmo shares this sense that the ability to look forward from the foundation of memory preserves order and temperance, especially in the face of change and unpredictability. In his chapter on memory, Guglielmo begins by asserting that "una perfetta memoria" is just as important to the successful dancer as an understanding of measure. If the music should change in the course of the dance, the dancer must be able to keep what he knows clear in his memory so that he is not found wanting "per pocha avertenza o per manchamento di memoria" (because of insufficient forethought or lack of memory). Memory allows the dancer to look ahead and adapt his execution of the dance to novelties introduced within the process of performance (Sparti 1993, 94).

The dance manuals' use of memory and anticipation speaks to a critical context that identifies memory's indispensability to the possibility of future performance. Throughout her work, Jody Enders explores memory and the idea of "protodrama," citing memory's mediation between invention and delivery. Rhetoric in this guise also fulfills an antici-patory function, "provid[ing] models and sketches of pre-performance, or virtual per-formance, or intentions of performance" (1999, 17).[6] Other theorizations of memory, anticipation, and performance find useful elaboration in Joseph Roach's device of the

---

[4] On the dancer's position as generating action by moving inside the dance, rather than watching it from outside, see Williams (1995, 55): "the dancer is often talking about self as that self exists in the dance—inside the action and generating it, not outside the action and watching it."

[5] On the way that dance relies on memory precisely because it is formalized movement, see Kaeppler (1991, 109).

[6] See also Enders (1999, 18, 18 n. 60, as well as 26 and 46) on protodrama and the anticipatory. See also Enders (1992) on the protodramatic. Enders's more recent point that "theatre is prone to accidents in ways that 'texts' are not; and those accidents are meaningful in light of intention" (2009, 12) also develops a dynamic of remembering and forgetting as related to the anticipation of what comes next in a performance.

"quotation" (to which I shall return later). Roach argues for the active role of memory in the constitution of performance. Part of the memory that we bring to bear on performance involves "kinesthetic imagination," and this imagination converges with memory, allowing the performer's awareness of movement to be "at once remembered and reinvented." In this understanding of performance and memory, Roach states that "[l]ike performance, memory operates as both quotation and invention, an improvisation on borrowed themes, with claims on the future as well as the past" (1996, 26–27, 33).[7]

Contemporary theories of dance specify how this effect resides in the body and therefore would play an important role in the reconstruction of *basse danse* and *bassadanza*. Erin Manning theorizes the process of danced movement as one that always contains what she calls an "interval," an incorporeal and yet substantial phenomenon in which the body experiences the potential of the movement that it is about to make. Central to Manning in her explication of this concept is the fact that movement is preceded by "pre-acceleration"; space itself is not static, but rather contributes to the production of movement (2009, 13–24). As a result, movement, memory, and forgetting must be triangulated. For Manning, the "becoming-event" that will result in movement "creates a memory that feeds into future movement" (2009, 25). At the same time, each new expression of movement involves both memory and a repeated "magic of forgetting that assures that every movement will begin anew" (18). As each movement is remade as though new, a somatic memory inhabits the space before the movement takes place. This memory projects itself into the future, and creates, in Manning's terms, a future anteriority always at play in the body's engagement with space (2009, 24).

Placing the textual accounts of early dance within the context of contemporary dance theory thus emphasizes the bodily, somatic nature of anticipation in the manuals' instructions for performing dance. The fifteenth-century manuals themselves use a language of ontological change in the body in order to instruct anticipatory techniques. Like the other manual writers, Cornazano specifies that memory is crucial to dancing because of the need to "remember the steps you are about to perform when you begin to dance" (Cornazano 1981, 18). Within this larger framework, he provides a specific description of the technique by which the dancer moves from the *ripresa* to *continenza* step in the *bassadanza*, a transition that requires delineating contrast between the large, or slower, step and the small, or quicker. Cornazano describes the transition from one movement to another as follows:

> Talhor tacere un tempo e star lo morte non e brutto ma entrare poi nel seguente con aeroso modo quasi come persona che susciti da morte a vita. In questo Misser Domenichino vostro bon servitore e mio maestro ha havuto evidentissimo guidicio dicendo che 'l dançare specialimente di misura larga vole essere simile ad ombra phantasmatica nella quale similitudine ad explicarla se intendono molte cose che non si sanno dire. (Smith 1995, vol. 1, 88, ll. 258–270)

---

[7]  Roach here builds upon Richard Schechner's idea that performance is always "twice-behaved behavior" (Schechner 1986, 36).

Sometimes to omit a tempo and stay in stillness is not ugly; but then, enter into the following step in an airy manner, almost like a person who has been resuscitated from death to life. In this, your good servant and my master, Misser Domenichino, has had the most evident judiciousness in saying that dancing, especially in the slow measure, should be similar to an illusory shadow, a simile in which [to explain it] many things that cannot be said are understood.

Cornazano first uses death as a metaphor ("star lo morte"), signifying stillness in the body. He then adjusts the figural force of this term, employing it as a simile but foregrounding a more literal and physical sense of death by contrasting it with life and associating it with resuscitation. In one sense, we might say that his simile simply provides a means to convey a shift in the tempo of the movement, from slower to faster. And yet, the abrupt and unexpected literality of death here creates a somewhat different effect. It suggests a qualitative change in the movement, rather than a quantitative one. As Nevile argues, the reference to death moves the dancer into a timeless state (2007, 305). Cornazano's description responds to and elaborates on Manning's concept of the interval. His imagery suggests that within the anticipatory dynamics that precede bodily movement, a shift potentially occurs in the dancer's sense of his own body. Not only is Cornazano asking the dancer to speed up in the transition; he is also asking the dancer to change his sense of being in his body during the anticipatory process—a body in death versus a body in life. If, for Manning, danced movement involves the entwinement of forgetting and remembering, for Cornazano it is a layering of memory's continuity with a change in ontological state, a propulsion from oblivion to knowing. Reading these manuals for instructions to reconstruct, one would have to take into account this aspect of the dance's physical experience as expressed figuratively.

Not only does figurative imagery elucidate the work of anticipation within a particular manual, but the manuals also anticipate each other in these forms of figuration. Cornazano's instructions elaborate upon his master Domenico's earlier text:

> fantasmata e una presteza corporalle la quale e mossa cum lo intelecto dela mexura dicta imprima disopra facendo requia acadauno tempo che pari haver veduto la capo di meduxa como dice el poeta cioe che facto el motto sii tutto di piedra in quello instante et in instante mitti ale como falcone che per paica mosso .... (Smith 1995, vol. 1, 12, ll. 60–65)

> (*fantasmata* is a bodily quickness which is moved by the understanding of the measure first spoken of above, making it necessary at one tempo that one appear to have seen the head of the Medusa as the poet says, that is, having made the motion, that you be all of stone in that instant, and in an instant have taken to wing like a falcon who has been moved by hunger.)

Cornazano was a pupil of Domenico's, and in that sense the latter might well have perceived himself as writing toward a future of further dance writing and dance instruction (Thomas 1978, 24). Domenico's depiction of the slow measure anticipates Cornazano's subtle use of bodily revival and the shape it gives to incipient movement. In the shift from the Medusa/falcon image to death/life, we see as well how one image can anticipate the potential meaning of another. Let us begin with Domenico's Medusa victim and falcon. A dancer instructed to replicate the condition of the petrified gazer, and then the hungry falcon, is in essence being instructed to replicate tropes from the classical and medieval past; to see these familiar cultural references out of the corner of his eye, so to speak, even as he tries to occupy the physical conditions of stony oblivion, followed by urgently forward-moving pursuit. The radical shift in the state of being exists as an intimation in Domenico's version through these metaphors. In Cornazano, however, we find a more extreme rendering in the command to be dead and then alive.

In the preceding example, anticipation structures the interlocution between master and pupil; but dance manuals make other uses of interlocution as well, and here again anticipation plays a crucial role in the instructional act. As Cornazano and Domenico suggest, dancing masters conducted implicit dialogues with each other, drawing the quotation (in Roach's sense) of the master forward in time to converse with the pupil. If such dialogue is implicit for Cornazano and Domenico, it becomes explicit for Guglielmo, who incorporates into his work an "Argumentum disciplinorum," a set of imagined objections and ripostes between himself and a student. This form is familiar from classical philosophical writing, and it appears as well in Arbeau's later *Orchésographie*, which is presented in its entirety as a dialogue between the pseudonymous Arbeau and a former pupil playfully named Capriol (Arbeau 1948, 11).[8] The two names possess an imaginative whimsicality: one a clever anagram of the author's real name (a dance of letters), and the other an allusion to a danced step. This exaggerated artifice emphasizes the location of this dialogue within the mind of a single author, rather than between two actual interlocutors. In the case of Guglielmo, as in the case of any dialogue imagined by one speaker, every utterance is foreseen. When Guglielmo's student challenges, for instance, "che ci bisogna memoria et misura? Ci pareno adoncha tutte cose superflue. Et senza esse potersi perfettamente ballare" ("what need is there for memory and measure? They thus seem to be all superfluous things, and it is possible to dance perfectly without them"), both Guglielmo and his readers surely know the reply: that all of the elements of dance are important, but "maxime la memoria & misura" ("most of all memory and measure") (Sparti 1993, 114). This dialogue of one functions as a kind of dance through its own use of memory in order to anticipate what will follow. Guglielmo possesses knowledge of the principles he wishes to deploy in his dance treatise. Because he is the only interlocutor in the scene, he can foresee the rhetorical steps and patterns the debate will trace, based on his own memory of both the relevant material and the conventional forms of philosophical dialogue. Engaging his memory, he can experience a sense of where he will move rhetorically before he enacts the movement. In fact, the dialogue of one means that Guglielmo never alights to rest, if we re-invoke Manning's formulation here. And

---

[8] Thoinot Arbeau is an anagram of Jehan Tabourot (Barker 1930, 2).

simultaneously, engaging with the form and momentum of the dialogue requires a forgetting of the kind Manning discusses, so that the rejoinder can appear to have the genuine force of debate, an urgent response to a newly introduced objection. Thus, when we read this text as instructional, the very technique of instruction embodies anticipation.

If anticipation asserts itself mainly through the Italian manuals' content and rhetoric, it does so in the French and Burgundian manual tradition through various formal devices. The two relevant texts are the manuscript known as KBR, Brussels 9085 (ca. 1470–1495) and Michel Toulouze's incunabulum *L'art et instruction de bien danser*, printed in the late 1480s.[9] Their dance notations, which consist of single letters as abbreviations designating steps, represent one of the earliest such notational systems recorded in the West (Closson 1912, 7). Toulouze's manual shares many features with Brussels 9085, including the notational technique. One difference, however, lies in the fact that *L'art et instruction* includes a narrative explanation of the abbreviations: "Et est a noter que pour plus facilement entendre les lettres que s'ensuyent apres les notes que pour. R. tu doibs entendre desmarche pour. B. branle, pour. S. pas simple et pour. D. tu doibs entendre pas double" (Jackman 1980) (And it is to be noted that to understand the letters that follow the notes more easily, for R you must understand "démarche," for B "branle," for S "simple step," and for D you must understand "double step"). The inclusion of this key might simply suggest a need for clarification. And yet, the age of terms like "branle," as well as their embeddedness within dance culture, makes it a little difficult to believe that these abbreviations were met with incomprehension.

I would suggest instead that Toulouze's elaboration makes manifest the way that the manual can anticipate a relationship between dance and text. The system of steps corresponding to individual letters looks forward to the unfolding of each inscribed sign into a narrative made up of such signs; the sight of the individual letters on the page contains within itself the possibility of a transformation into narrative. Brussels 9085, with only the letter code itself, and Toulouze, which elaborates upon that code, are thought to have a common source.[10] This implies that the memory technique of representing steps as letters—generated in that putative source—anticipates the possibility of multiplying the letters to form narrative text. We see this possibility realized in Toulouze. In characterizing this dynamic created between Brussels 9085 and Toulouze, we are speaking not of manuals whose content explicitly engages with anticipatory dynamics (as with the Italian texts), but rather of manuals whose anticipatory dynamics inhere within their

---

[9]  On the dating of Toulouze, see Ward (1976, 129). For a discussion of the dating of Brussels 9085, see Crane (1986, 5–7); and some more recent proposals concerning a later date (in the 1490s) in Wilson (2012, 77). A printed facsimile exists in Closson 1912. (Note Crane's caution that the facsimile introduces some engraver error [1986, 7].) Closson suggests that the manuscript was originally owned by Marie de Bourgogne (1912, 6).

[10]  On the possibility of the common source, see Crane (1986, 10). Bukofzer specifies that the absence of a melody from one text and not the other suggests they are not directly related, but rather derive from either parallel sources or a common source (1950, 193).

very form. Despite the multiplicity of dance traditions, the instructional tradition more broadly construed appears united in its dependence upon mechanisms of anticipation, and a forward-looking vision of time.

These analyses all suggest that when we read these manuals—both their content and their form—as instructions with which to reconstruct dances, we will find a particular understanding of the temporality of *basse danse* and *bassadanza*. In their articulations of the dancer's bodily orientation, time is anticipatory; the temporal experience of the dance builds itself upon looking forward. This anticipatory orientation lies so deeply within the grain of the manual tradition that it asserts itself at levels as diverse as narrative content, metaphor, mode of narration (dialogue), and even the very presentation of the text on the page. If we use these instructions to realize the physicality and material detail that represent one aspect of historical understanding, we uncover this version of time in the dance.

## Reenactment and Temporal Turning

But if the instructional techniques, rhetorics, and form of the manuals privilege this kind of anticipatory time, I would contend that another kind of time inheres within the experience of the dances when we look at the evidence differently. *Basse danse* and *bassadanza* produce for their performers and viewers an experience of temporality that works against a linear forward drive, or the anticipatory impulse that uses the past to look forward into the future. If we move away from thinking about reconstructing the dance by following its associated instructions, we discover instead that the time of its performance is recursive and multidirectional, and that it embodies intersecting trajectories, not just the impulsion forward. In this section, I will experiment with a few methods of reading the evidence that circumvent the activity of attempting to translate instructions into steps. This more peripheral gaze at the manual traditions reveals that the dances theorize their own performance time in a manner that differs from what they convey as instructions to follow.

One way to refocus one's look at the manuals is to consider what is around them. Of course, any attempt at reenactment, even the most traditional type of reconstruction, involves looking toward a larger matrix of the dance traditions in question as they relate to each other. Dance historians often rely on evidence external to the manuals in order to decipher the nature of the steps. But I propose here the goal of seeking out conceptual organization, rather than trying to refine our understanding of specific steps through knowledge of their international context. What we discover, following this alternate path, is that this evidence complicates from the outset the way that the dances occupy time. Some readings have interpreted *basse danse* and *bassadanza* as themselves embodying a model of progression, with a simpler form giving way to a more sophisticated one (Brainard 1979, 7; Gombosi 1941, 301–303), creating the perception of one tradition anticipating the other. But other scholars have seen this relationship differently.

Frederick Crane, for instance, views the dances as differing and autonomous forms, rather than as participating in an evolutionary scenario:

> Although the *basse danse* shows some common features over the long period of its history, and throughout its geographical distribution, three divisions can be distinguished . . . : the French *basse danse* of the fifteenth century, the Italian *bassadanza* of the fifteenth century, and the *basse danse* of the sixteenth century. (1986, 1)

Crane uses both space and time to counteract the narrative of progression. Other critics instead identify resonances existing between the northern European and Italian traditions. These resonances, however, replace the model of progressive continuity not with separation, but rather with shared and overlapping elements. One of the *bassadanza* melodies, for instance, appearing in Cornazano's Italian treatise also exists in Michel Toulouze's French incunabulum (Bukofzer 1950, 193). As David Wilson attests in discussing the French tradition, while certain dances may seem characteristic of the fifteenth versus the sixteenth century, "the transition from one to the other was achieved gradually, with different features being adopted in succession until a new style has been formed" (1984–1985, 11). Wilson later distinguishes between an evolution in musical tradition from the fifteenth to sixteenth centuries and the less linear development of the dance itself (2012, vii). Furthermore, while Italian *bassedanze* might, on the one hand, be perceived as more advanced than their French counterparts, Jennifer Nevile has argued that certain *bassedanze* deliberately altered their structures so as to be able to imitate, and incorporate elements of, French *basse danse* (Nevile 2011, 234–235). Conversely, Ingrid Brainard notes that the Burgundian manuscript Brussels 9085 was influenced by earlier Italian dance tradition (Brainard 1956, cited in Franko 1986, 5 n. 11). These structures of allusion indicate an interest in self-conscious gestures toward traditions removed in both space and time. Such phenomena suggest that the fifteenth-century practitioners of these dances did not necessarily see them in terms of a teleology of increased sophistication. Rather, the development of the dance tended to step forward and backward in time, as the dance itself does in space.

In other words, developments in these dance forms occur across multiple and interweaving temporalities. As David Lawton argues, "Whatever the period that contains us, our lives contain many different periods" (2007, 485). Seeing these dances as containing different periods of dance within themselves would allow them to exist both simultaneously and in sequence with one another. Frances Rust suggests that change in dance practices during the fifteenth century was slow (1969, 36). Kathi Meyer-Baer asserts that the form of *basse danse* "changed considerably" in the sixteenth century and that "forms of dances sometimes change quickly"; in this case, the rhythm changed, while the character of the step might have remained similar (1955, 274–275).[11] While it is possible to imagine the rate of change suddenly accelerating upon the move

---

[11]  A dance from 1529 has the 3/2 rhythm characteristic of the fifteenth century, but by 1530, 2/4 rhythm begins to appear, and by the end of the sixteenth century, we find 2/4 and 2/8 rhythm. "The

into the sixteenth century, it is equally possible to suppose that rates of change varied within themselves and varied for different aspects of the dance, and that over a broader expanse of time this phenomenon might take on the appearance that Meyer-Baer describes.

This account is important because it illuminates the experience of time in the performance. To reenact these dances would require the creation of this multi-temporal consciousness. To be sure, even at the level of reconstructing steps, a complex understanding of time is required for dances in this period. Nevile has suggested that the "temporal aspects" of Italian dance relate to "the deliberate creation of different rhythmic patterns between the steps and the accompanying music" (2007, 301, 308– 310); she also argues that the cessation of movement in this dance created the effect of the cessation of time (305, 308). But beyond the *tempi* dictating the dance's technique, the overlapping heritages of this dance tradition suggest that what one heard, what one saw, what one felt in forming a step with one's foot in a *basse danse* or *bassadanza* all placed one within a cultural moment at the same time that they unmistakably echoed other times and places. Thus the experience of temporal variation in the performance of these dances involves awareness not only of technique and physical execution, but also of the dance's interaction with its own history and stages of development.

Another way to shift one's focus toward the dance's conceptual stakes might be to consider the way that the dance as a pattern might look to its participants and observers. Again, this formulation admittedly muddies the binary of detail and concept: such a pattern could be considered a physical detail with which to reconstruct the dance, as much as a key to its ideational content. I will contend here, however, that the process of engaging in this perspectival shift reveals the dance's ability to theorize and conceptualize its own relationship to, and place in, time. As much as the linear shape of *basse danse* might reinforce the perception of its progressive impulse, aspects of performing *basse danse* also undo such progression. The incremental nature of the steps, combined with the spectacle of a horizontal line of dancers, casts into relief the element—almost the essence—of directionality itself. *Basse danse* choreography both advances and retreats, and it uses this forward and backward directional motion to represent and theorize temporal structure. As motion forward and back fills, empties, and refills the space of the dance, it suggests an element of recursion in the dance's time. Advancing and retreating patterns of movement are integral to this dance. The French tradition "recorded *basses danses* with only forward and backward motion relieved with occasional steps to the side (*branles*) until well into the fifteenth century" (Thomas 1978, 25). We see evidence of this characteristic in the well-known fifteenth-century *Basse danse du roy despaingne*'s measures:

only characteristic which might have been kept and was perhaps the reason that these dances were still called *bassas* may have been the use of our low bending step" (Meyer-Baer 1955, 275). See also Jennifer Nevile's suggestion that the writing down of dances contributed to increased rate at which they changed (2008, 306).

Rb /ssdddrrrb / ssdddrb / ssdddrrrb / ssdrdrb / ssdddrrrb / ssdrdrb/[12]

The *simple* (s) and *double* (d) steps move forward, while the *démarche* or *reprise* (r) steps move back; the *branle* (b) shifts to the side. In this choreography, as in many *basses danses*, the variation of steps primarily affects the relationship of forward to backward motion. The second measure contains fewer *reprises* than the first, and the fourth and sixth measures more rapidly alternate between forward and backward movement than do the others. These features make it possible to see *basse danse* as foregrounding the relationship between forward and backward motion. Emphasizing the prominence of this orientation is the fact that *basse danse* is related to *estampie*, one of the early dance forms possessing a "front," which involved dancing forward toward a person or point, and then back.[13] Thus, from the viewer's perspective as well, the steps involve a dynamic of forward and backward motion, and the processional and linear orientation of the dancing group accentuates the presence of advancing and retreating (punctuated at intervals by the sideways *branle*) in the constitution of the dance and its aesthetic. In such a dance, I would suggest, this multidirectionality in space evokes an analogous multidirectionality in time.[14] When they recede, the dancers reinhabit a spatial plane that they had already delineated in the past. Thus, it becomes possible in the backward step to revisit an earlier point in time through its delineation in space. The movement provides both viewer and participant with a visualization of time's passage in more than one direction.

*Basse danse* thus theorizes its own operations by opening up questions about the experience of time that its performance makes possible. If, as Sarah Kay has argued, it is a hallmark of late-medieval intellectual practice to explore the possibility of physical space to accommodate and engage metaphysical truth (2007, 7), then *basse danse* as a medieval cultural production asserts itself as generating a physical space that outlines and reflects a conceptual insight. *Basse danse* as performance produces a kinetic space capable of accommodating a nonverbal theory of how its time questions the structures of its own progression. Franko has suggested that "if the practice of the ideal dance is meant to 'represent' anything, that object to be represented would be its own theory"

---

[12] Transcribed from high-resolution images, produced by the Alamire Foundation, of MS Brussels 9085, consulted at the Koninklijke Bibliotheek van België, Brussels, Belgium, in July 2013.

[13] The *estampie*'s relationship to *basse danse* is suggested in the fact that the latter emerged as the former ceased to be recorded as performed; both dances are "stately" in character, the *estampie* uniquely so for its time (McGee 1989, 21). McGee appears to see *bassadanza* and *basse dance* as part of one tradition; the sentence preceding the one on *estampie* reads: "But where did the fifteenth-century *bassadanza/basse danse* come from?" (1989, 21); he goes on to hazard a guess (acknowledging the speculative nature of his comments) that French and Italian *estampies* differed from each other in a way that mimicked the difference between *basse danse* and *bassadanza* (1989, 22). On the *estampie* and the "front," see Rimmer (1991, 64).

[14] In certain other spheres, movements oriented in front of and behind the body have, in Western culture, traditionally been associated, respectively, with forward and backward progress in time. Brenda Farnell states that in American Sign Language, for instance, "past time signs use the space behind the line of the body, present time signs are located at the body, and future time signs are in front, consistent with the way in which the English language locates time spatially" (1995, 97).

(1986, 29).[15] In the performance of *basse danse*, the dancer therefore not only engaged in a complex experience of time but also had the opportunity to recognize in the performance of the dance a nonlinguistic theoretical discourse concerning its uses of time. If, again, we are aiming to reenact a more fully dimensional understanding of this dance than what simply realizing its instructions and notations would produce, it also becomes important to recognize this component of the performance experience that engages the dancer in a meditation on time, even as it moves the dancer around in time.

This perception reveals that even the textual instructions so invested in linear progression cannot entirely occlude this more shifting and dialectical temporal model. Domenico's invocation of *fantasmata*, which we examined earlier, makes this fact clear:

> fantasmata e una presteza corporalle la quale e mossa cum lo intelecto dela mexura dicta imprima disopra facendo requia acadauno tempo che pari haver veduto la capo di meduxa como dice el poeta cioe che facto el motto sii tutto di piedra in quello instante et in instante mitti ale como falcone che per paica mosso . . . . (Smith 1995, vol. 1, 13, ll. 60–65)

> (*fantasmata* is a bodily quickness which is moved by the understanding of the measure first spoken of above, making it necessary at one tempo that one appear to have seen the head of the Medusa as the poet says, that is, having made the motion, that you be all of stone in that instant, and in an instant have taken to wing like a falcon who has been moved by hunger.)

Both Domenico's and Cornazano's passages attempt to put into language the effect of the transition between a slow and fast tempo, or else—in a more extreme sense—between stillness and motion. As Franko argues in his reading of Domenico's passage, "*fantasmata* is not a quality peculiar to either movement . . . but rather one inherent in their interplay"; it is a "dialectical" transition between movement and pose "in which each seems about to become the other" (Franko 1986, 64–65). This dialectical reading of *fantasmata* suggests that the dance relies not simply on progression through time and an orientation to the future, but rather on a less linear kind of interplay between movement and pose. Giorgio Agamben's account of the development of "phantasm" through Aristotelian theory and medieval literary culture also has implications for the temporal experience of the phantasm. As a mental image vital to thought process, the classical and medieval phantasm of cognitive and memory theory overlaps with Domenico and Cornazano's usages. In all cases, it is an image in the mind that enables understanding, sensation, and memory (Agamben 1993, 76–77). As Agamben

---

[15]  Mark Franko finds a different kind of theoretical discourse—one concerning civility and good conduct—within the steps of early court dance. But his method of seeing the symbolic resonances of movement as theorizing the movement enacted relates to my discussion here (1986, 29): "The ideal dance excludes imitation inasmuch as it shows a 'theory-in-act,' the adequacy of movements with the image of their own principles."

suggests, while the phantasm is subjected to a "progressive 'disrobing' " of its material components in the process of intellection, it is also—particularly in its involvement with medieval theories of love—implicated in the dynamics of mirroring. Images of the vitreous eye, of water, of fountains, of Narcissus all inform the function and operation of the phantasm (79, 80–83).[16] These reflective motifs imply an experience of the phantasm that is dialectical and obsessively recursive, as much as it is included in a progression of mental steps moving forward and anticipating an endpoint.

Finally, if we shift from reconstructing steps to considering the material features of the dance manual manuscript, we find a similarly complex temporality. The manuscript Brussels 9085 provides striking evidence of this claim. I viewed this manuscript under the guidance of Michiel Verweij; I am grateful to the Koninklijke Bibliotheek van België for granting me exceptional permission to view this manuscript, which has been barred from consultation. Brussels 9085 was produced on black-tinted parchment, in a fashionable Burgundian style of the late fifteenth century, with its text, music, and notations copied in gold and silver inks. The luxurious character of this manuscript suggests that it is especially important to consider the reader's encounter with it beyond its use as an actual performance guide or script. It seems too valuable to have been used in this capacity, and therefore the reader's experience with it would have involved instead a detailed sensory engagement with the object's own material aspects. While black parchment was prestigious and sought after in this period, particularly among Burgundian nobility (Smith 1937, 103), the black dye rendered the parchment extremely fragile (Wieck 1997, 83). Examination of this manuscript revealed that its folios are composite in character, incorporating different materials. Verweij suggests that repair work had to be done on the original pages quite early in the manuscript's history, perhaps at the very end of the fifteenth century or the beginning of the sixteenth.[17] Thus for much of its history, Brussels 9085 has been an object that incorporates different times into itself; the experience of holding and looking at these strange pages necessitated a recursive, mobile, palimpsestic understanding of the nature of time. Certainly Brussels 9085 is not unique in encompassing its evidence of encounter at different temporal moments. But the makeup of the pages is somewhat unusual. Reenactment must encompass the processes by which such performances occur, in this case the perusal of the manual.[18] Thus the bodily confrontation of an object like this becomes relevant to my taxonomy of reenactment here, and this object further reinforces the sense of time that I argue characterizes the conceptual experience of the dance.

At more than one level, then, if we think outside the reconstructive act of following the manuals' instructions, we find evidence of an alternative experience of time in the

[16] Agamben notes that the Middle Ages "conceived of love as an essentially phantasmatic process, involving both imagination and memory in an assiduous, tormented circling around an image painted or reflected in the deepest self" (1993, 81). Agamben goes on to discuss the seer's union with his own image and the phantasm's mediating function in this dynamic (1993, 84).

[17] Michiel Verweij's suggestions concerning the manuscript are drawn from our converstion and a subsequent email exchange in July 2013; they appear here with his permission.

[18] See also Chapter 14 by VK Preston in this volume.

dance's performance as reenactment. In this temporal experience, the dance meditates upon reenactment itself. First, the choreographic overlap among the various traditions suggests the dancer's awareness of his own peregrinations back and forth in historical time, through the process of executing different steps and patterns, from tradition to innovation and back, perhaps, to conscious archaisms in gesture. Second, *basse danse* choreography makes visible a model of time in which moving back and moving forward balance each other in elaborate patterns. Third, even *bassadanza* manuals, at one level so invested in the humanist model of a temporality that anticipates progress, cannot entirely excise the recursive impulses of the dance from their accounts. Finally, the embodied experience of dance includes not only performance itself but also holding and perusing the manuals. In this context, we have Brussels 9085, a composite object that layers different times within its folio construction. The very artifact that communicates this dance to its audiences—past and present—embodies the dance's own temporal model: one that rebuts impulses toward prolepsis or a narrative of increasing sophistication. Thus, differing visions of time mark the distinction between the dance as physical reconstruction, on the one hand, and as a conceptually based reenactment that theorizes its own execution, on the other.

We must still consider how reenactment might or might not contribute to historical understanding, or what else it might accomplish. My remarks here are intended to establish some parameters around the binaries of historical understanding—interior/exterior, physical detail/concept—by assigning particular views of temporality to each of these terms. I must certainly acknowledge, at the same time, that any boundaries drawn here are far from impermeable; one could easily make the case that these different levels of the dance's operation, like the terms in all these binaries, are more deeply intertwined than I allow for here. My strategy, however, is to offer, through time, a method of provisional categorization that might lend some clarity to what are often problematic dichotomies. And my further aim in doing so is to address the still broader question of the work of reenactment as historical understanding in light of the historical body's specificity. Collingwood's reenactment model is critiqued (Agnew 2004, 335; Steuber 2002, 37–38, 42) because the historical body's contingency makes it impossible to inhabit and understand fully and with romantic sympathy (1977, 87) the agency of the historical subject, to "re-enac[t] . . . past thought in the historian's own mind" (1977, 215, 282). But I will suggest in closing that perhaps understanding the temporal experience of a historical subject does not require the kind of habitation of that subject that we would consider so problematic. In having argued, for taxonomic purposes, that the bodily mastering of the steps and the cognitive experience of dance involve two different kinds of time, I have also demonstrated that temporal experience itself emerges as shared by body and mind, detail and concept; as an experience, it transcends the binaries that make the historical subject so difficult to access. A historical subject's experience of time might therefore be more available to our understanding than other kinds of thoughts, agencies, and bodily experiences from the past.

It is also finally important that these temporal experiences derive from the genre of the instruction manual for performance. As Jasper Bernes has argued, reading Ashbery's

"The Instruction Manual" (1997, 8–10), the manual's speaker is "both the commander and executor of commands"; the manual inevitably creates an effect of doubling as one watches oneself undergo experience (Bernes, 2017, 66). A similar doubleness adheres to the reader of such a text: the doubleness of reading and doing, present and future. The double perspective of the instruction manual parallels the double perspective that Susan Foster has identified in the historian's body, which finds resonance with the bodies of the past, changing both past and present bodies (1995, 10) to embody and explicate across time. This parallel raises the interesting possibility that we are dealing not simply with the problem of the present historian trying to understand the past. Rather, the manuals, in their temporally animated capacity, are themselves looking forward to a dynamic of historical understanding, working out in their own way their occupation of time and their relationship to what is not in their immediate moment. As we saw, anticipatory memory in the manuals makes possible compositional creativity; in this sense, the manuals imagine forward in time. This formulation perhaps relieves some of the pressure generated by our anxieties around the historical agent's inaccessibility: instruction manuals gesture speculatively forth to us as much as we gesture speculatively back toward them. In these ways, some of the most ancient witnesses to Western dance contribute uniquely to the theorization of reenactment.

## Works Cited

Agamben, Giorgio. 1993. *Stanzas: Word and Phantasm in Western Culture*. Translated by Ronald L. Martinez. Minneapolis: University of Minnesota Press.

Agnew, Vanessa. 2004. "Introduction: What Is Reenactment?" *Criticism* 46(3): 327–339.

Arbeau, Thoinot. 1948. *Orchesography: A Treatise in the Form of a Dialogue*. Translated by Mary Stewart Evans. New York: Kamin Dance Publishers.

Arena, Antonius. 1986. "Rules of Dancing." Translated by John Guthrie and Marino Zorzi. *Dance Research: The Journal of the Society for Dance Research* 4(2): 3–53.

Ashbery, John. 1997. "The Instruction Manual." In *The Mooring of Starting Out*, 1st ed. New York: Ecco.

Barker, E. Phillips. 1930. "Some Notes on Arbeau." *Journal of the English Folk Dance Society* 3: 2–12.

Bernes, Jasper. 2017. *The Work of Art in the Age of Deindustrialization*. Stanford, CA: Stanford University Press. Remove the phrase "Cited with the author's permission."

Brainard, Ingrid. 1956. *Die Choreographie der Hoftänze in Burgund, Frankreich und Italien im 15. Jahrhundert*. PhD dissertation, Göttingen Phil. Fak. of Georg August Universität.

Brainard, Ingrid. 1979. "Bassedanse, Bassadanza and Ballo in the Fifteenth Century." In *Dance History Research: Perspectives from Related Arts and Disciplines*, edited by Joann W. Kealiinohomoku, 64–97. New York: CORD.

Bukofzer, Manfred. 1950. *Studies in Medieval and Renaissance Music*. New York: Norton, 1950.

Butterfield, Ardis. 2002. *Poetry and Music in Medieval France: From Jean Renart to Guillaume de Machaut*. New York: Cambridge University Press.

Carruthers, Mary. 2008. *The Book of Memory*, 2nd ed. New York: Cambridge University Press.

Chaganti, Seeta. 2012. "Proleptic Steps: Rethinking Historical Period in the Fifteenth-Century Dance Manual." *Dance Research Journal* 44(2): 29–47.

Closson, Ernest, ed. 1912. *Le Manuscrit dit de basses danses de la Bibliothèque de Bourgogne*. Brussels: Société des Bibliophiles et Iconophiles de Belgique.

Collingwood, R. G. 1977. *The Idea of History*. New York: Oxford University Press.

Copeland, Rita, and Ineke Sluiter, eds. 2009. *Medieval Grammar and Rhetoric: Language Arts and Literary Theory, AD 300–1475*. New York: Oxford University Press.

Cornazano, Antonio. 1981. *The Book on the Art of Dancing*. Translated by Madeleine Inglehearn and Peggy Forsyth. London: Dance Books.

Crane, Frederick. 1986. *Materials for the Study of the Fifteenth-Century Basse Danse*. New York: Institute of Mediaeval Music.

Dray, William H. 1995. *History as Re-enactment: R. G. Collingwood's Idea of History*. New York: Oxford University Press.

Enders, Jody. 1992. *Rhetoric and the Origins of Medieval Drama*. Ithaca, NY: Cornell University Press.

Enders, Jody. 1999. *The Medieval Theater of Cruelty*. Ithaca, NY: Cornell University Press.

Enders, Jody. 2009. *Murder by Accident: Medieval Theater, Modern Media, Critical Intentions*. Chicago: University of Chicago Press.

Farnell, Brenda. 1995. "Where Mind Is a Verb: Spatial Orientation and Deixis in Plains Indian Sign Talk and Assiniboine (Nakota) Culture." In *Human Action Signs in Cultural Context: The Visible and the Invisible in Movement and Dance*, edited by Brenda Farnell, 82–111. Metuchen, NJ: Scarecrow.

Fermor, Sharon. 1987. "On the Question of Pictorial 'Evidence' for Fifteenth-Century Dance Technique." *Dance Research Journal* 5(2): 18–32.

Foster, Susan Leigh. 1995. "Choreographing History." In *Choreographing History*, edited by Susan Leigh Foster, 3–24. Bloomington: Indiana University Press.

Franko, Mark. 1985. "Renaissance Conduct Literature and the Basse Danse: The Kinesis of Bonne Grace." In *Persons and Groups: Social Behavior as Identity Formation in Medieval and Renaissance Europe*, edited by Richard C. Trexler, 55–66. Binghamton: Medieval & Renaissance Texts & Studies.

Franko, Mark. 1986. *The Dancing Body in Renaissance Choreography (c. 1416–1589)*. Birmingham, AL: Summa.

Franko, Mark. 1989. "Repeatability, Reconstruction and Beyond." *Theatre Journal* 41(1): 56–74.

Gombosi, Otto. 1941. "About Dance and Dance Music in the Late Middle Ages." *The Musical Quarterly* 27(3): 289–305.

Howard, Skiles. 1998. *The Politics of Courtly Dancing in Early Modern England*. Amherst: University of Massachusetts Press.

Jackman, James L., ed. 1980. *Fifteenth-Century Basse Dances*. New York: Arno Press.

Kaeppler, Adrienne L. 1991. "Memory and Knowledge in the Production of Dance." In *Images of Memory: On Remembering and Representation*, edited by Susanne Küchler and Walter Melion, 109–120. Washington, DC: Smithsonian Institution Press.

Kay, Sarah. 2007. *The Place of Thought: The Complexity of One in Late Medieval French Didactic Poetry*. Philadelphia: University of Pennsylvania Press.

Lawton, David. 2007. "1453 and the Stream of Time." *JMEMS* 37(3): 469–491.

Manning, Erin. 2009. *Relationscapes: Movement, Art, Philosophy*. Cambridge, MA: MIT Press.

McCalman, Iain, and Paul A. Pickering, eds. 2010. *Historical Reenactment: From Realism to the Affective Turn*. New York: Palgrave Macmillan.

McGee, Timothy J. 1989. *Medieval Instrumental Dances*. Bloomington: Indiana University Press, 1989.

Meyer-Baer, Kathi. 1955. "Some Remarks on the Problems of the Basse-Dance." *Tijdschrift der Vereeniging voor Noord-Nederlands Muziekgeschiedenis* 17(4): 51–77.

Nevile, Jennifer. 2007. "Dance and Time in Fifteenth-Century Italy." In *Art and Time*, edited by Jan Lloyd Jones, 300–314. Melbourne: Australian Scholarly Publishing.

Nevile, Jennifer. 2008. "Dance Performance in the Late Middle Ages: A Contested Space." In *Visualizing Medieval Performance: Perspectives, Histories, Contexts*, edited by Elina Gertsman, 295–310. Burlington, VT: Ashgate.

Nevile, Jennifer. 2011. "Dance and Identity in Fifteenth-Century Europe." In *Music, Dance, and Society: Medieval and Renaissance Studies in Memory of Ingrid G. Brainard*, edited by Ann Buckley and Cynthia J. Cyrus, 231–248. Kalamazoo, MI: Medieval Institute Publications.

Payne, Ian. 2003. *The Almain in Britain, c. 1549–1675: A Dance Manual from Manuscript Sources*. Burlington, VT: Ashgate.

Rimmer, Joan. 1991. "Medieval Instrumental Dance Music." *Music & Letters* 72(1): 61–68 (review of McGee).

Roach, Joseph R. 1996. *Cities of the Dead: Circum-Atlantic Performance*. New York: Columbia University Press.

Rust, Frances. 1969. *Dance in Society*. London: Routledge & Kegan Paul.

Schechner, Richard. 1986. *Between Theater and Anthropology*. Philadelphia: University of Pennsylvania Press.

Schneider, Rebecca. 2011. *Performing Remains: Art and War in Times of Theatrical Reenactment*. New York: Routledge.

Smith, A. William, trans. 1995. *Fifteenth-Century Dance and Music: Twelve Transcribed Italian Treatises and Collections in the Tradition of Domenico da Piacenza*, vol. 1. Stuyvesant, NY: Pendragon Press, 1995.

Smith, Margaret Dean. 1937. "A Fifteenth-Century Dancing Book: 'Sur L'Art et Instruction de Bien Danser.'" *Journal of the English Folk Dance and Song Society* 3(2): 100–109.

Sparti, Barbara, ed. and trans. 1993. *Guglielmo Ebreo of Pesaro's On the Practice or Art of Dancing*. Oxford: Clarendon.

Steuber, Karsten R. 2002. "The Psychological Basis of Historical Explanation: Reenactment, Simulation, and the Fusion of Horizons." *History and Theory* 41: 25–42.

Thomas, Emma Lewis. 1978. "Music and Dance in Boccaccio's Time Part II: Reconstruction of *Danze* and *Balli*." *Dance Research Journal* 10(2): 23–42.

Ward, John M. 1976. "The Maner of Dauncying." *Early Music* 4(2): 127–140, 142.

Weymans, Wim. 2004. "Michel de Certeau and the Limits of Historical Representation." *History and Theory* 43(2): 161–178.

Wieck, Roger S. 1997. *Painted Prayers: The Book of Hours in Medieval and Renaissance Art*. New York: George Braziller.

Williams, Drid. 1995. "Space, Intersubjectivity, and the Conceptual Imperative: Three Ethnographic Cases." In *Human Action Signs in Cultural Context: The Visible and the Invisible in Movement and Dance*, edited by Brenda Farnell, 44–81. Metuchen, NJ: Scarecrow.

Wilson, David. 1984–1985. "The Development of French Basse Danse." *Historical Dance* 2(4): 5–12.

Wilson, David. 2012. *The* Basse Dance *Handbook: Text and Context*. Hillsdale, NY: Pendragon Press.

........................................................................

# CHAPTER 26

# TIME LAYERS, TIME LEAPS, TIME LOSS

## *Methodologies of Dance Historiography*

........................................................................

### CHRISTINA THURNER

"Dance historians! The past is now!" (Hutchinson Guest 2000, 71). This is historian and dance reconstructor Ann Hutchinson Guest's mantra as she fights for the preservation of dance's present within its future. But we can also read her call to action as a paradoxical assertion about our access to history. She urges us to handle the past with careful attention to its presence, and in so doing makes it clear that all historians start from the present when they move toward the past. She formulates here a certain notion of (dance) history according to which history is always a construction of the past, one that is constructed in the "now" and whose end is to better understand the past in the light of the events of the present, as well as the reverse.

Meanwhile, dance *history* has established itself as an essential component of dance *studies* and as part of this kind of historical consciousness in general. This is also what Alexandra Carter (among others) discovered in *Rethinking Dance History* in 2004, in which she acknowledges that "[p]aradoxically, the traditional discipline of history has come under attack from critical and cultural theories which question the very nature and status of knowledge, and how that knowledge is retrieved, organized, recorded, and received" (Carter 2004, 10). Just as historical epistemological interest asserts itself in dance research, so are we—according to Carter—prepared by other disciplines pertaining to postmodern theory to scrutinize this fundamental idea, to interrogate and to deconstruct it. Are we limping rather than marching forward because of our object of study—"Dance"? Or does dance as art and theory reflect on the problem of history in its own way? And, finally, where is, or where might be, the potential of a critical reworking, accounting, or narration of a history or histories proper to dance? These questions are our starting point here, and the first steps toward an answer are presented and sketched in this chapter.

Something general must (first and foremost) be said about the symptoms of the crisis we are noticing in historiography. Following from that, I came upon the category of "simultaneity of the nonsimultaneous" as a stage for assessing the unique opportunities and limitations involved with speaking about the history of dance. I will discuss alternative models of historiography taken from other disciplines (especially literary theory) as they relate to dance and ultimately lay the foundation of a nonvectorial, "spatialized" historiography of dance of the twentieth century. As such, our subject is thus specifically foundational and not (at least for now) the presentation of a finished "product" ready to endure critical deconstruction. The sensible starting point here is to reflect on the epistemological premises we take for granted before taking the plunge into the "manufacture" itself of historiography.

## THE CRISIS OF HISTORIOGRAPHY

"With the temporalities and movement structures of what once was a unified History," in the words of Burkhart Steinwachs, we no longer have adequate tools with which to study "the complexity of societal processes" (1985, 317). This is typical of the broad skepticism toward historiography that has persisted throughout the twentieth century. Theories of periodization in particular, as Niklas Luhmann points out, come in for criticism in that certain of its premises, "for example, linearity, irreversibility, continuity, necessity" are contested concepts (Luhmann 1985, 13). Alongside this critical attitude one can note a "growing trend of historical studies (for example New Historicism)" (Pechlivanos 1995, 171). This trend, under closer scrutiny, is frequently illustrative of such a critical attitude and reflective of a paradigmatic shift in our understanding of history. Reinhardt Koselleck knew, possibly as early as the 1970s, what Hegel already knew: "*History* unites the objective with the subjective side, and denotes quite as much the *historia rerum gestarum*, as the *res gestae* themselves; on the other hand it comprehends not less what has *happened*, than the *narration* of what has happened" (Hegel, cited in White 1987, 11–12). Thus do we become aware of the constructive character of historiography, which would not draw up a mimetic discourse mapping onto some true reality, but rather construct or constitute the written narrative of history(/ies) from epistemological interests, known or unknown (see also Koselleck 1985).

We would have "had" history in a form none other than a series of already interpreted stories accelerated into one continuous story, says Uwe Japp: "That is to say we never have them in a precise sense, but are always working on them" (Japp in Pechlivanos 1995, 177). Seen in this way, there can be no *single* comprehensive, chronological history in the manner that historicism has self-deceptively sought to make us believe since the end of the eighteenth century and the beginning of the nineteenth. In this way was the "older, plural form of history" expressed by "a singular guiding concept" of the "collective singular" (Pechlivanos 1995, 175). In contrast to "major history," Jean-François Lyotard was instead a proponent of the idea of "little narratives" as opposed to "grand narratives"

(1984, 60). The ramifications of this reframing for historical knowledge include prioritizing partiality over totality, plurality and diversity over homogeneity, contingency over teleological necessity, as well as discontinuities over linear progressions.

Assuming we are to take these general modifications to our epistemology seriously, which questions and insights relevant to dance history would surface? June Layson labels the dance historian as "both chronicler and interpreter," referring to the both constructive and inexact nature of their findings, which moreover "are always amenable to reinterpretation" (Layson and Adshead-Lansdale 1994, 4). The aesthetic canon of dance does a remarkable job of supporting itself given the vagueness of the material at its foundations. Performance, the true index, is something that is simply not available to the historian. Especially in the case of dance, each historiography not only hinges on what materials are at its disposal, but what sort of materials those are (illustration, description, notation, physically registered memories, electronic recordings, etc.)

# THE CONTEMPORANEITY OF THE NONCONTEMPORANEOUS

That the idea of a single and unified history of the arts cannot hold water must be taken into account when dance recurs to periodization (i.e., the romantic preceding the classic in ballet). Gratuitous distinctions and fabricated continuities imposed on dance history give off a false sense of historiographical lucidity, even as compared to other more traditionally historiographic disciplines, such as literature or the visual arts. The various currents running through and out of twentieth-century theatrical dance certainly evade linear organization and straightforward classification. They all the more comprise a complex network of contemporaneities of the noncontemporaneous that invites comparisons, prefers interpretations to be open, and is conducive to contingency, plurality, and difference. The so-called ballet, for example, exists surrounded by various forms of modern dance, which together constitute a heterogeneity that is prior to their respective influences on genre demarcations.

The category of *the contemporaneity of the noncontemporaneous* also plays a role in general history "as an indication of a growing difficulty with the idea of periodization" (Gumbrecht 1985, 35). Koselleck writes, "A differential classification of historical sequences is contained in the same naturalistic chronology. Within this temporal refraction is contained a diversity of temporal strata, which are of varying duration, according to the agents or circumstances in question, and which are to be measured against each other" (1985, 94). *Contemporaneity of the noncontemporaneous* can be seen as an alternative to the notion of the vectorial model of the chronologically progressing (developmental) history. The "temporal layers" that Koselleck is talking about store up much more in, around, and through themselves than any single agent could encompass. This becomes clearer in context of the following example, from a day in the history of dance.

Serge Diaghilev brought the Ballets Russes to Paris as the first decade of the twentieth century drew to a close. Writings on this event unanimously interpret it as the inauguration of modern ballet, and it certainly seems so in hindsight. Owing to this, it is easy to overlook the fact that the Ballets Russes' major players are not all grounded within the same layer of time. Mikhail Fokine choreographed both for the Ballets Russes and for the Marijnsky Ballet in St. Petersburg, and Vaslav Nijinsky danced for both companies; this is the first temporal layer of modern ballet, as well as a tradition-centric repertoire. At the same time, American ballet pioneers Loïe Fuller, Isadora Duncan, and Ruth St. Denis, who had already spent years revolutionizing free dance in Europe, voyaged back to their homeland. Fuller visited a handful of states for two years starting in 1910, St. Denis returned promptly to New York, and Duncan began her nationwide tour. That same timeframe saw the death of Marius Petipa, the birth of Birgit Cullberg and José Limón, and the displacement of Gret Palucca and family from California back to Dresden, where she later decided to reawaken German expressionist dance before a new audience. These decidedly arbitrarily compiled events together form a snapshot of a certain moment, a cross section of several layers of time. Their correlation is synchronic, yet diachronic in that they—to stay within Koselleck's terminology—indicate various "conditions," staggered backward and forward in time, as if to suggest meaning at a geographical level.

"Writing about the past," writes dance historian Lynn Garafola, "one has many [. . . .] gaps to fill, places to imagine, people to resurrect, and frames of reference to inhabit" (2005, ix). In a sense, historiography does nothing more than leap across the gaps between distinct time layers, creating a bridge over that which is otherwise populated only by the imagination. A large part of this operation is giving the relevant individuals or "actors" new life in a new and more or less explicitly defined frame of reference. Stephanie Jordan goes so far as to qualify this process as a "political manoeuvre to establish a power base for cultural identity as well as for art itself" (2000, n.p.) that emanates directly out of dance as an art form. Consequently an art establishes its presence *in* and *upon* its own historical writing. How art effectively does this with respect to its meaningfulness and perhaps also its politicality will be the theme of the next section of this chapter.

## ALTERNATIVE MODELS OF (SPATIAL) HISTORY

I must take yet another leap of faith here as I tread upon other venerated and well-cultivated disciplines of aesthetics so that I might finally return to the subject of dance. Literary theory, for example, has focused in large part since the 1980s on the search for historiographic methodologies adequate for the shaping and recording of its assertions. In the wake of this focus, one comes across various projects that seem to reject the vectorial model of time in favor of a *spatially* oriented one. Miltos Pechlivanos introduces two such projects in his essay "Historie(s) of Literature." One such project he mentions was

*The Columbia Literary History of the United States* (1988); the second is *A New History of French Literature* (1989) with Denis Hollier (among others) as editor. The latter received the Modern Language Association's James Russell Lowell Prize. Both are the team efforts of numerous authors, editors, and publishers, consisting of a series of chapters and essays against prevailing systems of representation within literary history. Offering neither an alphabetized encyclopedia nor a continuous narrative, they instead focus, as mentioned earlier, on notions of spatiality. *The Columbia Literary History of the United States* draws on architecture to find its metaphor, as Pechlivanos describes it:

> The construction of new history should take as its model the library or art gallery; it should have multiple doors leading in that each make us aware of the respective corridors they open onto. In contrast with old literary histories, which strive to be "monumental" and linear, a unified representation of the past, it makes foundational principles of complexity and contradiction and seeks to avoid the impression both of completeness and of homogeneity amongst its core values. [ . . . ] The reader should thus have [Pechlivanos here cites Elliot et al., xiii] the "paradoxical experience of seeing both the harmony and the discontinuity of materials." (Pechlivanos 1995, 172)

*A New History of French Literature* subscribes to a similar structure, making explicit reference to discontinuity, heterogeneity, and fragmentation. The spatial metaphor we see at the foundation here is "a historical and cultural field seen from a wide spectrum of contemporary critical perspectives" (Pechlivanos 1995, 174). The pressure points of history lie fanned out in planar space like historical landmarks, clusters of stories and proceedings. About two hundred essays deal in these terms, each marked with a date that automatically contextualizes them within the set of archived episodes that relates them to each other. In keeping with Pechlivanos's example, Proust's life story is never told from start to finish, from birth all the way through to death. It is rather told through a series of diverse articles, each contributing fragments of detail to the overall aspect we come to attribute to this author's life and work. Known chronological quantities are indispensable to this process, which also has the power to draw parallels between its subject and events or actors that appear in distant layers of the temporal cross section.

Certainly these projects are open to criticism. On the one hand, one can see a certain randomness in the points of view and information that come through heterogeneity and contingency as respectively advertised. On the other hand, the distancing from traditional systems of order tends to create new categories, which are just as untrustworthy as the earlier categories regarding periods, movements, schools, and generations. We cannot overstate the point that this work of historical writing emerges not only from new epistemological premises, but also from the affordances of new media. The arguably spatial connectivity enabled by the Internet leads not only to an everyday experience that is at odds with temporally linear ways of thinking and writing, but also acts as a new entry point into scientific methodology. Another logical consequence surely arises when we begin to question whether the book is (still) an optimal medium for such pursuits or whether electronic, let alone even more spatially oriented, media have become preferable.

This brings me to the conclusion of my own project. These preliminary consider-ations for theory are crucial to my attempts here to instigate the writing of an alternative history of dance that takes as its starting point the enmeshed model of a network, or a choreographic contemporaneity of the noncontemporaneous, rather than a straight line emerging from one starting point. On the form of the eventual final product, I cannot yet comment. It could be a DVD, a database, an installation, a lecture-demonstration, a danced reenactment, or some hybrid thereof. Dance, as a form that moves and is moved in living space, insists, in my assessment, on being mediated spatially or at least through spatial metaphor. The alternative is to lose all sense of its aesthetic history and con-text. I conclude by aligning myself with Helen Thomas, who, in turn, referencing Mark Franko, postulated that "[t]he construct of tradition with which I would want to work is one that lives and breathes through embodied textual practice (on or off stage), not one that is locked up in 'performance museums'" (Thomas 2004, 42)—nor, as we can safely extrapolate, from strictly chronological books of dance history.

The "new" governing principles of historical writing such as partiality over totality, plurality and difference over homogeneity, and contingency over teleological necessity, as well as discontinuity over linear progression, have long been the consensus among the modernists and especially among the postmodernists, at least for dance as *art*. Numerous works have since broken with a totalizing point of view and have reached for wider diversities instead of the easy harmony of the singular. These reject overdeter-mined viewpoints, opening perception rather than catering to the desire for straight-forward, affirmative views. Ultimately, they reflect critically on artistic traditions. The contemporaneity of the noncontemporaneous, understood as the choreographic juxta-position of moving scenes, could well be regarded both as the data that historical writing on dance seeks to chart *as well as the very model* for charting it. Such a history of dance would take its subject seriously and would not lag behind in finding possible answers to the questions it asks of the critical movement in historiography—moreover, it could even be exemplary of a historiography that is spatial in senses beyond the metaphorical.

I would like to conclude this chapter by indicating in a preliminary way that reenact-ments can be understood and described as a form of historiography. Reenactments in concrete spatial settings such as stages and museums furnish multilayered spatiotempo-ral constellations. These constellations are based, on the one hand, on critical reflection, as I have set it forth in this chapter, but on the other hand, reenactments resituate these critical reflections in present action. In this way, they take up historical events but don't render them directly as events; rather, they create purposeful relations (see Franko, Chapter 24 in this volume). That is to say, these relations are not side effects of histor-ical narrative: instead they are constitutive elements of events as reenactments evoke them—events, which are once again perceived by the actor and the recipient. It is these relations between a then and a now, between loci some of which could be considered historical and others of which could be considered present, that also negotiate between subject and object.

Contemporaneousness as distinguished from the noncontemporaneousness, spatial diversities, contingencies and pluralities—as distinct from the linear and chronological, as well as periodizing historical description—such phenomena are neither passed over nor called to order, neither obliterated nor overwritten. Instead, they are accepted as the constitutive elements and the productive condition of a form of historical accounting as reflected in a spatiotemporal, embodied, enacted, and so—for the public—also experienced phenomenon. The trend we see today in danced reenactment is in this way—and I shall conclude with this thought—a direct reaction to the crisis in historiography (both general historiography and dance historiography): danced reenactment is possibly a response to this crisis, one that provides an alternative paradigm for the writing of history in space and time as well as between spaces and times.

Translated from the German by Alessio Franko

## WORKS CITED

Carter, Alexandra, 2004. "Destabilising the Discipline: Critical Debates About History and the Impact of their Study on Dance." In *Rethinking Dance History: A Reader*, edited by Alexandra Carter, 10–19. London: Routledge.

Elliot, Emory, et al., eds. 1988. *Columbia Literary History of the United States*. New York: Columbia University Press.

Garafola, Lynn. 2005. *Legacies of Twentieth-Century Dance*. Middletown, CT: Wesleyan University Press.

Gumbrecht, Hans-Ulrich. 1985. "Posthistorie Now." In *Epochenschwellen und Epochenstrukturen im Diskurs der Literatur- und Sprachhistorie*, edited by Hans-Ulrich Gumbrecht and Ursula Link-Heer, 34–49. Frankfurt am Main: Suhrkamp.

Hollier, Denis, et al., eds. 1989. *A New History of French Literature*. Cambridge, MA: Harvard University Press.

Hutchinson Guest, Ann. 2000. "Is Authenticity to Be Had?" In *Preservation Politics: Dance Revived, Reconstructed, Remade*, edited by Stephanie Jordan, 65–71. London: Dance Books.

Jordan, Stephanie, ed. 2000. *Preservation Politics: Dance Revived, Reconstructed, Remade*. London: Dance Books.

Koselleck, Reinhardt. 1985. "History, Histories, and the Structure of Time." In *Futures Past: On the Semantics of Historical Time*. Translated by Keith Tribe, 92–104. Cambridge, MA: MIT Press.

Layson, June, and Janet Adshead-Lansdale, eds. 1994. *Dance History: An Introduction*. London: Routledge.

Luhmann, Niklas. 1985. "Das Problem der Epochenbildung und die Evolutionstheorie." In *Epochenschwellen und Epochenstrukturen im Diskurs der Literatur- und Sprachhistorie*, edited by Hans-Ulrich Gumbrecht and Ursula Link-Heer, 11–33. Frankfurt am Main: Suhrkamp.

Lyotard, François. 1984. *The Postmodern Condition: A Report on Knowledge*. Translated by Geoff Bennington and Brian Massumi. Minneapolis: University of Minnesota Press.

Pechlivanos, Miltos. 1995. "Literaturgeschichte(n)." In *Einführung in die Literaturwissenschaft*, 170–181. Stuttgart: Verlag J. B. Metzler.

Steinwachs, Burkhart. 1985. "Was leisten (literarische) Epochenbegriffe? Forderungen und Folgerungen." In *Epochenschwellen und Epochenstrukturen im Diskurs der Literatur- und Sprachhistorie*, edited by Hans-Ulrich Gumbrecht and Ursula Link-Heer, 312–323. Frankfurt am Main: Suhrkamp.

Thomas, Helen. 2004. "Reconstruction and Dance as Embodied Textual Practice." In *Rethinking Dance History: A Reader*, edited by Alexandra Carter, 32–45. London: Routledge.
White, Hayden. 1987. *The Content of the Form: Narrative Discourse and Historical Representation*. Baltimore, MD: Johns Hopkins University Press.

# PART IX

REENACTMENT
IN/AS GLOBAL
KNOWLEDGE
CIRCULATION

...................................................................................................

# CHAPTER 27

# (IN)DISTINCT POSITIONS

*The Politics of Theorizing Choreography*

...................................................................................................

JENS RICHARD GIERSDORF

I grew up in a society with a centralized power structure that pretended to be built upon the utopia of decentralized agency. My interest in the political labor of dance stems from the loss of and subsequent restructuring of my native culture after the fall of the Berlin Wall nearly thirty years ago, which required, on my part, radical shifts between different institutional and national approaches to dance. Since then, I have come to see agency as strategically and temporarily located, rather than a centralized or decentralized locus of power. These geographical and cultural shifts have drawn my interest to the ontological and epistemological potential of "in-between-ness"—the being between political systems (from socialism to global capitalism), between discursive traditions (continental philosophy versus US identitarian politics), between different institutional constructions of dance practice and theory (at research institutions, teaching colleges, or vocational training institutions), and between the disciplined social body and its breakdown in moments of instinctual and autonomic physical response. In-between-ness interests me for the co-presence of different positions or a Foucaultian Heterotopia, but most importantly for the impossibility of inhabiting it. In other words, I am mostly interested in the temporariness of a stable position and hence the potential of in-between-ness to destabilize agency as neither decentralized nor centralized. This raises the following questions: When one works against or inside a dominant system and that system collapses, can there really be a momentary opportunity for the reinvention of agency itself? Or does the collapse leave only room for other agents to rush in and occupy the empty space, thus canceling out the potential for a momentary state of in-between-ness? What does agency become after the collapse has yielded change? What is thus the price for evacuating the center or dispelling the myth of the inherent democratic value of decentralization?

In my past work, I investigated the first three shifts and the in-between-ness that I named earlier. These include, for instance, the unrecognized shared investigation of modernism and socialist realism in my book *The Body of the People*; the structural relationship of choreography and contemporary war in my work with Gay Morris in *Choreographies of 21ˢᵗ Century Wars*; different functions of emerging dance studies discourses in relation to national educational systems, or an alternative structuring of dance in relation to canonicity in articles in *Dance Research Journal*; and the understanding of the complex space created by a rethinking of the impact of US identity politics and universalizing continental philosophy in my ongoing collaboration with Yutian Wong (Giersdorf 2009a, 2009b, 2010, 2013; Giersdorf and Wong 2016; Morris and Giersdorf 2016). I was nearly ready to move on to new investigations that would have allowed me to partly move away from or to question the validity of dance studies as a disciplinary discourse, when I experienced what I would consider a very "destabilizing" career hiccup. I was invited by a dance scholar to present at a multidisciplinary conference in Basel, Switzerland, specifically to talk about my work on the epistemology of dance studies. I decided to present on the destabilization of the in-between space left by the inability of abstract philosophical European dance discourse and identity-based US dance studies to talk to each other. I imagined myself talking from the stability of my discipline to the mostly German-speaking scholars from media studies, theater history, and German studies about the politics of the choreography of this in-between and vacated space. I decided to present in German for this interdisciplinary audience, something I normally don't do, because all my higher education and professional work has been conducted in English.

I thought I was talking about the in-between space of the two different national dance discourses in order to make a destabilizing disciplinary intervention. However, the participants thought I was attacking them for not doing identity politics and then assured me that we all have moved on. I suddenly realized that I was getting "tomatoed." The interdisciplinary scholars did not understand my challenge to the power that dance studies can wield over dance by constructing it as an object of study or a method; rather, they viewed it as a national attack.[1] I had assumed that in this moment of our discipline's evolution, I could build on its stability and impact on other disciplinary discourses, and criticize dance studies' hegemonic national politics in relation to its object of investigation in order to expose the power of the different centers of a multinational dance studies. The interdisciplinary scholars experienced the mismatch between the theoretical models I used, which situated me in a North American discourse, and my German appearance and speech as confusing; they just wanted to hear a German dance analysis focusing on aesthetics and philosophical and historical questions, and utilizing the newest politico-aesthetic theories. There I was in a villa on the outskirts of Basel, where money was no object, where even the statues of little deer surrounding the pool had penises, where German media and theater scholars talked about the "ontologization of ontology" and said things like "art has nothing to do with culture" in response to my

---

[1] I am referring in this assessment to my own work on the national differences in dance studies and how dance and choreography are structured into an object of research or a method. The first approach centralizes dance into a tangible object, the second decentralizes it to be applied to any kind of dance (2009a).

talk, and I realized that what I thought was very stable and could be decentered was not. In other words, dance studies is fairly stable in a single national context and its disciplinary boundaries, but when you shift it out of our disciplinary discourse or national system, then it might not always be able to sustain its centrality, and other disciplinary approaches will take its place. I thus decided that I need to clarify my understanding of in-between-ness and its productive potential across disciplines and national discourses, which I am endeavoring to accomplish in this chapter.

Even though this chapter was born out of a not so pleasant experience of in-between-ness at the conference, I want to turn it into a productive investigation of two exclusive approaches for the theorization of dance, which I will label for the purposes of illustration as German philosophical conceptualization and US identity politics. Caused by incompatible methodologies, international communication within the field of dance studies often only takes place at the level of information—excluding critical engagement with the opposing positions. Such inability to critically engage reinforces local academic norms of national models of dance studies. Using the example of Trajal Harrell's unique reenactment of historical choreographic material and physicalization of dance theoretical positions in his choreography *Antigone Sr./Twenty Looks or Paris Is Burning at The Judson Church (L)*, I want to propose it as a productive model of in-between-ness that not only engages with both approaches to dance studies, but also provides a critical reenactment of them. Before I explain the nature of the differences between the two national models of dance studies, it is important to stress how these two positions reenact or reiterate historical developments in theorization in academia in Germany and the United States more generally, in respect to the way that the object of investigation is shaped and its power is exercised. Thus, the question of how scholars in their distinct national contexts and disciplinary discourses reenact either educational history seems to be at the core of their differing control over dancing and bodies.[2]

I start with three observations in a consciously non-chronological order in order to justify my assessment of national dance discourses' inability to critically engage with positions outside their national academic norms and artistic traditions.

1. The influential German dance researcher was sitting next to me while we listened to the keynote address of a large US dance conference with international participation, held in London in 2010. Over the last few days, she and I had exchanged much information about the different disciplinary structures, contents, and methods in dance studies in Germany and the United States. The speaker, one of the most famous African-American dance scholars, tried to convey to the audience his theorization of the concept of a black aesthetic in dance. Just the fact that he

---

[2] I use reenactment informed by Rebecca Schneider's (2011) exploration of the concept to allow for not only a reviving of historical structures in the present, but also a non-chronological restructuring for future potentiality. Such reenactments are nostalgic and emphasize simultaneity. In contrast to Schneider, I am exploring Harrell's choreography as a reenactment of utopian histories and theoretical models.

used the term "black beauty" in almost every other sentence seemed to point out that it was a difficult concept to define.[3] After some fifteen minutes, the German scholar leaned over and asked, "Why does he use the term 'black beauty'? He's brown." A quick glance on my part seemed to assure me that she wasn't making a politically incorrect joke, but that her question was apparently serious. To be honest, I could not answer. With this chapter, I hope to break my silence.

2. In 1986, Susan Manning described in her article "An American Perspective on *Tanztheater*" an exchange between protagonists of the US and the German dance scene at a symposium held at the Goethe House in New York City (1986). The American dance critic of the *New York Times*, Anna Kisselgoff, turned to Reinhild Hoffmann, with despair in her voice: "But why aren't you more interested in dance vocabularies?" Without answering, Hoffmann turned to the New York choreographer Nina Wiener and asked, "But why aren't you more interested in the social problems in a city like New York?" Wiener didn't reply either (1986, 57). Manning looked at this exchange of questions, neither of which received a response, as an indicator of the divergence of so-called postmodern or contemporary dance in the United States and Germany. While "American choreographers basically stressed the expressivity of pure movement" and not narrative and representational structures, German choreographers seemed to deal with content. As Manning stated, it seemed dance critics and dance theorists also emphasized this contrast, because Americans questioned the neo-expressionist approach to dance in *Tanztheater* and turned more toward dance description than the interpretation of dance; while at the same time the Germans assessed US dance as insignificant and formalist.[4]

3. In 1956, Theodor W. Adorno gave a lecture, "Some Aspects of a Comparison between German and American Culture," at the Historical Society of the Third Armored Division of the US Army in Hanau. Two years later, he gave this lecture again, in German, with the title "Kultur and Culture," during the "University Weeks for Continuing Education in Political Science in Hesse" in Bad Wildungen

---

[3] "Black aesthetic" and "black beauty" are concepts of strategic affirmation and essentialization of African-American attributes historically related to the civil rights movement and the Harlem Renaissance. They are not so much tools for an abstract investigation of aesthetics as for an exploration and celebration of specific African-American expressions and contributions to US culture and society. Stemming from investigations in art history and music and direct engagement with modernism, these cultural approaches to an understanding of such constructs as race, ethnicity, migration, and postcolonization influence larger social developments and artistic expressions, such as dance. See Manning (2006) and DeFrantz (2007).

[4] Revisiting her argument of 1986, Manning later used the differentiation of formalism and neo-expressionism to connote differences between the US and German positions (2010, 10). Interestingly enough, Manning placed Gerhard Bohner's reconstruction (1977) of Oskar Schlemmer's *Triadisches Ballett* (*Triadic Ballet*, 1922) outside of this binary structure. Important for the distinction between the American formalistic and the German conceptual approach to choreography and dance studies is also the dichotomy between theory and practice that seems to inform both approaches. However, an exploration of this important dichotomy goes beyond my investigation here. For a short analysis of this dichotomy in relation to dance education, see Giersdorf (2009a).

(1958). In both versions of the lecture, Adorno, who lived in the United States for eleven years as a privileged immigrant, tried to transcend the "fatal antitheses of *Kultur* and Culture" (2003). In particular, he wanted to question the German "anti-civilization" traditions, which fostered belief in the superiority of one continent over another, because the North American continent had produced nothing but refrigerators and automobiles, whereas Germany had created the "culture of mind" (2003).[5]

Based on the Latin root word *colere* (meaning to farm, cultivate the land, or care for livestock), Adorno defines culture as the relationship to and understanding of nature. Without privileging either side, Adorno builds his argument on the assumption that the United States and Europe fundamentally differ from each other regarding their mindset about nature and, therefore, use nature differently. One side tries to master and control the outer nature or environment (which comprises also the inner nature, or the subconscious) through exploitation and technology. The other side tries to preserve the outer nature or environment, and if using nature, still conserves its core (Adorno 2009, 146). It is not surprising that Adorno equates the first side with the United States and the second with Europe, particularly with Germany. Adorno argues that the different attitudes and the different uses of nature are based on completely different social systems. He looks at the United States as a fully developed capitalist society, or as Fredric Jameson calls it, "Monopole Capitalism," and as Lenin calls it "Imperialism," which defines itself through celebrating the shaping of reality and, therefore, the act of controlling it, rather than any reflection on that act (Jameson 2009, 141; Lenin 1960, 191). Germany, as Adorno sees it, is not a fully developed bourgeois society after its failed bourgeois revolutions during its nineteenth century nation building, and hence is a country that characterizes itself through a self-reflexive glorification of an *eigenartige Vergeistigung* and *Geisteskultur* ("peculiar spiritualization" and culture of the mind) (Adorno 2009, 147). In other words, American culture is an applied culture, while the German culture is abstract and therefore universal.

Adorno's speculations can easily be rejected as obscure or old-fashioned. Yet, national differences in production and reception (or in Adorno's terminology, consumption), especially in the historiography and the theorizing of culture and art, which the field of dance studies has been increasingly confronted with over the past ten years, make it difficult to disregard Adorno's analysis.[6] Even though I agree with Adorno's apparent practice of not privileging one definition of culture over another, the reality often looks different. I would like to critically illuminate and analyze the use of different concepts of the cultural and how the power of these different concepts are reenacted in academic

---

[5] Even though Adorno seemed to contradict his *Dialektik der Aufklärung* (*Dialectic of Enlightenment*) in his lectures about the analysis of the United States, his explanations still intererst me because in them he deals not only with the culture industry, but culture itself. See also Kalbus (2009).

[6] Art is of course not the same as culture. Yet, given that art is an important part of culture and that it is important to analyze the overlapping structures and functions, I am discussing them together.

and artistic systems. By highlighting the different strategies for a politicization of dance as either an activist or aesthetic category, I hope to ask which approaches become dominant as institutional paradigms that determine how dance is placed inside disciplinary and political boundaries. Building on my earlier analysis of the disciplinary discourses in dance studies in East Germany, the United Kingdom, and the United States, I don't trace historical development in our field, but rather categorize more broadly (Giersdorf 2009a). In other words, I discuss for dance studies what Foucault calls the "discursive formations" of disciplinary objects and fields inside a discipline, in conjunction with Bourdieu's understanding of the academic habitus of a discipline for the production and sustaining of cultural capital (Bourdieu 1988; Foucault 1972). With this, I hope to begin to discuss Harrell's choreography as an example that creates an embodied negotiation through a reenactment of different stances toward historical knowledge, aesthetics, politics, and dance. Harrell's choreographic practice reenacts distinct national models for a theorization of dance and simultaneously destabilizes them.

But for now, back to the three observations, which in spite of their congruent differentiations evoke diverse qualities. In the first case, the successful dance scholar inside the German university, who therefore herself is a product and producer of *Bildung* in Schiller's sense, wanted the African-American professor to be more specific in his theorization as assertion of his identity politics and corporeality (Schiller 2000). Coming from an educational tradition of abstract, rational reflection as a cornerstone of her *Bildung* and knowing about the impact of identity politics on US dance studies, the German scholar expected the American professor to execute an educational position of empirical affirmation of his identity. Already in 1797, in *Streit der Fakultäten* (*The Conflict of the Faculties*), Immanuel Kant accredited rationality, and not empirical knowledge in the service of religious institutions, with the capacity for critical reflection (Kant 2005). As a consequence, concepts of aesthetic education, or *Bildung*, from Friedrich Schiller and Wilhelm Humboldt look at culture and art not only as anthropological or aesthetic structures, but as knowledge systems that are important forces and adjusting control mechanisms in human evolution. Culture and art prevent negative side effects of human development, such as the destruction of nature and civilization (Humboldt 1986). In this understanding, culture is of course nationally connoted; its educational and cultural institutions, with their academic disciplines and art productions, support the construction of a national identity and the creation of citizens as national subjects. As Lauren Berlant pointed out, these national subjects require a dialectic between an abstraction from an individual corporeality and the embodiment of a standard body of the state (1993). The German dance scholar understood her own subjectivity in such abstract terms, due to her specific *Bildung*, and required the US scholar to embody his country's educational history in its specificity.

As Bill Reading has asserted, the function of educational institutions recently shifted in the United States strongly to that of global corporations (1996). Education works here more in the sense of professional education, a mission to which the so-called land-grant institutions had already committed themselves by the end of the nineteenth century. Identity politics was first established in 1969 in one of these institutions by the foundation of a department for ethnic studies after a long-lasting student protest at the University of California, Berkeley. From that point, it found its way as an academic discipline into all other educational institutions in the United States. Identity politics, which is a strong influence for all human, social, and art studies in the United States, never quite lost its activist roots, despite fusion with originally British Cultural Studies from the Birmingham School and advancement into postcolonial studies.[7] In these approaches to the theorizations of identity and embodiment, strategic essentialism, an intentionally reductive ontology, communicates with social constructivism.[8] This seems to be the background from within which the German dance scholar assumed that the African-American professor, despite his attempt to rethink an abstract European concept of aesthetics within US identity politics, was not applied enough. Her assumptions about his national educational system and physical identity determined for her his theorization of body, dance, and movement. Two different educational politics not so much clashed as moved incongruously next to each other. That might also be the reason for the American professor's difficulty in defining the black aesthetic. Moreover, this inability to communicate across national educational systems explains my own silence, as my transnational educational history places me at the intersection of German *Bildung* and US identity politics.

It is no surprise, either, that the questions from 1986 at the Goethe House were never answered. Different definitions of agency in Germany and the United States only allow digression and evasion. Agency, in American human and social studies, defines the potential for an activity of an individual within society, or as Anthony Appiah defines it, emphasizes less the moral basis or autonomy than the political condition for action (2005). American choreographers present at the Goethe House situated agency in spatiotemporal experiments and in choreographic potential. To come back to Adorno's differentiation, he would label this a fully developed "bürgerliche Geste" (bourgeoise gesture). By the second half of the twentieth century, postmodern dance in the United States questioned theatrical structures in its choreographic emphasis on movement experimentation, improvisation, and ostensible erasure of the theatrical relationship between performer and audience. German choreographers at the time of the exchange at the Goethe House remained in a theatrical structure that was historically much more important for German nation building and the creation of bourgeois citizenship than it has been in the United States, and questioned the institution of theater (and with it citizenship) from within, through repetitive and spectacularized pedestrian vignettes. Here, agency is situated in the creation of a temporary collective body, which emerges through the juxtaposition of audience and dancer in the theatrical space, as explained by Erika Fischer-Lichte (2004). This means that movement (or not-moving) establishes a relationship that then enables a reflection on social structures. Whereas movement executed by individual bodies is primarily a method of investigation in the United States, in

---

[7] Jill Dolan illuminates the relationship between education, theater, and political activism (2001).

[8] Even though Gayatri Spivak coined the term "strategic essentialism," she has since turned away from the concept (Ray and Spivak 2009).

Germany it is mostly utilized to create an abstracted relationship that could be used to understand social structures, such as citizenship. The kinetics of so-called postmodern dance in America is pitted against the abstract corporeal relationship between audience and performer in contemporaneous German choreography. Of course, these different approaches reflect themselves in the theorizing of dance, which I have explored elsewhere (2009). Rather than an exhaustive genealogy of the two models of dance theorization and how they connect, negate, and question each other, I am interested in this chapter in the in-between spaces created by them, and if there is a way to move in them constructively, without assigning a permanent place in them, but rather creating a simultaneity of different politics of dance theory. Here I think a discussion of Trajal Harrell's choreographic reenactments can be productive, since it not only refers to both positions, but also effectively interrogates them.

Although not recognizable distinctly as such, I do see Harrell's choreography as a variation on the lecture performance that has been increasingly appearing in the past couple of years in Europe. Maaike Bleeker postulates that "lecture performances emerge as a genre that gives expression to an understanding of dance as a form of knowledge production—knowledge not (or not only) about dance but also dance as a specific form of knowledge that raises questions about the nature of knowledge and about practices of doing research" (2012, 233). Bleeker considers self-reflection as the modus operandi of the lecture performance. Pirkko Husemann sees in the lecture performance a merging of production and reception and a self-reflection that turns particularly toward alternative forms, which reconsider familiar practices, expectations, opinions, and institutions, to imply the potential of one's own field of work and influences, as well as the unknown and the forgotten. It is this definition of Husemann that demands we consider Harrell's choreography as lecture performance (2004).

*Antigone Sr./Twenty Looks or Paris Is Burning at The Judson Church (L)* is a sequence in Harrell's diverse reenactments of a fictitious exchange between the voguing scene in Harlem and downtown postmodern dance of the 1960s (Huffington Post 2012). These two dance scenes, which took place only a few miles apart, did not connect, of course, not only because of their different participants—voguing was mainly developed by lower-class African Americans and Latinos, while the more privileged white participants rebelled with postmodern dance against established norms of modern dance and society. The postmodern rebellion is still celebrated in the New York dance scene as an important force in local and national dance history, as for instance during city-wide celebrations of the fiftieth anniversary of Judson Church. In addition, postmodern dance receives some international attention—interestingly, though, mainly outside of the environment of dance, in museums or fine arts institutions.[9] In the beginning of the 1990s, voguing had a short but far more global high point, when Madonna made the public familiar with the vocabulary of voguing with her hit *Vogue*.

---

[9] With *Platform 2012: Judson Now*, DanceSpaceProject celebrated the fiftieth anniversary of the first "concert" at the Judson Memorial Church and its impact on the contemporary dance scene. In Germany, I saw Yvonne Rainer and Trisha Brown's work performed at Documenta 12 in Kassel in 2007.

In the same year, Jennie Livingston provided a glance into ball culture with its houses and balls as consciously choreographed structures of social organization and protection in her film *Paris Is Burning*. Voguing is still used by a predominantly Latino/a and African-American LGBTQ community as an important tool for identification, self-fulfillment, and representation.

The crucial distinction between the now canonized higher culture of postmodern dance and the almost invisible subculture of voguing lies in their contrary utilization of form and dance. For Harrell, it is mainly different definitions of representation in performance that, while apparently incompatible, get reenacted and superimposed in his choreographies. While Judson Church choreographers refused any kind of theatricality and only critically engaged with authenticity, for the voguing house members, "realness" was at the center of their performances. "Realness" defines highly stylized imitation of particular social roles (e.g., that of the supermodel), but also more profane roles, like that of the businessman, crossing borders of gender and race. The defined vocabulary, the different styles, and the imitation of gender, racial, and social roles construct "realness" as a consciously non-naturalistic form of representation that defines itself through the simultaneous presence of signifier and referent and the conscious performance of the gap between them. Harrell expands the complexity of the conglomerate of these two concepts of representation by using the Greek tragedy of *Antigone* as a loose narrative structure. He describes the Greek theater and its male actors as the reason for the all-male cast for his version of *Antigone Sr./Twenty Looks or Paris Is Burning at The Judson Church (L)*.[10]

The performance begins with Harrell's diagnosis that the stage is actually too small for this work and that he, the actors, and stage designers are still in the process of finishing it. In Judson Church tradition, this underlines the creative process and makes the audience a participant in an investigation, rather than a consumer of a theater product. At the same time, this strategy references the lecture performance, with its explanation of the process of dance exploration and establishes Harrell as author and moderator. This role, which Harrell reenacts throughout the evening in different incarnations, demands a simultaneous seeing and being seen, which again becomes more complicated due to Harrell's repeatedly evoked African-American identity, and the way he harmonizes the seemingly white dancers in his orbit like satellites. Thereby, Harrell manages simultaneously to be the object of the theatrical structure and its creator, a position that permits a sophisticated comprehension of choreography as resistance and model for social resistance.[11]

Even though executed throughout the evening, the double structure becomes most apparent one hour after the beginning of the piece, when Harrell sits on a podium

[10] There are also Jr, S, M, and Made to Measure (M2M) versions as solo or mixed performances, and an XL version is released as a book.

[11] See André Lepecki, *Dance and (In)difference: Towards a Kinetic Critique of Communication*. http://blip.tv/dancetechtvbliptv/andr-lepecki-dance-and-in-difference-towards-a-kinetic-critique-of-communication-4663973.

covered with loose fabric in the middle of the stage and four dancers around him show off different costumes on imaginary catwalks in the voguing tradition. In the past hour, the audience had to rise to listen to the "anthem of the house" sung in a cappella, which the audience soon recognized as Britney Spears's first hit, "Baby One More Time." The dancers had then moved as if improvising, like introverted soloists in three different lit squares, looking more like dancers in a disco than actors on stage. Harrell eventually interrupted the events on stage from the auditorium by screaming, "Stop the fucking show! Stop the motherfucking show!" and then rapped in voguing style, "Give me legendary face! There is an icon in the house! That's *Antigone*, bitch! The house of Thebes is in the house!" Andrew Boynton of *The New Yorker* magazine saw these diverse elements merge and make sense under Harrell's direction. Harrell furthermore embraced the story of *Antigone*, a strong woman in a male-dominated society, in a Greek theater tradition of male representation of female roles, and with that also the similarities of the stylization of the Greek theater and voguing culture (Boynton 2012). Stylization is used here as strategy to reenact historical material across cultural, temporal, and spatial borders. Therefore, it is radically different from, for example, Martin Nachbar's engagement with Dore Hoyer's choreography or Fabián Barba's work with Wigman's. Harrell's choreography does not deal with the possibility or inability to control historical material, but instead questions established temporalities or even newly creates them. Reenactment produces new theatrical and historical structures, instead of functioning as archival practice. Harrell uses the reenactment of Greek theater practice, voguing culture, and postmodern dance against any fetishization of dance's ephemerality because he not only reanimates the past in the present, but also, as Mark Franko suggests, points to the future as a revised reenactment. As Harrell describes it, ". . . performance can be a way in which we collectively reimagine the impossibilities of history and thus make room for new possibilities in the world we make today" (2013, n.p.).

But now back to Harrell on stage, who sits in a vaguely feminine position with folded legs and an overlong T-shirt on the podium, surrounded by catwalks. "When I lose I find, my identity," the end of the ballad *The Darkest Side* by the Australian band *The Middle East*, to which Harrell, together with dancer Thibault Lac, emphatically sang along, still hung in the room. Lac now diligently tightens a string on Harrell's finger, which he then unreels and, after climbing over the audience, gives to a spectator. By repeating this action multiple times, Harrell is eventually directly connected with the audience. Many people can now move Harrell through a quick tug of the string. Furthermore, the strings symbolize the gaze of the audience that is directed toward Harrell. While Harrell changes the music from a laptop next to him, the dancers change costumes behind him, partly covered by curtains but once in a while visible to the audience.

Harrell explains that the first category is "The King's Speech vs. The Prince of Tides," a little later rapping "Prince of the runway, prince of the runway" and referencing the male protagonists in *Antigone*. Now, Harrell and his dancers display a network of references, hints, and allusions, which is stunning in its complexity. Harrell and dancer Rob Fordeyn, who flounces back and forth in high heels and an overlong T-shirt that looks like a little black dress, competitively comment on the events on the catwalk. Harrell and Fordeyn explain the outfits, while the other three dancers change into increasingly incredible costumes. Their outfits vaguely recall ethnic and historic variations on royal regalia, and the dancers present them like models, while respecting the strings that bind Harrell to the audience. Their position fluctuates between being hosts who explain that "Jil Sander is back in the house" and commentators who point out that parts of a presented outfit with a golden bag as headdress could also be converted into furniture ("This hat can become a chair. You saw it here first!"). They are lecturers who culturally and historically explain the "black ass" and ask themselves if the "mythical black ass" is also of importance to black male embodiment; they define the concept of realness and its subcategory "cunty realness," and become members of a voguing ball when calling out "Fake Hermés!" as a dancer appears, dressed with only two Hermés scarfs over his shoulders. Dance practice gets evoked repeatedly, for example when the dancer Stephen Thompson performs variations of ballet dressed in an oriental cape, or just by means of a column in the background of which Isamu Noguchi, Martha Graham's stage designer, would have been proud. Finally, we return to *Antigone*, when Harrell repeatedly sings "Prince of the runway" and the dancer Ondrej Vidlar appears, saying, "I am the prince of Preservation" after he gets introduced as Haimon, prince of Thebes. While Harrell adds one explanation after the other in the first-person perspective with exaggerated pathos in his voice, Vidlar collapses in an increasingly theatrical way. In the end, Vidlar explains that he is dead, and all the other dancers collapse "dying" around him, while they sing, "I want your love" in a choir with Harrell. Finally, Harrell releases himself from the audience by cutting the strings with scissors.

In a theatrical space, this sequence allows the audience simultaneous access to the history of *Antigone* and the tradition of the Greek theater, the history and practice of voguing with its multifaceted obsession for "realness," and further to what Mark Franko calls the complex relationship between emotionality and expressivity in modern dance and the seeming solution of this problem by the critical analysis of authenticity in postmodern dance (1995). Historical loci, which are normally separated temporarily and locally, are superimposed, questioned, and negated by parody. Furthermore, Harrell allows the audience to experience the theatrical space as a construction and institution by making theatrical labor, technique, and technology visible. At the same time, history, especially dance history, gets reenacted, created, and aestheticized, without the establishment of any hierarchy. Contents are choreographically analyzed; choreography itself is questioned regarding its function and representation of identity-structures and its potential for political actions by making a collective theater body visible.

The strings between Harrell and the audience not only materialize and expand Laura Mulvey's feminist concept of the gaze by adding Harrell's African-American body as an object to the observer's gaze; more important, identity-categories are exposed and complicated, not only by reenacting them, but also by commenting on them and contextualizing them (Mulvey 1999). The male dancers, on the other hand, represent the categories of kings and princes like participants in a voguing competition. Their attitude is not so much referencing camp as an analytical understanding of gender roles. Harrell uses historical material as form, which offers itself up for conceptual re-evaluation in the new context of the reenactment. Simultaneously, he gestures toward the material as part of an embodied cultural knowledge. The abstract choreographic investigation is connected with the embodiment of a concrete history without favoring either. Two different comprehensions and creations of culture are reenacted. The in-between-ness is choreographically staked out without occupying it.

Time and again, expression, rather than emotionality, is emphasized, often through separation and reuniting of voice and body. For example, in one scene Vidlar represents the body of Haimon's fight with himself and the political decision of his father, and Harrell offers the associated exaggerated voice. Excess in all forms is applied as an instrument of alienation. Whereas other lecture performances consciously try to be "normal," blurring the border between performance and everyday lecture, or to casually intellectualize dance, Harrell reenacts and creates a choreographic spectacle, which enables a new analysis of social structures and theorizing through dance. Taking an opposite direction to previous models of lecture performances enables the different national positions I described at the start of this chapter to coexist and to reveal their politics. While being more familiar with US identity politics, Harrell also understands, at the same time, how to transform self-reflexive abstract concepts of this applied theorizing into movement, and thus knows how to simultaneously assume the European position described earlier. The choreography of this positioning, as simultaneously identitarian and abstract, not only shows that both sides always work at the same time, but also reveals them as two forms of essentialism. Harrell and his dancers not only constantly and partly visibly change costumes behind the stage and in the audience, but also reenact these costume changes as part of the voguing spectacle. Thus, the conceptualization of a gesture simultaneously creates identity, and Harrell and his dancers choreograph the heterotopic access to discrepant national models of theorizing dance while simultaneously destabilizing them.

## ACKNOWLEDGMENTS

I am grateful to the participants of the Reenactment workshop at the University of California, Santa Cruz, for their invaluable feedback. I would also like to thank Constanze Schellow for her impact on an earlier German presentation of this material and Mark Franko for his conscientious dialogue and edits on the current text.

## WORKS CITED

Adorno, Theodor W. 1958. "Kultur und Culture." In *Hessische Hochschulwochen für staatswissenschaftliche Fortbildung*, 246–259. Bad Homburg: Max Gehlen.

Adorno, Theodor W. 2003. "Auf die Frage: Was ist deutsch?" In *Gesammelte Schriften*. Bd. 10, 691–701. Frankfurt am Main: Suhrkamp Taschenbuch Wissenschaft.

Adorno, Theodor W. 2009. "Kultur and Culture." *Social Text* 27 (2, 99): 145–158.

Appiah, Kwame Anthony. 2005. *The Ethics of Identity*. Princeton, NJ: Princeton University Press.

Berlant, Lauren. 1993. "National Brands/National Body: Imitation of Life." In *Phantom Public Sphere*, edited by Bruce Robbins, 173–208. Minneapolis: University of Minnesota Press.

Bleeker, Maaike. 2012. "Lecture Performance as Contemporary Dance." In *New German Dance Studies*, edited by Susan Manning and Lucia Ruprecht, 233. Urbana: University of Illinois Press.

Bourdieu, Pierre. 1988. *Homo Academicus*. Stanford, CA: Stanford University Press.

Boynton, Andrew. 2012. *When Drag and Modern Dance Collide*. The New Yorker, May 1.

DeFrantz, Thomas F. 2007. "Donald Byrd: Re/making 'Beauty.'" In *Dance Discourses: Keywords*, edited by Susanna Franco and Marina Nordera, 221–235. London: Routledge.

Dolan Jill. 2001. *Geographies of Learning: Theory and Practice. Activism and Performance*. Middletown, CT: Wesleyan University Press.

Fischer-Lichte, Erika. 2004. *Ästhetik des Performativen*. Frankfurt am Main: Suhrkamp Verlag.

Foucault, Michel. 1972. *The Archeology of Knowledge*. New York: Pantheon.

Franko, Mark. 1995. *Dancing Modernism/Performing Politics*. Bloomington: Indiana University Press.

Giersdorf, Jens Richard. 2009a. "Dance Studies in the International Academy: Genealogy of a Disciplinary Formation." *Dance Research Journal* 41(1): 23–44.

Giersdorf, Jens Richard. 2009b. "*Trio A* Canonical" *Dance Research Journal* 41(2): 19–24.

Giersdorf, Jens Richard. 2010. "Unpopulärer Tanz als Krise universeller Geschichtsschreibung oder Wie Yutian und ich lang anhaltenden Spaß mit unseriöser Historiographie hatten." In *Original and Revival*, edited by Christina Thurner, 91–100. Zurich: Chronos Verlag.

Giersdorf, Jens Richard. 2013. *The Body of the People: East German Dance since 1945*. Madison: University of Wisconsin Press.

Giersdorf, Jens Richard, and Yutian Wong. 2016. "Remobilizing Dance Studies" *Dance Research Journal* 48(3): 70–84.

Harrell, Trajal. 2013. "Artist Statement." http://newyorklivarts.org/artist/Trajal-Harrell (accessed June 19, 2013).

Huffington Post. 2012. http://www.huffingtonpost.com/julie-chae/trajal-harrell-photos_b_1946973.html

Humboldt, Wilhelm von. 1986. "Theorie der Bildung der Menschen. Bruchstücke. I. Klassische Problemformulierung." In *Allgemeine Bildung. Analysen zu ihrere Wirklichkeit. Versuche über ihre Zukunft*, edited by Heinz-Elmar Tenorth, 32–38. Weinheim/München: Juventa-Verlag.

Husemann, Pirkko. 2004. "The Absent Presence of Artistic Working Processes: The Lecture as Performance." Lecture Performance presented in Frankfurt, May 8, 2004. Text (English version, update March 2005) available at http://www.unfriendly-takeover.de/f14_b_eng.htm (accessed September 6, 2009).

Jameson, Fredric. 2009. *A Singular Modernity*. London: Verso.

Kalbus, Mark. 2009. "A Short Introduction to Adorno's Meditation between Kultur and Culture." *Social Text* 99(27, 2): 140.

Kant, Immanuel. 2005. *Der Streit der Fakultäten*. Hamburg: Felix Meiner Verlag.

Lenin, Wladimir Iljitsch. 1960. "Der Imperialismus als höchstes Stadium des Kapitalismus (1917)." In *Werke*, Bd. 22, 191–309. Berlin: Dietz Verlag.

Lepecki, André. *Dance and (In)difference: Towards a Kinetic Critique of Communication*. http://blip.tv/dancetechtvbliptv/andr-lepecki-dance-and-in-difference-towards-a-kinetic-critique-of-communication-4663973.

Manning, Susan Allene. 1986. "An American Perspective on Tanztheater." *The Drama Review* 30(2) (Summer): 57–79.

Manning, Susan. 2006. *Modern Dance, Negro Dance: Race in Motion*. Minneapolis: University of Minnesota Press.

Manning, Susan Allene. 2010. "Pina Bausch 1940–2009." *The Drama Review* 54(1) (Spring): 10–13.

Morris, Gay, and Jens Richard Giersdorf. 2016. *Choreographies of 21st Century Wars*. New York: Oxford University Press.

Mulvey, Laura. 1999. "Visual Pleasure and Narrative Cinema." In *Feminist Film Theory: A Reader*, edited by Sue Thornham, 58–69. New York: New York University Press.

Ray, Sangeeta, and Gayatri Chakravorty Spivak. 2009. *In Other Words*. Hoboken, NJ: Wiley-Blackwell.

Readings, Bill. 1996. *University in Ruins*. Cambridge, MA: Harvard University Press.

Schiller, Friedrich, 2000. *Über die ästhetische Erziehung des Menschen in einer Reihe von Briefen*. Ditzingen: Reclam.

Schneider, Rebecca. 2011. *Performance Remains: Art and War in Times of Theatrical Reenactment*. London: Routledge.

CHAPTER 28

....................................................................................................

# SCENES OF REENACTMENT/ LOGICS OF DERIVATION IN DANCE

....................................................................................................

## RANDY MARTIN

REENACTMENT would at first seem only to have regard for the past, but move a bit closer and it becomes apparent that these returns draw us toward the future. The neat temporal distinction between past, present, and future may itself belong to a certain history—in which case the more challenging question becomes how this encounter of times is staged under particular historical circumstances. Clearly not all of the past can be acted upon, and only traces of what is to come bear on our present. What might appear as repetition, then, is in practice a parsing of certain attributes of what we have found and what we are looking for. These moments from far and near are bundled together and unleashed on the world through a particular sensibility of how we move together, of bodies in circulation whose effects occasion further performance. Monuments may fall to ruin, but the detritus is repurposed, and openings amidst the rubble become, precisely, scenes of reenactment. Focusing on these emergent sensibilities for and of movement, an expanded field of bodily practices that links Euro-American professional dance to popular culture can render these scenes of change legible.

These spatial, temporal, and kinesthetic features of reenactment also apply to what is perhaps the most creative and destructive figure of our times: the derivative, which was disclosed in the aftermath of the 2008 financial bailout to be a vast, liquid, volatile, and extensive form of wealth, one that discloses openings among the ruins. Derivatives are known as financial contracts that manage the risks of an uncertain future, of volatilities of movements in markets that seek to reenact past opportunities apparently lost for economic gain to come. Quite literally, derivatives restage past performance as a prospect of future gain, they seek profits from sudden shifts in equilibrium, they mine present volatility for inventive returns. As avatars of the ways in which value is realized in movement, derivatives invite consideration of what dance knows so well. Dance, of course, relies upon risk, but also engenders other ways of valuing the creation of the unexpected. Whereas finance insists upon obligatory movement, it lacks a language of motion that dance discloses. In short, if reenactment today assumes the body of a derivative, we should turn to risk-generating movement practices to grasp our social kinesthetic in order the make plain that finance is not the only source of risk orientation that we might prize or that might capture our ways of moving together.

The derivative, as a social relation that assembles bits of what can be found around us into moving assemblages of embodied activity, allows us to nestle these kinesthetic worlds. Returning to the scene of ruin that financial crises continuously reenact, and looking for the creative movement sensibilities that arise there, positions dance in a larger surround that makes legible the cultural, historical, and political stakes of amplifying our capacities to move otherwise in the face of what is given and what we desire to make happen. As an investment strategy, the derivative shares with reenactment the capacity to see the new in the old, which Mark Franko calls "reinvention" (Franko 1989, 58), and the "creative returns" that André Lepecki denotes as a "will to re-enact". (Lepecki 2010, 43). The project here is to revisit the scene of what came to be called the postmodern and to reenact its derivative logic. The focus will be on the contexts and effects of allied movement practices: postmodern dance, hip-hop, and skateboarding. These three ways of moving connect not in a direct genealogical or aesthetic fashion, but by means of a derivative logic expressed kinesthetically. They, in turn, emerge by reenactments on the scene of the ruins of modernity's utopian spatial forms of industrialization or economic growth, social engineering or political progress, and suburbanization or cultural development.

Cultural scenes are made from people in movement. They come and go, etch pathways, leave traces, inhabit and abandon, deposit and withdraw their treasures. The action of population, to populate (*populare*), bears this double meaning: to fill spaces with people and leave them to ruin. Such movements have been described as starting and stopping (as in a historical period), rising and falling (as in a cycle), or ebbing and flowing (as in a wave). Yet there is more to movement than presence or absence; certain qualities, orientations, dispositions, and organizing principles may reign under particular circumstances. Kinesthetics are the ways in which movements incorporate sensibilities among some aggregate of bodies. These particular sensibilities toward movement, prior to or more general than any specific stylistic manifestation, constitute what can be considered a social kinesthetic. If an episteme describes a way of knowing that frames what will count, what will be valued, and what will direct the trajectory of further knowledge, social kinesthetics form kinesthemes, or embodied forms of sovereignty or rule.

Whereas an episteme is an array of rules by which knowledge is validated, or regularities within which it is produced, a kinestheme is the regularization of bodily practices, the moment of power by and through which bodies are called—but also devise responses—to move in particular ways. Epistemic movement has been thought in terms of temporal succession of spatially delineated way of knowing, what Michel Foucault famously described as an archaeology, an order of things from which the very category of the human would be derived. The classical episteme, which articulates all that is knowable in representational taxonomies, is followed by the modern, where abstraction ascends as language and is emancipated from representation, and the postmodern, which Foucault anticipates but does not name, as the rupture from these universalizing ideological schemas (Foucault 1970, 1972). While kinesthemes also have a history, they generate and occupy more of a spatial configuration, a medium of motional transmission. As such, various social kinesthetics can coexist at the same time, or even in the same place.

These ephemeral moments of ongoing reenactment whereby the bodies of dancers and audience encounter one another are the media through which pass the distributed links and mutual debts that may be paid for but can never be repaid. There is no direct and contained exchange between what dancers impart in performance and what audiences leave the scene with. Mark Franko insists that for dance, "metakinetic 'exchange'—the transfer of expression and interpellation to its audience—was its labor" and that "dance is also political because of the ways in which its models proliferated throughout the social world" (2002, 167).[1] What is engendered in performance is an embodied empathy, which, as Susan Foster describes it, "demonstrate[s] the many ways in which the dancing body in its kinesthetic specificity formulates an appeal to viewers to be apprehended and felt, encouraging them to participate collectively in discovering the communal basis of their experience" (2011, 218).

In terms of a social kinesthetic, the postmodern break that culminates in the new financial order of the 1970s figures a shift from the vertical to the horizontal, a promissory decolonization of the body that suddenly brings to notice troves of movement riches once consigned to the periphery.[2] Certainly the desires for the innocence of nature and the exoticism of the orient had been worthy fodder for the classical and modern kinesthemes. Now choreographic appropriation would have to contend with a cacophony of bodily practices that erupted in this dispersed and lateral topography. Just as third world liberation movements were delivering forms of national sovereignty that jostled against colonial claims to have the word, the bodily mobilizations that issued from the ruins of financial sovereignty bore their own demands of what debt should deliver. These practices turn out to be more generatively derivative in their expressions, more assertive about what can rise from the ruins of progress, able to deal with alacrity when confronted by indifference and enclosure.

---

[1] Franko is here speaking of the particular affinity between modern dance and labor movements in the 1930s of the United States, but his notion of a non-reflective performative economy located in the refusal of a laboring body to submit to industrial rationalization resonates with a more supple approach to discerning the work of dance in a range of circumstances.

[2] The decenterings of modernism's aesthetic universalism have been undertaken by postcolonial dance studies. See, for example, Marta Savigliano, *Tango and the Political Economy of Passion* (Boulder, CO: Westview, 1995); Ananya Chatterjea, *Butting Out: Reading Resistive Choreographies through Works by Jawle Willa Jo Zollar and Chandralekha* (Middletown, CT: Wesleyan University Press, 2004); Yutian Wong, *Choreographing Asian American* (Middletown, CT: Wesleyan University Press, 2010); Susan Leigh Foster, *Worlding Dance* (New York: Palgrave MacMillan, 2009); Yvonne Daniel, *Caribbean and Atlantic Diaspora Dance* (Urbana: University of Illinois Press, 2011); Priya Srinivasan, *Sweating Saris: Indian Dance as Transnational Labor* (Philadelphia: Temple University Press, 2011).

What is now called financialization emerges from the ruins of the Bretton Woods agreements in which the postwar sovereignty of the dollar is undone. What begins to be ruined in this moment as well is the very dreamscape by which America can be imagined. Innovations like mortgage-backed securities respond to a real estate market gone south. More broadly, the breakup of that enclosure around the privacy of the home pointed to what a house could no longer hold. What was released was taken to the streets. Such is the setting for the movement examples here—Trisha Brown's postmodern dance, breakdancing (hip-hop), and skateboarding—each figuring a capitalist promise of utopia that is subsequently abandoned. Liquidating these grounds is the basis for lateral mobility that suffuses a decentered social kinesthetic, and for derivative mobilizations that do not require unity to move together. The socialities carried by these movement practices are derived from other forms: what is called the pedestrian in the case of the postmodern; African American movement for the emergence of hip-hop; and skateboarding's reenactment of surfing in a different medium. Against the indifference to how movement is made and where it might lead us—the ruination that the compulsory drive of finance leaves in its wake—we can look carefully at those ruins of modernity's promise to see what else arises from them.

## TRISHA BROWN RETAKES SOHO

On April 18, 1970, Joseph Schlicter stepped off the roof and went down the side of a building at 80 Wooster Street in Soho, New York. A terrestrial being and not a sylph, he did not fall, but walked deliberately down the face of the building, altering the rate but not the weight of gravity's force. The building face is not smooth, but full of architectural detail—large metal shutters, some open, others shut, beckon like so many craters, while a fire escape suggests a road down not taken. Awaiting Schlicter at the bottom is a small band of onlookers who clap and cheer when he touches earth. The premiere is filmed, the descent captured in a grainy textured black and white long shot from below that detail what appears to be his gradual approach from the horizon of the building's edge. All manner of devices had made this unusual stroll possible. He was strapped inside a harness and assisted in his descent by accomplices on the roof and ground with pulleys and ropes. Unlike the romantic ballet machineries that conceal the artifice of defying gravity, the harness and cords appear as a kind of mobile spider's web, prominently displayed as he labors in and with them, submitting to capture in order to brave the wall. Each footfall seems carefully placed, making the effort of relinquishing his mass to gravity apparent with each step.

He was also performing a choreographic work by his then wife Trisha Brown called *Man Walking Down the Side of a Building*. The three-minute premiere remains part of the Trisha Brown Company repertory. Brown herself had performed a similar piece walking down the ladder of a water tower on the rooftop of a neighborhood building around the corner at 130 Greene Street (1973), and had created other works like *Roof*

*Piece* (1971), which arrayed dancers across the tops of several Soho buildings, increasing the scale and blending body and cityscape.[3] Forty years later, the 1970 work was reenacted by Liz Streb, self-described "extreme action choreographer" on the side of the Whitney Museum. Streb, who maintains a company and school that includes trapeze instruction in Williamsburg, Brooklyn (the urban cognate of Soho several decades later), described the sensation of grappling with gravity and architectural and mechanical elements to accomplish the performance. "The first time I walked down, my balance was so precarious that I was on the head of a pin and everything I did dislodged that balance . . . . I feel like each walk that I took there was nothing that became familiar" (Streb 2010).[4]

This spectacle of defamiliarization, of taken for granted movement reoriented so as to render it remarkable, points to a special treatment of the pedestrian. The walk down the wall is at once utterly utilitarian, determined by the necessity of circumstances, and transformative, denying the ordinariness of everyday movement while still making the extraordinary possible. The dangers seem to be an insistence of the harnessed body, but still require the assistance of others. The precariousness relies upon a double capture in harness and on film, with an eye toward witnesses present and absent, which are the conditions for placing this body at risk. Needless to say, the risk proves productive, and is here featured in its zero degree. The expectation is of falling and harm, and the dance defers this outcome while relying upon it. The performance records a debt to its accomplices and to its memorialization, to the apparatuses that would momentarily capture and release its value. This unlikely activity combines basic pedestrian elements that are the choreographer's ambient circumstances—walking, a residence, a husband, some friends with equipment, and no place else to perform but one's own backyard—and repurposing these as performance.

Just a few blocks south of Judson Church, Brown, Schlicter, and their son were residing illegally at 80 Wooster where *Man Walking Down the Side of a Building* was performed. She found "Soho some kind of a ghost town, desolate beautifully so" (Brown 1993). Her dance interests were "in collaboration with architecture and equipment" and she acquired the mountain climbing rigging from some climbers who taught her how to use it. In 1970 she decided to "make a formal organization and develop a language of movement" (1993.) She saw herself as excluded from the proscenium, given the absence of venues for choreographers under thirty-five; the reasons were "economic and by invitation and there were no invitations" (1993). Given these economic limitations and parental responsibilities, "I worked at my pace as I could and couldn't go on doing dangerous dances without support" (1993). Her work with Judson and music, sculpture, and

---

[3] Documentation of the complete Trisha Brown reparatory from the 1960s to the present can be found at the Trisha Brown Company website, http://www.trishabrowncompany.org/?section=20#main (accessed July 13, 2012).

[4] Elizabeth Streb discusses Trisha Brown's "Man Walking Down the Side of a Building" Whitney Museum of Modern Art (2010), http://www.youtube.com/watch?v=9kxWm31jh3Q (accessed June 14, 2012).

other visual arts amounted to an "intense bath in contemporary art" (1993). She views her work as a series of cycles, and advises that "you have to take me in parts" with "permission to take from whatever part of my body I want in making choreography" (1993). The cycles of work she described began with the equipment-based work of the early 1970s; mathematically based systems of accumulation; unstable molecular structures, elusive structures of movement joined by choreography; interruptions to non-fluid collages; and working with the unconscious (Brown 1993).

As she has aged, Brown has turned over teaching to her company members who "share concepts" and "internalize an information process through the body which comes out through exercises they design" (1993). If release technique describes a decentralized intelligence in the body, it also pertains to the distributed authority for cultivating dance knowledge. Brown's company in the 1980s included Irene Hultman, Eva Karczag, Diane Madden, Stephen Petronio, Vicky Shick, Randy Warshaw Lance Gries, Nicole Juralewicz, Gregory Lara, Carolyn Lucas, Lisa Schmidt, Shelley Senter, Wil Swanson, and David Thomson. While Robert Dunn's workshops assembled dancers in one place to experiment together, Brown afforded company members the opportunity to prepare privately and arrive at rehearsal to share what they had discovered. Lance Gries, who joined the company in 1985 and continues to teach release technique internationally, observed: "You the dancer are creating the system, and you are articulating your thought process" (Gries, cited in Wittmann et al. 2011, 269) This prepares each dancer so that "body and thought are working in multi-directions" (270). Teaching and composition would parallel this process of putting information into a room for all to work with, on the model of research. This distribution of authority for generating movement follows the interior logic of multiple sources within the body for initiating movement impulses. Gries notes that "[t]he initiation, or the key to a sensation of release, can start in many different places, and it is different for different people." (270) Rather than fixing the image of ideal movement in the reflection of the external source (whether the mirror, the teacher/choreographer, or notational scheme), this interior investigation focuses on generating conditions of "flow" that "unblock energy to use in new ways" (274).

Release could therefore be considered the arbitrage moment of movement, where the path between equivalents in different spaces is blocked and an initiating impulse needs to be introduced to affect the circulation that creates equilibrium. In release technique, this moment of pure interaction with other bodies in motion is termed "presence," which describes the maximum openness to influence by the information that is available in the environment. Rather than being taut and vigilant to respond accurately to an external movement command from an upright position, much release technique training begins with the body lying with the back on the floor and the knees bent and feet gently placed on the floor, a posture known as constructive rest—not simply a mode of relaxation in opposition to taut vigilance, but an alert receptivity that enhances the capacity to respond to information coming from all around. Modern dance technique honed the swing of the limbs and fall to the floor centered in a potent pelvic core. But release technique reverses the polarities of up and down; starting on the floor, the movement problem is not gravity but levity, or how to move up from the base.

The formalism of release technique resonates with other technical practices like the mathematical modeling of derivatives. The expansion of research capacity, the dissemination of arbitrage as an orientation to a field of difference, the scanning and rapid processing of information, the search for means to generate flow, constitute a kinesthetic alignment between dancers and financiers; so, too, the exploration of the relation between risk and uncertainty, the seizing of a moment of stability whose consequence is a generative instability or volatility, which becomes productive of further instruments of value. The vocabulary of dance may indeed go further in articulating how these associations are crafted:

> Stability/instability has been an area of interest in modern, later also in contemporary dance, since Doris Humphrey. Trisha Brown was interested in specific variations during the middle phase of her creative work in the 1980s, for example in *Set and Reset*, in which, along with falling principles, appear *tossing* (throwing individual body parts into space), *dropping* (letting individual body parts fall), *breaking* (allowing a shape to explode outwards with its energy), and *organizing* (bringing individual body parts into stable organization, aligned on top of one another). In those years, execution always focused on what is "real": with Gries tossing does not lead to a fully executed and perfected swing, nor does a breaking arm hold back its energy. It is necessary to really and truly hit the middle: execute simply and clearly the real energy expenditure of a tossing motion originating from the joint. (Wittman, Scheidl, and Siegmund 2011, 285)

Here, as with finance, we get the sense that properly applied technique accurately distills all available information, models it effectively in a decision (a sale that is also executed as a move or action), and that to "truly hit the middle" is to catch that very moment where value is made, and therefore to capture a fragile alignment between the technical device and the "execution always focused on what is "real." This career narrative of invitations from others that never arrive or are deferred (to have her work accepted, to join dance companies, to be produced in dance venues) drives her to generate the internal organizational infrastructure, occasions, and materials that will generate her body of work. Neither that body, nor the work, turns out to be one, and her interest in examining her own body in pieces and her work in cycles yields movement that follows the circuits of the body through elegant yet disjoint and unexpected articulations. While her movement is a careful exploration of what bodies can do when unleashed from their own kinesthetic conventions, her creative process is constantly decentering that capacity from her own body, incurring debts to her dancers and passing on the means of training to them. Assembling attributes that do not initially appear together, walk and wall, she provides other modalities by which their value appears that magnify the effects and the attentions of what bodies can achieve.

In this she was not alone. The "post" in postmodern did not stand upright, demarcating an absolute difference or break, but opened spaces that seemed uninhabitable or from which others would only have fallen to a deliberate transit along a dangerous path. Postmodern dancers were not simply conquering new spaces for performances; after all, what they claimed for their art was not theirs to keep. More provocatively, they can be seen as decolonizing the places and reenacting the conditions under which their art was made. Brown's ways of working certainly relied upon the unsanctioned space, but also displaced, albeit without removing, the figure of mastery at the center of choreographic organization. Her reenactments of pedestrian movement did not cite the work of other choreographers, as much as they repurposed the bodies and spaces she dwelled among. These bodies would constantly be slipping away from themselves, finding movement in the spaces—large and small—between the mimetic unities of self and world.

# HIP-HOP CITY

Buildings fall where once they stood, but urban ruins continually displace. The implosion of public housing and the funneling of public monies to monumental centers of trade was not simply a moment internal to a marquee architect's career, but came to figure prominently in the ruination of one path of urban development and the emergence of another. Artists like Brown who repurposed jettisoned industrial spaces would find themselves unwitting hinges of gentrification as much as they were articulating the movement that would make such shifts possible.[5] Hip-hop stars would shine still more brightly in this reconstellated urban galaxy, even as they embodied a deepening paradox of racial divides in the United States—revering the celebrities of popular culture while denigrating the culture of the popular. Some keys to this paradox can be found in the roots of hip-hop in the abandonment of social housing during the urban renewal of the 1970s. For far more poor urban youths of color, the projects remained home, even as they could not house them.

The streets had long served as urban playgrounds, but now they would become workshops in cultural production that would transit around the city and then around the world. In New York City, it was not a single housing complex that was exploded, but a massive destruction of housing stock—some one million units in all concentrated in the Bronx, Brooklyn, Harlem, and the Lower East Side—that comprised the urban ruins of progressive social housing from which hip-hop emerged. Landlords' abandonment of properties that were depreciating in value was one source for the amalgamation of finance, insurance, and real estate (FIRE) that would come to rule the city (Fitch 1993; Moody 2007). Fire was also an instrument of destruction, employed by these same absent owners to collect insurance in lieu of rent. Against this derivation of housing stock for other values that was a kind of predicate for securitization, hip-hop engaged its own forms of spreading other currencies of rule and territorial logic across the face of

---

[5]  On the broader strokes of gentrification in New York, see Neil Smith, *The New Urban Frontier: Gentrification and the Revanchist City* (New York: Taylor and Francis, 1996); for a focus on the dynamics of artists in residence in Soho, see Sharon Zukin, *Loft Living: Culture and Capital in Urban Change* (New Brunswick, NJ: Rutgers University Press, 1989).

the city. Tagging was not confined to the sides of buildings, but took the principal means of connecting work and home, mass transit, as its canvas in a context where that link was being severed through the kind of desindustrialization that had made Soho possible. Just as postmodern dance came from an immersive bath in the whole sea of the arts at a time when their disciplinary differentiation was a hallmark of modernist professionalization, hip-hop culture was distributed across music, visual art, and dance, and the corollary self-organization of youth into their own forms of collectives, whether these were named as gangs, posses, or crews.

The movement of hip-hop was no less derived than the pedestrian sources and environmental inputs of the postmodern. It too featured a reorientation of the body in relation to the forces of gravity, the vertical orientation of the body, the capacities for lateral movement, and the processes of collaborative invention. Breakdancing itself is a consummate iterative and citational derivative practice, with each boast of betterment referencing its sources and rivals and grabbing hold of the tight place that differentiates it from what others might value, very much in the manner of arbitrage. The first breakdancing to emerge in the Bronx in the early 1970s was an upright form that was inspired by a television broadcast in 1972 of James Brown's "Get on the Good Foot." Brown's quick lateral shuffles and spins, combined with sudden vertical drops to the knees and down to the floor in splits, displayed the juxtaposition between elaborate upright stepping and dropping down to dramatic low positions that would characterize b-boying. "Toprock" was the term for the precision rhythmic stepping that a dancer took into the circle and was composed of distinctive combinations and remixes of steps familiar to all in attendance, but that showed the mastery and ingenuity of the dancer. To this was added "uprock," the wide stance horizontal steps, and "downrock," the drops to the floor and held freeze positions that demonstrated athletic agility and dangerous movement. The floor-oriented movement required the ability to displace the base of movement from feet to the head, shoulders, or back, freeing the legs to twist and torque in order to generate the force of momentum with these other parts of the body on the ground that a James Brown might create on his feet.

While the breakdance groups or crews would perform in competitively framed knock-downs or slams, with each group trying to outdo the other in their kinesthetic accomplishment, as judged by the audience members who would attend the performances, movement was developed iteratively within the ensemble, much as it would be for a postmodern collective. The Rock Steady Crew claimed for itself a large number of distinct moves. Many of these involved reorienting the axis of the body and the process of locomotion from the movement of the feet to spinning on the top of the head, or twisting the pelvis and quickly uncorking this spiral to generate a rotation on the back, or leaping on the hands, or supporting the rest of the bodily weight with them. The mobility of this movement, the ease with which a performing platform made from a flattened cardboard box could be installed in any playground or street corner, comprised its own version of taking opportunity without invitation. The musical sources, large boom boxes that broadcast outsized portability, became the instrument of choice at a moment when New York City public schools had abandoned their instrumental music programs to fiscally induced budget cuts. Movement and music shared a highly inter-active sensibility of sampling, where bits and pieces of each would be assembled from the whole field of the popular forms and traditions that were available to them. Aram Sinnreich refers to the shift from origination to the mash-up as a culture of configurabil-ity (Sinnreich 2010).

The circle or cipher is a basic way in which hip-hop is arrayed in space. According to choreographer Rennie Harris, the circle can be understood as a form of protection and support, with each dancer facing one another, absent hierarchy, a momentary enclo-sure that sustains the ground for individual stylistic differences to emerge. The circle, as well as the genealogy of hip-hop itself, is, as Moncell Durden documents, contested in its origins and influences, and while widely disseminated, generates ongoing debates as to whether the term is a transliteration of Woloof "xippi" for being aware, or from early twentieth-century popular dance references to "hep cats" in the know (Durden and Harris 2009). This politics of authenticity, of untraceable origins, of indeterminate links, but also of widespread appropriation that effaces sources and influences, stages hip-hop on derivative ground, without certainty of underlying value yet consistently released to circuits of innovation and dispersion that affiliate while complicating lines of affiliation. Hip-hop is at once the circulation of black identity as an attribute of popular culture the world around, and a medium for rendering that identification volatile, mobile, and in transit.

That the value of hip-hop is continuously under scrutiny, that a battle is an internal means of assessment that can go either way, aligns the critical disposition of hip-hop with hedging, and the ongoing appraisal of minor differences with a kind of arbitrage. As with other dance forms, the challenges persist for translating movement into revenue streams for those who make it. Still, hip-hop dance moves are thoroughly mediated at their point of derivation, especially from other dance moves, and through their dissem-ination. Television, boom boxes, turntables, and other devices of mediated reproducible audio and visual images were prime tools for assembling the vast array of inputs that would be continually mixed and remixed to reenact the form. While the dance party elongated the space and time of musical reception, the creation of the short form music video became just as crucial in the dissemination and innovation that sustained hip-hop, as well as temporarily reinvigorating a flagging commercial recording sector.[6]

Hip-hop circles, with individual dancers jumping into the center to take a turn before being replaced by another featured mover, were reminiscent of African-derived slave movement and singing practices. Most recognizable among these was the ring shout, in which people moved counterclockwise in a circle and engaged in call-and-response exchanges, and foot stomps and body-slaps as a kind of corporal drumming. Thought to have come from the Congo and widely dispersed by slaves through the Caribbean

---

[6] For an emblematic volume of cultural criticism on these issues, see, Tricia Rose and Andrew Ross, *Microphone Fiends: Youth Music and Youth Culture* (New York: Routledge, 1994); on the impact of rap music on the music video, see Lisa Lewis, *Gender Politics and MTV* (Philadelphia: Temple University Press, 1990).

and the United States, the ring shout was practiced in black churches but also as a form of fugitivity, as among free settlements of the Carolina Gullahs, or among slaves taking refuge in the woods and claiming the night as their own in an exhausting dance until dawn. House parties, or Jooks, of the 1940s incorporated some of these elements of physical ardor, self-production, reclamation of space, but also the relinquishing of the body to gravity's pull that characterizes dances celebrating deities located in the ground rather than in the heavens. Rock and roll, in the pelvic gyrations of Chuck Berry or Little Richard, maintained a debt to these africanist roots as it recapitulated the migration of attentions from black to white audiences that is a persistent topoi of popular culture in the United States, going back to minstrelsy and tap dance. Sixties soul, motown, rhythm and blues continued to unleash the pelvic girdle, and the addition of the televisual, as in the pioneering show *Soul Train*, allowed the host, Don Cornelius, to spotlight and call upon one couple after another in this oscillation between the soloist and the ensemble.[7]

Its own embrace of released pelvis, reversed polarities of hands and feet, flying low to the ground, risk as reward, and the posse or ensemble that sustains it organizationally bear overtones of what will become contact improvisation in a parallel development over this same period. Breaking describes a body disarticulated from its normal posture and isolated into parts, as most evident in the perscussive explosions from the neck, shoulders, and pelvis called popping. This is a literal decentering of the impetus or locomotion for movement with a muscle-torqued release of energy in a wave that moves from right to left finger tips, or through the length of the body. For youthful practitioners, the urban environs would join these movements' risk profiles. Flips, somersaults, head spins, and walk-overs are all more dangerous and potentially deleterious when concrete or pavement is the surface. The desire named hip-hop could not be reduced to an escape fantasy, but was also a claim on a global abundance of movement, an entangled dance visible everywhere that afforded no single vantage point from which all could see what they had together. Drilling down into the earth, torquing and twisting the body in order to release it into an accelerating spiral, isolating movements that might emanate from anywhere, provided a rich firmament for creative expansion of a sociality for its own sake, and not for the measures by which it would be taken. That it provoked all manner of affiliations, weak and strong, also abetted its movement, crafting the uneven landscape, the jagged frontiers on which it would continue to circle and spin.

---

[7]  On the ring shout, see Sterling Stuckey, *Slave Culture: Nationalist Theory and the Foundations of Black America* (New York: Oxford University Press, 1987); on the rhythmic lineages, see Gary Stewart, *Breakout: Profiles in African Rhythm* (Chicago: University of Chicago Press, 1992); on black musicality, see Fred Moten, *In the Break: The Aesthetics of the Black Radical Tradition* (Minneapolis: University of Minnesota Press, 2003); on jookin' and the history of house parties, see Katrina Hazzard Gordon, *Jookin': The Rise of Social Dance Formations in African American Culture* (Philadelphia: Temple University Press, 1990); and on genealogies of blackness in dance see Brenda Dixon Gottschild *The Black Dancing Body: A Geography From Coon to Cool* (New York: Palgrave MacMillan, 2005) and Brenda Dixon Gottschild, *Digging The Africanist Presence in American Performance: Dance and Other Contexts* (Westport, CT: Praeger Publishers, 1996).

# BOARDING CULTURE

That the projects would become but a partial reprieve from the sordid conditions of the tenement slum inspired the fantasy of the urban getaway, like the waterfront pleasure zones of Coney Island and Rye Playland. The notion that a pastoral realm of leisure and consumption could become the organizing principle for laboring masses that left their workplaces behind was no small inspiration for the suburbs.[8] With water diverted from agriculture, Southern California real estate developers of the 1950s wanted to make a strong run on this dreamscape, although the mass entertainments of the West Coast had a longer history. Tobacco magnate Abbot Kinney opened Venice of America on July 4, 1905, on canal-drained swampland and within five years, the miniature railroad, gondolas, and amusement ride–laden piers drew over one hundred thousand visitors.

Annexed by the City of Los Angeles twenty years after it opened, the area had grown beyond its infrastructure, canals were paved over, and the remaining ones polluted with oil that had been discovered in the area in 1929, extracted by hundreds of rigs until the 1970s. African Americans who worked the oil fields settled in Oakwood through a racially segregated real estate covenant characteristic of the time. After the tourists departed and the piers burned, and were shut down in the 1940s, Venice, with its cheap ocean-front bungalows and edgy clubs, like the Gas House, Venice West, and later, the Cheetah Club, became a magnet for Beat poets of the 1950s and Jim Morrison, who would form the Doors in the 1970s. The Venice Shoreline Crips and Latino Venice 13, African American and Latino gangs, became potent neighborhood forces at this time (Stanton 2005). The seaside precincts of Santa Monica and Venice would be augmented by the fantastical Pacific Ocean Park, or P.O.P (1958–1967), which, perched atop what had been the old Lick and Ocean Park pier, could serve as a port of call for suburban bliss. What started as a drive by a joint venture of CBS and horse-racing Santa Anita Park to compete with Disneyland quickly became ensnared in Santa Monica's program of urban renewal in 1965, which closed the streets that led into the park and prevented access. But the pier itself fell to ruin over the next ten years, its rides sold off, buildings burned, pieces falling into the sea, until it was finally finished off by demolition early in 1975. The main ride of the park, the Sea Serpent roller coaster, took passengers on a rising and falling wave, where speed and sudden turns, near-death experiences shared with others, were the source of great delight.

The futurist engines were sputtering, the massive machineries falling from the skies, the wells dry, the hulking factories empty of labor, the masses de-agglutinated their brawny frame—agile, angry, and precarious. Certainly the will to thrill was still there,

---

[8] For an account of suburban pastoralism, see John R. Stilgoe, *Borderland: Origins of the American Suburb: 1820–1939* (New Haven, CT: Yale University Press). The gendered and labor relations to the emergence of amusement parks are detailed in Kathy Peiss, *Cheap Amusements: Working Women and Leisure in Turn-of-the-Century New York* (Philadelphia: Temple University Press, 1986)

and the rides would rise again, not with their gaze fixed upon the future, but with a wink to the past. The steel horses would be replaced by fiberglass, the smooth chrome by geometric graffiti, and the enthusiastic crowds by ensembles of outcasts. Once again, the mysterious blight that descended on this paradise issued from a toxic mix of real estate market collapse, development-induced drought, and deindustrializing job loss. The futurist vision relied upon a secure place for spectacle, a gap that would enable the crowd to witness what was to come.

The collective fantasy of a flight to the future was propelled by its opposite number: a fear of falling into the past. The mass witness of the one who might defy the downward pull, what Garrett Soden calls the gravity hero—a rebel who rises from the masses to confront the pulls of nature and sovereign authority—has captivated public attention for over two hundred years. Soden notes that by the end of the 1970s, "the old world that had admired his kind of gravity heroics was long gone. In its place was a youth culture that admired antiheroes and saw gravity not as a fearful threat but as a convenient plaything" (Soden 2003, 247). The board that slid across water, land, and ice would transcribe gravity's pull into a wave form and rotate falling from vertical sheer to horizontal face (even where heights were still being scaled). Allowing the rider to stay close to the surface, whatever the orientation, rendered the board "the wheel of gravity play" (Soden 2003, 247).

In the passage from the spectacle of risk as a theater, where the singular feat of the lone individual would be played against the perils of an overwhelming natural or social world, to participation in a world where danger was made intimate, a crumbling edifice of the future wound its way through multiple sites and circumstances. The conjuncture of risk and ruin was a cauldron for cultural creativity. Certainly this was the case for the decaying seaside pleasure arenas. As the Santa Monica pier itself fell into ruin, it drew the attentions of surfers. Like towers in sudden need of fording and brick walls demanding a languid pedestrian descent, the jagged pilings of the old pier provoked the breakers to swell their amplitude and beckoned the boarders to cluster together and catch them just at the right moment, with room for but one at a time.[9]

While danger, heroism, individualism, and nonconformity are frequent tropes to describe the values of boarding culture, the collectivism, ensemble, and cooperation are crucial features of the practice that complicate the common narratives of loners and outcasts. Whereas the waves were caught alone, there was usually someone there to witness the feat, an accomplice who might take the next wave, still sitting on his board to take the measure of success. There were no mirrors here, but all movement was closely observed. Like amphibians emerging from the sea, the basic moves of sweeping low off-center, gathering lateral momentum, and customizing equipment with neighborhood tags propelled the migration of ocean-going boards to landed planks on wheels, and eventually to other platforms such as snowboards as well. To speak of boarding culture,

[9] For an account that entertains multiple indigenous sources (Hawaiian and Peruvian) of surfing and outlines major developments, see Matt Warshaw, *The History of Surfing* (San Francisco: Chronicle Books, 2010).

then, is a reference to a movement across various kinds of landscape but with a shared disposition. As one commentator said of snowboarding, it is "an expansion of surfing and skateboarding, a way to explore different terrain with the same mind-set" (Brisick 2004, 69; Thorpe 2011, 23).[10]

Skateboarding is attributed with not only multiple origins, but also a pattern of fluorescence and disappearance, described as a "concrete wave" (Brooke 1999; Hawk 2000; Louison 2011; Weyland 2002). It appeared on the national scene as an innocent novelty item that had first been developed by surfers in the 1950s who put roller-skate wheels on wooden planks, and was then marketed to wholesome white youth in the 1960s by companies like Jack's, Hobie, and Makaha. The boards were ridden down a hilly street or along slalom, and the riders remained upright like an ice skater or ballet dancer, gliding along a frictionless surface. By 1965, what fit the advertising exuberance of a craze, which had been fueled by media attention, competitions, and some stars like Torger Johnson, Woody Woodward, and Danny Berrer, dissipated and, along with hula hoops and pogo sticks, went the way of P.O.P. itself. But what, from a commercial perspective, could be considered a fad did not go quietly. The notion that the pleasures of youthful movement could be dangerous to childhood led to the banning of skateboarding in some twenty cities, along with the association of sidewalk surfing as a public nuisance to others who might claim pedestrian spaces. The association of youthful transgressions as a causeless rebellion certainly appeared quaint and unsustainable in relation to more explicit anti-establishment challenges of student and countercultural social movements of the time.

Skateboarding was also characterized by the persistent introduction of new instruments in the boards and stylistic approaches to riding. The polyurethane wheels created by Frank Nasworthy, introduced in 1972, afforded more lateral control and feel that accompanied the skaters' expansion of the surfaces, angles, and tricks they undertook. Backyard swimming pools, the icons of suburban success, were left as fetid waters when residents were mandated to leave their pools empty in response to water conservation measures. The artifice of unsustainable water and land use rendered these concrete holes the equivalent of the broken windows and abandoned walls of urban streets. The curving surfaces of the kidney bean shaped pools emulated the ocean waves' geometries, but arrested the motion of the sea.

Teams of skateboarders, most notoriously the Zephyr Boys, drained the pools and rode the undulating surfaces of concrete. From the lip of the pool, Tony Alva would drop in and recreate the wave form of the aquatic cognate, deriving the same off-center movement, speed, and balance on the land-based platforms. Rather than standing upright as in 1960s freestyle, these skaters would crouch low and touch the pavement in a move called a Burt that they took from surfer Larry Burtleman, who would let his hand ride on the surface of the wave. Jeff Ho, Skip Engblom, and Craig Stecyk opened Zephyr Surfboard Productions in 1972 in the area between the Santa Monica Pier and Venice

---

[10] Thorpe's book, based on her own participation, complicates some of the masculinist and homosocial frameworks that frequently inform boarding culture.

known as Dogtown. Ho hand-shaped the boards, and Stecyk appropriated local graffiti iconography into the designs and started the eponymous surf team that soon became a band of skateboarders that included Stacy Peralta, Tony Alva, Wentzl Ruml, a number of other young men, and one women, Peggy Oki. The Zephyr Boys represented a generation who were the children of manufacture whose future would be canceled by the flight of oil, tire, automobile, and finally aerospace industries out of the state.

The Z-Boys bore the image of the deindustrialized white precariat. Their days were their own, and schools were less sites to mine their intellectual depths than expanded playgrounds to provide the surfaces for their kinesthetic explorations. The local elementary schools in the precincts around Dogtown were all built into hills with asphalt slopes. The Z-Boys local surround, broken of promises for upward movement in work or home, was recast as an expansive arbitrage opportunity. The daily regimen was to take to the streets to compare sites—pools, playgrounds, hills—to see which might be most advantageous for riding. Some research was required to ascertain whether anyone was onsite to chase them off, or whether they could get a few rides in before police came and shut them down. The team required a scout for sites, but also a lookout for the police. The inward gaze was matched by an outward imagination. Stacy Peralta brought his super-8 movie camera to the pool parties and captured the footage that would be the core of the 2004 documentary he produced with the shoe manufacturer Vans, called *Dog Town and Z-boys* (Peralta 2001). Stecyk's photos and early articles like "Aspects of the Downward Slide," published in 1975, abetted the group's fame, which was crystallized in the competition they won at Del Mar, California, that year.

In 1978, Alan Gelfand, nicknamed "Ollie," is credited with creating a move that came to bear his name and with distributing skateboarding from its designated haunts in pools and skateparks to a wide range of sites. An "ollie" begins with the rider's foot stomping on the back of the board in order to send both body and platform into the air, then sliding the front foot forward to reorient the board's movement to a forward horizontal plane, and then landing both feet back down on the moving surface, allowing the board itself to simulate the effects of the wave form and launch the rider into low lateral flight. The ollie is skateboarding's version of flying low, but it also opened the various surfaces of the city—a park bench, a stair railing, a retaining wall—to become available for repurposing as a means for exploring movement and treating those surfaces as a sketchbook on which lines of urban flight might be inscribed. These etchings were as much sonic as visual, the rhythms of wheels, trucks, or axles and boards grinding against metal and concrete echoing and reverberating into one another (Borden 2011).

As with postmodern dance and hip-hop, boarding culture engages a population deemed at risk of disappearance with activity considered to be extreme. Unlike the Owl of Minerva, these Black Swans do not wait for midnight to take flight, but depart at all hours. All three will make for themselves a kind of global audience and a long cast of participants who move between scenes and glean value in the lateral spaces that comprise their respective domains of arbitrage. Each claims a certain specialization and combination, and refers to cultural practices that maintain volatility now as a condition of risk-based sustainability. In hip-hop that larger sensibility is sampling, and for boarding culture the context it draws from is that of extreme sports. Here, too, a kind of derivation takes place that effectively decolonizes the extreme sports of the 1950s—big game hunting, sports car racing, mountain climbing—from the precincts of the very rich to the quotidian spheres of a populace faced with creating scenes of movement through its own ruins.

The logic of appropriation, a modernist idiom of reenactment, is complicated from the unidirectional incorporation that was evident in ballet's use of folk idioms or Graham and other modernists' orientalist, African, and Native American sources. Decentering both distributes and disburses kinesthetic practices of risk, but also yields its concentrations at the extremes. One measure of this would be the costs of entry and access, as in the equipment- and transport-laden forays for the wealthy. But the drive to exceed the performance of others, to locate value that others have overlooked or missed, does not simply drive the creation of new platforms for novel environments (like the volcano), but reaches back to preexisting practices and transforms them as well.

For all this, the decentered kinesthetic practices emerge at the point at which some upward mobility is blocked, and where some scene of ruin has been repurposed for its promises of risk-based creativity. Urban ruins, conventionally figured as a kind of trap, an enclosure from which racialized poverty has no escape, are, by means of these practices, restaged as a ground to rupture enclosure while transvaluing areas abandoned or of depreciating worth. This rupture of various spaces of enclosure signals precisely the shift from the disciplinary societies described by Michel Foucault to what Gilles Deleuze terms societies of control based upon coding and surfing. "The disciplinary man was a discontinuous producer of energy, but the man of control is undulatory, in orbit, in a continuous network. Everywhere *surfing* has already replaced the older *sports*" (Deleuze 1995, 181).

Just as Foucauldian bodies were not only docile but resistant, the encoding of control is met with a continuous decoding and recoding of lateral, decentered, and distributed mobilizations. The wave, the undulation, unfolds and circulates through an array of sense-making, affiliative, and intercommensurable practices. Yet these movements never converge; they may be used variously, but are never taken over, something is always spilling out, more bodies move in and take the generative place of what was left behind. Through the gaps in the ruins, the tears in the urban fabric, small spaces are opened from which larger volatilities emerge.

# GENERATIVE RISK

These clouds rising from the ruins, so many particles giving form to one another, reveal the kinesthetic forces of a derivative social logic. Unleashed are partial yet pervasive affinities for moving together and multiplying. Dance and other specialized movement practices bring these derivative socialities to notice, open the paths of assembly of what can be valued socially, point to ways in and out of our current predicaments, shift the principles by which our bodies are ruled. A decentered social kinesthetic runs on sentience in a world marked by spectacle. The conception of a society of the spectacle was articulated by Guy Debord in the 1960s as a colonization of public attention by means of a saturation of daily life by a unidirectional broadcast of radio, television, cinema, advertising, mass sporting events, and the like (Debord 1995). Spectacle is here seen as a suspension of critical attention as viewers are rendered passive and live variously through the actions of others. This chasm between performance and audience is both violated and bridged in these decolonizing movement practices, which in turn elicit and amplify various modes of participation. Spectacle would stand as an aesthetic reduction, a collapse of the senses onto a flat screen of the visual, a loss of the ability to make sense of and for oneself.

The risky movements of postmodern dance, hip-hop, and boarding culture do not fit in the same image, nor do they descend from the same line. They all decenter bodies' relation to their surroundings, reorienting what is up and down; they prize flying low and moving laterally, shifting suddenly, in the midst of a dangerous situation in which one has placed oneself. A gap, a break, an opening allows the body to move otherwise, to seize a moment where a minor difference prevails and to accelerate through, cleaving what had once been safely apart. Releasing, dropping, verticality—moments of danger for each of these practices—suspend the mover as arbitrager, between spaces of value, cutting into that space to leave it stitched anew with a residue of value behind. The value is both the accomplishment and the desire, the expanded sense of what is possible.

The iterative process of rehearsal, of taking turns doing movement for one another, amounts to a continuous shuttling between viewer and actor so as to render the spectacular internal to performance. Watching does not substitute for but enables doing. Nor is the rest of the ensemble merely watching. The crew, posse, team, company, are a first audience bearing witness, as much as they are baring their bodies' inventive means to come up with their next moves. They are securing the space, documenting the event, serving as critics and publicists, showing, comparing, appropriating what others are doing. The long-interview form that Trisha Brown undertakes throughout her career, the insider-accounts of a Stacy Peralta for boarding or Afrikaa Baambata for bombing, rest upon intimacy with creation of the form that undoes the separation between critical utterance and creative activity. But contemporary stages and streets are now noisy with the boasts, ruminations, accompaniments, and critical appraisals of practitioners, who have claimed the representational prowess of choreography as their own.

Hip-hop, boarding culture, and postmodern dance have made their way around the world, carried through all manner of commerce circuits, from contests to cinema, concerts with pricey tickets, to broadcast, print, and other mass media. The sampling techniques that have been so integral to the composition of these forms have also been a key factor in their dissemination. Capture technologies for the decentered kinesthetic are handheld—from the super-8 movie camera, to the video camcorder, to the smartphone. These eyes do not aggregate the masses in one place, but disperse bundles of attention through media of distribution—the social in social media, which has generalized access to the means of reenactment through sampling and dissemination. Granted, YouTube and Vimeo are commercial sites purchased by Google and IAC/InterActiveCorp, respectively, in 2006 that by 2011 claimed nearly half a billion visitors worldwide to their sites (Power 2011).

As with investors' clubs and other digital fantasies of open access, much of what is free is the labor and content that participants provide to the revenue streams of these large corporations (Terranova 2004). But what is neglected in such considerations is the widespread capacity for composing and editing these materials, for positioning them, and for commenting and reflecting on their significance. The surfeit of memory storage, of archives placed in repertories of reception, of file-sharing, of practical expertise in placement, indicates a different array of capacities for engagement than that pictured in the mollified masses of earlier spectacles. Like the movement itself, much of this reception is unabsorbable to specific instrumental use; rather, it serves as a kind of medium of circulation through which cultural values are engendered.

The emphasis in these three movement practices on flying low, off-center release to gravity, reversing position, and purpose of hands and feet (for mobility and balance) all serve to reorient the motional drive of the body from vertical lift to horizontal propulsion. These kinesthetic conditions do not form a stylistic unity, but could be said to express the lateral mobility by which derivative logics themselves become so prominent a feature of movement. The underlying sources of pedestrian, slave, and indigenous bodily practices are decolonized from their initial terms and settings to refigure those who by tradition would be assigned to the populations at risk into crafting corporal economies where risk counts as its own reward. A risky move is granted immediate value by the creative ensemble; it need not await final delivery, precisely in the manner that a derivative affords a price on a good or service that has not yet been made or come due. Derivatives promise continuous and real-time assessment of value that moves the constant calibration of the market into the hitherto hidden abode of production. The streets, pools, and walls on which these decolonizing bodies move are exposed already to the prospects of evaluative surveillance (whether cops chasing out boarders and taggers from illicit grounds, or cameras capturing the deed itself for further distribution). The question of who owns a given move may certainly be an object of spirited contention, but the insinuation of these lateral, risk-making maneuvers across so many ruinous sites eclipses the proprietary claims of possessive individualism by which celebrity may be measured, replacing it with a distributed possession by which participation in these practices multiplies. The measure of these risks taken is to reappraise which attributes will get bundled together given excess capacity.

The past forty years in which finance emerged from one ruined ground to plow through yet another have reoriented some senses by which what can be done, what is available for doing, and what wealth exists for have been subject to particular regimes of evaluation. It is no doubt easier to trace what formed this conjuncture than to entertain what might follow its undoing. The year 2008 has been taken as the ruination of a larger dreamscape, an abandonment of security toward the generalization of precarity, a cancellation of a promised future by diminishing access to higher education and professional occupations, home ownership that appreciates over time or similarly financed retirement accounts that sustain the end of life, or health care that would make lives per se sustainable. How the affiliated sensibilities of a decentered social kinesthetic activate the capacities for life-making from movement is by no means a straightforward or assured path to pursue. But what is now apparent is that the proclamations of scarcity that structure the prevailing schemes of valuation and mandate deficit reduction and budget cuts, wars against cultures and populations whose riskiness is unbearable, must confront a super abundance of capacity to move together, to assemble riches, to decide what to do next, to find uses for the creative endowments of others, to place ourselves in positions of mutual indebtedness. These emergent sovereignties animate and sustain the pleasure in danger, the openness to where the known meets what is not, that begins to cross from creative to social and political mobilization.

Derivatives came to stand for vast aggregates of wealth, unmoored from any particular purpose. The imperial power that has historically underwritten financial sovereignty has also morphed into a kind of discretionary intervention, easy to enter but difficult to sustain justification for. Yet what is also clear is that among these imperatives to be driven by risk, other sensibilities of what it means to make more or other out of what we have are also to hand (and foot). The derivative logic as presented here plays inside and outside of these dance practices, allowing them to shuttle between the ground they inhabit and the world that they ripple through. Difference is realized immediately in the risk well taken, and is deferred to other connections that remain promissory notes—a lateral move teetering on a wing and a prayer. The derivative logic might also help dance out of its own trap of ephemerality and location. Performances are, after all, derived from many other times, of rehearsal, of training, of touring; and they gather together movements from myriad locales, experiences, and sources, and recalibrate and recompose them for a given intervention. Seen from this expanded field, dance is already everywhere. Rather than appearing merely fleeting and ephemeral in performance, dance is the concatenation of varying durations, of reaches near and far that nestle among the moving bodies.

Conversely, finance has touted vast abundance that leaves scarcity for others in its wake. But like the hands and feet of decentered movement practices, the polarities of value can readily be reversed and the extremes of movement possibility mined to point to what else we might be and do together. Lateral mobility lives with what it has. If capital has jettisoned its own utopian promises, emerging social logics of the derivative point us in different directions. Utopia as an end we touch through our own means of intervention, a present and persistent staging for reenactments of futurity. These reenactments stage a larger capacity for transmitting the desire to move otherwise, toward different futures that avert the enclosures of intellectual property that rest upon claims to authorship or imperiled oral traditions for transmission. The ruins left are not sources of poverty, depletion, and shame, but the very roots of what could make a population assemble for its own sake, to establish its own terms of tenancy, to value its ensemble capacities as creative choreographies.

## WORKS CITED

Borden, Iain. 2011. "Another Pavement, Another Beach: Skateboarding and the Performative Critique of Architecture." In *Reclaiming the Streets*, edited by Ariadne Urlus and Clint Van Der Hartt, 31–51. Rotterdam: Post Editions.

Brisick, Jamie. 2004. *Have Board Will Travel: The Definitive History of Surf, Skate, and Snow.* New York: Harper Collins.

Brooke, Michael. 1999. *The Concrete Wave: The History of Skateboarding.* Toronto: Warwick Publishing.

Brown, Trisha. 1993. "Trisha Brown: Speaking on Dance." Directed by Douglas Rosenberg. Choreographed by Trisha Brown. Performed by Charles Reinhart and Trisha Brown. American Dance Festival 1996. http://daiv.alexanderstreet.com/View/571055.

Chatterjea, Ananya. 2004. *Butting Out: Reading Resistive Choreographies through Works by Jawle Willa Jo Zollar and Chandralekha.* Middletown, CT: Wesleyan University Press.

Daniel, Yvonne. 2011. *Caribbean and Atlantic Diaspora Dance.* Urbana: University of Illinois Press.

Debord, Guy. 1995. *Society of the Spectacle.* New York: Zone Books.

Deleuze, Gilles. 1995. "Postscript on Control Societies." In *Negotiations, 1972–1990.* Translated by Martin Joughin, 177–182. New York: Columbia University Press.

Dixon Gottschild, Brenda. 1996. *Digging the Africanist Presence in American Performance: Dance and Other Contexts.* Westport, CT: Praeger Publishers.

Dixon Gottschild, Brenda. 2005. *The Black Dancing Body: A Geography from Coon to Cool.* New York: Palgrave MacMillan.

Durden, Moncell, and Rennie Harris. 2009. "History and Concept of Hip Hop." Dancetime Publications. http://daiv.alexanderstreet.com/View/1630501.

Fitch, Robert. 1993. *The Assassination of New York.* London: Verso.

Foster, Susan Leigh. 2009. *Worlding Dance.* New York: Palgrave MacMillan.

Foster, Susan Leigh. 2011. *Choreographing Empathy: Kinesthesia in Performance.* London: Routledge.

Foucault, Michel. [1966] 1970. *The Order of Things: An Archeology of the Human Sciences.* New York: Random House.

Foucault, Michel. 1972. *Archaeology of Knowledge.* New York: Pantheon.

Franko, Mark. 1989. "Repeatability, Reconstruction and Beyond." *Theatre Journal* 41(1): 56–74.

Franko, Mark. 2002. *The Work of Dance: Labor, Movement and Identity in the 1930s.* Middletown, CT: Wesleyan University Press.

Hawk, Tony. 2000. *Hawk: Occupation Skateboarder.* New York: Harper Collins.

Hazzard Gordon, Katrina. 1990. *Jookin': The Rise of Social Dance Formations in African American Culture.* Philadelphia: Temple University Press.

Lepecki, André. 2010. "The Body as Archive: Will to Re-Enact and the Afterlives of Dances." *Dance Research Journal* 42(2): 28–48.

Lewis, Lisa. 1990. *Gender Politics and MTV.* Philadelphia: Temple University Press.

Louison, Cole. 2011. *The Impossible: Rodney Mullen, Ryan Scheckler and the Impossible History of Skateboarding.* Guilford, CT: Lyons Press.

Moody, Kim. 2007. *From Welfare State to Real Estate: Regime Change in New York City, 1974– Present.* New York: New Press.

Moten, Fred. 2003. *In The Break: The Aesthetics of the Black Radical Tradition.* Minneapolis: University of Minnesota Press.

Peiss, Kathy. 1986. *Cheap Amusements: Working Women and Leisure in Turn-of-the-Century New York*. Philadelphia: Temple University Press.

Peralta, Stacy. 2001. *Dogtown and Z-Boys*. Film. Directed by Stacy Peralta. Culver City, CA: Columbia Tri-Star.

Power, Don. "YouTube vs. Vimeo: Which Video Site Is Best for Business?" *Sprout Social*, August 31, 2011. http://sproutsocial.com/insights/2011/08/youtube-vs-vimeo-business/ (accessed July 2012).

Rose, Tricia, and Andrew Ross. 1994. *Microphone Fiends: Youth Music and Youth Culture*. New York: Routledge.

Savigliano, Marta. 1995. *Tango and the Political Economy of Passion*. Boulder, CO: Westview.

Sinnreich, Aram. 2010. *Mashed Up: Music, Technology and the Rise of a Configurable Culture*. Amherst: University of Massachusetts Press.

Smith, Neil. 1996. *The New Urban Frontier: Gentrification and the Revanchist City*. New York: Taylor and Francis.

Soden, Garrett. 2003. *Falling: How Our Greatest Fear Became Our Greatest Thrill—A History*. New York: W. W. Norton.

Srinivasan, Priya. 2011. *Sweating Saris: Indian Dance as Transnational Labor*. Philadelphia: Temple University Press.

Stanton, Jeffrey. 2005. *Venice, California: Coney Island of the Pacific*. Venice, CA: Donahue Publishing.

Stewart, Gary. 1992. *Breakout: Profiles in African Rhythm*. Chicago: University of Chicago Press.

Stilgoe, John R. 1988. *Borderland: Origins of the American Suburb: 1820–1939*. New Haven, CT: Yale University Press.

Streb, Elizabeth. 2010. *Streb: How to Become an Extreme Action Hero*. New York: Feminist Press.

Streb, Elizabeth. 2010. "Man Walking Down the Side of a Building." Whitney Museum of Modern Art. http://www.youtube.com/watch?v=9kxWm31jh3Q (accessed June 14, 2012).

Stuckey, Sterling. 1987. *Slave Culture: Nationalist Theory and the Foundations of Black America*. New York: Oxford University Press.

Terranova, Tiziana. 2004. *Network Culture: Politics for the Information Age*. London: Pluto Press.

Thorpe, Holly. 2011. *Snowboarding Bodies in Theory and Practice*. Houndmills, Basingstoke, UK: PalgraveMacMillan.

Warshaw, Matt. 2010. *The History of Surfing*. San Francisco: Chronicle Books.

Weyland, Jocko. 2002. *The Answer Is Never: A Skateboarder's History of the World*. New York: Grove Books.

Wittmann, Gabriele, Sylvia Scheidl, and Gerald Siegmund. 2011. "Lance Gries—Release and Alignment Oriented Techniques." In *Dance Techniques 2010 Tanzplan Germany*, edited by Inigo Diehl and Friederike Lampert, 269–270. Leipzig: Henschel.

Wong, Yutian. 2010. *Choreographing Asian American*. Middletown, CT: Wesleyan University Press.

Zukin, Sharon. 1989. *Loft Living: Culture and Capital in Urban Change*. New Brunswick, NJ: Rutgers University Press.

CHAPTER 29

....................................................................................

# A PROPOSITION FOR REENACTMENT

## Disco Angola *by Stan Douglas*

....................................................................................

### CATHERINE M. SOUSSLOFF

In the arts, the meaning of reenactment differs according to disciplinary conventions and methods. This apparently simple, even simplistic statement bears particular consideration here given the multiplicity of choreographies that have undertaken to explore the dimensions of the concept of reenactment since the beginning of this century. So, too, the field of dance studies has explored the wide range of approaches taken by dancers and choreographers to issues of reenactment and reconstruction, where the dancing body overtly lends itself to thinking about issues of history, memory, and time.[1] The situation is very different in the field of the visual arts, where art history has a particularly distant relationship to reenactment due to the objects of its study. No one has called Rembrandt's series of self-portraits undertaken throughout his career "reenactments," although they contain many of the elements identified with "historical reenactments": the same "scene" repeated—that is, the self-portrait of the sitter-painter, the same character (the artist) presented and often wearing the same items of clothing, and a living audience presumed for the finished work.[2] As the Rembrandt example illustrates, in the case of the traditional media and genres of the visual arts—such as painting and portraiture—reenactment has not usually been associated with visual representation.[3]

[1] I am grateful for the generosity of the artist, Stan Douglas, for his permission to reproduce his photographs and for his interest in my work on reenactment. All statements by Douglas used in this chapter come from email correspondence with the author, except where otherwise cited. For a remarkably early examination of dance in regard to reconstruction, memory, and history, see Franko (1989). More recently on the same issues, see Bleeker (2012).
[2] See the components of reenactment discussed by Schneider (2011).
[3] Portraiture, however, has been understood in recent years as "a performance," thus raising interesting issues for reenactment in that genre, which I cannot pursue here. On Rembrandt's portraits as performative, see Berger (2000).

No matter how realistically or accurately portrayed, figurative representations of people and events from the past could not be seen as the "live" agents required by performed reenactments in dance and theater. Indeed, beginning in the early Renaissance, the conventions of so-called history painting dictated that the reconstructed moment portrayed in the picture assume the veracity of historical (often biblical) figures depicted in it, while these same conventions concurrently denied the actual model(s) in and situation of the artist's studio. Thus, in art history and theory, the second order, integrated composition of the history painting—with its attendant narrative and moral significance—took precedence over the primary order of the actions of composing, including the use of studio models and the replication of clothing from an earlier era, using props and costumes.[4] In history painting, the priority of the second order in such images worked hand in hand with the moralizing narratives of the subject matter itself to prevent a place for a concept of reenactment in the methods and conceptual frameworks found in the discipline of art history. If art historians are among "scholars [that] have generally been slow to engage with the possibilities and problems posed by reenactment," as Vanessa Agnew contended in 2004, there are good, disciplinary reasons for this that speak to the conventions of visual media (see Agnew 2004).

This historiographical constraint in art history presents both artists and interpreters with significantly challenging opportunities, where the use of hybrid forms and methods and their subsequent interpretation can yield insight into prevailing concepts of reenactment in dance and theater studies.[5] Using the work of the contemporary Vancouver artist Stan Douglas, this chapter considers the significance raised by the dancing body for the disciplines of dance studies and art history when *imagined* historical reenactment plays a major role. To what aspects of history and fiction does the photograph of the dancing body *as* "historical reenactment" belong? Douglas presents an outstanding exception to the foregoing statements concerning reenactment and the visual arts. Since the mid-1980s—whether in photography, installation video, television, or film—Douglas has asserted the centrality of these media to thinking through the conceptual issues pertaining to and raised by reenactment, particularly the differences between historical and fictional representation (see Michael 1996).

---

[4] The problems involved in representing history in the visual arts were addressed at the beginning of the modern period by the artist Gustave Courbet in his 1855 masterpiece entitled *The Artist's Studio, a real allegory summing up seven years of my artistic and moral life* (Paris, Musée d'Orsay). Courbet famously commented on the impossibility of showing actual history in the modern easel painting by assembling in the picture a large and incongruous grouping of close contemporaries and historical figures who are portrayed in his studio, but who are not represented in the painting depicted at the center of the composition. There, the artist holds forth in front of a landscape, while the nude model at his side appears to have been forgotten or misplaced. In *The Artist's Studio*, Courbet comments on many aspects of the art of his day, but foremost among them is that the representation of history—with its imperative of idealized figuration—had come to an end. On what might be represented in lieu of history, see the 1863 essay by Charles Baudelaire, "Le Peintre de la Vie Moderne," in *Écrits sur l'art*, edited by Francis Moulinat (Paris: Librairie Générale Française, 1999), 503–552.

[5] For more on the problems for the discipline of art history presented by the temporality of performance, see Soussloff (2014).

FIGURE 29.1. *Disco Angola* by Stan Douglas (2012). Series of eight color photographs. Digital C-print mounted on Dibond aluminum. Edition of five.

In his suite of eight large-scale digital photographs entitled *Disco Angola* (2012) (Figure 29.1), Douglas conjoins aspects of historical reenactment and the dancing body, specifically the choreography of social dance. In *Capoeira, 1974* (Figure 29.2), actors dressed as Angolan rebels surround a central figure who enacts the martial art/dance form that originated in Angola and flourished in Brazil among former slaves, where it came to be used as a form of resistance to the colonial regime. Transported back to Angola in 1974, as imagined in Douglas's photograph, capoeira reenacts its connotation with resistance in the context of the Angolan civil wars that followed independence from Portugal. In the *Disco Angola* suite, the picture pairs with another photograph called *Kung Fu Fighting, 1975* (Figure 29.3), where the *mise en scène* is the corner of a large mirrored ballroom. With fists clenched, an athletic black dancer performs the martial arts–based disco dance for a single, seated male onlooker. Capoeira/Kung-fu, Angola/New York City, outside/inside, wartime revolutionaries/peacetime counter-culture rebels: the two photographs mark the significance that "social dance" has for embodied African warriors and ballroom buddies.

At the diegetic level, the history told by *Disco Angola* takes place contemporaneously in two locations separated geographically and culturally, as seen in the paired comparison of *Two Friends* (Figure 29.4) and *A Luta Continua* (Figure 29.5). In the original gallery installation, each of four photographs with Angola content hung opposite its New York City disco ballroom counterpart. This paired "hang," which emphasized issues of identification and alienation between two photographs, called attention to the contrasts between war and social dancing in the 1970s: between the parched and desolate African landscape and the urban grand ballroom discotheque; between the camaraderie of the African freedom-fighters and the diverse and alienated youth in the disco. However, the associative and contrastive relationships raised by the images are not contained in any one set of two photographs.[6]

For example, *Capoeira 1974* suggests dancing as a "break" in the otherwise serious activity of war, but one that also emphasizes, in its physicality and athleticism, the correspondences between bodies that dance and bodies that fight. In contrast, the photograph of the disco scene entitled *Kung Fu Fighting, 1975* references a disco dance taken from a martial art form and danced to the song of the same title released as a single by Carl Douglas in 1974. Due to its eventual rise to the top of the charts, this song has often been understood as the moment that disco came out from underground to become part of popular culture. Carleton "Carl" George Douglas was born in Kingston, Jamaica, in 1942 and emigrated to Great Britain, where he found success as a songwriter and performer. Here, in *Disco Angola*, the reference to *Kung Fu Fighting* also alludes to the many African diasporas responsible for the worldwide disco movement that proliferated in urban club scenes in Europe and North America beginning around 1970.[7]

---

[6]  For another view on what follows here, see Kealy (2014).

[7]  A further level of identificatory association could arguably be found between the younger artist named Douglas and the elder disco songwriter and performer named Douglas.

**FIGURE 29.2.** *Capoeira, 1974.* 142.2 × 213.4 cm. Cast: Chukwuemeka Amene, Akanni Ayodeji, JaQuan Coleman, Darell Davie, Jamell Evans, Lamont Hendrix, Gordon James Jr., D. K. Uzoukwu, Monti Washington, Cheke Whitfield.

**FIGURE 29.3.** *Kung Fu Fighting, 1975.* 91.4 × 137.2 cm. Cast: Martin Sancho Macek, Andrew Powell.

**FIGURE 29.4.** *Two Friends, 1975.* 106.7 × 142.2 cm. Cast: Joseph Bayard, Emily Blong, Paul Cram, Kyle Merryman, Jesus Rodriguez, Steve Turner, Janna Van Heertum, Martin Villareal.

**FIGURE 29.5.** *A Luta Continua*, 1974. 120.7 × 181 cm. Cast: Jorienne Green.

According to dance scholar Tim Lawrence, the fusion of African diasporas and African-American music in the forms that disco dancing took led to "a new expressive freedom" for the youth culture of the 1970s (Lawrence 2009). In the critical press of that era, this freedom was represented as a kind of "double marginality," the term used by historian Kai Fikentscher to characterize the black and gay modalities of disco culture (2000, 93–94).[8] In this interpretation, disco dance, disco music, and disco venues represented the freedoms of a "counterculture," especially when disco appropriated economic outlets, such as nightclubs and record labels, that had formerly been the territory of big music companies.[9] At the same time, disco was also represented as "underground culture" when the homosexual and African roots in disco music and dance were made visible to the public: dancers parodied the dominant social mores of the larger and straighter public in the music and the discotheque, seen in *Two Friends, 1974* (Figure 29.4), and *Club Versailles, 1974* (Figure 29.6).[10]

In *Disco Angola*, Stan Douglas makes the analogy between the sexual and cultural freedoms of the club scene and the idea of political freedom expressed by the Angolan freedom fighters against their colonizers. At the level of identification, the photos reveal congruencies between African fighters, the Afro-beat of disco music, and the African-American roots of disco culture; between dressing for war and dressing up (including masking and cross-dressing) for disco; between the theater of war and the theatrics of disco dancing; between the homosocial behaviors on view in Angola and the homosexual roots of disco culture.[11] In the photograph *Club Versailles, 1974* a dancer without pants mixes it up with the multi-ethnic group of dressed up disco clubbers. Douglas has spoken about these photographs in terms of the "visual rhymes between one situation and another, between post-colonial Angola and post-industrial New York, where certain freedoms were coincident with certain dangers" (Szewczyk 2015, 56).

Art historian Hal Foster has described Douglas's oeuvre as an example of "the staging of *nonsynchronous* forms," among which he counts reenactment (2002, 137). Although Foster does not expand on this useful concept of nonsynchronous forms in the visual arts, I take him to mean something complex: nonsynchronous forms in the visual arts do not adhere to the kinds of temporality usually assumed for historical agents in representation, that is, in portraiture and history painting. Rather, these contemporary forms propose other temporalities that call upon reenactment and alternative approaches to historical representation.[12] As many of the chapters in this volume suggest, dance scholars find such

[8] Whether or not "disco" represented a cultural "style" comes up often in the literature on it; see Thornton (1996). On the issue of popular culture and style, the seminal discussion is Hebdige (1979).

[9] My assessment here is based on extensive reading in the popular press of the period, but for a good recent summary discussion of the contemporary media view of disco, see Robinson (2010), to be supplemented by the comments in Straw (1993).

[10] The case for the association of a "disco style" with male homosexuality has been made most extensively by Hughes (1994).

[11] On these points about the intersection of race and sexuality in disco, see Thomas (1995).

[12] For a recent approach to temporalities in the visual arts using mainly approaches found in analytic philosophy and the philosophy of language and with different conclusions than I reach here, see Ross (2012). For views closer to mine, see Moxey (2013).

**FIGURE 29.6.** *Club Versailles, 1974.* 151.1 × 226.7 cm. Cast: Sethward Allison, Ryan Beard, Kohen Bennett, Teri Bocko, Jon Crow, Courtney Felix, Kelly Garcia, Ann Hadlock, Jamila Istanbulian, Annie Kassamanian, Natalia Kepler, Hanna Krauchanka, Jake Krickhan, Trip Langley, Myron McGuire, Keddric McNeil, Sam Muhaidly, Natalie Popovic, Reginald Span, Jazmine Thompson.

© Stan Douglas. Courtesy of the artist, David Zwirner, New York/London and Victoria Miro, London.

alternative temporalities in the history of dance.[13] For example, Seeta Chaganti has used the evidence of early modern dance manuals to posit "mechanisms of anticipation" as inherent in the *bassadanze* of the period (2012, 40).[14] She has argued that these alternative temporalities present themselves in contradistinction to the "given" theorizations of time found in the discipline of history (and here one might add art history).[15] At the same time, so she suggests, the different strategies for dealing with the past in the dances and dance manuals extend the possibilities for the meanings of reenactment today.

Unlike the situation in the field of dance, however, Hal Foster's view of nonsynchronous forms in the visual arts does not depend on a prior historiography. While he alludes to alternative suggestions about historical time found in the early twentieth-century writings of Walter Benjamin and Ernst Bloch, Foster finds alternative temporalities worked out in contemporary art itself.[16] In the gallery or museum, these works

[13]  Susan Leigh Foster (1995) first suggested such possibilities for an approach to history through dance.

[14]  See also Chaganti, Chapter 25 in this volume.

[15]  Historians who have explored the theoretical aspects of the function of time in historical representation include Collingwood (1977), de Certeau (1988), and Veyne (1984).

[16]  A recent excellent series of essays and artworks taking account of reenactment in both performance and art works can be found in Lütticken (2012) and Caronia, Janša, and Quaranta (2009). The most

occur in two modes: first, in installation works, which can combine various media (mainly sculpture, photography, video, film) with performances of all kinds; second, in the time-based media of digital photography and film, where an idea of the representation of a new concept of historical time converges with the characteristics and the constraints of existing technologies. Both questioning and augmenting these mediatizations of reenactment, *Disco Angola* (2012) emphasizes the significance of historical situation in a nonsynchronous temporality. Unlike Foster, my interest does not lie primarily in the artist's strategies that have employed a concept of reenactment through moving image and sound remixing, looping, montage, repetition, and redo, although it should be recognized that throughout his career Douglas has brilliantly exploited time-based media to provide "recombinant narratives," as he calls them. In these, the montage of individual fragments of sound and image controlled by a "live algorithm" create[s] a seemingly incomprehensible number of variations . . ." (Dressler 2008, 13).[17] In the *Disco Angola* suite, on the other hand, the artist uses still photography and the subject matter of disco dance and war to restage history, calling attention to how the juxtaposition and pairing of fictional images of dance and war transform historical understanding. The *Coat Check, 1974* of the disco ballroom (Figure 29.7), with its discarded outerware and street shoes, contrasts with the haphazard collection of baggage belonging to the fleeing white settlers of a contemporaneous Angola in *Exodus, 1975* (Figure 29.8). Douglas' wordplay between the titles of the photographs creates further resonances and unexpected insights into the significance of clothing left behind in times of dance and the belongings of refugees.

Four photographs that purportedly portray scenes from the theater of war in Angola confront four other photographs that purportedly capture contemporaneous moments in a New York City discotheque. In the photographs, Douglas sets up correspondences between "disco" and the rebel insurgency in Angola to suggest that *fictional reenactments* in art can bring the aesthetic and the ethical domains closer in our consciousness.[18] While Schneider (2011) has argued for the significance of the pairing of war and dance for performative reenactments, Douglas brings war and dance into a form of contestation through the active forms of social dance. The two nouns in the title *Disco Angola* announce both difference and comparison. The title conflates different places and actions together with a simultaneous temporality and suggests to the viewer the productivity of disorientation in reading the images.

Further, Douglas's creation of the persona of a fictitious photographer supposedly responsible for the photographs in the suite calls for a reconceptualization of the historical

wide-ranging exhibition on reenactment in the visual arts to date was *Life Once More: Forms of Reenactment in Contemporary Art*, Rotterdam, Witte de Witte, January 27–March 27, 2005. See also Arns and Horn (2007). For good overviews of reenactment in contemporary art, see Blackson (2007); Jones (2011).

[17] On the topic of "remake" in Douglas's films, which situates the problem of time specifically in the form of the film medium, see Lütticken (2004).

[18] For the most extensive discussion of the meaning of the term "disco," see Fikentscher (2000); see also Hughes (1994).

**FIGURE 29.7.** *Coat Check, 1974.* 120.7 × 181 cm.

© Stan Douglas. Courtesy of the artist, David Zwirner, New York/London and Victoria Miro, London.

**FIGURE 29.8.** *Exodus, 1975.* 180.3 × 257.8 cm. Cast: Tieasha Baker, Karina Castillo, Raymond Christian, Timothy Cooley, Susan Costell, Telisa Craig, Max Gomez, Dustin Green, Caitlyn Lombardo, Alondra Mendoza, Nicholas Mirante, Cindy Nieto, David O'Donnell, Bill Porter, Marcella Rodriguez, Ronald Rose, Mike Rubio, Gregory Salazar, Alicia Spillias, Cesar Tarquino, Christian Tolbert, Desary Vailencour, Dominique Washington.

© Stan Douglas. Courtesy of the artist, David Zwirner, New York/London and Victoria Miro, London.

and the fictional in photography: if a documentary or news photographer took these pictures, then surely, the events they depict must be real. Yet, these compositions are constructions of what might have been. The fictional photographer-photojournalist figured large in the press release for the opening at the David Zwirner Gallery in New York City:

> For this exhibition, titled *Disco Angola*, Douglas has again assumed the fictional Character of a photojournalist, this time a regular in the burgeoning disco underground of the early 1970s New York. For Douglas's alter ego, the new scene offered a cathartic respite from urban grittiness in a city on the verge of bankruptcy. Evolving out of funk and soul, the disco lifestyle mobilized the gay community in particular, and its self-conscious embrace of glamour and fashion represented a departure from the previous decade's counterculture. Cameroonian saxophonist Manu Dibango is widely credited for writing the first disco hit, the song "Soul Makossa" from 1972, and the movement as a whole took much of its inspiration from the African continent. Douglas's photographer traveled frequently to Angola, where civil war broke out in 1974 following a bloodless coup d'état to end Portuguese rule. His photographs reveal subtle parallels between the burgeoning disco culture and the Angolan liberation struggles. The exhibition presents eight works from the project: four based in Angola, and four in the photographer's native New York.

If the artist-photographer takes on the role of the photojournalist, as Douglas asserts, his persona also magnifies the effects of reenactment by doubling the events represented: the war in Angola and disco in New York City. It is important to emphasize that even in these "journalistic" photographs, the artist operates differently from the historian. Douglas rejects a responsibility both to narrative temporality and to what historian Paul Ricoeur has called "that fundamental noetic vision of history," which can be understood as "historical intentionality" because it involves that which the viewer essentially knows through the senses (Ricoeur 1984, 229). Both Ricoeur and Hayden White have argued that historical explanation differs most significantly from fictional narrative on the basis of intentionality, such that in the former the viewer can "see for herself" what really happened (Bal 2009; Ricoeur 1984, 175–225; White 1987, 1–25). But in *Disco Angola*, where all the images are fictions portrayed as history, *how* can the viewer assess on the basis of evidentiary facts the truth-value of the narrative in relation to itself and to other competing and fictional accounts? The location shot of an Angolan rebel checkpoint, *Checkpoint 1975* (Figure 29.9), is as staged as *Coatcheck, 1974*. With these reenactments Douglas asks the viewer to reevalute the truth of war, the meaning of dance. Importantly, Ricoeur and White have also maintained that the truth-value of a historical narrative pertains "only when it can be opposed to the deliberate suspension of the true/false alternative, characteristic of the fictional narrative" (Ricoeur 1984, 226). Thus, for example, narrative fiction film serves as the primary exemplar of "the false alternative" that gives documentary film its veridical status. In contrast, the doubling of fictional histories in *Disco Angola* proposes that history be read *associatively* through the nonsynchronous forms that are constructed in and by photography, rather than oppositionally to an already constructed version of the past.

**FIGURE 29.9.** *Checkpoint, 1975.* 132.1 × 303.5 cm. Cast: Paul Akumbu, Kamal Cooper, Braxton Mitchell, Joshua Shannon.

Moreover, this mode of picturing associatively proposes fictional reenactment as the means necessary to overcome the burdens of historical representation that have been posited for the medium of documentary photography (Tagg 1988, 2009). The staged and composed photographs in *Disco Angola* suspend a straightforward historical narrative, while simultaneously asserting that a fictional representation gets us closer to the truth of the past than does a history based on the perception of objectivity. The flexible relationship to form and composition may be considered intrinsic to the medium of digital photography, which manipulates rather than simply records. In *Disco Angola*, the photographs are neither "stills" nor the so-called journalistic "snapshots" they pretend to reference. Rather, they are digitally manipulated composites. While the still photograph counteracts to a large degree our grasp of the movement of time provided by the moving image and the narrative film, the digital photograph allows for the manipulation of temporal experience both in its composition and its reception. Thus, while the figures in these photographs appear as if frozen in the moment—an effect emphasized by the monumental scale of the compositions—the images, in fact, have been edited or moved using multiple shots. Douglas explains: "The digital compositing of photographs is pretty standard stuff although like any medium, every photographer makes their own particular use of it. I approach it like editing a film, although what are temporal relationships in moving pictures are spatial ones in stills." Douglas's method also presents a substantive visual challenge to earlier and more static representational media—such as history painting—used for the narrative presentation of the past. When these innovations in media combine with the diegetic strategies used in them, the digital photographic still gives both a conception of time that stands without apparent movement in a place and a temporality that moves in the service of a history that can be reenacted with the viewing of it.

While the photographs that make up *Disco Angola* are composed of composited images, the figures in the frame reference the potential for the freedom of movement in dance poses and dispositions. The apparent authenticity of the figures relies on the historically accurate recreation of the dances, costumes, and *mise en scène*. In this sense, Douglas makes visible his extensive historical research into the photographic archives of the war in Angola and the disco era. These hundreds of "reference images," as the artist calls them, inform the history of the fictional photographs obliquely, rather than through the usual and more obvious tropes of the historical reconstruction of the archive in art, where an exact quotation of preexisting documents or the juxtaposition of the actual archive with the work are exposed (Enwezor 2008). Douglas's photographs cannot be historical reenactments because none of these people or places actually existed prior to their appearance in *Disco Angola*. Perversely, by suppressing the visibility of "reference images," Douglas extends our awareness of the possibility of the fictional history on view.

In the end, this fiction suggests a utopian outcome that the actual history of the time did not live up to. The desire to relive the past that is so much a part of historical reenactment transforms in *Disco Angola* into a desire for a past that never existed: a period of time when Angolan rebels were fighting the cause of freedom and youth could "act out" freedom in underground discotheques through social dance. The potentials of these fictional histories were both overtaken by the grim realities of "true" history: Angola descended into a perpetual battlefield, while disco was impugned for its commercialization and "bad" music. Whether reaction or resolution, the utopian aspects of both the scene of war and the disco scene were lost to history. Their realization could only come through a fictionalized history, one that relies on a new form of mediated reenactment, which refuses to bring the past up again.

My analysis of the *Disco Angola* suite suggests that the way to counteract the reenactment of an actual history in the future is to re-present its fictional potential *as* art in the present. This suggestion resonates with one that Walter Benjamin made regarding Proust's idea of the past: people with better memories—or more "accurate" histories—have more to forget and a greater need for the liberatory potential of a fictionalized past, such as that represented in *Disco Angola* (Benjamin 1999a, *The Arcades Project*, 389). When Benjamin characterized Proust's approach to the past as "involuntary recollection" (*mémoire involontaire*), he made a distinction between the actual past and the remembered past that better served the present: "We know that in his work Proust described not a life as it actually was but a life as it was remembered by the one who had lived it" (Benjamin 1999b, *Selected Writings*: Vol. 2, 237). According to Benjamin, the *mémoire involontaire* functioned to aid in forgetfulness so that, in Proust's words, "the incurable imperfection in the very essence of the present" could be ignored (Benjamin 1999b, 239). Benjamin criticized an "elegiac form of happiness" that transformed existence into a preserve of memory" (Benjamin 1999b, 239–240). Using a similar critique of historical memory, in *Disco Angola*, Douglas casts a negative eye on the reconstruction of an actual past. In his images of dance and war, Douglas makes an intentional fiction of the past for purposeful use in the present. The intentionality of the reconstruction of the past through fictional images relies on the visual and historical associations between disco and the imagined life of the Angolan rebels in order to instill in the viewer a disequilibrium mimetic to the visual images in the photographs. *Disco Angola* exposes straightforward historical reenactment as another tool used "to distort the world into similarity." (Benjamin 1999b, 240) The moral lesson is clear: history will be repeated if it is always performed in the way it was reperformed.

According to Benjamin, Proust's approach to the past came about as a result of the increasing separation of art from life in modernity (Benjamin 1999b, 237). Douglas offers a somewhat different message for contemporary times. First, it should be observed that *Disco Angola* attempts to overcome the alienation from the present that much modern and contemporary art conveys. In the co-temporal and spatial images of disco dance and the Angolan war, Douglas posits redemption from the recent past through fictional reenactment. Reenactment in art—experienced spatially and imagistically—gives the lie to the temporality imposed on history by narrative and the traditional forms and methods of historical explanation. *Disco Angola* suggests that fictional reenactment can provide an understanding of the past required in our postmodern and post-historicist times. Harnessing the modalities and technologies of digital photography together with a recuperation of historical accuracy in dress and location provides us with images that in their choreographed crossings and associations fulfill Benjamin's requirements for historical representation: "To approach, in this way, 'what has been' means to treat it not historiographically, as heretofore, but politically, in political categories" (Benjamin 1999a, 392). In *Disco Angola*, reconstructed social dance provides the hinge for a politics of change envisioned for a better future.

## Works Cited

Agnew, Vanessa. 2004. "What Is Reenactment?" *Criticism* 46: 327–339.

Arns, Inke, and Gabriel Horn, eds. 2007. *History Will Repeat Itself: Strategies of Reenactment in Contemporary (Media) Art and Performance.* Dortmund: Hartware MedienKunstVerein and Berlin: SW Institute for Contemporary Art.

Bal, Mieke. 2009. *Narratology: Introduction to the Theory of Narrative.* Translated by Christine Van Boheemen. Toronto: University of Toronto Press.

Baudelaire, Charles. 1999. "Le Peintre de la Vie Moderne." In *Écrits sur l'art*, edited by Francis Moulinat, 503–552. Paris: Librairie Générale Française.

Benjamin, Walter. 1999a. *The Arcades Project.* Translated by Howard Eiland and Kevin McLaughlin. Cambridge, MA, and London: Harvard University Press.

Benjamin, Walter. 1999b. "On the Image of Proust." In *Selected Writings*: Vol. 2, *1927–1934*, edited by Michael W. Jennings, Howard Eiland, and Gary Smith; translated by Rodney Livingstone and others, 237–247. Cambridge, MA: Harvard University Press.

Berger, Harry, Jr. 2000. *Fictions of the Pose: Rembrandt against the Italian Renaissance.* Stanford, CA: Stanford University Press.

Blackson, Robert. 2007. "Once More with Feeling: Re-enactment in Contemporary Art and Culture." *Art Journal* 66: 28–40.

Bleeker, Maaike A. 2012. "(Un) Covering Artistic Thought Unfolding." *Dance Research Journal* 44: 13–25.

Caronia, Antonio, Janez Janša, and Domenico Quaranta, eds. 2009. *Reakt!: Reconstruction, Re-enactment, Re-reporting.* Brescia: FP Editions.

Certeau, Michel de. 1988. *The Writing of History*. Translated by Tom Conley. New York: Columbia University Press.

Chaganti, Seeta. 2012. "Proleptic Steps: Rethinking Historical Period in the Fifteenth-Century Dance Manual." *Dance Research Journal* 44: 29–47.

Collingwood, R. G. 1977. *The Idea of History*. New York: Oxford University Press.

Dressler, Iris. 2008. "Specters of Douglas." In *Stan Douglas, Past Imperfect: Works 1986–2007*, edited by Hans D. Christ and Iris Dressler, 9–24. Ostfildern: Hatje Cantz Verlag.

Enwezor, Okwui. 2008. *Archive Fever: Uses of the Document in Contemporary Art*. New York: International Center for Photography and Göttingen: Steidl.

Fikentscher, Kai. 2000. *'You Better Work!': Underground Dance Music in New York City*. Hanover, NH, and London: Wesleyan University Press.

Foster, Hal. 2002. *Design and Crime and Other Diatribes*. London: Verso.

Foster, Susan Leigh. 1995. *Choreographing History*. Bloomington: University of Indiana Press.

Franko, Mark. 1989. "Repeatability, Reconstruction and Beyond." *Theatre Journal* 41: 56–74.

Hebdige, Dick. 1979. *Subculture: The Meaning of Style*. London and New York: Routledge.

Hughes, Walter. 1994. "In the Empire of the Beat: Discipline and Disco." In *Microphone Fiends: Youth Music, Youth Culture*, edited by Andrew Ross and Tricia Rose, 147–156. New York and London: Routledge.

Jones, Amelia. 2011. "Performance, Live or Dead." In *Art Journal* 70(3): 32–38.

Kealy, Seamus. 2014. "Disco Angola 2012." In *Stan Douglas: Mise en Scène*, edited by Leon Krempel, 120. New York and London: Prestel.

Lawrence, Tim. 2009. "Beyond the Hustle: Seventies Social Dancing, Discotheque Culture and the Emergence of the Contemporary Club Dance." In *Ballroom, Boogie, Shimmy Sham, Shake: A Social and Popular Dance Reader*, edited by Julie Malnig, 199–214. Urbana and Chicago: University of Illinois Press.

Lütticken, Sven. 2004. "Planet of the Remakes." *New Left Review* 25: 117–119.

Lütticken, Sven. 2012. "General Performance." *e-flux journal* 31: 1–12.

Lütticken, Sven, and Jennifer Allen. 2005. *Life, Once More: Forms of Reenactment in Contemporary Art*. Rotterdam: Witte de With Center for Contemporary Art.

Michael, Linda. 1996. "Introduction," In Stan Douglas, *Real Fictions: Four Canadian Artists*, n.p. Sydney: Museum of Contemporary Art.

Moxey, Keith. 2013. *Visual Time: The Image in History*. Durham, NC: Duke University Press.

Ricoeur, Paul. 1984. *Time and Narrative*, Vol. 1. Translated by Kathleen McLaughlin and David Pellauer. Chicago and London: University of Chicago Press.

Robinson, Lisa. 2010. "Boogie Nights." *Vanity Fair*. New York: Condé Nast. Retrieved from www.vanityfair.com/culture/features/2010/02/oral-history-of-disco.

Ross, Christine. 2012. *The Past Is Present: The Temporal Turn in Contemporary Art*. London and New York: Continuum.

Schneider, Rebecca. 2011. *Performing Remains: Art and War in Times of Theatrical Reenactment*. New York: Routledge.

Soussloff, Catherine M. 2014. "Art History's Dilemma: Theories for Time in Contemporary Performance/Media Exhibitions." *Performance Research Journal* 19: 93–100.

Straw, Will. 1993. "The Booth, the Floor and the Wall: Dance Music and the Fear of Falling." In *Public 8: The Ethics of Enactment*, edited by Marc deGuerre and Kathleen Pirrie Adams, 169–182. Toronto: Public Access.

Szewczyk, Monika. 2015. "Midcentury Disco: Stan Douglas Interviewed by Monika Szewczyk." *Mousse* 32: 54–65.

Tagg, John. 1988. *The Burden of Representation: Essays on Photographies and Histories.* London: MacMillan.

Tagg, John. 2009. *The Disciplinary Frame: Photographic Truths and the Capture of Meaning.* Minneapolis: University of Minnesota Press.

Thomas, Anthony. 1995. "The House the Kids Built: The Gay Black Imprint on American Dance Music." In *Out in Culture*, edited by Corey K. Creekmur and Alexander Doty, 437–445. Durham, NC, and London: Duke University Press.

Thornton, Sarah. 1996. *Club Cultures: Music, Media and Subcultural Capital.* Hanover: Wesleyan University Press.

Veyne, Paul. 1984. *Writing History: Essay on Epistemology.* Translated by Mina Moore-Rinvolucri. Middletown, CT: Wesleyan University Press.

White, Hayden. 1987. *The Content of the Form: Narrative Discourse and Historical Representation.* Baltimore, MD, and London: Johns Hopkins University Press.

# CHAPTER 30

# DANCE IN SEARCH OF ITS OWN HISTORY

## On the Contemporary Circulation of Past Knowledge

### SABINE HUSCHKA

AT present, contemporary dance finds itself occupied with the question of where its own history might be stored. As part of a wider enthusiasm for history[1] that pervades many areas of society, contemporary dance also displays a clear interest—internationally as well as nationally speaking (in the German context)—in the historicity of its own form (Assmann 2006, 2007). Intensive research into this subject, as well as experimentation with memory as an artistic tool, has exposed the uncertainties within dance historicity. A wide range of transnational productions—for example, Fabián Barba's reconstructive work on Mary Wigman, the rereading of Steve Paxton's *Satisfyin' Lover* (1967/1996) by the Albrecht Knust Quartet, and the solo *Untitled* by Tino Seghal—despite their differences from one another, have all resonated with political questions about dance's retention within memory, its material basis, and its trajectory through media.

This may express the central desire of dance's far-reaching memory culture: to explore methods of appropriating and reactivating past knowledge, to seek out the remains of historicity across digital media, and, through these pieces of cultural memory, to reawaken historical works and styles. As of the 1990s, above all in Europe, different methods and practices have been developed—conceived as reconstruction or as reenactment—which seek to actualize dancerly and choreographic knowledge of the past. With funding from the national subsidy program *Tanzfonds Erbe* from the *Kulturstiftung des Bundes*, Germany has, since the second decade of the twenty-first century alone, been home to over forty productions that explicitly interrogate the possibilities and conditions for, and function of, a dance heritage. According to the *Kulturstiftung des Bundes*,

---

[1] Aleida Assmann has extensively shown that European societies are deeply interested in keeping the past present and creating cultural (and ritual) sites of remembrance.

its diverse program of productions "grapples with heritage" in the interest of achieving, as they programmatically refer to it, "an exemplary reappraisal of contemporary dance in Germany," which "is expressed in the topicality of modern dance and is anchored in the here-and-now."[2] Implicit in this mission statement is a temporally located transmission of historical knowledge, which brings the experience of history into a contemporary dialogue. Yet the question remains unresolved of how the implicit time interval separating the past from the present flows into the reenactment. On the other hand, intuition seems to tell us that this interval is irrelevant to the visualization of past dance in the present.

Numerous independent dancers and choreographers, independent curators, and ballet companies in German municipal theaters thus have been working toward a "living memory culture" of historical knowledge and are setting many different forms of reflection into motion. This work on memory, sometimes accompanied by round table discussions and symposia (e.g., *Archive/Practice* [2009] Tanzarchiv Leipzig; *tanzkongress* Düsseldorf, 2013), has focused predominantly on dance's twentieth-century luminaries, such as Isadora Duncan, Loïe Fuller, Anita Berber, Valeska Gert, Kurt Jooss, Mary Wigman, Gertrud Bodenwieser, Rudolf von Laban, Oskar Schlemmer, Jean Weidt, Yvonne Georgi, Clotilde and Alexander Sacharoff, Dore Hoyer, Gerhard Bohner, and Uwe Scholz, and on individual pieces by these artists, but also has included postmodern approaches to improvisation (Judson Dance Theater) and bodywork (Anna Halprin). As such, the overall socio-artistic project has been especially concerned, first, with the preceding figures and second, with the prevailing, institutionally grounded procedures for passing down dances and dance styles, as they exist within a repertoire,[3] to realize an appropriation of modern choreography, dance styles, and approaches that differ from the participant's own training, thus making the re-enactor, in a fairly literal sense, a stranger to them.

Standing somewhere between enshrinements and fabrications, between classically functioning reconstruction and recontextualizing arrangement of source materials, each production contrives its own unique format. Varied as they are, dance performances, lecture-demonstrations, installations, exhibitions, films, concerts, textual documentation, websites, talks, and drawings all offer fresh and relevant perspectives on the history of modern dance, which for its own part has taken on the tension between methods of inheritance and dissemination of its intellectual framework as a central concern. Dance history presents itself as a space for aesthetic reflection, recalls the remnants of an

[2] *Tanzfonds Erbe* (*Dance Heritage Fund*), a federal program funded by the *Kulturstiftung des Bundes* (*German Federal Cultural Foundation*) follows the aims of the UNESCO Convention for the Safeguarding Intangible Cultural Heritage. "TANZFONDS ERBE does not create a museum of work and people from the past, but rather a lively commemorative culture that reveals the topicality of modern day dance." http://tanzfonds.de/en/about-us/ (accessed May 2, 2017).
[3] Traditionally aesthetic and cultural dance memory is preserved through three types of processes: (1) the body-memory of the dancers, which means mimetically passing on dances and techniques from one generation of dancers to the next; (2) a set canon of dances in a company's repertoire, creating a tradition; and (3) the gathering of different types of materials in archives.

accessible kinetic knowledge, activates memories of spectatorship, brings together choreographic artifacts in the form of notation and images, and periodically overhauls its
own understanding of aesthetics by means of highly specialized research and interviews
with dancers, their pupils, and their contemporaries. Dance's past seeks to present itself
as both up-to-date and reiterant, paradoxical as it may sound: as overwrought as it is
expansive, simultaneously (re)discovered and (re)invented. Eyeing three distinct productions through this lens—namely, Jochen Roller's *The Source Code* (2012), Christina
Ciupke and Anna Till's *undo, redo and repeat* (2013), and Henrietta Horn's rendition
of Mary Wigman's *Le Sacre du Printemps* (2013)—I would like to bring to light what
space for reflection we have already developed for dance history, as well as to reconsider
the heavily ingrained procedure we have for tapping into adopted historical knowledge. Which reflective possibilities disclosed by reenactment comprise the extent of my
inquiry? Which spaces of remembering is dance able to incorporate into its art? What
makes a unit of historical knowledge susceptible to reactivation, and how does memory find its correspondence to choreography? How can historical knowledge of moving
bodies be reactivated?

Where will the art form of dance find itself at the end of its pursuit of an unattainable target (the past)? Which techniques and dynamics constitute the spaces in which it
stages its remembrance, and which spaces reflective of historicity could enable a work
of appropriating the past? These questions in particular propel Ciupke and Till's *undo,
redo, repeat* (2013) and Jochen Roller's *The Source Code* (2012) forward, reverberating
with renewed complexity when expressed through a reenactment and a mediated reflection on a digital project, respectively. A definitive work on conceptualizing reconstruction, Henrietta Horn's *Le Sacre du Printemps* (Wigman) (2013) contends with gaps in its
own source material to point out and nuance the way in which mediation complicates
the intellectual frameworks we apply to dance of the past.

## REENACTING BODY-KNOWLEDGE: ENCOUNTERING THE GAP

Having said this, how does contemporary dance actually go about revealing its past? Or
to phrase it somewhat absurdly, how does one get the past to present itself?

We can say that a conceptual setting has established itself when we understand the
actionable connection between the past and the present in and as an intervallic relationship that is open to negotiation.[4] This is the realm of notions such as *revival, remaking,*

---

[4] This has led to bizarre statements like one made by André Lepecki: "Jérôme Bel shows how the
past is not that which vanishes at every second that passes, but rather that which presents itself in the
present as a forceful absence, a set of references, signs, lines of forces, all traversing the body on stage, and
defining the ground on where dance (all of us) stands" (Lepecki 2004a, 176).

*restaging, reanimating,* and *replaying,* which proliferate conceptual and, by extension, analytical ambiguity (Krutschkova 2010). Discussing practices of historical memory within the German-speaking spheres of theory reveals a conceptual disequilibrium between *reconstruction* and *reenactment,* which has, for example, been explicitly drawn out in dialogue between dance scholars Claudia Jeschke and Nicole Haitzinger. Even when Jeschke questions the validity of the very idea of reconstruction, since she relies historiographically on repertoire practices, faithfulness to the original, and authenticity, she prefers nonetheless to isolate the notion of writing as *reconstruction,* through which she makes a distinction between documentation and witness (Jeschke 2010).[5] Jeschke remains skeptical of the kinds of conceptual perspectives on the past that Haitzinger tends toward with *reenactment.* For her, reenactment fails to identify any "tools adequate to generate past knowledge" (Jeschke 2009, 57). Haitzinger, on the other hand, recognizes *reenactment* as a form of *reinvention,* precisely as "contemporary artistic perspectives, in order to discover and visualize history" ("zeitgenössische künstlerische Perspektivierung, der (Er-)Findung und Visualisierung von Geschichte"), while vehemently opposing the practice of reconstruction, which she deems to be "as true to the original as possible in its repetition" (Haitzinger 2010, 181). The common thread between all these theoretical approaches lies in the recurring character of the "re," a *reminder,* as it were, an indicator of a practice dedicated to its own repetition (Foellmer 2014).[6] Nevertheless, "repetition" as a strategy for embodied memory has neither distinguished itself within theory nor proven itself to be analytically productive. Repetition per se is bankrupt.

# THE PROMISES AND POLITICAL DIMENSIONS OF REENACTMENT

The underlying practical and theoretical position on how dance's styles and aesthetic positions of the past will be remembered, how their intellectual frameworks should be addressed, and how knowledge of them should be called forth—all these are, as it were, interrogations of the aesthetics of dance. Without a doubt, contemporary dance's attempt to appropriate the past represents a substantial undertaking, wrought with tensions—all the more so, given the creative consequences for this campaign, which

---

[5] Jeschke points out that reconstructions based on oral histories rely on communicative memory, whereas reconstructions based on documentation rely on cultural memory.

[6] In regard to the theoretical figure of *repetition,* Susanne Foellmer, for example, differentiates between reconstructions as a "critical, distanced approach to deal with past representations, pieces or performances" (Foellmer 2014, 70) in contrast to reenactments as "an attempt to replicate past representation events and performances as faithfully as possible" (72) since reenactments seek to "reanimate an event as closely and in as much detail to the original event" [trans. footnote editor] (70).

seeks to secure the past as a mine of as yet undiscovered possibilities for export to the present, as recently illustrated in "Engagements with the Past in Contemporary Dance" (Hardt 2012).[7] What is more, the first glimpse of that which has been lost bursts open a mine of questions about the historicity of dance that is as irresistible as it is inexhaustible. This constitutive withdrawal of the past from the present is indubitably experienced as such. It is too late to fill in the gaps in dance's memory that have thus far gone unnoticed. What sort of space for memory would best allow us to encounter the past and convey it to the present when the bodily knowledge of that past has long since been buried?

In each appropriation of bygone choreography and style there nests a gaping wound unable to be closed: knowledge of movement dies with the dancers whose muscles remembered it. The repercussions of death, the "Faktum brutum" of historiography, as Günther Heeg calls it, is especially radical in the case of dance because of its dependence on the transient body (2006, 177). Choreographers and dancers who reach toward the past grope around for it in the emptiness left behind by an ephemeral materiality. Historical dancing bodies have, by definition, been evacuated from time. A dialogue with their long since extinguished phenomenal domain, from the perspective of the present moment, is divided between movement that is their own and movement they must find foreign. The resulting gaps become the site of a new work of remembering, as the losses they mark necessitate, structure, motivate, hinder, and enable a circumstantial appropriation of the past. Only with the intercession of outsiders and third parties can a path to the becoming-present be trod, can the past be brought into presently relevant dialogue. These are the conditions necessary to *stage* an afterlife for the deceased moving body.

Although the *ontological condition* of bodily movement may be a superficial consideration, the vacancies associated with it nonetheless demand that any reconstructive work of recall situate itself within a clear practical domain, which in turn determines its attitude toward the aesthetics and politics of dance. Because the friction between artistic technique and the past seems caught up precisely in those vacancies, which are precisely what makes dance, according to its own modern aesthetic self-image, an art in the form of body/movement and its ephemeral body of knowledge. The confrontation with such an evident and even trivial loss is, in a sense, a confrontation with dance's own foundational condition which is, to be ephemeral. Any recalling of the past in dance is contingent not only on the state of dance's aesthetic substance—namely, corporeality— but also on the status attributed aesthetically to the ephemeral, upon which our understanding of all of its characteristics and features rests. Since modernity, dance has been

---

[7]  Cf. Hardt 2012, in which she reflects on "a present that is highly reflective of the inescapability of the past" (218). Also cf. Lepecki: "With the expression, will to archive in contemporary dance, I am proposing an alternative affective, political, and aesthetic frame for recent dance Reenactments—as well as for their relations to archival forces, impulses, or systems of command. [ . . . ] I am suggesting that the current will to archive in dance, as performed by Reenactments, derives neither exclusively from 'a failure in cultural memory' (Foster 2004, 21–22) nor from 'a nostalgic lens' (Santone 2008, 147). I am proposing 'will to archive' as referring to a capacity to identify in a past work still non-exhausted creative fields of 'impalpable possibilities' (to use an expression from Brian Massumi [2002, 91])" (Lepecki 2010, 31).

considered an ephemeral and, more pointedly, fleeting form,[8] whose actual cultural and theoretical impact has withered under the nefarious effects of the "glorification, trivialization, and marginalization of dance as an apolitical activity" (Franko 1995, 206). As American dance scholarship has made plain, it is on that sort of discourse that the looming specter of "absolute untranslatability" subsists (Foster 1995, 9). The ontological determination to theorize the ephemeral or fleeting event reduces live dance, barely hanging on to its relevance as it is, to the status of isolated incident whose textures cannot be safely mapped onto any matrix of spatial or temporal references.

This radically presentist construal unabashedly obliterates dance's history and its historicity along with it. Yet this plain misunderstanding of the ontological disposition of dance's ephemeralities marks an aesthetic formulation, which through the appointed practices surrounding reenactment could potentially embody a critical intervention: The transmission of the fleeting/ephemeral disposition of dance occurs through a specific memory technique, through which pieces of dance history seem to find themselves reincarnated on stage. Reenactment has the power to transpose the aesthetic gaps in dance's memory—which themselves have no history—into a dimension of choreographic outlines for various visualization strategies. I will attempt to demonstrate in the following how these practices of reincorporation and appropriation of the past, and the collection of moves they represent, travel through constellations of space and time. Pictures, notes, observations, reviews, and memories, which make the historicity of a past dance tangible, are the components of a network that lead us to practices of embodied memory.

# RESCUING PAST KNOWLEDGE: "OCCUPYING THE VACANCIES"

The limits of this kind of knowledge of dance become materially evident when the techniques we have for recalling dance, themselves bound to the body, come up against glaring vacancies. The death of each modern dancer and choreographer, and the subsequent disappearance of their bodily knowledge from the world, bears heavily on the amount of space (both spatial and temporal) left to bridge between the past and its reproduction. An absence of bodily knowledge and a lack of most of the details of the techniques for transfer of knowledge from teachers to students leave us in the precarious position

---

[8] The ephemeral classifies the transience of dance as a short-lived act, a fleeting moment, inherently inhabited by an aura of disappearance. Modern discourses have basically inscribed the ontological characteristic of *ephemeron* into dance. Thus, it has become the differentiating criterion of this specific form of art and knowledge. Cf. Lepecki 2004b, 126ff. The terminology of the ephemeral became an ontological concept even before Paul Valéry; it goes back to the early 19th century, to a revised edition of *Lettres* (1803) by Jean Georges Noverre. On the difference between the transitory nature of dance and its ephemera in a historical context, cf. Huschka 2012.

of having to consider new strategies for finding dance knowledge in the current media landscape. The intensified search for novel paths toward a collective dance memory leads to a desperate search for any source, from inherited notebooks to performance recordings to photographs, that might be able to serve as a satisfying starting point for the faithful reproduction of an individual piece, or for the recapturing of a certain movement technique. Henrietta Horn's challenging reconstruction of Mary Wigman's *Le Sacre du Printemps* (1957), created along with Susan Barnett and Katharine Sehnert, is the culmination of tireless effort in the archives of the *Akademie der Künste Berlin*, collating copious previously unsorted source material, supplemented by conversations with Wigman's former dancers (Emma Lewis Thomas, Brigitta Hermann) and injecting a wealth of knowledge into the rehearsal process at Osnabrück Theater and Bielefeld Theater.

The equally thorough documenting material points out yet another outstanding absence: the central dance of The Chosen One was mysteriously missing from notes on the piece, which otherwise accounted for each scene in movement-by-movement detail. Save for a few photographs of rehearsals with Dore Hoyer, who singlehandedly fashioned and danced this role within Wigman's choreography, the entire solo passage, including its core movements, was lost. The team of reconstructionists approached this gaping vacancy from a middle ground between general contextual knowledge of then-prevalent styles of movement and specific historical knowledge of the original scenery and costumes. This practical approach to leaving the gaping holes open in the interest of a homogenous reconstruction is based on the idea that with the knowledge of the original dancers, "the choreographic gaps can be filled in reconstructing the piece."[9] These contemporaries *qua* "witnesses" have in their personal experience of dancing the piece a degree of authority with which to advise on its choreography. This affords them, in a certain sense, the status of a living archive, but does not take into account their own working process of remembering, which obviates the possibility of working at recollection. Instead, one must be mindful of the fragility of memory. (See Foellmer, Chapter 13 in this volume). What arose in this process of working with the "witnesses" were the kind of drastic issues of divergence and contradiction inherent in any system engaging multiple modes of recordkeeping.[10] The reconstructive work here takes as its premise the idea that an "intact" performance of *Le Sacre du Printemps* is producible, and that immediate, felicitous reference to the original should be enough to recreate the experience of it. As dramaturge Patricia Stöckemann puts it, the gaps ask "not to be left alone" but to be filled "in the spirit of the work of reconstruction and in the spirit of engagement with Mary Wigman and her style" (Stöckelmann 2013, project documentation).

---

[9] Stöckelmann in a video which is part of the project documentation 2013 (in German): http://tanzfonds.de/en/project/documentation-2013/le-sacre-du-printemps/ (accessed May 2, 2017).

[10] Cf. extracts from an interview with Wigman students Brigitta Herrmann and Katharine Sehnert (video documentation in German): "Mary Wigman: 'Kreise ohne Frontveränderung'. Ein Gespräch mit Brigitta Herrmann und Katharine Sehnert zur Rekonstruktion von 'Le Sacre du Printemps'" http://tanzfonds.de/en/project/documentation-2013/le-sacre-du-printemps/ (accessed May 2, 2017).

The united yet frequently divergent recollections of the former dancers were ultimately averaged out within Henrietta Horn's decision to choreograph the part of The Chosen One, originally choreographed and danced by Dore Hoyer. This act of reinvention remained unmarked by the aesthetic of the production. The tension-filled negotiation between the multifaceted memories of the former dancers were in the final analysis homogenized within the decision making process of Henrietta Horn such that she could create Hoyer's dance of sacrifice out of whole cloth without it registering as a break in the performance aesthetic. The multiplicity of sources and their frictions within the choreography did not resonate. What is more, this performative act tries to illuminate the timelessness of the choreography and seeks to manifest an eternal image of Wigman's aesthetic despite these problems.

## DANCING ACROSS MEDIA

European choreographers had already been working on various approaches to past dance pieces prior to this well-funded moment. These include Martin Nachbar, whose *Urheben Aufheben* (2008) recalls Dore Hoyer's *Affectos Humanos* (1962), Jérôme Bel with *Véronique Doisneau* (2006), *Lutz Förster* (2009), and *Cédric Andrieux* (2009), as well as Boris Charmatz with *Twenty Dances for the Twentieth Century* (2009). Despite the difference in historical reference points and performance format (they span dance piece, performance, and lecture-performance), they share a reflective and nevertheless occasionally fractured relationship with the past. The focus of historical memory is not on restoration, or on reaching some pure reconstruction of historical material, but rather on modes of reenacting, on new arrangements and reincorporations. The tools currently at their disposal for engaging with the past are critical ones—ones that are always open to reconsidering the status of given historical material. All material is treated as a stand-alone source or archive of dance and has been dissected and investigated accordingly. At the heart of this system lie questions of the extent to which the "leftovers"[11] of dance pieces and physical techniques contain memory (even in their respective materialities), how to jolt these memories back to life today, and whether they should be reactivated to begin with.

An excellent example of this in action is the long-standing tension in Martin Nachbar's work on Dore Hoyer's *Affectos Humanos* (1967) between physical material (including film clips) and the memories of her dancer and heir Waltraud Luley, which reveals how idiosyncratic the entire work of remembering is. In attempting to transfer a constitutive foreign source of movement material from an absent body onto a present one—formed differently at the level of history and stylistics—one discovers that in order

---

[11]  Cf. DFG-Projekt *On Remnants and Vestiges. Strategies of Remaining in the Performing Arts* (*ÜberReste. Strategien des Bleibens in den darstellenden Künsten*) led by Dr. Susanne Foellmer, Reader of Dance at Conventry University, GB.

for dance history to resolve these discrepancies, in effect to deal with the historicity of the individual body on its own technical and biographic-historical terms, reconstruction must work with and through constitutive difference, which is at odds with its project. Given the insurmountable technical difficultness of seamlessly embodying Dore Hoyer's established, expressionist style, Nachbar found that decoding it successfully depended on his ability to "confront the inaccessible" (Siegmund 2010, 21). A modern, uncostumed man, dancing without the music Hoyer's choreography was set to, Nachbar plainly exposes a gender-specific and historical difference between the two body *gestalts*, yet he retains the material basis of the choreography as well as Hoyer's expressive dance style. With *Urheben Aufheben* (2008), he attained yet a new level of reflective possibility: Standing before a blackboard, Nachbar expounds on dance's ability to serve as an act of recall, which is crucial for the historicity of his work and process, and goes on to choreographically illustrate and develop this point using the full stage area. Against this modest backdrop, he arrives at a choreographically reflexive and corporeally self-reconstructive performance of memory of an absence: a *counter*[12]-embodiment with no etiological agenda.

Larger, international dance companies have also taken notice of the intensive work in the aesthetic culture of memory. The deaths of such prominent modern choreographers as Pina Bausch and Merce Cunningham (who both passed away in 2009) have also inspired major interventions in dance epistemology as it had been practiced until that time. Death opens up urgent questions regarding the legacy of works and the possibility of their inheritance, for example, whether the repertory is in the best position to preserve them, and whether the distinctive styles and techniques on which they are based should continue to be taught. In the face of this very real withdrawal of living, of embodied dance knowledge from the world, companies and the theatrical community at large must contend with the importance of established wisdom and consider how it can now be passed down. Faced with this loss, an altered status of the knowledge of dance becomes obvious through which different types of practice are developed. The status of dance knowledge as cultural knowledge also thereby changes.[13]

The former companies of deceased choreographers have, for their own part, responded quite differently to the question of how dances and techniques can be conveyed and mediated while cut off from the embodiment of its authors. The Cunningham Trust, founded in 2009, views itself as subject to some aesthetic as well as sociopolitical imperative "to preserve, enhance, and maintain the integrity of that choreographic and other artistic work, and make such works available for the benefit of the public" (see Noland 2013).[14] In contrast, the Pina Bausch Foundation takes up the task of "retaining the artistic heritage of prominent dancers and choreographers both to treasure in

---

[12]  Translator's note: In German, the word "counter" (*wider*) is a homonym of "again" (*wieder*).

[13]  These trusts and foundations have established varying policies on how estates are to be managed and the forms of preserving and passing on dance knowledge they seek.

[14]  Also cf. http://www.mercecunningham.org/trust as well as a documentary on Cunningham directed by Marie-Hélène Rebois, *Merce Cunningham, A Legacy of Dance* (2012).

the present and to carry with us into the future" (Pina Bausch Foundation, "Mission"). Befitting the differences in their cultural and social politics, the two institutions pursue opposite practices: while *Tanztheater Wuppertal* reveres Pina Bausch's repertory of work and the aesthetic she developed over its course and wants to keep them "alive" by retaining the company and its veteran members, the Merce Cunningham Dance Company dissolved in 2011, in accordance with his will. It has opted instead to place his choreography in the hands of other dance companies, with the Cunningham Trust as steward of his repertory. These institutions do pursue comeasurable, intensive practices of archiving. The Cunningham Trust and the Pina Bausch Foundation both compile important production information and properties (such as costumes, props, and scenery), and digitize them alongside existing records (photographs, films, notes, etc.), effectively putting together a road map for proliferating these works into practice. And despite the stark difference in their perspectives on how dance as an embodied artform is best transmitted at the level of both aesthetics and politics, the sum of data and material—released in a centralized media packet[15]—will be rewound and replayed time and time again in the service of subsequent production processes.

The functional approaches to conservation and application point to an interesting facet of this pursuit: the tenuous status of embodied knowledge opens up other practical gateways newly mindful of dance's developing body of knowledge. Since the choreographer—as authority, guardian, and tangible vessel of this knowledge—has died, the knowledge apparatus upon which dance and choreography depend migrates elsewhere. Sources and materials resulting from and anchored in both dance practice and performance event, cumulatively constituting a transmedial network of notes, transcripts, photographs, costumes, scenic design blueprints, and films, become the vehicles for the transfer of knowledge. From this point on, knowledge of choreography and dance style emerges from negotiating with information and materials, which then become the definitive building blocks of knowing dance.

In this sense, dance knowledge is precisely post-bodily, and deploys various techniques and procedures to extract knowledge from bodies already in their own aftermaths. Nevertheless, the threshold of irretrievability for living dance knowledge that death marks is itself evidence of the absence of its embodied occurrence at exactly those moments at which the bodily, aesthetic, and cultural practices of transference become conceivable. The creation of a transmedial network of information and materials, along with the practices of appropriation that constitute this network, pave the way toward a nuanced framework for understanding where and how to invest the knowledge we have as manifestation of our intellectual culture across media. Only then will dance knowledge be recognizable as a materialized, mediatized system and process.

It therefore seems hasty to limit our understanding of dance knowledge to its position as the *topos* of embodied being. Implicitly, its complex disposition, embedded in

---

[15] Cf. for details on the archiving process in the *Cunningham Trust*: http://dancecapsules. mercecunningham.org/?8080ed and for the Pina Bausch Foundation: http://www.pinabausch.org/en/ archive (accessed May 2, 2017).

processes of embodying and imparting that are themselves dependent on our frame of media reference, unfolds between bodies and words, between bodies and writing, between bodies and images (both drawn and mental), and between bodies and bodies. This web of aesthetic knowledge rests on the active bodily implementation of verbal or textual directives, and on measurements of space, time, and image, both imagined and reasoned (Huschka 2017, forthcoming). These, above all, are the results of practicing reenactment.

# JOCHEN ROLLER'S *THE SOURCE CODE*

Appropriation of the past assumes dance's access to a library of interlocking reference materials spanning a significant time frame that speaks to the theoretical demands of its practice and their potential for reflecting history. This requisite entering into dialogue with the past calls attention to the historicity of the deceased, estranged body and to the mortality of knowledge and, likewise, in a less direct sense, to the historicity of the particular bodies involved in these practices (see Nachbar, Chapter 2 in this volume). A tangible distancing effect becomes legible with respect to that which now exists in the present, out of which effect the temporality between present and past can be grasped through a movement of appropriation. Acknowledging this distancing effect, with which memory processes for dancers and choreographers can be set into motion, sheds an especially bright light on reenactment's true potential, which Jochen Roller ruminates on in *The Source Code* and Christina Ciupke and Anna Till aim for in *undo, redo repeat*. Both productions accomplish their memories through an interactive relationship to various source materials, which is a targeted, mediatized way of achieving the reflective status for knowledge of dance. Their goal is to make contact with "others" that our distance from the past holds at bay, while resisting the impulse to fill any gaps or absences, to be frank and transparent about the temporal obstacles at play.

With *The Source Code*, Roller sets his sights on the conceptual two-step of engaging with Gertrud Bodenwieser's legacy of expressionist dance in the context of Australia, where she emigrated in 1938. Roller and his team of four dancers, journalist Elisabeth Nehring, and video artist Andrea Keiz first reconstructed Bodenwieser's choreography for *Errand into the Maze* (1954),[16] an appropriation which they termed a "recreation," but never performed for the public. The second phase of the project saw Roller edit all materials from the research and working periods for presentation on a website—including film clips of himself and his team in training sessions with Carol Brown and Barbara Cookson of the Bodenwieser School as a means of learning Bodenwieser's technique, some short showings of piecemeal reconstructions of choreographic fragments,

---

[16] Roller's *Errand into the Maze* does not carry any references to the eponymous piece by Martha Graham.

discussions from the three-week workshop, along with interviews with the former Bodenwieser dancers, and articles from newspapers and journals. The processes and problems of appropriation of the past[17] were logged on this website, which also contained the photos, emails, letters, and more that they had accumulated from over eight weeks of Roller's prior research. As the locus of all significant research material throughout work on appropriating *Errand into the Maze*, this website became an end in itself: http://www.thesourcecode.de. Far from an early change of course, the decision to forgo performing the reconstruction in favor of a digital product was the core conceit of the project. Rather than sit the public in front of a live imagining of a dance, the idea was instead to let it discover and work through the unavoidable, if implicit, problems and tensions within a transcontinental and temporally complicated process of remembering. Roller explains:

> For me, it's about making the reconstruction process completely transparent, to publish everything, or as much as possible, that documents our route, even the false paths taken, as I believe that ultimately the attempt and failure to reconstruct something says as much about the choreography as succeeding in copying it perfectly.[18]

At first glance, the website comes across as a hodgepodge of materials, without any chronological or other organizing structure that would identify it as completed research. The menu offers links to ten pages containing source material, such as historical photos, newspaper articles, theater programs, archival scripts laid out next to film clips of rehearsals that serve as clear introductions to the basic movement aesthetics of "Bodenwieser Technique," and journal interviews that outline the central aesthetics and themes of Bodenwieser's work at length, as well as spotlight her career in Australia after emigrating there to form her own company. The site assigns the visitor a marathon looking and reading tour of the material and the team's annotations of it from their discussions. After a certain amount of browsing, the visitor may store all the properties and links as his or her personal research path and may emerge with a brand new set of principles for appropriating the past. Roller puts it this way:

> By accessing rehearsal footage, interviews, photos, letters, and other testimonies, I invite the Online audience to make their own version of the 60-year old dance piece. The re-creation process was full of errors, contradictions, analogies, theories, assumptions, and interpretations. The structure of the website mirrors the structure of that process—it's a complex web of references, comparisons, and links.[19]

---

[17]    Interestingly, Roller and his team faced remarkable legal difficulties in their project. It was extremely complicated to gain access to a single film recording of *Errand in the Maze*. The recording in question was made in 1960, at a memorial concert commemorating Bodenwieser's death in 1959, which technically makes it a reconstruction as well.

[18]    Roller (2012) in interviews on the work process of the production: http://tanzfonds.de/en/project/documentation-2012/the-source-code/ (in German, but incl. English transcript) (accessed May 2, 2017).

[19]    Roller (2012) on the home page of the project's website. http://www.thesourcecode.de/ (accessed May 2, 2017).

The question of the modalities of the process of remembering follows visitors to the site, as they take up the mantle of researcher, sorting, interpreting, and appraising the source material collected before them. In so doing, they bring to the fore production-oriented issues of the meaning and purpose of the appropriation of a dance context, which is unfamiliar to all participants in the reconstruction. Paradoxically, Roller's team finds motivation in a baseline skepticism toward reconstruction as a pursuit. Their skepticism comes—interestingly enough—not from the implicit imperative to trigger a genuine moment of contact with the inaccessible. The reasoning behind this critical intervention is rather revealing of the differences between knowledge of historical movement and of the contemporary body. Even down to specific gestures and energy flow, the movements cannot perfectly recapture the aesthetic result of a body (of a former student of Bodenwieser) that contained that historical knowledge. Until the bitter end of an intense training process, the movements remained foreign to the team. At the same time, dancers in the team undertaking this reconstructive work may find it essential to take stock in re-embodiment as a bona fide exercise in reflecting across bodies.

## CIUPKE AND TILL'S *UNDO, REDO AND REPEAT*

In their own similarly in-depth research, Christina Ciupke and Anna Till probe for strategies of appropriation suited to unfamiliar styles of dance applicable to five major twentieth-century aesthetic touchstones: Mary Wigman, Kurt Jooss, Dore Hoyer, Pina Bausch, and William Forsythe. To that end, these two dancers ask explicitly which options exist for processing memory and plumb the practices of transferring dance knowledge. The search for potential carriers of and approaches to historical dance knowledge and bodily knowledge is always at the forefront of this research.

*Undo, redo and repeat* also features a tripartite structure—website, performance, and installation[20]—composing an interpersonal, transmedia structure for thinking through past dance styles and pieces. The question of passing and transferring dance knowledge emerges clearly as the chief concern. The production finds its key outlet in an interview with select people meaningfully connected to the aforementioned protagonists of the theater scene. These were Irene Sieben, who personally studied in Mary Wigman's dance class, Reinhild Hoffman, who was a student of Kurt Jooss at the Folkwang Hochschule Essen, Martin Nachbar, who amassed an encyclopedic knowledge of Dore Hoyer through his reconstructions (see Chapter 2 in this volume), and Thomas McManus, former dancer and current ballet master at the Forsythe Company, and a chosen group of people who were, as former visitors, familiar with Pina Bausch's work at *Tanztheater*

---

[20] The various production formats are entwined as the website serves as a source for research and for the documentation of an installation at *Heidelberger Kunstverein* and a performance at *Sophiensaele Berlin*.

*Wuppertal.* Before beginning the exercise in memory with these "witnesses,"[21] Ciupke and Till issued them the following request:

> . . . convey to us one physical memory that you unmistakably associate with their work. It can be a fragment you experienced as a spectator that you would like to pass on, such that it can survive historically and be remembered in the present. You provide this in the form of specific movement material, a part of a dance, a movement principle, choreographic material, an improvisational technique, a score, or anything else. (Ciupke and Till 2012)[22]

Irene Sieben subsequently conveyed a "physical memory of Mary Wigman's lessons" in which she demonstrated Wigman's signature circular motif as a choreographic figuration. Martin Nachbar gave Christina and Anna a movement task to perform under the title *Shaken and Stirred* (*Geschüttelt und gerührt*), a self-affective movement scale in order to affect the audience. The task was to perform a single movement sequence in different emotionally colored modes, following the orders and the observation of the partner. Thomas McManus asked Ciupke and Till to research five images on their own and referred them to the CD of *Improvisation Technologies* for study. Reinhild Hoffman ultimately declined their request "to deliver the material to be reinterpreted in the form of a set of instructions, a score, or written directives for performance such that they can be remembered in today's context."[23] She wanted to instead forward Ciupke and Till her piece *VOR ORT* (1997).[24] The former visitors of Pina Bausch provided a challenge to the choreographers, who had to choose from a diverse collection of accounts. This process whereby the "witnesses" formulated their tasks as scores was a sort of pre-hearsal in which students, colleagues, coworkers, friends, and spectators projected their experiences and body-knowledge of the key figures onto the production work to follow. These transmitted scores and movement tasks were the starting point for the deep dives into historical reference materials on the key figures that began Ciupke and Till's rehearsal process, through which they sought to dredge up the long-untouched sediment underneath and transpose it. The witnesses, who were, by then, acting like teachers, became integral to the intense rehearsal process that followed, which included lessons on reverse-engineering movements from the close study of a formidable portfolio of films, images, and notes, as well as (documented) interviews and abundant conversation with the "witnesses." Through time, their historicized dance knowledge brought about a re-embodied appropriation that does not suggest physical similitude. Rather, the rehearsals

[21] Ciupke and Till refer to these agents as "witnesses." Most of them also became active in the production, for example working as teachers.

[22] Unpublished production material. I would like to extend my thanks to Christina and Anna for generously sharing their material with me.

[23] Unpublished production material.

[24] *VOR ORT* is a solo performance by Reinhild Hoffmann, first performed September 28, 1997 in Berlin. See Chapter 13 in this volume.

paved the way for a transcorporeal process of transference and appropriation of historically marked positions, moving into a space of difference.

As the title *undo, redo and repeat* already suggests, *repeating* is the unfailing sys-
temic linchpin enabling the appropriation of movement, the physical requisite for a
*redo*. When dance history follows the corridor of memory all the way, *repeat* is what it
finds standing at the far end. At the near end is the practically far plainer *remake*: a *redo*
that rather comes level with a mimetically driven repetition. Yet the success of both of
these operations and modes of appropriation—*redo* and *repeat*—rests on a prior *undo*;
this much is clear from their work with their witness-teachers, whose presence shifted
their overall vocabulary of the past toward the language of *undoing: untied, unraveled,
unleashed,* and *unmoored*. The witnesses act as intermediaries given their, as it were,
relatively immediate connection to the aesthetic knowledge of the past. Their unique,
embodied historicity severs the stalemating reciprocity between that state of being
*erased* and of being *opened up, abstracted, done*,[25] long since obliterated and recalled in
our consciousness. In their version of the memory and appropriation process, Ciupke
and Till work right on the fault line between present and past, upon which they are able
to play into and away from the process of a remembered visualization in rehearsal as
well as on stage.

## STAGING EMBODIMENT

Placing its acts of recall between the past and the present and an awareness of how transmission is the constitutive process of any repetitious appropriation of the past, *undo,
redo and repeat* elucidated the necessary way to handle the historical coordination of
corporeality. These acts of re-embodiment traverse a transmedia landscape of dance
knowledge, which adherence to one's own appropriation of body knowledge has long
placed into question. This is apparent from the moment the performance starts. In a
sustained sequence of repetitions, figured choreographically as a simultaneous cycle,
Ciupke and Till demonstrate the central motifs of Mary Wigman's movement style,
"turning and circling," which come off quite differently in the present, far from the
superhuman ideal of Wigman's own body. These scenes carve out a visual-actual space,
in which Irene Sieben's lexical adjustments resonate, echoing also an audio recording of
Wigman discussing the principle of "dance composition." *Undo, redo and repeat* strips
away nearly every pretense surrounding reconstruction and reenactment, letting an
unstable dance historicity play out in a reactive, volatile theatrical space. The performance carries on in this expansive fashion, covering an increasing number of surfaces
in the theater with rotating projections, construing the space of historical performance

---

[25] Undo covers a wide semantic range, it can mean: untie, unravel, unleash, agitate, ail, alarm,
unnerve, paralyze, take back, delete, etc. https://www.merriam-webster.com/thesaurus/undo (accessed
May 2, 2017).

as a layered, transmedial screening of memory. Constantly flanked with images, text designs, audio clips, and objects, the performers exhibit the expressionist circles, the choreographic patterning behind a Polonaise, the aforementioned piece *VOR ORT*, performed as a duet, the development of an emotional scene about fear, and finally an improvised sequence with live commentary. The differences between each of the protagonists' techniques, down to the very paradigms they suggest, are palpable, and yet have long since become sources and materials of reconstructive appropriations in the same vein as the passing down of memories. The result is a spontaneous, performed choreographic reflection on how the past becomes embodied, how memories become tangible in choreographic spaces that interpellate the dances of both performers into an audio-visual networking of perception, mapped out over audio recordings (corrective reminders from the witnesses recorded during rehearsals and historical clips of the protagonists themselves), projections of text designs (letters from Pina Bausch's audience), and film excerpts (interviews with the witnesses).

To hand down historical dance knowledge, one must be able, as *undo, redo and repeat* makes plain, to go beyond the domain of the physical body. The audience experiences the past in performance, first as a passage through memory: a deliberate reconstitution within an intermedial order of knowledge, in which the past finds itself reflected in a choreographic apparatus of perception. Embodied memory seems best understood as a choreographic and theatrical spacing of body and scene that spreads out across the arena of the present. We can invoke the past intellectually, but choreography is the key to experiencing the past as profoundly and irremediably unfamiliar. This realization is tantamount to the unveiling of a dialogical terrain capable of summoning up the past, while staying in the present and revealing the site of appropriative work to be directly on those fissures where the past is most volatile.

## LOGIC AND GESTURES OF MEMORY

It would behoove one who desires to construe reenactment as a critical practice of *recalling history* to take note of how protocols of staging and techniques of perception themselves reflect relational structures between the past and the present.[26] Despite the wide range of practical fields included under the umbrella of established procedure for reenactment, which conducts one into the culturally, historically, and aesthetically transpired event through an apparatus of perception that is fundamentally conjoined with the present, there is an unmistakable specificity to how reenactment shines a light on the past: either as illumination, irritation, or conjuration. The past is transported to an

---

[26] Reenactments have become a global form of entertainment and private hobby within our prevailing event culture. Reenacting historical scenes through the lens of today's experiences has led to an idiosyncratic form of memory culture, particularly in the (performative) arts. Cf. Arns 2007; Heeg et al. 2014; and Schlehe et al. 2010.

arena of presentness, manifested in the overall restaging and rendered through a work of representation as performed by the body. The reality of the transpired real asserts itself within the staging strategy and nestles into a spatiotemporal suspension of the present moment.[27]

With respect to academic discourse as well as reenactment as it is practiced in the performing arts, the physical state of the body in repetition does not necessarily represent any aesthetic act of critical reflection on the past. The stated horizon of an experience for an image-critical-practice of enlivening and inserting the past into the "here and now," as Inka Arns and Steve Rushton stress for the arts, essentially does not occur in dance with the particular demands for visualization it imposes. The function of the bodily as enlivening instantiation of the past is largely irrelevant unless staged as such, not unlike in Fabián Barba's *A Mary Wigman Dance Evening* (2010), which brought the Wigman image archive to life before the audience's very eyes. In dance, embodiment is the reckoning with an escaping past, and the escape from a suffocating present.

Reenactment's gestural vocabulary lies rather in the appointment of a re-embodied act of staging of historiographic appropriations of the past. (See Franko, Chapter 1 in this volume). These acts of staging do not animate history in the way Jerome de Groot qualifies reenactment (De Groot 2009, 129). History is not a truth that needs to come out, but an appropriation of the past that needs to be acted out over media, bodies, and stagings. The reminiscent act of re-embodiment transports the past into a concrete perceptual field, in which something becomes present, while retaining its potency as past. This is, in effect, the logic of reenactment: a staged act of activated memory continually carrying out the work of its own self-assertion.

## WORKS CITED

Arns, Inke, ed. 2007. *History Will Repeat Itself*. Frankfurt am Main: Revolver, Archiv für Aktuelle Kunst.

Assmann, Aleida. 2006. *Der lange Schatten der Vergangenheit. Erinnerungskultur und Geschichtspolitik*. München: Beck

Assmann, Aleida. 2007. *Geschichte im Gedächtnis. Von der individuellen Erfahrung zur öffentlichen Inszenierung*. München: Beck

Carter, Alexandra, ed. 2004. *Rethinking Dance History: A Reader*. London: Routledge.

Foellmer, Susanne. 2014. "Re-enactment und andere Wieder-Holungen in Tanz und Performance." In *Zitieren, Appropriieren, Sampeln. Referenzielle Verfahren in den Gegenwartskünsten*, edited by Frédéric Döhl and Renate Wöhrer, 69–92. Bielefeld: Transcript.

Foster, Hal. 2004. "An Archival Impulse." *October* 110: 3–22.

Foster, Susan. 1995. *Choreographing History*. Bloomington and Indianapolis: Indiana University Press.

---

[27] Ludger Schwarte proposes the term "vergegenwärtigen" which translates as calling to mind; literally: bringing into the present (Schwarte 2013, 139).

Franko, Mark. 1995. "Mimique." In *Bodies of the Text: Dance as Theory, Literature as Dance*, edited by Ellen Goellner and Jaqueline Shea Murphy, 205–216. New Brunswick, NJ: Rutgers University Press.

De Groot, Jerome. 2009. *Consuming History*. London: Routledge.

Haitzinger, Nicole. 2010. "Re-Enacting Pavlova. Re-enacting Wiesenthal. Zur Erinnerungskultur(en) und künstlerischen 'Selbst'-Inszenierungen." In *Original und Revival Geschichts-Schreibung im Tanz: Geschichts-Schreibung im Tanz*, edited by Christina Thurner and Julia Wehren, 181–196. Zürich: Chronos.

Hardt, Yvonne. 2012. "Engagements with the Past in Contemporary Dance." In *New German Dance Studies*, edited by Susan A. Manning and Lucia Ruprecht, 217–231. Urbana: University of Illinois Press.

Heeg, Günther. 2006. "Die Beschreibung eines Zerfalls der Intentionen ist für die Theater-Geschichte von großer Bedeutung." Interview mit Günther Heeg am 14. Juli 2005. In *The atergeschichtsschreibung: Interviews mit Theaterhistorikern*, edited by Jens Ilg and Thomas Bitterlich, 176–187. Marburg: Tectum.

Heeg, Günther, Micha Braun, Lars Krüger, and Helmut Schäfer, eds. 2014. *Reenacting History: Theater & Geschichte*. Berlin: Theater der Zeit.

Huschka, Sabine. 2012. "Bewegung auf-lesen—Blicke ordnen. Wahrnehmungs- und Erinnerungsräume schaffen." In *Bewegung Lesen | Bewegung Schreiben*, edited by Isa Wortelkamp, 77–97. Berlin: Revolver.

Huschka, Sabine. 2017. *Tanz/Wissen: Choreografierte Körper im theatron. Auftritte und Theoria ästhetischen Wissens*. München: Epodium.

Jeschke, Claudia. 2010. "'Updating the Updates'. Zum Problem der 'Identität' in der Geschichts-Vermittlung vom Tanz(en)." In *Original und Revival: Geschichts-Schreibung im Tanz*, edited by Christina Thurner and Julia Wehren, 69–79. Zürich: Chronos.

Jeschke, Claudia. 2009. "Re-Konstruktion: Tänzerische Entzeitlichungs-Strategien und Reenactment." *Tanz & Archiv Forschungsreisen* 1: 51–57. München: Epodium.

Krutschkova, Krassimira. 2010. "Tanzgeschichte(n): wieder und wider. Re-enactment, Referenz, révérence." In *Original und Revival: Geschichts-Schreibung im Tanz*, edited by Christina Thurner and Julia Wehren, 39–45. Zürich: Chronos.

Lepecki, André. 2004a. "Concept and Presence: The Contemporary European Dance Scene." In *Rethinking Dance History. A Reader*, edited by Alexandra Carter, 170–181. London [u.a.]: Routledge,

Lepecki, André. 2004b. "Inscribing Dance." In *Of the Presence of the Body: Essays on Dance and Performance Theory*, edited by André Lepecki, 124–139. Middletown, CT: Wesleyan University Press.

Lepecki, André. 2010. "The Body as Archive: Will to Re-Enact and the Afterlive of Dances." *Dance Research Journal* 42(2) (Winter): 28–48.

Massumi, Brain. 2002. *Parables for the Virtual*. Durham, NC: Duke University Press.

Noland, Carrie. 2013. "Inheriting the Avant-Garde: Merce Cunningham, Marcel Duchamp, and the Legacy Plan." *Dance Research Journal* 45(2): 85–122.

Pina Bausch Foundation. 2011. "Mission." Pina Bausch Foundation. http://www.pinabausch.org/en/foundation/mission (accessed May 2, 2017).

Roller, Jochen. 2012. "Interview on the Work Process of the Production." http://tanzfonds.de/en/project/documentation-2012/the-source-code/ (in German, but incl. English transcript) (accessed May 2, 2017).

Santone, Jessica. 2008. "Marina Abramovic's *Seven Easy Pieces*: Critical Documentation Strategies for Preserving Art's History." *Leonardo* 41(2): 147–152.

Schlehe, Judith, Michiko Uike-Bormann, Carolyn Oesterle, and Wolfgang Hochbruck, eds. 2010. *Staging the Past: Themed Environments in Transcultural Perspectives*. Bielefeld: Transcript.

Schwarte, Ludger. 2013. "Die Architektur der Zeit." In *Zeitstrukturen: Techniken der Vergegenwärtigung in Wissenschaft und Kunst*, edited by Johannes Myssok and Ludger Schwarte (Hg.), 135–147. Berlin: Reimer.

Siegmund, Gerald. 2010. "Affekt, Technik, Diskurs. Aktiv passiv sein im Angesicht der Geschichte." In *Original und Revival: Geschichts-Schreibung im Tanz*, edited by Christina Thurner and Julia Wehren, 15–26. Zürich: Chronos.

Stöckelmann, Patricia. 2013. "Interview of the Documentation of the Project." http://tanzfonds. de/projekt/dokumentation-2013/le-sacre-du-printemps (accessed December 10, 2015).

# AFTERWORD

## *Notes after the Fact*

### LUCIA RUPRECHT

"For the postface," Gérard Genette writes in *Paratexts,* "it is always both too early and too late" (1997, 239). It is too late, Genette argues, because the postface cannot any more perform the functions of a preface, which holds the reader's interest, sets out what is to come, and provides a guide through the text; and too early, because it cannot yet respond to critical reactions that are bound to occur after a book's publication. The postface—or afterword—is an untimely genre. An afterword is imbued with the generic flaw of the supplement, of that which remains exterior to "real," "original," or "timely" contents. But its supplementary character also bears a promise, questioning notions of realness, originality, and timeliness. Reflecting upon contents that always will have happened already, the genre of the afterword corresponds to the out-of-time topic of this *Handbook:* reenactment. What follows, then, are a number of short supplementary notes on significant theoretical concepts that are part of the artistic and scholarly field of reenactment. These notes take up themes that run through the contributions to this volume, and their after-the-fact status is visible in their headings: "Postface," "Restance," "Temporality," and "Archive." They are succeeded by a longer note on the potential of danced reenactment to reshape the historiography of dance.

## POSTFACE

Post- and prefaces belong to what Jacques Derrida calls the *hors livre* or "outwork," those texts or not-quite texts that dwell at the margins of what is usually considered the main body of a book. The preface or outwork of Derrida's *Dissemination* includes the following passage:

> The *pre* of the preface makes the future present, represents it, draws it closer, breathes it in, and in going ahead of it puts it ahead. The *pre* reduces the future to the form

of manifest presence. This is an essential and ludicrous operation: not only because writing as such does not consist in any of these tenses (present, past, or future insofar as they are all modified presents); not only because such an operation would confine itself to the discursive effects of an intention-to-mean, but because, in pointing out a single thematic nucleus or a single guiding thesis, it would cancel out the textual displacement that is at place "here." (Here? Where? The question of the here and now is explicitly enacted in dissemination). (1981, 7)

Conversely, the *post* of the postface might then ideally (or ludicrously) attempt to make the past present, representing that which has already been written, drawing it closer, breathing it in, but also, by returning to it, assigning it its place in a "there." "Is not the question of the 'there' the ultimate question of reenactment?" Mark Franko asks in Chapter 24 of this volume. It is the fanning-out and complicating of this question that makes the theoretical and conceptual approaches that are assembled in this *Handbook* so rich and engaging. A firm assignment of place is of course impossible with regard to the many locations of this book's contributions. There is more than a single thematic nucleus or a single guiding thesis in *The Oxford Handbook of Dance and Reenactment*, and its textual displacement affects and is affected by the range of conceptual coinages. Terms are not fully stabilized. The notion of reenactment itself is not concerned to convey a definitive viewpoint on what is still a very diverse phenomenon. Franko notes in Chapter 1 that the artistic field of reenactment engenders a multifold vocabulary, including "re-performance, remake, citation, the distributed body, alternative histories, acheiropoietics, restructuring touch, re-actualization, the derivative, cover"; in Chapter 14, VK Preston extends this field to a heuristic reenacting of archival material by the scholar, which she calls "research-spectatorship." The heuristic and the performative are closely aligned in reenactment. It is therefore a privileged space for conversation between dancers (who are often also researchers) and researchers (who are often also dancers), which is evident in the selection of contributors to this volume who share an interest in questions of revitalization and return from various practical and discursive positions.

# RESTANCE

Speaking of the "resistance" of "reducing" a phenomenon or "a text as such to its effects of meaning, content, thesis, or theme," Derrida proposes to call this resistance *restance*, and explains: "coined from the verb *rester* (to remain)," *restance* means "'the fact or act of remaining or of being left over'" of a "sort of writing that can neither adapt nor adopt such a reduction" (1981, 7–8). In this light, the phenomenon of reenactment cannot be firmly pinned down by the semantics of its vocabulary. What is more, its own conceptual work of the "re-" also follows this logic.[1] Reenactments remain marked by the resistant

---

[1] See Franko, Chapter 24, in this volume.

traces of what their synthesis must reduce or erase. Retrospective covers of that which went before are molded by omissions. Concurrently, an afterword's analeptic reenactment of a collection of chapters, which brings back certain aspects of past writing while passing over others, does not assume the status of an exhaustive reconstruction. It still resounds, however, with the restance of that which it does not retrieve. Restance, then, is yet another term to be added to the list of reenactment nomenclature.

Restance affects reenactments in various ways. It can be most powerful if construed as an advertent effect of latency, as in Stan Douglas's fictional histories that are the object of his photographs for *Disco Angola* (2012).[2] Catherine Soussloff writes in Chapter 29 that actual history, the fact that "Angola descended into a perpetual battlefield, while disco was impugned for its commercialization and 'bad' music," is left out in Douglas's utopian reenactments, thus making obvious the constructed nature of *Disco Angola*'s redemptive élan, and its politically motivated refusal to reactivate the historical past.[3] In this case, such a refusal must be seen as an emancipatory act. In other words, Douglas ensures in this work that the actual past's absence is a conspicuous one. By contrast, restance can have a more problematic value when operating inadvertently, as revealed by Susanne Franco's discussion in Chapter 7 of Valerie Preston-Dunlop's "recreations" of Rudolf Laban's choreographies. Here the deliberate neglect of the fascist aspect and context of Laban's work leads to restance of a more haunting nature. The absence of an obvious and well-researched political burden casts a shadow on Preston-Dunlop's choreographies, adding unease to their allegedly neutral status. Making complex the question of "thereness" in reenactment, restance thus forces us to think about the politics of outspoken and unspoken retrieval.[4]

## TEMPORALITY

If the vocabularies of reenactment are unstable, multiple, and open to new additions, so too are reenactment's temporalities. "[D]anced reenactment places the dance work in a set of asymmetrical historical temporalities; it is hence likely to unsettle our assumed grounding in a linearly progressive past," Franko states in Chapter 1. In Chapter 25, writing on fifteenth-century *basse danse* and *bassadanza* manuals, Seeta Chaganti speaks of a kind of time that is "recursive and multidirectional [ ... ] ." As Christel Stalpaert's discussion of William Kentridge's video installations in Chapter 19 shows, such an approach to temporality might constitute a strategic statement, refusing clock time that

---

[2] On fictional reenactment, see also the chapters by Anna Pakes, Branislav Jakovljević, and Susan Jones in this volume (Chapters 5, 11, 22).

[3] Compare Ramsay Burt's discussion in Chapter 17 in this volume of the "utopian ideas that reconstructions, reenactments, reperformances, and related projects can offer by blasting performances out of the pigeonholes into which normative historical processes have consigned them".

[4] See Part IX in this volume.

is associated with capitalism and colonialism. Here Dada Masilo's reenactment of Loïe Fuller's *Serpentine Dance*, which is shown in reverse, literally re-embodies time, showing how to perform it otherwise.[5]

But the archival investments of current reenactment practices also include what Kate Elswit in Chapter 9 calls their "'future' potential." The recovery of past dances has come to constitute a new contemporary choreographic and performative activity with a forward-looking dimension, associating reenactment with a future impregnated with recovery. Or, in the words of performance scholar João Florêncio, member of the new Future Advisory Board of *Performance Studies International*, "at a critical time when so much of what has heretofore been taken for granted is melting, burning or fading away, *rethinking* the future is of the utmost urgency [italics added]."[6] Those who create, think, and comment about danced reenactments contest the presumed untouchable nature of the future, even when accepting the limits of their projections; and they doubt the presumed knowability of the past, even when piecing it together or reconstructing it. They accept that there is "an impossible element" within their efforts, Gerald Siegmund writes in Chapter 23, but they also take on the challenge and joy of hybrid temporality. Kate Elswit's work with Rani Nair is called *Future Memory* (Chapter 9); Chaganti discusses an "anticipatory" agency in the historical manuals that she is investigating (Chapter 25); Frédéric Pouillaude observes that Isidore Isou's 1960 lettrist ballet scores "document [ . . . ] in advance" the choreographic present (Chapter 8).[7] In a reversal of Walter Benjamin's thought image (or in fact, movement image) of the *Angelus Novus*, whose gaze is directed toward a (catastrophic) past while he is driven toward a future that lies behind his back, reenactments are facing the future in its double shape as both past and present futurity; yet at the same time, going backward, they also recede from it. Whereas we must advance through time—Benjamin's angel is irresistibly propelled into the future—we do not have to, but we decide to go back to the past. There is no "archival impulse," André Lepecki argues, but a "will to archive" (2010, 28).

# ARCHIVE

This will to archive has much in common with what Sigmund Freud, who devoted himself to the ways in which individual, unconscious pasts can be made available for analysis, calls "working-through," a mode of conscious remembering and appropriation of former experience that he contrasts to an unconscious mode of compulsive repetition. In Freud, however, conscious remembering cannot happen in the "motor sphere," which is the site where unconscious impulses are repetitively acted out or "discharge[d] in action." In the Freudian setting, remembering must take place in the "psychical field"

---

[5] Stalpaert (Chapter 19).
[6] http://www.psi-web.org/about/future-advisory-board/
[7] On "Past Futures," see also Richard Move (Chapter 4) and Randy Martin (Chapter 28) in this volume.

in order to become a precondition of working-through (2001, 153). Danced reenactment takes to task Freud's theory. Transposing this theory onto the territory of performance, it demonstrates how the bodily labor of choreography is actually able to work through collective, and sometimes also personal, pasts. Martin Nachbar points out in Chapter 2 that the "therapeutic aspect" of his *Repeater—Dance Piece with Father* (2007) consisted in recognizing that he and his father both display the same "line of tension" along shoulder and arm, and that the work on *Repeater* enabled him to accept this line as a gift from his father, as a mutual bond, as opposed to an unwanted restriction of his physical flexibility.

If the psychoanalytic notion of working-through becomes a physical one in reenactment, so too does the notion of archive or of archival practice. Taking into account current archival theories, this notion has a literal and a metaphorical dimension; it implies both "a body of documents and the institutions that house them" and "a metaphoric invocation for any corpus of selective collections and the longings that the acquisitive quests for the primary, originary, and untouched entail" (Stoler 2009, 45). Archival dance, by contrast, goes beyond textual sources and material objects. As an embodied practice, it is also always more than metaphorical. Dance bestows an archival function to the body and its movement. Dancers "re-member knowledge through their movements as the body acts" (Foster 2009, 8). They thus enter the archive in more than one way: like scholars, they engage in archival inquiry; but they also perform what they have found, and they perform how they relate to their archive, questioning their desire for authenticity.

Following Rebecca Schneider, to refer to the live acts of bodily movement as archival findings or documents unsettles the distinction between documents on the one side and performance acts on the other. As Schneider argues, "crossing the wires of this long-sedimented binary" effectuates an important theoretical shift, providing "a fertile way to interrogate the very privilege that document, inscription, and textuality have held over incorporation" (2011, 197). This theoretical shift not only affects ontological categorization, such as the insistence on performance's transience; it also pertains to the ethical and political relevance of performance. If the body itself becomes document, record, or evidence, and the dancer the archival agent or subject rather than object, hierarchical allocations that are entwined with the dichotomy of textual documents (as standing for the same) and embodied acts (as standing for the other) are no longer tenable. Often, dance deconstructs this dichotomy between embodiment and recording even further. Archival performances of the body-as-document are visually or textually recorded in turn, making documentation a genuine part of the performative event.[8]

---

[8]  See Philip Auslander, "The Performativity of Performance Documentation," *Performance Art Journal* 84 (2006): 1–10; Amelia Jones: "'Presence' in Absentia: Experiencing Performance as Documentation," *Art Journal* 56 (Winter 1997): 11–18; see also my discussion of Jochen Roller's *The Source Code* later in this afterword.

# HISTORIOGRAPHY

Reenactments are anti-positivistic and skeptical about accurate reconstructions of the past, but they also work toward new forms of approaching historical knowledge. They have an "investigative dimension [ . . . ] contributing to our understanding of the works, practice, or historical moment concerned" (Pakes, Chapter 5 in this volume); they uncover and in this sense also "produce" tradition or genealogy (Siegmund, Chapter 23 in this volume).[9] If one is able through reenactment to "grasp[] the logic of thought" embodied in the dance (Bleeker, Chapter 10 in this volume), this may also imply that one salvages aspects that have fallen to the wayside in previous processes of historiographical preservation. Carrie Noland in Chapter 6 considers Jennifer Goggans's 2014 reconstruction of Merce Cunningham's *Crises* (1960) part of the larger aesthetic realm of reenactment, and she explores how this reconstruction by a dancer with intimate knowledge of the original directs attention to affective and dramatic potentials that are usually denied in approaches to Cunningham's choreography.[10] Noland also argues that a reconstruction like Goggans's brings to the fore choreographic processes that show how ostensibly originary or even totalitarian agencies—a choreography that is imposed onto dancers' bodies, a source piece that determines its reconstruction—are shaped by that which they might seem to govern. *Crises* emerged from a process in which the choreographer's body gave in to being transformed by the movement qualities of one of his dancers, in this case Viola Farber. Likewise, a historical choreography will not remain unaffected by its reconstruction or reenactment. "It is as though a work," Noland writes,

> conceived originally for a different audience, discursively framed in a different way, bore in its very DNA the possibility of evolving along other lines. The aesthetic of the reconstructor, the kinetic particularities of the dancers, and the attitude of the contemporary audience all pull the choreography further in a direction latent in the choreography. (Chapter 6)

What, then would be the direction latent in the artistic field of reenactment, and how can we pull it further? This *Handbook* suggests an intrinsic or latent relationship between reenactment and historiography, whereby the performed histories of reenactments do not necessarily replace traditional historiography, but rethink its terms.[11] Referring to Vanessa Agnew's theorization of popular reenactments in Chapter 3, Timmy De Laet reminds us that this scholar detects a general emphasis in the field on affective historiography, and therefore ultimately doubts "whether reenactment has the 'capacity to

---

[9]  Pakes; see also Huschka's chapter in this volume.

[10]  For a detailed discussion of the problematic status of the witness of an original choreography, see Susanne Foellmer (Chapter 13) in this volume.

[11]  See also Ramsay Burt (Chapter 17) in this volume.

further historical understanding', precisely because of its 'emphasis on affect' " (Agnew, cited in Chapter 3)." But De Laet also asserts that the focus on affect alone does not capture the self-reflective dimension of new archival performance:[12] "The common equation of reenactment in dance with a search for affect has fostered a rather one-sided perspective that disregards how it also stimulates epistemic faculties and provokes critical reflection on how it is we come to know the past."

Franko is also wary to leave unchallenged claims that too readily conflate reenactment with historiography. If the discipline of history, as Michel Foucault has it, was for a long time deemed to be "a practice disengaged from the present," reenactment's allegiances to the body's here and now would preclude that it can act on this discipline's behalf. What if, however, reenactment were not primarily considered to perform a physical kind of historiography, but to stage the tension or the conflict between history and memory? In Chapter 30, Sabine Huschka speaks of a "staged act of activated memory," emphasizing that we do not aim to approach the truth of the past, but rather appropriate a mediated—and therefore precisely not immediate—version of it;[13] and we do so to create specific effects, restoring a certain operative dimension to that which is (no longer) gone. These views suggest that reenactment is not just bodily or mental recollection but a recalling to action of the past as event. Reenactment testifies to a new sense of agency in relationships with the past. This sense of agency is representative of a larger shift in theoretical concerns. There is an intimate link between the focus during the 1990s on ephemerality in performance studies and the insistence in trauma studies on the erasure of the event which is at the heart of painful experience.[14] That which Franko calls, significantly, the "post-ephemeral era" (Chapter 1) of reenactment shifts theoretical attention from a kind of eventness that exists through compulsive erasure and return, to one that exists through deliberate—if not uncomplicated—forms of reclaim.

The performative recalling to action of the past as event can also have a refreshing effect on the habits and conventions of traditional historiography. This is what Christina Thurner proposes in Chapter 26. Thurner considers danced reenactment a "form of historiography" which offers "a response" to "the postmodern crisis" of the writing of history, one that provides an "alternative paradigm," which she associates with the "enmeshed model of a network, or a choreographic contemporaneity of the noncontemporaneous, rather than a straight line emerging from one starting point" (Chapter 26 in this volume).[15] Or, as Franko puts it, reenactments and their multiple temporalities adopt

---

[12]  On affect, see also Anna Pakes (Chapter 5) and Gerald Siegmund (Chapter 23) in this volume.

[13]  On memory, see also Yvonne Hardt (Chapter 12) and P. A. Skantze (Chapter 16) in this volume.

[14]  See Cathy Caruth, *Unclaimed Experience: Trauma, Narrative, and History* (Baltimore, MD: Johns Hopkins University Press, 1996); Peggy Phelan, *Unmarked: The Politics of Performance* (London: Routledge, 1993), and *Mourning Sex: Performing Public Memories* (London: Routledge, 1997).

[15]  Julia Wehren echoes Thurner's position. Wehren explores the historiographical aspects of current performance practice by Olga de Soto, Foofwa d'Imobilité, Thomas Lebrun, and Boris Charmatz and argues that "their choreographic rethinking of history [ . . . ] represents dance history in meaningful and adequate ways," in *Körper als Archiv in Bewegung. Choreographie als historiografische Praxis* (Bielefeld: Transcript, 2016), 220 (my translation).

"the project of historiography by *acting on* that which seemed to belong forever more to the register of language (the *writing* of history)" (Chapter 1 in this volume). Reenactment not only takes something away from the field of writing, the present afterword would like to add, but is also able to give back to this field. It recalls to action, acts on, and thus reintroduces impact in the present to that which has been said and done. Kentridge's *The Refusal of Time* "questions time regimes that support a chronological, modernist conception of time and (dance) history," writes Stalpaert, making us aware of this performance's repercussions on our understanding of historiography (Chapter 19 in this volume). By casting a black performer and filmically intervening into a canonical dance piece, Kentridge may not rewrite, but does revisualize a prominent example of Western dance heritage, repossessing it to powerful effect for those whom this heritage excluded.

Pulling further the relationship between reenactment and historiography means, then, not to do away with or replace written historiographies by performed ones; but to complete the transfer of knowledge between the written and the performed by allowing the insights of performance to feed back into the sites of writing. Situated at the theoretically self-reflexive end of a continuum of archival practice in dance, the rethinking of methods for approaching the past is part of the performance of reenactments. Resounding with Judith Butler's model of performativity, reenactments reiterate rather than repeat, thinking with, but not within, the prescriptions of the past. In doing so, they indeed reflect upon historiography; they engage in theoretical as much as practical concerns. Reenactments can thus provide impulses for an academic practice of dance historiography that is at the height of current (performed) theorizing.

These impulses pertain, above all, to the meshwork of what I would like to call the inter-temporal and globally interconnected aspects of the project of reenactment.[16] *Inter-temporality* is used as an umbrella term here, encompassing not only the unsettlement of linear time in archival performance, but also the hybrid or aesthetic temporalities that currently receive much critical attention both within and beyond the field of dance.[17] Reenactment's temporal theorizing is in touch with cross-disciplinary debates, such as the discussion on the multiple temporalities of contemporaneity in art theory.[18] It also speaks to what Georgina Born, with reference to music, calls "the multiplicity of time in cultural production" (2015, 362), and to the new interest in literary history in the "transtemporal movement" of "[p]olychronic parallax in multiple historical dimensions," which breaks open firm allocations of literary context (Tucker 2011, x).

In addition, arguing for a globally interconnected dance history means acknowledging that dance brings together not only multiple times, but also multiple places; one might think of spatialized histories, and also of a "poetics of space and time" (Chapter 24). Styles of movement, dance pieces, and dancers migrate; forms of dance

---

[16] See Part VIII in this volume.
[17] See Michael Gamper and Helmut Hühn, *Was sind ästhetische Eigenzeiten?* (Hannover: Wehrhahn, 2014).
[18] See Terry Smith, "Contemporary Art and Contemporaneity," *Critical Inquiry* 32(4) (2006): 681–707.

adapt elements from each other; they fuse and branch out.[19] Erika Fischer-Lichte calls this interconnectedness "interweaving," and she points out that it "does not result in homogenization but generates diversity." She holds that

> moving within and between cultures is celebrated as a state of in-betweeness that will change spaces, disciplines and the subject as well as her/his body in a way that exceeds what is currently imaginable. By interweaving performance cultures without negating or homogenizing differences but permanently de/stabilizing and thus invalidating their authoritative claims to authenticity, performances, as sites of in-betweeness, are able to constitute fundamentally other, unprecedented realities. (2014, 12–15)

Such other, unprecedented realities emerge in Elswit's and Nair's reenactment of Kurt Jooss's gift to Swedish-based Indian dancer Lilavati Häger, and in Beyoncé's "borrowing" of movement material by Anne Teresa De Keersmaeker, as discussed in Chapter 18 by Anthea Kraut;[20] they arise in Randy Martin's "logics of derivation" which he detects in Trisha Brown's postmodern dance, in breakdancing, and in skateboarding (Chapter 28), and in Janez Janša's subversive reappropriation during the 2007 *Exodos Festival* in Ljubljana of canonical contemporary dance works from the United States, Germany, and Japan.[21] They can be witnessed in Ecuadorian Fabián Barba's "illusions of authenticity" when performing Mary Wigman's dances (Chapter 20), and in Richard Move's "sonic incarnations" of Martha Graham (Chapter 4). However, the lens of reenactment also casts new light on dance forms that are not necessarily associated with the theoretical outlook of this term, such as the thirteenth-century ritual dance theater *Kaisika Natakam*, whose restagings are explored by Ketu H. Katrak and Anita Ratnam in Chapter 15.[22] Anurima Banerji in Chapter 21 introduces the philosophical, performative, and spatial distribution of the dancer's body in the Indian *mahari naach*, which cannot be reproduced in this dance's reenactment in the shape of Odissi.[23] Here, the acknowledgement of reenactment theory draws out impossibilities, rather than possibilities, of reproduction across historical gaps.

What, then, might a type of historiography that is mindful of performative practice look like? It might still follow a traditionally discursive model, but tell (hi)stories that reflect inter-temporality and global interconnectedness in their thematic reaches and approaches. But it might also reflect, in its methodology and form, reenactment's poetics of space and time. As we have seen, reenactment redefines the notion of the archive, or,

[19] See Ann Cooper Albright and Ann Dils, *Moving History/Dancing Cultures: A Dance History Reader* (Middletown, CT: Wesleyan University Press, 2001); Susan Leigh Foster, ed., *Worlding Dance* (Basingstoke: Palgrave Macmillan, 2011); Gabriele Klein, "Inventur der Tanzmoderne. Geschichtstheoretische Überlegungen zur tanzwissenschaftlichen Forschung," *Forum Modernes Theater* 23/1 (2008), 5–12.

[20] See Kate Elswit (Chapter 9) and Anthea Kraut (Chapter 18) in this volume.

[21] See Ramsay Burt (Chapter 17) in this volume.

[22] See Ketu H. Katrak and Anita Ratnam (Chapter 15) in this volume.

[23] See Anurima Banerji (Chapter 21) in this volume.

**FIGURE A.1.**  *The Source Code—A Moving Archive.*

as some contributors to this volume argue, sets an anarchival practice against an archival one. Jens Giersdorf holds that reenactment produces "new theatrical and historical structures, instead of functioning as archival practice" (Chapter 27); VK Preston considers anarchival critical research one in which, as Schneider has it, the archive becomes *"another kind of performance"* (Schneider, cited in Chapter 14). In staged reenactments, in turn, the performance often becomes another kind of archive. It is an example of such a kind of archive that I would like to introduce in conclusion, based on a reenactment project that may serve as an inspiring model for a type of academic historiography that is attentive to the rethinking of historiography in dance.

German dancer, dance researcher, and choreographer Jochen Roller's project *The Source Code—A Moving Archive* stores material from Roller's 2014 re-creation of Gertrud Bodenwieser's 1954 dance drama *Errand into the Maze*.[24] Roller undertook the re-creation together with Australian-based dancers Latai Taumoepeau, Matthew Day, Lizzie Thomson, and Nadia Cusimano, German dance researcher Elisabeth Nehring, and video artist Andrea Keiz. Results from this project are accessible on a website that puts at our disposal a set of historiographical tools.[25] These tools consist not only in the making available of archival material, but also in recordings of the physical production of such material. The project was never meant to lead to a full reconstruction or reenactment on stage, but to document reenactment as a research process; at the same time, it also reenacts documents, remixing corporeal, visual, and discursive traces of a past performance.

Bodenwieser is a major proponent of early twentieth-century *Ausdruckstanz*. As an Austrian Jew, she had to emigrate to Australia, where she introduced Germanic

---

[24] "Re-creation" is the term that Roller chose for his project. For a complementary discussion of *The Source Code*, see Sabine Huschka (Chapter 30) in this volume.

[25] http://www.thesourcecode.de/

expressionism to new audiences. Part of the global circulation of *Ausdruckstanz* that led to hybrid cultural geographies,[26] Bodenwieser's work now also belongs to Australia's dance heritage. Roller's digital archive opens up this heritage again, allowing it to travel back to Austria, Germany, and beyond. His project website is organized along ten levels, including different themes such as genealogies of Bodenwieser technique, the aesthetic of danced expressionism, Bodenwieser's status as refugee, her movement material, and also one level crucially entitled "The Non-Reconstruction." All themed levels contain twelve documents: photographs, interviews with witnesses, discussions among Roller's recreation team, historical letters and descriptions of performances, program leaflets, and video clips of rehearsals and classes in Bodenwieser technique. The documents are placed in slight disarray in front of background images of old archival boxes or suitcases, creating the appearance of mock-materiality superseded by digital click-culture, but also reminding the visitor that the digital interface relies upon a project stage at which the team engaged with people, handled physical materials, and familiarized themselves as dancers with an unfamiliar school of movement.

When visiting the website as a researcher and clicking on the various documents, one reenacts, as it were, the reenactment process: one thematic level is called "Constantly Moving," and this is what the digital interface encourages, interspersed with moments of halt and attentiveness, zooming in on a historical photograph, an audio recording of a former Bodenwieser dancer, or a studio clip. There is also a commentary function that highlights cross-references between the documents. At the end of one's pathway through the material, one can generate a map that traces the research trajectory. The performativity of the site depends on how it is performed upon by the scholar. The 120 documents are enough to satisfy our desire for knowledge, and yet they are also based on obvious selection. Their "attitude" is cautious so as not to lure us into a delusion of total proximity. The discussions among the team rest on a shared commitment to learning about something that remains far away and impossible to assimilate, but that is still traceable as a historical form of movement with its own psycho-choreographical qualities.[27]

A project like *The Source Code* activates the past not as event, then, but as process, showing us how the performance of a reenactment—which was not intended in this case—might come about, without displaying a result. The studio clips that are included on the website only ever present us with snippets of movement sequences, often framed with discursive passages. Here, dance is conducted in ways that are almost undistinguishable from scholarship: the performers consult archival

[26]  See also Fabián Barba (Chapter 20) in this volume.

[27]  At the thematic level entitled "Refugee Alien" on the *Source Code* website, we find the recording of a conversation of the *Errand into the Maze* re-creation team at Rozelle School of Visual Arts in Sydney in January 2013. Roller talks about a specific movement, a form of "withheld collapse" or "a collapse where you know you have to go on" as Barbara Cuckson, custodian of the Bodenwieser Archives, had explained to the team; and he suggests that it might be possible to read this movement as the manifestation of Bodenwieser's "biographical pain." http://www.thesourcecode.de/refugee-alien. html#function-of-movement.

material, conduct interviews with witnesses, sit down and discuss. But they also add an embodied dimension to their research, engaging physically with a movement language that belongs to the past. The new archive that grew out of this range of activities retains their processual character. However, the creation of an archive does not seem to have been the single or most important aim of *The Source Code*. Rather, the archival structure facilitated—and still facilitates for us—that which appears to have been the project's initial driving momentum. At some point in one of the recorded conversations among the *Errand into the Maze* re-creation team, Roller talks about his motivations for embarking on *The Source Code*. He asks, "How much can you [ ... ] delve into another person's movement language, trying to understand what this person was concerned with?"[28] This, then, is yet another intriguing and perhaps the most fundamental question posed not only by Roller's project, but also by the extensive and multiple field of danced reenactment as a form of performative and scholarly inquiry.

## WORKS CITED

Auslander, Philip. 2006. "The Performativity of Performance Documentation." *Performance Art Journal* 84: 1–10.

Born, Georgina. 2015. "Making Time: Temporality, History, and the Cultural Object." *New Literary History* 46: 361–386.

Caruth, Cathy. 1996. *Unclaimed Experience: Trauma, Narrative, and History*. Baltimore, MD: Johns Hopkins University Press.

Cooper Albright, Ann, and Ann Dils. 2001. *Moving History/Dancing Cultures: A Dance History Reader*. Middletown, CT: Wesleyan University Press.

Derrida, Jacques. 1981. *Dissemination*. Translated by Barbara Johnson. London: The Athlone Press.

Fischer-Lichte, Erika. 2014. "Introduction: Interweaving Performance Cultures—Rethinking 'Intercultural Theatre:' Toward an Experience and Theory of Performance Beyond Postcolonialism." In *The Politics of Interweaving Performance Cultures: Beyond Postcolonialism*, edited by Erika Fischer-Lichte, Torsten Jost, and Saskya Iris Jain, 1–24. New York: Routledge.

Florêncio, Joao. 2016. http://www.psi-web.org/about/future-advisory-board/.

Foster, Susan Leigh. 2009. "Worlding Dance: An Introduction." In *Worlding Dance*, edited by Susan Leigh Foster, 1–14. Basingstoke, UK: Palgrave Macmillan.

Freud, Sigmund. 2001. "Remembering, Repeating and Working-Through." In *The Standard Edition of The Complete Psychological Works of Sigmund Freud*. Translated by James Strachey, vol. 12, 145–157. London: Vintage Books.

Gamper, Michael, and Helmut Hühn. 2014. *Was sind ästhetische Eigenzeiten?* Hannover: Wehrhahn.

Genette, Gérard. 1997. *Paratexts: Thresholds of Interpretation*. Translated by Jane E. Lewin. Cambridge: Cambridge University Press.

[28] Ibid.

Jones, Amelia. 1997. "Presence" in Absentia: Experiencing Performance as Documentation." *Art Journal* 56 (Winter): 11–18.

Klein, Gabriele. 2008. "Inventur der Tanzmoderne. Geschichtstheoretische Überlegungen zur tanzwissenschaftlichen Forschung." *Forum Modernes Theater* 23(1): 5–12.

Lepecki, André. 2010. "The Body as Archive: Will to Re-Enact and the Afterlives of Dances." *Dance Research Journal* 42(2): 28–48.

Phelan, Peggy. 1993. *Unmarked: The Politics of Performance*. London: Routledge.

Phelan, Peggy. 1997. *Mourning Sex: Performing Public Memories*. London: Routledge.

Roller, Jochen. 2014. http://www.thesourcecode.de/.

Schneider, Rebecca. 2011. *Performing Remains: Art and War in Times of Theatrical Reenactment*. New York: Routledge.

Smith, Terry. 2006. "Contemporary Art and Contemporaneity." *Critical Inquiry* 32(4): 681–707.

Stoler, Ann. 2009. *Along the Archival Grain: Epistemic Anxieties and Colonial Common Sense*. Princeton, NJ: Princeton University Press.

Tucker, Herbert F. 2011. "Introduction." *New Literary History* 42: vii–xii.

Wehren, Julia. 2016. *Körper als Archiv in Bewegung. Choreographie als historiografische Praxis*. Bielefeld, Germany: Transcript.

# INDEX

......................

Note: Page numbers followed by '*f*' and '*t*' refers to figures and tables

contemporary dance
  advent of new scene in, 483
  Brussels scene and, 401, 407
  digital revolution and, 483
  Duncan and, 492n11
  freelance dancers in, 472
  historicizing modes of 1980s, 489, 492–94
  history exclusion of communist
    countries', 340
  institutional support for companies
    of, 471
  interest in own history of, 587–89,
    587n1, 588n2
  linear evolution view of, 340, 408
  1990s reconstructions, 472, 473
  oppressed past and, 340
  originality notion as rejected by, 473
  political dimensions of appropriation
    efforts in, 590–92
contemporary Indian dance
  Nair's reconstructions and, 178, 197, 204,
    204n26, 206f
  Neo-Bharatam and, 320
*Continuous Project-Altered Daily (CP-AD)*, 257
  first performance of, 250
  performance modes of, 255–56
*Continuous Project-Altered Daily (CP-AD)*,
  appropriation of Rainer's
  as case study, 259–61
  improvisation scores and educational
    setting, 248–49, 256–58
  Judson Dance Theater and, 250n6
  performance score challenges, 255–58
  project introduction, 249n4
  rehearsal mode and self-reflexivity
    challenge in, 261–62
  skills involved in, 259–61
  surprise element in, 262
conventions, reactivation of, 409
Cook, Alexander, 92, 219–20
copyright, 356, 357, 364n19
Cornazano, 510–11, 515, 518
corporeality, 542
  Barba and, 13, 79, 93–96
  identity politics and, 540
"Countdown" video, Beyoncé, 357
  alternate version of, 363–64, 364n18

De Keersmaeker's choreography sequence
  in, 359
  lyrics and aesthetic of, 358–59
  music track leak before release of, 361
  referents for, 359–61
  "Snuggie" version of, 368–69, 369n31
  white experimental dance and,
    362–63, 362n14
"Couples" in *CP-AD*, 259, 260
Courbet, Gustave, 572n4
*CP-AD. See Continuous Project-Altered Daily*
Cramer, Franz Anton, 41
Crane, Frederick, on *basse danse* and
  *bassadanza*, 515
Crary, 457, 457n6
Craske, Margaret, 132
*Crises*
  allegory perception of, 124
  arch-walk from, *120*
  atypical qualities of, 105
  audience reaction to, 106
  autobiographical narrative speculation
    for, 117–18
  bonds and bondage in, 124–31, 127n60
  chance operations in, 113n39, 126–27
  choreography as contagion in,
    118–22, 125n57
  creative process behind choreography of,
    104–6, 127
  crisis alluded to by title, 105, 111, 118
  decontextualization discourse and, 107
  drama in, 101n1, 103, 105–6, 109
  duets in, 107–8, 111, 112–16, *114, 115,* 119, *120*
  elastic bands in, 108, 109, 109n29, 113,
    118, 126–29
  gamut of movements in, 104–5,
    104n8, 111–12
  gender and, 121, 121n46
  Martha Graham Dance Company interest
    in, 140
  motivated movement in, 139
  movement vocabulary of, 112
  music choice for, 104, 104n8
  *pas de deux* in, 111, 117, 121, 125
  photo of Farber and Cunningham in,
    113, *114*
  prop significance question, 118, 129–30